THE
LITERARY WORKS OF
Matthew Prior

MATTHEW PRIOR
From the painting by Jonathan Richardson, the elder, at Welbeck Abbey

THE
LITERARY WORKS OF
Matthew Prior

EDITED BY

H. BUNKER WRIGHT

AND

MONROE K. SPEARS

Volume I

OXFORD

AT THE CLARENDON PRESS

1959

Oxford University Press, Amen House, London E.C.4

GLASGOW   NEW YORK   TORONTO   MELBOURNE   WELLINGTON
BOMBAY   CALCUTTA   MADRAS   KARACHI   KUALA LUMPUR
CAPE TOWN   IBADAN   NAIROBI   ACCRA

PRINTED IN GREAT BRITAIN

NR 1-16-67

PREFACE

IN this edition Prior's complete literary works (prose as well as verse, Latin as well as English) are presented in a critical text based upon collation of all the extant manuscripts and early publications. Forty-one works are here published for the first time: three prose essays (*To Isaac Bickerstaff*, *Observations on Homer*, and *Observations on Ovid's Metamorphoses*), two fragmentary plays (*Ladislaus* and *Britanicus*), five epigrams, and thirty-one Latin works; much other material from Prior's unpublished manuscripts is incorporated into the Commentary. In addition, fourteen published works that have not been included in any previous edition of Prior are here first collected. On the other hand, a thorough investigation of the canon has resulted in the relegation of sixty titles to a section of Works Wrongly Attributed and the classification of eighteen others as Works of Doubtful Authenticity.

The plan and method of the edition are explained in the Introduction, which also contains a description of the manuscript and printed sources. The works themselves are arranged in chronological order according to dates of composition, and are accompanied by full textual apparatus. The Commentary provides much new information concerning the sources, the occasions, the historical context, and the bibliography of the works.

This edition is the product of a long and intimate collaboration by the two editors. The labour that it required has been shared equally, and each of us has participated in every phase of its preparation.

Of our numerous debts of gratitude, the greatest is due to the owners of the three principal collections of Prior manuscripts: the Duke of Portland, the Marquis of Bath, and the Miami University Library. Without their kind permission to examine, to photograph, and to print from the manuscripts in their possession we could not have undertaken this edition. For helping to make these manuscripts available to us, and for many other favours, we are grateful to Mr. F. R. D. Needham, formerly librarian at Welbeck Abbey; Miss Dorothy Coates, librarian at Longleat; and Mr. Edgar W. King, Director of Libraries, Emeritus, at Miami University. We also owe thanks to the officials of the British Museum, the Bodleian Library, the Public Record Office, St. John's College Library (Cambridge), Worcester College Library (Oxford), Harvard University Library, and the Pierpont Morgan Library for permission to print from manuscripts owned by these institutions; and to the University of Texas Library for permission to print from photostats of printed material in the Wrenn collection.

For permission to reproduce published and copyright material, we owe the following acknowledgements: to H.M. Stationery Office for quotation from various *Reports* of the Historical Manuscripts Commission; to the Oxford Bibliographical Society for quotation from Col. C. H. Wilkinson's 'The Library of Worcester College' in its *Proceedings and Papers*; to the *Essex Review* for quotation from Alfred Hills's 'Matthew Prior in Essex'; to the *Huntington Library Quarterly* for quotation from H. T. Swedenberg's 'George Stepney, My Lord Dorset's Boy'; to G. Bell & Sons for quotation from F. Elrington Ball's edition of Swift's *Correspondence*; to John Murray Ltd. for quotation from S. Arthur Strong's *Catalogue* of documents at Welbeck Abbey; to the Yale University Press for quotation from C. Kerby-Miller's edition of *Memoirs of . . . Martinus Scriblerus*; and to the Clarendon Press for quotation from George Sherburn's edition of Pope's *Correspondence*.

Professor A. Brandon Conron, of the University of Western Ontario, has devoted much time and expert knowledge to the Latin works, which we could not have edited without his help. The textual apparatus for these works is entirely his production, and he has made extensive contributions to the commentary on them. We are also indebted to Dr. Conron for allowing us to make full use of his unpublished dissertation, 'The Classical Influence in Matthew Prior's Poetry' (Harvard, 1951); we have drawn on this work often without specific acknowledgement.

So many scholars, librarians, booksellers, and others have assisted us that there is unfortunately not space to name them all here. Many particular debts are acknowledged in the Commentary. For general or extensive help, we are grateful to Professors George Sherburn, Brice Harris, Fredson T. Bowers, Allan H. Stevenson, and John D. Ralph; to Sir Harold Williams, Col. C. H. Wilkinson, Dr. L. G. Wickham Legg, Miss Frances Mayhew, Mr. F. Percy White, and Mr. W. J. Cameron. For allowing us to use their unpublished first-line indexes to miscellanies and songbooks, we owe thanks to Professors Richard C. Boys and Arthur M. Mizener and to Mr. W. N. H. Harding.

It is a pleasure to acknowledge the courteous and valuable help provided by the staffs of the libraries in which we have been privileged to work, especially the British Museum, the Bodleian Library, the Library of Congress, the Folger Shakespeare Library, the Henry E. Huntington

Library, the Newberry Library, and the libraries of Cambridge University, St. John's College (Cambridge), Harvard University, Yale University, Northwestern University, Miami University, Vanderbilt University, the University of the South, the University of Chicago, and the University of Cincinnati.

A period of intensive work on the edition was made possible by leaves of absence given to H. B. Wright by Miami University and to M. K. Spears by Vanderbilt University. Grants from the research funds of these universities, of the University of the South, and of the Modern Language Association of America, and substantial help from the Carnegie Foundation and from the Penrose and Reserve Funds of the American Philosophical Society, have made possible the travel required for our research and the extensive use of photography and other aids.

We are indebted to the Delegates of the Clarendon Press for their encouragement of this edition and to the officers on their staff who have aided in its publication.

H. B. W.
M. K. S.

June, 1957

CONTENTS

VOLUME II

LATIN WORKS

Edited with the assistance of A. Brandon Conron

INTRODUCTION

I. *Scope and Plan*

THIS edition contains all Prior's literary works. It does not include his memorials and other state papers or his journals, diaries, and voluminous correspondence. Of the numerous uncompleted pieces found among the manuscripts, we present as independent works only those that are clearly intended as such and are reasonably coherent and finished. Other fragmentary material that seems worth preserving is printed in the commentaries on works to which it is related.

The works are arranged chronologically, according to date of composition. When the exact date is unknown the work is placed under the latest possible date. On the other hand, when Prior has indicated, by sending a version to friends or by publishing it, that he considered a piece complete by a certain time, we have placed the work under that date even if our text is a later revision. When poems that first appeared in one of Prior's authorized collections cannot be assigned an earlier date of composition, we have placed them under the year in which the collection was compiled, in the order they had in the printed volume.

We have placed the English poetry and prose in the same sequence in the belief that an attempt to separate the two would produce needless difficulties and inconsistencies, for a number of the pieces include both. Similarly, we have not segregated the few pieces written by Prior in conjunction with others from those of single authorship. We have, however, placed the Latin works together in a separate section because they differ from the English both in interest and in editorial problems. We have also provided a separate section for Works of Doubtful Authenticity. In the list of Works Wrongly Attributed we have included every attribution, however foolish or tentative, that we can discover. Though we cannot hope that this list, long as it is, is complete, we hope that it will lay many ghosts and eliminate much of the confusion on the fringes of the Prior canon.

The commentary for each work consists of a tabular heading, followed when necessary by comment on the work as a whole and notes to specific passages. The heading contains: 1. A list of the manuscripts in which the work occurs, abbreviated according to the table given in section II of this introduction. 2. A condensed account of the publications of the work, in which the first publication, the first inclusion in a collected edition, and every other version of textual significance are listed. (Collected editions are referred to by italicized date, according to the list given in section IV of this introduction. Wherever possible, other books are identified by short title together with a reference to a standard bibliography.) 3. A statement of the copy-text and of the texts collated.

The comment on the work as a whole first gives the evidence for date of composition and describes the occasion, if known. We have followed the general practice of dating events in England Old Style, those on the continent New Style, but normalizing year divisions, invariably treating the new year as beginning on 1 January rather than on 25 March. Where confusion seems possible, we give both forms of the date. With one exception (see *An English Ballad*, 1695), we place poems by others that Prior answers or imitates—even those that Prior printed with his own—in the commentary rather than the text. Sources and parallels are printed in full only if they are particularly close to the work and are not readily accessible. Whenever we state that a certain book was owned by Prior, our authority is the catalogue of his library in the Welbeck MS. of the executors' reports. Books frequently referred to are cited according to the abbreviated references listed in section VII of this introduction; references to Prior's works employ the short titles used as headings for the commentaries, and each is regularly followed by the date under which the work is here printed. If a poem was set to music, we call attention to that fact and usually list the early settings; but we do not attempt to give complete information about the musical settings.

Finally, the notes to specific passages have been kept to a minimum. Allusions to classical myths are not explained unless they are particularly obscure; obsolete words, and obsolete uses of words still current, are explained only if they are very unusual. Cross-references have been given to show Prior's extensive self-borrowings and other similarities among his works.

II. *Manuscripts*

Manuscripts are extant for over half of Prior's literary works, and for many works there are two or more. The scattered copies found in various libraries, chiefly in the British Museum and the Bodleian Library, are dealt with in the commentaries; but the three major collections, which contain almost all of the known manuscripts, must be described here.

Welbeck Abbey, Worksop, Notts., the library of the Duke of Portland

W Poems and Drafts

A large volume of 171 leaves, which were until about 1930 kept in a loose bundle. When they were bound together, the various items were numbered and a typewritten table of contents supplied. Most of the manuscripts are rough drafts in Prior's hand, some are fair copies in the hand of his secretary, Adrian Drift, and others are Drift's copies emended and expanded by Prior.

Wm Miscellanies in Prose and Verse

A quarto volume labelled on the spine: 'Prior's Miscellan: &c Vol. IV'. It is item V B 1 in S. A. Strong's *Catalogue*, where it is described as a 'commonplace book'. Of its 153 leaves, three-fourths are blank. The entries, almost entirely in Prior's hand, consist of 'Annales of remarkable Occurences, from 1690 to 1691', 'Brouillons of Verse', and 'Characters, and Remarks on the different behavior of Mankind &c.'.

Longleat, Warminster, Wilts., the library of the Marquis of Bath

Prior Papers. Of the thirty volumes in this collection, the following are those that contain most of the manuscripts of literary works:

L 21 Vol. xxi, fols. 131v–162. Fragments on several subjects

This 'Commonplace for Prose', as it is called on fol. 161, is a confused mixture of two different series of numbered sheets. It is almost entirely in Prior's informal hand.

L 25 Vol. xxv. Essays and Dialogues of the Dead

A volume of 236 leaves. It consists partly of copies in Drift's cursive hand with emendations and additions in Prior's hand, and partly of fair copies in Drift's hand or in the hand of an anonymous copyist.

L 26 Vol. xxvi. Essays and Dialogues of the Dead

A volume of 180 leaves containing Drift's fair copies of the works in *L 25*.

L 27 Vol. xxvii. Poems on Several Occasions

A volume of 80 leaves containing fair copies in Drift's hand of twenty poems omitted from *1718* or written later.

L 28 Vol. xxviii. Poetical Miscellanies

A volume of over 300 leaves, sometimes numbered by pages but usually by leaves, only the rectos of which are used. It contains English works omitted from *1718* or written later, Latin works, and many fragments. Almost all of it is in Drift's fair hand, but there are some insertions in Pope's hand, and a few of the works are represented by printed copies of early editions.

L 29   Vol. xxix. Miscellaneous pieces in prose and verse

A volume of 120 leaves recently put together from the loose leaves described in the Historical MSS. Commission's *Third Report*, 1872, p. 193. It includes, besides letters, records, and printed copies of poems, a 'Commonplace Book for prose and verse, 1720 and 1721', and rough drafts and fragments in Prior's hand with fair copies by Drift.

L 30   Vol. xxx. Alma: or The Progress of the Mind

A fair copy in the manuscript printing of a professional scribe. Eighty leaves of vellum in tooled morocco binding.

Portland Papers. Of the twenty-four volumes in this collection, all of which once belonged to the daughter of Edward Lord Harley, the following contain a few Prior manuscripts among much other material:

Lpo 11   Vol. xi. Political Pieces in Prose and Verse, 1589–1769
Lpo 17   Vol. xvii. Scrapbook
Lpo 18   Vol. xviii. Scrapbook

Miami University Library, Oxford, Ohio

M   Prior MSS.

A bundle of 85 folio leaves, containing fair copies of fifty-six of Prior's works and an Index that lists these and forty-four other titles. The Index and most of the extant texts are in Drift's hand; five works show both Drift's hand and that of the anonymous copyist whose hand appears also in *L 25*; twelve are entirely in the hand of this copyist. On the leaves of text, there are pencilled folio numbers that correspond to the entries in the Index. The titles listed are all of works omitted from *1718* or written later.

Md   Drift's *Book of Common Prayer* with manuscript additions

The insertions in Drift's fair hand include copies of two of Prior's poems and information on the Drift family.

In the Introduction and Commentary these manuscripts are referred to by the initials that here precede the titles. The lists of manuscripts in the commentary headings identify the hand in each by the following system of abbreviations:

(P)	*Prior*
(D)	*Drift*
(D & P)	*Drift with revisions or additions by Prior*
(A)	*Anonymous copyist of M and L 25*
(X)	*Unknown*

The entry '(Index to M)' in a heading indicates that, although there is now no copy of the work in M, the title is listed in the table of contents.

The relation of the manuscripts in the three collections can best be explained by reviewing what is known of their history. Prior's will specified: 'All my Manuscripts, Negociations, Commissions and all papers whatsoever, whither of my public employments, or private studies I leave to my Lord Harley, my Executors or either of Them, having first burned such as may not be proper for any future inspection.' The executors whom he nominated, Edward Lord Harley and Adrian Drift, took care that none of the papers should be seen by anyone else until they had been carefully inspected (Welbeck MSS., *Executors' Reports*, i. 146, 159). Whether they eventually destroyed any of them in accordance with Prior's instructions is not known, but Drift asserted that the locked chest that he sent to Harley's London house in January 1722 contained 'all Mr: Prior's Manuscripts &ca: as well those found in his Study as his Scrutoire' (fol. 170).

Drift had for many years been Prior's secretary and amanuensis, writing sometimes in a cursive hand as if from dictation, sometimes making from Prior's original rough draft a careful transcript for further revision, and sometimes producing beautiful fair copies in italic script. After Prior's death, Drift began to transcribe the unpublished pieces he found among the poet's papers. Some of this work may have been done before the chest was sent to Lord Harley, but a note in *L 29*, 116, shows that Drift was still making copies of the manuscripts as late as April 1724. At times, he was assisted by the anonymous copyist whose clear but irregular hand occurs occasionally in the transcripts, and between them they created the copies we now have in *L 26*, *L 27*, *L 28*, *M*, and parts of *L 25* and *L 29*. A close examination of these fair copies reveals many indications of their posthumous production. They contain mistakes that would not have escaped Prior's supervision, and some of them have such significant labels as 'Brouillon of a poem begun at Wimpole in August 1721', and 'Fragments written at Down-Hall', or are marked with such notes as 'Query: if this has not been finished and printed?'

Of the original manuscripts from which Drift and his assistant copied, we have today only those in *W* and parts of *L 25* and *L 29*. The numerous cross-references on the transcripts, however, identify some of the sources now missing.[1] Many of the works in *L 28* that were not taken from *W* were derived from volumes i, ii, and iii of a '4° Miscellan.', of which we now know only volume iv (*Wm*); volume i, the source of

---

[1] These references show that for four poems, *L 28* is a transcript of published texts: *Enigma* (1693), *A New Answer* (1697), *A Fable* (1700), *To a Child of Quality* (1700).

seventy-six works written by 1690, was the most important in this series. There are also two references in *L 28* to a 'Folio Book of MS. Poems', which is now lost. In *M*, each work is marked with a page reference either to 'large folio' or to 'Smal folio'. The large folio is readily identified as *L 28*, and the texts in *M* as copies made from it. The small folio, from which *M* copied thirty works, has disappeared; it may have been the same as the lost folio referred to in *L 28*, or it may have been, like *L 28*, a volume of Drift's transcripts. A listing of all the references we have to the lost folio indicates that it contained at least seventy pages of which there are no known manuscript copies.

In 1723 Lord Harley entrusted his friend Pope with the transcripts by Drift that are in *L 28*, in order to have his opinion on the eventual publication of these works. Pope reported:

> The greater part I think are very good (& correct for the most part) but some of the very best written, I believe your Lordship will judge with me, ought not to be publishd. I mean some Satyrs on the French King, & some that touch people yet living, or their fathers. Some others Mr Prior himself thought it prudent to dis-own, when surreptitiously printed by Curll, & methinks it would make a wrong figure to ascribe 'em to him after such a publick denial, tho really his. But of this your Lordship, (who have doubtless considerd all this) will, & ought to be, the Determinate Judge, who shew the same Goodness & tenderness to the memory, that you did to the Person, of the Friend. . . .
>
> I have markd with a D. the beginning of every Poem which I think should be omitted, both such as I mentiond just now; & any which seem'd to me inferior to the rest, or not so fit for the publick. As to alterations here & there of particular lines, or the like, those will easily be made as the sheets are at the press. (Pope, *Correspondence*, ed. George Sherburn, Oxford, 1956, ii. 203.)

Pope did more than mark D's on the manuscript. He inserted titles for some of the fragmentary pieces, made some perfunctory emendations, filled in a few blanks, and in one instance supplied an entire stanza.[1]

There were others besides Pope, Harley, and Drift who were at this time engaged in preparing the manuscripts for the press, for a note in Drift's hand (*L 29, 91*) makes reference to 'the Collection intended for Publication, to be revised by Dr: Friend &ca.'.

These men, except for Pope, seem to have done little tampering with

---

[1] See commentary on *The Old Gentry* (1721). We are indebted to Professor George Sherburn for confirming our identification of Pope's hand in these insertions. At some later time Pope examined the lost small folio (*L 29, 91*); he also saw the four prose dialogues, but he did not alter the manuscripts of them (Joseph Spence, *Anecdotes*, ed. Singer, 1820, pp. 48–49).

Prior's text, and what they did is made obvious by comparison with the manuscripts copied—or, where these are lacking, by erasures and the intrusion of a foreign hand. Their attention was, it appears, directed primarily toward making a discreet choice of works to be published. Someone, taking the table of contents for *L 28*, marked titles to be omitted with *d*'s, which do not always agree with Pope's *D*'s in the text. Some of these *d*'s were later crossed out, and some titles, apparently those that were thought especially worthy of publication, were marked *x* and *xx*. We have evidence that it was these marks in the Contents of *L 28* that guided the selection of the 'Collection intended for Publication'. The page references in Drift's note referring to that collection identify it as the bundle of manuscripts, of which we now have the remnants in *M*. There are some ambiguities in the markings and in the titles given in both tables of contents, but, with one possible exception, no title definitely marked *d* in the Contents of *L 28* is listed in the Index to *M*; all of the titles marked *x* or *xx* seem to have been included as well as all of those titles opposite which a *d* has been crossed out. Of the titles unmarked in *L 28*, some are included in the Index to *M*; some are omitted. The texts that *M* took from *L 28* regularly adopt the revisions that Pope made in that volume.

If this collection had been published, it would have given to the world some 180 years sooner the four prose dialogues, the essays on *Learning* and *Opinion*, and a score of poems that did not see print until 1907; it would also have included the letter *To Isaac Bickerstaff* (1709) and three epigrams now published for the first time.

It was Lord Harley who stood in the way of the projected edition. Although he had co-operated in its preparation, he was reluctant to see it carried through. On 12 December 1728 Drift wrote to him:

I have Been, and am Still mightily Blamed for not Publishing My late Dear Masters Posthumous Works. . . . To which Complaints I Answer the Best I can, But can Never Doe it to Purpose Until Your Lordship is Pleased to Enable Me to do it Better When again Called upon by Mr Prior's Friends, Who have Reproached me Too Often with a Neglect of the Duty Owing to the Memory of That Great Man. (Welbeck MSS., *Executors' Reports*, ii. 39.)

When Drift died on 28 February 1737,[1] this edition had not appeared, and it never was to appear. Exactly what happened to all of the

---

[1] His funeral is dated 5 March 1736/7 in *The Marriage, Baptismal, and Burial Registers of the . . . Abbey of St. Peter, Westminster*, ed. J. L. Chester, 1876, p. 348. Bancks is therefore wrong in stating that Drift's death 'happened at the Beginning of the Year 1738' (*1740 History*, p. vi).

manuscripts is not known. Presumably, those later found at Welbeck and Longleat were at this time returned to Harley, if they were not already in his hands. Other copies were, however, retained among Drift's papers. The Preface to the first volume of the 1740 collection, *Miscellaneous Works of . . . Matthew Prior. . . . Now first published from His Original Manuscripts. Revised by Himself, and Copied fair for the Press By Mr. Adrian Drift, His Executor*, asserts that these copies passed from Drift to Charles Forman, who died in April 1739, before he could carry out his intention to publish them, and that they were thereupon delivered to John Bancks, who saw to it that they were in print within a few months.

This account may well be true, because there is no doubt that Bancks did have in his hands manuscripts derived from those now extant. For two-thirds of the works he published for the first time there are authentic manuscripts in *L 27*, *L 28*, or *M*, and his text for some of the poems reflects the alterations that Pope made in *L 28*. Yet it is probable that Bancks did not have access to any of these manuscripts themselves.[1] Judging by what he published, we conclude that Bancks did not have the 'Collection intended for Publication' (*M*), for his edition lacks two-thirds of the titles in the Index to that collection; nor did he have *L 28* with its careful system of markings and its numerous works not published until 1907. And although Bancks's edition did include all twelve of the unpublished poems among the works in *L 27*, these are short pieces (chiefly songs and epigrams), of which he most likely had other copies.

The lost manuscripts from which *1740* was printed included twenty-five poems of which we have no other copies. These may have derived from the missing small folio to which *M* refers or from other manuscripts of which we have no record. The same is true of the twenty-four songs that comprised *Lyric Poems 1741*, for which no manuscript is now extant. The only other large group of works for which manuscripts are lacking is the contents of *1718*; for over a hundred of the poems Prior published in this folio edition there are no manuscript copies, and there is no hint as to whether he preserved such copies after he saw the volume

---

[1] Bancks in his dedication of vol. i to Harley (then Earl of Oxford) does not make any pretence of having received his lordship's permission to publish, and there is evidence that Harley was displeased by the issuing of the edition (*H.M.C. Dartmouth*, 1887, i. 329). Bancks's statement that Drift gave the papers to Forman 'soon after the Decease of Mr. Prior, with a strict Injunction not to publish them till after the Death of Him, the said Mr. Drift', is, as we have seen, certainly not true of the literary works. It might, however, apply to the historical and biographical prose that Bancks used in the first volume, containing the *History of His Own Time*.

through the press. There are also about twenty scattered works that are not represented by manuscripts.

How *M* came to have a separate career both from the collections in Harley's possession and from the papers that Bancks acquired is not known, nor do we know the history of *M* for a century or more. The first that we hear of it is that it turned up in its present state, 'at a garden fête or similar event held on the Rectory lawn at either Dereham or Sheringham in Norfolk', where it was bought by an anonymous lady whose son much later (on 29 June 1948) put it up for sale at Sotheby & Co.[1] It was there purchased by Percy Dobell & Son, from whom it was acquired by the Miami University Library.

The Prior papers in Lord Harley's possession passed to his daughter, Lady Margaret, who married the second Duke of Portland in 1734 and subsequently kept them at Bulstrode. Upon the marriage in 1759 of her eldest daughter, Lady Elizabeth, to the third Viscount Weymouth (later created Marquis of Bath), almost all of these manuscripts and a large portion of the Portland papers were transferred to Longleat (*H.M.C. Bath*, i, p. v). Those that were not then removed have remained in the possession of the dukes of Portland. Until 1950 they were preserved at Welbeck Abbey, but since then they have been on deposit at the British Museum.

III. *The Problem of Authenticity*

Since Prior collected or otherwise acknowledged much less than half his work, and since publishers and hack writers of his day, as well as collectors of our own, found it profitable to attribute poems to him,[2] it is not easy to determine the canon of his works. We have nevertheless been able to show that sixty attributions are erroneous or unfounded, and so to reduce the number of doubtful attributions to eighteen. The evidence of authenticity for works that we accept as genuine varies in kind and in degree of authority. We have, however, been guided by certain general conclusions regarding the chief manuscript and printed sources, and these may be briefly explained.

First, we accept as genuine everything in the three major collections of Prior manuscripts (Longleat, Welbeck, and Miami), unless there is definite evidence to the contrary. Three poems, two certainly not by

---

[1] Letter from Sotheby & Co. to the editors.
[2] See J. Sutherland's notes to his edition of Pope's *Dunciad*, 1943, pp. 110 n., 113 n.; and see the comments on T. J. Wise in our list of Works Wrongly Attributed.

Prior and the other one probably not, do occur in Prior's hand in *W*, 84–85 (see commentary on *An Epitaph*, under Works of Doubtful Authenticity, 1703). These appear, however, on a single sheet, which may have been included in these papers by mistake. In *L 29*, 47 and 57, there are transcripts by Drift of *Epigram* ('Like a True Irish Marlin'), which is probably not Prior's (see under Works of Doubtful Authenticity, 1704). These four poems are probably all by Dorset, and Prior may well have transcribed them in order to preserve the work of his patron; presumably Drift failed to recognize them as Dorset's. In *M*, 70, Drift transcribed *On a F . . t*—later published in *1740*—which is definitely not Prior's; see under Works Wrongly Attributed. Finally, there is in *L 29*, 31, in an unidentified hand, *Epigram* ('To Richmond and Peterburgh'), which is probably not by Prior; see under Works of Doubtful Authenticity, 1714.

It is possible, therefore, that other works in the manuscripts are not Prior's. But we have not been able to find a shred of evidence to justify our doubting the authenticity of any of the other works. We conclude that the presence among the manuscripts of these poems—three certainly, and three probably, not by Prior—is an anomaly.

Second, we accept as genuine, works acknowledged by Prior in any way. This means that *A Satyr on the modern Translators* (1685)—acknowledged in a letter—and *Satyr on the Poets* (1687), which has a signed continuation in *L 28*, are changed from their traditional doubtful status. We consider signed publication during Prior's lifetime, if not repudiated by him or dubious for any other reason, as equivalent to acknowledgement by him; thus we accept *A Pindarique on His Maiesties Birth-Day* (1690) as genuine.

Third, we accept works published in two posthumous collections—*1740* and *Lyric Poems 1741*—that seem to have been printed from authentic manuscripts. We also accept two poems on the authority of *1727*. The reasons for considering these collections authentic are explained in the section on the History of the Canon, below.

Other manuscript or printed sources have been considered as individual cases and are fully discussed in the commentaries. Throughout, we have based our decisions primarily upon the provenance; other criteria, such as stylistic evidence and contemporary testimony, have been used only to supplement this one. The next section consists of a list of collected editions, not complete, but including all editions of any significance or interest. This list is discussed in the section following it.

IV. *Principal Collected Editions*

1707 Poems on Several Occasions ... London: Printed for R. Burrough, and J. Baker, ... and E. Curll, ... 1707.

1709 Poems on Several Occasions. London: Printed for Jacob Tonson, ... 1709. [Second Edition, Tonson, 1709. Reprinted by Tonson in 1711, 1713, and 1717.]

1716 A Second Collection of Poems on Several Occasions ... London, printed for J. Roberts, ... 1716.

1718 Poems on Several Occasions. London: Printed for Jacob Tonson ... and John Barber ... 1718. [Numerous reprints,[1] herein referred to by the abbreviation *P.S.O.* followed by date of publication.]

1722 A Supplement to Mr. Prior's Poems. Consisting Of such Pieces as are Omitted in the late Collection of his Works, and Others, now first Published, from his Original Manuscripts, in the Custody of his Friends ... London: Printed for E. Curll, ... MDCCXXII. [Reissued in 1722, together with Curll's Some Memoirs of the Life and Publick Employments of Matthew Prior, Esq ..., with new title page: Memoirs of the Life of Mr. Prior, etc. With a Supplement to his Poems. Rptd., with *1718*, Dublin, 1723 and 1728 (vol. ii misdated 1732 and 1738), G. Grierson.]

New Collection 1725 A New Collection of Poems on Several Occasions. By Mr. Prior, and Others ... London: Printed for Tho. Osborne, ... MDCCXXV. [Case 334. Often bound as a third volume to *P.S.O. 1725*.]

1727 Poems on Several Occasions, ... Volume III. The Second Edition ... London: Printed in the Year, MDCCXXVII. [No publisher given; *The Hind and the Panther Transvers'd* has a separate title-page, London, Printed for J. Hooke, M.DCC.XX.VII.]

1733 Poems on Several Occasions ... Volume the Third, and Last. The Third Edition. To Which is Prefixed The Life of Mr. Prior, By Samuel Humphreys, Esq; ... London, Printed: And sold by S. Birt ... and W. Feales ... MDCCXXXIII. [Reissued in 1734, with a new title-page, as third volume of the *P.S.O. 1733*.]

1740 Miscellaneous Works of His late Excellency Matthew Prior Esq; Consisting of Poems on Several Occasions, Viz. Epistles, Tales, Satires, Epigrams, &c. With some Select Latin Performances. Now first published from His Original Manuscripts. Revised by Himself, and Copied fair

---

[1] Dublin, 1719, J. Hyde *et al.*; London, 1720, T. Johnson (advs. in the vol. describe Johnson as 'Bookseller in the Hague'); London, 1721, J. Tonson and J. Barber (2 vols.); London, 1725, J. Tonson and J. Barber (2 vols.); London, 1733, R. Knaplock, J. Round, and J. Tonson ('The Fifth Edition', 2 vols.; reissued 1734 with new t.p., S. Birt and W. Feales); London, 1741, H. Lintot and J. and R. Tonson ('The Sixth Edition'); Glasgow, 1751, R. and A. Foulis (2 vols.; rptd. 1759, 1771); London, 1754, J. and R. Tonson *et al.*; Aberdeen, 1754, F. Douglass and W. Murray (2 vols.); London, 1766, J. and R. Tonson *et al.*; Berwick, 1766, R. Taylor (2 vols.); Edinburgh, 1773, A. Kincaid *et al.* (vols. xvii and xviii of The British Poets, ed. H. Blair); Cambridge, 1905 (ed. A. R. Waller).

for the Press By Mr. Adrian Drift, His Executor. London: Printed for the Editor. MDCCXL. [Normally described as vol. ii of *Miscellaneous Works* (vol. i being *History of His Own Time*); some copies contain a general title-page for both volumes, so describing them. The Second Edition of both volumes, 1740, differs only in title-pages. A pirated edition was published in Dublin, 1739, Printed by S. Powell for G. Risk *et al.*]

Lyric Poems 1741 Lyric Poems; Being Twenty Four Songs (Never before Printed:) by the Late Matthew Prior Esqr.; Set to Music by Several Eminent Masters. Printed for and Sold by Sam: Harding, . . . MDCCXLI. Publish'd Janry. 1st. 1740/1.

1742 Poems on Several Occasions . . . Volume the Second. The Fourth Edition. To which is Prefixed, The Life of Mr. Prior, By Samuel Humphreys, Esq; . . . London: Printed for C. Hitch . . . and J. Hodges . . . MDCCXLII. [Case 436 (d). Rptd.: London, 1754 (t.p. unchanged except for date. Companion vol. to *P.S.O. 1754*); London, 1767, W. Strahan *et al.* (Companion vol. to *P.S.O. 1766*).]

Eighteen Canzonets 1745? Eighteen Canzonets for Two, and three Voices; (The Words chiefly by Matthew Prior Esqr.) Set to Musick by John Travers Organist of his Majesty's Chapel Royal And of St. Paul Covent Garden. London Printed for the Author . . . N.D. [1745?]

1768 Poems on Several Occasions With a Supplement . . . Dublin: Printed for W. and W. Smith, P. and W. Wilson, Booksellers in Dame-street, 1768. [2 vols.]

1777 The Poetical Works of Matthew Prior. In Three Volumes. With the Life of the Author . . . Edinburg: At the Apollo Press, By the Martins. Anno 1777. [Bell's Edition. The Poets of Great Britain Complete from Chaucer to Churchill (vols. 47–49).] [2nd ed., 1784. Rptd.: London, 1797, G. Cawthorn (first and second vols. only).]

Evans 1779 The Poetical Works of Matthew Prior: Now First Collected, With Explanatory Notes, And Memoirs of the Author, In Two Volumes . . . London: Printed for W. Strahan, T. Payne, J. Rivington and Sons, J. Dodsley, T. Lowndes, T. Cadell, T. Caslon, J. Nichols, and T. Evans in the Strand. MDCCLXXIX.

Johnson 1779 The Poems of Prior. [The Works of the English Poets. With Prefaces, Biographical and Critical, by Samuel Johnson . . . (vols. 30–31). London: Printed by J. Nichols; for C. Bathurst, J. Buckland, W. Strahan . . . MDCCLXXIX.] [Rptd.: London, 1790 (vols. 32–34 of Works of the English Poets); Chiswick, Press of C. Whittingham, 1822 (vols. 30–31 of The British Poets).]

1793 The Poetical Works of Matthew Prior . . . To which is prefixed The Life of the Author . . . Edinburgh: Printed by Mundell and Son . . . Anno 1793. [The Works of the British Poets. With Prefaces, Biographical and Critical, by Robert Anderson, M.D. Volume Seventh . . .

London: Printed for John & Arthur Arch; and for Bell & Bradfute, and J. Mundell & Co. Edinburgh. 1795.]

1807 The Poetical Works of Matthew Prior. Collated with the Best Editions: by Thomas Park . . . London: Printed . . . for J. Sharpe . . . 1807. [Works of the British Poets, vols. xi–xii.]

1810 The Works of the English Poets . . . The Additional Lives By Alexander Chalmers . . . Vol. X . . . London: Printed for J. Johnson; . . . and Wilson and Son at York. 1810.

1825 The Poetical Works of Matthew Prior . . . London: Published by Jones & Company . . . 1825. [2 vols.]

1835 The Poetical Works of Matthew Prior London William Pickering 1835. [The Aldine Edition of the British Poets, vols. 36–37; 'Life' by the Rev. John Mitford. Rptd.: London, 1866, 1872, 1885; Boston, 1853, 1854, 1860, 1866, 1870, 1878, 1880, N.D.]

1858 The Poetical Works of Matthew Prior. With Memoir . . . By the Rev. George Gilfillan. Edinburgh: James Nichol . . . London: James Nisbet & Co. Dublin: W. Robertson. M.DCCC.LVIII. [Rptd.: Edinburgh, 1863, 1866, 1868, 1869; London, 1879.]

1889 Selected Poems of Matthew Prior With an Introduction and Notes by Austin Dobson . . . London   Kegan Paul, Trench & Co MDCCCLXXXIX.

1892 The Poetical Works of Matthew Prior   A New Edition Revised with Memoir by Reginald Brimley Johnson . . . London   George Bell & Sons 1892. [2 vols.; Aldine Edition. Rptd.: London, 1907.]

1907 Matthew Prior   Dialogues of the Dead and Other Works in Prose and Verse   The Text edited by A. R. Waller, M.A. Cambridge: at the University Press 1907. [The companion volume, a reprint of *1718*, was published in 1905. General title-page: Cambridge English Classics   The Writings of Matthew Prior.]

v. *History of the Canon*

This account deals only with the canon as represented in and formed by collected editions. Other publications of individual works are considered in the commentaries; questionable and unacceptable attributions are discussed in the sections on Works of Doubtful Authenticity and Works Wrongly Attributed.

1707, published 31 January 1707 (adv. *Daily Courant*), is an unauthorized edition, repudiated before publication by Tonson (*Daily Courant*, 24 January) and immediately after by Prior (*Daily Courant*, 6 February). The seventeen poems it contains had all—with the possible exception of *A Simile* (1707)—been published before and were all genuine. Prior objected, for diplomatic reasons, to the republication under his name of *To Mr. Fleetwood Shepherd* (1689), *A Satyr on the modern Translators* (1685), and *Satyr on the Poets* (1687), and also to numerous unauthorized changes in the texts.

1709, published 3 December 1708 (adv. *Daily Courant*), is Prior's first authorized collection. It contains fifty-one poems, of which nineteen were published for the first time. For bibliographical description, see R. W. Chapman, 'Prior's Poems, 1709', *R.E.S.* iii (1927), 76. The second edition, published 29 March 1709, is a complete resetting of the first as corrected by four cancels.

1716, published 20 March 1716 and repudiated by Prior in the *London Gazette* of 20–24 March, contains nine poems, all of which had previously been published. Curll, for whom Roberts published *1716*, again included the three poems to which Prior had objected in 1707.

1718, published 17 March 1719 (adv. *Daily Courant*), contains all the poems in *1709*—some of them extensively revised—together with one poem (*Charity*) published in 1703 but not included in *1709*. It also collects eight poems published since 1709, and adds fifty-one poems never before printed. This edition (discussed more fully in the next section) was supervised and corrected by Prior with great care. The numerous reprints of it are of no textual significance.

1722, published 10 November 1721 (adv. *Daily Post*), includes five poems which had been previously collected. In fact, Curll used the remainder sheets of *1716*, removing in most copies the first sixteen pages of *1716*, which contain poems published in *1718*. For these he substituted a new set of pages 1–14, containing one genuine poem—*To the Countess Dowager of Devonshire* (1689)—and two doubtful ones: *Upon Lady Katherine H—de's first appearing* and *The Judgment of Venus* (in Works of Doubtful Authenticity, 1718 and 1720). These three poems had all been printed before, but the last of them had not been attributed to Prior in print. Apart from this, the volume is of no significance for text or canon, but it is historically important as the first of a series of volumes intended as 'supplements' to *1718* and its many reprints. Curll's *Some Memoirs of the Life and Publick Employments of Matthew Prior, Esq; . . .* (published soon after *1722*, and often combined with it, with a general title-page) is a reprint, with slight revisions, of the life in Giles Jacob's *Historical Account of the Lives and Writings of Our most Considerable English Poets . . .* MDCCXX.

New Collection 1725 consists of *1722*—omitting the two *Satyrs*—and eight additional poems (six published separately since 1718; *Epitaph*,

1702, from the newspaper accounts of Prior's death; and *The Hind and the Panther Transvers'd*, 1687).

1727 is intended as a second edition of *New Collection 1725*, as the title-page indicates. The B.M. Catalogue describes it as edited by Samuel Humphreys, but there is no evidence for this; the prefatory matter is quite different from that in Humphreys's *1733*. The dedication, 'To Sir Henry Hussey, Bart.', is virtually identical to that in *New Collection 1725*, where it is signed, 'Philo-Musis'. In most copies of *1727* it is unsigned; but in at least one copy (in the Bodleian) it is signed 'E. Curll'. The volume reprints *New Collection 1725*, and adds three hitherto uncollected poems. One of these (*Ad . . . Samuelem Shaw*, Latin Works, 1692) had been published in 1692, with Prior's signature, and is further attested by the existence of a manuscript at Longleat. There is no such definite evidence of authenticity for the other two: *On Bishop Atterbury's Burying the Duke of Buckingham* (1721) and *The Remedy, Worse than the Disease* (1714). The first of these, however, fits in with Prior's other epigrams on Atterbury so well as to create a strong presumption of his authorship; both are the sort of personal epigram that might well circulate unpublished for some time; and we can discover no reason to doubt the authenticity of either. We therefore accept them as genuine, assuming that the editor of *1727* obtained them from manuscripts now lost.

1733 is simply a reprint of *1727*, with different preliminaries by the editor, Samuel Humphreys. A haphazard combination of *1733* with *1718* provided the text of *1768*.

1740, published in October 1739 (*Gentleman's Magazine*, ix, 1739, 556), is an important edition, and must be considered in some detail. There are many variations in the binding of this and vol. i (*The History of His Own Time*)—the plates, dedications, and prefaces being found in various combinations—but these raise no textual problems. The second edition of both volumes (1740) is, except for title-pages, identical with the first; it seems to be a re-issue of the same sheets. *1740* was edited and published by John Bancks or Banks (1709–51; see *D.N.B.*), formerly a weaver and bookseller, and author of two volumes of poetry (*Miscellaneous Works*, London, 1738) strongly imitative of Prior and expressing great admiration for him. As has been explained in section II, Bancks printed from authentic manuscripts that had been in Drift's possession and that were delivered to him after the death of Charles Forman, who had intended to publish them. Bancks had been concerned with the editing even before Forman's death on 28 April 1739, for the volume contains a letter from John Morley (Jr.) dated 16 April 1739, answering an inquiry from Bancks about Prior manuscripts. There is no way of telling how much editing Bancks did and how much had already been done by Drift and by Forman; but there are several indications that he was honest and conscientious.

The volume contains seventy-three English poems and thirteen Latin works. The Latin pieces are all published for the first time; of the English poems, only eleven had been published before. In the table of contents, Bancks marks with an asterisk the poems previously published. As far as we can discover, these asterisks are complete and correct, with two exceptions: *The Third Ode of Anacreon* is not starred, though it was published in 1703, and *Snuff* (unknown date) is starred, though we can find no earlier publication. Since the two titles are in roughly corresponding positions on facing pages, it is possible that the asterisk intended for *The Third Ode* was transferred to *Snuff* through a printer's error.

Although the general authenticity of *1740* seems well attested, the volume poses a major problem. Because of one of the most curious episodes in the history of the canon, a group of poems first published in *1740* was not again printed as Prior's for over 150 years. Since the arrangement of the volume is the basis of the problem, it must be explained. Through *A Letter* (1720), p. 134, we have manuscript evidence of authenticity for all but ten poems, and the absence of manuscripts for these ten does not appear to be significant. We have no manuscripts for any of the English poems from this point on. Through p. 134, the only poems signed by other authors are Dryden's translation of Ovid and Stanley's of Anacreon, given as parallels to Prior's versions. On p. 135 a poem by Edward Harley, Jr., is inserted, evidently as a companion-piece to Prior's two poems, immediately preceding it, to members of the Harley family. The two following poems—*Truth and Falshood* (1720) and *Nelly's Picture* (unknown date)—are accepted by all later editions. However, the next two poems (*Prologue*, unknown date —followed by Buckingham's verses on what Bancks took to be the same occasion—and *Amaryllis*, unknown date) are placed by *1742* in a section of 'Original Poems by Several Hands' and are omitted by later editions until *1892*. All these editions, however, accept the next two poems: *Upon Playing at Ombre* and *Cupid's Promise* (both unknown date).

After these poems occur three signed by other authors (Sir Harry Sheers, W. Walsh, and the Earl of Dorset); there seems to be no particular reason for their insertion at this point. They are followed by ten unsigned poems—*Dorinda, To Leonora, To Leonora. Encore, On a Pretty*

Madwoman, Absence, The New-Year's Gift, A Song ('For God's-sake'), *Snuff, To Celia,* and *Upon a Friend* (all unknown date). These ten poems were placed in the miscellany section in *1742* and were omitted by all subsequent editors until *1892*. It is possible that these poems, following the three signed by others, were intended in *1740* to form the kind of miscellany section so common in similar collections. Apparently the editor of *1742*, and perhaps later editors, did interpret the poems as constituting such a miscellany, and therefore concluded that they were not Prior's.

Since we do not have the manuscript collection from which *1740* was printed, we are unable to determine what part Forman and Bancks played in selecting and arranging the manuscripts passed on by Drift. It is possible, of course, that they chose to add some poems by other authors, but there is nothing to suggest this. The footnote to Dorset's *The Antiquated Coquette* (*1740*, p. 175) indicates that it was printed from manuscript, and that Bancks was conscientiously trying to establish authorship. (This is the first printing of the poem, and the basis of its attribution to Dorset; see Harris, *Dorset*, p. 235.) The natural inference is that the poems signed by others were in the manuscript collection, and not added by Forman or Bancks. As to the significance of the arrangement, it seems unlikely that Bancks would present these poems in this way if he knew or suspected them to be not by Prior: his editing is careful, and he separates Shelton's translations and the verses to Prior from Prior's poems.

The editor of *1742* is unknown: Humphreys's prefatory matter is reprinted from *1733*, but Humphreys had died in 1738. Whoever he was, he had access to no manuscripts, and there is no indication that he had any special knowledge of the authorship of the poems. If he took his cue from the arrangement of *1740*, his reasons for placing *Prologue* and *Amaryllis* in the miscellany section, while printing as Prior's the poems immediately preceding and following them in *1740*, are highly mysterious. Four poems in *1740* he omitted completely: *The Lame and the Blind* (1720), *Human Life* (unknown date), *A Letter* (1720), and *To my Lord* (1717). If he doubted their authenticity, he should have placed them in the miscellany section; though the last two are signed 'M.P.' in *1740*. This indication of carelessness makes it almost certain that his classification was based upon a casual and arbitrary interpretation of the arrangement of *1740*, and not upon knowledge of authorship.

As the first edition to bring together all the posthumous collections, *1742* acquired a fortuitous and wholly undeserved authority. *1777*

follows it but omits the entire miscellany section; it follows *1742* also in
the careless omission of the four other poems. *Evans 1779* also omits the
miscellany section (hence omitting the twelve poems in question), but
restores two of the four others carelessly omitted in *1742*—these are the
two signed 'M.P.'. Evans was a comparatively careful editor, and he
did go back to *1740* rather than depend entirely on *1742*. It seems clear,
however, that he was led by *1742* or its successors to omit these fourteen poems, since it is most unlikely that he had special knowledge of
their authorship. Evans does say that *1740* contains 'poems by himself
[Prior] and his friends, some of which must be considered as doubtful...'
(i, p. xvi). But probably he considered them doubtful only because of
their classification in *1742* and later editions. All subsequent editions,
based on either *Evans 1779* or *1777*, omitted the poems in question until
R. B. Johnson restored them in *1892*.

The omissions resulting from oversight require no discussion. The
fact that the other twelve poems (the last ten in *1740*, with *Prologue*
and *Amaryllis*) were rejected from the canon from 1742 to 1892, though
startling, seems to be without significance. We have not found any
clue to other authorship than Prior's, and we therefore accept them as
genuine. The only poems in *1740* that we do not accept are two that
do not affect the foregoing discussion, since we know that they were
included in the manuscript collection used by Bancks: see the discussion
of *On a F . . t*, in Works Wrongly Attributed, and the commentary on
The Mice (Works of Doubtful Authenticity, 1709).

Lyric Poems 1741, with which we may return to our chronological
account of the formation of the canon, is the last collection (until *1907*)
to add a substantial number of poems to Prior's works. The statement
in the title that the songs were 'Never before Printed' seems to be
correct, with one possible exception (see commentary on *A Two part
Song*, unknown date); of the two known composers, Smith was born in
1712 and Defesch came to England in 1731; so the settings were probably done not long before the book was published. Samuel Harding,
who published and sold the book, was a friend of Drift's. After Prior's
death, he assisted Drift in cataloguing Prior's library, later helped
appraise it, and sold it at his shop on 20 April 1724. (The printed sales
catalogue is in the British Museum, shelf mark S.C. 392 [12].) Drift
wrote to Harley on 29 November 1721:

Mr: Harding, My Lord, who was Assisting to me in taking the Catalogue
of Books, is an Ingenious & understanding Young Man, and is Master of
a good Trade & business, and has Managed several Auction of Books of his

own with good Success: Mr: Calcutt is of Opinion as well as Mr: Sanderson that he will be a fit Person when the Books comes to be Appraised to be Assisting in that Work. He is a very Honest Man, and an Old Acquaintance of Mine. (Welbeck MSS., *Executors' Reports*, i. 160v.)

Harding, then, would hardly attribute the volume to Prior as a bookseller's trick; and the connexion with Drift explains how the manuscripts could have come into his possession. The probability is strong that the songs are genuine, and we accept them as Prior's.

1742 is an expanded version of *1733*, and is intended as a companion volume to *P.S.O. 1741*. Although, as we have seen, it was carelessly edited, it was extremely influential because it was the first edition to bring together all the posthumous collections. It includes everything in *1733* (except *The Hind and the Panther Transvers'd*), the twenty-four songs from *Lyric Poems 1741*—adding four songs from *1740* (*Song*, 'Hast my Nannette', *Song*, 'Whither wou'd my Passion', *Nelly's Picture*, all three of unknown date, and *Song. Sett by Mr: Abell*, 1701) to make a section of 'twenty-eight songs' which was reproduced by all editions until *1907*—and most of the English poems in *1740*. (All Latin works in *1740* are omitted, except *Preamble to the Duke of Dorsets Patent*, which is included in the prefatory matter.) The significance of the omission of some poems from *1740*, and the relegation of others to a miscellany section, has already been discussed.

Eighteen Canzonets 1745? includes musical settings of eleven poems by Prior, all of them taken from *1740*. One of them—*To Leonora. Encore*—is among the group omitted by *1742* and later editions.

1777 combines *1718* and *1742*, omitting the twelve poems placed in the miscellany section by *1742*, and following *1742* in the careless omission of four other poems. To these *1777* adds one more careless omission: *On the Taking of Huy* (1694). It is of interest as the first edition to arrange the poems in a classified order: Odes, Songs and Ballads, Tales, Prologues and Epilogues, Epistles, Hymns, Epigrams, and Miscellaneous Poems. *1777* had some influence, since a few later editions are based on it, the Jones *1825* without change, the Park *1807* adding four poems from later editions and carelessly omitting several.

Evans 1779 is an important edition, since all subsequent editions for over a century (except the few that followed *1777*) were based on it. Evans combines *1718*, *1740*, and *1742*. His omission of fourteen poems in *1740* because of the influence of *1742* has already been discussed. In addition, he omits *Colin's Mistakes* (1721), which had been in *1722* and all the later 'supplementary' volumes. He restores ten of the Latin works omitted by *1742*, but omits the other two, as well as the one Latin work that *1742* did reprint from *1740* (the *Preamble to the Duke of Dorsets Patent*, 1720). Evans added to the Prior canon ten poems and an epitaph and a memorial in prose. Seven of these were collected by Evans from various scattered publications: *Epitaph on True* (1693), *To the Bishop of Ely. On his departure* (1685), *To the Bishop of Ely* (1685), *Epitaph for Sir Thomas Powys* (1720), *Epitaph* ('Meek Franco', 1721), *Thos: Britton, Small-Coal-Man* (1714), and *Epigram* ('I Stood, Sir', doubtful, 1712). All these except the last are proved authentic by manuscript or other evidence; the last one we classify as doubtful because the authority of the source from which Evans took it is questionable, and it does not appear that Evans had anything but the printed source to go on. Four poems and a prose memorial were published by Evans for the first time. Evans states that he took the memorial (which we print with *Engraven on a Column*, 1717) from the tablet in the church at Halstead. His source for the four poems—*Verses in Lady How's Ovids Epistles* (unknown date), the two *Epistles* (1717), and *Epigram* ('To Richmond and Peterburgh', doubtful, 1714)—was evidently *B.M. MS. Harl. 7316*, though he does not state this. (The same manuscript must have been his authority for attributing *An Epitaph on True* to Prior.) This seems to have been the only manuscript that Evans used; he remarks (i, p. xvi): 'Many Poems are said to remain still in MSS. in the possession of the Dutchess Dowager of Portland.' Evans was a scholarly and cultivated man (see John Nichols, *Literary Anecdotes of the Eighteenth Century*, vi, 1812, 434 n.–36 n.). Although, unfortunately, he gave no account of his sources or editorial methods, he provided a well-informed, though very brief, new Life of Prior, and—in a highly sporadic fashion—annotations for a good many poems. Most later editions reprint Evans's notes, some of which are valuable and many wildly erroneous. Evans also supplied new and altered titles freely; though they have become traditional because followed by later editions, we have generally ignored them.

Johnson 1779 is a reprint of *Evans*, identical in contents; the only difference is that the order of poems is changed and sometimes improved. All nine of the publishers of *Evans* are among the thirty-six publishers of *Johnson*, and there must have been some kind of trade agreement to permit the reprinting of *Evans* so quickly. The *Johnson* edition, sold as part of a set of sixty volumes, would hardly offer any competition to *Evans*. We use the inaccurate label, *Johnson*, simply because it is traditional; Johnson remarked with indignation, 'It is great impudence to put *Johnson's Poets* on the back of books which Johnson neither recommended nor revised. . . . This is indecent' (*Lives*, i, p. xxvi n.); in a note to John Nichols, he speaks of 'your edition, which is very impudently called mine' (ii. 65 n.). *1793* and *1810*, among subsequent editions, adopt the order of *Johnson*; *1835* and *1858* follow the order as well as the text of *Evans*.

All these editions add to *Evans 1779* the eight poems attributed to Prior by John Nichols in his *Select Collection of Poems*, 1780–2. These were all taken by Nichols from earlier publications. Two of them are undoubtedly genuine: the 1692 version of *To the Honourable Charles Montague* and the Latin poem (1683) *On the Marriage of George Prince of Denmark, and the Lady Anne*. Of the other six, two are demonstrably by other authors (*An Apology to a Lady* and *Against Modesty in Love*), two are attributed on wholly insufficient grounds (*On a young Lady's going to Town* and *A Paraphrase on the French*), and two represent early vague attributions repeated by Nichols (*When the Cat's away* and *A Fable of the Widow and her Cat*). Only the last of these merits classification as doubtful; the other five will be found under Works Wrongly Attributed. Nichols was a very careless editor: while attributing *An Apology* and *Against Modesty* to Prior, he printed them elsewhere in his *Collection* with correct ascriptions! Curiously, he attributes *Colin's Mistakes* to Dr. Samuel Croxall, and prints *The Third Ode of Anacreon* as anonymous.

Austin Dobson's volume of selections, *1889*, is included in our list because of the importance of its introduction and notes. Dobson went back to the original sources, quoted extensively from Sir James Montagu's *Memorandums* at Longleat and from other contemporary documents, and cast much light on Prior's literary career. For the first time, some of Prior's poems were edited with care.

R. B. Johnson in *1892* was the first editor to reconsider the canon of Prior's works and thereby correct some of the errors of his predecessors. His edition is a revision of Mitford's 'Aldine', *1835*, but Johnson went back to the earlier collections to restore the fourteen poems from *1740* which had been omitted by later editions and *Colin's Mistakes*, for the omission of which Evans was responsible. He was the first editor to question Nichols's attributions: he rejected three of these (*An Apology*, *Against Modesty*, and *On a young Lady's going to Town*), but printed the others. Johnson collected for the first time seven poems from various scattered publications: *Ad Regios Fratres* (Latin, 1685), 'Spare Dorsett's sacred life' (1694), 'Fame counting Thy books' (1720), the quatrain on Queen Mary's death that we print in the commentary on *An Ode. Presented to the King, 1695*, and three that we classify as doubtful

(*Epigram*, 'Like a True Irish Marlin', *Song in Prison*, and *Couplets*). Johnson had access to no manuscripts, and printed nothing not previously published. Most of his notes derive ultimately from *Evans 1779*, but he contributes a new and well-informed Life. In his Appendixes, Johnson prints *A Satyr on the modern Translators* (1685) and *Satyr on the Poets* (1687), which had not been included in collected editions since *1722*, and *The Hind and the Panther Transvers'd* (1687), which had not been included since *1733*.

1907 was a major contribution, since in it Waller printed for the first time six prose pieces and fifty-nine poems from the Longleat manuscripts. Eleven additional poems printed from the manuscripts had been published previously (Waller was aware that five of them had been published), but had never been collected. The volume contains: *The Hind and the Panther Transvers'd*, printed from the first edition; *1722*, complete; the poems added in *New Collection 1725*; all the English poems from *1740*; *The Examiner. Numb. 6* from the *1740 History*; from *Evans 1779*, the 'twenty-four songs' (with emendations from *Lyric Poems 1741*) and the twelve poems that Waller thought were first published by Evans (actually, eight of these had been published before); the pieces from the Longleat manuscripts; 'Fragments from Prior's Letters, Etc.'—three short pieces selected from those collected in *1892*; and an appendix of 'Poems Attributed to Prior', consisting of six of the poems attributed by Nichols (the Latin poem is omitted, and the early version of *To the Honourable Charles Montague* placed in the notes) and three other poems, which had not previously been printed as attributed to Prior. The companion volume, *P.S.O. 1905*, was the first edition of *1718* in which any attempt was made to collate earlier publications of the poems.

VI. *Text*

For each work, we have made a separate study of all extant manuscripts and early publications in order to determine which text is most likely to display Prior's final intentions. As a result, our copy-text for a great many of the works is more authoritative than that followed by previous collected editions. Ninety works are here printed from manuscripts heretofore unused, half of these being Prior's holographs or copies corrected in his hand. Over fifty works that other editors have taken from unreliable reprints are here printed directly from the original publications.

Our copy-text for all the works included in *1718* is Prior's own copy of that folio. For the works that made their first appearance in this collection, it is, of course, the only authorized publication. For the works that had been previously printed, *1718* presents Prior's final revision. We have given serious consideration to the question whether the works that the folio republished should not be printed in the form of their first publication with the insertion of authorial revisions present in *1718*. We found, however, that there is the strongest evidence that, even as to mechanical details, the *1718* text of these works is the one that had Prior's approval. His correspondence shows that he spent over a year in the preparation of copy for this collection and that he read proof for it, with attention to 'commas, semicolons, italic and capital'.[1] There is, on the other hand, no reason to believe that he took such pains with any earlier publication. The reason we have chosen to print from the copy of *1718* that was owned by Prior and bequeathed by him to St. John's College, Cambridge, is that it is one of the two known copies that are proved by bibliographical analysis to be entirely authoritative. Both this copy and the other one, which is in the Library of Congress, are of the extra large size that is distinguished by inner margins of over three inches; and collation of numerous copies of *1718* has revealed that only the folios of this size will display throughout the setting for which Prior read proof and will also contain all of the press corrections.[2]

Our copy-text for other works printed in Prior's lifetime is usually that of their first publication. In thirteen instances, however, we have chosen to follow an authoritative manuscript. Five of these are works that first appeared in the unreliable and sometimes incomplete text of a song-book or an engraved plate. Two are Latin epitaphs that were printed from the inscriptions on the monuments, and one is a Preamble printed inaccurately from the original document, which is itself our copy-text. Three are poems for which the manuscripts display Prior's revision of the text after publication: *An Ode in Imitation of Horace* (1692), *Considerations* (1693), *On the Taking of Huy* (1694). For one poem, *Advice to the Painter* (1685), the first publication (the basis of the text in all previous editions) was printed in 1703 from a redaction that shows the effects of eighteen years of manuscript transmission through many hands. One poem of doubtful authenticity (*An Epitaph*, 1703), we

---

[1] *H.M.C. Bath*, iii. 454; see also pp. 455, 459–60; *L 14*, pp. 180–1; *B.M. MS. Harl. 3780*, fols. 342, 344; Swift, *Correspondence*, ed. F. Elrington Ball, 1910–14, iii. 4–5, 8–9.
[2] H. B. Wright, 'Ideal Copy and Authoritative Text: The Problem of Prior's *Poems on Several Occasions*, 1718', *M.P.* xlix (1952), 234–41. The medium-sized copies, one of which Waller reproduced in *P.S.O. 1905*, are corrupted by the irregular distribution of sheets printed from a careless resetting.

print from the copy in Prior's autograph because of the importance of that document to the discussion of attribution. In only a single instance (apart from the contents of *1718*) have we chosen a later publication as our copy-text in preference to the first; this is the *Satyr on the Poets* (1687) where the 1694 text is clearly a late alteration of the text presented in the second publication, 1698, and is without authority.

Our copy-text for a work first published since Prior's death is always an authoritative manuscript when any exists; otherwise it is the earliest publication. For instance, we follow the text of *1740* only when a work it publishes for the first time is not found in such a manuscript. Although it is true, as has been shown in section II, that the editors of *1740* possessed authentic manuscripts now lost, these were copies derived from manuscripts to which we have access or were copies made by the same people from the same sources. Furthermore, a comparison with the extant manuscripts shows that either the editors or the printers of *1740* exercised a great deal of freedom in altering the details of their sources, and, even when they did not corrupt the text, imposed upon it a typographical style that did not come into fashion until after Prior's death.

Our copy-text for works that we publish from manuscript is, whenever possible, the most finished copy for which there is evidence of Prior's participation or supervision. Thus we always prefer a manuscript in which Prior's hand appears to a transcript of it which Drift made after Prior's death. Since this is the opposite of Waller's practice in *1907*, many of the works he published from the Longleat manuscripts are here presented in a new text. The difference is sometimes great, as in the instance of three poems of unknown date (*To a Painter*, and the two songs that follow it), which he printed as unfinished fragments. When we have only posthumous transcripts to choose from, we follow the one which gives evidence of being closest to Prior's original. Thus we prefer a text in *L 28* to one in *M* which is labelled as a copy from that volume, and we prefer a text in *M* that is marked as a transcript from the lost small folio to one in *L 27* which has no indication of its source and may therefore be derived from *M*.

The copy-text selected for each work is named in the commentary, which includes a discussion of the choice if the application of the above principles is not obvious. Editorial emendation has been conservative. We have not attempted to normalize the spelling, capitalization, or punctuation of the works, and have made alterations in them only when it was necessary to correct scribal or printing blunders, to expand abbreviations, or to supply essential full stops and initial capitals, and occasionally, internal punctuation required for clarity. Very few verbal emendations have been found necessary or justifiable. Our rule has been to introduce them only when we are convinced that they represent an authoritative reading distorted by a copyist or compositor. In so far as possible, the emendations we make are based on one of the texts we collate. In each instance, the apparatus notes the source of the substitute reading and gives the reading of the copy-text.

A few formal matters have been adjusted without annotation. Turned letters are reversed, characters in the wrong fount are rectified, and 'ʃ' is regularly changed to 's'. Titles are relined and supplied with terminal full stops; the type-style of titles and initial words is normalized; and accidental irregularities in the form and punctuation of stanza numbers, names of speakers, and marginal references are corrected. In printing from manuscripts, interlinear words and superior letters are brought down to the line and frequent contractions such as the following are spelled out: y^r, y^t, y^e, w^t, w^{th}, w^{ch}, ag^t, S^r, $friend^{sp}$, Honble, $fr\bar{o}$, $acct$, $\&$, and q (for *que*).

Every copy-text has been compared with all other texts referred to in the heading of the commentary, but only the texts listed as 'Collated' are reported in the critical apparatus. This list has in each case been restricted to those manuscripts and publications that may possibly have some textual authority. We always collate all the manuscripts in the Welbeck, Longleat, and Miami collections and also those in two volumes at the British Museum—*Lansdowne 852* and *Harley 7316*—which were owned by Edward Lord Harley and annotated by him. Other manuscript copies are collated only if there is some special reason for doing so. Late miscellany collections are ignored. Although we usually collate any first publication that is not here used as copy-text, we disregard those that are known to be derived from sources available to us for direct collation. For instance, we do not collate the *1907* text of the works published there from the Longleat MSS. All publications that are mere reprints are excluded from the reported collation.

The critical apparatus cites every significant variant in the collated texts, differences in spelling, punctuation, and other formal matters being disregarded unless they affect the meaning. When texts are listed as collated but no variants are given, the texts are in agreement.

Although our collation includes all authoritative manuscript versions, we have not attempted to give in the textual notes full information conce͏rning the steps of composition represented in Prior's rough drafts. Interesting though this might be, even a much more elaborate apparatus than is permissible in this edition would necessarily fail to give an accurate picture of the confused state of these manuscripts with their deletions, substitutions, interlineations, and reordering of lines. Consequently, the footnotes do not cite variants within such *brouillons* except when they are of significance in the determination of the text. In a few instances, readings rejected by Prior while composing his draft are printed in the commentary because they throw light upon the finished work.

All passages from manuscript that are quoted in the commentary have been subjected to the same editorial procedure as the texts of the literary works themselves. Since there is no critical apparatus in the commentary, however, we do not usually attempt there to point out the places at which we have found it necessary to add punctuation, to expand contractions, and to choose between alternative readings.

VII. *Abbreviated References*

(For abbreviations referring to *manuscripts* and to *collected editions* of Prior's works, see Introduction, Sections II and IV)

Bickley — Francis Bickley, *The Life of Matthew Prior*. London: Pitman & Sons, 1914.

Case — Arthur E. Case, *A Bibliography of English Poetical Miscellanies, 1521–1750.* Oxford: The Bibliographical Society, 1935.

Day & Murrie — Cyrus L. Day and Eleanore B. Murrie, *English Song-Books, 1651–1702: A Bibliography.* London: The Bibliographical Society, 1940.

D.N.B. — *The Dictionary of National Biography*, ed. Sir Leslie Stephen and Sir Sidney Lee. London: Oxford University Press, 1921–2.

Dryden — John Dryden, *Works*, in four volumes. London: Jacob Tonson, 1701. (Macdonald 108.) [Quotations from Dryden are from this first folio collection unless otherwise specified.]

Eves — Charles Kenneth Eves, *Matthew Prior: Poet and Diplomatist*. New York: Columbia University Press, 1939.

Ewing, 'Musical Settings' — Majl Ewing, 'Musical settings of Prior's Lyrics in the Eighteenth Century', *E.L.H.*, x (1943), 159–71.

Frey — Engelbert Frey, *Der Einfluss der englischen, französischen, italienischen und lateinischen Literatur auf die Dichtungen Matthew Priors.* Strassburg: Karl J. Trübner, 1915.

Greek Anthology — *The Greek Anthology*, with an English translation by W. R. Paton (The Loeb Classical Library). London: William Heinemann, 1918–27.

Harris, *Dorset*	Brice Harris, *Charles Sackville, Sixth Earl of Dorset, Patron and Poet of the Restoration.* Urbana (Ill.): University of Illinois Press, 1940.
1740 History	*The History of His Own Time. Compiled from the Original Manuscripts Of His late Excellency Matthew Prior Esq*; Revised and Signed by Himself, and Copied fair for the Press by Mr. Adrian Drift, His Executor. [Ed. J. Bancks.] London: Printed for the Editor, 1740. [Published as vol. i of *Miscellaneous Works of His late Excellency Matthew Prior.* . . . London: Printed for the Editor, 1740. And Sold by C. Corbett.]
H.M.C. Bath, iii	Historical Manuscripts Commission, *Calendar of the Manuscripts of the Marquis of Bath. Preserved at Longleat, Wiltshire*, vol. iii (Prior Papers). Hereford: His Majesty's Stationery Office, 1908. [Other volumes issued by the Historical Manuscripts Commission are referred to in the same manner.]
Johnson, *Lives*	Samuel Johnson, *Lives of the English Poets*, ed. G. Birkbeck Hill. Oxford: Clarendon Press, 1905.
Luttrell	Narcissus Luttrell, *A Brief Historical Relation of State Affairs, from September 1678 to April 1714.* Oxford: The University Press, 1857.
Macaulay	Thomas Babington Macaulay, 1st baron, *The History of England, from the Accession of James the Second*, ed. Charles H. Firth. London: Macmillan & Co., 1913–15.
Macdonald	Hugh Macdonald, *John Dryden: A Bibliography of Early Editions and of Drydeniana.* Oxford: Clarendon Press, 1939.
1722 Memoirs	*Some Memoirs of the Life and Publick Employments of Matthew Prior, Esq; with A Copy of his Last Will and Testament.* . . . London: Printed for E. Curll, 1722.
Montaigne	Michel Eyquem de Montaigne, *Les Essais*, ed. Pierre Villey. Paris: F. Alcan, 1930–1.
M.P.	*Modern Philology.*
N. & Q.	*Notes and Queries.*
O.E.D.	*A New English Dictionary on Historical Principles*, ed. Sir James A. H. Murray. Oxford: Clarendon Press, 1888–1933.
Pascal	Blaise Pascal, *Pensées*, ed. Léon Brunschvicg. Paris: Hachette, 1904.
P.O.A.S.	*Poems on Affairs of State.* [Vol. and ed. specified in each reference.]
R.E.S.	*Review of English Studies.*
Strong, *Catalogue*	S. Arthur Strong, *A Catalogue of Letters and Other Historical Documents Exhibited in the Library at Welbeck.* London: J. Murray, 1903.
Swift, *Poems*	Jonathan Swift, *Poems*, ed. Sir Harold Williams. Oxford: Clarendon Press, 1937.
Wickham Legg	L. G. Wickham Legg, *Matthew Prior: A Study of His Public Career and Correspondence.* Cambridge: The University Press, 1921.
Wise, *Catalogue*	Thomas James Wise, *The Ashley Library. A Catalogue of Printed Books, Manuscripts and Autograph Letters.* London: for private circulation, 1922–36.

1685

On the Coronation of the Most August Monarch K. James II. and Queen Mary.

The 23rd. of April, 1685.

I.

NO, 'tis in vain. What Limits can controul
The Rovings of my active Soul?
That Soul that scorns to be to Place confin'd,
But leaves its dull Companion *Earth* behind;
  Whilst *Fancy* with unbounded flight,   5
  Enjoys that Object of Delight,
Which envious distance would conceal from Sight:
   And doth by thought supply
   The weaker Prospect of the Eye,
    Giving *Poets* to partake   10
    (Like those *Deities* they make)
    Of Infinite Ubiquity.

II.

  Thus methinks I see the *Barge*,
Pleas'd with the Sacred weight of its Majestick charge;
  Argo a less Glorious Freight,   15
  From impov'rish'd *Colchos* brought;
The *Cretan* Sea now vanquish'd, must confess
Its Burthen meaner, and its Tryumph less;
Since richer *Thames* doth *James* and *Mary* bear,
HE great as *Jove*, SHE as *Europa* Fair.   20

  They come! Joy doubles Strength to ev'ry *Oar*,
   Ecchoes fill the wondring Shore,
   The Waves with an unusual Pride,
    Pay Homage to the *Lord*

Title: of the ... 1685.] *om. L 28* *23rd edd.: 23th 1685* *1 can*] *shal L 28*
3 that] *which L 28* *4 But*] *And L 28* *8–9*] *om. L 28* *15 Argo ... Freight,*
edd.: Argos ... Freight, 1685: Old Argo with a weight less glorious fraught L 28 *16*
From] *The treasure from L 28* *brought; edd.: brought L 28, 1685* *17 The*
Cretan Sea] *And Hellespont L 28* *18 Its ... its*] *His ... his L 28* *22 Ecchoes*
... wondring] *Resounding Ecchoes ... crowded L 28*

Of our asserted Main,   25
And calmly as they Glide,
Auspiciously afford
An *Omen* of His Reign.

III.

See, Glorious as the *Eastern* Sun,
Our *Monarch* from the Waters rise,   30
Whilst Zealous Crowds, like *Persians* run
To own the Blessing by their Sacrifice.
He comes, Religious Shouts proclaim Him near,
    JAMES and HOSANNA bless the Ear;
      Delighted Heav'n confirms the Joys,   35
And in glad sounds reflects the Image of the Voice.

IV.

Tryumphant *CÆSAR* in less Tryumph rode,
Though from a *Victor* to be made a *God*,
When Captive *Monarchs* trembled by His side,
    And by their shame increas'd His Pride;   40
      No private Sorrows here allay
    The common transports of the day,
    But in each exalted Breast
    (Of Happiness and JAMES possest)
      Is Evidently shown,   45
His People's Blessing's greater than His Own,
And he that gives the *Tryumph*, *Tryumphs* least.

V.

With weaker Shouts did *Israel* Ring,
Less esteem'd the Heavenly Choice,
Less approv'd the *Prophets* Voice   50
That Crown'd their wishes in a King.
    For wandring *Asses* did bestow
On *Saul* that Title to a Throne,
Which Providence to JAMES doth owe
For His Fore-fathers Virtues, and His own.   55

31 Zealous Crowds, like] Crowds like Zealous *L 28*   32 by] of *L 28*   34 the] each
L 28   35 the Joys,] the mighty Joys *L 28*   37 Tryumph] glory *L 28*   38] When
heighten'd from a Victor to a God *L 28*   39 Captive] captiv'd *L 28*   42 the day]
the happy Day *L 28*   48–55] *om. L 28*

VI.

Next, Fancy, to the *Altar* bring,
Second to him we there Adore; the *King*
By the Anointing *Prelate* met,
And Rising, where the mighty Brother Set.
But (Oh,) forbid the *Omen* Heav'n,   60
And Guard the Blessing you have giv'n,
Late He Possest, long may he fill the Throne,
And for the Nations Bliss, defer his own.

To the E of D. upon His Marriage.

THE scorching Dogstar and the Suns fierce ray
Conspir'd with mingl'd flames to vex the day
When by young Damon Lycidas was laid
Beneath a spacious Oaks obliging shade
And thus with harmless strife the emulous Shepherds plaid.   5

DAMON.

Let this bless'd day our fruitless Quarrels end
Soften the Rival to the friend
And make our kindness not our skil contend.

LYCIDAS.

Begin, raise Thou thy tuneful Voice
So may my Muse approve thy happy choice.   10

DAMON.

May Venus so my choice approve
As I begin with mighty things and Love.
When first Heav'ns Eldest offspring Light,
Sprang from the fertile Womb of solid night;
What made the melancholy discord cease   15
And charm'd the warring Elements to peace?

---

56 VI. Next,] V. Now *L 28*   57 him] what *L 28*   61 And Guard] Protect *L 28*
62 Possest] ascends *L 28*   63 *Followed in L 28 by:*
Whilst Marys charms unbend the care
Of that rich load his sacred temples wear
(Herself the brightest Jewel there.)
Title: E of D.] Earl of Dorset '*Contents*' *of L 28*, '*Index*' *of M*   8 contend. *edd.*:
contend *L 28*   10 choice. *edd.*: choice *L 28*

From what great cause what brooding influence came
This well proportion'd frame?
From Thee, blest Queen of Harmony and Love;
Thou greatest pow'r on Earth, thou brightest star above. 20

LYCIDAS.

When Loves great Dictates were obey'd,
And Heav'ns last noblest Master Piece was made
To make the new form'd Monarch truly blest
And in one richer Gift compleat the rest
What secret pow'r unlock'd his pregnant side, 25
To the soft Yoak bow'd his delighted mind
Taught the unpractic'd Lover to be kind
And bless the wound whilst he embrac'd the Bride?
'Twas Thou Almighty King of Heav'n and Love
That Govern'st all below, and blessest all above. 30

DAMON.

'Twas Love subdu'd the noble Daphnis heart
Love gave the welcome happy wound,
And with this triumph all his Conquest crown'd
Whilst Daphnis blest the wound and met the Dart
Pleas'd with the grateful bondage more 35
Then with his early spoyls, and boasted Liberty before.

LYCIDAS.

'Twas Love subdu'd the fair Dorinda's breast
Love to her heart a secret warmth convey'd
With pleasing Pain surpris'd the wond'ring Maid
And kindly for her Joys disturb'd her rest. 40
Whilst Daphnis stronger charms with Love's conspire
To make her own the Diety and fan the growing fire.

DAMON.

But thy rude Music Swain, my ruder Tongue
The glories they shou'd reach wou'd wrong,
For Daphnis Love 45
Shou'd only prove
The Theam of Daphnis' Song.

28 Bride? *edd.*: Bride *L 28*   30 blessest *edd.*: blesse'st *L 28*   42 fire. *edd.*: fire *L 28*

LYCIDAS.

Nor can the Joys of Angells be exprest.
Nor know we ought of Heav'n above yon Skies
Which yet we bless with Pray'rs and please with Sacrifice.   50

DAMON.

Lett's then the hasty Sun arrest
Time will stay till they are blest;

LYCIDAS.

Nay rather blame the Suns too hasty flight
Bid him withdraw his tedious light
And kindly send the wish'd for night.   55

DAMON.

May Daphnis wound her with a Cure,

LYCIDAS.

And may Dorinda's flames endure
Like Vesta's fires..............

DAMON.

............for these like them are pure.

LYCIDAS.

Let Heaven its utmost Care employ   60
To make Their life but one continu'd Joy.

DAMON.

Let Nature all her Tribute bring
To make their Year but one continu'd Spring,

LYCIDAS.

With softest Violetts strow her bed,

DAMON.

With freshest Myrtill crown his head.   65

55 wish'd *edd.*: wish *L 28*, *M*   night. *M*: night *L 28*   56 Cure *M*: lure *or* Cure(?)
L 28   59 pure. *edd.*: pure *L 28*, *M*   60 utmost] uttermost *M*   61 Joy. *edd.*:
Joy *L 28*, *M*   63 Spring, *edd.*: Spring *L 28*, *M*

LYCIDAS.

With Hymens Tree Apollo's joyn,
And round his brow their mingl'd honors twine;
Their mingl'd honors sure to him are due
Who with the Nymph has gain'd the Lawrel too.

DAMON.

The Joys of Harvest crown their Cares,   70
And stil encrease their Plenty with their Years.

LYCIDAS.

The Joys of Vintage swell their Bowers,
And if they overflow, o'erflow on Ours:

DAMON.

Fly swift the smiling Hours, let each glad Morn
The fruitful pleasures of the last return.   75

LYCIDAS.

Fly smiling Hours, let each succeeding Night
Improve the transports of the first delight.

DAMON.

In glad Procession let each rolling Year
  See the joyful Mother bear
A beauty Second only to her own.   80

LYCIDAS.

Or if the kinder Gods conspire to crown
  Her stronger wishes with a Son
His Parents great Perfections let him share
And prove her beauties, and his Virtue's Heir.

---

67 twine; *edd.*: twine *L 28, M*   70 Cares *L 28 (Pope?) over illegible word, M*   72
The Joys of] The Joys *M (written by D over an erasure)*   73 overflow *L 28 (Pope?)*,
M: o'erflow *L 28 (D)*   77 delight. *edd.*: delight *L 28, M*   84 beauties *L 28 (D)*:
Beauty's *L 28 (Pope?), M*

To the Countess of D....t walking in a Garden.

YES I did stubernly believe
　　The place no added Beauty cou'd receive
'Till bright Dorinda's passing by
Convinc'd my Infidelity.

Where e'er She came new Glories fell　　　　　　5
The dullest Plant grew Sensible
　　Its willing branches every Tree
　　By grateful instinct spread
　　And round the fair Divinity
Cast the glad shade of its protecting head.　　10

The opening Flowers where e'er She went
Diffus'd their tributary scent
Crowding beneath her beauteous feet
　　Officiously they bow'd
With pleas'd Humility to meet　　　　　　　　15
The fresher beauties of their sacred Load.

　　Nature seem'd to serve and woo
As she wou'd make her Queen of Seasons too;
　　The Sun for her prolongu'd the Day
　　Kindly stop'd his setting light.　　　　　20
She went, that only cou'd engage his stay
　　And all was gloomy, all was Night.

Ah shou'd the God returning show
The wonders he has seen below
The amazing Truth his am'rous Sire wou'd move　　25
　　　　Make him confess
　　　　His Thunder less
　　Then are the Shafts of Love.
Descending, his transform'd Divinity
　　He'd to your bosom pour　　　　　　　　30
　　And Poets once might hope to see
　　An other Golden Shower.

Title: D....t] *M* Dorset '*Contents*' *of L 28*　　3 'Till] The *M*　　18 too; *edd.*: too
L 28, M　　20 light. *edd.*: light *L 28, M*　　28 Love. *edd.*: Love *L 28, M*　　29 Descending, *edd.*: Descending *L 28, M*

Advice to the Painter.

On the happy defeat of the Rebels in the West, and the Execution of the late Duke of Monmouth.

— Pictoribus atque Poetis
Quidlibet —

SINCE by just Flames the guilty Piece is Lost,
(The noblest Work thy fruitless Art could boast,)
Imploy thy faithfull Pains a second time,
From the DUKE's ashes raise the KING of LYME
And make thy Fame eternall as his crime.   5

The Land, (if such it may be counted,) draw,
Where Int'rest is Religion; Treason, Law;
Th' ungratefull Land whose treacherous Sons are foes
To the kind Monarchy by which they rose,
And by instinctive hatred dread the Power   10
Joyn'd in our KING, and in their Conquerour;
Amidst the councills of that close Divan,
Draw the misled, aspiring, wretched Man,
His Sword maintaining what his Fraud began.
Draw Treason, Sacrilege, and Julian nigh,   15
(The curst Achitophel's kind Legacy:)
And least their horrid force too weak should prove
Add tempting Woman's more distructive Love.
Give the Ambitious Fair—

*Except as indicated, all texts agree with Rawl. Variants from Rawl that all other texts
have in common are given as found in 1703. Title: the Painter] a Painter Firth 15 & 16,
Sloane, Wood   On the happy] Upon the All others   1 Piece is] Picture's
Wood   3 Imploy] Renew All others   4 KING] Prince All others   5 thy]
his Wood   his] thy Firth 15   6 counted] called Wood   7 Where]
Whose 1703, L 28, Firth 16   Int'rest edd.: Inte'rest Rawl: Interest 1703, L 28,
Firth 15, Sloane, Wood: Intrest Firth 16   8 Th' L 28, Firth 15, Sloane, Wood: The'
Rawl: Th 1703: The Firth 16   ungratefull] ingrateful 1703, Firth 15 & 16, Sloane,
Wood   whose] where Wood   9 the] that Firth 15, Sloane   they] it Wood
10 instinctive] intestine Wood   dread] tread Firth 15   the] that All others   12
councills] Councell Firth 15   that close] this black 1703, L 28, Firth 15 : the black Sloane,
Wood: that black Firth 16   13 Draw] Paint Firth 15, Sloane   misled, aspiring]
aspireing, misled Wood   15 Julian nigh] Perfidy 1703, L 28, Firth 15, Sloane, Wood:
Julian by Firth 16   16 Followed in 1703, by this couplet:*
        Three direful Engins of a Rebel's hate,
        Fit to perform the blackest work of Fate.
*All other texts insert these verses, with the following variants: dreadful Engines Firth 15,
Sloane: Mighty Engins Firth 16: The dreadfull Engine...workes Wood   17 And]
But All others*

All Natures gifts refin'd by subtlest Art,   20
(Too able to betray his easy heart,)
And with worse Charms than Helen's to destroy
That other hope of our mistaken Troy.

The Scene from Dulness and Dutch Plotts bring o'er,
And sett the hopefull Parricide a-shoar,   25
Fraught with the blessings of each boorish friend,
And the kind helps their pray'rs and brandy lend,
With those few crowns—
Some English Jews and some French Christians send.

Next in the blackest Colours paint the Town,   30
For old Hereditary Treasons known,
Whose Infant sons in early mischeifs bred,
Swear to the Cov'nant they can hardly read,
Brought up with too much Charity to hate
Ought but their Pray'r-book and their Magistrate,   35
Here let his gaudy banner be displaid,
Whilst the kind Fools invoke their neighbours aid,
T' adore the Idol which themselves have made,
And Peasants from neglected Plows resort,
To fill his Army, and adorn his Court: 40

Near these exalted on a Drum unbrac'd
Let Heav'ns and James's enemy be plac'd.
The Wretch that hates (like his Arguile) the Crown,
The Wretch that (like our Oates) defames the Gown;
And through the Speaking-trumpet of his Nose   45
Blasphemously Heav'ns sacred Word expose,

---

20 subtlest Art] Subtle Arts *Firth 15*   21 his] that *All others*   22 worse] more
1703, L 28, Firth 15, Sloane   24 Dutch] dull *Firth 15*   27 helps] help *Firth 15*
pray'rs *edd.*: pray'ers *Rawl*: Prayers *Firth 16, Sloane*: Pray'rs *1703, L 28, Firth 15, Wood*
30 the blackest] thy darkest *1703, L 28, Firth 16, Sloane, Wood*: thy blackest *Firth 15*
31 Treasons] Treason *All others*   32 mischeifs] Mischeif *Firth 15, Wood*   33
the] that *Firth 15 & 16, Sloane*   Cov'nant *1703, L 28, Sloane*: Cove'nant *Rawl*:
Covenant *Firth 15 & 16, Wood*   35 Pray'r-book *edd.*: Pray'er-book *Rawl*: Bible *1703,
L 28, Firth 16, Sloane, Wood*: Bibles *Firth 15*   and their] and the *Firth 15*   36 his]
the *All others*   banner] banners *Sloane*   37 Whilst] While *All others*   38 T'
1703, L 28, Sloane, Wood: To' *Rawl*: To *Firth 15 & 16*   the] that *All others*   which]
they *All others*   39 Plows] Fields *1703, L 28, Firth 15, Sloane, Wood*   41 these
exalted] this, erected *1703, L 28, Firth 15, Sloane, Wood*: these erected *Firth 16*   42
Heav'ns *Firth 15*: Heav'ens *Rawl*: Heav'n *L 28*: Heaven's *1703, Sloane*: heaven *Firth 16*:
Heav'n's *Wood*   enemy] Enemyes *Firth 15*   43 his] false *All others*   44 our]
vile *1703, L 28, Firth 15, Sloane, Wood*: vild *Firth 16*   defames] defiles *Firth 15*   46]
Heav'ns sacred Word profanely does expose, *All others*

Bidding the Long-ear'd rout "With one accord
"Stand up, and fight the Battels of the Lord."

Then near the Pageant Prince, (alass! too nigh,)
Draw Gray with a Romantic constancy,   50
"Resolv'd to conquer or resolv'd to—fly."
And let there in his guilty Face appear
The Rebel's malice and the Cowards fear,
That future ages in thy Piece may see,
Not his Wife falser to his bed, then to his party He.   55

Now let the curst Triumvirate prepare
For all the glorious Ills of Horrid war;
Let zealous Lust the dreadfull Work begin,
Back't with a sad variety of Sin,
Let Vice in all its num'rous Shapes be shown,   ⎫ 60
Crimes which to milder Brennus were unknown,   ⎬
And innocent Cromwell would have blusht to own: ⎭
Their Arms from pillag'd Temples let 'em bring,
And rob the Deity to wound the KING.

Excited thus by their Camp-preist's long prayer,   65
Their Countries curses, and their own despair,
Whilst Hell combines with it's black offspring night,
To hide their Treach'ry, or Secure their flight,
The watchfull Troops with cruell hast come on,
Then shout, look terrible, discharge, and run.   70

Fal'n from his short-liv'd power, and flatter'd hopes,
His friends destroy'd by Hunger, Swords or Ropes,

47 Long-ear'd] large-ear'd *1703, L 28*   48 Battels] Battel *All others*   Lord." *edd.*:
Lord. *Rawl, 1703, L 28, Firth 15*: Lord *Firth 16, Sloane*: Lord: *Wood*   49 near] nigh
1703, L 28, Firth 15, Sloane, Wood   50 Draw Gray] Paint *G. 1703, Sloane*: Paint Gray
L 28, Firth 15 & 16, Wood   a Romantic] the old Roman *Sloane, Wood*: his old
Roman *Firth 15*   51 fly." *edd.*: fly. *Rawl, Firth 15*: fly *Firth 16*: Fly; *1703*: Fly *Sloane*:
fly; *L 28, Wood*   54 thy Piece] thy Face *1703, L 28*: this peice *Wood*   55 his
party] all Parties *1703, L 28, Wood, Firth 15*   57 glorious] baneful *1703, L 28, Firth 15,
Sloane, Wood*   Horrid] Rebells *Wood*: Rebell *Firth 15, Sloane*   58 zealous Lust]
zealous Rage *1703, L 28*: rampant Lust *Wood*: Lawless Lust *Firth 15, Sloane*   59 Back't]
Blackt *Firth 16*   a] the *All others*   60 num'rous *edd.*: num'erous *Rawl*: Numer-
ouse *Firth 16*: numerous *1703, L 28, Firth 15, Sloane, Wood*   61 to] to the *Firth 16*
62 innocent *L 28, Firth 15, Wood*: inno'cent *Rawl*: Innocent *1703, Firth 16, Sloane*
blusht] blest *Firth 16*   65 Excited] Erect *Wood*   thus] then *1703, L 28, Firth
15, Sloane, Wood*   their] the *Firth 15, Wood*   66 curses] Cryes *Firth 15*
67 Whilst] While *1703, L 28, Firth 15 & 16, Sloane*   black] vile *1703, L 28*: sad
Firth 15, Sloane, Wood   68 Treach'ry *edd.*: Treache'ry *Rawl*: Treachery *All others*
or] and *Firth 15, Sloane*   69 The] Their *Firth 15, Sloane*   70 shout] shoot *Wood*
72 Swords] Sword *Firth 16*   or] and *All others*

To some near Grove the WESTERN MONARCH flyes,
In vain;—the Grove her innocent Shade denyes,
The juster Trees—   75
Which, when for refuge Charles and Virtue fled,
By gratefull instinct their glad branches spread,
And round the sacred Charge cast their enlarged head,
Soon as the outcast Absolom comes nigh,
Drop off their trembling Leaves, and blasted dye.   80

Not Earth itself would hide her guilty Son,
Thô he for refuge to her bowells run:
Seditious Corah to her arms she took,
When angry Heav'n his *good old cause* forsook,
But now provok't with a more just disdain   85
She shrinks her frighted Head, and gives our Rebell back again.

Now, Artist, let thy juster Pencil draw
The sad effects of necessary Law,
In painted Words and speaking Colours tell
How the great, pittied, stubborn Traytour fell.   90
On the sad Scene the glorious Rebel place,
His Pride and Sorrow strug'ling in his face;
Describe the labours of his tortur'd Breast,
(If by thy Imag'ry thought can be exprest,)
Show with what diff'rence Two vast passions move,   95
And how the Heroe with the Christian strove:

Then draw the sacred Prelate by his side,
To raise his sorrow and confound his pride,
With the dear dreadfull thought of a God crucified.

---

74 Grove her innocent] innocent Grove her *All others*   76 Which,] Who *All others*
78 the] their *Wood*   enlarged] sacred *Wood*   79 Soon as] Straight when *All others*   comes] was *Firth 15, Sloane*   80 trembling] fading *All others*   81 Not] Nor *1703, L 28*   itself] her self *1703, L 28, Firth 15, Wood*   would] will *All others*   83 Seditious] Rebellious *1703, L 28, Firth 15 & 16, Sloane*: Rebelling *Wood*   arms] Arm *1703*   84 angry...good] Heav'n, and *Israel* his *All others* 85 with] by *All others*   86 shrinks] shrunck *Firth 16*   89 tell] Show *Firth 15, Sloane*   90] The dismal Exit this sham Prince befel; *1703, L 28, Wood*: This Tragedies last Act the fatal Blow, *Firth 15, Sloane*: How the great Stuborne pityed Traytor fell. *Firth 16* 92 His] With *All others*   93 labours . . . tortur'd] Pangs . . . distracted *All others* 94 Imag'ry] Labours *1703, L 28, Firth 15 & 16, Sloane*: colours *Wood*   95 diff'rence *edd.*: diffe'rence *Rawl*: difference *1703, L 28, Firth 15, Sloane, Wood*: differance *Firth 16* vast] strong *Firth 15, Sloane, Wood*   97 draw] place *All others*   Prelate] Prelates *Firth 15, Sloane*   98 confound] depress *Firth 15, Sloane*   99 thought] Thoughts *1703, L 28, Firth 15, Wood*

Paint (if thou can'st) the powerfull Words which hung,   } 100
Upon the holy Man's persuasive Tongue,
Words sweet as Moses writ, or Asaph sung,   }
Words whose prevailing Influ'nce might have won
All but the haughty, hard'ned Absolon.

At distance, round the weeping Mother, place   105
The too unmindfull Father's beuteous race,
But (like the Grecian Artist) spread a vail,
O'er the sad Beuties of fair Annabel,
No Art, no Muse those sorrows can express
Which would be render'd by Description less.   110

Now close the dismal Scene, conceal the rest—
—That the sad Orphan's Eyes can teach us best,
Thy guilty Art might raise our ill-plac'd grief too high
And make us whilst We pitty Him, forgett our Loyalty.

To the Lord Bishop of Rochester,

on His History of the Plot written by His late Majesties command. And an Apologie for these Verses call'd the Advice to a Painter, by the same Author.

My Lord,

WITH humble hope your goodness will excuse
The hasty zeal of an aspiring Muse;
I with unequal pace your steps persue,
And thought I trod securely following you,
Repenting now, like *Phaeton*, too late   } 5
I feebly sink beneath the Glorious weight.
And own the work for all but you too great: }

100 powerfull Words which] Heavenly Words that *1703*, *L 28*, *Firth 16*, *Sloane*, *Wood*: Heavenly work that *Firth 15*   101 the] each *Firth 15*   Man's] Mens *1703*, *Sloane* 102 writ] wrote *Firth 15*, *Sloane*, *Wood*: wrott *Firth 16*   103 Influ'nce *edd.*: Influ'ence *Rawl*: Influence *1703*, *L 28*, *Firth 15 & 16*, *Wood*: Infleuence *Sloane*   105 the] their *All others*   108 O'er] On *Firth 15*   111 Now] Here *All others*   conceal] disclose *Firth 15*   112 can] will *All others*   113 ill-plac'd] ill-tim'd *1703*, *L 28*, *Firth 16*, *Wood*: ill tun'd *Firth 15*, *Sloane*   114 whilst] while *All others*
     Title] To the B. of R. Upon His Account of the Whiggish Conspircy by His late Majesty's order. *L 28*   1 hope] Hopes *L 28*   3 pace your steps] steps Your pace *L 28*   7 own] find *L 28*

The hand that rivall'd Heaven took thence its fire
Er'e he the sensless Machin cou'd inspire;
And the rash Author wou'd attempt in vain,   10
Unless he borrow'd your diviner Pen;
To imitate or praise with equal flight
What only *Charles* cou'd Dictate, only you cou'd Write.

  If trouble past by repetition please,
Thô meaner tongues the grateful tale reherse,   15
What mighty Raptures must these Ills create,
Which bravely, as he conquer'd, you relate;
Our joys without our sufferings had been less,
And for the remedy, the wound we bless.
So did not *Catilines* defeated rage   20
Your much-lov'd *Tullies* daring Pen engage,
His Rome wou'd want one Glory of his tongue,
The World a Master-peece, and Fame a Song.

Not Writing to K. P.

S o from Divinity and things above
  The Zealots thoughts have sometimes chanc'd to rove
'Till on his life he does with grief reflect,
Compares Heav'ns goodness with his own neglect,
Abhors his crime and vows he'l now begin   5
With double Penitence to clear his Sin.
Then sighing trembling doubting he draws near,
His Piety stil vanquish'd by his fear,
Till Heav'n beholds and Pittys what he feels
And with glad Omens his wish'd Pardon Seals   10
Pleas'd with the truth of his repentence more
Then with his constant Pray'rs and drudging Zeal before.

14 trouble] Troubles *L 28*   15 the...reherse,] Your...express *L 28*   16
mighty...these] Joys, what...those *L 28*   19 the remedy,] Your Remedy *L 28*
   Title] Not writing to Katharine Prior '*Contents*' *of L 28*   3 reflect, *edd.*: reflect *L 28*
4 neglect, *edd.*: neglect. *L 28*   6 Sin. *edd.*: Sin *L 28*   7 near, *edd.*: near *L 28*
8 fear, *edd.*: fear. *L 28*

To the right Reverend Father in God Francis Lord Bishop of Ely. &c.

On his Lordship's departure from Cambridge soon after I had the Honour to be made known to Him.

Damon: TELL, dear Alexis, tell thy Damon why
    Dost Thou in mournfull Shades obscurely lye?
   Why dost Thou sigh? why strike thy panting breast?
   And steal from life the needfull Hour's of rest?
   Are thy Kidds starv'd by Winter's early frost?   5
   Are any of thy bleating Stragglers lost?
   Have strangers Cattle trod thy new-plow'd ground?
  Has great Joanna, or her greater Shepheard frown'd?

Alexis: See! my Kidds browse; my Lambs securely play;
   (Ah! were their Master unconcern'd, as They!)   10
   No beasts (at Noon I look't) had trod my ground;
   Nor has Joanna or Her Shepheard frown'd.

Damon: Then stop the lavish fountain of your Eyes,
   Nor let those sighs from your swoln bosom rise,
   Chase Sadness, Friend, and Solitude away,   15
  And once again rejoice, and once again look Gay.

Alexis: Say what can more our tortur'd Souls annoy,
   Than to behold, admire, and lose our Joy?
   Whose Fate more hard then those who sadly run
   For the last Glimps of the departing Sun?   20
   Or what Severer Sentence can be given,
   Then having Seen, to be excluded Heaven?

Damon: None Shepheard none—[Alexis:] Then ceace to chide my cares,
   And rather pitty then restrain my Tears;
   Those Tears, my Damon, which I justly Shed,   25
   To think how great my Joys, how soon they fled.
   I told Thee, Friend, (now bless the Shepheards name
   From whose dear Care the kind occasion came)

Title] The First Copy to My Lord of Ely. *L 28* 4 Hour's] hour *L 28* 5 Winter's early] rig'rous Winters *L 28* 11 (at...look't) *edd.*: [at...look't] *Rawl*: (at...look'd) *L 28* 12 Her Shepheard] her greater Shepherd *L 28* 13 Eyes,] Tears *L 28* 14 those] these *L 28* rise, *L 28*: rise *Rawl* 17 Souls] Soul *L 28* 19–20] *om. L 28* 21 Or] Say, *L 28* 23 Then *L 28*: then *Rawl*

That I, ev'n I, might happily receive,
The sacred Wealth which Heav'n and Daphnis give.   30
That I might See the lovely awfull Swain
Whose holy Crosier guides our willing plain:
Whose pleasing Pow'r, and ruling goodness keep
Our Souls, with equal care as We our Sheep.
Whose Praise excites each Lyre, employes each Tongue   35
Whilst only he that caus'd dislikes the Song.
To this Great, Humble, parting Man I gain'd
Access, and happy for an Hour I reign'd.
Happy, as new form'd Man in Paradice,
'Ere Sin debaucht his inoffensive bliss: 40
Happy as Heroes after Battells won;
Prophets entranc't; or Monarchs on the Throne—
—But (oh!, my Freind,) those Joys with Daphnis flew,
To them these tributary Tears are due.
Damon: Was He soe Humble then? those Joys soe vast?   45
Cease to admire that both so quickly past.
Too happy should We be would smiling Fate
Render one blessing durable and great:
But (oh! the sad vicissitude), how soon
Unwelcome night succeeds the cheerfull Noon!   50
And rigid Winter nips the flowry pomp of June!
Then greive not, Friend, like Thee Since all mankind,
A certain change of Joy and Sorrows find.
Suppress thy sighs, thy down-cast Eye-lids raise,
Whom present thou ador'dst, him Absent praise.   55

---

29 ev'n *edd.*: eve'n *Rawl*: even *L 28*   30 Heav'n *L 28*: Heave'n *Rawl*   33 Pow'r *edd.*: Pow'er *Rawl*: pow'r *L 28*   35 Tongue *L 28*: Tong. *Rawl*   42 the] their *L 28*   43] But Daphnis, Friend, and happyness are fled *L 28*   44 are due] I shed *L 28*   45 He . . . then?] Daphnis then so kind, *L 28*   49 oh] ah *L 28* 54 *Preceded in L 28 by:*

Come, give thy anxious Soul its wonted Peace
And from this Hour let all sad troubles cease

thy sighs, thy] thy Sighs, those *L 28*   55 thou ador'dst, *edd.*: thou ador'dst *Rawl*: Thou adore'dst *L 28*

To Madam K: P.

A Pastoral Dialogue.

DAMON.

SEE Strephon see what a refulgent ray
Dispells yon Clouds, and gilds the rising day
The smiling Feilds their early Treasures bring
And warbling Birds proclaim the coming spring
Young tender Plants and swelling buds appear   5
Whilst Nature smiling seems to bless the Year.
Lively the Nymphs and sportive are their Swains,
All Sorrows Banish'd from the cheerful Plains
Save only what Thy troubl'd Soul contains.
Then tell me Strephon, prythee tell me why   10
Dost Thou in mournful shades obscurely lye?
Why dost Thou sigh, why strike Thy panting breast
And steal from life the needful hours of rest?
Are thy Kids starv'd by rig'rous Winter's frost?
Are any of thy bleating straglers lost?   15
Have Strangers Cattle trod thy new Plow'd ground
Or (what is worst) has great JOANNA frown'd?

STREPHON.

ON yonder Hills my bleating straglers play
(Ah! were their Master unconcern'd as they)
No beasts (at Noon I look'd) had trod my ground   20
Nor have I lost my Kids, nor has Joanna frown'd.

DAMON.

THEN stop the lavish fountains of your Eyes
Nor let those Sighs from your swoln bosom rise,
Send all these melancholy thoughts away
And once again rejoice, and once again look gay.   25

STREPHON.

AH Damon what can add to Sorrows more
Then thoughts of happyness enjoy'd before?

Title] To Madam Katharine Prior. A Pastoral 'Contents' of L 28   6 Year. edd.: Year
L 28   7 Swains, edd.: Swains L 28   9 contains. edd.: contains L 28   17
frown'd? edd.: frown'd. L 28

What more disturbs the slighted Lovers breast
Then sad remembrance how he has been bless'd
What kind reception once his Passion found   30
And how he flourish'd e'er his fair one frown'd?
What more the wretched Exil's soul annoys
Then recollection of his former Joys?
Or what severer Sentence can be giv'n
Then having seen, to be excluded Heav'n?   35

DAMON.

NONE Shephard None——

STREPHON.

——then cease to chide my Cares
And rather pitty then restrain my Tears,
Those tears, my Damon, which I justly shed
To think how great my Joys, how soon they fled;   40
I told thee, Friend (when I forsook those Sheep
Which Thou the while with equal care didst keep)
That I wou'd visit fair Celinda's Shrine,
And pay those Vows which gratitude enjoyn.
Since then how happy did thy Strephon live.   45
Happy........
In all kind Heav'n or kinder She cou'd give
Happy as new form'd Man in Paradice
E'er Sin debauch'd his inoffensive bliss
Happy as Heroes after Battles won,   50
Prophets entranc'd or Monarchs on their Throne.
Then chide not if I sometimes drop a Tear
When I remember how I triumph'd there
And with past pleasures present woes compare.

DAMON.

BUT were those pleasures so extremely vast?   55
Wonder not then that they so quickly past.
Too happy shou'd we be wou'd smiling Fate
Render one blessing durable and great.

31 frown'd? *edd.*: frown'd *L 28*   35 seen,...Heav'n? *edd.*: seen...Heav'n. *L 28*
41 thee *edd.*: the *L 28*   44 enjoyn. *edd.*: enjoyn *L 28*   50 won, *edd.*: won *L 28*
58 great. *edd.*: great *L 28*

917.27   C

But (Ah! the sad Vicisitude) how soon
Unwelcome Night succeeds the chearful Noon   60
And rigid Winter nips the flow'ry pomp of June.
Then grieve not Friend, like Thee since all Mankind
A certain change of Joy and sorrows find
Come give thy anxious Soul its wonted peace
And from this Hour let all sad troubles cease;   65
Suppress thy Sighs, those down cast Eyelids raise,
Tune thy neglected Harp, and sing the Goddess' praise.

To the Reverend Father in God Francis,
Lord Bishop of Ely &c.

I F Poets, e're they cloath'd their infant Thought,
   And the rude Work to just perfection brought,
Did still some God or Godlike Man invoke,
Whose mighty Name their sacred Silence broke;
Your Goodness, Sir, will easily excuse   5
The bold requests of an aspiring Muse;
Who with your blessing would Your Aid implore
And in her weakness justifie Your Power:
From Your fair Pattern, Sir, she strives to write,
And, with unequall Strength, pursues your flight   10
Yet hopes She ne'r can Err that follows You,
Led by Your blest Commands, and great Example too:
Then Smiling an aspiring Influ'nce give,
And make the Muse and her Endeavours live;
Claim all her future Labours as Your due,   15
Let every Song begin and end with You;
So to the blest retreat She'l gladly goe,
Where the Saints Palm, and Muses lawrell grow;
Where kindly Both in glad embraces joyn'd,
And round Your Brow their mingled Honours twin'd;   20

---

62 Thee *edd.*: The *L 28*   65 cease; *edd.*: cease *L 28*   66 raise, *edd.*: raise *L 28*
    Title] To my Lord of Ely at Christmas. *L 28*   9 strives] learnt *L 28*   11 Yet
hopes...follows] And sure...Follow *L 28*   12 Commands,] command *L 28*   13
Influ'nce *edd.*: Influe'nce *Rawl*: influence *L 28*   14 And] To *L 28*   17 the] that
L 28   18 and] the *L 28*   19 kindly...in] closely...with *L 28*   20 twin'd; *edd.*:
twin'd *Rawl L 28*

Both to the Virtue due which could excell
As much in Writing as in Living Well:
So shall she proudly press the tunefull string,
And mighty Things in mighty Numbers sing;
Nor doubt to strike Prudentius' daring Lyre,   25
And humbly bring the Verse which You inspire.

A Satyr on the modern Translators.

Odi imitatores servum pecus, &c.

SINCE the united cunning of the Stage,
Has balk'd the hireling Drudges of the Age:
Since *Betterton* of late so thrifty's grown,
Revives old Plays, or wisely acts his own:
Thum'd *Rider* with a Catalogue of Rhimes,   5
Makes the compleatest Poet of our Times:
Those who with nine months toil had spoil'd a Play,
In hopes of Eating at a full Third day,
Justly despairing longer to sustain
A craving Stomach from an empty Brain,   10
Have left Stage-practice, chang'd their old Vocations,
Atoning for bad Plays, with worse Translations,
And like old *Sternhold* with laborious spite,
Burlesque what nobler Muses better write:
Thus while they for their Causes only seem   15
To change the Channel, they corrupt the Stream.
So breaking *Vintners* to increase their Wine,
With nauseous Drugs debauch the generous Vine:
So barren *Gipsies* for recruit are said,
With Strangers Issue to maintain the Trade;   20
But lest the fair Bantling should be known,
A daubing Walnut makes him all their own.
    In the head of this Gang too *John Dryden* appears,
But to save the Town-censure and lessen his Fears,
Join'd with a Spark whose Title makes me civil,   25
For *Scandalum Magnatum* is the Devil:

21 the ... which] Your ... that *L 28*   26 humbly ... Verse] bring the sacred Song *L 28*
    Title] om. *Sloane*   3 thrifty's] thrifty *Sloane*   15 while ... Causes] whilst for their
excuse they *Sloane*   21 the fair] the fairer [the *blotted*] *Sloane*   24 Town-censure]
towns Censure, *Sloane*   25 a] the *Sloane*

Such mighty Thoughts from *Ovid*'s Letters flow,
That the Translation is a work for two;
Who in one Copy joyn'd their shame have shewn,
Since *T—e* could spoil so many, though alone: 30
My Lord I thought so generous would prove,
To scorn a Rival in affairs of Love:
But well he knew his teeming pangs were vain,
Till Midwife *Dryden* eas'd his labouring Brain;
And that when part of *Hudibras*'s Horse   35
Jogg'd on, the other would not hang an Arse;
So when fleet *Jowler* hears the joyfull halloo,
He drags his sluggish Mate, and *Tray* must follow.
But how could this learn'd brace employ their time?
One construed sure, while th'other pump'd for Rhime: 40
Or it with these, as once at *Rome*, succeeds,
The *Bibulus* subscribes to *Cæsar*'s Deeds:
This, from his Partners Acts, ensures his Name,
Oh sacred thirst of everlasting Fame!
That could defile those well cut Nails with Ink,   45
And make his Honour condescend to think:
But what Excuse, what Preface can atone,
For Crimes which guilty *Bayes* has singly done?
Bayes, whom *Rose Alley* Ambuscade injoyn'd,
To be to Vices which he practic'd kind,   50
And brought the venome of a spitefull *Satyr*,
To the safe innocence of a *dull Translator*.
Bayes, who by all the Club was thought most fit ⎫
To violate the *Mantuan Prophet*'s wit,   ⎬
And more debauch what loose *Lucretius* writ.   ⎭ 55
When I behold the rovings of his Muse,   ⎫
How soon *Assyrian* Ointments she would lose   ⎬
For Diamond Buckles sparkling at their Shoes.   ⎭
When *Virgil*'s height is lost, when *Ovid* soars, ⎫
And in Heroics *Canace* deplores   ⎬ 60
Her Follies, louder than her Father roars,   ⎭

27 mighty] wieghty *Sloane*   28 the Translation] to translate 'em *Sloane*   30
T—e] Tate *Sloane*   36 other would] tother coud *Sloane*   37 *Jowler*] Fowler
Sloane   40 while th'other] whilst tother *Sloane*   49 whom *Sloane*: whose *1697*
Alley] alleys *Sloane*   52 a] *om. Sloane*   57 Ointments] *oyntment Sloane*   would]
coud *Sloane*

I'd let him take *Almanzor* for his Theme;
In lofty Verse make *Maximin* blaspheme,
Or sing in softer Airs St. *Katharine*'s Dream.
Nay, I could hear him damn last Ages Wit,   65
And rail at Excellence he ne'er can hit;
His Envy shou'd at powerfull *Cowley* rage,
And banish Sense with *Johnson* from the Stage:
His Sacrilege should plunder *Shakespear*'s Urn,
With a dull Prologue make the Ghost return   70
To bear a second Death, and greater pain,
While the Fiend's words the Oracle prophane;
But when not satisfy'd with Spoils at home,
The Pyrate wou'd to foreign Borders roam;
May he still split on some unlucky Coast,   75
And have his Works, or Dictionary lost;
That he may know what *Roman* Authors mean,
No more than does our blind Translatress *Behn*.
     The Female Wit, who next convicted stands,
Not for abusing *Ovid*'s Verse but *Sand*'s: 80
She might have learn'd from the ill borrow'd Grace,
(Which little helps the ruine of her Face)
That Wit, like Beauty, triumphs o're the Heart,
When more of Nature's seen and less of Art:
Nor strive in *Ovid*'s Letters to have shown,   85
As much of Skill, as Lewdness in her own:
Then let her from the next inconstant Lover,
Take a new Copy for a second Rover:
Describe the cunning of a Jilting Whore,
From the ill Arts her self has us'd before;   90
Thus let her write, but Paraphrase no more.
     R—*mer* to *Crambo* privilege does claim,
Not from the Poet's Genius, but his Name;
Which Providence in contradiction meant,
Though he Predestination cou'd prevent,   95
And with bold dulness translate Heavens intent.
Rash Man! we paid thee Adoration due,
That ancient Criticks were excell'd by you:

---

63 Verse *edd.*: Verses *1697*: vers, *Sloane*   72 While] whilst *Sloane*   80 Not *Sloane*:
Nor *1697*   82 ruine] ruins *Sloane*   92 R—*mer*] Rymer *Sloane*   96 translate]
frustrate *Sloane*

Each little Wit to your Tribunal came
To hear their doom, and to secure their Fame: 100
But for Respect you servilely sought Praise,
Slighted the Umpire's Palm to court the Poet's Bayes;
While wise Reflexions and a grave Discourse,
Declin'd to Zoons a River for a Horse.
So discontented *Pemberton* withdrew,   105
From sleeping Judges to the noisie Crew;
Chang'd awefull Ermin for a servile Gown,
And to an humble fawning smooth'd his frown:
The *Simile* will differ here indeed;
You cannot versify, though he can plead.   110

To painfull *Creech* my last Advice descends,
That he and Learning would at length be Friends;
That he'd command his dreadfull Forces home,
Not be a second *Hannibal* to *Rome*.
But since no Counsel his Resolves can bow,   115
Nor may thy fate, O *Rome*, resist his Vow;
Debarr'd from Pens as Lunaticks from Swords,
He shou'd be kept from waging war with Words.
Words which at first like Atoms did advance,
To the just measure of a tunefull Dance,   120
And jumpt to Form, as did his Worlds, by chance.
This pleas'd the Genius of the vicious Town;
The Wits confirm'd his Labours with renown,
And swore the early Atheist for their own.
Had he stopt here—— But ruin'd by Success,   125
With a new Spawn he fill'd the burthen'd Press,
Till, as his Volumes swell'd, his Fame grew less.
So Merchants flattered with increasing Gain,
Still tempt the falshood of the doubtfull Main;
So the first running of the lucky Dice,   130
Does eager Bully to new Bets intice;
Till Fortune urges him to be undone,
And *Ames-Ace* loses what kind *Sixes* wone.

---

100 and] or *Sloane*   102 court] catch *Sloane*   103 While] whilst *Sloane*   104
Declin'd] descend *Sloane*   106 sleeping] *Sloane* ye grave *Alt. reading in Sloane*
114 Not] nor *Sloane*   120 measure] measures *Sloane*   124 swore *Sloane*: swear
1697   125 Success *edd.*: Succcss *1697*: success *Sloane*   126 fill'd] fills *Sloane*

Witness this Truth *Lucretia*'s wretched Fate,
Which better have I heard my Nurse relate;   135
The Matron suffers violence again,
Not *Tarquin*'s Lust so vile as *Creech*'s Pen;
Witness those heaps his Midnight Studies raise,
Hoping to rival *Ogilby* in Praise:
Both writ so much, so ill, a doubt might rise,   140
Which with most Justice might deserve the Prize;
Had not the first the Town with Cutts appeas'd,
And where the Poem fail'd the Picture pleas'd.

   Wits of a meaner rank I wou'd rehearse,
But will not plague your Patience nor my Verse: 145
In long oblivion may they happy lie,
And with their Writings may their Folly die.
Now why should we poor *Ovid* yet pursue,
And make his very Book an Exile too,
In words more barbarous than the place he knew?   150
If *Virgil* labour'd not to be translated,
Why suffers he the only thing he hated?
Had he foreseen some ill officious Tongue,
Wou'd in unequal Strains blaspheme his Song;
Nor Prayers, nor Force, nor Fame shou'd e'er prevent   155
The just Performance of his wise intent:
Smiling he'd seen his martyr'd Work expire,
Nor live to feel more cruel Foes than Fire.

   Some Fop in Preface may those Thefts excuse,
That *Virgil* was the draught of *Homer*'s Muse: 160
That *Horace*'s by *Pindar*'s Lyre was strung,
By the great Image of whose Voice he sung;
They found the Mass, 'tis true, but in their Mould
They purg'd the drossy Oar to current Gold:
Mending their Pattern, they escap'd the Curse,   165
Yet had *they* not writ better, they'd writ worse.
But when we bind the Lyric up to rhime,
And lose the Sense to make the Poem chime:
When from their Flocks we force *Sicilian* Swains,
To ravish Milk-maids in our *English* Plains;   170

137 *Creech*'s *edd.*: *Chreech*'s *1697*: Creech's *Sloane*   142 the Town with Cutts] with
Cuts the town *Sloane*   144 wou'd] coud *Sloane*   147 Folly] follyes *Sloane*   157
he'd *Sloane*: h'had *1697*   170 in] on *Sloane*

And wandring Authors, e'er they touch our shore,
Must, like our Locust *Hugonots*, be poor.
I'de bid th'importing Club their pains forbear,
And traffick in our own, tho' homely ware,
Whilst from themselves the honest Vermin spin,   175
I'de like the Texture, tho' the Web be thin;
Nay, take *Crown*'s Plays, because his own, for wit;
And praise what *D'urfey*, not translating, writ.

1686

A Hymn to the Spring.

I.

FAIREST Child of flowing time,
   Earths refreshment, Heav'ns delight,
Beauties honor, Natures Prime
Joy of our Soul, and glory of our sight!
   O bridle in the posting hours;   5
      Thy too precipitated course restrain,
   Cast out thy blossoms, spread thy flow'rs,
Augment our pleasure, and prolong thy reign.
      For t'were impiety to wish Thee gone,
Tho Summer next and all her fruits come on.   10

II.

   All, thy absent Deity
   With repeated Pray'rs implore;
   All rejoice, thy Presence nigh,
Behold thy Miracles, and bless thy Pow'r.
      The Farmer from thy looks receives   15
   The blooming promise of a fruitful Year:
      The Lover from thy bounty weaves
An early Honor for his Mistress' hair:

173 their *Sloane*: thier *1697*
   Title] *M* A Song in praise of the Spring *B.M.*   4 of our Soul,] *M om. B.M.*   5
the] thy *M, B.M.*   6 precipitated] *M* swift flying *B.M.*   7 Cast out] *M* Protect
B.M.   8 our pleasure, and] *M* and still *B.M.*   9 t'were impiety to] *M* oh we
cannot *B.M.*   10 next and all] *M* with *B.M.*   11–30] *M om. B.M.*

The sullen Warrior smiles, to see thee spread
The future Pride of his ennobled head.   20

III.

Senseless as the Year we lye,
'Till kind spring's enlivening fires
Wakens our activity,
Improves our Joys, and heightens our desires.
     For thee ev'n Venus we'l despise   25
Thou brighter Queen of Harmony and Love!
     And Thee too born above the skies
     Without a fictious Metaphor we'l prove:
For what is Heav'n but bright recesses, where
A constant Spring inriches all the Year?   30

1687

To the E of D. on the Birth of His Son.

I.

WAKE Goddess wake Thy drousy Lyre
     Let the neglected Chords to louder Strains be strung,
And raise Thy voice, and swell thy numbers higher,
     No common Theme requires Thy Song.
For loe! from old Eternities glad Womb   5
The promis'd day, the glorious Birth is come:
'Tis come; the noble Babe securely lies
On his fair Mothers joyful breast;
(Happy his Age whose Infancy enjoys
A Seat of Plenty and a Heav'n of rest.)   10
But, Oh! what Clouds of glory, clouds of light
Too strong for feeble Mans external Eye
Roll round the noble Babe, and mock my drowned Sight:
     That Light, that glory I wou'd see;
     Hear, Goddess, hear thy Votary: 15

24 heightens] heighten *M*
  Title] To the Earl of Dorset on his Birth Day '*Contents*' *of L 28*   15 Votary: *edd.*:
Votary *L 28*

The meanest of thy Sons inspire
Come to my breast, and with Thy pow'rful ray
Drive dimm Humanity away
Wake, Goddess, wake thy Lyre.

II.

Hark the quicken'd Lyre awakes,   20
Each willing string melodious tremblings makes:
        And see! the appeas'd Air, and opening sky
        Proclaim the Goddess nigh.
She's here, I feel the generous rage within
        Enliven each extended vein.   25
I feel the kind the cruel Goddess roll
All through each part of my exalted Soul
And prest with Joy and pain'd with extacy
        Loe! what mighty things I see.

III.

Mid'st a fair Troop of smiling Deities: 30
Grave Janus with Majestic pace draws near
The sacred place where the blest Infant lies.
Janus with pleasing Care and easy Joy
        Does all his happy Eyes imploy
        The lovely Babe to view   35
Employs 'em all, and thinks them all too few.
        Pleas'd and ravish'd with the sight
He wings the coming Hours with new delight
        No more looks backward now, but here
From this blest Birth dates the enobl'd Year.   40

IV.

Jocund Hymen next appears
His fragrant head with chearful joy he rears
        With freshest wreaths his hair was bound
        With brightest flames his torch was crown'd.
Onward he came and coming smil'd   45
And saw and kist and blest the happy Child

20 awakes, *edd.*: awaks(?) *L 28*   32 lies. *edd.*: lies *L 28*   44 crown'd. *edd.*:
crown'd *L 28*

He saw and kist and blest, and laugh'd aloud
  Whilst all the little lovely crowd
  Who with officious Joy stood hov'ring by
Laugh'd aloud with Him, and blest the Augury.   50

v.

  Wanton and gay came Venus by
    Venus saw Dorinda's Son
    Smil'd and took him for her own
And much She wou'd have said of flames and darts
  Of sighing Maids and yeilding hearts   55
  But Pallas with majestic gravity
Reprov'd the light discourse, and Know, she crys,
This Child is born to nobler Victories:
Arms and the dusky field shal be his care
'Tis he shal lead the gen'rous Britain forth   60
  To hazardous encounter and hard war,
He shal renew his fam'd forefathers worth
  And bid the wond'ring Soldier imitate
    His Virtue and be great.
She said, and reverently low deprest   65
Her armed head down to the Lovely Child;
The lovely Child with Ominous gallantry
Threw his young Arms around her glittring Crest
  And claspt it to him close and smil'd
Whilst all the greater Gods that waited by   70
Bow'd to the Babe, and blest the Augury.

With mild Magnificence and humble State
  See Jove Himself vouchsafes to wait.

---

57 Know, she crys, *edd.*: know she crys *L 28*   58 Victories: *edd.*: Victories *L 28*
60 gen'rous *edd.*: gene'rous *L 28*   61 war, *edd.*: war *L 28*   66 Child; *edd.*:
Child *L 28*

Satyr on the Poets.

In Imitation of the Seventh Satyr of Juvenal.

Et Spes, & Ratio Studiorum, &c.

ALL my Endeavours, all my Hopes depend
  On you, the Orphans, and the Muses Friend:
The only great good Man, who will declare
Virtue, and Verse the Objects of your care,
And prove a Patron in the worst of times: 5
When Hungry *Bayes* forsakes his empty Rhymes,
Beseeching all true Catholicks Charity
For a poor Proselyte, that long did lye
Under the Mortal Sins of Verse and Heresie.

    Shadwell and starving *Tate* I scorn to Name;   10
Poets of all Religions are the same:
Recanting *Settle*, brings the tuneful Ware,
Which wiser *Smithfield* damn'd to *Sturbridge* Fair:
Protests his Tragedies and Lybels fail
To yield him Paper, penny Loaves and Ale;   15
And bids our Youth, by his Example fly
The love of Politicks, and Poetry.
And all Retreats, except *Newhall*, refuse
To shelter starving *Durfey*'s Jocky Muse:
There to the Butler, and her Graces Maid,   20
He turns like *Homer*, Sonnettier for Bread:
Knows his just Bounds; nor ever durst aspire
Beyond the swearing Grooms, and Kitchin Fire.

Title] A Satyr upon the Poets, being a Translation out of ... *Juvenal. 1703*: A Satyr
against *Poetry. In a Letter to the Lord D.——— 1694   Motto*] *1703 om. 1694*   1 *Preceded in 1703 by salutation: SIR,*   ALL ... all] *1703* Let ... as *1694*   2 Orphans, and]
1703 Orphan's Trust, *1694*   3] *1703* The Great good Man, whose kind Resolves declare
1694   4 Objects of your] object of his *1703*: Object of your *1694*   5–6] *1703*
When hungry Poets now abdicate their Rhimes,
For some more darling Folly of the Times. *1694*
7–9] *om. 1694*   8 Proselyte, that] Prostitute which *1703*   10 *Shadwell* ... scorn]
Shadwell, ... T——— I cease *1703*: S———l and ——— I here forbear *1694*   11] Condemn'd
to Lawrel, tho' unknown to Fame: *1694*   Religions *1703*: Religion *1698*   12
Settle] *1703* S———tle *1694*   19 starving *Durfey*'s] *Durfey*, and his *1703*: tuneful
D———'s *1694*   20–23] *om. 1694*   20 her] his *1703*   23 Grooms] Groom *1703*

Is there a Man to these Examples blind,
To Clinking Numbers fatally design'd,　　　　　　　25
Who, by his Parts wou'd purchase Meat and Fame,
And in next Miscellanies plant his Name?
Were my Beard grown, the wretch I'd thus advise;
Repent fond Mortal, and be timely wise;
Take heed, nor be by guilded Fops betray'd　　　　30
Clio's a Jilt, and *Pegasus* a Jade.
By Verse you'l starve; *John Saul* cou'd never live,
Unless the Bell-Man made the Poet thrive:
Go rather, in some little Shed by *Pauls*,
Sell *Chivy Chase*, and *Baxter*'s Salve for Souls.　　35
Cry Rara Shows, sing Ballads, Transcribe Votes,
Be *Care*, or *Ketch*, or any thing, but *Oates*.

Hold Sir, some Bully of the Muses Cryes,
Methinks you're more Satyrical, than Wise:
You rail at Verse indeed; but rail in Rhime;　　　40
At once incourage, and condemn the Crime.

True Sir, I write, and have a Patron too,
To whom my Tributary Songs are due;
Yet with your leave I'de honestly dissuade
Those wretched Men from *Pindus* barren Shade:　　45
Who, tho they tire their Muse and rak their Brains,
With blustring Heroes, and with piping Swains,
Can no Great patient giving Man engage
To fill their Pockets, and their Title Page.
Were I like these unhappily Decreed　　　　　　50
By penny Elegies to get my Bread;
Or want a Meal, unless *George Croom* and I
Cou'd strike a Bargain for my Poetry:
I'd damn my Works, to wrap up Soap and Cheese ⎫
Or furnish Squibs for City Prentices;　　　　　 ⎬ 55
To burn the Pope, and Celebrate Queen *Bess*.　 ⎭

25 Clinking...design'd,] *1703* chinking...enclin'd; *1694*　　26 Parts] *1703* Muse *1694*
Meat *1694, 1703*: Meal *1698*　　27 next] *1703* th' next *1694*　　30 nor be...Fops]
nor be...Hopes *1703*: be not...Baits *1694*　　33 Unless...made] *1703* Did not...
make *1694*　　34 in...by] *1703* to...near *1694*　　35 and] *1694* or *1703*　　36
sing] *1694* sell *1703*　　Votes,] *1703* Vote: *1694*　　37 Care] *1703* Carr *1694*
46 tire] *1694* fire *1703*　　50 unhappily] *1703* by angry Fate *1694*　　52 Or] *1703*
And *1694*

But on; your ruin stubbornly pursue;
Herd with the hungry little Chiming Crew,
Obtain the empty Title of a Wit,
And be a free-cost Noisie in the Pit,   60
Print your dull Poems, and before 'em place
A Crown of Laurel, and a Meager Face:
And may just Heav'n thy hated Life prolong,
'Till thou blest Author! See'st thy deathless Song
The dusty Lumber of a *Smithfield* Stall,   } 65
And find thy Picture starch'd to Suburb Wall,
With *Jony Armstrong*, and the Prodigal.

And, to compleat the Curse,
When Age, and Poverty comes faster on,
And sad Experience tells thou art undone: 70
May no kind Country Grammar School afford
Ten Pound a year, for Lodging, Bed and Board,
Till void of any fix'd Employ, and now
Grown Useless to the Army, and the Plow,
You've no Friend left, but Trusting Landlady,   } 75
Who stows you in hard Truckle Garret high,
To dream of Dinner, and Curse Poetry.

Sir, I've a Patron, you reply; 'tis true,
Fortune and Parts, you say may get one too:
Why Faith, e'en try; Write, Flatter, Dedicate,   80
My Lord's and his Fore-fathers Deeds relate;
Yet know, he'll wisely strive ten thousand ways
To shun a needy Poet's fulsom Praise:
Nay, to avoid thy Importunity,
Neglect his State, and condescend to be   } 85
A Poet, tho perhaps he's worse than thee.

Thus from a Patron, he becomes a Friend;
Forgetting to Reward, learns to Commend:

---

58 Herd *1694, 1703*: Her'd *1698*   hungry little] *1703* little hungry *1694*   59 empty]
1703 airy *1694*   60 a] *1703* on *1694*   63 Heav'n *1694, 1703*: Hea'vn *1698*   66
find . . . to] findst . . .'gainst *1703* : findst . . . to *1694*   69 comes] *1703* come *1694*
70 thou art] *1703* thee thou 'rt *1694*   72 Pound . . . Lodging,] pound a Year to
pay for *1703*: Pounds a Year for Lodging, *1694*   75 You've *1694, 1703*: Youv'e *1698*
76 in hard] on hard *1703*: in kind *1694*   77 Dinner] *1703* Dinners *1694*   78 Sir,]
1703 Still *1694*   79 Fortune and] *1703* Fate, and good *1694*   81 My *1703* Your
1694   86 he's] a *1694, 1703*

Receives your twelve long Months successful Toil,
And talks of Author's Energy and Stile;   90
Damns the dull Poems of the Scribling Town,
Applauds your Writing, and Esteems his own:
Whil'st thou in Complaisance oblig'd must sit
To extol his Judgment, and admire his Wit;
And wrapt with his Essay on Poetry,   } 95
Swear *Horace* writ not half so strong as he,
But that we're partial to Antiquity.
Yet this Authentick Peer perhaps scarce knows,
With Jingling Sounds to tag insipid Prose,
And shou'd be, by some Honest *Manly*, told   100
H'ad lost his Credit, to secure his Gold.

But if thou'rt bles'd enough to write a Play,
Without the hungry hopes of kind Third-day,
And he presumes that to thy Dedication
Thou'lt fix his Name, not bargain for the Station;   105
My Lord his useless Kindness then assures,
And to the utmost of his power, he's Yours:
How fine your Plot! how exquisite your Scene!
And play'd at Court, 'twould strangely please the Queen!
And you may take his Judgment sure, for he   110
Knows the true Spirit of good Poetry,
And might with equal Justice, have put in
For Poet Laureat, as Lord Chamberlain.
All this you see and know, yet cease to shun,
And seeing, knowing, strive to be Undone.   115
So Kid-napp'd Dutchess, once beyond *Graves-end*,
Rejects the Council of recalling Friend;
Is told the dreadful Bondage she must bear
And sees, unable to avoid the Snare.

89 twelve...successful] twelve...successless *1703* : long six Months succesless *1694*   90
Author's Energy] Authors, Energy, *1703* : Authors Energies *1694*   92 Writing, and
Esteems] Writings, and repeats *1694, 1703*   93 Whil'st thou] *1703* Thou Wretch, *1694*
94 To extol] T' extol *1703* : Extol *1694*   95–97] *1703 om. 1694*   98 Yet this
Authentick] *1703* Tho' this Poetic *1694*   100 be, by *edd.* : be by, *1698* : be by *1694, 1703*
101 H'ad *1703* : H' had *1698* : He'd *1694*   104 presumes...to] believes...in
1703 : presumes...in *1694*   105 not...the] *1703* nor...his *1694*   107 to the]
1703 vows to th' *1694*   108] How...each Scene! *1703* : Likes the whole Plot, and
praises e'ery Scene, *1694*   109 'twould] *1694* would *1703*   112–13] *om. 1694*
112 Justice] Judgment *1703*   113 Chamberlain] Ch——in *1703*   116 Dutchess]
1703 Slave, when *1694*   118 told the...she] *1703* sold to...he *1694*

So practic'd Thief, oft Taken, ne'er dismay'd,   120
Forgets the Sentence, and pursues the Trade;
Tho yet he almost feels the Smoking Brand,
And sad *T. R.* stands fresh upon his Hand.

   The Author then, whose daring hopes wou'd strive
With well built Verse, to keep his Fame alive,   125
And something to Posterity present,
That's very New, and very Excellent,
Something beyond the uncall'd drudging Tribe,
Beyond What *Bays* can write, or I describe,
Shou'd in substantial Happiness abound,   130
His Mind with Peace, his Board with Plenty crown'd:
No early *Duns* should break his learned Rest,   ⎫
No sawcy Cares, his nobler Thoughts molest;   ⎬
Only the God within should shake his lab'ring Breast.   ⎭

   In vain we from our Sonnettiers require   135
The height of *Cowley*'s and *Anacreon*'s Lyre:
    "In vain we bid 'em fill the Bowl,
    "Large as their capacious Soul,
Who since the King was Crown'd, ne'er tasted Wine,
But rise at Eight, and know not where to Dine.   140
In vain, we bid dejected *Settle* hit
The Tragick Flights of *Shakespear*'s towring Wit;
He needs must miss the Mark, who's kept so low
He scarce has strength enough to draw the Bow.
Sidley indeed and *Rochester* might Write,   145
For their own Credit, and their Friends Delight,
Shewing how far they cou'd the rest out-do,
As in their Fortunes, so their Writings too;
But shou'd Drudge *Dryden* this Example take,
And *Absaloms* for empty Glory make,   150

120 oft...dismay'd] oft...afraid *1703*: if...dismay'd *1694*   123 T. R. *1694, 1703*:
J. R. 1698   stands] *1703* stand *1694*   124 whose] *1703* with *1694*   127
That's *1694, 1703*: Tha'ts *1698*   129 *Bays* can] *1703 BEN* cou'd *1694*   133
Thoughts] *1703* Thought *1694*   134 the God within] *1703* th' ent'ring God *1694*
135 *Preceded in 1694 by ll. 141–4 of the present text*   we... Sonnettiers] *1703* from
our starv'd *Songsters* we *1694*   137 'em *1703*: him *1698*: them *1694*   140 rise
at Eight] write at sight *1703*: write at Eight *1694*   141–4] *In 1694, these lines are inserted
before l.* 135 *of the present text*   141 *Settle*] *1703* S——*tle 1694*   142 *Shakespear*'s
towring] *1703* Tow'ring *Shakespear*'s *1694*   144 scarce has] has not *1694, 1703*
145 *Sidley...Rochester*] *Sedley...Rochester 1703*: D——*t...*R——*r 1694*   148 so]
1703 in *1694*   149–54] *om. 1694*   149 this *1703*: his *1698*

He'd soon perceive his Income scarce enough,
To feed his Nostrils with Inspiring Snuff,
Starving for Meat, nor surfeiting on Praise,
He'd find his Brain as barren as his *Bays*.
There was a time When *Otway* Charm'd the Stage;   155
Otway the Hope, the Sorrow of our Age!
When the full Pitt with pleas'd attention hung,
Wrap'd with each Accent from *Castalio*'s Tongue:
With what a Laughter was his Soldier read!
How Mourn'd they, when his *Jaffier* Struck and Bled!   160
Yet this best Poet, tho with so much ease,
He never drew his Pen, but sure to please:
Tho Lightning were less lively than his Wit,
And Thunder-claps less loud than those o'th' Pit,
He had of's many Wants, much earlier dy'd,   165
Had not kind Banker *Betterton* supply'd,
And took for Pawn, the Embrio of a Play,
Till he could pay himself the next Third-day.

Were *Shakespear*'s self alive again, he'd ne'er
Degenerate to a Poet from a Player.   170
Carlile i'th' new rais'd Troops preferr'd we see,
And chatt'ring *Montfort* in the *Chancery*:
Montfort how fit for Politicks and Law,
That play'd so well Sir *Courtly* and *Jack Daw*!
Dance then Attendance in slow *Mulgrave*'s Hall,   175
Read Mapps, or count the Sconces till he call;
One Actor's Commendation shall do more,
Than Patron now, or Merit heretofore.
Some Poets I confess, the Stage has fed,
Who for Half-crowns are shown, for two pence read;   180

152 Nostrils] Nostril *1703*   153 nor] not *1703*   154 Brain] Brains *1703*
156 Hope *1694, 1703*: Hopes *1698*   the Sorrow of our] *1703* and Sorrow of the
1694   158 Wrap'd with...from] *1703* Charm'd on...of *1694*   *Castalio*'s *1694*,
1703: *Castalia*'s *1698*   160 they] *1703* we *1694*   161 best Poet, tho] *1703* great
Poet, who *1694*   162 He never...but] *1703* Still...and still was *1694*   163 Tho
...were] *1703* The...is *1694*   164 Pit, *1703*: Pit. *1698*: Pit: *1694*   165 He had
of's] *1703* Had of his *1694*   166 Had not...*Betterton*] *1703* But that...B——n
1694   168 the next] *1703* next full *1694*   Third-day. *edd.*: Third-day *1698*: third
Day. *1694, 1703*   169 alive] *1694* to live *1703*   170 to...from *1694, 1703*: from
...to *1698*   171–83] *om. 1694*   171 *Carlile 1703: Cartel 1698*   Troops preferr'd we] Troop we *1703*   175 *Mulgrave*'s *edd.*: *Mougrave*'s *1698*: M——ves *1703*
176 count *edd.*: court *1698, 1703*   180 shown *1703*: thrown *1698*

But these not envy thou, nor imitate,
But rather Starve in *Shadwell*'s silent Fate,   )
Than new vamp Farces, and be Damn'd with *Tate*.   )
For now no *Sidney* will three hundred give,
That needy *Spencer*, and his Fame may live.   185
None of our Nobility will send
To the *King's-Bench*, or to his *Bethlem* Friend.
Chymists and Whores, by *Buckingham* were fed,
Those by their honest Labours gain'd their Bread
But he was never so expensive yet,   190
To keep a Creature meerly for his Wit:
And *Cowley*, from all *Clifden*, scarce cou'd have
One Grateful Stone, to show the World his Grave.

Pembrook lov'd Tragedy, and did provide
For Butchers Dogs, and for the whole Bank-side: 195
The *Bear* was fed; but Dedicating *Lee*
Was thought to have a larger Paunch than he.
More I cou'd say; but care not much to meet
A Crab-Tree Cudgel, in a narrow Street:
Besides, your Yawning prompts me to give o're,   200
Your humble Servant, Sir, not one word more.

    Thus far my Satyrist and angry Friend:
You, Sir, began the Verse; and You must end.
And may just Phœbus his wish'd Aid deny;
And my vex'd Strings in sullen Silence lye: 205
When they forget Your Name: for O! to You
My Song, my Thought, my very Soul is due.
Then O! receive my Thanks: O deign to take
The little Offering a poor Muse can make:
That pants and Strives and fain wou'd let Men see   210
How good her Patron and how grateful She.
Fain wou'd—but soon she finds the noble Song
A Theme too mighty for a Muse so Young;

181 nor] but *1703*   182 But] Much *1703*   183 Than] Then *1703*   184
Sidney] *Sidneys 1694, 1703*   186 Nobility will] new Nobility will *1703*: poor Nobility
can *1694*   187 the] *1703* his *1694*   188 *Buckingham*] *1703* this great Lord *1694*
189 Those...gain'd] *1703* These...earn'd *1694*   191 his] *1703* its *1694*   192–9]
om. 1694   194 *Pembrook*] *Pemb——— 1703*   200 Besides,] *1703* But now *1694*
201 Sir, *1703*: Sir— *1694*: *om. 1698*   not one word] *1703* I've done—no *1694*
202–18 L 28: *om. 1694, 1698, 1703*

Then owns her Weakness, wishes, rages, grieves;
And with mad trouble the wrong'd subject leaves: 215
Yet Vows her Labor She'l one day renew,
With Strengthn'd Wings the glorious Toil pursue;
And Sing of wondrous Piety and You.

The Hind and the Panther Transvers'd to the Story of The Country Mouse and the City-Mouse.

Much Malice mingled with a little Wit. *Hind. Pan.*
Nec vult Panthera domari. Quæ Genus.

PREFACE.

THE *Favourers of the* Hind *and* Panther *will be apt to say in its Defence,
That the best things are capable of being turn'd to Ridicule; that* Homer
has been Burlesque'd, and Virgil *Travested without suffering any thing in their
Reputation from that Buffoonry; and that in like manner, the* Hind *and the*
Panther *may be an exact Poem, though 'tis the Subject of our Raillery: But* 5
*there is this difference, that those Authors are wrested from their true Sense, and
this naturally falls into Ridicule; there is nothing Represented here as monstrous
and unnatural, which is not equally so in the Original. First as to the General
Design, Is it not as easie to imagine two* Mice *bilking Coachmen, and supping at
the* Devil; *as to suppose a* Hind *entertaining the* Panther *at a Hermits Cell,* 10
discussing the greatest Mysteries of Religion, and telling you her son Rodriguez
*writ very good Spanish? What can be more improbable and contradictory to the
Rules and Examples of all Fables, and to the very design and use of them? They
were first begun and raised to the highest Perfection in the* Eastern Countries;
where they wrote in Signs and spoke in Parables, and delivered the most useful 15
*Precepts in delightful stories; which for their Aptness were entertaining to the
most Judicious, and led the vulgar into understanding by surprizing them with
their Novelty, and fixing their Attention. All their Fables carry a double
meaning; the Story is one and intire; the Characters the same throughout, not
broken or chang'd, and always conformable to the Nature of the Creatures they* 20
introduce. They never tell you that the Dog *which snapt at a shadow, lost his
Troop of Horse, that would be unintelligible; a piece of Flesh is proper for him to
drop, and the Reader will apply it to mankind; they would not say that the* Daw
who was so proud of her borrow'd Plumes lookt very ridiculous when Rodriguez

came and took away all the book but the 17th, 24th, *and* 25th *Chapters, which* 25
she stole from him: But this is his new way of telling a story, and confounding the
Moral *and the* Fable *together.*

Before the Word was written, said the Hind,
Our Saviour Preacht the Faith to all Mankind.

What relation has the Hind *to our Saviour? or what notion have we of a* 30
Panther's *Bible? If you say he means the Church, how does the Church feed on
Lawns, or range in the Forest? Let it be always a Church, or always the cloven-
footed Beast, for we cannot bear his shifting the scene every Line. If it is absurd
in Comedies to make a Peasant talk in the strain of a* Hero, *or a Country Wench
use the language of the Court; how monstrous is it to make a Priest of a Hind,* 35
*and a Parson of a Panther? To bring 'em in disputing with all the Formalities
and Terms of the School? Though as to the Arguments themselves, those, we
confess, are suited to the Capacity of the Beasts, and if we would suppose a Hind
expressing her self about these Matters, she would talk at that Rate.*

As to the Absurdity of his expressions, there is nothing wrested to make 'em 40
ridiculous, the terms are sometimes alter'd to make the Blunder more visible;
Knowledg misunderstood *is not at all better sense than* Understanding
misunderstood, *though 'tis confest the Author can play with words so well, that
this and twenty such will pass off at a slight reading.*

There are other mistakes which could not be brought in, for they were too gross 45
for Bayes *himself to commit. 'Tis hard to conceive how any man could censure the*
Turks *for* Gluttony, *a People that debauch in* Coffee, *are voluptuous in a mess
of* Rice, *and keep the strictest* Lent, *without the Pleasures of a* Carnival *to
encourage them. But 'tis almost impossible to think that any man who had not
renounced his Senses, should read* Duncomb *for* Allen: *He had been told* 50
that Mr. Allen *had written a Discourse of Humility; to which he wisely
answers, That that magnified Piece of* Duncombs *was Translated from the*
Spanish *of* Rodriguez, *and to set it beyond dispute, makes the infallible Guide
affirm the same thing. There are few mistakes, but one may imagine how a Man
fell into them, and at least what he aim'd at; but what likeness is there between* 55
Duncomb *and* Allen? *do they so much as Rhime?*

*We may have this comfort under the severity of his Satyr, to see his Abilities
equally lessen'd with his Opinion of us; and that he could not be a fit Champion
against the* Panther *till he had laid aside all his Judgment. But we must applaud
his Obedience to his new Mother* Hind; *she Disciplin'd him severely, she com-* 60
manded him it seems, to Sacrifice *his darling Fame, and to do it effectually he*

publisht this learned Piece. This is the favourable Construction we would put on his faults, tho he takes care to inform us, that it was done from no Imposition, but out of a natural Propensity he has to Malice, and a particular Inclination of doing Mischief. What else could provoke him to Libel the Court, *Blaspheme* 65 Kings, *abuse the whole* Scotch Nation, *rail at the greatest Part of his own, and lay all the Indignities imaginable on the only establish'd Religion? And we must now Congratulate him this Felicity, that there is no Sect or Denomination of Christians, whom he has not abused.*

Thus far his Arms have with Success been crown'd.   70

Let Turks, Jews *and* Infidels, *look to themselves, he has already begun the War upon them. When once a Conqueror grows thus dreadful, 'tis the Interest of all his Neighbours to oppose him, for there is no Alliance to be made with one that will face about, and destroy his Friends, and like a second* Almanzor, *change sides meerly to keep his hand in ure. This Heroick temper of his, has created* 75 *him some Enemies, that did by no means affect Hostility; and he may observe this Candor in the Management, that none of his Works are concern'd in these Papers, but his last Piece; and I believe he is sensible this is a favour. I was not ambitious of Laughing at any Perswasion, or making Religion the Subject of such a Trifle; so that no man is here concern'd, but the Author himself, and nothing ridicul'd* 80 *but his way of arguing.*

But, Gentlemen, if you won't take it so, you must grant my Excuse is more reasonable than our Author's to the Dissenters.

The Hind and the Panther, Transvers'd to the Story of the Country and the City-Mouse.

Bayes. Johnson. Smith.

Johnson.

HAH! my old friend Mr. *Bayes*, what lucky chance has thrown me upon you? Dear Rogue let me embrace thee.

Bayes. Hold, at your peril, Sir, stand off and come not within my Swords point, for if you are not *come over to the Royal party, I expect neither fair war, nor fair quarter from you.*   5

Johns. How, draw upon your friend? and assault your old Acquaintance? O' my *conscience* my intentions were Honourable.

Bayes. Conscience! Ay, ay, I know the deceit of that word well enough, let me have the *marks* of your *Conscience* before I trust it, for if it be not of the same stamp with mine, Gad I may be *knockt down* for all your fair 10 promises.

Smith. Nay, prithee *Bayes*, what damn'd Villany hast thou been about that thou'rt under these apprehensions? upon my Honour I'm thy friend; yet thou lookest as sneaking and frighted as a dog that has been worrying sheep.   15

Bayes. Ay Sir, *The Nation is in too high a ferment for me to expect any mercy*, or I'gad, to trust any body.

Smith. But why this to us, my old friend, who you know never trouble our heads with National concerns till the third bottle has taught us as much of Politicks, as the next does of Religion?   20

Bayes. Ah Gentlemen, leave this prophaneness, I am alter'd since you saw me, and cannot bear this loose talk now; Mr. *Johnson*, you are a man of Parts, let me desire you to read *the Guide of Controversy*; and Mr. *Smith*, I would recommend to you *the Considerations on the Council of Trent*, and so Gentlemen your humble Servant.——*Good life be now* 25 *my Task.*

Johns. Nay Faith, we wont part so: believe us we are both your Friends; let us step to the *Rose* for one quarter of an hour, and talk over old Stories.

Bayes. I ever took you to be men of Honour, and for your sakes I will 30 transgress as far as one Pint.

Johns. Well, Mr. *Bayes*, many a merry bout have we had in this House, and shall have again, I hope: Come, what Wine are you for?

Bayes. Gentlemen, do you as you please, for my part he shall bring me a single Pint of any thing.   35

Smith. How so, Mr. *Bayes*, have you lost your pallat? you have been more curious.

Bayes. True, I have so, but *senses* must be *starv'd* that the *soul* may be *gratified.* Men of your Kidney make the *senses* the *supream Judg*, and therefore bribe 'em high, but we have laid both the use and pleasure 40 of 'em aside.

Smith. What, is not there good eating and drinking on both sides? you make the separation greater than I thought it.

Bayes. No, no, whenever you see a fat Rosie-colour'd fellow, take it from me, he is either a Protestant or a *Turk*.   45

Johns. At that rate, Mr. *Bayes*, one might suspect your conversion; methinks thou hast as much the face of an *Heretick* as ever I saw.

Bayes. Such was I, such by nature still I am. But I hope ere long I shall have drawn this *pamper'd Paunch* fitter for the *straight gate.*

Smith. Sure, Sir, you are in ill hands, your Confessor gives you more 50 severe rules than he practices; for not long ago a *Fat Frier* was thought a *true Character.*

Bayes. Things were misrepresented to me: I confess I have been unfortunate in some of my Writings: but since you have put me upon that subject, I'le show you a thing I have in my Pocket shall wipe off all that, 55 or I am mistaken.

Smith. Come, now thou art like thy self again. Here's the *Kings* Health to thee—— Communicate.

Bayes. Well, Gentlemen, here it is, and I'le be bold to say, the exactest Piece the world ever saw, a *Non Pareillo* I'faith. But I must 60 bespeak your pardons if it reflects any thing upon your perswasion.

Johns. Use your Liberty, Sir, you know we are no *Bigots.*

Bayes. Why then you shall see me lay the *Reformation* on its back, I'gad, and justifie our Religion by way of *Fable.*

Johns. An apt contrivance indeed! what do you make a *Fable* of 65 your *Religion?*

Bayes. Ay I'gad, and without *Morals* too; for I tread in no mans steps; and to show you how far I can out-do any thing that ever was writ in this kind, I have taken *Horace*'s design, but I'gad, have so out-done him, you shall be asham'd for your *old friend.* You remember in him the 70 *Story* of the *Country-Mouse,* and the *City-Mouse;* what a plain simple thing it is, it has no more life and spirit in it, I'gad, than a Hobbyhorse; and his *Mice* talk so meanly, such common stuff, so like *meer Mice,* that I wonder it has pleas'd the world so long. But now will I undeceive *Mankind,* and teach 'em to *heighten,* and *elevate a Fable.* I'le 75 bring you in the very same *Mice* disputing the depth of *Philosophy,* searching into the fundamentals of *Religion,* quoting *Texts, Fathers, Councils,* and all that, I'gad, as you shall see either of 'em could easily make an Asse of a *Country Vicar.* Now whereas *Horace* keeps to the dry naked story, I have more copiousness than to do that, I'gad. Here, 80 I draw you general *Characters,* and describe all the *beasts* of the *Creation;* there, I launch out into long *Digressions,* and leave my *Mice* for twenty Pages together; then I fall into *Raptures,* and make the finest *Soliloquies,* as would ravish you. Won't this do, think you?

Johns. Faith, Sir, I don't well conceive you; all this about two 85 *Mice?*

Bayes. Ay, why not? is it not great and Heroical? but come, you'l understand it better when you hear it; and pray be as severe as you can, I'gad I defie all *Criticks*. Thus it begins.

> *A milk-white* Mouse *immortal and unchang'd*,   90
> *Fed on soft* Cheese, *and o're the* Dairy *rang'd*;
> *Without, unspotted*; *innocent within*,
> *She fear'd no danger, for she knew no* Ginn.

Johns. Methinks Mr. *Bayes*, soft Cheese is a little too coarse Diet for an *immortal Mouse*; were there any necessity for her eating, you should 95 have consulted *Homer* for some *Cœlestial Provision*.

Bayes. Faith, Gentlemen, I did so; but indeed I have not the *Latin* one, which I have mark'd by me, and could not readily find it in the Original.

> *Yet had She oft been* scar'd *by bloody Claws*   100
> *Of winged* Owls, *and stern* Grimalkins *Paws*
> *Aim'd at her* destin'd *Head, which made her fly*,
> *Tho She was doom'd to Death, and fated not to dye.*

Smith. How came She that *fear'd no danger* in the line before, to be scar'd in this, Mr. *Bayes?*   105

Bayes. Why then you may have it *chas'd* if you will; for I hope a Man may run away without being *afraid*; mayn't he?

Johns. But pray give me leave; how was She *doom'd to Death*, if She was *fated not to dye*; are not *doom* and *fate*, much the same thing?

Bayes. Nay *Gentlemen*, if you question my skill in the Language, I'm 110 your humble Servant; the *Rogues* the *Criticks*, that will allow me nothing else, give me that; sure I that made the Word, know best what I meant by it: I assure you, *doom'd* and *fated*, are quite different things.

Smith. Faith, Mr. *Bayes*, if you were *doom'd* to be hang'd, whatever you were *fated* to, 'twould give you but small comfort.   115

Bayes. Never trouble your head with that, Mr. *Smith*, mind the business in hand.

> *Not so her young*; *their* Linsy-woolsy *line*,
> *Was* Hero's *make, half humane, half Divine*.

Smith. Certainly these *Hero's*, *half Humane, half Divine*, have very 120 little of the *Mouse* their *Mother*.

Bayes. Gadsokers! Mr. *Johnson*, does your Friend think I mean nothing but a *Mouse*, by all this? I tell thee, Man, I mean a *Church*, and these young Gentlemen her Sons, signifie *Priests, Martyrs* and *Confessors*, that were hang'd in *Oats's Plot*. There's an excellent *Latin* Sentence, which 125

I had a mind to bring in, *Sanguis Martyrum semen Ecclesiæ*, and I think I have not wrong'd it in the Translation.

> *Of these a slaughter'd Army lay in Blood,*
> *Whose sanguine Seed encreas'd the sacred* Brood;
> *She multipli'd by these, now rang'd alone,*   130
> *And wander'd in the Kingdoms once her own.*

Smith. Was She *alone* when *the sacred Brood was encreased?*

Bayes. Why thy Head's running on the *Mouse* again; but I hope a *Church* may be *alone*, tho the *Members* be *encreased*, mayn't it?

Johns. Certainly Mr. *Bayes*, a *Church* which is a *difusive Body of Men*, 135 can much less be said to be *alone*.

Bayes. But are you really of that Opinion? Take it from me, Mr. *Johnson*, you are wrong; however to oblige you, I'le clap in some *Simile* or other, about the *Children of Israel*, and it shall do.

Smith. Will you pardon me one word more, Mr. *Bayes?* What could 140 the *Mouse* (for I suppose you mean her now) do more then *range* in the *Kingdoms*, when they were her own?

Bayes. Do? why She *reign'd*; had a *Diadem, Scepter* and *Ball*, till they depos'd her.

Smith. Now her Sons are so *encreas'd*, She may try t'other pull for't. 145

Bayes. I gad, and so She may before I have done with Her; it has cost me some pains to clear Her Title. Well, but Mum for that, Mr. *Smith*.

> *The common Hunt,* She timorously past by,
> For they made tame, *disdain'd Her company*;
> *They grin'd,* She in a fright *tript* o're the Green,   150
> *For* She was *lov'd,* whereever She was *seen.*

Johns. Well said little *Bayes*, I'faith the Critick must have a great deal of leasure, that attacks those Verses.

Bayes. I gad, I'le warrant him, who ere he is, *offendet solido*; but I go on.

> *The Independent Beast.* ——   155

Smith. Who is that Mr. *Bayes?*

Bayes. Why a *Bear*: Pox, is not that obvious enough?

> ——*In groans Her hate exprest.*

Which I gad, is very natural to that *Animal*. Well! there's for the *Independent*: Now the *Quaker*; what do you think I call him?   160

Smith. Why, A *Bull*, for ought I know.

---

132 *encreased?* edd.: *encreased.* 1687

Bayes. A *Bull!* O Lord! A Bull! no, no, a *Hare*, a *quaking Hare.*——
Armarillis, because She wears *Armour*, 'tis the same Figure; and I am
proud to say it, Mr. *Johnson*, no man knows how to *pun* in *Heroics* but
my self. Well, you shall hear.   165

> She thought, and reason good, the *quaking Hare*
> Her cruel Foe, because *She would not swear*,
> And had *profess'd neutrality*.

Johns. A shrew'd Reason that, Mr. *Bayes*; but what Wars were there?
Bayes. Wars! why there had bin bloody Wars, tho they were pretty 170
well reconcil'd now. Yet to bring in two or three such fine things as
these, I don't tell you the Lyon's Peace was proclaim'd till fifty pages
after, tho 'twas really done before I had finish'd my Poem.

> *Next Her, the Buffoon Ape his body bent,*
> *And paid at Church a Courtier's complement.*   175

That Gauls somewhere; I gad I can't leave it off, tho I were cudgel'd
every day for it.

> *The brisl'd Baptist Boar, impure as he.*

Smith. As who?
Bayes. As the *Courtier*, let 'em e'n take it as they will, I gad, I seldom 180
come amongst 'em.

> *Was whiten'd with the foam of Sanctity.*
> *The Wolf with Belly-gaunt his rough crest rears,*
> *And pricks up.*——Now in one word will I abuse the whole Party
most damnably——*and pricks up.*——I gad, I am sure you'l Laugh——*his* 185
predestinating Ears. Prethee Mr. *Johnson*, remember little *Bays*, when next
you see a *Presbyterian*, and take notice if he has not *Predestination* in the
shape of his *Ear*: I have studied men so long, I'le undertake to know
an *Arminian*, by the setting of his Wig.

> *His predestinating Ears.* I gad there's ne're a *Presbyterian* shall dare to 190
show his Head without a Border: I'le put 'em to that expence.

Smith. Pray Mr. *Bays*, if any of 'em should come over to the *Royal
Party*, would their Ears alter?
Bayes. Would they? Ay, I gad, they would shed their *Fanatical Lugs*,
and have just such well-turn'd *Ears* as I have; mind this *Ear*, this is a true 195
Roman Ear, mine are much chang'd for the better within this two years.
Smith. Then if ever the Party should chance to fail, you might lose
'em, *for what may change, may fall.*

Bayes. Mind, mind——

> *These fiery* Zuinglius, *meagre* Calvin *bred.*   200

Smith. Those I suppose are some Out-Landish Beasts, Mr. *Bayes.*

Bayes. Beasts; a good Mistake! Why they were the chief *Reformers*, but here I put 'em in so bad Company because they were Enemies to my *Mouse*, and anon when I am warm'd, I'gad you shall hear me call 'em *Doctors, Captains, Horses* and *Horsemen* in the very same Breath. 205 You shall hear how I go on now,

> Or else reforming *Corah* spawn'd *this Class,*
> *When opening Earth made way for all to pass.*

Johns. For *all,* Mr. *Bayes?*

Bayes. Yes, They were *all* lost there, but some of 'em were thrown up 210 again at the *Leman-Lake*: as a Catholick *Queen* sunk at *Charing-Cross*, and rose again at *Queenhith.*

> *The Fox and he came shuffled in the dark,*
> *If ever they were stow'd in* Noah's *Ark.*

Here I put a Quære, Whether there were any *Socinians* before the *Flood,* 215 which I'm not very well satisfied in? I have been lately apt to believe that the World was drown'd for that *Heresy*; which among Friends made me leave it.

> *Quickned with Fire below, these Monsters breed*
> *In Fenny* Holland, *and in Fruitful* Tweed.   220

Now to write something new and out of the way, to elevate and surprize, and all that, I fetch, you see this *Quickning Fire* from the Bottom of *Boggs* and *Rivers.*

Johns. Why, Faith, that's as ingenious a Contrivance as the *Virtuoso's* making a Burning-Glass of Ice.   225

Bayes. Why was there ever any such thing? Let me perish if ever I heard of it. The Fancy was sheer new to me; and I thought no Man had reconcil'd those Elements but my self. Well Gentlemen! Thus far I have followed Antiquity, and as *Homer* has numbred his Ships, so I have rang'd my Beasts. Here is my *Boar* and my *Bear*, and my *Fox*, and my 230 *Wolf*, and the rest of 'em all against my poor *Mouse*. Now what do you think I do with all these?

Smith. Faith I do'nt know, I suppose you make 'em fight.

Bayes. Fight! I'gad I'd as soon make 'em Dance. No, I do no earthly thing with 'em, nothing at all, I'gad: I think they have play'd their 235

Parts sufficiently already; I have walk'd 'em out, show'd 'em to the Company, and rais'd your Expectation. And now whilst you hope to see 'em bated, and are dreaming of Blood and Battels, they sculk off, and you hear no more of 'em.

Smith. Why, Faith, Mr. *Bayes*, now you have been at such expence in 240 setting forth their Characters, it had been too much to have gone through with 'em.

Bayes. I'gad so it had: And then I'le tell you another thing, 'tis not every one that reads a Poem through. And therefore I fill the first part with Flowers, Figures, fine Language, and all that; and then I'gad sink 245 by degrees, till at last I write but little better than other People. And whereas most Authors *creep servilely* after the Old Fellows, and strive to grow upon their Readers; I take another Course, I bring in all my Characters together, and let 'em see I could go on with 'em; but I'gad, I wo'nt.   250

Johns. Could go on with 'em Mr. *Bayes!* there's no Body doubts that; You have a most particular *Genius* that way.

Bayes. Oh! Dear Sir, You are mighty obliging: But I must needs say at a *Fable* or an *Emblem* I think no Man comes near me, indeed I have studied it more than any Man. Did you ever take notice, Mr. *Johnson*, 255 of a little thing that has taken mightily about Town, a *Cat with a Top-knot?*

Johns. Faith, Sir, 'tis mighty pretty, I saw it at the Coffee-House.

Bayes. 'Tis a Trifle hardly worth owning; I was t'other Day at *Will's* throwing out something of that Nature; and I'gad, the hint was taken, 260 and out came that Picture; indeed the poor Fellow was so civil to present me with a dozen of 'em for my Friends, I think I have one here in my Pocket; would you please to accept it Mr *Johnson?*

Johns. Really 'tis very ingenious.

Bayes. Oh Lord! Nothing at all, I could design twenty of 'em in an 265 Hour, if I had but witty Fellows about me to draw 'em. I was proffer'd a Pension to go into *Holland*, and contrive their *Emblems*. But hang 'em they are dull Rogues, and would spoil my Invention. But come, Gentlemen, let us return to our Business, and here I'le give you a delicate description of a Man.   270

Smith. But how does that come in?

Bayes. Come in? very naturally. I was talking of a *Wolf* and that supposes a Wood, and then I clap an Epithet to't, and call it a *Celtic Wood*: Now when I was there, I could not help thinking of the *French Persecution,* and I'gad from all these Thoughts I took occasion to rail at 275

the *French King*, and show that he was not of the same make with
other Men, which thus I prove.

The Divine Blacksmith *in th' Abyss of Light,*
Yawning and lolling *with a careless beat,*
Struck out the mute Creation at a Heat.   280
But he work'd hard to Hammer out our Souls,
He blew the Bellows, and stir'd up the Coals;
Long time he thought and could not on a sudden
Knead up with unskim'd *Milk* this Reas'ning Pudding:
Tender, and mild within its Bag it lay   285
Confessing still the softness of its Clay,
And kind as Milk-Maids on their Wedding-Day.
Till *Pride of Empire, Lust,* and hot Desire
Did over-boile him, like too great a Fire,
And understanding grown, *misunderstood,*   290
Burn'd Him to th' Pot, and sour'd his curdled Blood.

Johns. But sure this is a little prophane, Mr. *Bayes.*

Bayes. Not at all: do's not *Virgil* bring in his *God Vulcan* working at
the *Anvil?*

Johns. Ay Sir, but never thought his Hands the fittest to make a   295
Pudding.

Bayes. Why do you imagin Him an Earthly dirty *Blacksmith?* 'Gad you
make it prophane indeed. I'le tell you there's as much difference
betwixt 'em, I'gad as betwixt my Man and *Milton*'s. But now, Gentlemen, the Plot thickens, here comes my t'other Mouse, the City Mouse.   300

A *spotted* Mouse, the prettiest next the White,
Ah! were her Spots wash'd out, as pretty quite,
With *Phylacteries* on her Forehead spred,
Crozier in Hand, and *Miter* on her Head.
Three Steeples Argent on her Sable Shield,   305
Liv'd in the *City,* and disdain'd the *Field.*

Johns. This is a glorious *Mouse* indeed! but, as you have dress'd her,
we do'nt know whether she be *Jew, Papist* or *Protestant.*

Bayes. Let me embrace you, Mr. *Johnson,* for that; you take it right.
She is a meer *Babel* of *Religions,* and therefore she's a *spotted Mouse* here,   310
and will be a *Mule* presently. But to go on.

This Princess——

Smith. What *Princess,* Mr. *Bayes?*

Bayes. Why this *Mouse,* for I forgot to tell you, an *Old Lyon* made a *left Hand Marriage* with her Mother, and begot *on her Body Elizabeth* 315 *Schism,* who was married to *Timothy Sacriledg,* and had Issue *Graceless Heresy.* Who all give the same Coat with their Mother, *Three Steeples Argent,* as I told you before.

> This Princess tho *estrang'd* from what was *best,*
> *Was* least Deform'd, because Reform'd the least.   320

There's *De* and *Re* as good I'gad as ever was.

> *She in a Masquerade of Mirth and Love,*
> *Mistook the Bliss of Heaven for Bacchinals above,*
> *And grub'd the* Thorns *beneath our tender Feet,*
> *To make the Paths of Paradise more sweet.*   325

There's a Jolly Mouse for you, let me see any Body else that can shew you such another. Here now have I one damnable severe reflecting Line, but I want a Rhime to it, can you help me Mr. *Johnson.*

> She——
> *Humbly content to be despis'd at Home,*   330

Johns. Which is too narrow Infamy for some.
Bayes. Sir, I thank you, now I can go on with it.

> *Whose Merits are diffus'd from Pole to Pole,*
> *Where Winds can carry, and where Waves can rowl.*

Johns. But does not this reflect upon some of your Friends, Mr. *Bayes?* 335
Bayes. 'Tis no matter for that, let me alone to bring my self off. I'le tell you, lately I writ a damn'd Libel on a whole Party, sheer Point and Satyr all through, I'gad. Call'd 'em Rogues, Dogs, and all the Names I could think of, but with an exceeding deal of Wit; that I must needs say. Now it happen'd before I could finish this Peice, the Scheme of Affairs 340 was altered, and those People were no longer Beasts: Here was a Plunge now: Should I lose my Labour, or Libel my Friend? 'Tis not every Body's Talent to find a *Salvo* for this: But what do me I but write a smooth delicate Preface, wherein I tell them that *the Satyr was not intended to them,* and this did the Business.   345
Smith. But if it was not intended to them against whom it was writ, certainly it had no meaning at all.
Bayes. Poh! There's the Trick on't. Poor Fools, they took it, and were satisfied: And yet it maul'd 'em damnably I'gad.
Smith. Why Faith, Mr. *Bayes,* there's this very Contrivance in the 350 *Preface* to *Dear Joys Jests.*

Bayes. What a Devil do you think that I'd steal from such an Author? Or ever read it?

Smith. I can't tell, but you sometimes read as bad. I have heard you quote *Reynard the Fox.*   355

Bayes. Why there's it now; take it from me, Mr. *Smith,* there is as good *Morality,* and as sound Precepts, in the *delectable History of Reynard the Fox,* as in any Book I know, except *Seneca.* Pray tell me where in any other Author could I have found so pretty a Name for a Wolf as *Isgrim?* But prithee, Mr. *Smith,* give me no more trouble, and let me go on with 360 my *Mouse.*

> *One Evening,* when she went away from Court,
> *Levee's and Couchee's past without resort.*

There's Court Language for you; nothing gives a Verse so fine a turn as an Air of good Breeding.   365

Smith. But methinks the *Levee's and Couchee's* of a *Mouse* are too great, especially when she is walking from Court to the cooler Shades.

Bayes. I'gad now have you forgot what I told you that she was a *Princess.* But pray mind; here the two Mice meet.

> She met the Country Mouse, whose *fearful Face*   370
> *Beheld from far the common watering Place,*
> *Nor durst approach——*

Smith. Methinks, Mr. *Bayes,* this Mouse is strangely alter'd, since she *fear'd no Danger.*

Bayes. Godsokers! Why no more she does not yet fear either Man or 375 Beast: But, poor Creature, she's afraid of the Water, for she could not swim, as you see by this.

> *Nor durst approach, till with an awful Roar*
> *The Soveraign Lyon bad her fear no more.*

But besides, 'tis above thirty Pages off that I told you she *fear'd no* 380 *Danger;* and I'gad if you will have no variation of the Character, you must have the same thing over and over again; 'tis the Beauty of Writing to strike you still with something new. Well, but to proceed.

> But when she had this sweetest Mouse *in view,*
> Good *Lord, how she admir'd her Heavenly Hiew!*   385

Here now to show you I am Master of all Stiles, I let my self down from the *Majesty* of *Virgil,* to the *Sweetness* of *Ovid.*

> Good *Lord, how she admir'd her Heavenly Hiew!*

What more easy and familiar! I writ this Line for the *Ladies*: The little
Rogues will be so fond of me to find I can yet be so tender. I hate such 390
a rough unhewen Fellow as *Milton*, that a Man must sweat to read
Him; I'gad you may run over this and be almost asleep.

>   Th'Immortal Mouse who saw the *Viceroy* come
>   So far to see Her, did invite her Home.

There's a pretty Name now for the *Spotted Mouse*, the *Viceroy!*   395
    Smith. But pray why d'e call her so?
    Bayes. Why! Because it sounds prettily: I'le call her the *Crown-
General* presently if I've a mind to it. Well.

>   ————did invite her Home
>   To smoak a Pipe, and o're a sober Pot   400
>   Discourse of *Oates* and *Bedloe*, and the *Plot*.
>   She made a Court'sy, like a Civil Dame,
>   And, being *much a Gentlewoman*, came.

Well, Gentlemen, here's my first part finish'd, and I think I have kept
my Word with you, and given it the *Majestick turn of Heroick Poesy*. The 405
rest *being matter of Dispute, I had not such frequent occasion for the magnificence
of Verse*, tho I'gad they speak very well. And I have heard *Men*, and
considerable Men too, talk the very same things, a great deal worse.
    Johns. Nay, without doubt, Mr. *Bayes*, they have received no small
advantage from the smoothness of your numbers.   410
    Bayes. Ay, ay, I can do't, if I list: though you must not think I have
been so dull as to mind these things my self, but 'tis the advantage of our
Coffee-house, that from their talk one may write a very good *polemical*
discourse, without ever troubling ones head with the Books of *Con-
troversie*. For I can take the slightest of their Arguments, and clap 'em 415
pertly into four Verses, which shall stare any *London Divine* in the face.
Indeed your knotty Reasonings with a long train of *Majors* and *Minors*,
and the Devil and all, are too barbarous for my stile; but 'i gad I can
flourish better with one of these twinkling Arguments, than the best of
'em can fight with t'other. But we return to our *Mouse*, and now I've 420
brought 'em together, let 'em 'en speak for themselves, which they will
do extreamly well, or I'm mistaken: and pray observe, Gentlemen, if in
one you don't find all the delicacy of a luxurious City-Mouse, and in the
other all the plain simplicity of a sober serious Matron.

>   *Dame, said the Lady of the Spotted Muff*,   425
>   Methinks your *Tiff* is sour, your *Cates* meer stuff.

403 came. *edd*.: came *1687*

There did not I tell you she'd be nice?

> Your Pipe's so foul, that I disdain to smoak;
> And the Weed worse than e're *Tom. I*——*s* took.

Smith. I did not hear she had a *Spotted Muff* before. 430

Bayes. Why no more she has not now: but she has a Skin that might make a *Spotted Muff*. There's a pretty Figure now unknown to the Ancients.

> Leave, leave (†*she's earnest you see*) this hoary *Shed* † *Poeta Lo-*
>   and lonely Hills, *quitur.* 435
> And eat with me at *Groleau*'s, smoak at *Will*'s.
> What Wretch would nibble on a Hanging-shelf,
> When at *Pontack*'s he may *Regale* himself?
> Or to the House of cleanly *Renish* go;
> Or that at *Charing-Cross*, or that in *Channel-Row?* 440

Do you mark me now? I would by this represent the vanity of a *Town-Fop*, who pretends to be acquainted at all those good Houses, though perhaps he nere was in 'em. But heark! she goes on.

> Come, at a Crown a Head our selves we'll treat,
> *Champain* our Liquor, and *Ragousts* our Meat. 445
> Then hand in hand we'll go to *Court*, dear *Cuz*,
> To visit *Bishop Martin*, and *King Buz*.
> With *Evening Wheels* we'll drive about the *Park*,
> Finish at *Locket*'s, and reel home i'th' Dark.
> Break clattering Windows, and demolish Doors 450
> *Of English Manufactures*—*Pimps, and Whores.*

Johns. Methinks a *Pimp* or a *Whore*, is an odd sort of a *Manufacture*, Mr. *Bayes.*

Bayes. I call 'em so, to give the *Parliament* a hint not to suffer so many of 'em to be exported, to the decay of Trade at home. 455

> With these Allurements *Spotted* did invite
> From *Hermits Cell*, the *Female Proselyte*.
> *Oh! with what ease we follow such a Guide,*
> *Where Souls are starv'd, and Senses gratifi'd.*

Now would not you think she's going? but I gad, you're mistaken; 460 you shall hear a long Argument about Infallibility, before she stirs yet.

> But here the *White*, by *observation wise*,
> *Who long on Heaven had fixt her* prying *Eyes*,

With thoughtful Countenance, and grave Remark,
Said, or my Judgment fails me, or 'tis dark.   465
Lest therefore we should stray, and not go right,
Through the *brown horrour* of the starless Night,
Hast thou *Infallibility, that Wight?*
Sternly the Savage grin'd, and thus reply'd:
That Mice may err, was never yet deny'd.   470
That I deny, said the immortal Dame,
There is a Guide—Gad I've forgot his Name,
Who lives in *Heaven or Rome*, the Lord knows where,
Had we but him, Sweet-heart, we could not err.
But heark you, Sister, this is but a Whim;   *Spotted*   475
For still we want a *Guide* to find out Him.   *Mouse,*
                                                    Loquitur.

Here you see I don't trouble my self to keep on the Narration, but
write *white Speaks* or *dapple Speaks* by the side. But when I get any noble
thought which I envy a *Mouse* should say, I clap it down in my own
Person with a *Poeta Loquitur*; which, take notice, is a surer sign of a 480
fine thing in my Writings, than a Hand in the Margent any-where else.
Well now says *White*,

What need we find Him, we have certain proof
That he is somewhere, *Dame*, and that's enough:
For if there is a *Guide* that knows the way,   485
Although we know not him, we cannot stray.

That's true, I Gad: Well said *White*. You see her Adversary has
nothing to say for her self, and therefore to confirm the Victory, she
shall make a *Simile*.

Smith. Why then I find Similes are as good after Victory, as after 490
a Surprize.

Bayes. Every Jot, I Gad, or rather better. Well, she can do it two ways,
either about *Emission* or *Reception* of Light, or else about *Epsom-waters*, but
I think the last is most familiar; therefore speak, my pretty one.

As though 'tis controverted in the *School*,   495
If *Waters* pass by *Urine* or by *Stool*.
Shall we who are *Philosophers*, thence gather
From this dissention that they work by neither.

And I Gad, she's in the right on't; but mind now, she comes upon
her swop!   500

All this I did, your Arguments to try.

467 Night, *edd.*: Night. *1687*

And I Gad, if they had been never so good, this next Line confutes 'em.

Hear, and be dumb, thou Wretch, *that Guide am I.*

There's a Surprize for you now! How sneakingly t'other looks? Was 505 not that pretty now, to make her ask for a *Guide* first, and then tell her she was one? Who could have thought that this little *Mouse* had the *Pope* and a whole *General Council* in her Belly? Now Dapple had nothing to say to this; and therefore you'll see she grows peevish.

Come leave your Cracking tricks, and as they say,   510
Use not, that Barber that trims time, delay
Which I gad is new, and my own.
I've Eyes as well as you to find the way.
Then on they jogg'd, *and since an hour of talk*
Might cut a Banter *on the tedious walk;*   515
As I remember said the sober Mouse,
I've heard much talk of the *Wits Coffee-House.*
Thither, says *Brindle,* thou shalt go, and see
Priests sipping *Coffee, Sparks* and *Poets Tea;*
Here rugged Freeze, there Quality well drest,   520
These bafling the *Grand-Seigniour;* those the *Test.*
And hear shrew'd guesses made, and reasons given,
That humane Laws were never made in Heaven.
But above all, what shall oblige thy sight,
And fill thy Eye-Balls with a vast delight;   525
Is the *Poetic Judge* of sacred *Wit,*
Who do's i' th' *Darkness of his Glory* sit.
And as the Moon who first receives the light,
With which she makes these neither Regions bright;
So does he shine, reflecting from a far,   530
The Rayes he borrow'd from a better Star:
For rules which from *Corneille* and *Rapin* flow,
Admir'd by all the scribling Herd below,
From *French Tradition* while he does dispence,
Unerring Truths, 'tis Schism, a damn'd offence,   535
To question his, or trust your private sense.

Hah! Is not that right, Mr. *Johnson?* Gad forgive me he is fast a sleep! Oh the damn'd stupidity of this Age! a sleep! Well, Sir, Since you'r so drousy, your humble Servant.

533 below, *edd.*: below. *1687*

Johns. Nay, Pray Mr. *Bayes,* Faith I heard you all the while. *The* 540
white Mouse.

Bayes. The white Mouse! ay, ay, I thought how you heard me. Your
Servant, Sir, your Servant.

Johns. Nay, Dear *Bayes,* Faith I beg thy Pardon, I was up late last
Night, Prithee lend me a little Snuff, and go on.   545

Bayes. Go on! Pox I don't know where I was, well I'll begin. Here,
mind, now they are both come to Town.

> But now at *Peccadille* they arrive,
> And taking Coach, t'wards *Temple-Bar* they drive;
> But at St. *Clement's Church,* eat out the Back;   550
> And slipping through the *Palsgrave,* bilkt poor *Hack.*

There's the *Utile* which ought to be in all Poetry, Many a *young
Templer* will save his shilling by this Stratagem of my Mice.

Smith. Why, will any *young Templer* eat out the back of a Coach?

Bayes. No, I gad, but you'll grant it is mighty natural for a Mouse. 555

> Thence to the *Devil,* and ask'd if *Chanticleer,*
> *Of Clergy kind,* or Councellour *Chough* was there;
> Or Mr. *Dove,* a Pigeon of Renown,
> *By his high crop, and corny Gizzard known,*
> Or *Sister* Partlet, *with the Hooded head;*   560
> No, Sir. She's *hooted hence,* said *Will,* and fled.
> Why so? *Because she would not pray a Bed.*

Johns. aside. 'Sdeath! Who can keep awake at such stuff? Pray, Mr.
Bayes, lend me your Box again.

Bayes. Mr. *Johnson,* How d'e like that Box? Pray take notice of it, 565
'twas given me by a *person* of *Honour* for looking over a Paper of Verses;
and indeed I put in all the lines that were worth any thing in the whole
Poem. Well, but where were we? Oh! Here they are, just going up
stairs into the *Apollo;* from whence my White takes occasion to talk
very well of *Tradition.*   570

> Thus to the place where *Johnson* sat we climb,
> Leaning on the same Rail that guided him;
> And whilst we thus on equal helps rely,
> Our Wit must be as true, our thoughts as high.
> For as an *Author* happily compares   575
> *Tradition* to a well-fixt pair of *Stairs,*

So this the *Scala Sancta* we believe,
By which his *Traditive Genius* we receive.
Thus every step I take my Spirits soar,
And I grow more a *Wit*, and more, and more.   580

There's humour! Is not that the liveliest Image in the World of a
Mouses going up a pair of Stairs. *More a Wit, and more and more?*

Smith. Mr. *Bayes*, I beg your Pardon heartily, I must be rude, I have a
particular Engagement at this time, and I see you are not near an end yet.

Bayes. Godsokers! Sure you won't serve me so: All my finest Discrip- 585
tions and best Discourse is yet to come.

Smith. Troth, Sir, if 'twere not an Extraordinary concern I could not
leave you.

Bayes. Well; but you shall take a little more, and here I'll pass over
two dainty *Episodes* of *Swallows, Swifts, Chickens,* and *Buzzards.*   590

Johns. I know not why they should come in, except to make yours
the longest *Fable* that ever was told.

Bayes. Why, the excellence of a *Fable* is in the length of it. *Æsop*
indeed, like a Slave as he was, made little, short, simple stories, with
a dry Moral at the end of 'em; and could not form any noble design. 595
But here I give you *Fable* upon *Fable*; and after you are satisfied with
Beasts in the first course, serve you up a delicate Dish of Fowl for the
second; now I was at all this pains to abuse one particular person; for
I gad I'll tell you what a trick he serv'd me. I was once translating a
very good *French Author*, but being something long about it, as you 600
know a Man is not always in the Humour; What does this *Jack* do, but
put's out an Answer to my Friend before I had half finished the
Translation: so there was three whole Months lost upon his Account.
But I think I have my revenge on him sufficiently, for I let all the World
know, that he is a *tall, broadback'd, lusty fellow*, of a *brown Complexion, fair* 605
Behaviour, a *Fluent Tongue*, and *taking* amongst the *Women*; and to top it
all that he's much a *Scholar*, more a *Wit*, and owns but *two Sacraments.*
Don't you think this Fellow will hang himself? But besides, I have so
nickt his Character in a Name as will make you split. I call him—I gad
I won't tell you unless you remember what I said of him.   610

Smith. Why that he was much a *Scholar*, and more a *Wit*—

Bayes. Right; and his name is *Buzzard*, ha! ha! ha.

Johns. Very proper indeed, Sir.

Bayes. Nay, I have a farther fetch in it yet than perhaps you imagine;
for his true name begins with a *B*, which makes me slily contrive him 615

this, to begin with the same Letter: There's a pretty device, Mr.
Johnson; I learn'd it, I must needs confess, from that ingenious sport,
I love my Love with an *A*, because she's *Amiable*; and if you could but
get a knot of merry Fellows together, you should see how *little Bayes*
would top 'em all at it, I gad.   620

   Smith. Well, but good Faith, Mr. *Bayes*, I must leave you, I am half an
hour past my time.

   Bayes. Well, I've done, I've done. Here are eight hundred Verses upon
a rainy Night, and a Birds-Nest; and here's three hundred more,
Translated from two *Paris Gazets*, in which the *Spotted Mouse* gives an 625
account of the Treaty of Peace between the *Czars* of *Muscovy*, and the
Emperour, which is a piece of News *White* does not believe, and this is
her Answer. I am resolv'd you shall hear it, for in it I have taken occasion to prove *Oral Tradition* better than *Scripture*. Now you must know,
'tis sincerely my Opinion, that it had been better for the World, if we 630
nere had any *Bibles* at all.

> E'er that *Gazet* was printed, said the *White*,
> *Our Robin* told another story quite;
> This *Oral Truth* more safely I believ'd,
> My Ears cannot, your Eyes may be deceiv'd.   635
> By word of Mouth unerring Maxims flow,
> And *Preaching's* best, if understood, or no.
> Words I confess *bound by, and trip so light*,
> *We have not time to take a steady sight*;
> Yet fleeting thus are plainer then when Writ,   640
> To long Examination they submit.

   Hard things—Mr. *Smith*, if these two lines don't recompence your
stay, ne'r trust *John Bayes* again.

> Hard things at the first Blush are clear and full,
> *God mends on second thoughts*, but Man grows dull.   645

   I gad I judge of all Men by my self, 'tis so with me, I never strove
to be very exact in any thing but I spoil'd it.

   Smith. But allowing your Character to be true, is it not a little too
severe?

   Bayes. 'Tis no matter for that, these general reflections are daring, 650
and savour most of a *noble Genius*, that spares neither *Friend* nor *Foe*.

   Johns. Are you never afraid of a drubbing for that *daring* of your *noble
Genius?*

Bayes. Afraid! Why *Lord* you make so much of a beating, I' gad 'tis no more to me than a Flea biting. No, No, if I can but be witty upon 655 'em, let 'em en lay on, I Faith, I'll ne'r baulk my fancy to save my Carkass. Well, but we must dispatch, Mr. *Smith.*

> Thus did they merrily carouse all day,
> *And like the gaudy fly their Wings display;*
> *And sip the sweets, and bask in great* Apollo's *ray.*   660

Well there's an end of the Entertainment; and Mr. *Smith*, if your affairs would have permitted, you would have heard the best *Bill of Fare* that ever was serv'd up in *Heroicks*: but here follows a dispute shall recommend it self, I'll say nothing for it. For *Dapple*, who you must know was a *Protestant*, all this while trusts her own Judgment, and 665 foolishly dislikes the Wine; upon which our *Innocent* does so run her down, that she has not one word to say for her self, but what I put in her Mouth; and I gad, you may imagine they won't be very good ones, for she has disoblig'd me, like an *Ingrate.*

> *Sirrah*, says *Brindle*, Thou hast brought us Wine,   670
> Sour to my tast, and to my Eyes unfine.
> Says *Will*, all *Gentlemen* like it, ah! says *White*,
> What is approv'd by them, must needs be right.
> 'Tis true, I thought it bad, but if the House
> Commend it, I submit, a private Mouse.   675

Mind that, mind the *Decorum*, and Defference, which our Mouse pays to the Company.

> Nor to their *Catholic* consent oppose
> My erring Judgment, and reforming Nose.

Ah! ah! there she has nick't her, that's up to the Hilts, I gad, and 680 you shall see *Dapple* resents it.

> Why, what a Devil shan't I trust my Eyes?
> Must I drink *Stum* because the *Rascal* lyes?
> And palms upon us *Catholic* consent,
> To give *sophisticated Brewings* vent.   685
> Says *White*, What ancient Evidence can sway,
> If you must Argue thus and not obey?
> *Drawers* must be trusted, through whose hands convey'd,
> You take the *Liquor*, or you spoil the *Trade.*
> For sure those *Honest Fellows* have no knack   690
> Of putting off *stum'd Claret* for *Pontack.*

How long, alas! would the poor Vintner last,
If all that drink must *judge*, and every *Guest*
Be allowed to have an understanding *Tast?*
Thus she: Nor could the Panther well inlarge,   695
With weak defence, against so strong a Charge.

There I call her a *Panther*, because she's spotted, which is such a blot
to the *Reformation*, as I warrant 'em they will never claw off, I Gad.

But with a *weary Yawn* that shew'd her pride,
Said, *Spotless* was a *Villain*, and she *lyed*.   700
White saw her *canker'd Malice* at that word,
And said her Prayers, and drew her *Delphic Sword*.
T'other cry'd *Murther*, and her *Rage restrain'd*:
And thus her passive Character maintain'd.
But now alas——   705

Mr. *Johnson*, pray mind me this; Mr. *Smith*, I'll ask you to stay no
longer, for this that follows is so engaging; hear me but two Lines, I
Gad, and go away afterwards if you can.

But now, alas, I grieve, I grieve to tell
What sad mischance these pretty things *befel*   710
These Birds of Beasts——

There's a tender Expression, *Birds of Beasts*: 'tis the greatest Affront
that you can put upon any *Bird*, to call it, *Beast of a Bird*: and a *Beast* is
so fond of being call'd a *Bird*, as you can't imagine.

These Birds of Beasts, these learned Reas'ning Mice,   715
Were separated, banish'd in a trice.
Who would be learned for their sakes, who wise?

Ay, who indeed? There's a *Pathos*, I Gad, Gentlemen, if that won't
move you, nothing will, I can assure you: But here's the sad thing I was
afraid of.   720

The *Constable* alarm'd by this noise,
Enter'd the Room, directed by the voice,
And speaking to the *Watch, with head aside*,
Said, *Desperate Cures must be to desperate Ills apply'd*.
These *Gentlemen*, for so their Fate decrees,   725
Can n'ere enjoy at once the *But and Peace*.
When each have separate Interests of their own,
Two Mice are one too many for a Town.

By *Schism* they are torn; and therefore, *Brother*,
Look you to one, and I'll secure the t'other.   730
Now whither *Dapple* did to *Bridewell* go,
Or in the *Stocks* all night her Fingers blow,
Or in the *Compter* lay, concerns not us to know.
But the *immortal Matron, spotless White*,
Forgetting *Dapple*'s Rudeness, Malice, Spight,   735
Look'd kindly back, and wept, and said, *Good Night*.
Ten thousand Watchmen waited on this Mouse,
With Bills, and Halberds, to her Country-House.

This last Contrivance I had from a judicious Author, that makes *Ten
thousand Angels* wait upon his *Hind*, and she asleep too, I Gad.—   740
Johns. Come, let's see what we have to pay.
Bayes. What a Pox, are you in such hast? You han't told me how you
like it.
Johns. Oh, extreamly well. Here, Drawer.

Epistle, to Lord ———.

THAT with much Wealth and large encrease, My Lord,
    Your happy Granaries are amply stor'd;
That You can boast a Noble race, and show
United Honors Center'd all in You;
That in all Turns of State Your word has stood,   5
To Your own Honor, and Your Countries Good;
That You write so that since great Strephons death
No daring brow claims ev'n the Second wreath:
Yet these Perfections, were my thoughts declar'd,
Nor ask that praise, nor merit that reward,   10
As that one good, which ev'n Your Foes confess
(If any such there can be) You Possess.
A real Judgment, and a Solid Mind
Expert to use these blessings in their kind,
As Prudence dictates, and as God design'd.   15

Thô I dont fancy an impartial dole
Of Sense distributed to every Soul;

Title: L 28 (Pope), 'Contents' *of L 28 (D), M: om. L 28 (D)*   7 write so *L 28 (D)*: so
sing, *L 28 (Pope), M*   11 ev'n *edd.*: ev'en *L 28, M*   16 Thô...fancy *L 28 (D)*: 'Tis
true, I think not *L 28 (Pope), M*

So that no Two, but can exactly say,
Each had his Measure, tho a diff'rent way:
Yet potent Nature frankly has bestow'd   20
Such various gifts amongst the mingl'd Crowd,
That I believe, the dullest of the kind,
Wou'd he but Husband and Manure his Mind,
Might find some Exc'llence there, which well-improv'd
At home might make him Pleas'd, in public Lov'd.   25

Some with grave Judgment can decide the Cause,
And govern Nations and Establish Laws.
Others in rougher Policy Excell,
Manage their Troops and wage the Battel well.
With useful Science, some, and wholsom rules,   30
Improve our Virtues, and exalt our Souls.
And some search cunning Nature, and declare
How all things did, and why they thus appear.
Some know to bound the Earth; and some to Guide
The lab'ring Bark above the impetuous Tyde.   35
Some can with Art alure the trembling string,
And happy wonders in apt Measures Sing.
Others can form the Hero or the Saint,
In breathing Stone, or animated Paint.
Thus some may Profit us, and some may Please;   40
All may have diff'rent Honors, diff'rent ways.

Some have large Wealth and may receive the guest
Others have Wit and Mirth to Crown the Feast.

Then all that Vice, and those absurdities,
Which every moment every body sees,   45
Arise, (might I declare my thoughts) from this;
Not that Men want, but use their Parts amiss:
Not One in Twenty their own Tallents know,
The Ox wou'd champ the bitt, the War horse plough:
The Coward Sieges and Campaigns recites,   50
The Cripple dances, and the Coxcomb writes.

---

24 Exc'llence *edd.*: Exce'llence *L 28*: Excellence *M*   35 the *L 28* (*D*): th' *L 28*
(*Pope?*), *M*   43 Feast. *edd.*: Feast *L 28*: feast. *M*   44–47 *See commentary*
48 One] *M* Two *L 28* (*164*): *Illegible in W*   Tallents] *M* Talent *W*, *L 28* (*164*)

    No Ancient Piece, much harder than the rest,
That by Translation scorns to be exprest,
But all those People who to Phillis chime,
And make *admiring* and *desiring* Rhime,   55
With Emu'lous Labour turn and tumble it,
And heads forthwith are scratch'd, and nailes are bitt.
No happy Picture, whose rich features show
Vandyke! Thy labour, or Thine, Angelo!
But whilst the Dawbers with joint pains combine   ) 60
To rival each inimitable line,   }
The great Original comes forth a *Sign*.   )
Painters and Poets any thing may dare—   )
I grant You, Sir, but with a previous Care   }
Of what their Strength denys, and what t'wil bear.) 65
Who after Waller sings the *Holland*-fight,
Tells but how Ill 'tis possible to write:
Who fain wou'd throughly show his want of Skill,
From Lely draws my Lady Cleveland ill.

    Is there a Man, on whom indulgent fate   70
Has smil'd, and thrown a competent Estate?
With Sense enough to use the blessing right,
To his own Pleasure, and his Friends delight.
On he shal run, where Nature never mean't,
Nor friends, nor force, nor Bedlam, shal prevent.   75
Perhaps his Whim runs to Divinity,   )
Not *Pulton* then, not Casuist *ABC*,   }
Or their new Converts, troublesome as he.   )
Perhaps to Law; his Cases then shal tire
A City Orphan, or a Norfolk Squire;   80
His unintelligible Talk shal put
A Widow, or a real Lawyer, out.
Take heed (crys all the Country) come not near!
'Tis Term-time at his Table all the Year.

    Is there another, with such moderate Sence   85
It just suffices not to give offence?

52–69 *In L 28, these follow l. 84, but are marked to be inserted at this point, as they are in M*
68 Who fain *L 28 (D)*: & Who *L 28 (Pope)*: And who *M*   70–84 *In L 28, these follow
l. 90, but are marked (by Pope?) to be inserted here, as they are in M*   77 Casuist] Casuists *M*
86 It *L 28 (D)*: As *L 28 (Pope)*, *M*

Tis odds but he shal Print his Poetry,
Thô such perhaps as *Higden* writes or I:
Nestles amongst the Criticks in the Pitt,
And talks at Will's, and wou'd be thought a Wit.   90

　The rough Tarpaulin when he Home has brought
Health, Strength, and Treasure, every thing but Thought:
Must needs turn Spark forsooth; and to be known
Keeps very High, is jilted, and Undon.
The Land-Commander, whose ill favor'd face   95
Might make him rail at Love, and break his glass;
If He 'as been once in France, affects to go
Odly ill-drest, and spruce as any Beau,
Ogles, and Combs, and Bows, and does not doubt
To raise his Fortunes by the Pettycoat.   100
The awkerd City Spark, who shou'd not Swear
But sneaking Shop-Oaths to put off bad Ware,
Nor drink but at the chusing of the May'r,
Getts very drunk, and with it very rude:
Some Suit their Inclinations, and are lewd;   105
On Vice, in him, 'tis Saucy to intrude.
Vice (says the Moralist, and wou'd dispute)
Which no Man's Nature realy can Suit.
It may Deceive us thô, Sir; but in these
It looks so ill, it scarse appears to Please.   110

　Well; most their business, their Discourse, their Cloaths,
Their very Vice, unfit for them they chuse.
The Squire from Mother sent unfleg'd and raw,
To learn good breeding and to read the Law,
Though he has little else to justify   115
His Parts, but Innocence and modesty,
Quitts these as soon as possibly he can,
And swears, and drinks, and fain wou'd be—

　But to my Theme—I firmly stil aver
Tis not through want of parts, but want of care,   120
To use those parts aright, so many err:

88 as *Higden* writes] a Higden write *M*   91–110 *In L 28 & M, these follow l. 118,*
where Drift inserted them from a facing page of his copy-text   102 off] of *M*   108
Which *L 28 (D)*: With *L 28 (Pope)*, *M*   110 Please. *edd.*: Please *L 28*: please, *M*
112 Their *edd.*: There *L 28*, *M*   they *L 28 (D)*: will *L 28 (Pope)*, *M*   114 the
L 28 (Pope), *M*: to *L 28 (D)*

They wont spare time to weigh the good or ill,
We blame their *Intellect*, the Fault lyes in their *will.*
I know a hopeful Youth about the Town,
Whose Friends and Parts design'd him for the Gown;   125
His body was but weak, his quiet mind
To gentle Peace seem'd happily enclin'd:
Yet Thoughtless He, and erring in this Care
Of his own strength is fall'n in love with War;
Herds with the Fighters, and with Pleasure feels   130
A long Toledo jarring at his Heels:
Talks ill of Sieges rais'd, and Armys led,
And wears his Cravat string, and Breeches red.
I met the Youth, and truly, far from spight,
Told him his Tallent never was to fight—   135
He frown'd, and said, "*Nor Yours perhaps to Write.*"

1688

To Mr Charles Montagu, on his Marriage with the Right Honorable the Countess of Manchester.

CHAMONT was absent, and Remembrance brought
Him and past Blessings thick upon my Thought:
Those but my Tortures now; whilst my vex't Heart
Beat quick, and throb'd, and sought its Nobler part,
Nor would have Rest; uneasy still Alone   5
I scorn'd the Wretch my Self, my Worth was gon.
In Company I strove for Ease in vain
Whilst Mirth in others but encreas't my Pain.
Med'cines from Books as vain I often took,
They that Writ best but told me how You spoke   10
In vain I saw; each Object thrô my Eye
Touch'd my Soul quick with Something still of Thee.

---

128 Care *L 28 (D)*: Care, *L 28 (Pope?)*: care *M*   136 *Write.*" *edd.*: *Write. L 28, M*
   Title] To a Friend on his Marriage. *L 28 (Pope), M*   4 sought *L 28 (Pope?), M*: saught
B.M., L 28 (D)

My Friend and I sat there; We that way mov'd;
There read, there talk't, and every where we lov'd.
  But when 'twas said, Thou ne'r must hope to See   15
That Friend return to Things below and Thee.
Happy He triumphs, happy has possest
A Seat of Glory, and a Heav'n of Rest:
'Twas base to sigh; and grew a Crime to moan;
So much I prize Your Joy beyond my Own.   20
  Theseus still lov'd and still desir'd his Friend
Whilst great Alcides yet on Earth remain'd:
But when the Hero to his Heav'n arriv'd
Most the Youth wanted Him, yet least He griev'd.
Pleas'd that the Friend was in the God improv'd   25
He learn'd to worship what before He Lov'd.

  Accept my first Oblation, thy own Heart,
(For Friendship shall be forc't to let it part.)
'Tis Love demands it, and I must resign,
Honoria gave Her own, and merits Thine.   30
And to return it thus I triumph more,
Than keeping it from all the Sex before.
Accept my wishes too: meet all the Charms
The Muses gave, in dear Honoria's Arms.
Her self a Muse more noble than the Nine   35
For when We Harmony it self would paint
Art does but in One gracefull Figure joyn
The lovely Woman and the pious Saint.
May all Thy Hours in glad Procession pass
Kind as Her look, and soft as her Embrace.   40
And every Hour new pleasures may'st Thou find
All Fair and Lovely as Thy Mistress' Mind.
And sure that's very lovely, very fair:
Nothing but Heav'n, and You, my Friend, are there.
May all Her future Minutes happy prove   45
As are Thy Numbers when Thou writ'st of Love.

14 There...there] These...these *L 28, M*   18, 23 Heav'n *L 28, M*: Heav'en *B.M.*
20 Joy] Bliss *L 28 (Pope), M*: [   ] *L 28 (D)*   21 still desir'd] *L 28, M* follow'd still
Bodl   22 yet on] *L 28, M* upon *Bodl*   23 to his Heav'n arriv'd] *L 28, M* was to
Heav'n receiv'd, *Bodl*   26 Lov'd *edd.*: Lov d *B.M.*: lov'd *L 28, M, Bodl*   29 must]
will *L 28, M*   35–38] *Deleted (by Pope?) in L 28*: *om. M*   43–44] *L 28 om. M*
44 Heav'n *L 28*: Heav'en *B.M.*   46 writ'st *M*: write'st *B.M.*: writst *L 28*

How strangely happy those well Beauty knew
She fled Apollo, but She ran to You.
May smiling Peace and gentle Concord spread
Their blooming sweets around Thy spotless Bed 　　　50
And may Mankind with pleasing Wonder see
Successive Hopes of thy great Progeny
Till dear Chamont's and Virgil's labours dye.

A Session of the Poets (imperfect.)

SINCE the King like a venterous Gamster at Loo
Threw by his old Courtiers, and took in for New
Till by shuffling and drawing the cards were so mix't
That those which Won this deal were laid aside next
The Sons of the Muses began to repine 　　　5
That who e'er was turn'd out John Dryden kept in
So, Numerous and Noisy to Phœbus they came
To ask why of All the Knaves he shou'd be Pam.

John Dryden appear'd at the head of the Gang,
And with a low bow and learned Harangue 　　　10
He said with Submission he thought t'wou'd be hard
If he of the Bays shou'd at length be debar'd
Who so well had writ and so frankly declar'd.
Declaring says Phœbus, concerns not this court;
They that set you at work let 'em e'en pay you for't. 　　　15
Whats Religion to Us, tis well known that many
Have manag'd the Place well without having Any.
For matter of Writing 'tis frankly confest
If we'l take your bare word for't You do it much best.

next that advances 　　　20
Is the Priest to the Sacrifice honest Sir Francis.
Ochanti, Huy Hannon, Rozarno, Tzinzummey
Bloody hands, blazing Comets, Priests devils and Mummy
Sure this will engage You? Apollo says No
All these pritty tricks Lee in Bedlam can show. 　　　25

47–48] *L 28 om. M*
　15 for't. *edd.*: for't *L 28*　　　21 Francis. *edd.*: Francis *L 28*　　　25 show. *edd.*: show
L 28

Why then (tho Despina and Tamerlane fail)
I'm my Lord Dorsets Friend, I hope that may prevail,
Apollo bow'd low at the name, and declar'd
What a just Veneration he had for my Lord.
But heark'yee Sir Knight, says the God, that wont do   30
For if he had the Bays whom his Honor best knew
W. R. has fairer pretences than You.

   Old Waller came next, and handsomly pleaded
That none writ so neat and so calmly as he did
That with very much Wit he no anger exprest   35
Nor sharpen'd his Verse with a venomous Jest.
And granting all this, said Apollo, old Friend
'Twil signify little to'th' business in hand
For as he that's dubb'd Hero, must first to the Wars
And bring home sore bruises and Hazardous Scars   40
So, he that wou'd rise and be prov'd a true Bays
(To be fitted in every respect to the Place)
Must be damn'd for his plays and for Satyr Sustain
Two beatings at least in a little By-Lane.

   Next little Tom Durfey demanded the Bays   45
For the sense of his Songs and the Plot of his Plays
A double pretence which I'l vow very Strong
But I've heard says Apollo a Scurrilous Song
In which You've affronted my friend Mrs. Long
And heark-yee Squire Durfey the Man that refuses   50
Respect to the Sex is no friend to the Muses.

   Next Maidwel who young Poetasters can bring
As some do tame Blackbirds, to Whistle and Sing,
His Tropes and his Figures most finely employs
To purchace the Wreath for himself and his Boys   55
Apollo inform'd him he shou'd be most glad
If from his own Works any Plea cou'd be made
But at present he thought his pretences but bad.
For if he that Taught best had most right to the Lawrel
Old Busby not he must determine the Quarrel.   60

32 You. *edd.*: You *L 28*   53 Sing, *edd.*: Sing *L 28*   59–60 *In L 28, these are*
misplaced before l. 56   60 Quarrel. *edd.*: Quarrel *L 28*

From the Island of Love with a Shipload of Verse
Comes Afra and asks the Court leave to Rehearse
Enjoyment and Raptures and pretty Devises
Enamell'd on Watches for Damon and Isis.
The Poetess Sung: at length swore She'd prove   65
That She and Jack Hoyle taught the whole Age to Love
And on with't She ran, nor had ended 'till now
But Phœbus reprov'd her, and gave her to know
That her Tongue went too fast, and her Love watch too Slow.

The next that put in for't was little Jo: Crown   70
He swore his Sir Courtly had ravish'd the Town.
Then Shadwel too sweated amain in the Praise
Of the language and Plott of his Squire of Alsace.
They both were put by, So were two or three more
That fell short of the Lawrel the SESSION before   75
For they cou'd no more their Pretensions repeat
Than a Horse thats once distanc'd may run Second heat.

With a bundle of Poetry Settle was there
Some brought from the Play-House, and some from the Fair.
But Apollo assur'd him, He never wou'd Chuse   80
The Lawrel from such Demi Poets as those
Who write Treason in Verse, and recant but in Prose.

Sir Ch: . . . . . that can write and better Translate
Was likewise Deny'd it for He'd an Estate
And from Homer to D. . . .n it never was known   85
That the Laureat had three Pence a Year of his own.

Tom Wicherly challeng'd the Bays as his Due
And brought the Plain Dealer to prove his words true.
I own says Apollo the Strength of Your Plea
But e'er You've the Place, there's one rub in Your way: 90
The Test, my Dear Friend, You must certainly take
Wou'd to God we cou'd get it repeal'd for your Sake.

After these a whole Gang with ill looks and hard Names
Thrust up to Apollo and forc'd in their Claims.

66 Hoyle *edd.*: Hogle *L 28*   70 *In L 28, preceded by:*
                If e'er he was found
      To chuse words for any thing else but the sound.
73 Alsace. *edd.*: Alsace *L 28*   90 way: *edd.*: way *L 28*

On Exodus iii. 14. I am that I am.
An Ode.

Written in 1688, as an Exercise at St. John's College, Cambridge.

I.

MAN! Foolish Man!
    Scarce know'st thou how thy self began;
Scarce hast thou Thought enough to prove Thou art;
Yet steel'd with study'd Boldness, thou dar'st try
To send thy doubting Reason's dazled Eye   5
Through the mysterious Gulph of vast Immensity.
Much thou canst there discern, much thence impart.
    Vain Wretch! suppress thy knowing Pride;
      Mortifie thy learned Lust:
Vain are thy Thoughts, while thou thy self art Dust.   10

II.

Let Wit her Sails, her Oars let Wisdom lend;
The Helm let politick Experience guide:
Yet cease to hope thy short-liv'd Bark shall ride
Down spreading Fate's unnavigable Tide.
    What, tho' still it farther tend?   15
    Still 'tis farther from its End;
And, in the Bosom of that boundless Sea,
Still finds its Error lengthen with its Way.

III.

With daring Pride and insolent Delight
Your Doubts resolv'd you boast, your Labours crown'd;   20
And, ʻEYPHKA! your God, forsooth is found
Incomprehensible and Infinite.

Title: An...Cambridge.] 1709 A Pindarique ODE. 1693   7 much thence] 1709 and much 1693   10 while] 1709 whilst 1693   11 In 1693, the present stanzas I and II are combined as stanza 1   11] 1709 Wisdom her Oars, and Wit her Sails may lend, 1693 16 farther] 1709 further 1693   18] 1709 Loses it self, and its increasing way. 1693 20 Your...boast] 1709 You boast your Doubts resolv'd 1693

But is He therefore found? Vain Searcher! no:
Let your imperfect Definition show,
That nothing You, the weak Definer, know.   25

IV.

Say, why shou'd the collected Main
It self within it self contain?
Why to its Caverns shou'd it sometimes creep,
And with delighted Silence sleep
On the lov'd Bosom of its Parent Deep?   30
Why shou'd its num'rous Waters stay
In comely Discipline, and fair Array,
Till Winds and Tides exert their high Commands?
Then prompt and ready to obey,
Why do the rising Surges spread   35
Their op'ning Ranks o'er Earth's submissive Head,
Marching thro' different Paths to different Lands?

V.

Why does the constant Sun
With measur'd Steps his radiant Journeys run?
Why does He order the Diurnal Hours   40
To leave Earth's other Part, and rise in Ours?
Why does He wake the correspondent Moon,
And fill her willing Lamp with liquid Light,
Commanding Her with delegated Pow'rs
To beautifie the World, and bless the Night?   45
Why does each animated Star
Love the just Limits of it's proper Sphere?
Why does each consenting Sign
With prudent Harmony combine
In Turns to move, and subsequent appear,   50
To gird the Globe, and regulate the Year?

---

25 nothing] *1709* nothing less than nothing *1693*   33 Till...their] *1709* Prepar'd to
meet its *1693*   Commands *1693*: Command *1709, 1718*   34–35] *1709* And with
diffus'd Obedience spread *1693*   37 Marching] *1709* And march *1693*   38 *In 1693,
the present stanzas IV and V are combined as stanza 3*   does] *1709* shou'd *1693*   43
fill] *1709* filling *1693*   44 Pow'rs] *1709* Power *1693*   46, 48 does] *1709* shou'd *1693*
50–51] *1709* To keep in order, and gird up the regulated Year? *1693*

VI.

Man does with dangerous Curiosity
  These unfathom'd Wonders try:
With fancy'd Rules and arbitrary Laws
Matter and Motion he restrains;   55
And study'd Lines and fictious Circles draws:
  Then with imagin'd Soveraignty
Lord of his new Hypothesis he reigns.
He reigns: How long? 'till some Usurper rise;
And he too, mighty Thoughtful, mighty Wise,   60
Studies new Lines, and other Circles feigns.
From this last Toil again what Knowledge flows?
    Just as much, perhaps, as shows,
    That all his Predecessor's Rules
Were empty Cant, all Jargon of the Schools;   65
That he on t'other's Ruin rears his Throne;
And shows his Friend's Mistake, and thence confirms his own.

VII.

On Earth, in Air, amidst the Seas and Skies,
  Mountainous Heaps of Wonders rise;
    Whose tow'ring Strength will ne'er submit   70
To Reason's Batteries, or the Mines of Wit:
Yet still enquiring, still mistaking Man,
Each Hour repuls'd, each Hour dare onward press;
And levelling at GOD his wandring Guess,
(That feeble Engine of his reasoning War,   75
Which guides his Doubts, and combats his Despair)
Laws to his Maker the learn'd Wretch can give:
Can bound that Nature, and prescribe that Will,
Whose pregnant Word did either Ocean fill:
Can tell us whence all Beings are, and how they move and live. 80

61 and other] *1709* new *1693*   62] *1709*
          On t' other's Ruine rears his Throne,
          And shewing his mistakes, maintains his own.
          Well then! from this *new toil* what *Knowledge* flows! *1693*
64–67] *1709*
          That former Searchers were but bookish Fools,
            Their choice Remarks, their Darling Rules,
          But canting Error all, and *Jargon* of the Schools.   *1693*
68] *1709* Through the aerial Seas, and watry Skies, *1693*   80 Can...whence] *1709*
And...how *1693*

Thro' either Ocean, foolish Man!
That pregnant Word sent forth again,
Might to a World extend each ATOM there;
For every Drop call forth a Sea, a Heav'n for every Star.

VIII.

Let cunning Earth her fruitful Wonders hide;   85
And only lift thy staggering Reason up
To trembling CALVARY's astonish'd Top;
Then mock thy Knowledge, and confound thy Pride,
Explaining how Perfection suffer'd Pain,
Almighty languish'd, and Eternal dy'd: 90
How by her Patient Victor Death was slain;
And Earth prophan'd, yet bless'd with Deicide.
Then down with all thy boasted Volumes, down;
     Only reserve the Sacred One:
         Low, reverently low,   95
     Make thy stubborn Knowledge bow;
Weep out thy Reason's, and thy Body's Eyes;
         Deject thy self, that Thou may'st rise;
To look to Heav'n, be blind to all below.

IX.

Then Faith, for Reason's glimmering Light, shall give   100
     Her Immortal Perspective;
And Grace's Presence Nature's Loss retrieve:
Then thy enliven'd Soul shall see,
That all the Volumes of Philosophy,
With all their Comments, never cou'd invent   105
     So politick an Instrument,
To reach the Heav'n of Heav'ns, the high Abode,
Where MOSES places his Mysterious God,

81–82] *1709*
       Vain Man! that pregnant Word sent forth again,
       Through either Ocean, *1693*

84 For every] *1709* And for each *1693*   89 Explaining how] Sustaining how *1709* : By telling thee, *1693*   90] *1709* An Eternal Essence dy'd; *1693*   91 How... Victor] *1709* Death's Vanquisher by vanquish'd *1693*   92 And... bless'd] *1709* The promis'd Earth prophan'd *1693*   99 To look to] *1709* And to see *1693*   100 *In 1693, the present stanzas VIII and IX are combined as stanza 6*   103 see,] *1709* know *1693*
107–12] *1709* So fit, as *Jacob's* Ladder was to scale the distant Skie. *1693*

As was that Ladder which old JACOB rear'd,
When Light Divine had human Darkness clear'd; 110
And his enlarg'd Ideas found the Road,
Which Faith had dictated, and Angels trod.

The Orange.

1. GOOD people I pray
 Throw the Orange away,
'Tis a very sower Fruit, and was first brought in play
When good *Judith Wilk*
In her pocket brought Milk, 5
And with Cushings and Warming-pans labour'd to bilk
    This same Orange.

2. When the Army retreats
And the Parliament sits
To Vote our K—— the true use of his Wits: 10
'Twill be a sad means
When all he obtains
Is to have his Calves-head dress'd with other mens Brains,
    And an Orange.

3. The sins of his Youth 15
Made him think of one Truth,
When he spawl'd from his Lungs, and bled twice at the mouth,
That your fresh sort of Food
Does his Carcass more good,
And the damn'd thing that Cur'd his putrefied blood 20
    Was an Orange.

4. This hopeful young Son
Is surely his own
Because from an O—— it cry'd to be gone
But the Hereticks say 25
He was got by Da——
For neither K—— nor the Nuncio dare stay
    Near an Orange.

Title] Answer to an Orange. *L 28* 24 O——] Orange *L 28* 26 Da——]
Dada *L 28*

5. Since *Lewis* was Cut
   From his Breech to the Gut,
   France fancies an open-arse delicate Fruit;   30
   We wiser than so
   Have two strings to our bow
   For we've a good Q—— that's an open-arse too,

                      And an Orange. 35

6. Till *Nanny* writ much
   To the Rebels the D——
   Her Mother, good Woman, ne're ow'd her a grutch
   And the box of the Ear
   Made the matter appear,   40
   That the only foul savour the Q—— could not bear

                      Was an Orange.

7. An honest old Peer
   That forsook God last year,
   Pull'd off all his Plaisters, and Arm'd for the War;   45
   But his Arms would not do,
   And his Aches throbb'd too,
   That he wish'd his own Pox and his M——s too

                      On an Orange.

8. Old Tyburn must groan,   50
   For *Jeffreys* is known
   To have perjur'd his Conscience to marry his Son;
   And *D——s* cause
   Will be try'd by Just Laws,
   And *Herbert* must taste a most damnable Sauce   55

                      With an Orange.

9. *Lobb*, *Penn*, and a score
   Of those honest men more
   Will find this same Orange exceedingly sowre;
   The Q—— to be seiz'd   60
   Will be very ill pleas'd,
   And so will K—— Pippin, too dry to be squeez'd

                      By an Orange.

37 D——] Dutch *L 28*   39 of] on *L 28*   48 M——s] M.......s *L 28*:
Majesties *MS. insertion in Bodl. copy of 1688*   53 D——s] Devonshires *L 28*   54
Will...Just] Must...the *L 28*   56 Orange. *L 28 and 2 issues of 1688*: Orange
Wrenn copy of 1688   57 *Lobb, Penn*] Penn, Lob *L 28*   59 Orange] Or....*L 28*
62 Pippin] P.....*L 28*

Journey to Copt-Hall.

THIRTY Six Miles—too far to walk a foot
    And Pegasus, God knows, will never do't:
Yet I will on—It is decree'd,
I'l hire a more substantial Steed.
Accoutrement of Sword and Coat   5
Useless Ornament I vote.
Thus borrowing Whip and Cordibeck,
Proceed we next to Tick for Hack.

With *Faith I'l pay*, and six pence earnest
I got my Quondam Coach-horse harnest: 10
I mount, and great as Hudibrass,
With unarm'd kick urge on my horse;
Whilst he by instinct stil approaches
His old acquaintance of the Coaches:

With whipping constant as his trott,   15
My Beast and I to *Eppin* gott,
From whence, with loss of Whip and Leather,
I brought my sober Machin heither.
I came I saw,—what once to see again
My Horse I'd pardon, and renew my Pain.   20

Here well-set Simile might shine
Of Pilgrimage to Power divine,
Of zealous Persian who wou'd run
To gaze on beams of distant Sun;
But th'are abus'd by franctic *Lee*   25
And sung to Stuttring *Durfey*'s *Ge sol re.*

Well then—to Supper admirable
I sit, near Matron grave and head of Table
Methodically She carves Cunney
Whilst Frenchman talks of blood and Mony.   30
Diff'rent Discourses crown the Meal
Much of Religion past, and much of Veal.

19 saw *edd.*: say L 28, M   30 Mony. *M*: Mony L 28   32 Veal. *M*: Veal L 28

But one thing spoilt my appetite
Monsieur till ten from Candle light
Extended Three Prodigious Lies— 35
Good night.

On Mr: F. S. Killing the French K...

Sir,

T HE joyful Slaves, whom your report set free
From Taxes, wooden Shoes, and Slavery;
Their Neighbours too, who by the Bully scar'd,
His Warlike Bombs and Politic Rats bane fear'd;
All that have *trembling shook at his Alarms,* 5
Dutch-Men and *Protestants that felt his Arms,*
And wisely hop'd, his less Religious Son
Wou'd tolerate the *Mass* or *Alcoran:*
Last, *German Bishops,* who began to think,
They now might see less Fighting, and more drink: 10
All these their humblest Thanks to S....... send,
France's Deliv'rer, and the Muses Friend.
S......... the glory of whose lasting Name
Shal *crack Time's Iron Teeth and swel the cheeks of fame*
S........ whose mighty *Monarch-murthering* word 15
Rivals the force of St: Raviliac's Sword.
Say, (*for Thou knowest,*) thou *Hero-heart'ning Muse!*
What wou'd his presence, what his Arms produce?
Whose bare Report has nobler Mischiefs done,
Then *Oates*'s Mustard Balls, or *Pickerin*'s gun: 20
That at more distance kills, and Ecchoes louder,
Than Aurum fulminans or German Powder?

Title] On Mr: Fleetwood Shephards killing the French King '*Contents*' *of L 28*: To
Mr. Shepherd: Upon his Reporting the French King to be dead:
The mighty Nine, in full Assembly, meeting,
To their Well-wisher, Fleetwood Shepherd, Greeting. *B.M.*
Some of the punctuation and some of the marks for italics in L 28 were inserted by another hand
(*Pope?*) 1 Sir, *L 28* (*D*), *B.M.*: *deleted in L 28 (by Pope?*) your] you *B.M.* 2
Slavery] Tyranny *B.M.* 4 Politic] polite *B.M.* 5 *trembling*] trembl'd and *B.M.*
9 Last,] The *B.M.* 11 humblest...S.......] humble...Shepherd *B.M.* 12
Deliv'rer *B.M.*: Deliv'erer *L 28* 13, 15 S.........] Shepherd, *B.M.* 19
Mischiefs] Mischief *B.M.* 22 German] Cannon *B.M.*

Say, how at Paris, free from zealous fear,
S........ and *Reformation* shal appear: ⎫
Brutus at Rome less honor'd than he there!   ⎬ 25
How the swift Bumpers shal with joy go round,   ⎭
Whilst every Bowl with S......'s Name is crown'd;
And to his Health the Mawdlin Protestants
Shal first drink *Bourdeaux* dry, then beggar *Nantz.*

There be Those that leave Their Names behind them.

Ecc: 44. 8.

In Praise of the Lady Margaret Foundress of St: John's.

I.

I F gilded flaggs and heaps of polish'd Stone
   Can make the Deads memorial known
If from the well-cutt brass will long appear
   The Just the Gen'rous the Good lies here
How long will Margaretta's Name be prais'd,   5
   Who spent her Wealth another way
   Who built what never will Decay
Who Living Pillars of Her Glory rais'd?

CHORUS

Margaretta's Name shal live
And lasting Tribute of just Fame receive   10
Long as the Sacred Walls she founded stand,
The Pride, the light, the glory of our Land.
Long as the learned Youth shal flourish there
Inspir'd with Thoughts of Heav'n and Her,
Shal press with pleasing force the grateful String   15
And thanks and Praises to their Godess sing.

24 S.........] Shepherd *B.M.*   27 Whilst...S......'s] While...Shepherd's *B.M.*
  4 Gen'rous *edd.*: Gene'rous *L 28*   14 Her, *edd.*: Her. *L 28*

II.

If charitable Acts alone
Best make their Pious Authors known
If to the chearful Giver Men shal raise
    Lasting Monuments of praise   20
    How long shal Margaretta's Name
Grace the bright Rolls of Piety and Fame?

CHORUS

Long as Three Nations gratefully shal show
The mighty Thanks they to her goodness owe
Long as the sacred Page shal be Carress'd   25
Which tells Us CHARITY and SHE are bless'd.

III.

If Charitable Acts alone
Can for a Multitude of Sins attone
    If at that great that dreadful day
    Beyond which Time shal be no more   30
Who cherish'd Orphans and reliev'd the Poor
    With holy Confidence shal stay
And see his Sins and Sorrows wash'd away,
    What then shal be to Margaretta giv'n?

CHORUS

One of the best the brightest Seats in Heav'n.   35
    With Saints and Martyrs she shal live
    Encircl'd round with lasting Joy
Which no mischance, no Sorrow can destroy
Which Man desires, and GOD alone can give.

---

26 bless'd. *edd.*: bless'd *L 28*   33 away, *edd.*: away *L 28*   35 Heav'n. *edd.*:
Heav'n *L 28*   36 Martyrs *edd.*: Marty'rs *L 28*

Many Daughters have done well, but Thou Excellest them all.

Prov: 31. 29.

As spoken in a Vision to the Lady Margaret Foundress of St: John's.

'T WAS night, the Drousy Diety began
To chain with sleep the buisy thoughts of Man,
When free from Noise and troubles of the Day
Our . . . Poet in those flow'ry Meadows lay
Where reverent Cham cuts out its famous way   5
When loe! O strange, an unexpected light
Dispers'd the Native darkness of the Night
And rais'd at once his wonder and delight.
But how, how welcome did that light appear
Which usher'd in a form all Heav'nly fair   10
A Form which lately left its Mansh'on there.
A Woman proper, beautiful and fine
Her garb was Noble and her Mein divine
Majestick greatness Triumph'd in her face
And every Limb had its peculiar grace.   15
With sober Pace the lovely Ghost drew near,
Her smiling seem'd to Chide His useless fear
At length he knows the venerable Shade,
Runs to meet that of which he was afraid.
And thus with reverence Thrice bowing said   20
Hail mighty Patroness! Hail great and Good!
Hail doubly fam'd for Virtue and for blood!
Hail Thou, whose Acts shou'd I presume to show
I shou'd blasphem by Epithets too low.
Hail Saint or Princess royal or Divine   25
Hail wonder of our Sex and Fame of Thine
Be Thou my Muse vouchsafe to look on me
The meanest of thy learned Progeny.

8 delight. *edd.*: delight *L 28*   16 near, *edd.*: near *L 28*   18 Shade, *edd.*: Shade *L 28*
25 Saint *edd.*: St: *L 28*   28 Progeny. *edd.*: Progeny *L 28*

Inspire my Soul that I may sing Thy fame
And raise a work eternal as my Theam   30
Inspire my Soul that I may loudly tell
How far Thou dost all Woman kind Excell
How Thou bless'd Shade——
When York had Lancaster so long withstood
And Englands face was stain'd with English blood   35
Did'st bless the Nation with a Godlike Son
Who recompenc'd the Ills their Arms had done
Who made all Faction all Rebellion cease
And gave Us Plenty, Liberty, and Peace.
You heard each Tongue with joy your glory sing   40
Each bless the Parents of so good a King
With all the Praises Gratitude cou'd bring.
But thought the Gift not worthy yet of You
Unless with Peace You gave Us Learning too.
Then, then indulgently both paps you drew   45
And rais'd Two fabricks which shal ever be
Great Monuments of Piety and Thee——
   Fain wou'd the cheerful Poet have gon on
To Sing the Works her Charity had done
But She who did like Heav'n her Gifts dispence   50
Without the Hopes of any recompence
Seem'd by a frown to chide his saucy Eloquence
And moving from him with a graceful Pace
Ascended to that bright that happy Place
Where Saints like Her enjoy an everlasting Peace.   55

1689

To My Lady Exeter, on New Years day.
Her Birth-Day.

I.

GREAT God of Time, whose early care
Ordain'd the first-born of the Year
   To wait the gentle Anna's birth
O stil that happy Care employ
And stil let all her Minutes fly   5
   All wing'd with Peace, and crown'd with Mirth.
With softest Slumbers bless her Nights
And wake her still to new Delights
Bless all her Days and bid the Year
To show'r it's blessings all on Her.   10

II.

If Autumn blasts or Winter Storms,
O turn on us the threaten'd harms.
   From all that ill her beauties guard,
For her let Spring diffuse its flowers
And Harvest spread its richer Stores,   15
   With all thats good her cares reward.
O let delight and Plenty spread
Their blooming Sweets around her Head
O let the Seasons all desire
To Shower their Blessings all on Her.   20

III.

In the dear Lord of her Desires
Bless Her, for all his Joys are hers:
   Bless Him Secure from noise and Harms
And O when Love appoints the Day
Enrich it with thy Noblest ray   25
   And bring him safe to her Arms.

6 Mirth *edd.*: Myrtle *L 28*   11 Storms, *edd.*: Storms *L 28*   13 guard, *edd.*: guard
L 28   15 Stores, *edd.*: Stores *L 28*   21 III. *edd.*: *om. L 28*   26 Arms. *edd.*:
Arms *L 28*

O let her all those Blessings know
That Men can ask or Gods bestow
Let Love and Heav'n and Earth conspire
To Shower their Blessings all on her.

30

To the Right Honourable the Countess Dowager of Devonshire, On a Piece of Wissin's; Whereon were all her Grandsons Painted.

WISSIN and *Nature* held a long Contest,
  If She *Created*, or He *Painted* best:
With pleasing Thought the wond'rous Combat grew,
She still form'd *Fairer*, He still *Liker* drew.
In these Seven Brethren, they contended last,   5
  With Art increas'd their utmost Skill they try'd,
And both well pleas'd they had themselves surpass'd,
  The Goddess *Triumph'd*, and the Painter *Dy'd*.
That both their Skill to this vast Height did raise,
Be ours the Wonder, and be yours the Praise: 10
For here as in some Glass is well discry'd,
Only your self thus often multiply'd.

When Heaven had You and Gracious *Anna* made,
What more exalted Beauty could it add?
Having no nobler Images in Store,   15
It but kept up to these, nor could do more
Than Copy well, what it well fram'd before.
If in dear *Burleigh*'s generous Face we see
Obliging Truth, and handsome Honesty;
With all that World of Charms, which soon will move   20
Reverence in Men, and in the Fair-Ones love:
His every Grace, his fair Descent assures,
He has his Mother's Beauty, She has yours.
If ever *Cecill*'s Face had every Charm
That Thought can fancy, or that Heaven can form;   25
Their Beauties all become your Beauty's Due,
They are all Fair, because they're all like You:

If every *Ca'ndish* great and charming Look,
From You that Air, from You the Charms they took.
In their each Limb your Image is exprest, 30
But on their Brow firm Courage stands confest;
There their great Father by a strong Increase,
Adds Strength to Beauty, and compleats the Piece.
Thus still your Beauty in your Sons we view,
Wissin seven Times one great Perfection drew, } 35
Whoever sate, the Picture still is You.
So when the Parent Sun with genial Beams,
Has animated many goodly Gems;
He sees himself improv'd, while every Stone,
With a resembling Light, reflects a Sun. 40
So when great *Rhea* many Births had given,
Such as might govern Earth, and People Heaven;
Her Glory grew diffus'd, and fuller known,
She saw the Deity in every Son:
And to what God soe'er Men Altars rais'd, 45
Honouring the Off-spring they the Mother prais'd.
In short-liv'd Charms let others place their Joys
Which Sickness blasts, and certain Age destroys:
Your stronger Beauty, Time can ne'er deface,
'Tis still renew'd, and stamp'd in all your Race. 50

 Ah! *Wissin*, had thy Art been so refin'd,
As with their Beauty to have drawn their Mind,
Thro' circling Years thy Labours would survive,
And living Rules to fairest Virtue give
To Men unborn, and Ages yet to live; } 55
'Twould still be wonderful, and still be new,
Against what Time, or Spight, or Fate could do,
'Till thine confus'd with Nature's Pieces lie,
And *Cavendish*'s Name, and *Cecill*'s Honour Die.

To the Countess of Exeter, Playing on the Lute.

WHAT Charms You have, from what high Race You sprung,
    Have been the pleasing Subjects of my Song:
Unskill'd and young, yet something still I writ,
Of CA'NDISH Beauty join'd to CECIL's Wit.
But when You please to show the lab'ring Muse,   5
What greater Theam your Musick can produce;
My babling Praises I repeat no more,
But hear, rejoice, stand silent, and adore.

The PERSIANS thus, first gazing on the Sun,
Admir'd how high 'twas plac'd, how bright it shone;   10
But, as his Pow'r was known, their Thoughts were rais'd;
And soon they worship'd, what at first they prais'd.

ELIZA's Glory lives in SPENCER's Song;
And COWLEY's Verse keeps Fair ORINDA young.
That as in Birth, in Beauty You excell,   15
The Muse might dictate, and the Poet tell:
Your Art no other Art can speak; and You,
To show how well you play, must play anew:
Your Musick's Pow'r your Musick must disclose;
For what Light is, 'tis only Light that shows.   20

Strange Force of Harmony, that thus controuls
Our Thoughts, and turns and sanctifies our Souls:
While with its utmost Art your Sex cou'd move
Our Wonder only, or at best our Love:
You far above Both these your GOD did place,   25
That your high Pow'r might worldly Thoughts destroy;
That with your Numbers You our Zeal might raise,
And, like Himself, communicate your Joy.

Title: the...Exeter,] *1709* A LADY of Quality's *1693*   2 pleasing...my] *1709*
Subject of our Daring *1693*   3-4] *1709 om. 1693*   5 please] *1709* pleas'd *1693*
6 Theam...can] *1709* Theams...could *1693*   7 My...I] *1709* Our...we *1693*   15
as...You] *1709* you in *Beauty*, and in *Birth 1693*   22 Thoughts, and turns] *1709* inmost
Thoughts *1693*   23 While] *1709* Whilst *1693*   25 above] *1709* beyond *1693*

917.27   G

When to your Native Heav'n You shall repair,
And with your Presence crown the Blessings there;   30
Your Lute may wind its Strings but little higher,
To tune their Notes to that immortal Quire.
Your Art is perfect here; your Numbers do,
More than our Books, make the rude Atheist know,
That there's a Heav'n, by what he hears below.   } 35

As in some Piece, while LUKE his Skill exprest,
A cunning Angel came, and drew the rest:
So, when You play, some Godhead does impart
Harmonious Aid, Divinity helps Art;
Some Cherub finishes what You begun,   40
And to a Miracle improves a Tune.

To burning ROME when frantick NERO play'd,
Viewing that Face, no more he had survey'd
The raging Flames; but struck with strange Surprize,
Confest them less than those of ANNA's Eyes: 45
But, had he heard thy Lute, He soon had found
His Rage eluded, and his Crime atton'd:
Thine, like AMPHION's Hand, had wak'd the Stone,
And from Destruction call'd the rising Town:
Malice to Musick had been forc'd to yield;   50
Nor could he Burn so fast, as Thou cou'dst Build.

Picture of Seneca dying in a Bath.
By Jordain.

At the Right Honourable the Earl of Exeter's at
Burleigh-House.

WHILE cruel NERO only drains
The moral SPANIARD's ebbing Veins,
By Study worn, and slack with Age,
How dull, how thoughtless is his Rage!

36 while] *1709* whilst *1693*   38 when] *1709* whilst *1693*   43 that] *1709* your *1693*
44 raging] *reigning 1693, 1709*   45 Confest them] *1709* Confess 'em *1693*   48
wak'd] *1709* rais'd *1693*   49 the rising] *1709* a Fairer *1693*

Heighten'd Revenge He should have took;   5
He should have burnt his Tutor's Book;
And long have reign'd supream in Vice:
One nobler Wretch can only rise;
'Tis he whose Fury shall deface
The Stoic's Image in this Piece.   10
For while unhurt, divine JORDAIN,
Thy Work and SENECA's remain,
He still has Body, still has Soul,
And lives and speaks, restor'd and whole.

A Flower, Painted by Simon Varelst.

WHEN fam'd VARELST this little Wonder drew;
FLORA vouchsaf'd the growing Work to view:
Finding the Painter's Science at a Stand,
The Goddess snatch'd the Pencil from his Hand;
And finishing the Piece, She smiling said;   5
Behold One Work of Mine, that ne'er shall fade.

To Mr. Fleetwood Shepherd.

WHEN Crowding Folks, with strange ill Faces,
Were making Legs, and begging Places;
And some with Patents, some with Merit,
Tired out my good Lord *D——t*'s Spirit:
Sneaking, I stood, among the Crew,   5
Desiring much to Speak with You.
I waited, while the Clock struck Thrice,
And Footman brought out fifty Lies;
Till Patience vext, and Legs grown weary,
I thought it was in vain to tarry: 10
But did Opine it might be better,
By Penny-post to send a Letter.

Title: *Simon*] *om. Lpo 18, Lansd*   6 One Work of Mine] at least One Flower
Lpo 18, Lansd
    Title] *A Petitionary Epistle: From Mr.* Prior, *to* Fleet Shepherd. *1706*   1 WHEN] While
1706   3 Patents] Patent *1706*   4 *D——t's*] *Dorset's 1706*   8 Footman] Footmen
1706   9 Till] But *1706*   10 thought] found *1706*   11 But] And *1706*

Now, if you miss of this Epistle,
I'm balkt again, and may go Whistle.
My business, Sir, you'll quickly guess,   15
Is to desire some little Place:
And fair Pretentions I have for't,
Much Need, and very Small Desert.
When e're I writ to you, I wanted;
I always begg'd, you always granted.   20
Now, as you took me up when little,
Gave me my Learning, and my Vittle
Askt for me, from my Lord, Things fitting,
Kind as I'd been your own begetting;
Confirm what formerly you've given,   25
Nor leave me now at Six and Seven
As S——d has left *Mun. St*——*n.*
No Family that takes a Whelp,
When first he Laps and scarce can Yelp,
Neglects or turns him out of Gate,   30
When he's grown up to Dogs Estate:
Nor Parish, if they once adopt
The spurious Barns that Strowlers dropt,
Leave 'em when grown up lusty Fellows,
To the wide World, that is, the Gallows: 35
No, thank 'em for their Love, that's Worse,
Than if they'd Throtled them at Nurse.
   My Uncle, rest his Soul, when Living,
Might have contriv'd me ways of Thriving;
Taught me with Cyder to replenish   40
My Fatts, or ebbing Tide of Rhenish.
So when for Hock I drew Prickt White-wine,
Swear't had the flaver, and was right Wine:
Or sent me with Ten Pounds to *Furney-*
Vall's-Inn, to some good Rogue Attorney;   45

13–14] *om. 1706*   18 Need] Want *1706*   19] I ne'er Writ to you, but I've wanted;
1706   20 I] And *1706*   21 *Preceded in 1706 by inserted lines:*
    To my old Custom I am true;
    For God's Sake, don't you get a New.
Now] But *1706*   23] And still Equipt me with things fitting, *1706*   27 S——d
...*Mun. St*——*n*] Sunderland...Munsteven *1706*   30 him out of] it out at *1706*
31 he's grown up] once 'tis grown *1706*   32 Nor] No *1706*   33] The helpless
Bearns which Strowls have dropt: *1706*   36 No, *edd.*: No *1697*: None *1706*   their]
such *1706*   41 or] at *1706*   42 So] And *1706*   44 sent] put *1706*   45
some good Rogue] eminent *1706*

Where now, by forging Deeds and Cheating,
I'd had some handsom ways of getting.
All this you made me quit to follow,
That sneaking Whey-fast God *Apollo*.
Sent me among a Fidling Crew   } 50
Of Folks, I'ad never seen or Knew,
Calliope, and God knows who.
To add no more Invectives to it,
You spoil'd the Youth to make a Poet.
In Common Justice, Sir, there's no Man   55
That makes the Whore but keeps the Woman.
Among all honest Christian People
Who e're breaks Limbs, maintains the Cripple.
  The Sum of all I have to say,
Is, that you'd put me in some way   } 60
And your Petitioner shall pray——
  There's one thing more I had almost slipt,
But that may do as well in Post-script;
My Friend *C——s M——ue*'s preferr'd,   }
Nor would I have it long observ'd,   } 65
That one Mouse eats, while t'other's starv'd.

An Epistle to Fleetwood Shephard, Esq;

Burleigh, May 14, 1689.

SIR,

As once a Twelvemonth to the Priest,
  Holy at ROME, here Antichrist,
The SPANISH King presents a Jennet,
To show his Love;—That's all that's in it:
For if his Holiness wou'd thump   5
His reverend Bum 'gainst Horse's Rump,
He might b' equipt from his own Stable
With one more White, and eke more Able.

48 All . . . quit] You made me leave all this, *1706*　　　50 a] the *1706*　　　54 You . . . a]
You've . . . the *1706*　　　56 makes] takes *1706*　　　57] And, amongst all honest
People, *1706*　　　60 you'd put] you'l let *1706*　　　61 shall pray ——] shall ever Pray,
&c. *1706*　　　63 that] it *1706*　　　66 t'other's *edd.*: to'ther's *1697*: th'other's *1706*
　　Title] *1709　A Letter from Mr.* Prior, *to Mr.* Fleetwood Sheppard. *1692*　　2] *1709*
Whom some call Pope, some Antichrist, *1692*　　3 King presents] *1709* Monarch sends
1692

Or as with Gondola's and Men, His
Good Excellence the Duke of VENICE   10
(I wish, for Rhime, 't had been the King)
Sails out, and gives the Gulph a Ring;
Which Trick of State, He wisely maintains,
Keeps Kindness up 'twixt old Acquaintance:
For else, in honest Truth, the Sea   15
Has much less need of Gold, than He.

Or, not to rove, and pump one's Fancy
For Popish Similies beyond Sea;
As Folks from Mud-wall'd Tenement
Bring Landlords Pepper-Corn for Rent;   20
Present a Turkey, or a Hen
To Those might better spare Them Ten:
Ev'n so, with all Submission, I
(For first Men instance, then apply)
Send You each Year a homely Letter,   25
Who may return Me much a better.

Then take it, Sir, as it was writ,
To pay Respect, and not show Wit:
Nor look askew at what it saith;
There's no Petition in it,—'Faith.   30

Here some would scratch their Heads, and try
What They shou'd write, and How, and Why;
But I conceive, such Folks are quite in
Mistakes, in Theory of Writing.
If once for Principle 'tis laid,   35
That Thought is Trouble to the Head;
I argue thus: The World agrees,
That He writes well, who writes with Ease:
Then He, by Sequel Logical,
Writes best, who never thinks at all.   40

Verse comes from Heav'n, like inward Light;
Meer human Pains can ne'er come by't:
The God, not we, the Poem makes;
We only tell Folks what He speaks.

12 Gulph] *1709* Sea *1692*   24 then] *1709* than *1692*   35 Principle] *1709*
Principles *1692*

Hence, when Anatomists discourse,   45
How like Brutes Organs are to Ours;
They grant, if higher Powers think fit,
A Bear might soon be made a Wit;
And that, for any thing in Nature,
Pigs might squeak Love-Odes, Dogs bark Satyr.   50

MEMNON, tho' Stone, was counted vocal;
But 'twas the God, mean while, that spoke all.
ROME oft has heard a Cross haranguing,
With prompting Priest behind the Hanging:
The Wooden Head resolv'd the Question;   55
While You and PETTIS help'd the Jest on.

Your crabbed Rogues, that read LUCRETIUS,
Are against Gods, You know; and teach us,
The God makes not the Poet; but
The Thesis, *vice-versâ* put,   60
Should *Hebrew-wise* be understood;
And means, The Poet makes the God.

ÆGYPTIAN Gard'ners thus are said to
Have set the Leeks they after pray'd to;
And ROMISH Bakers praise the Deity   65
They chipp'd, while yet in its Paniety.

That when You Poets swear and cry,
The God inspires; I rave, I die;
If inward Wind does truly swell Ye,
'T must be the Cholick in your Belly: 70
That Writing is but just like Dice;
And lucky Mains make People Wise:
That jumbled Words, if Fortune throw 'em,
Shall, well as DRYDEN, form a Poem;
Or make a Speech, correct and witty,   75
As you know who—at the Committee.

So Atoms dancing round the Center,
They urge, made all Things at a Venture.

56 While] *1709* Whilst *1692*   70 your] *1709* the *1692*   74 Shall,] *1709* Can
1692   78 made] *1709* form'd *1692*

But granting Matters shou'd be spoke
By Method, rather than by Luck;   80
This may confine their younger Stiles,
Whom DRYDEN pedagogues at WILL's:
But never cou'd be meant to tye
Authentic Wits, like You and I:
For as young Children, who are try'd in   85
Go-Carts, to keep their Steps from sliding;
When Members knit, and Legs grow stronger,
Make use of such Machine no longer;
But leap *pro Libitu*, and scout
On Horse call'd Hobby, or without: 90
So when at School we first declaim,
Old BUSBEY walks us in a Theme,
Whose Props support our Infant Vein,
And helps the Rickets in the Brain:
But when our Souls their Force dilate,   95
And Thoughts grow up to Wit's Estate;
In Verse or Prose, We write or chat,
Not Six-Pence Matter upon what.

'Tis not how well an Author says;
But 'tis how much, that gathers Praise.   100
TONSON, who is himself a Wit,
Counts Writers Merits by the Sheet.
Thus each should down with all he thinks,
As Boys eat Bread, to fill up Chinks.

Kind Sir, I shou'd be glad to see You;   105
I hope Y'are well; so God be wi' You;
Was all I thought at first to write:
But Things, since then, are alter'd quite;
Fancies flow in, and Muse flies high:
So God knows when my Clack will lye: 110
I must, Sir, prattle on, as afore,
And beg your Pardon yet this half Hour.

82 DRYDEN] *1709 Dr——n 1692*   99 an Author] *1709* a Writer *1692*   101 TONSON]
T——n *1692, 1709*   102 Writers] *1709* Authors *1692*   106 wi' You;] *1709* with
y', *1692*   107 I thought at first] *1709* at first I thought *1692*   108 then] *1709*
that *1692*

So at pure Barn of loud NON-CON,
Where with my Granam I have gone,
When LOBB had sifted all his Text,   115
And I well hop'd the Pudding next;
Now to apply, has plagu'd me more,
Than all his Villain Cant before.

For your Religion, first, of Her
Your Friends do sav'ry Things aver: 120
They say, She's honest, as your Claret,
Not sowr'd with Cant, nor stum'd with Merit:
Your Chamber is the sole Retreat
Of Chaplains ev'ry SUNDAY Night:
Of Grace, no doubt, a certain Sign,   125
When Lay-Man herds with Man Divine:
For if their Fame be justly great,
Who wou'd no Popish Nuncio treat;
That His is greater, We must grant,
Who will treat Nuncio's Protestant.   130
One single Positive weighs more,
You know, than Negatives a Score.

In Politicks, I hear, You're stanch,
Directly bent against the FRENCH;
Deny to have your free-born Toe   135
Dragoon'd into a Wooden Shoe:
Are in no Plots; but fairly drive at
The Publick Welfare, in your Private:
And will, for ENGLAND's Glory, try
Turks, Jews, and Jesuits to defy,   } 140
And keep your Places till You die.

For me, whom wandring Fortune threw
From what I lov'd, the Town and You;

113–14] *1709*
> So, where I've with my Gran'am gone,
> At Sacred Barne of pure Noncon——— *1692*

115 had] *1709* has *1692*   117] In *1692, preceded by:*
> The Rogue has cough'd up to'ther Hour,

Now] *1709* And *1692*   118 Cant] *1709* Stuff *1692*   119 first, of Her] *1709* then,
I hear *1692*   120] *1709* A very good Account of her; *1692*   127 great,] *1709* high,
who *1692*   128] *1709* Wou'd never treat the Pope's Nuncio, *1692*   129 greater]
1709 higher *1692*   131–2] *1709 om. 1692*

Let me just tell You how my Time is
Past in a Country-Life.—*Imprimis,*   145
As soon as PHOEBUS' Rays inspect us,
First, Sir, I read, and then I Breakfast;
So on, 'till foresaid God does set,
I sometimes Study, sometimes Eat.
Thus, of your Heroes and brave Boys,   150
With whom old HOMER makes such Noise,
The greatest Actions I can find,
Are, that they did their Work, and Din'd.

     The Books of which I'm chiefly fond,
Are such, as You have whilom con'd;   155
That treat of CHINA's Civil Law,
And Subjects Rights in GOLCONDA;
Of Highway-Elephants at CEYLAN,
That rob in Clans, like Men o' th' HIGHLAND;
Of Apes that storm, or keep a Town,   160
As well almost, as Count LAUZUN;
Of Unicorns and Alligators,
Elks, Mermaids, Mummies, Witches, Satyrs,
And twenty other stranger Matters;
Which, tho' they're Things I've no Concern in,   165
Make all our Grooms admire my Learning.

     Criticks I read on other Men,
And Hypers upon Them again;
From whose Remarks I give Opinion
On twenty Books, yet ne'er look in One.   170

     Then all your Wits, that flear and sham,
Down from DON QUIXOTE to TOM TRAM;
From whom I Jests and Punns purloin,
And slily put 'em off for Mine:
Fond to be thought a Country Wit: 175
The rest,—when Fate and You think fit.

     Sometimes I climb my Mare, and kick her
To bottl'd Ale, and neighbouring Vicar;
Sometimes at STAMFORD take a Quart,
'Squire SHEPHARD's Health,—With all my Heart.   180

147] *1709* I rise to Read, perhaps to Breakfast, *1692*   161 As . . . as] *1709* Better, perhaps than *1692*

Thus, without much Delight, or Grief,
I fool away an idle Life;
'Till SHADWELL from the Town retires,
(Choak'd up with Fame and Sea-coal Fires,)
To bless the Wood with peaceful Lyric;   185
Then hey for Praise and Panegyric;
Justice restor'd, and Nations freed,
And Wreaths round WILLIAM's glorious Head.

On Fleet: Shepheards takeing away
a childs bread and butter.

AT that so pleasant Season of the Year,
When fields and meadowes fresh and gay appear,
The tender infant of some neighb'ring Swaine,
Eat bread and butter upon Brentford plaine,
Grac'd with glasse windowes in the Diamond cutt;   5
Such was his nice indulgence to his gutt:
Smileing he sat, secure and unconcern'd,
When hungry Shepherd this poor child discern'd,
Resolv'd to make him his lov'd morsell yeild,
Or swore hee'd kill him in the open field.   10
Thrice hee prepar'd for this unequall fight;
As oft the child secur'd himself by flight.
Hunger, and rage, at once his Soul inspire;
His lookes were fierce, and his red eyes struck fire.
So sparkled Turnus eyes with furious rage,   15
When with Aeneas hee did once engage;
So Ajax look'd, when hee with Hector strove,
And so look'd Capaneus defying Jove.
The child stood trembling, almost dead with fear,
Whilst he run at him with a full carreer,   20
Luxurious brat, hee cry'd, give me the bread,
Each hour you are by tender mother fed;

---

181 without much Delight] *1709* far from Pleasure, Sir *1692*   183 *In 1692, preceded*
by:

> Till Mr. *Maidwell* cease to Teach,
> Then I'll Jerk Youth, and say *Inspeech*; *1692*

'Till] *1709* Or *1692*   185 Wood] *1709* Woods *1692*

Here, free from hunger, and from harm secure,
You think not what wee travellers endure—
Then, like a Heroe, seiz'd upon the prize, 25
Whilst floods of teares ran from the infants eyes,
And the plaine ecchoes with the mournfull cryes.

To Mr: K——s Tune of the
Prince's march.

G REAT Nassau rise from Beauty
 Leave Maria's softer Charms
Call the Soldier to his Duty
Bid the Trumpet sound Alarms.
To renown Love excites Thee 5
 O prepare
 Sudden War
Mary's injur'd Cause invites Thee
Love and Mary bless thy Arms.

Great Nassau rise to Glory 10
Rise to Save our sinking State
Truth and Justice march before Thee
Victory behind shal wait.
Death and Hell n'er shal vex Thee
 Faith and Laws 15
 Back thy Cause
All our Isle with Joy expects Thee
March to Conquer and be great.

Sound to France, spread Thy Banner
Hoist thy Sails and plow the Main 20
Guarded by Success and Honor
Vindicate thy own again

Title] Song *Harl*: *om. 1689*   1 from Beauty] *1689* to Glory *Harl*   3 his] *Harl*
their *1689*   4 Trumpet] Trumpets *1689* : Soldier *Harl*   6 O] *Harl* ah *1689*   8
Mary's] *1689* MARIA's *Harl*   12 march before Thee] *Harl* walk before you, *1689*
13 Victory *Harl*, *1689* : Vitory *L 28*   15 Faith] Truth *Harl*, *1689*   17 All...
with] *Harl* Thro' thy Toyls *1689*   19–27 *om. 1689*   19 France] Fame *Harl*

Fortune laughs, Fate is willing
    To Advance
    Thee o'er France   25
Court the Hours whilst yet they'r smiling
March to Overcome and Reign.

To Dr: F......... in a Letter to Beverley disswading him from drinking Waters.

To clear the Brain or purge the thought
  Your Waters are not worth a Groat,
The Spaw it self cou'd never do't
Unless Your Brain lay in your Gutt.
Your Costive fancy if You'd stir up,   5
Add to your Waters Pills or Syrrup.
So your loose Muse may chance to store yee
With Arguments a Posteriori
You (like the Spaniard) may be writing
Some handsom Tract of easy Sh....g—   10
Or making some clean Returnello
Of who Sh...s white or who Sh...s yellow.
But if some labour you design
Like all its Breth'ren fair and fine
Lay by your Element and rather   15
Drink (by my Lords good leave) Forefather.
When Jove his Godhead purg'd with water
He got some Sneaking Fountain Daughter.
   But for the Offspring of his brain
His head ak'd much, and he cry'd Alass!   20
   Twas Wine that brought the generous pain
The God drank hard, and out sprang Pallas.
To her pale Sons, insipid *Isis*
The draught of her own Stream advises;
But well We know, our *Alma-Mater*   25
Holds Claret wholsomer than Water:
And by her *Candle* and her *Cup*
Bids Sitt up late, and drink all up.

23 laughs, *edd.*: laughs *L* 28: Laughs, *Harl*   26 whilst] while *Harl*
7 yee] you *M*   20 and] *om. M*

1690

To Dr. Sherlock, on his Practical Discourse Concerning Death.

FORGIVE the Muse, who in unhallow'd Strains
The Saint one Moment from his GOD detains:
For sure, whate'er You do, where-e'er You are,
'Tis all but one good Work, one constant Pray'r:
Forgive Her; and intreat That GOD, to Whom   5
Thy favour'd Vows with kind Acceptance come,
To raise her Notes to that sublime Degree,
Which suits a Song of Piety and Thee.

Wond'rous good Man! whose Labours may repel
The Force of Sin, may stop the Rage of Hell: 10
Thou, like the BAPTIST, from thy GOD wast sent
The crying Voice, to bid the World repent.

Thee YOUTH shall study; and no more engage
Their flatt'ring Wishes for uncertain AGE;
No more with fruitless Care, and cheated Strife   15
Chace fleeting Pleasure thro' this Maze of Life;
Finding the wretched All They here can have,
But present Food, and but a future Grave:
Each, great as PHILIP's Victor Son, shall view
This abject World, and weeping, ask a New.   20

Decrepit AGE shall read Thee, and confess,
Thy Labours can asswage, where Med'cines cease:
Shall bless thy Words, their wounded Souls Relief,
The Drops that sweeten their last Dregs of Life:
Shall look to Heav'n, and laugh at all beneath;   25
Own Riches gather'd, Trouble; Fame, a Breath;
And LIFE an Ill, whose only Cure is DEATH.

Title: To Dr. Sherlock,] *1709* To the Reverend Dr. *SHERLOCK*, Dean of St. *Paul's*; *1693*:
om. *Md*   7 Notes...sublime] *1709*, *Md* Numbers...blest *1693*   8 Which] *Md*
That *1693*, *1709*   11 Thou...wast] *Md* Who...wert *1693*, *1709*   12 The
crying Voice, to] *1709*, *Md* To be the Voice, and *1693*   14 Their] *Md* His *1693*, *1709*
17 They] *Md* He *1693*, *1709*   19 Victor Son, shall] *1709*, *Md* Son, shall sit and *1693*
20 abject] *1709*, *Md* sordid *1693*

Thy even Thoughts with so much Plainness flow;
Their Sense untutor'd INFANCY may know:
Yet to such height is all That Plainness wrought;   30
WIT may admire, and letter'd PRIDE be taught:
Easie in Words thy Style, in Sense sublime:
   On it's blest Steps each Age and Sex may rise:
'Tis like the Ladder in the PATRIARCH's Dream,
   It's Foot on Earth, it's Height above the Skies.   35
Diffus'd it's Virtue, boundless is it's Pow'r:
'Tis Publick Health, and Universal Cure:
Of Heav'nly MANNA 'tis a second Feast,
A Nation's Food, and All to ev'ry Taste.

   To it's last Height mad BRITAIN's Guilt was rear'd: 40
And various DEATH for various Crimes She fear'd:
With your kind Work her drooping Hopes revive:
You bid Her read, repent, adore, and live:
You wrest the Bolt from Heav'ns avenging Hand;
Stop ready DEATH, and save a sinking Land.   45

   O! save Us still; still bless Us with thy Stay:
O! want thy Heav'n, 'till We have learnt the Way:
Refuse to leave thy destin'd Charge too soon:
And for the Church's Good, defer thy own.
O! live; and let thy Works urge our Belief;   50
Live to explain thy Doctrine by thy Life;
'Till future INFANCY, baptiz'd by Thee,
Grow ripe in Years, and old in Piety;
'Till CHRISTIANS, yet unborn, be taught to die.

   Then in full Age, and hoary Holiness   55
Retire, great Teacher, to thy promis'd Bliss:
Untouch'd thy Tomb, uninjur'd be thy Dust,
As thy own Fame among the future Just;
'Till in last Sounds the dreadful Trumpet speaks:
'Till JUDGMENT calls; and quick'ned NATURE wakes: 60
'Till thro' the utmost Earth, and deepest Sea
Our scatter'd ATOMS find their destin'd Way,

30 such] *1709, Md* that *1693*   35 above] *Md* beyond *1693, 1709*   41 DEATH]
1709, Md Deaths *1693*   42 Work] *1709, Md* Works *1693*   58 among] *1709, Md*
amongst *1693*   59 dreadful] *Md* dreaded *1693, 1709*   62 destin'd] *1709, Md*
hidden *1693*

In haste to cloath their Kindred Souls again;
Perfect our State, and build immortal Man:
Then fearless Thou, who well sustain'dst the Fight,   65
To Paths of Joy, and Tracts of endless Light
Lead up all those who heard Thee, and believ'd:
'Midst thy own Flock, great Shepherd, be receiv'd;
And glad all Heav'n with Millions Thou hast sav'd.

A Pindarique on His Majesties Birth-Day.

Sung before Their Majesties at Whitehall, The Fourth of November 1690.

A Prophecy by Apollo.

As through *Britania*'s Raging Sea,
  Our Great Defender Plowed his Glorious Way,
To make our Wishes, and his Fame compleat,
    To fix a new our sinking State,
    And fill the great Decrees of Fate,   5
    Apollo turn'd the Mistick Book,

In which Recorded lies the certain Doom
    Of Time unborn, and Years to come;
    Auspicious Omens thence he took,
Lawrel adorn'd his Brow, and Joy his Look;   10
    Aloud he Blest the happy Day,
    Whose lustre twice returned must see,
    Truth Restored, and *Albion* Free.
Aloud he bad the mighty Months proceed,
All Deck'd with fair Success, and Crowned with happy Deed.   15
    He Smil'd, and struck the Lyre and said,

Heaven has Revers'd *Britania*'s Doom:
Her promised Day appears, her better Fate is come.

---

65 fearless] *Md* fearless, *1693, 1709*   66 Tracts] *1709, Md* Worlds *1693*   67 who]
1693, Md that *1709*
  5 Fate, *edd.*: Fate. *1690*

The gentle Star, whose joyful Ray,
Enliven'd this Auspicious Day   20
When *Holland* blest the Hero's Birth,
Doth with diffusive Goodness shed,
It's larger Gifts, o're *Britain*'s rising Head,
And thence, around the Joyful Earth.

Ye Sacred Muses, whose Harmonious lays   25
Are destin'd to Record his Praise,
Prepare with Solemn Joy, prepare
The chearful Consort of the War:
Awake the Trumpets, rouze the Drums,
The King, the Conqueror, the Hero comes,   30
With shining Arms he decks the listed Fields,
IO Britannia! Then *JERNE* yeilds,
IO Britannia! Bless the Conqueror,
Put all thy Glory on, exert thy Power;
And greet thy *WILLIAM*'s happy Toil,   35
Assert the Sea, defend the Isles,
And on the lower World look safely down,
Thy Self a World alone.

See on the Continent appear,
Engaging Troops and ready War.   40
On Foreign Plains the British Armies shine,
WILLIAM leads on, and Victory pursues,
And on *Sein*'s Banks the Hero well renews
The Glories of the *Boyne*.
Deliver'd *Gallia* dreading now no more,   45
Tyrannick Might, and Lawless Power,
Obeys her Antient Conqueror.
O're *Europe* freed Victorious *WILLIAM* Reigns,
And sullen War, and vanquished Pride,
Behind his Chariot Wheels are Tyed   50
In Everlasting Chains.

Bid the Drums and Trumpets cease,
And Tune the softer Instruments of Peace;

20 Day *edd.*: Day. *1690*   26 Praise, *edd*: Praise. *1690*   31 decks *MS. alt. in*
B.M. copy: deck'd *1690*   32 Then *edd.*: They *1690*   50 Tyed *MS. alt.*: Tide *1690*

All that through Speaking Pipes convey
Sounds of Delight, and Images of Joy;   55
All that by Artful Charms, or Vocal Wires,
In happy Numbers gently can Express,
          All the Pleasure all the Bliss,
That *WILLIAM*'s Cares Deserve, or *MARY*'s Love Requires.

MARIA now no longer Fear   60
The doubtful Chance of horrid War;
No longer Arm thy Hero with thy Prayer;
          To Battle he no more shall Ride,
No more for Thee, and His *Britania* Bleed.
Saturnian Ages are renewed, and Golden Times succeed: 65
The shining Years begin their happy Race,
          With Concord Crown'd and Blest with Peace.

Fair Plenty opens wide her bounteous Hand,
And throws her Gifts o're all the Land.
Virtue does with Heaven conspire,   70
To make *Britania*'s Joys entire,
Whilst *WILLIAM*, and whilst *MARY* Reign.
Astrea has forsook the Stars,
And joyned her Throne to Theirs,
Nor shall return from Earth again,   75
Whilst *WILLIAM*, and whilst *MARY* Reign.

To a Lady Sleeping.

STILL Sleep stil fold those lovely Arms
     Stil be free from noise and Harms
Whilst all the Gods of Love defend Thee
(The Gods of Love which stil attend thee)
Whilst around in humble State   5
A Thousand wanton Angels wait
Whilst Gods officiously find
Pleasing Dreams to charm thy mind,
Dreams of things (if such there are)
Like your self Serene and fair,   10

55 Delight *MS. alt.*: Delights *1690*   59 Deserve *MS. alt.*: Deserves *1690*   62
Prayer; *MS. alt.*: Prayer, *1690*   65 succeed: *MS. alt.*: succeed *1690*   66 shining
edd.: shinning *1690*   67 Concord *edd.*: Conquer'd *1690*: Conquest *MS. alt.*
73 *Astrea edd.*: *Astr a 1690*

And when You open those bright Eyes
When Morpheus with the wel-cloath'd Vision flyes
May You that Happyness renew
And all the Pleasures of your Dream prove true.

Charity never faileth.

1: Cor: XIII. 8.

I.

SAY would'st Thou gain eternal Praise,
Go foolish Man thy great designs pursue,
   Go, try ten thousand ways;
Thy Toil like Sisyphus each hour renew
   Yet know that after all Thy Pain,   5
Like Him thou dost but roll a heavy Stone in vain.

II.

Rush, if thou wilt into the Camp, and try
   To purchace Fame by Victory,
Let Fortune stil against thy foes conspire
   Still on Thee, her Darling wait   10
   And kindly seem to make thee great,
Great as thy soaring wishes can require.
Yet when thy Troops return with Conquest crown'd
Thy recompence is only shouts and noise
(The Rabbles unintelligible voice)   15
And scarce a Lawrel-leaf for every wound.

III.

But say the Senate should thy Service own
And to thy Memory with comely Pride
   Erect a shining Pyramide:
By this Thou canst not be for ever known,   20
The Marble will decay, the Polish'd Iron rust,
And both will be as soon as Thou art, Dust.

---

3 ways; *edd.*: ways *L 28*   5 Pain, *edd.*: Pain *L 28*   11 thee *edd.*: her *L 28*
12 require. *edd.*: require *L 28*   19 Pyramide: *edd.*: Pyramide *L 28*

IV.

Then throw your Sword and Gauntlet by,
Change your Armour for a Gown
Read all the Secrets of Philosophy   25
And thus endeavor to obtain renown,
    Yet here thy Study will prove vain
    No glory can'st Thou hence obtain
Since Men the mighty Stagyrite disdain.

V.

Should'st Thou invoke the Muses then, and try   30
If honor can be gain'd by Poetry,
Alas! no glory will from hence arise
Tho (which is much improbable) thy Rhimes
Affect the Squeamish Criticks of these times.
What they Admire their Children may dispise   35
Homer is Censur'd, Ennius quite thrown by,
    Then how short-liv'd will be thy Praise:
Like what thou labour'st for, a sprig of Bayes,
'Twill with its Transitory Master Dye.

VI.

Hard fate! can nothing then secure our Name   40
    From Envys cruel rage
    And the devouring Teeth of Age
Can nothing Purchace everlasting Fame?
Yes, CHARITY will do't, 'tis This Alone
Will make its Author always known.   45
    The Charitable Man shal live
    Without what needless Art can give
    And every Tongue his Acts rehearse
Tho no Man built his Tomb, or sung his Praise in Verse.

VII.

Old Time and Envy shal his glory view   50
    Each vainly striving to pursue;

23 by, *edd.*: by *L 28*   34 times. *edd.*: times *L 28*   37 Praise: *edd.*: Praise *L 28*
38 labour'st *edd.*: labour'est *L 28*   Bayes, *edd.*: Bayes *L 28*   45 known. *edd.*: known
L 28   49 Verse. *edd.*: Verse *L 28*   51 pursue; *edd.*: pursue *L 28*

Whilst looking back he sees them fly behind
And scapes the fatal Gulph which swallows all Mankind.
    Nay even in that dreadful Day
When all Men else to Rocks and Caverns run   55
And desperately strive an angry GOD to shun
    When time it self shal be no more,
Who fed the Orphan, and reliev'd the Poor
    Shal with undaunted Courage stay
And Ten times more receive, then e'er he gave away.   60

Arria and Petus out of Martial.

Paraphrase.

WITH Roman constancy and decent pride
    The dying Matron from her wounded side
      Drawing forth the guilty blade
To her lov'd Lord the fatal gift convey'd.
But then in streams of blood and sorrow drown'd,   5
Pardon, she crys, an unbecoming Tear
      (The Womans weakness will appear)
Yet think not tis that I repent the Deed
      Or that my firm resolves give ground.
Witness just Heav'n 'tis nothing that I bleed   10
But that You must, there Petus, there's the Wound.

God is Love.

I.

ALMIGHTY Power!
    Whom Angells' Hymns, men's Prayers adore.
For whom no Speech, no thought cou'd frame
    A comprehensive Name;

53 Mankind. *edd.*: Mankind *L 28*   57 more, *edd.*: more *L 28*
4 convey'd. *edd.*: convey'd *L 28*   5 drown'd, *edd.*: drown'd *L 28*   6 Pardon,
... crys, *edd.*: Pardon ... crys *L 28*   9 ground. *edd.*: ground *L 28*
2 Angells' *edd.*: Angells *L 28, M*

'Till Thou from Heav'n vouchsafst a ray,   5
Thy glory and our knowledge to improve;
Thou mixt Thy beams with our exalted Clay,
And we, enlightened, learn to call thee *Love.*

II.

All was in Chaos and confusion laid
   'Till by Loves creating word   10
   The melancholy Mass was stir'd
And the commanded Elements with hasty joy obey'd.
      Then peaceful Sphears with wond'rous Music roll'd,
      Time his harmonious course began,
      The circling Years in glad Procession ran,   15
      Order and beauty blest the New born World.
         And every object strove to prove
That all was made and all preserv'd by love.

III.

When Heav'ns last noblest Masterpiece was made
Love, pow'rful love, unlockt his pregnant side   20
And kindly thence call'd forth the blushing Bride;
Love to his heart a secret was convey'd
And made him bless the wound   court the Maid.
      Love did the willing Souls unite
Whilst He became Her strength, She his delight   25
      This happy Pair more truly One
Then when both Sexes lay in Adams side alone.

IV.

   Thus they liv'd and thus they Lov'd.
   Each smiling Hour their bliss improv'd
But when for knowledge and Sins sake they stray'd   30
   When God and love were disobey'd
By God and love the mild decree was giv'n
Which threw them down from Paradise and rais'd them
      up to Heav'n.

21 Bride; *edd.*: Bride *L 28, M*   23 Maid. *edd.*: Maid *L 28, M*   25 strength,
M: strength *L 28*   28 Lov'd. *edd.*: Lov'd *L 28, M*

V.

Exalted Lyre thy tuneful sinews move
Teach Man divinity and love: 35
Forgetfull Man, in Bethlems poor abode
Behold new born Eternity
And hear the Thunderers voice chang'd to an Infants cry
Nourish'd like Thee with circulating blood
Compound like Thee with limbs and cloath'd with Skin, 40
Like Thee in every thing, but Sin.

VI.

Then cast (if Tears restrain not) cast thy Eye
Up to the dismal top of frighted Calvary
See whom thy Pray'rs so oft invok'd
To whom thy fatlings fell, thy Altars smoak'd 45
See to the fatal Cross He's ty'd,
The thorns his temples wound, the spear his side:
And to compleat his glorious Miserys,
Imperious Love, what wou'dst thou more? He *Dyes.*
What wou'dst Thou more? Thy Deity we own: 50
By thy mysterious Power alone
The *World* was fram'd, *Man* sav'd, *God* crucified.

Letter to *J* ....

MY little Wid: to you I send
Or as my Doctress or my Friend
Hoping these Lines may find You S.....g
As I am at this present writing.
I yesternight read Nendicks bills 5
Believ'd his lies and took his Pills;
No sooner was the Rascall swallow'd
Ah J...y can you guess what follow'd?
I'l swear I thought I shou'd have quicken'd,
And from that moment fondly reckon'd. 10

35 love: *edd.*: love *L 28, M*   36 Man, *edd.*: Man *L 28, M*   40 Skin, *edd.*: Skin *L 28, M*   46 ty'd, *edd.*: ty'd *L 28, M*   50 own: *edd.*: own *L 28, M*
4 writing. *edd.*: writing *L 28, M*   6 Pills; *edd.*: Pills *L 28, M*

At last my Physic like your Marriage
Brought nothing forth but a Miscarriage.
When I had suffer'd as I tell Yee
Those plaguey wamblings in my Belly
Backwards I much Dismist, and after   15
Indeed I scarse cou'd hold my Water.
Faith J..e those Pills are past enduring
That work at once by Stool and Urine;
I shou'd not, were you here, intreat Yee
To give me liberty to beat Yee;   20
For gentle walking will alone
Bring neighbor Nendick kindly down.
Thus having Thirty times I think
Drank your dear health in posset drink
I Answer to my Billet doux Require   25
And rest
                    Sweet J..e
                        Your stinking Friend
                        M Pr...r.

Cælia.

WERE Cælia absent and remembrance brought
      Her and past raptures thick upon my thought
The next kind She might meet my rais'd desire
And beastly Lust quench Loves disabl'd Fire.
But when I want my Friend, when my vex't heart   5
Beats short, and pants and seeks its nobler part,
For the sad Ill no med'cine can be found:
'Tis You that made, 'tis You must cure the Wound.

---

28 stinking *L 28 (D)*: filthy *L 28 (Pope), M*
  Title: 'Contents' of L 28: The same Varied, *L 28 (see commentary)*   1 Cælia *edd.*:
Cæclia *L 28*   6 part, *edd.*: part *L 28*   7 med'cine *edd.*: medi'cine *L 28*   found:
edd.: found *L 28*

Song Set by Messrs: Pickering and Tudway.

LOVE I confess I thought Thee but a Name
  The Painters fancy and the Poets Theme,
The old Wives Tale, the wishing Virgins dream,
    But if indeed Thou art a God
    Supreme in Goodness and in Pow'r   5
    Now make it clearly understood
    And I'l repent and I'l adore.
Or use thy Mercy, and withdraw the dart
Gently! Ah! gently, from my fester'd heart;
Or strike the weapon thrô my Cælia's breast—   10
And be Thy Godhead by thy Pow'r exprest.
For whilst I follow and my Cælia flies
    Whilst I entreat and She denys
I own my Self a harden'd Atheist stil
And must deny thy Power, or blame thy Will.   15

Song Set by Mr: K.

I.

LOVE, has often threaten'd War
  Beauty led up all the Fair
Yet stil my heart repell'd the Harms
    Their cruelty intended,
But when my Cælia took up Arms   5
Unable to resist her Charms
The Fort no longer I defended.

II.

Strength and Wisdom useless prove,
Once to see her is to Love;

---

3 dream, *edd.*: dream *L 28*   12 Cælia *edd.*: Cælias *L 28*
  Title] A Song set by Mr: King '*Index*' to *M*: *om. 1695*   3 stil] *om. 1695*   4 in-
tended, *1695*: intended *L 28*   5 Cælia] Silvia *1695*   8–14] *om. 1695*   8 prove,
L 28 (Pope): powr *L 28 (D)*

Others in Time a heart may gain   10
    By Treaty or Perswasion,
Their Conquests They by Siege obtain;
You o'er my heart were born to reign
And bravely took it by Invasion.

A Hymn to Venus, upon a Marriage.

I

ALMIGHTY pow'r of Harmony and Love
    That Governst all below and blessest all above
At whose command this well proportion'd frame
From the dark womb of empty Chaos came
    Whose smile bid wild confusion cease   5
    And charm'd the jarring Elements to peace,
Who life and joy to th' earliest beings gave
And stil with new supplies defeats the conquest of the Grave,
    Marriage I sing, be thou my Muse.
    To thy young Prophets Soul infuse   10
    Such vigorous heat such active fire
    As tun'd thy dear Anacreons Lyre
    That my officious Song may prove
Noble as was our Lovers first desire
Sweet as their Courtship lasting as their Love.   15

II

    Yes Venus your Divinity we own
Your pow'r and goodness equally are shown
    Since this happy pair you join.
    Forsake Cythera's crouded shrine
    Victims of vulgar hearts disclaim   20
Nor seek new Conquests but the last maintain
    Your last which has outdone
    All other glories which your Cupids won

---

7 earliest *edd.*: earliest, L 28   8 Grave, *edd.*: Grave L 28   9 sing, ... Muse.
edd.: sing ... Muse L 28   15 Love. *edd.*: Love L 28   18 join. *edd.*: join L 28
21 maintain *edd.*: mentain L 28

    Since yielding to your Godhead, Jove
Confest his Thunder less then were the Shafts of Love.   25
    Go let your darlings useless arms be broke
    Let his torch languish in enactive Smoak:
        His little Deity must now dispair
    To see such Lovers at his Altars crown'd
        Or vanquish with an equal wound   30
So great an Hero, and a Bride so fair.

III

    On these may all your Blessings flow
    On these your choicest Gifts bestow
    Let all their after minutes prove
    Kind as is your kindest Dove   35
And soft as down upon the wings of love:
    Still with their years encrease their joy
Stil be their raptures full yet never cloy
        Whilst each succeeding Night
Improves the Transport of the last delight.   40
In glad procession may each rolling Year
        See the joyful Parent bear
    A Beauty second only to her own
    Or if the smiling Gods conspire to crown
        Her stronger Wishes in a Son,   45
His Fathers Soul as Image let him share
And prove his Honors and his Virtues Heir.

24 Godhead, *edd.*: Godhead *L 28*   25 Love. *edd.*: Love *L 28*   27 Smoak: *edd.*:
Smoak *L 28*   40 delight. *edd.*: delight *L 28*

1692

To the Honourable Charles Montague, Esq;

I.

HOWE'ER, 'tis well, that while Mankind
Thro' Fate's perverse *Mæander* errs,
He can Imagin'd Pleasures find,
To combat against Real Cares.

II.

Fancies and Notions He pursues,   5
Which ne'er had Being but in Thought:
Each, like the GRÆCIAN Artist, woo's
The Image He himself has wrought.

III.

Against Experience He believes;
He argues against Demonstration;   10
Pleas'd, when his Reason He deceives;
And sets his Judgment by his Passion.

IV.

The hoary Fool, who many Days
Has struggl'd with continu'd Sorrow,
Renews his Hope, and blindly lays   15
The desp'rate Bett upon to Morrow.

V.

To Morrow comes: 'tis Noon, 'tis Night;
This Day like all the former flies:
Yet on He runs, to seek Delight
To Morrow, 'till to Night He dies.   20

Title] *1709* In a Letter to the Honourable Mr. *Charles Montague. 1693*: *om. 1692*   1
while] *1709 whilst 1692, 1693*   2 perverse *Mæander*] *1709 Fantastick Mazes 1692,
1693*   5 He pursues] *1709 we pursue 1692, 1693*   7 Each, ... GRÆCIAN ... woo's]
1709 And ... doting ... woo, 1692, 1693   8 He himself has] *1709 we our selves have
1692, 1693*   9 He believes;] *1709 we believe, 1692, 1693*   10 He argues] *1709
And argue 1692, 1693*   11] *1709 Pleas'd that we can our selves deceive, 1692, 1693*
12 sets his ... his] *1709 set our ... our 1692, 1693*   18 This ... flies:] *1709 The ...
fled; 1692, 1693*   20 He dies] *1709 he's dead 1692, 1693*

VI.

Our Hopes, like tow'ring Falcons, aim
   At Objects in an airy height:
The little Pleasure of the Game
   Is from afar to view the Flight.

VII.

Our anxious Pains We, all the Day,   25
   In search of what We like, employ:
Scorning at Night the worthless Prey,
   We find the Labour gave the Joy.

VIII.

At Distance thro' an artful Glass
   To the Mind's Eye Things well appear: 30
They lose their Forms, and make a Mass
   Confus'd and black, if brought too near.

IX.

If We see right, We see our Woes:
   Then what avails it to have Eyes?
From Ignorance our Comfort flows: 35
   The only Wretched are the Wise.

X.

We weary'd should lye down in Death:
   This Cheat of Life would take no more;
If You thought Fame but empty Breath;
   I, PHILLIS but a perjur'd Whore.   40

23 The little] *1709 But all the 1692, 1693*   24 from afar] *1709 afar off 1692, 1693*
25–28] *1709*

> *The worthless Prey but only shows,*
> *The Joy consisted in the Strife;*
> *What-e'er we take, as soon we lose,*
> *In* Homer's *Riddle, and in Life.*
>
> *So whi[l]st in Fev'rish Sleeps we think*
> *We taste what waking we desire,*
> *The Dream is better than the Drink,*
> *Which only feeds the sickly Fire. 1692, 1693*

29–30] *1709 Order of lines reversed 1692, 1693*   31–32] *1709*

> *Bring but the flattering Objects near,*
> *They're all a senseless gloomy Mass. 1692, 1693*

33 If ... right] *1709 Seeing aright 1692, 1693*   36] *1692, 1693* And Sorrow from our
being wise. *1709*   39 empty] *1709 Stinking 1692, 1693*   40 I,] *1693, 1709 And 1692*

Song.

WHILST I am scorch'd with hot desire,
    In vain cold Friendship you return:
Your drops of Pity on my Fire
Alas! but make it fiercer burn.

Ah! would you have the Flame supprest   5
That kills the Heart it heats too fast;
Take half my Passion to your Breast,
The rest in mine shall ever last.

An Ode.

I.

WHILE blooming Youth, and gay Delight
    Sit on thy rosey Cheeks confest,
Thou hast, my Dear, undoubted Right
To triumph o'er this destin'd Breast.
My Reason bends to what thy Eyes ordain;   5
For I was born to Love, and Thou to Reign.

II.

But would You meanly thus rely
    On Power, You know I must Obey?
Exert a Legal Tyranny;
    And do an Ill, because You may?   10
Still must I Thee, as Atheists Heav'n adore;
Not see thy Mercy, and yet dread thy Power?

Title: M: om. 1692, 1695   1 *hot*] warm *M (written over an erasure), 1695*   6
heats] *1695* heals *M*
    Title] *1693, 1709* Verses by Mr. *Prior. 1692*   1 WHILE] *1709* Whilst *1692, 1693*
blooming] *1693, 1709* Beauty, *1692*   2] *1709 In all thy Looks and Gestures shine, 1692,
1693*   4] *1709 To rule this destin'd Heart of mine. 1692, 1693*   5 thy] *1709 your
1692, 1693*   6 Thou] *1709 you 1692, 1693*   7 thus] *1709 then 1692, 1693*   8
Obey?] Obey: *1709 : obey, 1692 : obey; 1693*   9 Exert] *1709 It is but 1692 :* 'Tis but
1693   10 And] *1709 To 1692, 1693*   may?] *1709 may 1692 :* may. *1693*   11 Still]
1709 Why *1692, 1693*   12 yet] *but 1692, 1693, 1709*

III.

Take Heed, my Dear, Youth flies apace;
    As well as CUPID, TIME is blind:
Soon must those Glories of thy Face   15
    The Fate of vulgar Beauty find:
The Thousand Loves, that arm thy potent Eye,
Must drop their Quivers, flag their Wings, and die.

IV.

Then wilt Thou sigh, when in each Frown
    A hateful Wrinkle more appears;   20
And putting peevish Humours on,
    Seems but the sad Effect of Years:
Kindness it self too weak a Charm will prove,
To raise the feeble Fires of aged Love.

V.

Forc'd Compliments, and formal Bows   25
    Will show Thee just above Neglect:
The Heat, with which thy Lover glows,
    Will settle into cold Respect:
A talking dull Platonic I shall turn;
Learn to be civil, when I cease to burn.   30

VI.

Then shun the Ill, and know, my Dear,
    Kindness and Constancy will prove
The only Pillars fit to bear
    So vast a Weight, as that of Love.
If thou canst wish to make My Flames endure,   35
Thine must be very fierce, and very pure.

13 Heed] *1693, 1709* Care *1692*   14 As ... TIME] *1709* Time equally with Love *1692,*
1693   15 those] *1693, 1709* these *1692*   16 Beauty] *1693, 1709* Beauties *1692*
19 wilt Thou] *1709* thou wilt *1692, 1693*   20 A] *1693, 1709* One *1692*   23 Kindness it self] *1709* Ev'n Kindness, then, *1692, 1693*   24] *1709* To reinflame the Ashes of
my Love. *1692* : To raise the Ghost of my departed Love. *1693*   31 the] *1693, 1709*
that *1692*   35 canst] *1693, 1709* wouldst *1692*

VII.

Haste, CELIA, haste, while Youth invites,
   Obey kind CUPID's present Voice;
Fill ev'ry Sense with soft Delights,
   And give thy Soul a Loose to Joys: 40
Let Millions of repeated Blisses prove,
That Thou all Kindness art, and I all Love.

VIII.

Be Mine, and only Mine; take care
   Thy Looks, thy Thoughts, thy Dreams to guide
To Me alone; nor come so far,   45
   As liking any Youth beside:
What Men e'er court Thee, fly 'em, and believe,
They're Serpents all, and Thou the tempted EVE.

IX.

So shall I court thy dearest Truth,
   When Beauty ceases to engage;
So thinking on thy charming Youth,   50
   I'll love it o'er again in Age:
So TIME it self our Raptures shall improve,
While still We wake to Joy, and live to Love.

An Ode in Imitation of the Second Ode of the Third Book of Horace.

(1)

How long Enchanted *Albion* wilt thou lye
   In the Lethargic Dream, the Sad repose
By which thy close thy constant Enemy
   Has softly lull'd thee to thy Woes?

37 while Youth] *1709 whilst Love 1692, 1693*   38 kind CUPID's present] *1709 the gentle Godhead's 1692*: the Godhead's gentle *1693*   42 all Kindness art] *1709 art Kindness all 1692, 1693*   44 Thy Looks, thy Thoughts, thy] *1709 Thy Words, thy Looks, thy 1692*: Your Looks, your Thoughts, your *1693*   47 'em] *1693, 1709 them 1692*   49 shall] *1693, 1709 will 1692*   51 So] *1709 And, 1692, 1693*   charming] *1693, 1709 pleasing 1692*   52] *1693, 1709 I'le love thee on in spite of Age: 1692*   53 Raptures] *1693, 1709 Transports 1692*   54 While ... We] *1709 And ... we'le 1692, 1693*   Joy] *1693, 1709 Joys 1692*
  1 Enchanted] deluded *1692*   2 Dream, *edd.*: Dream *L* 29: Sleep, *1692*

Or wake, degenerate Isle, or cease to own   5
What thy Old Kings in *Gallic* Camps have done,
The Wreaths they purchas'd, and the Spoils they won:
Behold the Nations are again alarm'd
William, so Fate requires, again is Arm'd,
     Thy Father to the Feild is gone: 10
Again *Maria* weeps Her absent Lord:
     The softer Honour of thy Throne
For *Albion*'s Good consents to Rule alone.
Oh! be thy Courage and thy Fame restor'd,
Mov'd by Her Tears, excited by His Sword.   15

(2)

     See, the Repenting Isle awakes,
With happy Strength her vicious Chains She breaks:
The Clouds which hung around Her beauteous head
     Down to their parent Night are fled:
Looks forth the Goddess, and sees Belgia Stand   20
Prepar'd to meet their common Lords Command;
Her Lions roaring by Her side, Her Arrows in her hand;
She Blushes to have been so long witheld,
And weeps Her Crime, and hastens to the Feild:
Henceforth Her Youth shal be inur'd to bear   25
     Hazardous Toil and active War:
To march beneath the Dog-Starrs raging Heat,
Patient of Summers Drought, and Martial Sweat;
And only grieve in Winter Camps to find,
The Sun too fleeting for the Work design'd: 30

7 Wreaths ... Spoils] Spoils They brought Thee back, the Crowns *1692*   won: *1692* : won
L 29   8] *om. 1692*   Behold *edd.*: behold *L 29*   12] *om. 1692*   13 *Albion*'s
Good consents] Thy Repose content *1692*   14-15]

       Are Thy Enervate Sons not yet Alarm'd?
       When *WILLIAM* Fights, dare they look tamely on,
       So slow to get their Ancient Fame Restor'd,
       As nor to melt at Beauties Tears, nor follow Valours Sword? *1692*

17-20]

       Her Vicious Chains the generous Goddess breaks:
       The Foggs around Her Temples are Dispell'd;
       Abroad She Looks, and Sees Arm'd *Belgia* stand *1692*

23 She Blushes] And Blushing *1692*   24 And weeps] Weeps off *1692*   30
Its Days too short for Labours They design'd: *1692*

All Night beneath hard heavy Arms to Watch;
All Day to mount the Trench, to Storm the Breach;
And every rugged Path to tread,
Where *William* and His Virtue lead.

(3)

As when the thundering Brass prepares to breath   35
Collected Anger and emissive Death,
In the try'd Mettle the close Dangers glow,
And now too late the Dying Foe
Perceives the Flame, yet cannot ward the Blow;
So whilst in *William*'s Breast ripe Councils lye,   40
Secret and Sure as Brooding Fate,
No more of His Design appears
No more can *Gallia* penetrate
Than what augments her fears,
And vanquisht Loüis can discry   45
Only a long unmeasur'd Ruin nigh.

(4)

See Great *Britannia!* near the Norman Shore
And Coasts of Old Submissive to thy Power
See thy Arm'd Navies plow their glorious way
And with bold Prows assert their Masters Sea,   50
In vain the Hostile Fleets retire
And run to Shipwrack from the Briton's fire.

33 every... Path] all... Paths *1692*   35–36]
          Silence is the Soul of War;
          Deliberate Counsel must prepare
          The Mighty Work, which Valour must compleat:
          Thus *WILLIAM* Rescued, thus Preserves the State;
          Thus Teaches Us to Think and Dare;
          As whilst his Cannon just prepar'd to Breath
               Avenging Anger and swift Death, *1692*
43–44]
          Than what Awakens *Gallia*'s Fears;
          And (though Guilts Eye can sharply penetrate) *1692, Earlier reading in*
L 29 *(the first line not deleted)*   44 fears, *edd.*: fears L 29   45 And *edd.*: & L 29: *om.*
1692   vanquisht] Distracted *1692*   46 nigh. *1692*: nigh, L 29   47–50]
          On *Norman* Coasts and Banks of frighted *Seine*,
               Lo! the Impending Storms begin:
          Britannia safely through her Masters Sea
               Plows up her Victorious Way.
          The *French Salmoneus* throws his Bolts in vain,
          Whilst the true Thunderer asserts the Main: *1692*
51 In ... Hostile] 'Tis done! to Shelves and Rocks his *1692*   52 And ... from the
Briton's] They ... to avoid our *1692 (where it follows l. 54)*

Swift Victory in vengeful Flames
Burns down the Pride of their presumptuous Names;
And the torn Ships that reach the *Gallic* Coast   55
Are but sad Marks to Show the rest are lost.
This, mighty William, this thy Queen has done
Thy Softer half has shook thy Rivals Throne.
Equal to thine Her Fame as Her command:
To Her 'tis given from Her Paternal Sea   60
To drive the Foe; 'tis given to Thee
To drive th'Invader from thy Native Land.
Io Britannia! loose thy Oceans Chains
Whilst *Russel* Strikes the Blow thy Queen Ordains:
Thus Rescu'd, thus Rever'd, for ever Stand,   65
And bless the Council and reward the Hand,
Io! Britannia! thy *Maria* Reigns.

(5)

From *Marys* Conquest and the rescu'd Main
Let *France* look forth to *Sambres* armed Shoar
And boast those Joys for *Williams* Death no more   70
Which speak Her Terror of his Life too plain.
The Fatal Day alas! draws nigh
When o'er the plains from Distant Towers on high,
Casting around her mournful Eye,
Loüis Friend or Wife shal cry: 75

54 presumptuous *edd.*: presumptious *L 29*: Presumptuous *1692*   55 Ships ... *Gallic*]
Vessels that regain their *1692*   57–62]

> All this the Mild, the Beauteous, Queen has done,
> And *WILLIAM*'s softer half shakes *Lewis*' Throne:
>   *MARIA* does the Sea command
> Whilst *Gallia* flies her Husband's Arms by Land,
> So, the Sun absent, with full sway, the Moon
> Governs the Isles, and rules the Waves alone;
> So *Juno* thunders when her *Jove* is gone. *1692*

59 command: *edd.*: command *L 29*   68 Conquest] Conquests, *1692*   70 those
Joys] her Joy *1692*   *In 1692 followed by:*

> He lives, let *France* confess, the Victor lives:
> Her Triumphs for his Death were vain,

71 Which speak] And spoke *1692*   72–73]

> The mighty years begin, the day draws nigh,
> In which *That One* of *Lewis*' many Wives,
> Who by the baleful force of guilty Charms,
> Has long enthraul'd Him in Her wither'd Arms,
> Shall o're the Plains from distant Towers on high *1692*

74 Casting] Cast *1692*   75] And with Prophetick Sorrow cry: *1692*

Why dos my ruin'd Lord retard his Flight?
Why dos dispair provoke his Age to fight?
As well the Wolf may venture to engage
  The Angry Lions kindled rage.
The Ravenous Vultur, and the Bird of Night,   80
As safely tempt the Stooping Eagles flight,
As *Loüis* to unequal Arms defy
Yon' Hero, crown'd with blooming Victory
  Yet unbreath'd from Battles gain'd
And mad *Iernes* civil rage restrain'd,   85
See all yon' dusty Feilds quite cover'd o'er
With Hostile Troops, and *Orange* at their Head,
  (Fatal Name that Tyrants Dread!)
He comes, our ruin'd Empire is no more,
Down like the *Persian* goes the *Gallic* Throne,   90
Fainting *Darius* flys, pursues great *Ammons* Son.

(6)

Now from the dubious Battel's mingl'd heat
Let Fear look back, and stretch her hasty wing,
Impatient to secure a base retreat:
Let the pale Coward leave his Wounded King   95
  For the vile priviledge of breath,
To live with shame in dread of glorious Death.
In vain: the well directed Bolts of War
Are taught the charging Heros Head to spare
And Strike the Coward Sculking in the rear.   100
Confus'd and mad the Traytor bites the Ground,
His back transfixed with a Dishonest wound,
And owns that Fate has swifter Wings than Fear.

---

79 kindled] generous *1692*   84 Yet] And yet *1692* (*where this line follows l. 85*)
85] Just triumphing o're Rebel rage restrain'd, *1692*   87 *In 1692, followed by:*
     ORANGE destin'd to compleat
     The great Designs of labouring Fate,

88 Fatal] *ORANGE* the *1692*   89 more, *1692*: more *L 29*   90 Throne, *1692*:
Throne *L 29*   91] *Darius* flies, young Ammon urges on. *1692*   96 of] to *1692*
98–100]
    In vain: for Fate has swifter Wings than fear,
    She follows hard, and strikes Him in the rear, *1692*

101 Confus'd] Dying *1692*   103] *In 1692, used as variant of l. 98*

While, through the fiercest Troops, and thickest press
Undaunted Virtue carrys on Success;   105
While equal Heav'n guards the distinguish'd brave,
And Armies must not hurt whom Sheilding *Angels* Save.

(7)

Virtue to Verse the real Lustre gives,
Each by the others mutual Friendship lives:
The Heros Acts Sustain the Poets Thought,   110
Æneas suffer'd and *Achilles* fought,
Or *Virgils* Majesty and *Homers* rage
In vain had strove to Vanquish Envious Age.
While then your Hero drowns his rising fear
     With Drums Alarms and Trumpets Sounds,   115
In arm'd retreats Secure, and guarded Towns
While he from Danger as from Honour far
Declines the Combat and protracts the War;
     In vain Ye *Gallic* Muses Strive
With Labour'd Verse to keep his Fame alive.   120
Your costly Monuments in vain you raise
On the weak Basis of his mould'ring Praise.
Against his will you chain your frighted King
     To rapid Rhines divided Bed,
Whence in the Anguish of His Soul he fled;   125
     You mock your Hero whilst you Sing,
     The wounds for which he never bled:
Falsehood dos Poyson on your Verse infuse
And *Loüis* fear gives death to *Boileau*'s Muse.

104 While,] Whilst *1692*   105 Undaunted] *om. 1692*   106 While] Whilst *1692*
107 must ... Sheilding] cannot hurt whom *1692*   108 the real] immortal *1692*   gives,
1692: gives *L 29*   110 Sustain] enlarg'd *1692* (*where this line follows l. 111*)   113]
Had ne're like lasting Nature vanquish'd Age; *1692*   114] Whilst *Lewis* then his
rising Terrour drowns *1692*   116 In ... Secure,] Whilst hid in arm'd Retreats *1692*
117 While he] *om. 1692*   118] He bribes close Murder against open War: *1692*
119 Ye] you *1692*   121 costly] mouldring *1692*   122 his mould'ring] the Tyrants
1692   123 In *1692, preceded by:*

     Your Songs are sold, your Numbers are Prophane,
     'Tis Incense to an Idol given,
     Meat offer'd to *Prometheus*' Man,
     That had no Soul from Heaven.

124 To] On *1692*   125] *om. 1692*   126 You ... you] And ... ye *1692*   128
Verse infuse] Praise defuse, *1692*   129 Muse. *1692*: Muse *L 29*

(8)

But Virtue is her own Reward,   130
Thô neither Lyre were Strung, or Verse were heard,
In a Superior Orb the Goddess Rowles
Nor minds our Censure, nor desires our Praise,
Her Acts no human Accident controuls,
Nor Envy can depress, nor Flatt'ry raise: 135
Thô none Shou'd injure her, thô none Adore,
Thô Triumphs or Misfortunes were no more
She Seeks no Lustre and She fears no Night,
      But in her Self compleatly bright
      Not lessen'd thô repell'd by Fate   140
Rejects the mean Design, attempts the great
And in the Battel falls, or Saves the State.

When bound in double Chains poor Belgia lay
To foreign Arms, and inward Strife a Prey,
When Fortune basely with Ambition joyn'd   145
And all was lost, except the Patriots mind.
When the Impetuous Storm and raging wind
Just ready the torn Vessel to o'erwhelm
Forc'd not the Faithful Pilot from the Helm;
When Syrens voices danc'd upon the Seas   150
And fine Persuasion proffer'd seeming peace
      Yet stil the Hero great in Arms
      Stop't his wise Ear against their fatal Charms

---

130 *In 1692, preceded by:* On it's own Worth True Majesty is rear'd,   But] And *1692*
Reward, *1692*: Reward *L 29*   131–44]
            With solid Beams and Native Glory bright,
            She neither Darkness dreads, nor covets Light;
            True to Her self, and fix't to inborn Laws,
            Nor sunk by spight, nor lifted by Applause,
            She from Her settled Orb looks calmly down,
            On Life or Death, a Prison or a Crown.
            When bound in double Chains poor *Belgia* lay
            To foreign Arms, and inward strife a Prey,
            Whilst One Good Man buoy'd up Her sinking State,
                And Virtue labour'd against Fate; *1692*

146 lost, except] conquer'd but *1692*   147] When Storms let loose, and raging Seas
1692   149 the Helm;] his Helm, *1692*   150–3]
            Nor all the Syren Songs of future Peace,
            And dazling Prospect of a promis'd Crown,
                Could lure his stubborn Virtue down; *1692*

Against or Promisses or Threatnings Stood
   To that which was Severely good;   155
Then had no Trophies justify'd his Fame
No Poet blest his Song with Nassau's Name,
Yet o'er his head unblemish'd Glory Sat
Plain to the Soul and visible to Thought
Yet Virtue did as real Triumph bring   160
And Heav'n as plainly shew'd the future *King*
As when He at the Altar Stood, Confest
   In all his Types and Robes of Pow'r,
When Britain freed His Soveraign Honours blest,
And own'd him next to what we there Adore.   165

(9)

   Say, Joyful *Boynes* Victorious flood
   Stain'd by the warring Heroes blood
Say, when his Armies past, did he retire,
Or view the mingled Battles distant Fire?
Cou'd he believe His person was too dear?   170
Or with his Greatness did he cloath his fear?
   Intreating Friends and threat'ning Foes
   In vain the Warriors Speed oppose:
Thrô the first Waves He wing'd His vent'rous way,
   And on the adverse Shoar arose,   175
   Great as the Ruler of the Day
   Rises from the Morning Sea.
But long that Ruler had withdrawn his Light,
Long eas'd His Labours in Repose and Night

154] But against Charms, and Threats, and Hell, He stood, *1692*   Against *edd.*: against
L 29   158–9] *om. 1692*   160] Virtue alone did all that Honour bring, *1692*
161 shew'd the future] pointed out *The 1692*   162 Confest] *om. 1692*   164]
Whilst at His Feet Religious *Britain* bow'd, *1692*   165 there *1692*: the *L 29*
166 Joyful *Boynes*] joyful *Maese*, and *Boin's 1692*   167] (For each has mixt his Waves
with Royal Blood) *1692*   168 Say, when his] When *WILLIAM's 1692*   169
the mingled] from far the *1692*   171–3]
            Or use His Greatness to conceal His Fear?
            Could Prayers or Sighs the dauntless Heroe move?
            Arm'd with Heaven's Justice, and His People's Love, *1692*
176–81]
            (Ten thousand flying Death's in vain oppose)
               Like the great Ruler of the Day,
            With Strength and Swiftness mounting from the Seas:
            Like Him all Day He Toil'd, but long in Night
               The God had eas'd His wearied light,
               'Ere Vengeance left the stubborn Foes,
               Or *WILLIAM's* Labours found repose. *1692*

E'er from those Toils our Monarch knew to cease   180
Which were to give the troubled World its Peace.

(10)

Whence Ancient Rhine inverts his fruitful Urn
Or Maes and Waal with happy Error turn
To Belgia's sav'd Dominions, and the Sea
Whose righted Waves rejoice in Williams Sway,   185
Is there a Town where Children are not taught
Here Gallia trembl'd for here William fought?
      And when in the Ambiguous Feild
      Faint to pursue untaught to yeild
His Armies waver'd, Stept not he between?   190
      Restor'd the Dubious Fight again,
      Mark'd out the Coward that durst fly,
And led the panting Brave to Victory?
Stil as She fled Him, did he not o'ertake
Her doubtful course, and bring Her bleeding back?   195
By his keen Sword did not the Boldest fall?
Was He not King, Commander, Soldier, All——?
His Danger Such as with becoming Dread
His Subjects yet unborn Shal weep to read;

---

181 *In 1692, followed by ll. 190–204*   182–3]
      Where e're old *Rhine* his fruitful Water turns,
      Or fills his Vassals Tributary Urns; *1692*
187 Gallia trembl'd ... William] *Holland* Prosper'd, ... *ORANGE 1692*   *In 1692,*
followed by:
      Through Rapid Waters, and through flying Fire:
      Here rush'd the Prince, Here made whole *France* retire.
      By different Nations be this Valour blest,
         In different Languages confest,
           And then let *Shannon* Speak the rest:
      Let *Shannon* Speak, how on her wond'ring Shore,
      When Conquest hov'ring on his Arms did wait,
      And only ask'd some Lives to Bribe her o're.
      The God-like Man, the more than Conqueror,
      With high Contempt sent back the specious Bait,
      And Scorning Glory at a Price too great,
      With so much Power such Piety did joyn,
         As made a Perfect Virtue Soar
           A Pitch unknown to Man before,
      And lifted *Shannon*'s Waves o'er those of *Boyne.*
188–9] *om. 1692*   190 His Armies waver'd] When His Troops falter'd *1692*   Stept
edd.: Step *L 29*: stept *1692*   193 panting] fainting *1692*   194 o'ertake *edd.*: o'ertake,
L 29, 1692   195 and bring] still brought *1692*   back? *1692*: back *L 29*   198
Danger] Dangers *1692*   199 read; *edd.*: read *L 29*: Read; *1692*

And were not these the only Days   200
(Lett Envy conscious of the Heroes praise
     To late Posterity declare)
In which the Pious Prince refus'd to hear
His Friends Advices or his Subjects Pray'r.

(11)

Ye *Heros*, who have Fought your Countries Cause,   205
Redress'd Her Injuries, or Form'd Her Laws,
To my Advent'rous Song just Witness bear,
     And hear the Pious Goddess Swear,
That *William* Treasures up a greater Name
Than any of the *Nine* did e'er proclaim: 210
That He improves and gives with Int'rest back
All that Hereditary Stock of Fame
     He did from His forefathers take.
That in His Constellation he Unites
     Their scatter'd Rays, and fainter Lights: 215
That His full glory shal for ever Shine,
     Sublime its Sphere, it's ray Divine,
Above yon rolling Orbs and Azure Sky;
     Where nothing comes that knows to Dye.

200 these ... Days] those ... Days that ere *1692*   201–2] *om. 1692*   203 In
which] *om. 1692*   205 In *1692, this begins strophe XII, and is preceded by:*
        XI.
     Nor do his Subjects only share
     The Prosp'rous Fruits of His Indulgent Reign;
     His Enemies approve the Pious War,
     Which, with their Weapon, takes away their Chain:
     More than His Sword, His Goodness strikes His Foes;
     They Bless His Arms, and Sigh they must oppose.
     Justice and Freedom on his Conquests wait,
     And 'tis for Man's Delight that He is Great:
     Succeeding Times shall with long Joy contend,
     If He were more a Victor, or a Friend:
     So much His Courage and His Mercy strive,
     He Wounds, to Cure; and Conquers, to Forgive.
who] that *1692*   208]
     Assist the Pious Muse, and hear Her Swear,
     That 'tis no Poet's Thought, no Flight of Youth,
     But solid Story, and severest Truth, *1692*

210] Than any Country, any Age, can Boast: *1692*   211 That He improves] He has
improv'd, *1692 (where this line follows l. 213)*   212 All that Hereditary] And all that
Ancient *1692*   214 That ... he Unites] And ... does unite *1692*   215 and ...
Lights] of ... Light *1692*   216–17]
     Above or Envy's lash, or Fortunes Wheel,
     That settled Glory shall for ever dwell *1692*
218 yon ... Azure] the ... common *1692*   219 knows to] e'er shall *1692*

Thô whilst our Mortal Eye presumes to look   220
Into Mysterious Fates Eternal book
We own some points in fainter lights exprest
In Symbols figur'd and in Shadows drest;
Yet thrô the whole such obvious Truths at least
In general Characters engrav'd we find   225
As make the Justice of the God Confest
And to right Paths direct the Honest mind.
After the Virtuous Act the Just reward
Shal be return'd, however long defer'd:
    After the black and Impious Deed   230
The Punishment thô slow shal Sure Succeed:
Thus far at least we are indulg'd to read.
And thô thrô certain Years and destin'd Times
    Merit has lain confus'd with Crimes;
Jove has seem'd Negligent of human Cares,   235
Nor Scourg'd our Follies, nor return'd our Prayers;
Yet now his Justice lifts the Equal Scales,
Ambition is Suppress'd, and Right prevails:
Fate it's great Ends by slow Degrees Attains,
O'er *Europe* Free'd Victorious *William* Reigns,   240
    And sullen War and Captive Pride
    Behind his Chariot Wheels are ty'd
      In Everlasting Chains.

220–32]

XIII.

Where Roves the Muse? Where thoughtless to return
    Is her short liv'd Vessel Born,
By Potent Winds too subject to be tost?
And in the Sea of *WILLIAM*'s Praises lost?
Nor let her tempt that Deep, nor make the Shore
    Where our abandon'd Youth She sees
Shipwrackt in Luxury, and lost in Ease;
Whom nor *Britannia*'s Danger can alarm,
    Nor *WILLIAM*'s Exemplary Virtue warm:
Tell 'em howe'er the King can yet Forgive
Their Guilty Sloath, their Homage yet Receive,
    And let their wounded Honour live:
But sure and sudden be their just Remorse;
    Swift be their Virtues rise, and strong its Course; *1692*

223 drest; *edd.*: drest *L 29*   233 And thô thrô] For though for *1692*   235 Jove has]
Though *Jove 1692*   237 Yet ... lifts] His Justice now Demands *1692*   238 Ambition
... Right] Sedition ... Truth *1692*   240] And *Europe* is Redeem'd, and *WILLIAM*
Reigns. *1692*   241–3] *om. 1692*

1693

Considerations on part of the Eighty Eighth Psalme.

I.

HEAVY, O Lord, on me Thy Judgments lye,
Accurs't I am, while God rejects my Cry.
O'erwhelm'd in Darkness and Dispair I groan;
And ev'ry place is Hell; for God is Gone.
O Lord, arise, and let Thy Beams controll   5
Those horrid Clouds, that press my frighted Soul:
Save the Poor Wand'rer from Eternal Night,
        Thou that art the God of Light.

II.

Downward I hasten to my destin'd place;
There None obtain Thy Aid, or Sing Thy Praise.   10
Soon I shal lye in Deaths deep Ocean drown'd:
Is Mercy there; or sweet Forgiveness found?
O save Me yet, whilst on the brink I stand;
Rebuke the Storm and waft my Soul to Land.
O let Her rest beneath Thy Wing secure,   15
        Thou that art the God of Pow'r.

III.

Behold the Prodigal: To Thee I come,
To hail my Father, and to seek my Home.
Nor refuge cou'd I find, nor Friend abroad,
Straying in Vice and destitute of God.   20

Title: part of] *L 27, 1740 om. 1693 In 1740, title continues:* A College Exercise. 1690.
1 HEAVY, O Lord, *1693, 1740*: Heavy, O Lord *L 27*: Heavy O Lord *M*   2 Accurs't ...
while God rejects] *L 27, 1740* And curs'd ... for God neglects *1693*   3 O'erwhelm'd]
L 27, 1740 O Lord, *1693*   5 O Lord, arise, *L 27, 1693*: O! Lord, arise, *1740*: O Lord
arise *M*   7 Save ... Wand'rer] *L 27, 1740* O rise, and save me *1693*   10 or] *L 27,
1740* none *1693*   12 or] *L 27, 1740* is *1693*   14 waft my Soul] *L 27, 1740* set me
safe *1693*   15] *L 27, 1740* O make my Longings and thy Mercy sure, *1693*   17
Prodigal ... I] *L 27, 1740* wearied Prodigal is *1693*   18] *L 27, 1740* To Thee, his Hope,
his Harbour, and his Home *1693*   19 Nor ... nor] *L 27, 1740* No Father he cou'd find, no
1693   20 Straying in Vice] *L 27, 1740* Depriv'd of Joy *1693*

O let Thy Terrors, and my Anguish End!
Be Thou my Refuge, and be Thou my Friend:
Receive the Son Thou did'st so long reprove,
Thou that art the God of Love.

Enigma.

*B*Y *Birth I'm a Slave, yet can give you a Crown;*
I dispose of all Honours, my self having none:
I'm obliged by just Maxims to govern my Life,
Yet I hang my own Master, and lye with his Wife.
Where Men are a Gaming, I cunningly sneak,   5
And their Cudgels and Shovels away from 'em take.
Fair Maidens and Ladies I by the Hand get,
And pick off their Diamonds, tho' ne're so well set;
But when I have Comrades, we rob in whole Bands,
Then we presently take off your Lands from your Hands;   10
But this fury once over, I've such winning Arts,
That you love me much more than you doe your own Hearts.

An Epitaph on True, her Majesty's Dog.

*I*F *Wit or Honesty cou'd save*
Our mouldring Ashes from the Grave,
This Stone had yet remain'd unmark'd,
I still wrote Prose, and True *still bark'd:*
But envious Fate has claim'd its due,   5
Here lies the mortal Part of True;
His deathless Virtues must survive,
To better us that are alive.
His Prudence and his Wit were seen,
In that, from Mary's *Grace and Meen,*   10
He own'd the Pow'r, and lov'd the Queen.

21 my] *L 27, 1740* his *1693*   22 my Refuge . . . my] *L 27, 1740* his Father . . . his *1693*
  Title: *L 28*: ENIGMA I. by Mr. *Prior. 1693*: AN ENIGMA. *1740*   5 *Where*]
When *L 28, 1740*   cunningly *L 28, 1740:* cunning *1693*   6 *'em*] them *L 28, 1740*
8 *Diamonds L 28, 1740*: *Diamons 1693*   9 *But*] For *L 28, 1740*   10 *we*] *L 28 om.*
1740
  Title] True's Epitaph, by Prior *Lpo 18, Harl*   3 *yet*] still *Lpo 18, Harl*   4
wrote] writt *Lpo 18, Harl*

By long Obedience he confest,
That serving her was to be blest.
Ye Murmurers, let True *evince,*
That Men are Beasts, and Dogs have Sence.   15
His Faith and Truth all White-hall *knows,*
He ne're could fawn, or flatter those
Whom he believ'd were Mary's *Foes.*
Ne're skulk'd from whence his Soveraign led him,
Nor snarl'd against the Hand that fed him.   20

Read this ye Statesmen now in Favour,
And mend your own, by True's *Behaviour.*

Hymn to the Sun.

Set by Dr. Purcel, and Sung before their Majesties on New-Years-Day, 1694.

I.

LIGHT of the World, and Ruler of the Year,
   With happy Speed begin Thy great Career;
And, as Thou dost thy radiant Journies run,
   Through every distant Climate own,
     That in fair ALBION Thou hast seen   5
     The greatest Prince, the brightest Queen,
   That ever sav'd a Land, or blest a Throne,
Since first Thy Beams were spread, or Genial Power was known.

II.

   So may Thy Godhead be confest,
   So the returning Year be blest,   10
   As His Infant Months bestow
   Springing Wreaths for WILLIAM's Brow;

20 *Nor*] Or *Lpo 18, Harl*
   Title: *Hymn ... and*] *1709* FOR THE NEW YEAR: TO THE SUN. Intended To be
1694 1694] 1693/4 *1694, 1709*   3 Thou ... Journies] *1709* the Radiant Journey's
1694   4 *Preceded in 1694 by a version of the present l. 8*   every distant Climate] *1709*
all the distant Nations *1694*   7 Land, or blest] *1709* People, ever Grac'd *1694*   8]
1709 Where e're thy Beams are spread, where e're thy Power is known, *1694* (*where it is l. 4*)
11 His] its *1694, 1709*

As His Summer's Youth shall shed
Eternal Sweets around MARIA's Head:
From the Blessings They bestow,   15
Our Times are dated, and our *Æra's* move:
They govern, and enlighten all Below,
As Thou dost all Above.

III.

Let our Hero in the War
Active and fierce, like Thee, appear: 20
Like Thee, great Son of JOVE, like Thee,
When clad in rising Majesty,
Thou marchest down o'er DELOS' Hills confest,
With all Thy Arrows arm'd, in all Thy Glory drest.
Like Thee, the Hero does his Arms imploy,   25
The raging PYTHON to destroy,
And give the injur'd Nations Peace and Joy.

IV.

From fairest Years, and Time's more happy Stores,
Gather all the smiling Hours;
Such as with friendly Care have guarded   30
Patriots and Kings in rightful Wars;
Such as with Conquest have rewarded
Triumphant Victors happy Cares;
Such as Story has recorded
Sacred to NASSAU's long Renown,   35
For Countries sav'd, and Battels won.

V.

March Them again in fair Array,
And bid Them form the happy Day,
The happy Day design'd to wait
On WILLIAM's Fame, and EUROPE's Fate.   40

---

13 His] its *1694, 1709*   14 around MARIA's] *1709* round *Mary*'s *1694*   15 bestow]
1709 shall know *1694*   24 in] *1709* with *1694*   27] *1709*   *In* 1694, *in italics, and*
marked Cho.   28 fairest ... happy] *1709* Ancient Times Historic *1694*   30 Such as]
1709 All that *1694*   32 Such as] *1709* All that *1694*   33–34] *1709*

> His Great Fore-fathers Pious Cares,
> All that Story have Recorded *1694*

36 sav'd] *1709* Sack'd *1694*   37–44] *1709*   *In* 1694, *in italics, and marked* Cho.

Let the happy Day be crown'd
With great Event, and fair Success;
No brighter in the Year be found,
But That which brings the Victor home in Peace.

VI.

Again Thy Godhead We implore,   45
Great in Wisdom as in Power;
Again, for good MARIA's sake, and Ours,
    Chuse out other smiling Hours;
Such as with joyous Wings have fled,
    When happy Counsels were advising;   50
Such as have lucky Omens shed
    O'er forming Laws, and Empires rising;
Such as many Courses ran,
Hand in Hand, a goodly Train,
To bless the great ELIZA's Reign;   55
And in the Typic Glory show,
What fuller Bliss MARIA shall bestow.

VII.

As the solemn Hours advance,
Mingled send into the Dance
Many fraught with all the Treasures,   60
    Which Thy Eastern Travel views;
Many wing'd with all the Pleasures,
    Man can ask, or Heav'n diffuse:
That great MARIA all those Joys may know,
Which, from Her Cares, upon Her Subjects flow.   65

VIII.

For Thy own Glory sing our Sov'raign's Praise,
    God of Verses and of Days:

47 good MARIA's] *1709 Mary's 1694*   49 joyous] *1709* lucky *1694*   51 lucky] *1709*
glad *1694*   53 Courses] *1709* Lustres *1694*   57 What ... MARIA shall] *1709* The
... which *Mary* should *1694*   58 solemn] *1709* Graver *1694*   61 Thy] *1709* the
1694   64–65] *1709*
        To ease the Cares which for Her Subjects sake
        The Pious Queen does with glad Patience take.
     Cho.   *To let Her all the Blessings know*
        Which from those Cares upon Her Subjects flow. 1694

Let all Thy tuneful Sons adorn
    Their lasting Work with WILLIAM's Name;
Let chosen Muses yet unborn   70
Take great MARIA for their future Theam:
    Eternal Structures let Them raise,
    On WILLIAM's and MARIA's Praise:
Nor want new Subject for the Song;
    Nor fear they can exhaust the Store;   75
'Till Nature's Musick lyes unstrung;
'Till Thou, great God, shalt lose Thy double Pow'r;
And touch Thy Lyre, and shoot Thy Beams no more.

1694

'Spare Dorsett's sacred life, decerning fate'

SPARE Dorsett's sacred life, decerning fate,
And Death shall march thrô Courts and Camps in State,
Emptying his Quiver on the vulgar Great;
Round Dorsett's board lett Peace and Plenty dance.
Far off lett Famine Her sad reign advance,   5
And War walk deep in blood thrô conquer'd France.

Apollo thus began the Mystic Strain,
The Muses Sons all bow'd and sayd Amen.

---

71 great ... future] *1709* Mary's Goodness for their *1694*   73 MARIA's] *1709* on
Mary's *1694*   74 Subject] *1709* Subjects *1694*   77–78] *1709* Till Thou shalt shine
no more *1694*
    Title: edd.: om. St *J*, L *10*   2 State, L *10*: Sta St *J* (*where cropping has trimmed
ends of some lines*)   4 dance. L *10*: dance St *J*   5 advance, L *10*: advance St *J*
6 France. L *10*: Fran St *J*   8 Amen. L *10*: Amen St *J*

To My Lady Dursley, on Her Reading Milton's Paradise Lost.

HERE reading how fond ADAM was betray'd,
And how by Sin EVE's blasted Charms decay'd;
Our common Loss unjustly You complain;
So small that Part of it, which You sustain.

You still, fair Mother, in your Offspring trace   5
The Stock of Beauty destin'd for the Race:
Kind Nature, forming Them, the Pattern took
From Heav'n's first Work, and EVE's Original Look.

You, happy Saint, the Serpent's Pow'r controul:
Scarce any actual Guilt defiles your Soul: 10
And Hell does o'er that Mind vain Triumph boast,
Which gains a Heav'n, for earthly EDEN lost.

With Virtue strong as Yours had EVE been arm'd,
In vain the Fruit had blush'd, or Serpent charm'd:
Nor had our Bliss by Penitence been bought;   15
Nor had frail ADAM fall'n, nor MILTON wrote.

'That Heaven and Earth might witness bear'

THAT Heaven and Earth might witness bear
That Justice stood by Marie's throne,
Nor could They doubt if Right from Her
On others Subjects should be shown
When They reflected with what care   5
She ask'd it for Her own.

Title: 1694: TO THE LADY *DURSLEY*, On the same Subject. *1709, 1718 (see commentary)*   4 So small] *1709* Small is *1694*   6 the Race] *1709* our Race *1694*
7 Pattern] *1709* Features *1694*   8 first ... and] *1709* own ... in *1694*   10 Scarce any] *1709* Whilst scarce one *1694*   11 that ... Triumph] *1709* your ... Triumphs *1694*
13 Virtue ... had] *1709* equal Vertue had frail *1694*   14 or] *1709* the *1694*   15 Nor ... Penitence] *1709* Our Bliss by Penitence had neer *1694*   16 Nor ... nor] *1709*
Adam had never faln, or *1694*
    Titles edd.: *om. L 10*

On the Taking of Huy.

THE Town which Loüis bought, the King reclaims
  And brings instead of Bribes avenging Flames.
Now Louis take Thy Titles from above,
Boileau shal Sing and We'll believe Thee Jove.
Jove gain'd his Mistress with alluring Gold   5
But Jove like Thee was impotent and Old:
Active and Young he did like William stand,
And Stunn'd the Dame, his Thunder in his Hand.

1695

An Ode.

Presented to the King, on his Majesty's Arrival in Holland, After the Queen's Death. 1695.

*Quis desiderio sit pudor aut modus
Tam cari capitis? præcipe lugubres
Cantus, Melpomene.*

I.

AT MARY's Tomb, (sad, sacred Place!)
  The Virtues shall their Vigils keep:
And every Muse, and every Grace
In solemn State shall ever weep.

Title: *1694*: On the Taking Namur. *M*: ON THE TAKING OF NAMUR, 1692. *1740*: Upon the Kings taking Namur. *L 29*   1 the King reclaims] Nassau reclaims, *1740*: the King requires, *1694*: our King requires *L 29*   2] *1740* With Gold one brib'd, the other storm'd by Fires: *1694*: With ... stormes with fires *L 29*   3 above, *edd.*: above *M*, *L 29*: Above, *1740*: above! *1694*   4 Boileau ... We'll ... Jove. *edd.*: Boileau ... Wee'l ... Jove *M*: Boileau ... we'll ... Jove. *1740*: Let fawning *Boileau* sing his earthly Jove! *1694*: Let flattering ... jove *L 29*   5 gain'd] *1694, 1740* Bribed *L 29*   6 But Jove] *1740* When he, *1694*, *L 29*   Old: *edd.* : Old *M* : old : *1694*, *1740*: old, *L 29*   7 Active] *1694, 1740* Vigorous *L 29*
Title] *1709* TO THE KING, AN ODE ON His Majesty's ARRIVAL IN HOLLAND, *1695*. *1695*   *Motto: præcipe ... Melpomene.*] *1709* Hor. *1695*   1–4] *1709*
ON MARY's Tomb, thrô rowling Years,
The Mournful Graces all shall weep;
And, with fresh Lamps and flowing Tears,
The Virtues endless Vigils Keep. *1695*

II.

The future, pious, mournful Fair,   5
  Oft as the rolling Years return,
With fragrant Wreaths, and flowing Hair,
  Shall visit Her distinguish'd Urn.

III.

For Her the Wise and Great shall mourn;
  When late Records her Deeds repeat: 10
Ages to come, and Men unborn
  Shall bless her Name, and sigh her Fate.

IV.

Fair ALBION shall, with faithful Trust,
  Her holy Queen's sad Reliques guard;
'Till Heav'n awakes the precious Dust,   15
  And gives the Saint her full Reward.

V.

But let the King dismiss his Woes,
  Reflecting on his fair Renown;
And take the Cypress from his Brows,
  To put his wonted Lawrels on.   20

VI.

If prest by Grief our Monarch stoops;
  In vain the BRITISH Lions roar:
If He, whose Hand sustain'd them, droops;
  The BELGIC Darts will wound no more.

5–8] *1709 om. 1695*   9 Her . . . Great] *1709* MARY distant Lands *1695*   10
repeat:] *1709* relate, *1695*   13 faithful] *1709* watchful *1695*   16 And . . . her]
1709 To Cloath it in its *1695*   17 dismiss] *1709* forsake *1695*   21 *In 1695, pre-*
ceded by:

> The Lovely Dead, whom He regrets,
> Can know no Fear, can feel no Grief:
> The living World, whom He forgets,
> Would perish without His Relief.

21 If . . . our] *1709* While . . . their *1695*   21–24] *1709*   *In 1695, the lines are in this*
order: 22, 21, 24, 23

VII.

Embattel'd Princes wait the Chief, 25
  Whose Voice should rule, whose Arm should lead;
And, in kind Murmurs, chide That Grief,
  Which hinders EUROPE being freed.

VIII.

The great Example They demand,
  Who still to Conquest led the Way; 30
Wishing Him present to Command,
  As They stand ready to Obey.

IX.

They seek That Joy, which us'd to glow,
  Expanded on the Hero's Face;
When the thick Squadrons prest the Foe, 35
  And WILLIAM led the glorious Chace.

X.

To give the mourning Nations Joy,
  Restore Them Thy auspicious Light,
Great Sun: with radiant Beams destroy
  Those Clouds, which keep Thee from our Sight. 40

XI.

Let Thy sublime Meridian Course
  For MARY's setting Rays attone:
Our Lustre, with redoubl'd Force,
  Must now proceed from Thee alone.

---

25 the] *1709* their *1695*   28 EUROPE] *1709* EUROPE's *1695*   31 Wishing Him]
1709 And wish Him *1695*   37 To] *1709* Oh! *1695*   38–39] *1709*
           Break forth, great Sun, with usual Light:
           And let thy stronger Beams destroy *1695*

41–44] *1709*

           Advance in thy Meridian Course,
           And, since thy MARY's Light is gone,
           Rejoyce the World with double Force,
           Thy Beams all fixt in Thee alone. *1695*

XII.

See, Pious King, with diff'rent Strife   45
   Thy struggling ALBION's Bosom torn:
So much She fears for WILLIAM's Life,
   That MARY's Fate She dare not mourn.

XIII.

Her Beauty, in thy softer Half
   Bury'd and lost, She ought to grieve: 50
But let her Strength in Thee be safe:
   And let Her weep; but let Her live.

XIV.

Thou, Guardian Angel, save the Land
   From thy own Grief, her fiercest Foe;
Lest BRITAIN, rescu'd by Thy Hand,   55
   Should bend and sink beneath Thy Woe.

XV.

Her former Triumphs all are vain,
   Unless new Trophies still be sought;
And hoary Majesty sustain
   The Battels, which Thy Youth has fought.   60

XVI.

Where now is all That fearful Love,
   Which made Her hate the War's Alarms?
That soft Excess, with which She strove
   To keep her Hero in her Arms?

49–52] *1709*

     Her fair Delight, Her softer Half,
     Cold in the Grave with MARY lies,
     Unless in Thee her strength is safe,
     The frighted Nation wholly dies.   *95*

53 the] *1709* our *1695*   55 Lest BRITAIN,] *1709* Lest, rais'd and *1695*   56 Should]
1709 She *1695*   61 all That] *1709* BRITAIN's *1695*   63 That soft] *1709* Where
that *1695*

XVII.

While still She chid the coming Spring,   65
    Which call'd Him o'er his subject Seas:
While, for the Safety of the King,
    She wish'd the Victor's Glory less.

XVIII.

'Tis chang'd; 'tis gone: sad BRITAIN now
    Hastens her Lord to Foreign Wars: 70
Happy, if Toils may break his Woe;
    Or Danger may divert his Cares.

XIX.

In Martial Din She drowns her Sighs,
    Lest He the rising Grief should hear:
She pulls her Helmet o'er her Eyes,   75
    Lest He should see the falling Tear.

XX.

Go, mighty Prince, let FRANCE be taught,
    How constant Minds by Grief are try'd;
How great the Land, that wept and fought,
    When WILLIAM led, and MARY dy'd.   80

XXI.

Fierce in the Battel make it known,
    Where Death with all His Darts is seen,
That He can touch thy Heart with None,
    But That which struck the Beauteous Queen.

XXII.

BELGIA indulg'd her open Grief,   85
    While yet her Master was not near;

66 Him ... his] *1709* Thee ... thy *1695*   67 While] *1709* Whilst *1695*   68 less.]
1709 less? *1695*   69 chang'd; ... gone:] *1709* gone, ... chang'd; *1695*   73 Din]
1709 sounds *1695*   82 His] *1709* her *1695*   83 He can touch] *1709* she could
strike *1695*   84 which ... Beauteous] *1709* with which she struck the *1695*   85 *In*
1695, preceded by the present ll. 117–20 and by:
                Envy shall calm that useless Rage,
                By which Thy Glory brighter grows,

With sullen Pride refus'd Relief,
And sat Obdurate in Despair.

XXIII.

As Waters from her Sluces, flow'd
Unbounded Sorrow from her Eyes: 90
To Earth her bended Front She bow'd,
And sent her Wailings to the Skies.

XXIV.

But when her anxious Lord return'd;
Rais'd is her Head; her Eyes are dry'd:
She smiles, as WILLIAM ne'er had mourn'd: 95
She looks, as MARY ne'er had dy'd.

XXV.

That Freedom which all Sorrows claim,
She does for Thy Content resign:
Her Piety itself would blame;
If Her Regrets should waken Thine.   100

XXVI.

To cure Thy Woe, She shews Thy Fame;
Lest the great Mourner should forget,
That all the Race, whence ORANGE came,
Made Virtue triumph over Fate.

And Death, Thy Sorrows to asswage,
Shall turn her wrath, and wound Thy Foes.

87–88] *1709*

She hated Hope, She scorn'd Relief,
And triumph'd, Proud in full Despair. *1695*

89–92] *1709*

Her echo'd Wailings pierc't the Skyes,
To Earth her bended Forehead bow'd,
The Tears unbounded from her Eyes,
As Waters from her Sluces, flow'd. *1695*

93 when her anxious] *1709* soon as Thou her *1695*   94 Rais'd is her Head;] *1709* **Her**
Head is rear'd, *1695*   101 *In 1695, preceded by:*

Dissembling Ease, and forcing Joy,
She begs her Lord his Tears to dry:
Did BELGIA e're her prayers employ,
And ORANGE stand regardless by?

101 Woe] *1709* Woes *1695*

XXVII.

WILLIAM His Country's Cause could fight,   105
And with His Blood Her Freedom seal:
MAURICE and HENRY guard that Right,
For which Their pious Parent fell.

XXVIII.

How Heroes rise, how Patriots set,
Thy Father's Bloom and Death may tell: 110
Excelling Others These were Great:
Thou, greater still, must These excell.

XXIX.

That last fair Instance Thou must give,
Whence NASSAU's Virtue can be try'd;
And shew the World, that Thou can'st live   115
Intrepid, as Thy Consort dy'd.

XXX.

Thy Virtue, whose resistless Force
No dire Event could ever stay,
Must carry on it's destin'd Course;
Tho' Death and Envy stop the Way.   120

XXXI.

For BRITAIN's Sake, for BELGIA's, live:
Pierc'd by Their Grief forget Thy own:
New Toils endure; new Conquest give;
And bring Them Ease, tho' Thou hast None.

---

106 Her] *1709* its *1695*   108 Parent *1709*: Parents *1718*: Father *1695*   109–12] *1709*

> A second WILLIAM's Bloom could tell
> How Heroes rise, how Patriots set:
> As Theirs did Others Deeds excel,
> Excelling Theirs be Thine compleat. *1695*

116 Intrepid, ... Consort] *1709* As glorious ... MARY *1695*   117–20 *In 1695, these lines precede l. 85*   121] *1709* That Thou canst live for BELGIA's sake, *1695*   122 Their Grief] *1709* her Grief's *1695*   123 Conquest give;] *1709* Conquests make *1695*   124 And bring Them] *1709* To give her *1695*

XXXII.

Vanquish again; tho' She be gone,   125
 Whose Garland crown'd the Victor's Hair:
And Reign; tho' She has left the Throne,
 Who made Thy Glory worth Thy Care.

XXXIII.

Fair BRITAIN never yet before
 Breath'd to her King a useless Pray'r: 130
Fond BELGIA never did implore,
 While WILLIAM turn'd averse His Ear.

XXXIV.

But should the weeping Hero now
 Relentless to Their Wishes prove;
Should He recall, with pleasing Woe,   135
 The Object of his Grief and Love;

XXXV.

Her Face with thousand Beauties blest,
 Her Mind with thousand Virtues stor'd,
Her Pow'r with boundless Joy confest,
 Her Person only not ador'd: 140

XXXVI.

Yet ought his Sorrow to be checkt;
 Yet ought his Passions to abate:
If the great Mourner would reflect,
 Her Glory in her Death compleat.

125-44] *1709*

> To Keep from treach'rous Foes Her store,
> Thô all Thy Wealth be robb'd by Death;
> To vanquish, thô She lives no more
> Whose Hands prepar'd the Victor's Wreath.
>
> Oh, could Thy Griefs obdurate prove
> To BELGIA's Cries, to BRITAIN's Fears,
> Yet let them yield to MARY's Love,
> To NASSAU's Glory joyn'd in Her's. *1695*

132 averse] aside *1709*

XXXVII.

She was instructed to command,   145
  Great King, by long obeying Thee:
Her Scepter, guided by Thy Hand,
  Preserv'd the Isles, and Rul'd the Sea.

XXXVIII.

But oh! 'twas little, that her Life
  O'er Earth and Water bears thy Fame: 150
In Death, 'twas worthy WILLIAM's Wife,
  Amidst the Stars to fix his Name.

XXXIX.

Beyond where Matter moves, or Place
  Receives it's Forms, Thy Virtues rowl:
From MARY's Glory, Angels trace   155
  The Beauty of her Part'ner's Soul.

XL.

Wise Fate, which does it's Heav'n decree
  To Heroes, when They yield their Breath,
Hastens Thy Triumph. Half of Thee
  Is Deify'd before thy Death.   160

XLI.

Alone to thy Renown 'tis giv'n,
  Unbounded thro' all Worlds to go:
While She great Saint rejoices Heav'n;
  And Thou sustain'st the Orb below.

145–6] *1709*

   If MARY could so well command,
   It was by long obeying Thee; *1695*

150] *1709* Thy Fame o'er Earth and Water bears, *1695*   152] *1709* To Fix His Name
amidst the Stars. *1695*   155 Glory,] *1709* Glories *1695*   156 Beauty] *1709* Beauties
1695   159 Triumph.] *1709* Triumphs, *1695*   161 Alone ... Renown] *1709* And
to Thy Fame alone *1695*   163–4] *1709*

   While MARY reigns a Saint in Heaven,
   And Thou a Demi-God below. *1695*

AN ENGLISH BALLAD

With

Boileau's 'Ode Sur la Prise de Namur'

Ode Sur la Prise de Namur, Par les Armes du Roy, L' Année 1692.

Par Monsieur Boileau Despreaux.

I.

Q UELLE docte & Sainte yvresse
   Aujourd'huy me fait la loy?
Chastes Nymphes du *Permesse*,
N'est-ce pas vous que je voy?
Accourez, Troupe Sçavante: 5
Des sons que ma Lyre enfante;
Ces Arbres sont réjoüis:
Marquez en bien la cadence:
Et vous, Vents, faites Silence:
Je vais Parler de Louis.   10

II.

Dans ses chansons immortelles,
Comme un Aigle audacieux,
Pindare étendant ses aisles,
Fuit loin des Vulgaires yeux.
Mais, ô ma fidele Lyre,   15
Si, dans l'ardeur qui m'inspire,
Tu peux suivre mes Transports;
Les chesnes des Monts de *Thrace*
N'ont rien oüi, que n'efface
La douceur de tes accords.   20

III.

Est-ce Apollon & Neptune,
Qui sur ces Rocs Sourcilleux
Ont, compagnons de Fortune,
Basti ces Murs orgueilleux?

Title: Namur, . . . Despreaux.] NAMUR. *1695*: *NAMUR.* L'Année 1692. Par Monsieur *Despreaux de Boileau. 1709*   18 des *1695*: de *1709, 1718*

---

them in *France. 1695*   14 While] *1709* Whilst *1695*   15] *1709 Des Preaux*, a Vulture, only flies *1695*   16 shows] *1709* seeks *1695*   17 Honour] *1709* Conscience *1695*   18] *1709* His Measures soon from Truth will rove; *1695*   19 And ... eight] *1709* Give *Boileau* but Five *1695*   20 Makes ... take] *1709* And ... takes *1695*   24 Of *Marli* Wood,] *1709* At *Trianon 1695*

An English Ballad, On the Taking of Namur by the King of Great Britain, 1695.

Dulce est desipere in loco.

I. *and* II.

SOME Folks are drunk, yet do not know it:
  So might not BACCHUS give You Law?
Was it a Muse, O lofty Poet,
  Or Virgin of St. CYR, You saw?
Why all this Fury? What's the Matter,   5
  That Oaks must come from *Thrace* to dance?
Must stupid Stocks be taught to flatter?
  And is there no such Wood in *France*?
Why must the Winds all hold their Tongue?
  If they a little Breath should raise;   10
Would that have spoil'd the Poet's Song;
  Or puff'd away the Monarch's Praise?

PINDAR, that Eagle, mounts the Skies;
  While Virtue leads the noble Way:
Too like a Vultur BOILEAU flies,   15
  Where sordid Interest shows the Prey.
When once the Poet's Honour ceases,
  From Reason far his Transports rove:
And BOILEAU, for eight hundred Pieces,
  Makes LOUIS take the Wall of JOVE.   20

III.

NEPTUNE and SOL came from above,
  Shap'd like MEGRIGNY and VAUBAN:
They arm'd these Rocks; then show'd old JOVE
  Of *Marli* Wood, the wond'rous Plan.

Title: On ... Namur ... 1695.] On ... *NAMUR.* 1695. *1709*: On ... *NAMUR.* 1705.
Copies of 1709 with uncancelled leaf: In ANSWER to Mr. *DESPREAUX's* Pindarique
ODE On ... NAMURE. *1695*   1 SOME ... do] *1709* WAS you not drunk, and did
1695   2 So ... give] *1709* When you thought *Phœbus* gave *1695*   3–4] *1709*
                  Or was it not, good Brother Poet,
                  The chaste Nymph *Maintenon* you saw? *1695*

5 Why ... Fury?] *1709* She charm'd you sure, or *1695*   7 Must stupid Stocks ...
flatter?] *1709* If Stocks must needs ... flatter, *1695*   8] *1709* You'll find enough of
[*continued opposite*

De leur enceinte fameuse   25
La *Sambre* unie à la *Meuse*,
Deffend le fatal abord;
Et par cent bouches horribles
L'airain sur ces Monts terribles
Vomit le Fer, & la Mort.   30

IV.

Dix mille vaillans ALCIDES
Les bordant de toutes parts,
D'éclairs au loin homicides
Font petiller leurs Remparts:
Et dans son Sein infidele   35
Par tout la Terre y recele
Un feu prest à s'élancer,
Qui soudain perçant son goufre,
Ouvre un Sepulchre de soufre
A quiconque ose avancer.   40

V.

Namur, devant tes murailles
Jadis la *Grece* eust vingt Ans
Sans fruit veu les funerailles
De ses plus fiers Combattans.
Quelle effroyable Puissance   45
Aujourd-huy pourtant s'avance,
Preste à foudroyer tes monts?
Quel bruit, quel feu l'environne?
C'est JUPITER en Personne;
Ou c'est le Vainqueur de *Mons*.   50

... excell the *Greeks: 1709* : Are We then braver than the *Greeks? 1695*   46] *1709* What
Power Divine those Hills regain? *1695*   47 little WILL] *1709 Brittain's* KING *1695*
49–52] *1709*

His Arm shall keep your Victor under,
And *Europe's* Liberty restore;
Your *Jupiter* must quit his Thunder,
And fright the injur'd World no more. *1695*

Such Walls, these three wise Gods agreed,   25
    By Human Force could ne'er be shaken:
But You and I in HOMER read
    Of Gods, as well as Men, mistaken.
Sambre and *Maese* their Waves may join;
    But ne'er can WILLIAM's Force restrain: 30
He'll pass them Both, who pass'd the *Boyn*:
    Remember this, and arm the *Sein*.

IV.

Full fifteen thousand lusty Fellows
    With Fire and Sword the Fort maintain:
Each was a HERCULES, You tell us;   35
    Yet out they march'd like common Men.
Cannons above, and Mines below
    Did Death and Tombs for Foes contrive:
Yet Matters have been order'd so,
    That most of Us are still alive.   40

V.

If *Namur* be compar'd to *Troy*;
    Then BRITAIN's Boys excell'd the GREEKS:
Their Siege did ten long Years employ:
    We've done our Bus'ness in ten Weeks.
What Godhead does so fast advance,   45
    With dreadful Pow'r those Hills to gain?
'Tis little WILL, the Scourge of *France*;
    No Godhead, but the first of Men.
His mortal Arm exerts the Pow'r,
    To keep ev'n *Mons*'s Victor under: 50
And that same JUPITER no more
    Shall fright the World with impious Thunder.

---

27 You and I in] *1709 Boileau*, we who *1695*   28 Of]*1709* Find *1695*   36 out ...
common] *1709* they march'd but like other *1695*   38 Foes] *1709* Us *1695*   39–40]
1709

        Yet *WILLIAM* order'd matters so,
          That few were there but are alive. *1695*

41 If *Namur* be] *1709* Why is *Namure 1695*   42 Then ... excell'd the GREEKS:] Then
[*continued opposite*

VI.

N'en doute point: c'est luy-mesme.
Tout brille en luy; Tout est Roy.
Dans *Bruxelles* NASSAU blême
Commence à trembler pour Toy.
En vain il voit le *Batâve*,   55
Desormais docile Esclâve,
Rangé Sous ses étendars:
En vain au Lion *Belgique*
Il voit l'Aigle *Germanique*
Uni Sous les Leopards.   60

VII.

Plein de la frayeur nouvelle,
Dont ses sens sont agités,
A son secours il appelle
Les Peuples les plus vantéz.
Ceux-là viennent du rivage,   65
Où s'enorgueillit le *Tage*
De l'or, qui roule en ses eaux;
Ceux-ci des champs, où la neige
Des marais de la *Norvége*
Neuf mois couvre les roseaux.   70

VIII.

Mais qui fait enfler la *Sambre*?
Sous les *Jumeaux* effrayéz,
Des froids Torrens de *Decembre*
Les Champs par tout sont noyéz.
CERES s'enfuit, éplorée   75
De voir en proye à BOREE

66 Où *1695*: Ou *1709, 1718*

58–60]   One more, and then thy Fame is Crown'd,
                Perform thy Master's high Commission,
                For *William* ne'er will stand his Ground. *1695*

59 the] his *1709*   65–68] *1709 om. 1695*   69 the mighty VILL'ROY] *1709* this mighty
Marshall *1695*   70 Finds a small] *1709* But finds a *1695*   71 So] *1709* He *1695*
72 And ... prudent] *1709* Yet ... Prudence *1695*   73–74] *1709*
                Ban and *Arriereban*, all appear,
                Great Armies, would they march but faster; *1695*
75 Poor] *1709* But *1695*   76 We fancy'd all,] *1709* One would have thought *1695*
78 the Marshal's plain] *1709* a General's *1695*   79 the] *1709* this *1695*   81–84]
1709 om. 1695

VI.

Our King thus trembles at *Namur*,
 Whilst VILLEROY, who ne'er afraid is,
To *Bruxelles* marches on secure,   **55**
 To bomb the Monks, and scare the Ladies.
After this glorious Expedition,
 One Battle makes the Marshal Great:
He must perform the King's Commission:
 Who knows, but ORANGE may retreat?   **60**
Kings are allow'd to feign the Gout,
 Or be prevail'd with not to Fight:
And mighty LOUIS hop'd, no doubt,
 That WILLIAM wou'd preserve that Right.

VII.

From *Seyn* and *Loyre*, to *Rhone* and *Po*,   **65**
 See every Mother's Son appear:
In such a Case ne'er blame a Foe,
 If he betrays some little Fear.
He comes, the mighty VILL'ROY comes;
 Finds a small River in his Way: **70**
So waves his Colours, beats his Drums;
 And thinks it prudent there to stay.
The *Gallic* Troops breath Blood and War:
 The Marshal cares not to march faster:
Poor VILL'ROY moves so slowly here,   **75**
 We fancy'd all, it was his Master.

VIII.

Will no kind Flood, no friendly Rain
 Disguise the Marshal's plain Disgrace?
No Torrents swell the low *Mehayne*?
 The World will say, he durst not pass. **80**
Why will no *Hyades* appear,
 Dear Poet, on the Banks of *Sambre*?
Just as they did that mighty Year,
 When You turn'd *June* into *December*.

53 Our King thus] *1709* Whilst *WILLIAM 1695* 54 Whilst] *1709* Great *1695* 57
After] *1709* Add to *1695*

[*continued opposite*

Ses guerets d'epics chargéz,
Et Sous les Urnes fangeuses
Des *Hyades* orageuses
Tous ses Trésors submergéz.   80

IX.

Déployez toutes vos rages,
Princes, Vents, Peuples, Frimats;
Ramassez tous vos nuages;
Rassamblez tous vos Soldats.
Malgré vous *Namur* en poudre   85
S'en va tomber Sous la foudre
Qui domta *Lille, Courtray,*
Gand la Superbe Espagnole,
Saint Omer, Bezançon, Dole,
Ypres, Mastricht, & *Cambray.*   90

X.

Mes présages s'accomplissent:
Il commence à chanceler:
Sous les coups qui retentissent
Ses Murs s'en vont s'écrouler.
MARS en feu qui les domine,   95
Souffle à grand bruit leur ruine;
Et les Bombes dans les airs
Allant chercher le tonnere,
Semblent tombant sur la Terre,
Vouloir s'ouvrir les Enfers.   100

XI.

Accourez, NASSAU, BAVIERE,
De ces Murs l'unique espoir:
A couvert d'une Riviere
Venez: vous pouvez tout voir.

98 chercher *1695, 1709* : chercer *1718*   102 De] *1695* Des *1709*

93–96] *1709 om. 1695*   97–98] *1709*
Yet, *Boileau*, we'll take t'other Strain
In Honour of that greater Prince, *1695*

100 plunder'd] gutted *1709* : conquer'd *1695*   101–8] *1709 om. 1695*   109] *1709*
'Tis done, Great *Louis*, Troops advance, *1695*   110 Says MARS,] *1709 Mars* speaks *1695*
111 *Id est*] *1709* That is *1695*   112 can] *1709* dare *1695*   115] *1709* For you that saw it
best can say *1695*

The Water-*Nymphs* are too unkind   85
    To VILL'ROY; are the Land-*Nymphs* so?
And fly They All, at Once Combin'd
    To shame a General, and a Beau?

IX.

Truth, Justice, Sense, Religion, Fame
    May join to finish WILLIAM's Story: 90
Nations set free may bless his Name;
    And *France* in Secret own his Glory.
But *Ipres, Mastrich,* and *Cambray,*
    Besançon, Ghent, St. *Omers, Lysle,*
Courtray, and *Dole*——Ye Criticks, say,   95
    How poor to this was PINDAR's Style?
With Eke's and Also's tack thy Strain,
    Great Bard; and sing the deathless Prince,
Who lost *Namur* the same Campaign,
    He bought *Dixmude,* and plunder'd *Deynse.*   100

X.

I'll hold Ten Pound, my Dream is out:
    I'd tell it You, but for the Rattle
Of those confounded Drums: no doubt
    Yon' bloody Rogues intend a Battel.
Dear me! a hundred thousand *French*   105
    With Terror fill the neighb'ring Field;
While WILLIAM carries on the Trench,
    'Till both the Town and Castle yield.
VILL'ROY to BOUFFLERS should advance,
    Says MARS, thro' Cannons Mouths in Fire;   110
Id est, one Mareschal of *France*
    Tells t'other, He can come no nigher.

XI.

Regain the Lines the shortest Way,
    VILL'ROY; or to *Versailles* take Post:
For, having seen it, Thou can'st say   115
    The Steps, by which *Namur* was lost.

85 too] all *1695, 1709*   86] *1709* We hope the Land-Nymphs are not so: *1695*
87] These Ebb alas! fly they? Combin'd *1709* : Or Fortune sure with Love has join'd *1695*
88 shame ... Beau?] *1709* fail ... Beau. *1695*   91 set free] *1709* combin'd *1695*
[*continued opposite*

Considerez ces approches: 105
Voyez grimper sur ces roches
Ces Athletes belliqueux;
Et dans les Eaux, dans la Flame,
LOUIS à tout donnant l'ame,
Marcher, courir avecque eux.   110

XII.

Contemplez dans la tempeste,
Qui sort de ces Boulevars,
La Plume qui sur sa teste
Attire tous les regards.
A cet Astre redoutable   115
Toûjours un sort favorable
S'attache dans les Combats:
Et toûjours avec la Gloire
MARS amenant la Victoire
Vôle, & le suit à grands pas.   120

XIII.

Grands Deffenseurs de l'*Espagne*,
Montrez-vous: il en est temps:
Courage; vers la *Mahagne*
Voilà vos Drapeaux flottans.
Jamais ses ondes craintives   125
N'ont veû sur leurs foibles rives
Tant de guerriers s'amasser.
Courez donc: Qui vous retarde?
Tout l'Univers vous regarde.
N'osez vous la traverser?   130

XIV.

Loin de fermer le passage
A vos nombreux bataillons,
LUXEMBOURG a du rivage
Reculé ses pavillons.

---

134 *Namur*] *1709* The World *1695*   136 Shou'd shine near] *1709* May equal *1695*
137] He likes *Versailles*, his proper Station, *1709*: Safe *Louis* shines, knows his own Station,
1695   138 Nor cares for] *1709* He likes not *1695*   141–52] *om. 1695*   142
met them in their] left an open *1709*

The Smoke and Flame may vex thy Sight:
Look not once back: but as thou goest,
Quicken the Squadrons in their Flight;
And bid the D——l take the slowest.   120
Think not what Reason to produce,
From LOUIS to conceal thy Fear:
He'll own the Strength of thy Excuse;
Tell him that WILLIAM was but there.

XII.

Now let us look for LOUIS' Feather,   125
That us'd to shine so like a Star:
The Gen'rals could not get together,
Wanting that Influence, great in War.
O Poet! Thou had'st been discreeter,
Hanging the Monarch's Hat so high;   130
If Thou had'st dubb'd thy Star, a Meteor,
That did but blaze, and rove, and die.

XIII.

To animate the doubtful Fight,
Namur in vain expects that Ray:
In vain *France* hopes, the sickly Light   135
Shou'd shine near WILLIAM's fuller Day.
It knows *Versailles*, it's proper Station;
Nor cares for any foreign Sphere:
Where You see BOILEAU's Constellation,
Be sure no Danger can be near.   140

XIV.

The *French* had gather'd all their Force;
And WILLIAM met them in their Way:
Yet off they brush'd, both Foot and Horse.
What has Friend BOILEAU left to say?

117–20] *1709 om. 1695*   121 Reason] *1709* Reasons *1695*   122, 123 thy] *1709*
your *1695*   125 Now ... for] *1709* But where is now great *1695*   126] *1709*
That wav'd so glorious from afar? *1695*   127 get] *1709* come *1695*   128] *1709*
Without the Lustre of that Star. *1695*   129 O] *1709* Ah, *1695*   130 Hanging
the Monarch's] *1709* Since thou would'st hang his *1695*   131 dubb'd thy Star,] *1709*
call'd it but *1695*   132] *1709* That blaz'd a while, and then God b'y. *1695*

[*continued opposite*

Quoy? leur seul aspect vous glace?   135
Où sont ces chefs pleins d'audace,
Jadis si prompts à marcher,
Qui devoient de la *Tamise*,
Et de la *Drâve* Soûmise,
Jusqu'à *Paris* nous chercher?   140

XV.

Cependant l'effroy redouble
Sur les Remparts de *Namur*.
Son Gouverneur qui se trouble
S'enfuit sous son dernier mur.
Déja jusques à ses portes   145
Je voy monter nos cohortes,
La Flame & le Fer en main:
Et sur les Monceaux de piques,
De Corps morts, de Rocs, de Briques,
S'ouvrir un large chemin.   150

XVI.

C'en est fait. Je viens d'entendre
Sur ces Rochers éperdus
Battre un Signal pour se rendre:
Le Feu cesse. Ils sont rendus.
Dépoüillez vôtre arrogance,   155
Fiers Ennemis de la *France*,
Et desormais gracieux,
Allez à *Liege*, à *Bruxelles*,
Porter les humbles nouvelles
De *Namur* pris à vos yeux.   160

---

160 *In 1695, followed by an additional stanza:*

> Pour moy, que Phebus anime
> De ses transports les plus doux,
> Rempli de ce Dieu sublime,
> Je vais, plus hardi que vous,
> Montrer que sur le Parnasse,
> Des bois frequentés d'Horace
> Ma Muse dans son declin,
> Sçait encor les avenuës,
> Et des sources inconnuës
> A l'Auteur du Saint Paulin.*
>
> * *Poëme Heroïque du sieur P**.*

When his high Muse is bent upon't,   145
    To sing her King, that Great Commander,
Or on the Shores of *Hellespont,*
    Or in the Valleys near *Scamander;*
Wou'd it not spoil his noble Task,
    If any foolish *Phrygian* there is,   150
Impertinent enough to ask,
    How far *Namur* may be from *Paris?*

XV.

Two Stanza's more before we end,
    Of Death, Pikes, Rocks, Arms, Bricks, and Fire:
Leave 'em behind You, honest Friend: 155
    And with your Country-Men retire.
Your Ode is spoilt; *Namur* is freed;
    For *Dixmuyd* something yet is due:
So good Count GUISCARD may proceed;
    But BOUFFLERS, Sir, one Word with you.——   160

XVI.

'Tis done. In Sight of these Commanders,
    Who neither Fight, nor raise the Siege,
The Foes of *France* march safe thro' *Flanders;*
    Divide to *Bruxelles,* or to *Liege.*
Send, FAME, this News to *Trianon;*   165
    That BOUFFLERS may new Honours gain:
He the same Play by Land has shown,
    As TOURVILLE did upon the Main.
Yet is the Marshal made a Peer:
    O WILLIAM, may thy Arms advance;   170
That He may lose *Dinant* next Year,
    And so be Constable of *France.*

153–7] *1709*

     Of Death, Pikes, Rocks, Arms, Bricks, and Fire,
     We'll play three Stanza's, and have done;
     The Castle yields, the *French* retire,
     So keep your Powder in your Gun.
       Namure by *WILLIAM*'s Arms is freed; *1695*

161–2] *1709 om. 1695*   163 The ... safe] *1709* March, ... on *1695*   165–8] *1709*
     Nor fear the least these fierce Commanders,
     Who neither fight, nor raise the Siege. *1695*

169 Yet ... made] *1709* Losing *Namure, France* gains *1695*   170] *1709* Let *WILLIAM*'s
Armies but advance, *1695*   171 That He may] *1709 Bouffler*'s shall *1695*   172 so be]
1709 be made *1695*

To My Lord Buckhurst, Very Young, Playing with a Cat.

THE am'rous Youth, whose tender Breast
  Was by his darling Cat possest,
Obtain'd of VENUS his Desire,
Howe'er irregular his Fire:
Nature the Pow'r of Love obey'd: 5
The Cat became a blushing Maid;
And, on the happy Change, the Boy
Imploy'd his Wonder, and his Joy.

Take care, O beauteous Child, take care,
  Lest Thou prefer so rash a Pray'r: 10
Nor vainly hope, the Queen of Love
Will e'er thy Fav'rite's Charms improve.
O quickly from her Shrine retreat;
Or tremble for thy Darling's Fate.

The Queen of Love, who soon will see   15
  Her own ADONIS live in Thee,
Will lightly her first Loss deplore;
Will easily forgive the Boar:
Her Eyes with Tears no more will flow;
With jealous Rage her Breast will glow: 20
And on her tabby Rival's Face
She deep will mark her new Disgrace.

Title] *1709* TO A BOY Playing with his CAT. *1704*   7–10] *1709*
    And potent of his Vows and Joys,
    He thank'd the Gods, and blest his Choice.
      Ah! Beauteous Boy, take care least thou
    Renew the fondness of his Vow, *1704*
11 Nor vainly hope,] *1709* Take care to think *1704*   13–14] *1709*
    Shoud'st thou prefer so rash a Pray'r,
      The Queen of Love wou'd never hear.
      Ah! rather from her Altars run,
    Least thou be griev'd and she undone. *1704*
15 who soon will] *1709* will quickly *1704*   17 In *1704, preceded by:*
    And glances thrown upon a Beast,
    Which well might make a Goddess blest,
17 Loss] *1709* Love *1704*   19–20] *1709 om. 1704*   22 She deep] *1709* Enrag'd *1704*

A Prologue made for Lord Buckhurst to Speak at Westminster at Christmas 1695.

PISH, Lord, I wish this Prologue was but Greek,
    The Young CLEONIDES wou'd boldly speak:
But can Lord BUCKHURST in poor ENGLISH say,
Gentle Spectators pray Excuse the Play?
No, witness all ye Gods of Ancient GREECE,   5
Rather than Condescend to Terms like These
I'd go to Schole six Hours on Christmas Day
Or construe PERSIUS while my Comrades play.
Such Work by Hireling Actors shou'd be done
Who tremble when they see a Critic frown.   10
Poor Rogues that smart like Fencers for their Bread,
And if they are not wounded are not fed.
But, Sirs, Our Labour has more noble Ends
We Act our Tragedy to see our Friends.
Our generous Scenes are for pure Love repeated   15
And if You are not pleas'd, at least Y'are Treated.
The Candles and the Cloaths our Selves we bought,
Our Tops neglected and our Balls forgot.
To learn our Parts, we left our Midnight bed,
Most of You snor'd whilst CLEOMENES read;   20
Not that from this Confession we wou'd Sue
Praise undeserv'd; We know our Selves and You.
Resolv'd to Stand or Perish by our Cause
We neither Censure Fear or beg Applause,
For those are WESTMINSTER and SPARTA's Laws.   25
Yet if we see some Judgment well enclin'd,
To Young Desert and growing Virtue kind,
That Critick by ten thousand Marks shou'd know
That greatest Souls to Goodness only Bow;
And that Your little HERO does inherit   30
Not CLEOMENES more than DORSETS Spirit.

Title: A...Westminster] PROLOGUE SPOKEN BY Lord BUCKHURST AT *WEST-MINSTER*-SCHOOL, *At a Representation of Mr* DRYDEN's *CLEOMENES*, The Spartan HERO. *1740*   1 Greek, *edd.*: Greek *M*: GREEK, *1740*   2 The] Then *1740*   3 say, *1740*: say *M*   5 No, ... GREECE, *1740*: No ... GREECE *M*   16 pleas'd, *1740*: pleas'd *M*   Y'are] your *1740*   17 bought, *1740*: bought *M*   19 bed, *1740*: bed *M*   20 read; *1740*: read *M*   24 Applause, *edd.*: Applause *M*: applause, *1740*   26 enclin'd, *edd.*: enclin'd *M*: inclin'd, *1740*   27 kind, *1740*: kind. *M*

1696

Presented to the King, at his Arrival in Holland, after the Discovery of the Conspiracy 1696.

Serus in cœlum redeas; diuque
Lætus intersis populo Quirini:
Neve Te nostris vitiis iniquum
Ocyor aura
Tollat——   Hor. ad Augustum.

YE careful Angels, whom eternal Fate
  Ordains, on Earth and human Acts to wait;
Who turn with secret Pow'r this restless Ball,
And bid predestin'd Empires rise and fall:
Your sacred Aid religious Monarchs own;   5
When first They merit, then ascend the Throne:
But Tyrants dread Ye, lest your just Decree
Transfer the Pow'r, and set the People free:
See rescu'd BRITAIN at your Altars bow:
And hear her Hymns your happy Care avow: 10
That still her Axes and her Rods support
The Judge's Frown, and grace the awful Court:
That Law with all her pompous Terror stands,
To wrest the Dagger from the Traitor's Hands;
And rigid Justice reads the fatal Word;   15
Poises the Ballance first, then draws the Sword.

Title: *Presented ... Conspiracy 1696.*] *1709* VERSES Humbly presented ... late horrid CONSPIRACY Against His most Sacred Person. *1696, N.D.*   Motto: *Tollat*——] *1709*
Tollat, hic magnos potius triumphos
Hic ames dici pater atque Princeps,
Neu sinas Gallos equitare inultos
Te duce, CÆSAR. 1696, N.D.

4 predestin'd] alternate *1709*: determin'd *1696, N.D.*   5 Monarchs] *1709* Princes *1696, N.D.*   7 Ye] you *1696, N.D., 1709*   11 still] *1709* yet *1696, N.D.*   12 The Judge's Frown ... the] *1709* Her Judges hand ... her *1696, N.D.*   13 That] *1709* Where *1696, N.D.*   15 And] *1709* Where *1696, N.D.*

BRITAIN Her Safety to your Guidance owns,
That She can sep'rate Parricides from Sons;
That, impious Rage disarm'd, She lives and Reigns,
Her Freedom kept by Him, who broke Her Chains.   20

And Thou, great Minister, above the rest
Of Guardian Spirits, be Thou for ever blest:
Thou, who of old wert sent to ISRAEL's Court,
With secret Aid great DAVID's strong Support;
To mock the frantick Rage of cruel SAUL;   25
And strike the useless Jav'lin to the Wall.
Thy later Care o'er WILLIAM's Temples held,
On BOYN's propitious Banks, the heav'nly Shield;
When Pow'r Divine did Sov'reign Right declare;
And Cannons mark'd, Whom They were bid to spare.   30

Still, blessed Angel, be thy Care the same;
Be WILLIAM's Life untouch'd, as is his Fame:
Let Him own Thine, as BRITAIN owns His Hand:
Save Thou the King, as He has sav'd the Land.

We Angels Forms in pious Monarchs view: 35
We reverence WILLIAM; for He acts like You;
Like You, Commission'd to chastize and bless,
He must avenge the World, and give it Peace.

Indulgent Fate our potent Pray'r receives;
And still BRITANNIA smiles, and WILLIAM lives: 40

17] *1709* To your blest guidance She her safety owns, *1696, N.D.*   19 *In 1696 and N.D.,*
preceded by:
    And boldly give those Criminals their doom,
    Who would, like *Nero*, rip their Parents womb:
19 impious Rage] *1709* Death and Hell *1696, N.D.*   21–25] *1709*
    And thou, blest Guardian, destin'd to defend
    That Sacred Life on which all ours depend:
    Thou sure, whose charge of old was *Israel's* Court,
    When sent from Heav'n great *David's* strong support,
    Thy arm unseen eluded cruel *Saul, 1696, N.D.*
26 strike] *1709* struck *1696, N.D.*   29] *1709*
    When EUROPE pale betwixt two Armies stood,
    And trembling BRITAIN doubted to be good,
    Till Miracles did WILLIAM'S right declare, *1696, N.D.*
34 Save Thou] *1709* And save *1696, N.D.*   39–40] *1709*
    Our Prayers are heard, new Miracles are shown,
    The Powers that rescu'd will preserve the Throne: *1696, N.D.*

The Hero dear to Earth, by Heav'n belov'd,
By Troubles must be vex'd, by Dangers prov'd:
His Foes must aid to make his Fame compleat,
And fix his Throne secure on their Defeat.

So, tho' with sudden Rage the Tempest comes; 45
Tho' the Winds roar; and tho' the Water foams;
Imperial BRITAIN on the Sea looks down,
And smiling sees her Rebel Subject frown:
Striking her Cliff the Storm confirms her Pow'r:
The Waves but whiten her Triumphant Shore: 50
In vain They wou'd advance, in vain retreat:
Broken They dash, and perish at her Feet.

For WILLIAM still new Wonders shall be shown:
The Pow'rs that rescu'd, shall preserve the Throne.
Safe on his Darling BRITAIN's joyful Sea, 55
Behold, the Monarch plows his liquid Way:
His Fleets in Thunder thro' the World declare,
Whose Empire they obey, whose Arms they bear.
Bless'd by aspiring Winds He finds the Strand
Blacken'd with Crowds; He sees the Nations stand } 60
Blessing his Safety, proud of his Command.
In various Tongues He hears the Captains dwell
On their great Leader's Praise: by Turns They tell,
And listen, each with emulous Glory fir'd,
How WILLIAM conquer'd, and how FRANCE retir'd; 65
How BELGIA freed the Hero's Arm confess'd,
But trembl'd for the Courage which She blest.

43 aid ... compleat] *1709* contribute to make Him great *1696, N.D.* 44 Throne secure]
1709 Glory sure *1696, N.D.* 47 Imperial ... the] *1709* Fair BRITAIN on the angry *1696,*
N.D. 49 Striking ... Storm] *1709* Heav'n in assaulting Her *1696, N.D.* 53–54] *1709*
om. *1696, N.D.* (*see note for ll. 39–40*) 55 Safe ... Darling] *1709*' Tis done, once
more thro' *1696, N.D.* 56 Behold, the ... liquid] *1709* Her glorious ... Prosp'rous
1696, N.D. 57–61] *1709*

> Arm'd with those Fleets who have in thunder said
> To distant Worlds, whose Empire they obey'd:
> He lands, and sees united Nations stand,
> Their parts of Glory dealt by His command, *1696, N.D.*

62–63] *1709* om. *1696, N.D.* 64] *1709* Their glowing Brests with fresh Ideas fir'd,
1696, N.D. 66 *In 1696 and N.D., preceded by:*

> When fixt as Fate he stood in *Namurs* Field,
> Till Rocks and Floods and Fire were taught to yield,

66 How BELGIA] *1709* Till *Flanders 1696, N.D.*

O Louis, from this great Example know,
To be at once a Hero, and a Foe:
By sounding Trumpets, Hear, and ratl'ing Drums,   70
When William to the open Vengeance comes:
And See the Soldier plead the Monarch's Right,
Heading His Troops, and Foremost in the Fight.

Hence then, close Ambush and perfidious War,
Down to your Native Seats of Night repair.   75
And Thou, Bellona, weep thy cruel Pride
Restrain'd, behind the Victor's Chariot ty'd
In brazen Knots, and everlasting Chains.
(So Europe's Peace, so William's Fate ordains.)
While on the Iv'ry Chair, in happy State   80
He sits, Secure in Innocence, and Great
In regal Clemency; and views beneath
Averted Darts of Rage, and pointless Arms of Death.

In a Window in Lord V . . . . . . s house 1696.

I N Vain by Druggs and rules of Art
Poor Ratcliff wou'd my Lungs ensure
They lye too near a wounded heart
Whose sickness Death alone can cure.

68–83]
> He comes; pale Gallia dreads his Arms a-far,
> And bent on Parricide refuses War,
> But well she knows his Vengeance n'er will tread
> Those Paths of horrour which her guilt has led.
> The Trumpets Sounds shall tell the arming Foe
> When WILLIAM meditates the noble Blow,
> Before the foremost Troops in open fight
> The Hero's arm shall prove the Monarchs right.
>   'Tis done, and Europe freed must own his hand,
> Whilst Thames shall flow, or Britains Empire stand. *1696, N.D.*

70 Hear, and ratl'ing] mark, and surly *1709*   72–73 *In 1709, order reversed with these*
variants: And See ... Right,] Behold ... Right. *1709*   73 Fight. *Reset sheet in 1718:*
Fight, *1709, 1718*   75 Native] pristin *1709*
    Title: V . . . . . . s] Villiers '*Contents' of L 28*

Written in the Year 1696.

WHILE with Labour Assiduous due pleasure I mix
    And in one day attone for the Busyness of Six
In a little Dutch Chaise on a Saturday Night
On my left hand my Horace and   on my right
No Memoire to compose and no Post-boy to move   5
That on Sunday may hinder the softness of Love:
For her, neither Visits nor Parties of Tea
Nor the long winded Cant of a dull Refugée
This Night and the next shal be Hers shal be Mine
To good or ill Fortune the Third we resign: 10
Thus Scorning the World and superior to Fate
I drive on my Car in processional State.
So with *Phia* thrô *Athens Pisistratus* rode
Men thought her *Minerva* and Him a new God
But why shou'd I stories of Athens rehearse   15
Where People knew Love and were partial to Verse
Since none can with Justice my pleasures oppose
In *Holland* half drownded in Interest and Prose:
By *Greece* and past Ages what need I be try'd
When the *Hague* and the Present are both on my side   20
And is it enough for the Joys of the day
To think what *Anacreon* or *Sapho* wou'd say
When good *Vandergoos* and his provident Vrough
As they gaze on my Triumph do freely allow
That search all the province you'l find no Man there is   25
So blest as the *Englishen Heer* SECRETARIS.

Title: W (at end of poem), L 28 Verses written at the Hague. Anno 1696 '*Index*' *to M*:
WRITTEN at the HAGUE, In the year 1696. *1740*   2 Busyness *L 28* (Pope), *1740*:
pleasures *W*, *L 28* (D)   4 and   on] *L 28* a NYMPH on *1740*   6 Love: *L 28*: Love
W: love; *1740*   7 her, *1740*: her *W*, *L 28*   10 resign: *1740*: resign *W*, *L 28*   18
drownded] drowned *L 28*, *1740*   Prose: *edd.*: Prose *W*, *L 28*: prose: *1740*   25 you'l]
L 28 you'd *1740*

1697

'Who would, says Dryden, Drink this draught of Life'

WHO would, says Dryden, Drink this draught of Life
   Blended with bitter Woes and tedious Strife
But that an Angel in Some Lucky hour
Does healing Drops into the Goblet pour?
When wearied I would Spill the baleful cup   5
Some Sparkling Bubble of delight springs up:
My Sov'rein or my friend was heard to tell
I served Him faithfully, or loved Him well.
Then easy hope decieves my flatterd tast
One Joy attones ten thousand evils past;   10
New Scenes of thought I from this model frame,
Consent to Live, that I my part may claim
In Townshend's Friendship or in Williams fame.

A New Answer to An Argument against a Standing Army.

WOULD they, who have Nine Years look'd sow'r
   Against a *French*, and *Popish* Pow'r,
Make Friends with both in half an Hour:
         This is the Time.

Would they discreetly break the Sword,   5
By which their Freedom was restor'd,
And put their Trust in *Lewis*'s Word:
         This is the Time.

Title: edd.: om. L 10   4 Does ... pour? *edd.: does ... pour L 10*   6 up: *edd.: up*
L 10   10 past; *edd.: past L 10*   11 frame, *edd.: frame L 10*   13 Townshend's
edd.: Townshen's L 10
   5 discreetly] *N.D., M (where it is written in another hand over an erasure) directly L 28,*
1704   the] *L 28, M, 1704* that *N.D.*

Would they leave *England* Unprotected,
To shew how well they are Affected,   10
And get themselves next Bout Elected!
           This is the Time.

Against the Souldiers Lusts and Gullets,
Would they preserve their Wives and Pullets,
And break our Guns to save our Bullets: 15
           This is the Time.

Would they oblige a Winter Sea,
Their prudent Orders to obey,
Or keep a standing Wind in Pay,
           This is the Time.   20

Would they but say what th'are pursuing,
Who th'are advancing, who undoing,
Which pack of Knaves shall prove our Ruin:
           This is the Time.

A Gods Name let 'em shew their Games,   25
Fix us to one of their Extreams,
A Common-wealth, or else King *James*:
           This is the Time.

Upon this passage in Scaligerana.

Les Allemans ne se soucient pas quel Vin ils
boivent pourveu que ce soit Vin, ni quel Latin
ils parlent pourveu que ce soit Latin.

WHEN You with Hogh Dutch Heeren dine,
     Expect false Latin and Stum'd wine:
They never tast who always drink;
They always talk, who never think.

9 *In N.D., preceded by:*
       Would you turn Hero's into Pads,
       And crush the Sp'rits of our brave Lads,
       And make them look like *Bedlam* Mads?
           This is the Time.

13–14] *N.D.* Lines transposed in *L 28, M, 1704*   19 Or] *N.D.* And *L 28, M, 1704*
standing] *L 28, M, 1704* straying *N.D.*   21 th'are] *N.D.* they're *L 28, M, 1704*   22
Who th'are ... who] *N.D.* Whom they're ... whom *L 28, M, 1704*   23] What ... Ruin?
L 28, M, 1704: Which sort of Men do threaten ruin? *N.D.*   25 A Gods Name] *L 28, M,*
1704 I pray then *N.D.*   26 Fix us ... their] *N.D.* And fix ... these *L 28, M, 1704*   28
This is] *N.D.* For now's *L 28, 1704*: For now is *M*
     Title: *Scaligerana edd.*: Scaligerina *M*: Scaligeriana *L 27, 1740*   1 Hogh] *L 27* High *1740*

1699

Carmen Seculare, For the Year 1700.
To the King.

Aspice, venturo lætentur ut Omnia Sæc'lo:
O mihi tam longæ maneat pars ultima vitæ
Spiritus, & quantum sat erit tua dicere facta!
Virg. Eclog. 4.

I.

THY elder Look, Great JANUS, cast
Into the long Records of Ages past:
Review the Years in fairest Action drest
With noted White, Superior to the rest;
ÆRAS deriv'd, and Chronicles begun   5
From Empires founded, and from Battels won:
Show all the Spoils by valiant Kings achiev'd,
And groaning Nations by Their Arms reliev'd;
The Wounds of Patriots in Their Country's Cause,
And happy Pow'r sustain'd by wholesom Laws: 10
In comely Rank call ev'ry Merit forth:
Imprint on ev'ry Act it's Standard Worth:
The glorious Parallels then downward bring,
To Modern Wonders, and to BRITAIN's King:
With equal Justice and Historic Care   15
Their Laws, Their Toils, Their Arms with His compare:
Confess the various Attributes of Fame
Collected and compleat in WILLIAM's Name:

Title: Seculare, ... 1700.] 1700, 1709 *SÆCULARE* 1701   1-2] 1700, 1701, 1709
            Great Janus turn thy elder look
            Back into fates eternal book. *Wm*
3 Review] *1709* Call out *1700, 1701*   11 Rank call ev'ry] *1709* Order march each *1700,*
1701   12-13] *1709*
            Mark ev'ry Act with its intrinsic Worth:
            Then hast the Mighty Parallels to bring   *1700, 1701*

To all the list'ning World relate,
(As Thou dost His Story read)
That nothing went before so Great,   } 20
And nothing Greater can succeed.

II.

Thy Native LATIUM was Thy darling Care,
Prudent in Peace, and terrible in War:
The boldest Virtues that have govern'd Earth   25
From LATIUM's fruitful Womb derive their Birth.
    Then turn to Her fair-written Page:
From dawning Childhood to establish'd Age,
    The Glories of Her Empire trace: } 30
Confront the Heroes of Thy ROMAN Race:
And let the justest Palm the Victor's Temples grace.

III.

The Son of MARS reduc'd the trembling Swains,
And spread His Empire o'er the distant Plains:
But yet the SABINS violated Charms
Obscur'd the Glory of His rising Arms.   35
NUMA the Rights of strict Religion knew;
On ev'ry Altar laid the Incense due;
    Unskill'd to dart the pointed Spear,
Or lead the forward Youth to noble War.
Stern BRUTUS was with too much Horror good,   40
Holding his *Fasces* stain'd with Filial Blood.
FABIUS was Wise, but with Excess of Care:
He sav'd his Country; but prolong'd the War:
While DECIUS, PAULUS, CURIUS greatly Fought;
    And by Their strict Examples taught,   45

19 To] *1700, 1709* And round to *1701*   23 Thy Native] *1709 om. 1700, 1701*   27
Then ... Her] *1709* Turn thither the *1700, 1701*   29 Her] *1709* the *1700, 1701*   31
the justest ... Temples] *1709* fair Proof my bold Assertion *1700, 1701*   32 The Son of
MARS] *1709* If *Mars*'s Son *1700, 1701*   34 But yet] *1709 om. 1700, 1701*   36] *1709*
Strict Religion *Numa* knew, *1700, 1701*   40–41] *1709*
                    Sealing his Justice with his Childrens Blood
                    Stern *Brutus* was with too much Horror good.   *1700, 1701*

44 While DECIUS] *1709 Fabricius 1700, 1701*

How wild Desires should be controll'd;
And how much brighter Virtue was, than Gold;
They scarce Their swelling Thirst of Fame could hide;
And boasted Poverty with too much Pride.
Excess in Youth made SCIPIO less Rever'd: 50
And CATO dying seem'd to own, He Fear'd.
JULIUS with Honour tam'd ROME's foreign Foes:
But Patriots fell, e'er the Dictator rose.
And while with Clemency AUGUSTUS reign'd;
The Monarch was ador'd; the City chain'd.   55

IV.

With justest Honour be Their Merits drest:
  But be Their Failings too confest:
  Their Virtue, like their TYBER's Flood
Rolling, it's Course design'd the Country's Good:
But oft the Torrent's too impetuous Speed   60
From the low Earth tore some polluting Weed:
And with the Blood of JOVE there always ran
Some viler Part, some Tincture of the Man.

V.

  Few Virtues after These so far prevail,
But that Their Vices more than turn the Scale: 65
Valour grown wild by Pride, and Pow'r by Rage,
Did the true Charms of Majesty impair;
ROME by Degrees advancing more in Age,
Show'd sad Remains of what had once been fair:
Till Heav'n a better Race of Men supplies;   70
And Glory shoots new Beams from Western Skies.

VI.

Turn then to PHARAMOND, and CHARLEMAIN,
And the long Heroes of the GALLIC Strain;
Experienc'd Chiefs, for hardy Prowess known,
And bloody Wreaths in vent'rous Battles won.   75

46 wild Desires should] *1709* dang'rous Lusts must *1700* : dang'rous Lust must *1701*   48
They] *1709* But *1700, 1701*   53 But] *1709* Too many *1700, 1701*   54 while] *1709*
tho' *1700, 1701*   56 With justest ... Merits] With equal ... Merits *1709* : Let
their Deserts with mighty Praise be *1700, 1701*   58 Virtue, like] *1709* Virtue
rowling like *1700, 1701*   59 Rolling ... the] *1709* Its rapid Force design'd their *1700,
1701*   62 And] *1700, 1701* So *1709*   63 viler Part, some] *1709* small allaying
1700, 1701   75] *1709* And in fierce Battels Bloody Laurels won. *1700, 1701*

From the First WILLIAM, our great NORMAN King,
The bold PLANTAGENETS, and TUDORS bring;
Illustrious Virtues, who by turns have rose,
In foreign Fields to check BRITANNIA's Foes;
With happy Laws Her Empire to sustain;   80
And with full Power assert Her ambient Main:
But sometimes too Industrious to be Great,
Nor Patient to expect the Turns of Fate,
They open'd Camps deform'd by Civil Fight:
And made proud Conquest trample over Right: 85
Disparted BRITAIN mourn'd Their doubtful Sway;
And dreaded Both, when Neither would obey.

VII.

From DIDIER, and Imperial ADOLPH trace
The Glorious Offspring of the NASSAW Race,
Devoted Lives to Publick Liberty;   90
The Chief still dying, or the Country free.
Then see the Kindred Blood of ORANGE flow,
From warlike CORNET, thro' the Loins of BEAU;
Thro' CHALON next; and there with NASSAW join,
From RHONE's fair Banks transplanted to the RHINE.   95
Bring next the Royal List of STUARTS forth,
Undaunted Minds, that rul'd the rugged North;
'Till Heav'n's Decrees by rip'ning Times are shown;
'Till SCOTLAND's Kings ascend the ENGLISH Throne;
And the fair Rivals live for ever One.   100

VIII.

JANUS, mighty Deity,
Be kind; and as Thy searching Eye
Does our Modern Story trace,
Finding some of STUART's Race
Unhappy, pass Their Annals by: 105
No harsh Reflection let Remembrance raise:
Forbear to mention, what Thou canst not praise:
But as Thou dwell'st upon that Heav'nly Name,
To Grief for ever Sacred, as to Fame,

78 Virtues] *1709* Heroes *1700, 1701*   86 Disparted] *1709* Afflicted *1700, 1701*   89
Glorious ... the NASSAW] *1709* fruitful ... Great *NASSAW*'s *1700, 1701*   92 Then]
1709 Next *1700, 1701*   96 Bring next] *1709* Then call *1700, 1701*

Oh! read it to Thy self; in Silence weep;　　　　　　110
And Thy convulsive Sorrows inward keep;
Lest BRITAIN's Grief should waken at the Sound;
And Blood gush fresh from Her eternal Wound.

IX.

Whither would'st Thou further look?
Read WILLIAM's Acts, and close the ample Book:　　　115
Peruse the Wonders of His dawning Life;
　　How, like ALCIDES, He began;
With Infant Patience calm'd Seditious Strife,
And quell'd the Snakes which round his Cradle ran.

X.

Describe His Youth, attentive to Alarms,　　　　　　120
By Dangers form'd, and perfected in Arms:
When Conqu'ring, mild; when Conquer'd, not disgrac'd;
By Wrongs not lessen'd, nor by Triumphs rais'd:
　　Superior to the blind Events
　　Of little Human Accidents;　　　　　　　　　125
　　And constant to His first Decree,
To curb the Proud, to set the Injur'd free;
To bow the haughty Neck, and raise the suppliant Knee.

XI.

His opening Years to riper Manhood bring;
And see the Hero perfect in the King:　　　　　　　130
Imperious Arms by Manly Reason sway'd,
And Power Supreme by free Consent obey'd:
With how much Haste His Mercy meets his Foes:
And how unbounded His Forgiveness flows:
With what Desire He makes His Subjects bless'd,　　135
His Favours granted ere His Throne address'd:

113 fresh] *1701*, *1709* forth *1700*　　　116 dawning] *1709* blooming *1700*, *1701*　　117–
19] *1709*
　　　　　His Infant Patience calming Factious Strife,
　　　　　Quelling the Snakes that round his Cradle ran,
　　　　　For *WILLIAM* thus, *Alcides* thus began.　*1700*, *1701*
122 Conquer'd] *1709* Vanquish'd *1700*, *1701*　　　132 Power Supreme] *1709* happy Pow'r
1700, *1701*

What Trophies o'er our captiv'd Hearts He rears,
By Arts of Peace more potent, than by Wars:
How o'er Himself, as o'er the World, He Reigns,
His Morals strength'ning, what His Law ordains.   140

XII.

Thro' all His Thread of Life already spun,
Becoming Grace and proper Action run:
The Piece by VIRTUE's equal Hand is wrought,
Mix'd with no Crime, and shaded with no Fault:
No Footsteps of the Victor's Rage   145
Left in the Camp, where WILLIAM did engage:
No Tincture of the Monarch's Pride
Upon the Royal Purple spy'd:
His Fame, like Gold, the more 'tis try'd,
The more shall it's intrinsic Worth proclaim;   150
Shall pass the Combat of the searching Flame,
And triumph o'er the vanquish'd Heat,
For ever coming out the same,
And losing nor it's Lustre, nor it's Weight.

XIII.

JANUS be to WILLIAM just;   155
To faithful HISTORY His Actions trust:
Command Her, with peculiar Care
To trace each Toil, and comment ev'ry War:
His saving Wonders bid Her write
In Characters distinctly bright;   160
That each revolving Age may read
The Patriot's Piety, the Hero's Deed:
And still the Sire inculcate to his Son
Transmissive Lessons of the King's Renown:

138 Arts ... potent,] *1709* Moderation greater *1700, 1701*   140 Morals strength'ning,]
1709 Life enforcing *1700, 1701*   143 The ... Hand] *1709* By equal Virtues all the
Piece *1700, 1701*   156 faithful] *1709* future *1700, 1701*   157 Command] *1709* Bid
1700, 1701   158 To ... comment] *1709* Trace ev'ry Toil, and mention *1700, 1701*
160 In Characters] *1709* In shining Characters *1700, 1701*   161–84] *1709*

> Fair to be read, when all that we can give
> To make our Master's Glory live,
> Does of its self insensibly decay,
> When Time the Marble and the Brass devours,
> And envious Winters in sure Ruin lay
> The Pride of *Namur*'s Towers.

[*continued opposite*

That WILLIAM's Glory still may live;   165
When all that present Art can give,
The Pillar'd Marble, and the Tablet Brass,
    Mould'ring, drop the Victor's Praise:
When the great Monuments of His Pow'r
Shall now be visible no more: 170
When SAMBRE shall have chang'd her winding Flood;
And Children ask, where NAMUR stood.

XIV.

NAMUR, proud City, how her Towr's were arm'd!
How She contemn'd th'approaching Foe!
'Till She by WILLIAM's Trumpets was allarm'd,   175
And shook, and sunk, and fell beneath His Blow.
    JOVE and PALLAS, mighty Pow'rs,
Guided the Hero to the hostile Tow'rs.
    PERSEUS seem'd less swift in War,
    When, wing'd with Speed, he flew thro' Air.   180
    Embattl'd Nations strive in vain
    The Hero's Glory to restrain:
Streams arm'd with Rocks, and Mountains red with Fire
    In vain against His Force conspire.
Behold Him from the dreadful Height appear!   185
And lo! BRITANNIA's Lions waving there.

XV.

EUROPE freed, and FRANCE repell'd
The Hero from the Height beheld:

> *Namur's* Towers which War had arm'd
> Against what human Force cou'd do,
> By *WILLIAM's* Valour were alarm'd,
> Were subdu'd by *WILLIAM's* Blow:
> *WILLIAM* mounted *Namur's* Towers,
> Second him *Jove*, and *Pallas*, Mighty Powers;
> He flew like *Perseus* thro' the Air,
> The utmost dreadful height to gain,
> *WILLIAM* and the God of War
> Can only Toils like these sustain;
> Rocks, Rivers, Mountains, Armies, Fire,
> To stop his Glorious Course conspire:
> Why will they conspire in vain?
> What can *WILLIAM's* Force restrain?   *1700, 1701*

187 repell'd] *1709* dismay'd, *1700, 1701*   188 The Hero ... beheld:] *1709 WILLIAM*
...survey'd; *1700, 1701*

He spake the Word, that War and Rage should cease:
He bid the MAESE and RHINE in Safety flow;   190
   And dictated a lasting Peace
   To the rejoicing World below:
To rescu'd States, and vindicated Crowns
His Equal Hand prescrib'd their ancient Bounds;
Ordain'd whom ev'ry Province should obey;   195
How far each Monarch should extend His Sway:
Taught 'em how Clemency made Pow'r rever'd;
And that the Prince Belov'd was truly Fear'd.
Firm by His Side unspotted HONOUR stood,
Pleas'd to confess Him not so Great as Good: 200
His Head with brighter Beams fair VIRTUE deck't,
Than Those which all His num'rous Crowns reflect:
Establish'd FREEDOM clap'd her joyful Wings;
Proclaim'd the First of Men, and Best of Kings.

XVI.

   Whither would the Muse aspire   205
With PINDAR's Rage without his Fire?
Pardon me, JANUS, 'twas a Fault,
Created by too great a Thought:
Mindless of the God and Day,
I from thy Altars, JANUS, stray,   210
From Thee, and from My self born far away.
   The fiery PEGASUS disdains
To mind the Rider's Voice, or hear the Reins:
When glorious Fields and opening Camps He views;
   He runs with an unbounded Loose: 215
Hardly the Muse can sit the headstrong Horse:
Nor would She, if She could, check his impetuous Force:

189 spake the Word, that ... should] *1709* order'd ... to *1700, 1701*   190–3] *1700,
1701, 1709*

        Britain happy Isle rejoice.
        Let the rescu'd Nations all around
        Receive the Image of thy voice
        And mingle in the happy Sound.
        From the Danube to the Boyne
        Let Europe in the Triumph Joyn. *Wm*

197 Clemency made Pow'r] *1709* Grace made Majesty *1700, 1701*   198 that] *1709* how
1700, 1701   200] *1709* Confessing him less Great than Good: *1700, 1701*   201
VIRTUE] *1709* Glory *1700, 1701*   204 Proclaim'd ... and Best] *1709* Virtue proclaim'd
... and Fame the Best *1700, 1701*   205 *In 1700 & 1701, preceded by:* Whither is wild
Fancy brought?

With the glad Noise the Cliffs and Vallies ring;
While She thro' Earth and Air pursues the King.

XVII.

She now beholds Him on the BELGIC Shoar;   220
Whilst BRITAIN's Tears His ready Help implore,
Dissembling for Her sake his rising Cares,
And with wise Silence pond'ring vengeful Wars.
   She thro' the raging Ocean now
Views Him advancing his auspicious Prow;   225
Combating adverse Winds and Winter Seas,
Sighing the Moments that defer Our Ease;
Daring to wield the Scepter's dang'rous Weight,
And taking the Command, to save the State:
Tho' e'er the doubtful Gift can be secur'd,   230
New Wars must be sustain'd, new Wounds endur'd.

XVIII.

Thro' rough IERNE's Camp She sounds Alarms,
And Kingdoms yet to be redeem'd by Arms;
In the dank Marshes finds her glorious Theme;
And plunges after Him thro' BOYN's fierce Stream.   235
She bids the NEREIDS run with trembling Haste,
To tell old OCEAN how the Hero past.
The God rebukes their Fear, and owns the Praise
Worthy that Arm, Whose Empire He obeys.

XIX.

Back to His ALBION She delights to bring   240
The humblest Victor, and the kindest King.
ALBION, with open Triumph would receive
   Her Hero, nor obtains His Leave:
Firm He rejects the Altars She would raise;
And thanks the Zeal, while He declines the Praise.   245

219 the] *1709* her Godlike *1700, 1701*   222 Her sake] *1709* our sakes *1700, 1701*
225 auspicious] *1709* adventrous *1700, 1701*   226 Winter] *1700, 1709* Winters *1701*
232–34] *1709* Anon in *Irish* Camps she finds her Theme, *1700, 1701*   240–3] *1709*
     She thence to *Albion* does the Victor bring,
     Albion with Iö's greets her happy King; *1700, 1701*
244 Firm He rejects] *1709* But he declines *1700, 1701*   245 And thanks ... while He
declines] *1709* Accepts ... tho' he rejects *1700, 1701*

Again She follows Him thro' BELGIA's Land,
And Countries often sav'd by WILLIAM's Hand;
Hears joyful Nations bless those happy Toils,
Which freed the People, but return'd the Spoils.
In various Views She tries her constant Theme;   250
Finds Him in Councils, and in Arms the Same:
When certain to o'ercome, inclin'd to save,
Tardy to Vengeance, and with Mercy, Brave.

XX.

Sudden another Scene employs her Sight:
She sets her Hero in another Light: 255
Paints His great Mind Superior to Success,
Declining Conquest, to establish Peace:
She brings ASTREA down to Earth again,
And Quiet, brooding o'er His future Reign.

XXI.

Then with unweary'd Wing the Goddess soars   260
East, over DANUBE and PROPONTIS Shoars;
Where jarring Empires ready to engage,
Retard their Armies, and suspend their Rage;
'Till WILLIAM's Word, like That of Fate, declares,
If They shall study Peace, or lengthen Wars.   265
How sacred His Renown for equal Laws,
To whom the World defers it's Common Cause!
How fair His Friendships, and His Leagues how just,
Whom ev'ry Nation courts, Whom all Religions trust!

247 Countries] *1709* Nations *1700, 1701*   248–53] *1709*
         Ranges Confederate Armies on the Plains,
         And in pitch'd Battels bleeding Conquest gains;
         Thence to the Points of armed Rocks aspires,
         O'er hollow Mountains bellowing hidden Fires,
         Beholds the Rocks submit, the Mountains bow,
         And willing Nations Crown the Common Victor's Brow. *1700, 1701*
261 East, over] Eastward, to *1700, 1701, 1709*   265 lengthen] *1700, 1709* lengthens *1701*
267 whom] *1709* Him *1700, 1701*   268–9]
         The Turk consents to what your words decree
         He scarce trusts more in Mahomet than thee
         And all Religions And all nations trust
         The Man whom all acknowledge just. *Wm*
269] *1709* Him all Religions, Him all Nations trust. *1700, 1701*

XXII.

From the MÆOTIS to the Northern Sea,   270
    The Goddess wings her desp'rate Way;
Sees the young MUSCOVITE, the mighty Head,
Whose Sov'reign Terror forty Nations dread,
Inamour'd with a greater Monarch's Praise,
And passing half the Earth to His Embrace: 275
She in His Rule beholds His VOLGA's Force,
O'er Precipices, with impetuous Sway
Breaking, and as He rowls his rapid Course,
Drowning, or bearing down, whatever meets his Way.
But her own King She likens to His THAMES,   280
With gentle Course devolving fruitful Streams:
Serene yet Strong, Majestic yet Sedate,
Swift without Violence, without Terror Great.
Each ardent Nymph the rising Current craves:
Each Shepherd's Pray'r retards the parting Waves: 285
The Vales along the Bank their Sweets disclose:
Fresh Flow'rs for ever rise: and fruitful Harvest grows.

XXIII.

Yet whither would th'advent'rous Goddess go?
Sees She not Clouds, and Earth, and Main below?
Minds She the Dangers of the LYCIAN Coast,   290
And Fields, where mad BELEROPHON was lost?
    Or is Her tow'ring Flight reclaim'd
By Seas from ICARUS's Downfall nam'd?
Vain is the Call, and useless the Advice:
To wise Perswasion Deaf, and human Cries,   295
    Yet upward She incessant flies;
Resolv'd to reach the high Empyrean Sphere,
And tell Great JOVE, She sings His Image here;
To ask for WILLIAM an Olympic Crown,
To CHROMIUS' Strength, and THERON's Speed unknown: 300

278 He ... his] *1709* it ... its *1700, 1701*   rapid] violent *1700, 1701, 1709*   279
his] *1709* its *1700, 1701*   281] *1709 om. 1700, 1701*   282 Majestic yet Sedate]
1709 exempt from all Extreams *1700, 1701*   283] *1709* And with fair Speed devolving
fruitful Streams. *1700, 1701*   286 The ... Bank] *1709* Round either Bank the Vales
1700, 1701   288 Yet ... advent'rous] *1709* Whither wou'd the *1700, 1701*   292
tow'ring] *1709* daring *1700, 1701*   296 Yet] *1709 om. 1700, 1701*   297 the high
Empyrean] *1709* the high Empyreal *1700*: the Empyrean *1701*

Till lost in trackless Fields of shining Day,
  Unable to discern the Way
Which NASSAW's Virtue only could explore,
Untouch'd, unknown, to any Muse before,
She, from the noble Precipices thrown,   305
Comes rushing with uncommon Ruin down.
  Glorious Attempt! Unhappy Fate!
The Song too daring, and the Theme too great!
  Yet rather thus She wills to die,
Than in continu'd Annals live, to sing   310
A second Heroe, or a vulgar King;
  And with ignoble Safety fly
In sight of Earth, along a middle Sky.

XXIV.

To JANUS' Altars, and the numerous Throng,
  That round his mystic Temple press,   315
  For WILLIAM's Life, and ALBION's Peace,
Ambitious Muse reduce the roving Song.
  JANUS, cast Thy forward Eye
Future, into great RHEA's pregnant Womb;
  Where young Ideas brooding lye,   320
And tender Images of Things to come:
  'Till by Thy high Commands releas'd;
'Till by Thy Hand in proper Atoms dress'd,
In decent Order They advance to Light;
Yet then too swiftly fleet by human Sight;   325
And meditate too soon their everlasting Flight.

XXV.

Nor Beaks of Ships in Naval Triumph born,
Nor Standards from the hostile Ramparts torn,
  Nor Trophies brought from Battles won,
Nor Oaken Wreath, nor Mural Crown   330

301 trackless] *1709* ample *1700, 1701*   308–9] *1709*
          Too bold the Strong, the Hero was too Great;
          She chuses rather thus to die, *1700*:
Too bold the Song, ... die, *1701*   312 And] *1700, 1709* Then *1701*   315 mystic
Temple] bolted Temples *1700, 1701, 1709*   324 Light;] *1701, 1709* Fight, *1700*   328
Ramparts] Rampart *1700, 1701, 1709*   329–30]
          Not all the noble spoyls of glorious feilds
          Not all the Wreaths which conquests yields *Wm*
330 Nor ... nor] *1709* The Oaken Garland, nor the *1700, 1701*

Can any future Honours give
To the Victorious Monarch's Name:
The Plenitude of WILLIAM's Fame
Can no accumulated Stores receive.
Shut then, auspicious God, Thy Sacred Gate,   335
And make Us Happy, as our King is Great.
Be kind, and with a milder Hand,
Closing the Volume of the finish'd Age,
(Tho' Noble, 'twas an Iron Page)
A more delightful Leaf expand,   340
Free from Alarms, and fierce BELLONA's Rage:
Bid the great Months begin their joyful Round,
By FLORA some, and some by CERES Crown'd:
Teach the glad Hours to scatter, as they fly,
Soft Quiet, gentle Love, and endless Joy: 345
Lead forth the Years for Peace and Plenty fam'd,
From SATURN's Rule, and better Metal nam'd.

XXVI.

Secure by WILLIAM's Care let BRITAIN stand;
Nor dread the bold Invader's Hand:
From adverse Shoars in Safety let Her hear   350
Foreign Calamity, and distant War;
Of which let Her, great Heav'n, no Portion bear.
Betwixt the Nations let Her hold the Scale;
And as She wills, let either Part prevail:
Let her glad Vallies smile with wavy Corn: 355
Let fleecy Flocks her rising Hills adorn:

331–4] *1709*

> Can to Victorious *WILLIAM*'s Name
> Augmented Honours give:
> His is an ample Plenitude of Fame,
> Incapable Addition to receive. *1700, 1701*

335 Sacred] Mystic *1700, 1701, 1709*   338–43] *1700, 1701, 1709*

> Turn this Iron heavy page
> And give us a succeeding age
> Free from mad Bellona's rage.
> Give every Month eternal light
> From the action he has done
> Mark Every year distinctly bright
> For the Triumphs he has won. *Wm*

344 Teach the glad] *1709* Command the laughing *1700, 1701*   346 Lead forth the] *1709*
Distribute *1700, 1701* : *om. Wm*   347 From … and] *1709* And Times from *1700, 1701,*
Wm   350 adverse] *1709* other *1700, 1701*   352] *1709* Of which no Portion she
shall bear. *1700, 1701*   355 wavy] *1709* ripen'd *1700, 1701*

Around her Coast let strong Defence be spread:
Let fair Abundance on her Breast be shed:
And Heav'nly Sweets bloom round the Goddess' Head. }

XXVII.

Where the white Towers and ancient Roofs did stand,   360
Remains of WOLSEY's or great HENRY's Hand,
To Age now yielding, or devour'd by Flame;
Let a young PHENIX raise her tow'ring Head:
Her Wings with lengthen'd Honour let Her spread;
And by her Greatness show her Builder's Fame.   365
August and Open, as the Hero's Mind,
  Be her capacious Courts design'd:
  Let ev'ry Sacred Pillar bear
Trophies of Arms, and Monuments of War.
The King shall there in PARIAN Marble breath,   370
His Shoulder bleeding fresh: and at His Feet
  Disarm'd shall lye the threat'ning DEATH:
(For so was saving JOVE's Decree compleat.)
Behind, That Angel shall be plac'd, whose Shield
  Sav'd EUROPE, in the Blow repell'd: 375
On the firm Basis, from his Oozy Bed
  BOYN shall raise his Laurell'd Head;
  And his Immortal Stream be known,
Artfully waving thro' the wounded Stone.

359 And Heav'nly] And let Eternal *1700, 1701, 1709*   360 *In the 1700 & 1701 eds.,
stanzas XXXIII to XXXV of the present text are inserted at this point*   360] *1709* From
the wild Ruins of the ancient Court, *1700, 1701*   361–5] *1709*

    Let a new Phœnix her young Columns rear,
    As may the Greatness of this Reign support,
    An Object worthy *WILLIAM*'s Care; *1700*:
    Her Graceful Wings let a Young Phœnix rear,
    The Greatness of Our Empire to Support,
    And prove an Object worthy *WILLIAM*'s *Care*; *1701*

366] *1709* Open, yet Solid, as the Builder's Mind, *1700, 1701*   367 capacious Courts]
1709 spacious Rooms *1700, 1701*   370 The King shall there] *1709* There shall the KING
1700, 1701   372 Disarm'd ... threat'ning] *1709* Disarm'd and Stopt ... threatn'd *1700,
1701*   374–79] *1709*

    His Genius plac'd behind defends the Blow;
    Disembled Waters from the Basis flow,
      And *Boyn*'s Triumphant Flood is known,
      For ever in the Wounded Stone.
    Before the Palace, *Thames* shall softly glide,
    With dear Affection forming long delay,
      Unwilling to be forc'd away,
      Tho' all the Sister-Rivers chide,
    Fond of Her Lord, forgetful of Her Tide. *1700, 1701*

XXVIII.

And Thou, Imperial WINDSOR, stand inlarg'd,   380
    With all the Monarch's Trophies charged:
Thou, the fair Heav'n, that dost the Stars inclose,
Which WILLIAM's Bosom wears, or Hand bestows
On the great Champions who support his Throne,
    And Virtues nearest to His own.   385

XXIX.

Round ORMOND's Knee Thou ty'st the Mystic String,
That makes the Knight Companion to the King.
From glorious Camps return'd, and foreign Feilds,
Bowing before thy sainted Warrior's Shrine,
Fast by his great Forefather's Coats, and Shields   390
Blazon'd from BOHUN's, or from BUTLER's Line,
He hangs His Arms; nor fears those Arms should shine
With an unequal Ray; or that His Deed
    With paler Glory should recede,
Eclips'd by Theirs; or lessen'd by the Fame   395
Ev'n of His own Maternal NASSAW's Name.

XXX.

Thou smiling see'st great DORSET's Worth confest,
The Ray distinguishing the Patriot's Breast:
Born to protect and love, to help and please;
Sov'reign of Wit, and Ornament of Peace.   400
O! long as Breath informs this fleeting Frame,
Ne'er let me pass in Silence DORSET's Name;
Ne'er cease to mention the continu'd Debt,   ⎫
Which the great Patron only would forget,   ⎬
And Duty, long as Life, must study to acquit.   ⎭ 405

---

380 Imperial] *1709* Imperious *1700, 1701*   381 Monarch's Trophies] *1709* Stores of *Britain*'s Honour *1700, 1701*   383 or] *1709* His *1700, 1701*   384 On ... who] To ... that *1700, 1701, 1709*   388–96] *1709*
         Returning Glorious from the Foreign Field,
         In Thee he pays his Vows, and hangs his Shield. *1700, 1701*
398] *1709* In *1700 &* *1701, preceded by:* Transcendent Goodness in just Honours drest,
399–400] *1709 om. 1700, 1701*

XXXI.

Renown'd in Thy Records shall CA'NDISH stand,
Asserting Legal Pow'r, and just Command:
To the great House thy Favour shall be shown,
The Father's Star transmissive to the Son.
From Thee the TALBOT's and the SEYMOUR's Race   410
Inform'd, Their Sire's immortal Steps shall trace:
Happy may their Sons receive
The bright Reward, which Thou alone canst give.

XXXII.

And if a God these lucky Numbers guide;
If sure APOLLO o'er the Verse preside;   415
JERSEY, belov'd by all (For all must feel
    The Influence of a Form and Mind,
Where comely Grace and constant Virtue dwell,
Like mingl'd Streams, more forcible when join'd.)
    JERSEY shall at Thy Altars stand;   420
    Shall there receive the Azure Band,
That fairest Mark of Favour and of Fame,
    Familiar to the VILIER's Name.

XXXIII.

Science to raise, and Knowledge to enlarge,
    Be our great Master's future Charge;   425
To write His own Memoirs, and leave His Heirs
High Schemes of Government, and Plans of Wars;
By fair Rewards our Noble Youth to raise
To emulous Merit, and to Thirst of Praise;
To lead Them out from Ease e'er opening Dawn,   430
Through the thick Forest and the distant Lawn,

406–13] *1709*

    In Thee Great *Cavendish* Name shall long be known,
    The Father's Light transmitted to the Son.
    In Thee the *Seymours*, and the *Talbot*'s Line,
    With high Preheminence shall ever shine. *1700*:

In Thee ... The Father's Star transmitted ... shine. *1701*   415 Verse] *1709* Song *1700*,
1701   416 For all must feel] *1709* as well as Me *1700, 1701*   417–21] *1709* Shall
at thy Altars bow, shall own to Thee *1700, 1701*   422 That] *1709* The *1700, 1701*
425 our great Master's] *1709* her Heroes *1700, 1701*   428 By fair Rewards] *1709* To
hardy Feats *1700, 1701*   429 To ... to] *1709* And stimulate Desert, with *1700, 1701*

Where the fleet Stag employs their ardent Care;
And Chases give Them Images of War.
To teach Them Vigilance by false Alarms;
Inure Them in feign'd Camps to real Arms;   435
Practise Them now to curb the turning Steed,
Mocking the Foe; now to his rapid Speed
To give the Rein; and in the full Career,
To draw the certain Sword, or send the pointed Spear.

XXXIV.

Let Him unite His Subjects Hearts,   440
Planting Societies for peaceful Arts;
Some that in Nature shall true Knowledge found,
And by Experiment make Precept sound;
Some that to Morals shall recal the Age,
And purge from vitious Dross the sinking Stage;   445
Some that with Care true Eloquence shall teach,
And to just Idioms fix our doubtful Speech:
That from our Writers distant Realms may know,
    The Thanks We to our Monarch owe;
And Schools profess our Tongue through ev'ry Land,   450
That has invok'd His Aid, or blest His Hand.

XXXV.

Let His high Pow'r the drooping MUSES rear.
The MUSES only can reward His Care:
'Tis They that guard the great ATRIDES' Spoils:
'Tis They that still renew ULYSSES' Toils: 455
To Them by smiling JOVE 'twas giv'n, to save
Distinguish'd Patriots from the Common Grave;
To them, Great WILLIAM's Glory to recal,
When Statues moulder, and when Arches fall.
Nor let the MUSES, with ungrateful Pride,   460
    The Sources of their Treasure hide:

438 To ... in] *1701, 1709* Give all the Rein, and midst *1700*   439 To ... certain] *1701,*
1709 Draw the sure *1700*   440–1] *1709*
        To plant Societies for peaceful Arts,
        Increase our Learning and unite our Hearts; *1700, 1701*
448] That distant Realms may from our Authors know, *1700, 1701, 1709*   451 has]
have *1700, 1701, 1709*   454 the great ATRIDES'] *1709* Great *Agamemnon*'s *1700, 1701*
458] *1700, 1701, 1709* his praise recall *Wm*   459 moulder] *1700, 1701, 1709 om. Wm*
461 Sources ... Treasure] *1709* mutual Obligation *1700, 1701*

The Heroe's Virtue does the String inspire,
When with big Joy They strike the living Lyre:
  On WILLIAM's Fame their Fate depends:
With Him the Song begins: with Him it ends.   465
    From the bright Effluence of His Deed
    They borrow that reflected Light,
    With which the lasting Lamp They feed,
Whose Beams dispel the Damps of envious Night.

XXXVI.

Through various Climes, and to each distant Pole   470
In happy Tides let active Commerce rowl:
Let BRITAIN's Ships export an Annual Fleece,
Richer than ARGOS brought to ancient GREECE;
Returning loaden with the shining Stores,
Which lye profuse on either INDIA's Shores.   475
As our high Vessels pass their wat'ry Way,
Let all the Naval World due Homage pay;
With hasty Reverence their Top-Honours lower,
    Confessing the asserted Power,
To Whom by Fate 'twas given, with happy Sway   480
To calm the Earth, and vindicate the Sea.

XXXVII.

Our Pray'rs are heard, our Master's Fleets shall go,
As far as Winds can bear, or Waters flow,
New Lands to make, new INDIES to explore,
In Worlds unknown to plant BRITANNIA's Power;   485
Nations yet wild by Precept to reclaim,
And teach 'em Arms, and Arts, in WILLIAM's Name.

XXXVIII.

With humble Joy, and with respectful Fear
The list'ning People shall His Story hear,
The Wounds He bore, the Dangers He sustain'd,   490
How far he Conquer'd, and how well he Reign'd;

Shall own his Mercy equal to His Fame;
And form their Children's Accents to His Name,
Enquiring how, and when from Heav'n He came.
Their Regal Tyrants shall with Blushes hide   495
Their little Lusts of Arbitrary Pride,
  Nor bear to see their Vassals ty'd:
When WILLIAM's Virtues raise their opening Thought,
His forty Years for Publick Freedom fought,
  EUROPE by His Hand sustain'd,   500
  His Conquest by His Piety restrain'd,
And o'er Himself the last great Triumph gain'd.

XXXIX.

No longer shall their wretched Zeal adore
  Ideas of destructive Power,
Spirits that hurt, and Godheads that devour: 505
New Incense They shall bring, new Altars raise,
And fill their Temples with a Stranger's Praise;
When the Great Father's Character They find
Visibly stampt upon the Hero's Mind;
And own a present Deity confest,   510
In Valour that preserv'd, and Power that bless'd.

XL.

Through the large Convex of the Azure Sky
(For thither Nature casts our common Eye)
Fierce Meteors shoot their arbitrary Light;
And Comets march with lawless Horror bright: 515
These hear no Rule, no righteous Order own;
Their influence dreaded, as their Ways unknown:
Thro' threaten'd Lands They wild Destruction throw;
'Till ardent Prayer averts the Public Woe:
But the bright Orb that blesses all above,   520
The sacred Fire, the real Son of JOVE,

---

497 Nor bear] *1709* Nor longer bear *1700, 1701*   501] *1709* His own Stupendious
Victories restrain'd, *1700, 1701*   502 Himself ... great] *1709* the Righted World
Eternal *1700, 1701*   511] *1700, 1701, 1709*
                 Great in War and good in peace
                 Powerfull to avenge or bless: *Wm*

Rules not His Actions by Capricious Will;
Nor by ungovern'd Power declines to Ill:
Fix'd by just Laws He goes for ever right:
Man knows His Course, and thence adores His Light.   525

XLI.

O JANUS! would intreated Fate conspire
To grant what BRITAIN's Wishes could require;
Above, That Sun should cease his Way to go,
E'er WILLIAM cease to rule, and bless below:
    But a relentless Destiny   530
    Urges all that e'er was born:
Snatch'd from her Arms, BRITANNIA once must mourn
The Demi-God: The Earthly Half must die.
Yet if our Incense can Your Wrath remove;
If human Prayers avail on Minds above;   535
Exert, great God, Thy Int'rest in the Sky;
Gain each kind Pow'r, each Guardian Deity,
    That conquer'd by the publick Vow,
    They bear the dismal Mischief far away:
O! long as utmost Nature may allow,   540
    Let Them retard the threaten'd Day:
Still be our Master's Life Thy happy Care:
Still let His Blessings with His Years increase:
To His laborious Youth consum'd in War,
Add lasting Age, adorn'd and crown'd with Peace: 545
    Let twisted Olive bind those Laurels fast,
        Whose Verdure must for ever last.

525 Man ... thence] *1709* And Man, that knows his Course, *1700, 1701*   528 Above,
That ... his Way] *1709* That ... his Destin'd Way *1700, 1701*   529 rule, and bless]
1709 Govern all *1700, 1701*   532 Snatch'd from her Arms,] *1709* Her absent Lord *1700,
1701*   533 The Demi-God:] *1709* And of the Demi-God *1700, 1701*   534 Your
Wrath remove;] *1709* excite your Care, *1700, 1701*   535] *1709* If Heavenly Wills relent
to Human Pray'r, *1700, 1701*   537 each kind ... Guardian] *1709* ev'ry Tutelary *1700,
1701*   539 bear ... far] bear ... long *1709* : keep ... long *1700, 1701*   540 O! long
as utmost] O, far as utmost *1709* : And far as lengthn'd *1700, 1701*   541 Let Them
retard] *1709* Reject with happy Power *1700, 1701*   542–7] *1709*

                                Adorn Great Williams future Years
                                  With pleasures that shall ever last
                                  And recompense the heroes cares
                                  For all the labours of the past. *Wm*:

                                  Into the Ocean for his Life design'd,
                                  Throw, bounteous Heav'n, innumerable Hours,
                                  And that stern Fate its strict Account may find,
                                  Make up that Loss by taking them from Ours. *1700, 1701*

XLII.

Long let this growing ÆRA bless His Sway:
And let our Sons His present Rule obey:
On His sure Virtue long let Earth rely: } 550
And late let the Imperial Eagle fly,
To bear the Hero thro' His Father's Sky,
To LEDA's Twins, or He whose glorious Speed
On Foot prevail'd, or He who tam'd the Steed;
To HERCULES, at length absolv'd by Fate   555
From Earthly Toil, and above Envy great;
To VIRGIL's Theme, bright CYTHEREA's Son,
Sire of the LATIAN, and the BRITISH Throne;
     To all the radiant Names above,
     Rever'd by Men, and dear to JOVE.   560
     Late, JANUS, let the NASSAW-Star
New born, in rising Majesty appear,
     To triumph over vanquish'd Night,
     And guide the prosp'rous Mariner
With everlasting Beams of friendly Light.   565

1700

A Fable.

I N *Æsop's* Tales an honest Wretch we find,
  Whose Years and Comforts equally declin'd;
He in two Wives had two domestick Ills,
For different Age they had, and different Wills;

548–9] *1709*

> Deep in this Age let Him extend His Sway,
> And our late Sons with chearful Awe obey. *1700*:

> His Power let Subjects yet Unborn Obey,
> And let this Age grow Old beneath His Sway, *1701*

553–8] *1709*

> To Great *Æneas*, to *Themistocles*,
> To *Pollux, Theseus, Hercules*, *1700, 1701*

559 To] *1709* And *1700, 1701*   561 JANUS, let the] *1709* let the New-born *1700, 1701*
562 New ... rising] *1709* With dawning *1700, 1701*   564 prosp'rous] *1709 British 1700,*
1701
     Title] L *27*, L *28*, M The Fable of The old man with Tow Wives. *Lpo 11 : om. Stowe*
4] L *27*, L *28*, M, *Stowe* Various their Age, and diff'rent were their Wills; *Lpo 11*

One pluckt his Black Hairs out, and one his Grey,   5
The Man for quietness did both obey,
Till all his Parish saw his Head quite bare,
And thought he wanted Brains as well as Hair.

The Moral.

The Parties, hen-peckt *W——m*, are thy Wives,
The Hairs they pluck are thy Prerogatives;   10
Tories thy Person hate, the Whigs thy Power,
Tho much thou yieldest, still they tug for more,
Till this poor Man and thou alike are shown,
He without Hair, and thou without a Crown.

Ballad.

T HE factions that Each other claw
     By joint consent have both undone Thee
Thou like the Goat in Moses law
Hast all the Nations Sins upon Thee.

Whilst those upon thy faults discants   5
Harlay and Mountagu shall joyn
Not one but roars at Irish Grants
But all forgett you past the Boyne.

Five hundred Hams all pleas'd all proud
That they their fathers shame discover   10
But Not one Japhet in the crowd
To draw the decent Mantle over.

---

5 pluckt] *L 28, M, Lpo 11, Stowe* pick'd *L 27*   6 did] *L 28, M, Stowe* wou'd *L 27,
Lpo 11*   7 his Parish] *L 28, M, Stowe* the Parish *L 27, Lpo 11*   8 thought ...
Brains] *L 28* thought ... Sence *Stowe*: that ... Sense *L 27*: said ... Sense *M* (*in D's hand
over erasures*), *Lpo 11*   9 *The Moral.*] *L 27, L 28, M* Mor. *Lpo 11*: om. *Stowe*
The Parties] *L 27, L 28* (*D*), *Lpo 11, Stowe* Two Parties *L 28* (*Pope*), *M*   *W——m*]
W ...... L 28, M: William *L 27, Lpo 11, Stowe*   thy] *L 27, L 28, M, Stowe* the *Lpo 11*
10 pluck] *L 27, L 28, M, Lpo 11* pluckt *Stowe*   11 the] *L 28, M* and *L 27, Lpo 11, Stowe*
12 Tho] Too *L 28*: And *L 27, M* (*inserted in D's hand*), *Lpo 11, Stowe*   still *L 28*: till *1703*:
and *L 27, Lpo 11, Stowe*: yet *M* (*in D's hand over an erasure*)   13 this ... thou] *L 27,
L 28, M, Stowe* Thou and this Poor Man *Lpo 11*   are] *L 28, Lpo 11* art *M, L 27, Stowe*
14 Hair,] *L 27, L 28, M, Lpo 11* hairs *Stowe*
   Title: 'Contents' of L 28 (*D*), *Text of L 28* (*Pope*), *M*: om. *W*   *Initial capitals supplied
from L 28 and M for ll. 1, 2, 4, 9, 11, 12, 14–16, 21–24*   that] which *L 28, M*   4
Thee. *M*: Thee *W, L 28*   5 those *Uncertain reading in W*: H.. *L 28, M*   6 Harlay
and Mountagu] H ..... and M .... *L 28, M*   8 Boyne. *M*: Boyne *W, L 28*   12
over. *M*: over *W, L 28*

What in thy government is right
To Summers Name shall stand recorded
The Lawrells thou hast gain'd in fight   15
Let Ormonds merit be rewarded.

Thy Ministry supports the throne
With Prudence above all disasters
What proves Successfull is their own
And what miscarryes is their Masters.   20

Twas by a house of commons wrought
That preists and papists shan't alarm yee
But 'twas his Majestys own fault
That we have neither fleet nor Army.

A Song.

IN vain You tell your parting Lover,
You wish fair Winds may waft Him over.
Alas! what Winds can happy prove,
That bear Me far from what I love?
Alas! what Dangers on the Main   5
Can equal Those that I sustain,
From slighted Vows, and cold Disdain?

Be gentle, and in Pity choose
To wish the wildest Tempests loose:
That thrown again upon the Coast,   10
Where first my Shipwrackt Heart was lost,
I may once more repeat my Pain;
Once more in dying Notes complain
Of slighted Vows, and cold Disdain.

14 Summers] S......'s L 28 (D): So——r's L 28 (Pope), M   16 Ormonds] O......'s
L 28 (D): O.....d's L 28 (Pope), M   rewarded. M: rewarded W, L 28   18 above]
O...... L 28 (D): O.....d L 28 (Pope): O——d M   20 Masters. M: Masters W, L 28
23 Majestys L 28, M: Majsties W   24 Army. M: Army W, L 28
    Title] 1709 A New Song. 1700   4 bear Me far] 1709 makes me fly 1700   6 that]
1709 which 1700   10 thrown again upon] 1709 they may drive me on 1700   12]
1709 that I once more may tell my Pain, 1700

'This Man he took into his Bed'

THIS Man he took into his Bed
 An Old and Eke a Homely Wife;
He Swanked Soundly for his bread
An Honest but a painful Life.

Hans Carvel.

HANS CARVEL, Impotent and Old,
 Married a Lass of LONDON Mould:
Handsome? enough; extreamly Gay:
Lov'd Musick, Company, and Play:
High Flights She had, and Wit at Will: 5
And so her Tongue lay seldom still:
For in all Visits who but She,
To Argue, or to Repartée?

    She made it plain, that Human Passion
Was order'd by Predestination;   10
That, if weak Women went astray,
Their Stars were more in Fault than They:
Whole Tragedies She had by Heart;
Enter'd into ROXANA's Part:
To Triumph in her Rival's Blood,   15
The Action certainly was good.
How like a Vine young AMMON curl'd!
Oh that dear Conqu'ror of the World!
She pity'd BETTERTON in Age,
That ridicul'd the God-like Rage.   20

    She, first of all the Town, was told,
Where newest INDIA Things were sold:

Title: edd.: om. L 12   2 Wife; *edd.*: Wife *L 12*
  Title] Monsieur *De la Fontaine*'s *HANS CARVEL*, IMITATED. *1704, 1709 : De La*
Fontain's HANS CARVEL Imitated. *1701*: Hans Carvell De la Fountain imitated Adapted to
the E. of Ranelagh 1700. *Harl*   3 Handsome?] *1709* Handsome *1701, 1704, Harl*
12 Their Stars] *1701, 1704, 1709* The Gods *Harl*   15 Triumph in her] *1709* spill a
Hated *1701, 1704, Harl*   17 How] *1704, 1709, Harl* But *1701*   22 newest
INDIA Things] *1701, 1704, 1709* New East Indian Silks *Harl*

So in a Morning, without Bodice,
Slipt sometimes out to Mrs. THODY's;
To cheapen Tea, to buy a Screen:　　　　　　　　　25
What else cou'd so much Virtue mean?
For to prevent the least Reproach,
BETTY went with Her in the Coach.

But when no very great Affair
Excited her peculiar Care;　　　　　　　　　30
She without fail was wak'd at Ten;
Drank Chocolate, then slept again:
At Twelve She rose: with much ado
Her Cloaths were huddl'd on by Two:
Then; Does my Lady Dine at home?　　　　　　　　　35
Yes sure;—but is the Colonel come?
Next, how to spend the Afternoon,
And not come Home again too soon;
The Change, the City, or the Play,
As each was proper for the Day;　　　　　　　　　40
A Turn in Summer to HYDE-PARK,
When it grew tolerably Dark.

Wife's Pleasure causes Husband's Pain:
Strange Fancies come in HANS's Brain:
He thought of what He did not name;　　　　　　　　　45
And wou'd reform; but durst not blame.
At first He therefore Preach'd his Wife
The Comforts of a Pious Life:
Told Her, how Transient Beauty was;
That All must die, and Flesh was Grass:　　　　　　　　　50
He bought Her Sermons, Psalms, and Graces;
And doubled down the useful Places.
But still the Weight of worldly Care
Allow'd Her little time for Pray'r:

24 THODY's;] *1704, 1709 Tody's, 1701*: Toddys *Harl*　　　26 cou'd...Virtue] *1709* in Gods name could she *1701, 1704*: in Gods name cou'd they *Harl*　　　32 then slept again:] *1701, 1704, 1709* and slept at ten *Harl*　　　42 grew] *1701, 1704, 1709* grows *Harl*　　　43 Wife's Pleasure...Husband's Pain:] Wives Pleasure...Husbands Pain, *1701, 1704, 1709*: Wives Pleasures...husbands paines *Harl*　　　44 come...Brain:] *1701, 1704, 1709* comes... brains *Harl*　　　45 did] *1701, 1704, 1709* dare *Harl*　　　47 his] *1704, 1709* to's *1701, Harl* 49 Her] *1701, 1704, 1709 om. Harl*　　　50 That...was] *1701, 1704, 1709* How...is *Harl* 53 But] *1701, 1704, 1709* And *Harl*　　　Care] *1709* Cares *1701, 1704, Harl*　　　54 time] *1701, 1704, 1709* times *Harl*　　　Pray'r] *1709* Prayers *1701, 1704, Harl*

And Cleopatra was read o'er,   55
While Scot, and Wake, and Twenty more,
That teach one to deny one's self,
Stood unmolested on the Shelf.
An untouch'd Bible grac'd her Toilet:
No fear that Thumb of Her's should spoil it.   60
In short, the Trade was still the same:
The Dame went out: the Colonel came.

    What's to be done? poor Carvel cry'd:
Another Batt'ry must be try'd:
What if to Spells I had Recourse?   65
'Tis but to hinder something Worse.
The End must justifie the Means:
He only Sins who Ill intends:
Since therefore 'tis to Combat Evil;
'Tis lawful to employ the Devil.   70

    Forthwith the Devil did appear
(For name Him and He's always near)
Not in the Shape in which He plies
At Miss's Elbow when She lies;
Or stands before the Nurs'ry Doors,   75
To take the naughty Boy that roars:
But without Sawcer Eye or Claw,
Like a grave Barrister at Law.

    Hans Carvel, lay aside your Grief,
The Devil says: I bring Relief.   80
Relief, says Hans: pray let me crave
Your Name, Sir.—Satan.—Sir, your Slave:
I did not look upon your Feet:
You'll pardon Me:—Ay, now I see't:
And pray, Sir, when came You from Hell?   85
Our Friends there, did You leave Them well?
All well: but pr'ythee, honest Hans,
(Says Satan) leave your Complaisance:

57 That] *1701, 1704, 1709* To *Harl*   58 Stood] Lay *1701, 1704, 1709, Harl*   59
her] *1701, 1704, 1709* the *Harl*   60 Thumb] *1701, 1704, 1709* Thumbs *Harl*   69
Since] *1701, 1704, 1709* Time *Harl*   74 lies;] *1701, 1704, 1709* crys *Harl*   75 Nurs'ry]
1701, 1704, 1709 Buttry *Harl*   79 Carvel,] *1701, 1704, 1709* said he *Harl*   85 when
came] *1701, 1704, 1709* when you came *Harl*   86] *1701, 1704, 1709* Did you leave our
Friends there well *Harl*

The Truth is this: I cannot stay
Flaring in Sun-shine all the Day: 90
For, *entre Nous*, We Hellish Sprites,
Love more the Fresco of the Nights;
And oft'ner our Receipts convey
In Dreams, than any other Way.
I tell You therefore as a Friend,   95
E'er Morning dawns, your Fears shall end:
Go then this Ev'ning, Master CARVEL,
Lay down your Fowls, and broach your Barrel;
Let Friends and Wine dissolve your Care;
Whilst I the great Receipt prepare: 100
To Night I'll bring it, by my Faith;
Believe for once what SATAN saith.

Away went HANS: glad? not a little;
Obey'd the Devil to a Tittle;
Invited Friends some half a Dozen,   105
The Colonel, and my Lady's Cousin.
The Meat was serv'd; the Bowls were crown'd;
Catches were sung; and Healths went round:
Barbadoes Waters for the Close;
'Till HANS had fairly got his Dose: 110
The Colonel toasted to the best:
The Dame mov'd off, to be undrest:
The Chimes went Twelve: the Guests withdrew:
But when, or how, HANS hardly knew.
Some Modern Anecdotes aver,   115
He nodded in his Elbow Chair;
From thence was carry'd off to Bed:
JOHN held his Heels, and NAN his Head.
My Lady was disturb'd: new Sorrow!
Which HANS must answer for to Morrow.   120

In Bed then view this happy Pair;
And think how HYMEN Triumph'd there.

93 Receipts] *1704, 1709, Harl* Deceits *1701*   100 Whilst... great] *1701, 1704, 1709*
While... grand *Harl*   101 To] *1701, 1704, 1709* This *Harl*   103 glad?] *1709* glad
1701, 1704, Harl   108 Catches were sung;] *1701, 1704, 1709* Catchs, New Songs *Harl*
109 Barbadoes Waters] *1709* Modish Ratafia *1701, 1704, Harl*   112 mov'd] *1704, 1709*
went *1701, Harl*   114 or] *1701, 1704, 1709* and *Harl*   121 this] *1709* the *1701,*
1704, Harl   122 Triumph'd] *1701, 1704, 1709* triumphs *Harl*

HANS, fast asleep, as soon as laid;
The Duty of the Night unpaid:
The waking Dame, with Thoughts opprest,   125
That made Her Hate both Him and Rest:
By such a Husband, such a Wife!
'Twas ACME's and SEPTIMIUS' Life.
The Lady sigh'd: the Lover snor'd:
The punctual Devil kept his Word: 130
Appear'd to honest HANS again;
But not at all by Madam seen:
And giving Him a Magick Ring,
Fit for the Finger of a King;
Dear HANS, said He, this Jewel take,   135
And wear it long for SATAN's Sake:
'Twill do your Business to a Hair:
For long as You this Ring shall wear,
As sure as I look over LINCOLN,
That ne'er shall happen which You think on.   140

    HANS took the Ring with Joy extream;
(All this was only in a Dream)
And thrusting it beyond his Joint,
'Tis done, He cry'd: I've gain'd my Point.—
What Point, said She, You ugly Beast?   145
You neither give Me Joy nor Rest:
'Tis done.—What's done, You drunken Bear?
You've thrust your Finger G—d knows where.

Written at Paris, 1700. In the Beginning of Robe's Geography.

OF All that WILLIAM Rules, or ROBE
Describes, Great RHEA, of Thy Globe;
When or on Post-Horse, or in Chaise,
With much Expence, and little Ease,

128 SEPTIMIUS'] *1704, 1709, Harl* Septimia's *1701*   138 For long] *1701, 1704, 1709* For's
long *Harl*   143 his] *1704, 1709, Harl* the *1701*   144] *1701, 1704, 1709 om. Harl*
146 neither] *1701, 1704, 1709* never *Harl*   148 You've] *1701, 1704, 1709* You *Harl*

My destin'd Miles I shall have gone,   5
By THAMES or MAESE, by Po or RHONE,
And found no Foot of Earth my own;
GREAT MOTHER, let Me Once be able
To have a Garden, House, and Stable;
That I may Read, and Ride, and Plant,   10
Superior to Desire, or Want;
And as Health fails, and Years increase,
Sit down, and think, and die in Peace.
Oblige Thy Fav'rite Undertakers
To throw Me in but Twenty Acres: 15
This Number sure They may allow;
For Pasture Ten, and Ten for Plow:
'Tis all that I wou'd Wish, or Hope,
For ME, and JOHN, and NELL, and CROP.

Then, as Thou wil't, dispose the rest   20
(And let not FORTUNE spoil the Jest)
To Those, who at the Market-Rate
Can barter Honour for Estate.

Now if Thou grant'st Me my Request,
To make Thy Vot'ry truly blest,   25
Let curst Revenge, and sawcy Pride
To some bleak Rock far off be ty'd;
Nor e'er approach my Rural Seat,
To tempt Me to be Base, and Great.

And, GODDESS, This kind Office done,   30
Charge VENUS to command her Son,
(Where-ever else She lets Him rove)
To shun my House, and Field, and Grove:
Peace cannot dwell with Hate or Love.

Hear, gracious RHEA, what I say: 35
And Thy Petitioner shall Pray.

To a Child of Quality of Five Years Old, the Author suppos'd Forty.

Lords, Knights, and Squires, the num'rous Band
 That wear the Fair Miss *Mary*'s Fetters,
Were summon'd, by her high Command,
 To show their Passion by their Letters.

My Pen amongst the rest I took,   5
 Least those bright Eyes that cannot read
Shou'd dart their kindling Fires, and look
 The Pow'r they have to be obey'd.

Nor Quality, nor Reputation,
 Forbid me yet my Flame to tell,   10
Dear Five Years old befriends my Passion,
 And I may Write 'till she can Spell.

For while she makes her Silk-worms Beds
 With all the tender things I swear,
Whilst all the House my Passion reads,   15
 In Papers round her Baby's Hair.

She may receive and own my Flame,
 For tho' the strictest *Prudes* shou'd know it,
She'll pass for a most virtuous Dame,
 And I for an unhappy Poet.   20

Then too, alas, when she shall tear
 The Lines some younger Rival sends,
She'll give me leave to Write, I fear,
 And we shall still continue Friends.

For as our diff'rent Ages move,   25
 'Tis so ordain'd, wou'd Fate but mend it,
That I shall be past making Love,
 When she begins to comprehend it.

Title: of Five … Author suppos'd Forty.] *L 28, M* FIVE … AUTHOR Forty. 1704. *1740*
4 Passion] *L 28, M* passions *1740* 11 befriends] *L 28, 1740* befriend *M* 14 things]
L 28, M things, *1740*

1701

Les Estreines.

ACCEPT, my Love, as true a Heart
As ever Lover gave;
'Tis free (it vows) from any art,
And proud to be your Slave.

2

Then take it kindly, as 'twas meant, 5
And let the Giver live:
Who, with it, would the World have sent,
Had it been his to give.

3

And, that Dorinda may not fear,
I e're will prove untrue; 10
My vows shall, ending with the Year,
With it begin a-new.

Song. Sett by Mr: Abell.

READING ends in Melancholy;
Wine breeds Vices and Deseases;
  Wealth is but Care, and Love but folly;
Only Friendship truly pleases.
  My Wealth, my Books, my Flask, my Molly, 5
Farewell all, if FRIENDSHIP Ceases!

Title: Song ... Abell.] *M* A Song, ... Abell. *L 27, 1740* : The Second SONG. *1701*   **3**
Wealth is but ... but] *M, L 27, 1740* Bus'ness is ... is *1701*   4 Only ... truly] *M, L 27,*
1740 wholly ... only *1701*   5]*M, L 27, 1740* Flasks, Affairs, Books and *Dolly, 1701*

Ballad.

THE Crown once again
　　Its rights shall maintain
And the Nation shall make a good figure.
　　For our Glorious redeemer
　　Tells Harley and Seymour　　　　　　5
Tis time We should act with great Vigour.

　　When the hands of all pages
　　Find how sad a thing age is
In our little disperited fr——
　　Tis likely his Brain　　　　　　10
　　New fire should retain
And he'l Act with abundance of vigour.

　　His Majesties Actions
　　Shall soon suppress factions
And by May we shall Paris beleaguer　　15
　　For without Troops or Pence
　　Without counsells or Sence
The King has a fancy for vigour.

　　Whilst he lays his concern on
　　The Shoulders of Vernon　　　　　　20
His credit will surely grow bigger
　　And if Sunderland comes
　　Sound trompetts beat drums
No doubt but we'l act with great vigour.

　　Albemarle leads the way　　　　　　25
　　Drest like Mars in a play
With Cassie as fierce as a tyger
　　And Miremont the Prince
　　Shall his Country convince
That his Majesties favrites have vigour.　　30

Title: edd.: Another [Ballad] 'Contents' of L 28 : om. W, L 28　　Caps. supplied (as in L 28)
for first words of ll. 4, 8, 10, 12, 16, 20, 22, 25, 28, 30, 39　　Full stops (lacking in both W &
L 28) supplied for ll. 6, 12, 18, 24, 30, 36　　6 We] They L 28, Earlier reading in W
7 all] the L 28, Earlier reading in W　　10 Brain] Brains L 28　　15 we] he L 28
19 concern] concerns L 28　　23 trompetts] Trumpet L 28　　27 With Cassie as] L 28
and young Auverquerque Earlier reading in W

Vice Chamberlain Bartie
Is in the Court party
Lord Cutts for the Combat is eager
And from Jore and Laloe
Grand Louis shal know   35
What it is to be given to vigour.

But if Whigg getts the better
You'l see how he'l fetter
And hamstring our royal Intreger
If the Tory prevails   40
In comes little Wales
And have not We acted with vigour?

1702

To a Young Gentleman in Love.
A Tale.

FROM publick Noise and factious Strife,
  From all the busie Ills of Life,
Take me, My CELIA, to Thy Breast;
And lull my wearied Soul to Rest:
For ever, in this humble Cell,   5
Let Thee and I, my Fair One, dwell;
None enter else, but LOVE—and He
Shall bar the Door, and keep the Key.

To painted Roofs, and shining Spires
(Uneasie Seats of high Desires)   10
Let the unthinking Many croud,
That dare be Covetous and Proud:
In golden Bondage let Them wait,
And barter Happiness for State:

34 from] for *L 28*   37 Whigg getts] Whigs get *L 28*   41 Wales] W ...., *L 28*
42 not We] We not *L 28*   vigour? *edd.*: vigour *W*: Vigor? *L 28*
   3 CELIA] *Cloe 1702, 1709*

917.27   O

But Oh! My CELIA, when Thy Swain   15
Desires to see a Court again;
May Heav'n around This destin'd Head
The choicest of it's Curses shed:
To sum up all the Rage of Fate,
In the Two Things I dread and hate;   20
May'st Thou be False, and I be Great.

Thus, on his CELIA's panting Breast,
Fond CELADON his Soul exprest;
While with Delight the lovely Maid
Receiv'd the Vows, She thus repaid: 25

Hope of my Age, Joy of my Youth,
Blest Miracle of Love and Truth!
All that cou'd e'er be counted Mine,
My Love and Life long since are Thine:
A real Joy I never knew;   30
'Till I believ'd Thy Passion true:
A real Grief I ne'er can find;
'Till Thou prov'st Perjur'd or Unkind.
Contempt, and Poverty, and Care,
All we abhor, and all we fear,   35
Blest with Thy Presence, I can bear.
Thro' Waters, and thro' Flames I'll go,
Suff'rer and Solace of Thy Woe:
Trace Me some yet unheard-of Way,
That I Thy Ardour may repay;   40
And make My constant Passion known,
By more than Woman yet has done.

Had I a Wish that did not bear
The Stamp and Image of my Dear;
I'd pierce my Heart thro' ev'ry Vein,   45
And Die to let it out again.

15 CELIA] *Cloe 1702, 1709*   22 CELIA's] *Cloe's 1702, 1709*   37–42] *1709*
Can suffer Racks, and run thro' Flame,
Still contented, still the same;
Then trace me some unheard of way,
Thy constant Ardour to repay,
For I my Sense of it wou'd show,
In more than Woman e're cou'd do: *1702*

No: VENUS shall my Witness be,
(If VENUS ever lov'd like Me)
That for one Hour I wou'd not quit
My Shepherd's Arms, and this Retreat,   50
To be the PERSIAN Monarch's Bride,
Part'ner of all his Pow'r and Pride;
Or Rule in Regal State above,
Mother of Gods, and Wife of JOVE.

O happy these of Human Race!   55
But soon, alas! our Pleasures pass.
He thank'd her on his bended Knee;
Then drank a Quart of Milk and Tea;
And leaving her ador'd Embrace,
Hasten'd to Court, to beg a Place.   60
While She, his Absence to bemoan,
The very Moment He was gone,
Call'd THYRSIS from beneath the Bed;
Where all this time He had been hid.

MORAL.

WHILE Men have these Ambitious Fancies;   65
And wanton Wenches read Romances;
Our Sex will—What? Out with it. Lye;
And Their's in equal Strains reply.
The Moral of the Tale I sing
(A Posy for a Wedding Ring)   70
In this short Verse will be confin'd:
Love is a Jest; and Vows are Wind.

Epitaph.

NOBLES, and Heralds by Your leave,
Here lyes what Once was MATTHEW PRIOR,
The Son of ADAM and of EVE,
Can STUART, or NASSAW go higher.

55 O] *1709 om. 1702*   56 soon, alas!] *1709* Oh! how soon *1702*   62 The very
Moment] *1709* As soon as ever *1702*   65 WHILE] *WHILST 1702, 1709*   67
will—...it.] *1709 will be innur'd to 1702*   68 in equal Strains] *1709 instructed to 1702*
     Title: edd.: *Another Epitaph. L 27 (following 'For His own Epitaph'): om. 1721fp*   I
NOBLES,] Courtiers *1721fp*   2 What Once was] the Bones of *1721fp*   4 Can
STUART] Let *Bourbon 1721fp*

1703

A Song.

IF Wine and Musick have the Pow'r,
To ease the Sickness of the Soul;
Let PHOEBUS ev'ry String explore;
And BACCHUS fill the sprightly Bowl.
Let Them their friendly Aid imploy, 5
To make my CLOE's Absence light;
And seek for Pleasure, to destroy
The Sorrows of this live-long Night.

But She to Morrow will return:
VENUS, be Thou to Morrow great; 10
Thy Myrtles strow, Thy Odours burn;
And meet Thy Fav'rite Nymph in State.
Kind Goddess, to no other Pow'rs
Let Us to Morrow's Blessings own:
Thy darling LOVES shall guide the Hours; 15
And all the Day be Thine alone.

Adriani Morientis ad Animam Suam. Imitated.

POOR little, pretty, flutt'ring Thing,
Must We no longer live together?
And dost Thou prune thy trembling Wing,
To take thy Flight Thou know'st not whither?

Thy humorous Vein, thy pleasing Folly 5
Lyes all neglected, all forgot:
And pensive, wav'ring, melancholy,
Thou dread'st and hop'st Thou know'st not what.

---

6 my CLOE's] *1709* Calista's *1703*   13 Pow'rs] *1709 pow'r 1703*   14 Let us ...
Blessings] *1709* we...*Joys will 1703*
 Title: Suam] *1709 om. 1704*   *Imitated*] *1709 TRANSLATED 1704*   3
trembling] *1709* doubtful *1704*   6 all neglected, all] *1709* interrupted and *1704*

The Despairing Shepherd.

ALEXIS shun'd his Fellow Swains,
　Their rural Sports, and jocund Strains:
　　(Heav'n guard us all from CUPID's Bow!)
He lost his Crook, He left his Flocks;
And wand'ring thro' the lonely Rocks,　　　　5
　　He nourish'd endless Woe.

The Nymphs and Shepherds round Him came:
His Grief Some pity, Others blame;
　　The fatal Cause All kindly seek:
He mingled his Concern with Theirs;　　　　10
He gave 'em back their friendly Tears;
　　He sigh'd, but wou'd not speak.

CLORINDA came among the rest;
And She too kind Concern exprest,
　　And ask'd the Reason of his Woe:　　　　15
She ask'd, but with an Air and Mein,
That made it easily foreseen,
　　She fear'd too much to know.

The Shepherd rais'd his mournful Head;
And will You pardon Me, He said,　　　　20
　　While I the cruel Truth reveal?
Which nothing from my Breast shou'd tear;
Which never shou'd offend Your Ear,
　　But that You bid Me tell.

'Tis thus I rove, 'tis thus complain,　　　　25
Since You appear'd upon the Plain;
　　You are the Cause of all my Care:
Your Eyes ten thousand Dangers dart:
Ten thousand Torments vex My Heart:
　　I love, and I despair.　　　　30

Title] *1709*; *1704 adds:* A *PASTORAL.*　　2 jocund] *1709* sprightly *1704*　　14 And
She too] *1709* She too a *1704*　　21 While] *1709* Whilst *1704*

Too much, ALEXIS, I have heard:
'Tis what I thought; 'tis what I fear'd:
   And yet I pardon You, She cry'd:
But You shall promise ne'er again
To breath your Vows, or speak your Pain: 35
   He bow'd, obey'd, and dy'd.

The Lady's Looking-Glass.

CELIA and I the other Day
   Walk'd o'er the Sand-Hills to the Sea:
The setting Sun adorn'd the Coast,
His Beams entire, his Fierceness lost:
And, on the Surface of the Deep,   5
The Winds lay only not asleep:
The Nymph did like the Scene appear,
Serenely pleasant, calmly fair:
Soft fell her Words, as flew the Air.
With secret Joy I heard Her say,   10
That She wou'd never miss one Day
A Walk so fine, a Sight so gay.

But, oh the Change! the Winds grow high;
Impending Tempests charge the Sky;
The Light'ning flies; the Thunder roars;   15
And big Waves lash the frighten'd Shoars.
Struck with the Horror of the Sight,
She turns her Head, and wings her Flight;
And trembling vows, She'll ne'er again
Approach the Shoar, or view the Main.   20

Once more at least look back, said I;
Thy self in That large Glass descry:
When Thou art in good Humour drest;
When gentle Reason rules thy Breast;

---

33 And] *1709* But *1704*   34 But... promise] *1709* Provided you will *1704*   35 To
breath] *1709* Declare *1704*
   Title] *1709*; *1704 adds:* IN IMITATION OF A *GREEK IDYLLIUM.*   7–9] The
Prospect and the Nymph were gay, *1704*   8 pleasant] joyous *1709*   10 secret] *1709*
silent *1704*   11–12] *1709* That we shou'd walk there ev'ry Day. *1704*   13 grow]
1709 grew *1704*   19 She'll] *1709* she *1704*   20 Approach... view] *1709* Will press
... see *1704*   21 Once... back] *1709* Look back at least once more *1704*   22 large]
1709 great *1704*

The Sun upon the calmest Sea   25
Appears not half so bright as Thee:
'Tis then, that with Delight I rove
Upon the boundless Depth of Love:
I bless my Chain; I hand my Oar;
Nor think on all I left on Shoar.   30

But when vain Doubt, and groundless Fear
Do That Dear Foolish Bosom tear;
When the big Lip, and wat'ry Eye
Tell Me, the rising Storm is nigh:
'Tis then, Thou art yon' angry Main,   35
Deform'd by Winds, and dash'd by Rain;
And the poor Sailor, that must try
It's Fury, labours less than I.

Shipwreck'd, in vain to Land I make;
While Love and Fate still drive Me back: 40
Forc'd to doat on Thee thy own Way,
I chide Thee first, and then obey.
Wretched when from Thee, vex'd when nigh,
I with Thee, or without Thee, die.

To the Author of
Love and Friendship: A Pastoral.

B Y SILVIA if thy charming Self be meant;
If Friendship be thy Virgin Vows Extent;
O! let me in AMINTA's Praises join:
Her's my Esteem shall be, my Passion Thine.
When for Thy Head the Garland I prepare;   5
A second Wreath shall bind AMINTA's Hair:
And when my choicest Songs Thy Worth proclaim;
Alternate Verse shall bless AMINTA's Name:
My Heart shall own the Justice of Her Cause;
And Love himself submit to Friendship's Laws.   10

31 Doubt] Doubts *1704, 1709*
    Title: Love . . . Pastoral. edd. (taken from title of poem that precedes in 1718) : THE Foregoing
PASTORAL. *1709, 1718 :* THE PASTORAL, *Printed*, Page 378. *1704*   3, 6, 8
AMINTA's] *1709 Corinna's 1704*

But, if beneath thy Numbers soft Disguise,
Some favour'd Swain, some true ALEXIS lyes;
If AMARYLLIS breaths thy secret Pains;
And thy fond Heart beats Measure to thy Strains:
May'st thou, howe'er I grieve, for ever find   15
The Flame propitious, and the Lover kind:
May VENUS long exert her happy Pow'r,
And make thy Beauty, like thy Verse, endure:
May ev'ry God his friendly Aid afford;
PAN guard thy Flock, and CERES bless thy Board.   20

But, if by chance the Series of thy Joys
Permit one Thought less chearful to arise;
Piteous transfer it to the mournful Swain,
Who loving much, who not belov'd again,
Feels an ill-fated Passion's last Excess;   25
And dies in Woe, that Thou may'st live in Peace.

To a Lady:

She refusing to continue a Dispute with me, and leaving me in the Argument.

An Ode.

I.

SPARE, Gen'rous Victor, spare the Slave,
Who did unequal War pursue;
That more than Triumph He might have,
In being overcome by You.

14 beats] *1709* beat *1704*   17] *1709* May *Cytherea* make her Conquest sure, *1704*
18 make] *1709* let *1704*   21–23] *1709*
                  Yet, if amidst the Series of these Joys,
                  One sad Reflection should by chance arise,
                  Give it, in Pity, to the wretched Swain, *1704*
25 Feels] *1709* Felt *1704*   26 dies... may'st] *1709* dy'd... might'st *1704*
  Title] *1709* Disputing with a LADY, Who left me in the ARGUMENT. *1704*

II.

In the Dispute whate'er I said,   5
   My Heart was by my Tongue bely'd;
And in my Looks You might have read,
   How much I argu'd on your side.

III.

You, far from Danger as from Fear,
   Might have sustain'd an open Fight: 10
For seldom your Opinions err;
   Your Eyes are always in the right.

IV.

Why, fair One, wou'd You not rely
   On Reason's Force with Beauty's join'd?
Cou'd I their Prevalence deny,   15
   I must at once be Deaf and Blind.

V.

Alas! not hoping to subdue,
   I only to the Fight aspir'd:
To keep the beauteous Foe in view
   Was all the Glory I desir'd.   20

VI.

But She, howe'er of Vict'ry sure,
   Contemns the Wreath too long delay'd;
And, arm'd with more immediate Pow'r,
   Calls cruel Silence to her Aid.

VII.

Deeper to wound, She shuns the Fight: 25
   She drops her Arms, to gain the Field:
Secures her Conquest by her Flight;
   And triumphs, when She seems to yield.

14] *1709* On Force thus formidably join'd? *1704*   17–28]
        But quicker Arts of Death you use,
          Traverse your Ground to gain the Field,
        And, whilst my Argument pursues,
          With sudden Silence bid me yield. *1704*

22 Wreath] Gift *1709*

VIII.

So when the PARTHIAN turn'd his Steed,
    And from the Hostile Camp withdrew;   30
With cruel Skill the backward Reed
    He sent; and as He fled, He slew.

The Ladle.

THE Scepticks think, 'twas long ago,
    Since Gods came down *Incognito*,
To see Who were Their Friends or Foes,
And how our Actions fell or rose:
That since They gave Things their Beginning;   5
And set this Whirligig a Spinning;
Supine They in their Heav'n remain,
Exempt from Passion, and from Pain:
And frankly leave us Human Elves,
To cut and shuffle for our selves: 10
To stand or walk, to rise or tumble,
As Matter, and as Motion jumble.

The Poets now, and Painters hold
This *Thesis* both absurd and bold:
And your good-natur'd Gods, They say,   15
Descend some twice or thrice a-day:

31 With... backward] *1709* He backward sent the Fatal *1704*   32 He sent... fled,]
1709 Secure of Conquest as *1704*   *In 1704, followed by:*

Daunted, I dropt my useless Arms,
    When you no longer deign'd to Fight,
Then Triumph deck'd in all its Charms,
    Appear'd less beautiful than Flight.

Oh! trace again the Hostile Plains,
    My Troops were wounded in the War,
But whilst this fiercer Silence reigns
    They suffer, famish'd by Despair.

Capricious Author of my Smart,
    Let War ensue, or Silence cease,
Unless you find my Coward Heart
    Is yielding to a separate Peace. *1704*

8 Passion, and] *1709* Pleasure as *1704*   14 both absurd] *1709* dangerous *1704*

Else all these Things We toil so hard in,
Would not avail one single Farthing:
For when the Hero We rehearse,
To grace His Actions, and Our Verse;   20
'Tis not by dint of Human Thought,
That to his LATIUM He is brought:
IRIS descends by FATE's Commands,
To guide his Steps thro' Foreign Lands:
And AMPHITRITE clears his Way   25
From Rocks and Quick-sands in the Sea.

And if You see Him in a Sketch;
(Tho' drawn by PAULO or CARACHE)
He shows not half his Force and Strength,
Strutting in Armour, and at Length: 30
That He may make his proper Figure,
The Piece must yet be four Yards bigger:
The NYMPHS conduct Him to the Field:
One holds his Sword, and One his Shield:
MARS standing by asserts his Quarrel: 35
And FAME flies after with a Lawrel.

These Points, I say, of Speculation
(As 'twere to save or sink the Nation)
Men idly learned will dispute,
Assert, object, confirm, refute: 40
Each mighty angry, mighty right,
With equal Arms sustains the Fight;
'Till now no Umpire can agree 'em:
So both draw off, and sing *Te Deum.*

Is it in *Equilibrio,*   45
If Deities descend or no?
Then let th' Affirmative prevail,
As requisite to form my Tale:
For by all Parties 'tis confest,
That those Opinions are the best,   50
Which in their Nature most conduce
To present Ends, and private Use.

43 Umpire] *1709 Medium 1704*   44 *Deum. 1704, 1709 : Deum 1718 (corrected in reset sheet)*

Two Gods came therefore from above,
One MERCURY, the t'other JOVE:
The Humour was (it seems) to know,   55
If all the Favours They bestow,
Could from our own Perverseness ease Us;
And if our Wish injoy'd would please Us.

Discoursing largely on this Theme,
O'er Hills and Dales Their Godships came;   60
'Till well nigh tir'd at almost Night,
They thought it proper to alight.

Note here, that it as true as odd is,
That in Disguise a God or Goddess
Exerts no supernat'ral Powers;   65
But acts on Maxims much like Ours.

They spy'd at last a Country Farm,
Where all was snug, and clean, and warm;
For Woods before, and Hills behind
Secur'd it both from Rain and Wind: 70
Large Oxen in the Fields were lowing:
Good Grain was sow'd: good Fruit was growing:
Of last Year's Corn in Barns great Store;
Fat Turkeys gobbling at the Door:
And Wealth (in short) with Peace consented,   75
That People here should live contented:
But did They in Effect do so?
Have Patience, Friend; and Thou shalt know.

The honest Farmer and his Wife,
To Years declin'd from Prime of Life,   80
Had struggl'd with the Marriage Noose;
As almost ev'ry Couple does:
Sometimes, My Plague! sometimes, My Darling!
Kissing to Day, to Morrow snarling;
Jointly submitting to endure   85
That Evil, which admits no Cure.

58 would] *1709* might *1704*   69 Woods... Hills] *1709* Hills... Woods *1704*   71
Large] *1709* Fat *1704*   83 Sometimes] *1704* Sometime *1709*

Our Gods the outward Gate unbarr'd:
Our Farmer met 'em in the Yard;
Thought They were Folks that lost their Way;
And ask'd them civilly to stay: 90
Told 'em, for Supper, or for Bed
They might go on, and be worse sped.—

So said, so done: the Gods consent:
All three into the Parlour went:
They complement: They sit: They chat;   95
Fight o'er the Wars; reform the State:
A thousand knotty Points They clear;
Till Supper and my Wife appear.

JOVE made his Leg, and kiss'd the Dame:
Obsequious HERMES did the same.   100
JOVE kiss'd the Farmer's Wife, You say.
He did—but in an honest Way:
Oh! not with half that Warmth and Life,
With which He kiss'd AMPHITRYON's Wife.—

Well then, Things handsomly were serv'd: 105
My Mistress for the Strangers carv'd.
How strong the Beer, how good the Meat,
How loud They laught, how much They eat,
In Epic sumptuous would appear;
Yet shall be pass'd in Silence here: 110
For I should grieve to have it said,
That by a fine Description led,
I made my Episode too long,
Or tir'd my Friend, to grace my Song.

The Grace-Cup serv'd, the Cloth away,   115
JOVE thought it time to show his Play:
Landlord and Landlady, He cry'd,
Folly and Jesting laid aside,
That Ye thus hospitably live,
And Strangers with good Chear receive,   120

109] *1709* Wou'd gloriously in Verse appear, *1704*   113 Episode too] *1709* Epic very
1704

Is mighty grateful to your Betters,
And makes ev'n Gods themselves your Debtors.
To give this *Thesis* plainer Proof,
You have to Night beneath your Roof
A Pair of Gods: (nay never wonder)   125
This Youth can Fly, and I can Thunder.
I'm JUPITER, and He MERCURIUS,
My Page, my Son indeed, but spurious.
Form then Three Wishes, You and Madam:
And sure, as You already had 'em,   130
The Things desir'd in half an Hour
Shall all be here, and in your Pow'r.

Thank Ye, great Gods, the Woman says:
Oh! may your Altars ever blaze.
A Ladle for our Silver Dish   135
Is what I want, is what I Wish.—
A Ladle! cries the Man, a Ladle!
'Odzooks, CORISCA, You have pray'd ill:
What should be Great, You turn to Farce:
I Wish the Ladle in your A——.   140

With equal Grief and Shame my Muse
The Sequel of the Tale pursues:
The Ladle fell into the Room,
And stuck in old CORISCA's Bum.
Our Couple weep Two Wishes past,   145
And kindly join to form the last,
To ease the Woman's aukward Pain,
And get the Ladle out again.

MORAL.

THIS Commoner has Worth and Parts,
Is prais'd for Arms, or lov'd for Arts: 150
His Head achs for a Coronet:
And Who is Bless'd that is not Great?

Some Sense, and more Estate, kind Heav'n
To this well-lotted Peer has giv'n:

136 is] *1709* and *1704*   153 Sense] *1709 Parts 1704*

What then? He must have Rule and Sway: 155
And all is wrong, 'till He's in Play.

The Miser must make up his Plumb,
And dares not touch the hoarded Sum:
The sickly Dotard wants a Wife,
To draw off his last Dregs of Life.   160

Against our Peace We arm our Will:
Amidst our Plenty, *Something* still
For Horses, Houses, Pictures, Planting,
To Thee, to Me, to Him is wanting.
That cruel *Something* unpossess'd   165
Corrodes, and levens all the rest.
That *Something*, if We could obtain,
Would soon create a future Pain:
And to the Coffin, from the Cradle,
'Tis all a WISH, and all a LADLE.   170

Charity.

A Paraphrase on the Thirteenth Chapter of the First Epistle to the Corinthians.

DID sweeter Sounds adorn my flowing Tongue,
Than ever Man pronounc'd, or Angel sung:
Had I all Knowledge, Human and Divine,
That Thought can reach, or Science can define;
And had I Pow'r to give that Knowledge Birth,   5
In all the Speeches of the babling Earth:
Did SHADRACH's Zeal my glowing Breast inspire,
To weary Tortures, and rejoice in Fire:
Or had I Faith like That which ISRAEL saw,
When MOSES gave them Miracles, and Law: 10
Yet, gracious CHARITY, indulgent Guest,
Were not Thy Pow'r exerted in my Breast;

158 dares...hoarded] *1709 dare...gotten 1704*
2 Man...Angel] *Md* Men...Angels *1704*   5 had] *1704 om. Md*

Those Speeches would send up unheeded Pray'r:
That Scorn of Life would be but wild Despair:
A Tymbal's Sound were better than my Voice: 15
My Faith were Form: my Eloquence were Noise.

CHARITY, decent, modest, easy, kind,
Softens the high, and rears the abject Mind;
Knows with just Reins, and gentle Hand to guide,
Betwixt vile Shame, and arbitrary Pride.   20
Not soon provok'd, She easily forgives;
And much She suffers, as She much believes.
Soft Peace She brings where-ever She arrives:
She builds our Quiet, as She forms our Lives;
Lays the rough Paths of peevish Nature ev'n;   25
And opens in each Heart a little HEAV'N.

Each other Gift, which GOD on Man bestows,
It's proper Bounds, and due Restriction knows;
To one fixt Purpose dedicates it's Pow'r;
And finishing it's Act, exists no more.   30
Thus, in Obedience to what HEAV'N decrees,
Knowledge shall fail, and Prophecy shall cease:
But lasting CHARITY's more ample Sway,
Nor bound by Time, nor subject to Decay,
In happy Triumph shall for ever live,   35
And endless Good diffuse, and endless Praise receive.

As thro' the Artist's intervening Glass,
Our Eye observes the distant Planets pass;
A little we discover; but allow,
That more remains unseen, than Art can show: 40
So whilst our Mind it's Knowledge wou'd improve;
(It's feeble Eye intent on Things above)
High as We may, We lift our Reason up,
By FAITH directed, and confirm'd by HOPE:
Yet are We able only to survey   45
Dawnings of Beams, and Promises of Day.
HEAV'N's fuller Effluence mocks our dazl'd Sight;
Too great it's Swiftness, and too strong it's Light.

But soon the mediate Clouds shall be dispell'd:
The Sun shall soon be Face to Face beheld,   50
In all His Robes, with all His Glory on,
Seated sublime on His Meridian Throne.

Then constant FAITH, and holy HOPE shall dye,
One lost in Certainty, and One in Joy:
Whilst Thou, more happy Pow'r, fair CHARITY,   55
Triumphant Sister, greatest of the Three,
Thy Office, and Thy Nature still the same,
Lasting thy Lamp, and unconsum'd thy Flame,
Shalt still survive—
Shalt stand before the Host of HEAV'N confest,   60
For ever blessing, and for ever blest.

Celia to Damon.

Atque in Amore mala hæc proprio, summeque secundo
Inveniuntur—   Lucret. Lib. 4.

WHAT can I say, what Arguments can prove
My Truth, what Colours can describe my Love;
If it's Excess and Fury be not known,
In what Thy CELIA has already done?

Thy Infant Flames, whilst yet they were conceal'd   5
In tim'rous Doubts, with Pity I beheld;
With easie Smiles dispell'd the silent Fear,
That durst not tell Me, what I dy'd to hear:
In vain I strove to check my growing Flame,
Or shelter Passion under Friendship's Name: 10
You saw my Heart, how it my Tongue bely'd;
And when You press'd, how faintly I deny'd—

E'er Guardian Thought cou'd bring it's scatter'd Aid;
E'er Reason cou'd support the doubting Maid;
My Soul surpriz'd, and from her self disjoin'd,   15
Left all Reserve, and all the Sex behind:
From your Command her Motions She receiv'd;
And not for Me, but You, She breath'd and liv'd.

51 In] *Md* With *1704*
15 her] its *1704, 1709*

But ever blest be CYTHEREA's Shrine;
And Fires Eternal on Her Altars shine;   20
Since Thy dear Breast has felt an equal Wound;
Since in Thy Kindness my Desires are crown'd.
By Thy each Look, and Thought, and Care, 'tis shown,
Thy Joys are center'd All in Me Alone;
And sure I am, Thou woud'st not change this Hour   25
For all the White ones, Fate has in it's Pow'r.—

Yet thus belov'd, thus loving to Excess,
Yet thus receiving and returning Bliss,
In this great Moment, in this golden NOW,
When ev'ry Trace of What, or When, or How   30
Shou'd from my Soul by raging Love be torn,
And far on swelling Seas of Rapture born;
A melancholy Tear afflicts my Eye;
And my Heart labours with a sudden Sigh:
Invading Fears repel my Coward Joy;   35
And Ills foreseen the present Bliss destroy.

Poor as it is, This Beauty was the Cause,
That with first Sighs Your panting Bosom rose:
But with no Owner Beauty long will stay,
Upon the Wings of Time born swift away: 40
Pass but some fleeting Years, and These poor Eyes,
(Where now without a Boast some Lustre lyes)
No longer shall their little Honours keep;
Shall only be of use to read, or weep:
And on this Forehead, where your Verse has said,   45
The LOVES delighted, and the GRACES play'd;
Insulting Age will trace his cruel Way,
And leave sad Marks of his destructive Sway.

Mov'd by my Charms, with them your Love may cease,
And as the Fuel sinks, the Flame decrease: 50
Or angry Heav'n may quicker Darts prepare;
And Sickness strike what Time awhile wou'd spare.

---

29 Moment] *1709* Minute *1704*   42 Lustre] Beauty *1704, 1709*   43 Honours]
Lustre *1704, 1709*   44 Shall] *1709* And *1704*   48] *1709* And with indented
Furrows mark his sad extent of Sway. *1704*   52 awhile] a while *1704, 1709*

Then will my Swain His glowing Vows renew;
Then will His throbbing Heart to Mine beat true;
When my own Face deters Me from my Glass;   55
And KNELLER only shows, what CELIA was?

Fantastic FAME may sound her wild Alarms:
Your Country, as You think, may want your Arms.
You may neglect, or quench, or hate the Flame,
Whose Smoak too long obscur'd your rising Name: 60
And quickly cold Indiff'rence will ensue;
When You Love's Joys thro' Honour's Optic view.

Then CELIA's loudest Pray'r will prove too weak,
To this abandon'd Breast to bring You back;
When my lost Lover the tall Ship ascends,   65
With Musick Gay, and Wet with Jovial Friends:
The tender Accents of a Woman's Cry
Will pass unheard, will unregarded die;
When the rough Seaman's louder Shouts prevail;
When fair Occasion shows the springing Gale;   70
And Int'rest guides the Helm; and Honour swells the Sayl.

Some wretched Lines from this neglected Hand,
May find my Hero on the Foreign Strand,
Warm with new Fires, and pleas'd with new Command:
While She who wrote 'em, of all Joy bereft,   75
To the rude Censure of the World is left;
Her mangl'd Fame in barb'rous Pastime lost,
The Coxcomb's Novel, and the Drunkard's Toast.

But nearer Care (O pardon it!) supplies
Sighs to my Breast, and Sorrow to my Eyes.   80
Love, Love himself (the only Friend I have)
May scorn his Triumph, having bound his Slave.
That Tyrant God, that restless Conqueror
May quit his Pleasure, to assert his Pow'r;
Forsake the Provinces that bless his Sway,   85
To vanquish Those which will not yet obey.

53 renew;] renew, *1709* : renew? *1704*   54 true;] true, *1709* : true? *1704*   56 was?
1704, 1709 : was. *1718*   58] *1709* And Custom call you forth to distant Arms. *1704*
66 Jovial] *1709* Jolly *1704*   69 When] *1709* While *1704*   71 swells] fills *1704, 1709*
73 my Hero] my Lover *1709* : you landed *1704*   74 Warm Fill'd *1704, 1709*

Another Nymph with fatal Pow'r may rise,
To damp the sinking Beams of CELIA's Eyes;
With haughty Pride may hear Her Charms confest;
And scorn the ardent Vows that I have blest: 90
You ev'ry Night may sigh for Her in vain;
And rise each Morning to some fresh Disdain:
While CELIA's softest Look may cease to Charm;
And Her Embraces want the Pow'r to warm:
While these fond Arms, thus circling You, may prove   95
More heavy Chains, than Those of hopeless Love.

Just Gods! All other Things their Like produce:
The Vine arises from her Mother's Juice:
When feeble Plants, or tender Flow'rs decay;
They to their Seed their Images convey: 100
Where the old Myrtle her good Influence sheds;
Sprigs of like Leaf erect their Filial Heads:
And when the Parent Rose decays, and dies;
With a resembling Face the Daughter-Buds arise.
That Product only which our Passions bear,   105
Eludes the Planter's miserable Care:
While blooming Love assures us Golden Fruit;
Some inborn Poison taints the secret Root:
Soon fall the Flow'rs of Joy; soon Seeds of Hatred shoot.

Say, Shepherd, say, Are these Reflections true?   110
Or was it but the Woman's Fear, that drew
This cruel Scene, unjust to Love and You?
Will You be only, and for ever Mine?
Shall neither Time, nor Age our Souls disjoin?
From this dear Bosom shall I ne'er be torn?   115
Or You grow Cold, Respectful, and Forsworn?
And can You not for Her You love do more,
Than any Youth for any Nymph before?

The Wedding Night.

WHEN *Jove* lay blest in his *Alcmæna*'s Charms,
Three Nights in one he prest her in his Arms;
The Sun lay set, and conscious Nature strove
To shade her God, and to prolong his Love.
From that auspicious Night *Alcides* came,⁣ 5
What less could rise from *Jove*, and such a Dame?
May this auspicious Night with that compare,
Nor less the Joys, nor less the rising Heir,
He strong as *Jove*, she like *Alcmæna* Fair.

The Third Ode of Anacreon, Translated.

AT dead of Night, when Stars appear,
And strong *Boötes* turns the Bear;
When Mortals sleep their Cares away,
Fatigu'd with Labours of the Day,
Cupid was knocking at my Gate; 5
Who's there? said I: Who knocks so late,
Disturbs my Dream, and breaks my Rest?
O fear not me, a harmless Guest,
He said; but open, open pray;
A foolish Child, I lost my Way, 10
And wander here this Moonless Night,
All Wet and Cold, and wanting Light.
With due Regard his Voice I heard,
Then rose, a ready Lamp prepar'd
And saw a naked Boy below, 15
With Wings, a Quiver, and a Bow:
In haste I ran, unlock'd my Gate,
Secure, and thoughtless of my Fate;
I gave the Child an easie Chair
Against the Fire, and dry'd his Hair; 20

Title] CONSUMMATION. To a FRIEND. *1740*
Title] CUPID TURNED STROLLER. FROM *ANACREON*, ODE III. *1740* 6
said] says *1740* 7 Dream] dreams *1740* 10 I] I've *1740* 11 Moonless] moon-
light *1740* 19 gave] set *1740*

Brought friendly Cups of chearful Wine,
And warm'd his little Hands with mine.
All this did I with kind Intent;
But he, on wanton Mischief bent,
Said, Dearest Friend, this Bow you see;   25
This pretty Bow belongs to me:
Observe, I pray, if all be right,
I fear the Rain has spoil'd it quite:
He drew it then, and straight I found
Within my Breast a secret Wound.   30
This done, the Rogue no longer staid,
But leap'd away, and laughing said,
Kind Host adieu, we now must part,
Safe is my Bow, but sick thy Heart.

To a Lady that design'd going to a Fortune-Teller.

YOU, Madam, may with Safety go,
   Decrees of Destiny to know;
For at your Birth kind Planets reign'd,
And certain Happiness ordain'd:
Such Charms as yours are only giv'n   5
To chosen Favourites of Heav'n.

But such is my uncertain State,
'Tis dangerous to try my Fate:
For I wou'd only know from Art,
The future Motions of your Heart,   10
And what predestinated Doom
Attends my Love for Years to come;
No Secrets else that Mortals learn
My Care deserve, or Life concern;
But this will so important be,   15
I dread to search the dark Decree:
For while the smallest Hope remains,
Faint Joys are mingled with my Pains;

Title] THE FORTUNE-TELLER. TO A YOUNG LADY IN SEARCH OF HER
DESTINY. *1740*

Vain distant Views my Fancy please,
And give some intermitting Ease: 20
But shou'd the Stars too plainly show
That you have doom'd my endless Woe,
No Human Force, nor Art, cou'd bear
The Torment of my wild Despair.

This Secret then I dare not know,   25
And other Truths are useless now.
What matter, if unbless'd in Love,
How long or short my Life will prove?
To gratifie what low Desire,
Shou'd I with needless Haste enquire,   30
How Great, how Wealthy I shall be?
O! what is Wealth or Pow'r to me?
If I am happy, or undone,
It must proceed from you alone.

1704

Prologue, Spoken at Court before the Queen, on Her Majesty's Birth-Day, 1704.

SHINE forth, Ye Planets, with distinguish'd Light,
As when Ye hallow'd first this Happy Night:
Again transmit your Friendly Beams to Earth,
As when BRITANNIA joy'd for ANNA's Birth:
And Thou, propitious Star, whose sacred Pow'r   5
Presided o'er the Monarch's Natal Hour,
Thy Radiant Voyages for ever run,
Yielding to none but CYNTHIA, and the Sun:

27 matter] matters *1740*
   Title: Prologue...Birth-Day,] 1704t, 1709 PROLOGUE. *1704p   1704]* 1703/4 *1704t,*
1709: om. 1704p   5 propitious...sacred] *1709* kind...Tutelary *1704p, 1704t*   6
Presided o'er the] *1709* Guided the Future *1704p, 1704t*   8 Yielding...but] *1709*
Only less Bless'd than *1704p, 1704t*

With Thy fair Aspect still illustrate Heav'n:
Kindly preserve what Thou hast greatly giv'n: 10
Thy Influence for thy ANNA We implore:
Prolong One Life; and BRITAIN asks no more.
For Virtue can no ampler Power express,
Than to be Great in War, and Good in Peace:
For Thought no higher Wish of Bliss can frame,   15
Than to enjoy that Virtue STILL THE SAME.
Entire and sure the Monarch's Rule must prove,
Who founds Her Greatness on Her Subjects Love;
Who does our Homage for our Good require;
And Orders that which We should first Desire: 20
Our vanquish'd Wills that pleasing Force obey:
Her Goodness takes our Liberty away:
And haughty BRITAIN yields to Arbitrary Sway.

    Let the young AUSTRIAN then Her Terrors bear,
Great as He is, Her Delegate in War: 25
Let Him in Thunder speak to both his SPAINS,
That in these Dreadful Isles a Woman Reigns.
While the Bright Queen does on Her Subjects show'r
The gentle Blessings of Her softer Pow'r;
Gives sacred Morals to a vicious Age,   30
To Temples Zeal, and Manners to the Stage;
Bids the chaste Muse without a Blush appear,
And Wit be that which Heav'n and She may hear.

    MINERVA thus to PERSEUS lent Her Shield;
Secure of Conquest, sent Him to the Field: 35
The Hero acted what the Queen ordain'd:
So was His Fame compleat, and ANDROMEDE unchain'd.

    Mean time amidst Her Native Temples sate
The Goddess, studious of Her GRECIAN's Fate;

13] *1709* For what can Virtue more to Man express, *1704p*, *1704t*   14 Peace:] *1709*
Peace? *1704p*, *1704t*   15] *1709* What further Thought of Blessing can we frame, *1704p*,
1704t   16 to... Virtue... SAME.] *1709* that That Virtue shou'd be... Same? *1704p*,
1704t   28 While] Whilst *1704p*, *1704t*, *1709*   30 sacred] *1709* Glorious *1704p*, *1704t*
36–39] *1709*
                Told him how Barb'rous Rage should be restrain'd;
                And bid him Execute what she Ordain'd.
                Mean time the Deity in Temples sat,
                Fond of Her Native *Grecians* Future Fate; *1704p*, *1704t*

Taught 'em in Laws and Letters to excell,   40
In Acting justly, and in Writing well.
Thus whilst She did Her various Pow'r dispose,
The World was freed from Tyrants, Wars, and Woes:
Virtue was taught in Verse, and ATHENS' Glory rose.

An Ode. Inscribed to the Memory of
the Honble Col. George Villiers,

Drowned in the River Piava, in the
Country of Friuli. 1703.

In Imitation of Horace, Ode 28. Lib. 1.

Te Maris & Terræ numeroque carentis arenæ
Mensorem cohibent, Archyta, &c.

SAY, dearest VILLIERS, poor departed Friend,
(Since fleeting Life thus suddenly must end)
Say, what did all thy busie Hopes avail,
That anxious Thou from Pole to Pole didst sail;
E'er on thy Chin the springing Beard began   5
To spread a doubtful Down, and promise Man?
What profited thy Thoughts, and Toils, and Cares,
In Vigour more confirm'd, and riper Years?
To wake e'er Morning-dawn to loud Alarms,
And march 'till close of Night in heavy Arms?   10
To scorn the Summer Suns and Winter Snows,
And search thro' ev'ry Clime thy Country's Foes?
That Thou might'st Fortune to thy Side ingage;
That gentle Peace might quell BELLONA's Rage;
And ANNA's Bounty crown Her Soldier's hoary Age?   15

In vain We think that free-will'd Man has Pow'r
To hasten or protract th'appointed Hour.
Our Term of Life depends not on our Deed:
Before our Birth our Funeral was decreed.

---

42 She did Her various] *1709* the Goddess did Her *1704p, 1704t*   44 ATHENS' Glory]
1709 Athens *1704p, 1704t*
    Title: *1703.] om. 1709*   17 th'appointed] the pointed *1709*

Nor aw'd by Foresight, nor mis-led by Chance, 20
Imperious Death directs His Ebon Lance;
Peoples great HENRY's Tombs, and leads up HOLBEN's Dance.

Alike must ev'ry State, and ev'ry Age
Sustain the universal Tyrant's Rage:
For neither WILLIAM's Pow'r, nor MARY's Charms 25
Could or repel, or pacifie his Arms:
Young CHURCHILL fell, as Life began to bloom:
And BRADFORD's trembling Age expects the Tomb.
Wisdom and Eloquence in vain would plead
One Moment's Respite for the learned Head: 30
Judges of Writings and of Men have dy'd;
MECÆNAS, SACKVILLE, SOCRATES, and HYDE:
And in their various Turns the Sons must tread
Those gloomy Journeys, which their Sires have led.

The ancient Sage, who did so long maintain, 35
That Bodies die, but Souls return again,
With all the Births and Deaths He had in Store,
Went out PYTHAGORAS, and came no more.
And modern AS——L, whose capricious Thought
Is yet with Stores of wilder Notion fraught, 40
Too soon convinc'd, shall yield that fleeting Breath,
Which play'd so idly with the Darts of Death.

Some from the stranded Vessel force their Way;
Fearful of Fate, they meet it in the Sea:
Some who escape the Fury of the Wave, 45
Sicken on Earth, and sink into a Grave:
In Journeys or at home, in War or Peace,
By Hardships Many, Many fall by Ease.
Each changing Season does it's Poison bring;
Rheums chill the Winter, Agues blast the Spring: 50
Wet, Dry, Cold, Hot, at the appointed Hour,
All act subservient to the Tyrant's Pow'r:
And when obedient Nature knows His Will,
A Fly, a Grape-stone, or a Hair can kill.

21 His] the *1709*

For restless PROSERPINE for ever treads 55
In Paths unseen, o'er our devoted Heads;
And on the spacious Land, and liquid Main
Spreads slow Disease, or darts afflictive Pain:
Variety of Deaths confirms her endless Reign.

On curst PIAVA's Banks the Goddess stood, 60
Show'd her dire Warrant to the rising Flood;
When What I long must love, and long must mourn,
With fatal Speed was urging his Return;
In his dear Country to disperse his Care,
And arm himself by Rest for future War; 65
To chide his anxious Friends officious Fears,
And promise to their Joys his elder Years.

Oh! destin'd Head; and oh! severe Decree;
Nor native Country Thou, nor Friend shalt see;
Nor War hast thou to wage, nor Year to come: 70
Impending Death is thine, and instant Doom.

Hark! the imperious Goddess is obey'd:
Winds murmur; Snows descend; and Waters spread:
Oh! Kinsman, Friend,—Oh! vain are all the Cries
Of human Voice; strong Destiny replies: 75
Weep You on Earth; for He shall sleep below:
Thence None return; and thither All must go.

Whoe'er Thou art, whom Choice or Business leads
To this sad River, or the neighb'ring Meads;
If Thou may'st happen on the dreary Shoars 80
To find the Object which This Verse deplores;
Cleanse the pale Corps with a religious Hand
From the polluting Weed and common Sand;
Lay the dead Hero graceful in a Grave;
(The only Honour He can now receive) 85
And fragrant Mould upon his Body throw;
And plant the Warrior Lawrel o'er his Brow:
Light lye the Earth; and flourish green the Bough.

So may just Heav'n secure thy future Life
From foreign Dangers, and domestic Strife: 90

And when th'Infernal Judges dismal Pow'r
From the dark Urn shall throw Thy destin'd Hour;
When yielding to the Sentence, breathless Thou
And pale shalt lye, as what Thou buriest now;
May some kind Friend the piteous Object see,   95
And equal Rites perform, to That which once was Thee.

A Letter to Monsieur Boileau Despreaux; Occasion'd by the Victory at Blenheim, 1704.

—*Cupidum, Pater optime, vires*
Deficiunt: neque enim Quivis horrentia Pilis
Agmina, nec Fractâ pereuntes cuspide Gallos—
Hor. Sat. 1. L. 2.

SINCE hir'd for Life, thy Servile Muse must sing
Successive Conquests, and a glorious King;
Must of a Man Immortal vainly boast;
And bring him Lawrels, whatsoe'er they cost:
What Turn wilt Thou employ, what Colours lay   5
On the Event of that Superior Day,
In which one ENGLISH Subject's prosp'rous Hand
(So JOVE did will; so ANNA did command:)
Broke the proud Column of thy Master's Praise,
Which sixty Winters had conspir'd to raise?   10

From the lost Field a hundred Standards brought
Must be the Work of Chance, and Fortune's Fault:
BAVARIA's Stars must be accus'd, which shone,
That fatal Day the mighty Work was done,
With Rays oblique upon the GALLIC Sun.   } 15
Some DÆMON envying FRANCE mis-led the Fight:
And MARS mistook, tho' LOUIS order'd right.

Title: Boileau Despreaux] *Boileau Depreaux 1704: Boileau 1709   Blenheim, 1704.*] *1709*
BLENHEIM. *1704*   1 Servile] *1709* Servant *1704*   2 glorious] *1709* happy *1704*
3 vainly] *1709* loudly *1704*   12 be...Fortune's] *1709, W* certainly be Fortune's lasting
1704   15 With] *1709* And darted *1704*   16] *In 1704, preceded by:* Or shall our
Muse essay a higher Flight?   16 DÆMON...mis-led] *1709* erring Deities disturb'd *1704*
17 MARS] *1709* Fate *1704*

When thy young Muse invok'd the tuneful Nine,
To say how LOUIS did not pass the RHINE,
What Work had We with WAGENINGHEN, ARNHEIM, 20
Places that could not be reduc'd to Rhime?
And tho' the Poet made his last Efforts,
WURTS—who could mention in Heroic—WURTS?
But, tell me, hast thou reason to complain
Of the rough Triumphs of the last Campaign? 25
The DANUBE rescu'd, and the Empire sav'd,
Say, is the Majesty of Verse retriev'd?
And would it prejudice thy softer vein,
To sing the Princes, LOUIS and EUGENE?
Is it too hard in happy Verse to place 30
The VANS and VANDERS of the RHINE and MAES?
Her Warriors ANNA sends from TWEED and THAMES,
That FRANCE may fall by more harmonious Names.
Can'st thou not HAMILTON or LUMLY bear?
Would INGOLDSBY or PALMES offend thy Ear? 35
And is there not a Sound in MARLBRÔ's Name,
Which Thou and all thy Brethren ought to claim,
Sacred to Verse, and sure of endless Fame?

 CUTTS is in Meeter something harsh to read:
Place me the Valiant GOURAM in his stead: 40
Let the Intention make the Number good:
Let generous SYLVIUS speak for honest WOOD.
And tho' rough CHURCHILL scarce in Verse will stand,
So as to have one Rhime at his Command;
With Ease the Bard reciting BLENHEIM's Plain, 45
May close the Verse, rememb'ring but the DANE.

 I grant, old Friend, old Foe (for such We are
Alternate, as the Chance of Peace and War)

29 and] or *1704, 1709* 34–36] *1709*
    Hamilton, Lumley, Palmes, or Ingoldsby,
    May tolerably well with Verse agree.
    And MALBRÔ, Poet, MALBRÔ has a Name *1704*
37 ought to claim] *1709* may proclaim *1704* 38 Sacred to Verse] *1709* Elected to
immortal Lays *1704* 42 Let...speak] *1709* And...stand *1704* 43–46] *1709*
    Churchil, if that rough Sound offend the Strain,
    Be true to Glorious Worth, and sing the *Dane*. *1704*

That we Poetic Folks, who must restrain
Our measur'd Sayings in an equal Chain,   50
Have Troubles utterly unknown to Those,
Who let their Fancy loose in rambling Prose.

 For Instance now, how hard it is for Me
To make my Matter and my Verse agree?
In one great Day on HOCHSTET'*s fatal Plain*   55
FRENCH *and* BAVARIANS *twenty thousand slain;*
Push'd thro' the DANUBE *to the Shoars of* STYX
Squadrons eighteen, Battalions twenty six:
Officers Captive made and private Men,
Of these twelve hundred, of those thousands ten.   60
Tents, Ammunition, Colours, Carriages,
Cannons, and Kettle-Drums—sweet Numbers these.
But is it thus You ENGLISH Bards compose?
With RUNICK Lays thus tag insipid Prose?
And when you should your Heroes Deeds rehearse,   65
Give us a Commissary's List in Verse?

 Why Faith, DEPREAUX, there's Sense in what You say:
I told You where my Difficulty lay:
So vast, so numerous were great BLENHEIM's Spoils,
They scorn the Bounds of Verse, and mock the Muse's Toils.   70
To make the rough Recital aptly chime,
Or bring the Sum of GALLIA's Loss to Rhime,
'Tis mighty hard: What Poet would essay
To count the Streamers of my Lord Mayor's Day?
To number all the several Dishes drest   75
By honest LAMB, last Coronation Feast?
Or make Arithmetic and Epic meet;
And NEWTON's Thoughts in DRYDEN's Stile repeat?

 O Poet, had it been APOLLO's Will,
That I had shar'd a Portion of thy Skill;   80

63–66] *1709*
    AVE APOLLO!—Sir—one Moment's Ease.
    Tell me, is this to reckon or rehearse?
    A Commissary's List, or Poet's Verse? *1704*
69–70] *1709 om. 1704* 71 To ... aptly chime] *1709* He that can ... chime *1704* 72
GALLIA's] *Lewis' 1704, 1709* 73–76] *1709 om. 1704* 77 Or] *1709* May *1704*
78 Thoughts] *1709* Books *1704* 79 Poet] *1709* BOILEAU *1704*

Had this poor Breast receiv'd the Heav'nly Beam;
Or could I hope my Verse might reach my Theam;
Yet, BOILEAU, yet the lab'ring Muse should strive,
Beneath the Shades of MARLBRÔ's Wreaths to live:
Should call aspiring Gods to bless her Choice;   85
And to their Fav'rites Strain exalt her Voice,
Arms and a Queen to Sing; Who, Great and Good,
From peaceful THAMES to DANUBE's wond'ring Flood
Sent forth the Terror of her high Commands,
To save the Nations from invading Hands,   90
To prop fair Liberty's declining Cause,
And fix the jarring World with equal Laws.

    The Queen should sit in WINDSOR's sacred Grove,
Attended by the Gods of War and Love:
Both should with equal Zeal Her Smiles implore,   95
To fix Her Joys, or to extend Her Pow'r.

    Sudden, the NYMPHS and TRITONS should appear;
And as great ANNA's Smiles dispel their Fear,
With active Dance should Her Observance claim;
With Vocal Shell should sound Her happy Name.   100
Their Master THAMES should leave the neighb'ring Shoar,
By his strong Anchor known, and Silver Oar;
Should lay his Ensigns at his Sov'raign's Feet,
And Audience mild with humble Grace intreat.

    To Her his dear Defence he should complain,   105
That whilst He blesses Her indulgent Reign;
Whilst furthest Seas are by his Fleets survey'd,
And on his happy Banks each INDIA laid;

---

82 Or...reach] *1709* And were my Numbers equal to *1704*   83–84] *1709 om. 1704*
85–86] *1709*
               To noblest Strains I'd raise my serious Voice,
               And calling ev'ry Muse to bless my Choice, *1704*

87 to] *1709* I'd *1704*   91 prop...declining] *1709* vindicate a sinking Empire's *1704*
93 The...sit] *1709* I'd place the QUEEN *1704*   96 To...or] *1709, W* These prompt
to...those *1704*   98 great...dispel] *1709* Her Looks may dissipate *1704*   99–100]
1709 With active Dance shou'd please Her Eye, with vocal Shells Her Ear. *1704*   105
To...he] *1709* With Pious Speech the River *1704*   106 Her indulgent] *1709*
ANNA's careful *1704*

His Breth'ren MAES, and WAAL, and RHINE, and SAAR
Feel the hard Burthen of oppressive War: 110
That DANUBE scarce retains his rightful Course
Against two Rebel Armies neighb'ring Force:
And All must weep sad Captives to the SEIN,
Unless unchain'd and freed by BRITAIN's Queen.

The valiant Sov'reign calls Her Gen'ral forth;   115
Neither recites Her Bounty, nor His Worth:
She tells Him, He must EUROPE's Fate redeem,
And by That Labour merit Her Esteem:
She bids Him wait Her to the Sacred Hall;
Shows Him Prince EDWARD, and the conquer'd GAUL;   120
Fixing the bloody Cross upon His Breast,
Says, He must Dye, or succour the Distress'd:
Placing the Saint an Emblem by His Side,
She tells Him, Virtue arm'd must conquer lawless Pride.

The Hero bows obedient, and retires: 125
The Queen's Commands exalt the Warrior's Fires.
His Steps are to the silent Woods inclin'd,
The great Design revolving in his Mind:
When to his Sight a Heav'nly Form appears:
Her Hand a Palm, her Head a Lawrel wears.   130

Me, She begins, the fairest Child of JOVE,
Below for ever sought, and bless'd above;
Me, the bright Source of Wealth, and Power, and Fame;
(Nor need I say, VICTORIA is my Name:)
Me the great Father down to Thee has sent: 135
He bids Me wait at Thy distinguish'd Tent,
To execute what ANNA's Wish would have:
Her Subject Thou, I only am Her Slave.

Dare then; Thou much belov'd by smiling Fate:
For ANNA's Sake, and in Her Name, be Great: 140
Go forth, and be to distant Nations known,
My future Fav'rite, and My darling Son.

---

116 Neither recites...nor His] *1709* Nor names...nor proclaims his *1704*   132] *1709*
Courted by Men below, and bless'd by Gods above, *1704*   140] *1709* 'Tis *ANNA*'s
Glory, and Thou shalt be Great: *1704*

At SCHELLENBERG I'll manifest sustain
Thy glorious Cause; and spread my Wings again,
Conspicuous o'er Thy Helm, in BLENHEIM's Plain.   } 145

The Goddess said, nor would admit Reply;
But cut the liquid Air, and gain'd the Sky.

His high Commission is thro' BRITAIN known:
And thronging Armies to His Standard run.
He marches thoughtful; and He speedy sails: 150
(Bless Him, ye Seas! and prosper Him, ye Gales!)
BELGIA receives Him welcome to her Shores;
And WILLIAM's Death with lessen'd Grief deplores.
His Presence only must retrieve That Loss:
MARLBRÔ to Her must be what WILLIAM was.   155
So when great ATLAS, from these low Aboads
Recall'd, was gather'd to his Kindred-Gods;
ALCIDES respited by prudent Fate,
Sustain'd the Ball, nor droop'd beneath the Weight.

Secret and Swift behold the Chief advance;   160
Sees half the Empire join'd, and Friend to FRANCE:
The BRITISH General dooms the Fight; His Sword
Dreadful He draws: The Captains wait the Word.
ANNE and St. GEORGE, the charging Hero cries:
Shrill Echo from the neighb'ring Wood replies   165
ANNE and St. GEORGE.—At That auspicious Sign
The Standards move; the adverse Armies join.
Of Eight great Hours, Time measures out the Sands;
And EUROPE's Fate in doubtful Balance stands:
The Ninth, VICTORIA comes:—o'er MARLBRÔ's Head   } 170
Confess'd She sits; the Hostile Troops recede:—
Triumphs the GODDESS, from her Promise freed.

143–5] *1709*
       At *Schellenberg* I'll visit Thee again,
         And sit propitious on Thy Helm in *Blenheim*'s glorious Plain. *1704*
147 the Sky] *1709* her native Sky *1704*   148 is thro' BRITAIN] *1709* thro' the Land is
1704   149 Armies] *1709* Countries *1704*   152 Shores;] *1709, W* Coast, *1704*
153] *1709, W* And almost ceases to weep WILLIAM lost. *1704*   154–9] *1709, W*
       Since that Great *Hercules* resign'd to Fate,
       The *Atlas* This, who must support her State. *1704*
161] *1709* He sees half GERMANY combin'd with FRANCE; *1704*   162 The BRITISH...
His] The *English*... His *1709* : Combin'd in vain—He draws the fatal *1704*   163] *1709*
The Troops obedient wait the Master Word: *1704*   164 Hero] *1709* Gen'ral *1704*
167 adverse] *1709* threat'ning *1704*

    The Eagle, by the BRITISH Lion's Might
Unchain'd and Free, directs her upward Flight:
Nor did She e'er with stronger Pinions soar   175
From TYBER's Banks, than now from DANUBE's Shoar.

    Fir'd with the Thoughts which these Ideas raise,
And great Ambition of my Country's Praise;
The ENGLISH Muse should like the MANTUAN rise,
Scornful of Earth and Clouds, should reach the Skies,   180
With Wonder (tho' with Envy still) pursu'd by human Eyes.

    But We must change the Style.—Just now I said,
I ne'er was Master of the tuneful Trade.
Or the small Genius which my Youth could boast,
In Prose and Business lies extinct and lost.   185
Bless'd, if I may some younger Muse excite;
Point out the Game, and animate the Flight.
That from *Marseilles* to *Calais* FRANCE may know,
As We have Conqu'rors, We have Poets too;
And either Laurel does in BRITAIN grow.   190
That, tho' amongst our selves, with too much Heat,
We sometimes wrangle, when We should debate;
(A consequential Ill which Freedom draws;
A bad Effect, but from a Noble Cause:)
We can with universal Zeal advance,   195
To curb the faithless Arrogance of FRANCE.
Nor ever shall BRITANNIA's Sons refuse
To answer to thy Master, or thy Muse;
Nor want just Subject for victorious Strains,
While MARLBRÔ's Arm Eternal Laurel gains;   200
And where old SPENCER sung, a new ELISA reigns.

173–6] *1709*
     The *Roman* Eagle on the *Danube* Shoars
     Hears how the *British* Lion Victor roars,
     She claps her joyful Wings, and high to *Julian* Glory soars. *1704*
179 ENGLISH] *British 1704, 1709*   182 But We must] *1709* But, Goddess, *1704*   189
Conqu'rors,] *1709* Victors *1704*   190] *1709 om. 1704*   197–8] *1709*
     Our Muses as our Armies can agree,
     To humble LEWIS, and reply to Thee. *1704*
199 Nor...victorious] *1709* Nor shall we...our *1704*   200 While] *1709* Whilst *1704*
201 where old] *1709* in the Land where *1704*

An English Padlock.

MISS DANAE, when Fair and Young
(As HORACE has divinely sung)
Could not be kept from JOVE's Embrace
By Doors of Steel, and Walls of Brass.
The Reason of the Thing is clear;   5
Would JOVE the naked Truth aver:
CUPID was with Him of the Party;
And show'd himself sincere and hearty:
For, give That Whipster but his Errand;
He takes my Lord Chief Justice' Warrant: 10
Dauntless as Death away He walks;
Breaks the Doors open; snaps the Locks;
Searches the Parlour, Chamber, Study;
Nor stops, 'till He has CULPRIT's Body.

Since This has been Authentick Truth,   15
By Age deliver'd down to Youth;
Tell us, mistaken Husband, tell us,
Why so Mysterious, why so Jealous?
Does the Restraint, the Bolt, the Bar
Make Us less Curious, Her less Fair?   20
The Spy, which does this Treasure keep,
Does She ne'er say her Pray'rs, nor sleep?
Does She to no Excess incline?
Does She fly Musick, Mirth, and Wine?
Or have not Gold and Flatt'ry Pow'r,   25
To purchase One unguarded Hour?

Your Care does further yet extend:
That Spy is guarded by your Friend.—
But has This Friend nor Eye, nor Heart?
May He not feel the cruel Dart,   30
Which, soon or late, all Mortals feel?
May He not, with too tender Zeal,

Title: An] *1705t, 1709* The *1705dp*   1 MISS DANAE] *1705t, 1709* THE forward Dame
1705dp   8 show'd himself sincere] *1709* acted vigorous *1705dp, 1705t*   9 For, give]
1705t, 1709 Forgive *1705dp*   20 Curious] *1705t, 1709* Owners *1705dp*   21 which...
Treasure] who does the Fair One *1705dp*: who...Treasure *1705t, 1709*   29 This] that
1705dp, 1705t, 1709   nor Eye] *1705t, 1709* no Eye *1705dp*

Give the Fair Pris'ner Cause to see,
How much He wishes, She were free?
May He not craftily infer   35
The Rules of Friendship too severe,
Which chain Him to a hated Trust;
Which make Him Wretched, to be Just?
And may not She, this Darling She,
 Youthful and healthy, Flesh and Blood,   } 40
Easie with Him, ill-us'd by Thee,
 Allow this Logic to be good?

 Sir, Will your Questions never end?
I trust to neither Spy nor Friend.
In short, I keep Her from the Sight   45
Of ev'ry Human Face.—She'll write.—
From Pen and Paper She's debarr'd.—
Has She a Bodkin and a Card?
She'll prick her Mind.—She will, You say:
But how shall She That Mind convey?   50
I keep Her in one Room: I lock it:
The Key (look here) is in this Pocket.
The Key-hole, is That left? Most certain.
She'll thrust her Letter thro'—Sir MARTIN.

 Dear angry Friend, what must be done?   55
Is there no Way?—There is but One.
Send Her abroad; and let Her see,
That all this mingled Mass, which She
Being forbidden longs to know,
Is a dull Farce, an empty Show,   60
Powder, and Pocket-Glass, and Beau;
A Staple of Romance and Lies,
False Tears, and real Perjuries:
Where Sighs and Looks are bought and sold;
And Love is made but to be told: 65
Where the fat Bawd, and lavish Heir
The Spoils of ruin'd Beauty share:

34 He] *1705t, 1709* she *1705dp* 51–54] *1709*
  I lock her fast, I keep the Key;
  The Key-hole,—Fool, take that away: *1705dp, 1705t*
55 must] *1705t, 1709* may *1705dp* 57 abroad] *1705t, 1709* aboard *1705dp* 62 Stayl]e
1705t, 1709 Steeple *1705dp* 63 Tears] *1705t, 1709* Fears *1705dp*

And Youth seduc'd from Friends and Fame,
Must give up Age to Want and Shame.
Let Her behold the Frantick Scene,   70
The Women wretched, false the Men:
And when, these certain Ills to shun,
She would to Thy Embraces run;
Receive Her with extended Arms:
Seem more delighted with her Charms: 75
Wait on Her to the Park and Play:
Put on good Humour; make Her gay:
Be to her Virtues very kind:
Be to her Faults a little blind:
Let all her Ways be unconfin'd: 80
And clap your PADLOCK—on her Mind.

1706

Pallas and Venus. An Epigram.

THE TROJAN Swain had judg'd the great Dispute;
And Beauty's Pow'r obtain'd the Golden Fruit;
When VENUS, loose in all Her naked Charms,
Met JOVE's great Daughter clad in shining Arms.
The wanton Goddess view'd the Warlike Maid   5
From Head to Foot, and Tauntingly She said:

Yield, Sister; Rival, yield: Naked, You see,
I vanquish: Guess how Potent I should be;
If to the Field I came in Armour drest;
Dreadful, like Thine, my Shield, and terrible my Crest.   10

The Warrior Goddess with Disdain reply'd;
Thy Folly, Child, is equal to thy Pride:

72 these certain] *1705t, 1709* those monst'rous *1705dp*   73 would] *1705t, 1709* should
1705dp
    5 The wanton Goddess] *1709* From Head to Foot she *1706*   6–8] *1709*
                      And tauntingly the wanton Goddess said;
                      Alas, since naked I cou'd vanquish Thee,
                      How more successful, *Pallas,* shall I be, *1706*
9 If...came] *1709* When...come *1706*   10 Crest.] Crest? *1706, 1709*   11 Dis-
dain] *1709* a Smile *1706*

Let a brave Enemy for once advise,
And VENUS (if 'tis possible) be Wise.
Thou to be strong must put off every Dress: 15
Thy only Armour is thy Nakedness:
And more than once, (or Thou art much bely'd)
By MARS himself That Armour has been try'd.

An Ode, Humbly Inscrib'd to the Queen. On the Glorious Success of Her Majesty's Arms, 1706.

Written in Imitation of Spenser's Stile.

Te non paventis funera Galliæ,
Duræque tellus audit Iberiæ:
Te cæde gaudentes Sicambri
Compositis venerantur Armis. Hor.

THE PREFACE.

*W*HEN *I first thought of Writing upon this Occasion, I found the* Ideas *so great and numerous, that I judg'd them more proper for the Warmth of an* Ode, *than for any other sort of Poetry: I therefore set* HORACE *before Me for a Pattern, and particularly his famous Ode, the Fourth of the Fourth Book,*

Qualem ministrum fulminis Alitem, *&c.*   5

which He wrote in Praise of DRUSUS *after his Expedition into* GERMANY, *and of* AUGUSTUS *upon his happy Choice of That General. And in the following Poem, tho' I have endeavor'd to Imitate all the great Strokes of that* Ode, *I have taken the Liberty to go off from it, and to add variously, as the Subject and my own Imagination carry'd Me. As to the Style, the Choice I made of* 10 *following the* Ode *in Latin, determin'd Me in* English *to the Stanza; and herein it was impossible not to have a Mind to follow* Our great Countryman SPENSER; *which I have done (as well at least as I could) in the Manner of my Expression, and the Turn of my Number: Having only added one Verse to his*

15] *1709* To be more Strong abandon ev'ry Dress; *1706*
   Title: the Glorious . . . Arms, 1706.] 1709 THE Late Glorious . . . ARMS. *1706*   6
wrote] Writ 1706, 1709   8 endeavor'd to Imitate] 1709 Imitated 1706   9 to add] add 1706, 1709   the Subject] 1709 my Subject 1706   10 my own] 1709 om. 1706   Style] 1709 Matter of Stile 1706   12 follow] 1709 Imitate 1706   14 Number] Numbers 1706, 1709   added . . . to] 1709 chang'd . . . in 1706

Stanza, which I thought made the Number more Harmonious; and avoided such 15
of his Words, as I found too obsolete. I have however retain'd some few of them,
to make the Colouring look more like SPENSER'*s.* Behest, Command; Band,
Army; Prowess, *Strength;* I weet, *I know;* I ween, *I think;* whilom, *hereto-*
fore; and Two or Three more of that Kind, which I hope the Ladies *will pardon*
me, and not judge my MUSE *less handsome, though for once she appears in a* 20
Farthingal. I have also, in SPENSER'*s Manner, used* Cæsar *for the Emperor,*
Boya *for* Bavaria, Bavar *for that Prince,* Ister *for* Danube, Iberia *for*
Spain, *&c.*
   That Noble Part of the Ode *which I just now mention'd,*

   Gens, quæ cremato Fortis ab *Ilio*   25
   Jactata *Tuscis* æquoribus, *&c.*

where HORACE *praises the* Romans, *as being Descended from* ÆNEAS, *I have*
turn'd to the Honor of the BRITISH *Nation, descended from* BRUTE, *likewise a*
TROJAN. *That this* BRUTE, *Fourth or Fifth from* ÆNEAS, *settled in* ENG-
LAND, *and built* LONDON, *which he call'd* Troja Nova, *or* Troynovante, *is* 30
a Story which (I think) owes it's Original if not to GEOFFRY *of* Monmouth,
at least to the Monkish *Writers; yet is not rejected by Our great* CAMDEN,
and is told by MILTON, *as if (at least) He was pleas'd with it; though possibly*
He does not believe it: However it carries a Poetical Authority, which is sufficient
for our Purpose. It is as certain that BRUTE *came into* ENGLAND, *as that* 35
ÆNEAS *went into* ITALY; *and upon the Supposition of these Facts,* VIRGIL
wrote the best Poem that the World ever read, and SPENSER *paid Queen*
ELIZABETH *the greatest Compliment.*
   I need not obviate one piece of Criticism, that I bring my Hero

   From burning *Troy,* and *Xanthus* red with Blood: 40

whereas He was not born, when That City was destroy'd. VIRGIL, *in the Case*
of His own ÆNEAS *relating to* DIDO, *will stand as a sufficient Proof, that a*
Man in his Poetical Capacity is not accountable for a little Fault in Chronology.
   My Two Great Examples, HORACE *and* SPENSER, *in many Things resemble*
each other: Both have a Height of Imagination, and a Majesty of Expression in 45
describing the Sublime; *and Both know to temper those Talents, and sweeten the*
Description, so as to make it Lovely as well as Pompous: Both have equally That

15 *which . . . Harmonious*] *1709 om. 1706*   15–16 *such . . . obsolete*] *1709 his Obsolete*
Words 1706   24 *which*] *om. 1706, 1709*   31 *if not*] *om. 1706, 1709*   32 *at least to*] *and*
1706, 1709   32–33 *yet is . . .* MILTON] *yet Our Great* Cambden *does not reject it, and* Milton
tells it 1706, 1709   34 *However it carries*] *It carries however 1706, 1709*   37 *wrote . . .*
Poem] *writ one of the best Poems 1706 : writ . . . Poem 1709*   38 *the greatest Compliment*]
1709 one of the greatest Compliments 1706   39–43] *1709 om. 1706*   44 *in*] *1709 do,*
I think, in 1706

agreeable Manner of mixing Morality with their Story, and That Curiosa
Felicitas *in the Choice of their Diction, which every Writer aims at, and so very
few have reach'd: Both are particularly Fine in their Images, and Knowing in* 50
*their Numbers. Leaving therefore our Two Masters to the Consideration and
Study of Those, who design to Excel in Poetry, I only beg Leave to add, That it
is long since I have (or at least ought to have) quitted* PARNASSUS, *and all the
flow'ry Roads on that Side the Country; tho' I thought my self indispensably
obliged, upon the present Occasion, to take a little Journey into Those Parts.*   55

An Ode, Humbly Inscrib'd to the Queen.

I.

W HEN Great AUGUSTUS govern'd Antient ROME,
  And sent his Conqu'ring Bands to Foreign Wars;
Abroad when Dreaded, and Belov'd at Home,
He saw his Fame encreasing with his Years;
HORACE, Great Bard (so Fate ordain'd) arose;   5
And Bold, as were his Countrymen in Fight,
Snatch'd their fair Actions from degrading Prose,
And set their Battels in Eternal Light:
High as their Trumpets Tune His Lyre he strung;
And with his Prince's Arms He moraliz'd his Song.   10

II.

   When bright ELIZA rul'd BRITANNIA's State,
Widely distributing Her high Commands;
And boldly Wise, and fortunately Great,
Freed the glad Nations from Tyrannick Bands;
An equal Genius was in SPENSER found: 15
To the high Theme He match'd his Noble Lays:
He travell'd ENGLAND o'er on Fairy Ground,
In Mystic Notes to Sing his Monarch's Praise:
Reciting wond'rous Truths in pleasing Dreams,
He deck'd ELIZA's Head with GLORIANA's Beams.   20

51 *Leaving therefore*] 1709 *So leaving* 1706   52 *add, That*] *add, (as to my own Part)
That* 1706, 1709   53 *at least*] 1709 om. 1706   54 *indispensably*] 1709 om. 1706
55 *Parts.*] *Parts: And hereupon I declare, that if the* Reader *will be good enough to Pardon me
this Excursion, I will neither trouble him with Poem or Preface any more, 'till my Lord Duke
of* Marlborough *gets another Victory greater than those of* Blenheim *and* Ramillies. 1706:
Parts: Now if the Reader ... *Excursion, I declare I will not trouble him again in this kind, 'till ...*
Marlborough *gains ...* Ramillies. 1709
  2 *Conqu'ring Bands*] *Conqu'ring Troops* 1706: *Legions forth* 1709   19 *Reciting*]
1709 *And telling* 1706

III.

But, Greatest ANNA! while Thy Arms pursue
Paths of Renown, and climb Ascents of Fame,
Which nor AUGUSTUS, nor ELIZA knew;
What Poet shall be found to sing Thy Name?
What Numbers shall record, what Tongue shall say   25
Thy Wars on Land, Thy Triumphs on the Main?
O Fairest Model of Imperial Sway!
What Equal Pen shall write Thy wond'rous Reign?
Who shall Attempts and Feats of Arms rehearse,
Not yet by Story told, nor parallel'd by Verse?   30

IV.

Me all too mean for such a Task I weet:
Yet if the Sovereign Lady deigns to Smile,
I'll follow HORACE with impetuous Heat,
And cloath the Verse in SPENSER's Native Style.
By these Examples rightly taught to sing,   35
And smit with Pleasure of my Country's Praise,
Stretching the Plumes of an uncommon Wing,
High as OLYMPUS I my Flight will raise:
And latest Times shall in my Numbers read
ANNA's Immortal Fame, and MARLBRÔ's hardy Deed.   40

V.

As the strong Eagle in the silent Wood,
Mindless of warlike Rage, and hostile Care,
Plays round the rocky Cliff, or crystal Flood;
'Till by JOVE's high Behests call'd out to War,
And charg'd with Thunder of his angry King,   45
His Bosom with the vengeful Message glows:
Upward the Noble Bird directs his Wing;
And tow'ring round his Master's Earth-born Foes,
Swift He collects his fatal Stock of Ire;
Lifts his fierce Talon high, and darts the forked Fire.   50

29 Feats of Arms] *1709* Victories *1706*   30 Not...parallel'd] *1709* By Story yet untold,
unparallell'd *1706*   32 deigns] *1706* daign'd *1709*   33 I'll] *1706* I'd *1709*   38
will] would *1706, 1709*   39 shall] should *1706, 1709*   42] *1709* Nor seeking Battel,
nor intent on Harms, *1706*   44 War] *1709* Arms *1706*

VI.

Sedate and calm thus Victor MARLBRÔ sate,
Shaded with Laurels, in his Native Land;
'Till ANNA calls Him from his soft Retreat,
And gives Her Second Thunder to his Hand.
Then leaving sweet Repose, and gentle Ease,   55
With ardent Speed He seeks the distant Foe:
Marching o'er Hills and Vales, o'er Rocks and Seas,
He meditates, and strikes the wond'rous Blow.
Our Thought flies slower than Our General's Fame:
Grasps He the Bolt? (We ask) when He has hurl'd the Flame. 60

VII.

When fierce BAVAR on JUDOIGN's spacious Plain
Did from afar the BRITISH Chief behold;
Betwixt Despair, and Rage, and Hope, and Pain,
Something within his warring Bosom roll'd:
He views that Fav'rite of Indulgent Fame,   65
Whom whilom He had met on ISTER's Shoar:
Too well, alas! the Man He knows the same,
Whose Prowess there repell'd the BOYAN Pow'r;
And sent Them trembling thro' the frighted Lands,
Swift as the Whirlwind drives ARABIA's scatter'd Sands.   70

VIII.

His former Losses He forgets to grieve;
Absolves his Fate, if with a kinder Ray
It now would shine, and only give Him leave
To Balance the Account of BLENHEIM's Day.
So the fell Lion in the lonely Glade,   75
His Side still smarting with the Hunter's Spear,
Tho' deeply wounded, no way yet dismay'd,
Roars terrible, and meditates new War;

51] *1709* In Council Calm and in Discourse Sedate, *1706*   52 Shaded with Laurels,] *1709*
Under his Vineyard *1706*   53] *1709* Quiet and safe thus Victor *Marlb'rough* sate, *1706*
54 And gives Her Second] *1709* 'Till *Anna* gives Her *1706*   55 sweet] *1709* soft *1706*
56 ardent Speed He] *1709* swift Impatience *1706*   57 Marching] *1709* Flying *1706*
59–60] *1709*
    Quicker than Thought he takes his destin'd Aim,
    And Expectation flies on slower Wings than Fame. *1706*
61] *1709* Untam'd *Bavar*, when on *Ramillia*'s Plain *1706*   62 Did from afar] *1709* Afar
he did *1706*

In sullen Fury traverses the Plain,
To find the vent'rous Foe, and Battel Him again.   80

IX.

Misguided Prince! no longer urge Thy Fate,
Nor tempt the Hero to unequal War;
Fam'd in Misfortune, and in Ruin Great,
Confess the Force of MARLBRÔ's stronger Star.
Those Laurel Groves (the Merits of thy Youth)   85
Which Thou from MAHOMET didst greatly gain,
While bold Assertor of resistless Truth,
Thy Sword did Godlike Liberty maintain,
Must from thy Brow their falling Honors shed;
And their transplanted Wreaths must deck a worthier Head.   90

X.

Yet cease the Ways of Providence to blame,
And Human Faults with Human Grief confess:
'Tis Thou art chang'd; while Heav'n is still the same:
From Thy ill Councils date Thy ill Success.
Impartial Justice holds Her equal Scales;   95
'Till stronger Virtue does the Weight incline:
If over Thee thy glorious Foe prevails;
He now Defends the Cause, that once was Thine.
Righteous the War, the Champion shall subdue;
For JOVE's great Handmaid POWER, must JOVE's Decrees pursue.   100

XI.

Hark! the dire Trumpets sound their shrill Alarms:
AUVERQUERQUE, branch'd from the renown'd NASSAWS,
Hoary in War, and bent beneath his Arms,
His Glorious Sword with Dauntless Courage draws.

82 the Hero] *1709* thy Rival *1706*   85 Those... Merits] *1709* That Laurel Grove, that
Harvest *1706*   87 While] *1709* Whilst *1706*   89–90] *1709*
     Must shed, I ween, its Honours from thy Brow;
     And on another Head another Spring must know. *1706*
94 From... Councils date] *1709* In... Conduct seek *1706*   99–100] *1709*
     Jove's Handmaid *Pow'r* must *Jove*'s Behests pursue,
     And where the Cause is Just, the Warrior shall Subdue. *1706*
102 branch'd] *1709* sprung *1706*   104–10] *1709*
     With an Intrepid Hand and Courage draws
     That Sword, Immortal *William* at his Death

[*continued next page*

When anxious BRITAIN mourn'd her parting Lord,   105
And all of WILLIAM that was Mortal Dy'd;
The faithful Hero had receiv'd This Sword
From His expiring Master's much-lov'd Side.
Oft from it's fatal Ire has LOUIS flown,
Where-e'er Great WILLIAM led, or MAESE and SAMBRE run.   110

XII.

But brandish'd high, in an ill-omen'd Hour
To Thee, proud GAUL, behold thy justest Fear,
The Master Sword, Disposer of thy Power:
'Tis That which CÆSAR gave the BRITISH Peer.
He took the Gift: Nor ever will I sheath   115
This Steel, (so ANNA's high Behests ordain)
The General said, unless by Glorious Death
Absolv'd, 'till Conquest has confirm'd Your Reign.
Returns like these Our Mistress bids us make,
When from a Foreign Prince a Gift Her BRITONS take.   120

XIII.

And now fierce GALLIA rushes on her Foes,
Her Force augmented by the BOYAN Bands:
So VOLGA's Stream, increas'd by Mountain Snows,
Rolls with new Fury down thro' RUSSIA's Lands.
Like two great Rocks against the raging Tide,   125
(If Virtue's Force with Nature's We compare)
Unmov'd the Two united Chiefs abide,
Sustain the Impulse, and receive the War.
Round their firm Sides in vain the Tempest beats;
And still the foaming Wave with lessen'd Pow'r retreats.   130

(Who could a fairer Legacy bestow?)
Did to the Part'ner of his Arms bequeath:
That Sword well *Loüis* and his Captains know;
For they have seen it drawn from *William*'s Thigh,
Full oft as he came forth, to Conquer, or to Die. *1706*

111 in... Hour] *1709* and waving in the Air, *1706*   112–13] *1709*

Behold, unhappy Prince, the Master Sword,
Which perjur'd *Gallia* shall for ever fear: *1706*

114 Peer] *1709* Lord *1706*   116 This Steel] *1709* He said *1706*   117 The General
said] *1709* This Glorious Gift *1706*   118 Conquest has confirm'd] *1709* I by Conquest
fix *1706*   127] *1709* The Two great adverse Chiefs unmov'd abide, *1706*

XIV.

The Rage dispers'd, the Glorious Pair advance,
With mingl'd Anger, and collected Might,
To turn the War, and tell aggressing FRANCE,
How BRITAIN's Sons and BRITAIN's Friends can fight.
On Conquest fix'd, and covetous of Fame,   135
Behold Them rushing thro' the GALLIC Host.
Thro' standing Corn so runs the sudden Flame,
Or Eastern Winds along SICILIA's Coast.
They deal their Terrors to the adverse Nation:
Pale Death attends their Arms, and ghastly Desolation.   140

XV.

But while with fiercest Ire BELLONA glows,
And EUROPE rather Hopes than Fears Her Fate;
While BRITAIN presses Her afflicted Foes;
What Horror damps the Strong, and quells the Great?
Whence look the Soldiers Cheeks dismay'd and pale?   145
Erst ever dreadful, know They now to dread?
The Hostile Troops, I ween, almost prevail;
And the Pursuers only not recede.
Alas! their lessen'd Rage proclaims their Grief!
For anxious, lo! They croud around their falling Chief!   150

XVI.

I thank Thee, Fate, exclaims the fierce BAVAR;
Let BOYA's Trumpet grateful Iö's sound:
I saw Him fall, their Thunderbolt of War:—
Ever to Vengeance sacred be the Ground—
Vain Wish! short Joy! the Hero mounts again   155
In greater Glory, and with fuller Light:
The Ev'ning Star so falls into the Main,
To rise at Morn more prevalently bright.

131 Rage...Glorious] *1709* Shock sustain'd, the Friendly *1706*   135 On Conquest fix'd]
1709 Fix'd on Revenge *1706*   140 Arms] *1709* Deed *1706*   141 while...Ire] *1709*
oh! while mad with Rage *1706*   143] *1709* While with large Steps to Conquest *Britain*
goes, *1706*   145 Whence...Cheeks] *1709* Why do those Warriors look *1706*   146
Erst...now] *1709* That, ever Dreadful, never knew *1706*   147 The...ween,] *1709* Why
does the charging Foe *1706*   149 Alas!...proclaims] *1709* Their Rage, alas! submitting
to *1706*   150 For...They] *1709* Behold, they weep, and *1706*   153 their] *1709* that
1706   154] *1709* I saw Their *Marlb'rough* stretch'd along the Ground— *1706*   155
Wish] *1709* Hope *1706*   the Hero] *1709* for *Marlb'rough 1706*

He rises safe: but near, too near his Side,
A good Man's grievous Loss, a faithful Servant dy'd.   160

XVII.

Propitious MARS! the Battel is regain'd:
The Foe with lessen'd Wrath disputes the Field:
The BRITON fights, by fav'ring Gods sustain'd:
Freedom must live; and lawless Power must yield.
Vain now the Tales which fab'ling Poets tell,   165
That wav'ring CONQUEST still desires to rove!
In MARLBRÔ's Camp the Goddess knows to dwell:
Long as the Hero's Life remains her Love.
Again FRANCE flies: again the Duke pursues:
And on RAMILLIA's Plains He BLENHEIM's Fame renews.   170

XVIII.

Great Thanks, O Captain great in Arms! receive
From thy Triumphant Country's public Voice:
Thy Country greater Thanks can only give
To ANNE, to Her who made those Arms Her Choice.
Recording SCHELLENBERG's, and BLENHEIM's Toils,   175
We dreaded lest Thou should'st those Toils repeat:
We view'd the Palace charg'd with GALLIC Spoils;
And in those Spoils We thought thy Praise compleat:
For never GREEK, We deem'd, nor ROMAN Knight,
In Characters like these did e'er his Acts indite.   180

XIX.

Yet mindless still of Ease, Thy Virtue flies
A Pitch to Old and Modern Times unknown:
Those goodly Deeds which We so highly prize,
Imperfect seem, great Chief, to Thee alone.

---

161 Propitious MARS! the] *1709* And lo! the dubious *1706*   162 Wrath] *1709* Rage *1706*
164 Freedom] *1709* And *Liberty 1706*   lawless Power must] *1709 Gallia 1706*   169–70]
1709
                    The Foe retires, the Victor urges on,
                    And *Blenheim's* Fame again is in *Ramillia* known. *1706*
176 We...should'st] *1709* We wish'd Thou wou'dst no more *1706*   177 GALLIC] *1709*
Gallia's 1706   181 Ease,] *1709* Rest *1706*

Those Heights, where WILLIAM's Virtue might have staid,   185
And on the Subject World look'd safely down,
By MARLBRÔ pass'd, the Props and Steps were made,
Sublimer yet to raise his Queen's Renown:
Still gaining more, still slighting what He gain'd,
Nought done the Hero deem'd, while ought undone remain'd.   190

XX.

When swift-wing'd RUMOR told the mighty GAUL,
How lessen'd from the Field BAVAR was fled;
He wept the Swiftness of the Champion's Fall;
And thus the Royal Treaty-Breaker said:
And lives He yet, the Great, the Lost BAVAR,   195
Ruin to GALLIA, in the Name of Friend?
Tell Me, how far has Fortune been severe?
Has the Foe's Glory, or our Grief an End?
Remains there, of the Fifty Thousand lost,
To save our threaten'd Realm, or guard our shatter'd Coast?   200

XXI.

To the close Rock the frighted Raven flies,
Soon as the rising Eagle cuts the Air:
The shaggy Wolf unseen and trembling lyes,
When the hoarse Roar proclaims the Lion near.
Ill-starr'd did We our Forts and Lines forsake,   205
To dare our BRITISH Foes to open Fight:
Our Conquest We by Stratagem should make:
Our Triumph had been founded in our Flight.
'Tis Our's, by Craft and by Surprize to gain:
'Tis Their's, to meet in Arms, and Battel in the Plain.   210

XXII.

The ancient Father of this Hostile Brood,
Their boasted BRUTE, undaunted snatch'd his Gods
From burning TROY, and XANTHUS red with Blood,
And fix'd on Silver THAMES his dire Abodes;

188] *1709* To lift Great *Anna*'s Glory further on; *1706*   190 Nought...deem'd] *1709*
Nothing was done, He thought *1706*   202 the...cuts] *1709* he sees the Eagle cut *1706*
203 trembling] *1709* fearful *1706*   205 Ill-starr'd] *1709* Why then *1706*   206 our...
Foes] *1709* the...Foe *1706*

And this be TROYNOVANTE, He said, the Seat   215
By Heav'n ordain'd, My Sons, Your lasting Place:
Superior here to all the Bolts of Fate
Live, mindful of the Author of your Race,
Whom neither GREECE, nor War, nor Want, nor Flame,
Nor Great PELEIDES' Arm, nor JUNO's Rage could tame.   220

XXIII.

Their TUDOR's hence, and STUART's Off-spring flow:
Hence EDWARD, dreadful with his Sable Shield,
TALBOT, to GALLIA's Pow'r Eternal Foe,
And SEYMOUR, fam'd in Council, or in Field:
Hence NEVIL, Great to Settle or Dethrone,   225
And DRAKE, and CA'NDISH, Terrors of the Sea:
Hence BUTLER's Sons, o'er Land and Ocean known,
HERBERT's, and CHURCHILL's Warring Progeny:
Hence the long Roll which GALLIA should conceal:
For, oh! Who vanquish'd, loves the Victor's Fame to tell?   230

XXIV.

Envy'd BRITANNIA, sturdy as the Oak,
Which on her Mountain-Top She proudly bears,
Eludes the Ax, and sprouts against the Stroke;
Strong from her Wounds, and greater by her Wars.
And as Those Teeth, which CADMUS sow'd in Earth,   235
Produc'd new Youth, and furnish'd fresh Supplies:
So with young Vigor, and succeeding Birth,
Her Losses more than recompens'd arise;
And ev'ry Age She with a Race is Crown'd,
For Letters more Polite, in Battels more Renown'd.   240

XXV.

Obstinate Pow'r, whom Nothing can repel;
Not the fierce SAXON, nor the cruel DANE,
Nor deep Impression of the NORMAN Steel,
Nor EUROPE's Force amass'd by envious SPAIN,

222 Sable] *1709* azure *1706*

Nor FRANCE on universal Sway intent,   245
Oft breaking Leagues, and oft renewing Wars,
Nor (frequent Bane of weaken'd Government)
Their own intestine Feuds, and mutual Jars;
Those Feuds and Jars, in which I trusted more,
Than in My Troops, and Fleets, and all the GALLIC Pow'r.   250

XXVI.

To fruitful RHEIMS, or fair LUTETIA's Gate
What Tidings shall the Messenger convey?
Shall the loud Herald our Success relate,
Or mitred Priest appoint the Solemn Day?
Alas! my Praises They no more must Sing;   255
They to my Statue now must Bow no more:
Broken, repuls'd is their Immortal King:
Fall'n, fall'n for ever is the GALLIC Pow'r—
The *Woman Chief* is Master of the War:
Earth She has freed by Arms, and vanquish'd Heav'n by Pray'r. 260

XXVII.

While thus the ruin'd Foe's Despair commends
Thy Council and Thy Deed, Victorious Queen,
What shall Thy Subjects say, and what Thy Friends?
How shall Thy Triumphs in Our Joy be seen?
Oh! daign to let the Eldest of the NINE   265
Recite BRITANNIA Great, and GALLIA Free:
Oh! with her Sister SCULPTURE let her join
To raise, Great ANNE, the Monument to Thee;
To Thee, of all our Good the Sacred Spring;
To Thee, our dearest Dread; to Thee, our softer KING.   270

XXVIII.

Let EUROPE sav'd the Column high erect,
Than TRAJAN's higher, or than ANTONINE's;
Where sembling Art may carve the fair Effect,
And full Atchievement of Thy great Designs.

246 Oft... oft] *1709* Still... still *1706*   247 frequent] *1709* usual *1706*   256
They... now] And... they *1706, 1709*   261 While] Whilst *1706, 1709*
917.27   R

In a calm Heav'n, and a serener Air,   275
Sublime the QUEEN shall on the Summit stand,
From Danger far, as far remov'd from Fear,
And pointing down to Earth Her dread Command.
All Winds, all Storms that threaten Human Woe,
Shall sink beneath Her Feet, and spread their Rage below.   280

XXIX.

There Fleets shall strive by Winds and Waters tost;
'Till the young AUSTRIAN on IBERIA's Strand,
Great as ÆNEAS on the LATIAN Coast,
Shall fix his Foot: and This, be This the Land,
Great JOVE, where I for ever will remain   285
(The Empire's other Hope shall say) and here
Vanquish'd, Intomb'd I'll lye, or Crown'd I'll Reign—
O Virtue, to thy BRITISH Mother dear!
Like the fam'd TROJAN suffer and abide;
For ANNE is Thine, I ween, as VENUS was His Guide.   290

XXX.

There, in Eternal Characters engrav'd,
VIGO, and GIBRALTAR, and BARCELONE,
Their Force destroy'd, their Privileges sav'd,
Shall ANNA's Terrors, and Her Mercies own:
SPAIN, from th'Usurper BOURBON's Arms retriev'd,   295
Shall with new Life and grateful Joy appear,
Numb'ring the Wonders which That Youth atchiev'd,
Whom ANNA clad in Arms, and sent to War;
Whom ANNA sent to claim IBERIA's Throne;
And made Him more than King, in calling Him Her Son.   300

XXXI.

There ISTER pleas'd, by BLENHEIM's glorious Field
Rolling, shall bid his Eastern Waves declare
GERMANIA sav'd by BRITAIN's ample Shield,
And bleeding GAUL afflicted by her Spear:

---

280 spread] *1709* spend *1706*   287 Vanquish'd…Crown'd] *1709* Intomb'd I'll
Slumber, or Enthron'd *1706*   295 th'Usurper] *1709* the Rival *1706*

Shall bid Them mention MARLBRÔ, on that Shore   305
Leading his Islanders, renown'd in Arms,
Thro' Climes, where never BRITISH Chief before
Or pitch'd his Camp, or sounded his Alarms:
Shall bid Them bless the QUEEN, who made his Streams
Glorious as those of BOYN, and safe as those of THAMES.   310

XXXII.

BRABANTIA, clad with Fields, and crown'd with Tow'rs
With decent Joy shall her Deliv'rer meet;
Shall own Thy Arms, Great QUEEN, and bless Thy Pow'rs,
Laying the Keys beneath Thy Subject's Feet.
FLANDRIA, by Plenty made the Home of War,   315
Shall weep her Crime, and bow to CHARLES restor'd;
With double Vows shall bless Thy happy Care,
In having drawn, and having sheath'd the Sword.
From these their Sister Provinces shall know
How ANNE supports a Friend, and how forgives a Foe.   320

XXXIII.

Bright Swords, and crested Helms, and pointed Spears
In artful Piles around the Work shall lye;
And Shields indented deep in ancient Wars,
Blazon'd with Signs of GALLIC Heraldry;
And Standards with distinguish'd Honors bright,   325
Marks of high Pow'r and National Command,
Which VALOIS' Sons, and BOURBON's bore in Fight,
Or gave to FOIX', or MONTMORANCY's Hand:
Great Spoils, which GALLIA must to BRITAIN yield,
From CRESSY's Battel sav'd, to grace RAMILLIA's Field.   330

XXXIV.

And as fine Art the Spaces may dispose,
The knowing Thought and curious Eye shall see
Thy Emblem, Gracious QUEEN, the BRITISH Rose,
Type of sweet Rule, and gentle Majesty:

311 BRABANTIA] *1709* There *Brabant 1706*   312 With] *1709* In *1706*   314 the]
her *1706, 1709*   315 FLANDRIA] *1709* Flanders *1706*   318 and] or *1706, 1709*
319 From... Provinces] *1709* Her Sister Provinces from her *1706*   320 and] or *1706,*
1709   324 Signs] *1709* Marks *1706*   326 Marks] *1709* Types *1706*   332 shall]
should *1706, 1709*   333 Gracious] *1709* happy *1706*   334 Type... Rule] *1709*
Sign... Pow'r *1706*

The NORTHERN Thistle, whom no Hostile Hand   335
Unhurt too rudely may provoke, I ween;
HIBERNIA's Harp, Device of Her Command,
And Parent of Her Mirth, shall there be seen:
Thy vanquish'd Lillies, FRANCE, decay'd and torn,
Shall with disorder'd Pomp the lasting Work adorn.   340

XXXV.

Beneath, Great QUEEN, oh! very far beneath,
Near to the Ground, and on the humble Base,
To save Her self from Darkness, and from Death,
That MUSE desires the last, the lowest Place;
Who tho' unmeet, yet touch'd the trembling String;   345
For the fair Fame of ANNE and ALBION's Land,
Who durst of War and Martial Fury Sing:
And when Thy Will, and when Thy Subject's Hand
Had quell'd those Wars, and bid that Fury cease;
Hangs up her grateful Harp to Conquest, and to Peace.   350

1707

A Simile.

D EAR THOMAS, didst Thou never pop
   Thy Head into a Tin-man's Shop?
There, THOMAS, didst Thou never see
('Tis but by way of Simile;)
A SQUIRREL spend his little Rage,   5
In jumping round a rowling Cage?
The Cage, as either Side turn'd up,
Striking a Ring of Bells a-top—?

---

336 rudely may provoke] *1709* nearly may approach *1706*   337 HIBERNIA's ... Her] *1709*
And *Ireland*'s Harp, her Emblem of *1706*   338 Parent ... shall] Instrument of Joy,
should *1706*: Parent ... should *1709*   339] *1709* And *Gallia*'s wither'd Lillies pale, and torn,
1706   340 Shall ... Pomp] Should, here and there dispers'd, *1706*: Should, ... Pomp, *1709*
348 Will, ... Subject's] Will appointed *Marlb'rough*'s *1706*: Will, ... *Marlbrô*'s *1709*
349 Had ... bid] *1709* To end those Wars, and make *1706*   350 Hangs] *1706* Hung *1709*
Conquest, and to] Everlasting *1706, 1709*
   1, 3 THOMAS] *1707p, 1709* WILLIAM *1707*   6 rowling] *1709* rouling *1707p*: rolling
1707   8 a-top—?] *1709* a top—; *1707p*: at top, *1707*

Mov'd in the Orb; pleas'd with the Chimes;
The foolish Creature thinks he climbs: 10
But here or there, turn Wood or Wire,
He never gets two Inches higher.

So fares it with those merry Blades,
That frisk it under PINDUS' Shades.
In noble Songs, and lofty Odes,   15
They tread on Stars, and talk with Gods.
Still Dancing in an airy Round:
Still pleas'd with their own Verses Sound.
Brought back, how fast soe'er they go:
Always aspiring; always low.   20

Epilogue to Phædra.

Spoken by Mrs. Oldfield, who acted Ismena.

LADIES, to Night your Pity I implore
For One, who never troubled You before:
An OXFORD-Man, extreamly read in GREEK,
Who from EURIPIDES makes PHÆDRA speak;
And comes to Town, to let Us Moderns know,   5
How Women lov'd two thousand Years ago.

If that be all, said I, e'en burn your Play:
I' gad! We know all that, as well as They:
Show Us the youthful, handsome Charioteer,
Firm in his Seat, and running his Career;   10
Our Souls would kindle with as gen'rous Flames,
As e'er inspir'd the antient GRECIAN Dames:
Ev'ry ISMENA would resign her Breast;
And ev'ry dear HIPPOLYTUS be blest.

But, as it is, Six flouncing FLANDERS Mares   15
Are e'en as good, as any Two of Theirs;
And if HIPPOLYTUS can but contrive
To buy the gilded Chariot; JOHN can drive.

9 the Orb;] the Orb, *1707p, 1709*: this Orb, *1707*   11 turn] *1707p, 1709* turns *1707*
14 PINDUS'] *1709* Pindus *1707p*: PINDAR'S *1707*
  4 EURIPIDES] *1709* Eu----ripides *1707*

Now of the Bustle You have seen to Day,
And PHÆDRA's Morals in this Scholar's Play,   20
Something at least in Justice should be said:
But this HIPPOLYTUS so fills One's Head—
Well! PHÆDRA liv'd as chastly as She cou'd,
For she was Father JOVE's own Flesh and Blood.
Her aukward Love indeed was odly fated: 25
She and her POLY were too near related:
And yet that Scruple had been laid aside,
If honest THESEUS had but fairly dy'd:
But when He came, what needed He to know,
But that all Matters stood in *Statu quo?*   30
There was no harm, You see; or grant there were:
She might want Conduct; but He wanted Care.
'Twas in a Husband little less than rude,
Upon his Wife's Retirement to intrude—
He should have sent a Night or two before,   35
That He would come exact at such an Hour:
Then He had turn'd all Tragedy to Jest;
Found ev'ry Thing contribute to his Rest;
The *Picquet*-Friend dismiss'd, the Coast all clear,
And Spouse alone impatient for her Dear.   40

But if these gay Reflections come too late,
To keep the guilty PHÆDRA from her Fate;
If your more serious Judgment must condemn
The dire Effects of her unhappy Flame:
Yet, Ye chaste Matrons, and Ye tender Fair,   45
Let Love and Innocence engage your Care:
My spotless Flames to your Protection take;
And spare poor PHÆDRA, for ISMENA's sake.

1708

Preface.

*T*HE Greatest Part of what I have Written having already been Published, either singly or in some of the Miscellanies, it would be too late for Me to make any Excuse for appearing in Print. But a Collection of Poems has lately appeared under my Name, tho' without my Knowledge, in which the Publisher has given Me the Honor of some Things that did not belong to Me; and has 5 Transcribed others so imperfectly, that I hardly knew them to be Mine. This has obliged Me, in my own Defence, to look back upon some of those lighter Studies, which I ought long since to have quitted, and to Publish an indifferent Collection of Poems, for fear of being thought the Author of a worse.

Thus I beg Pardon of the Public for Reprinting some Pieces, which, as they 10 came singly from their first Impression, have (I fancy) lain long and quietly in Mr. TONSON's Shop; and adding others to them, which were never before Printed, and might have lain as quietly, and perhaps more safely, in a Corner of my own Study.

The Reader will, I hope, make Allowance for their having been written at very 15 distant Times, and on very different Occasions; and take them as they happen to come, Public Panegyrics, Amorous Odes, Serious Reflections, or idle Tales, the Product of his leisure Hours, who had Business enough upon his Hands, and was only a Poet by Accident.

I take this Occasion to thank my good Friend and School-fellow Mr. DIBBEN, 20 for his excellent Version of the Carmen Seculare, though my Gratitude may justly carry a little Envy with it; for I believe the most accurate Judges will find the Translation exceed the Original.

I must likewise own my self obliged to Mrs. SINGER, who has given Me Leave to Print a Pastoral of Her Writing; That Poem having produced the Verses 25 immediately following it. I wish She might be prevailed with to publish some other Pieces of that Kind, in which the Softness of Her Sex, and the Fineness of Her Genius, conspire to give Her a very distinguishing Character.

---

1 *Written*] *Writ* 1709   2 *or in*] *or else in* 1709   12 *adding . . . them,*] *with others* 1709   15 *Reader will*] *Reader as he turns them over, will* 1709   *written*] *writ* 1709 18 *had Business*] *had commonly Business* 1709

Dedication. To the Right Honorable Lionel, Earl of Dorset and Middle-sex.

I T looks like no great Compliment to Your Lordship, that I prefix Your Name to this Epistle; when, in the Preface, I declare the Book is publish'd almost against my Inclination. But, in all Cases, My Lord, You have an Hereditary Right to whatever may be called Mine. Many of the following Pieces were written by the Command of Your Excellent 5 Father; and most of the rest, under His Protection and Patronage.

The particular Felicity of Your Birth, My Lord; The natural Endowments of Your Mind, (which, without suspicion of Flattery) I may tell You, are very Great; The good Education with which these Parts have been improved; and Your coming into the World, and seeing Men very 10 early; make Us expect from Your Lordship all the Good, which our Hopes can form in Favour of a young Nobleman. *Tu Marcellus eris,*— Our Eyes and our Hearts are turned on You. You must be a Judge and Master of Polite Learning; a Friend and Patron to Men of Letters and Merit; a faithful and able Counsellor to Your Prince; a true Patriot to 15 Your Countrey; an Ornament and Honor to the Titles You possess; and in one Word, a Worthy Son to the Great Earl of DORSET.

It is as impossible to mention that Name, without desiring to Commend the Person; as it is to give Him the Commendations which His Virtues deserved. But I assure my self, the most agreeable Compliment 20 I can bring Your Lordship, is to pay a grateful Respect to Your Father's Memory. And my own Obligations to Him were such; that the World must pardon my Endeavoring at His Character, however I may miscarry in the Attempt.

A Thousand Ornaments and Graces met in the Composition of this 25 Great Man; and contributed to make Him universally Belov'd and Esteem'd. The Figure of His Body was Strong, Proportionable, Beautiful: and were His Picture well Drawn, it must deserve the Praise given to the Pourtraits of RAPHAEL; and, at once, create Love and Respect. While the Greatness of His Mein inform'd Men, they were approaching 30 the Nobleman; the Sweetness of it invited them to come nearer to the Patron. There was in His Look and Gesture something that is easier conceived than described; that gain'd upon You in His Favor, before He spake one Word. His Behavior was Easie and Courteous to all; but

Title: Dedication. Supplied from the running title in 1709 & 1718   5 written] writ 1709   14 of Polite] of all Polite 1709   34 spake] spoke 1709

Distinguished and Adapted to each Man in particular, according to his 35 Station and Quality. His Civility was free from the Formality of Rule, and flowed immediately from His good Sense.

Such were the Natural Faculties and Strength of His Mind, that He had occasion to borrow very little from Education: and He owed those Advantages to His own Good Parts, which Others acquire by Study 40 and Imitation. His Wit was Abundant, Noble, Bold. Wit in most Writers is like a Fountain in a Garden, supply'd by several Streams brought thro' artful Pipes, and playing sometimes agreeably. But the Earl of DORSET's was a Source rising from the Top of a Mountain, which forced it's own way, and with inexhaustible Supplies, delighted 45 and inriched the Country thro' which it pass'd. This extraordinary Genius was accompany'd with so true a Judgment in all Parts of fine Learning, that whatever Subject was before Him, He Discours'd as properly of it, as if the peculiar Bent of His Study had been apply'd That way; and He perfected His Judgment by Reading and Digesting 50 the best Authors, tho' He quoted Them very seldom.

Contemnebat potiùs literas, quàm nesciebat:

and rather seem'd to draw His Knowledge from His own Stores, than to owe it to any Foreign Assistance.

The Brightness of His Parts, the Solidity of His Judgment, and the 55 Candor and Generosity of His Temper distinguish'd Him in an Age of great Politeness, and at a Court abounding with Men of the finest Sense and Learning. The most eminent Masters in their several Ways appeal'd to His Determination. WALLER thought it an Honor to consult Him in the Softness and Harmony of his Verse: and Dr. SPRAT, in 60 the Delicacy and Turn of his Prose. DRYDEN determines by Him, under the Character of *Eugenius*; as to the Laws of Dramatick Poetry. BUTLER ow'd it to Him, that the Court tasted his *Hudibras*: WICHERLEY, that the Town liked his *Plain Dealer*: and the late Duke of BUCKINGHAM deferr'd to publish his *Rehearsal*; 'till He was sure (as He expressed it) 65 that my Lord DORSET would not *Rehearse* upon Him again. If We wanted Foreign Testimony; LA FONTAINE and S^T· EVREMONT have acknowledg'd, that He was a Perfect Master in the Beauty and Fineness of their Language, and of All that They call *les Belles Lettres*. Nor was this Nicety of His Judgement confined only to Books and Literature; 70 but was the Same in Statuary, Painting, and all other Parts of Art. BERNINI would have taken His Opinion upon the Beauty and Attitude

50 His] this *1709*

of a Figure; and King CHARLES did not agree with LELY, that my Lady
CLEVELAND's Picture was Finished, 'till it had the Approbation of my
Lord BUCKEHURST. 75

As the Judgement which He made of Others Writings, could not be
refuted; the Manner in which He wrote, will hardly ever be Equalled.
Every one of His Pieces is an Ingot of Gold, intrinsically and solidly
Valuable; such as, wrought or beaten thinner, would shine thro' a
whole Book of any other Author. His Thought was always New; and 80
the Expression of it so particularly Happy, that every body knew immediately, it could only be my Lord DORSET's: and yet it was so Easy
too, that Every body was ready to imagine himself capable of writing
it. There is a Lustre in His Verses, like That of the Sun in CLAUDE
LORAINE's Landskips; it looks Natural, and is Inimitable. His Love- 85
Verses have a Mixture of Delicacy and Strength: they convey the Wit
of PETRONIUS in the Softness of TIBULLUS. His Satyr indeed is so
severely Pointed, that in it He appears, what His Great Friend the
Earl of ROCHESTER (that other Prodigy of the Age) says He was;

> *The best good Man, with the worst-natur'd Muse.* 90

Yet even here, That Character may justly be Applied to Him, which
PERSIUS gives of the best Writer in this Kind, that ever lived:

> *Omne vafer vitium ridenti* Flaccus *amico*
> *Tangit, & admissus circum præcordia ludit.*

And the Gentleman had always so much the better of the Satyrist, that 95
the Persons touched did not know where to fix their Resentments; and
were forced to appear rather Ashamed than Angry. Yet so far was this
great Author from Valuing himself upon His Works, that He cared not
what became of them, though every body else did. There are many
Things of His not Extant in Writing, which however are always 100
repeated: like the Verses and Sayings of the Ancient DRUIDS, they
retain an Universal Veneration; tho' they are preserved only by
Memory.

As it is often seen, that those Men who are least Qualified for Business, love it most; my Lord DORSET's Character was, that He certainly 105
understood it, but did not care for it.

Coming very Young to the Possession of two Plentiful Estates, and
in an Age when Pleasure was more in Fashion than Business; He turned
his Parts rather to Books and Conversation, than to Politicks, and what

73 LELY] *Lilly 1709*   79 beaten] Beat *1709*

more immediately related to the Public. But whenever the Safety of 110
His Countrey demanded His Assistance, He readily entred into the
most Active Parts of Life; and underwent the greatest Dangers, with
a Constancy of Mind, which shewed, that He had not only read the
Rules of Philosophy, but understood the Practice of them.

In the first *Dutch* War He went a Voluntier under the Duke of YORK: 115
His Behavior, during That Campaigne, was such, as distinguish'd the
SACKVILLE descended from that HILDEBRAND of the Name, who was
one of the greatest Captains that came into ENGLAND with the Conqueror. But His making a Song the Night before the Engagement (and
it was one of the prettiest that ever was made) carries with it so sedate 120
a Presence of Mind, and such an unusual Gallantry, that it deserves as
much to be Recorded, as ALEXANDER's jesting with his Soldiers, before
he passed the GRANICUS: or WILLIAM the First of ORANGE, giving
Order over Night for a Battel, and desiring to be called in the Morning,
lest He should happen to Sleep too long. 125

From hence, during the remaining Part of King CHARLES's Reign,
He continued to Live in Honorable Leisure. He was of the Bed-chamber
to the King; and Possessed not only His Master's Favor, but (in a great
Degree) His Familiarity; never leaving the Court, but when He was
sent to That of FRANCE, on some short Commissions and Embassies of 130
Compliment: as if the King designed to show the FRENCH, (who would
be thought the Politest Nation) that one of the Finest Gentlemen in
EUROPE was His Subject; and that We had a Prince who under-
stood His Worth so well, as not to suffer Him to be long out of His
Presence. 135

The succeeding Reign neither relish'd my Lord's Wit, nor approved
His Maxims: so He retired altogether from Court. But as the irretriev-
able Mistakes of That unhappy Government, went on to Threaten the
Nation with something more Terrible than a *Dutch* War: He thought
it became Him to resume the Courage of His Youth, and once more to 140
Engage Himself in defending the Liberty of His Countrey. He entred
into the Prince of ORANGE's Interest; and carried on His Part of That
great Enterprise here in LONDON, and under the Eye of the Court; with
the same Resolution, as His Friend and Fellow-Patriot the late Duke of
DEVONSHIRE did in open Arms at NOTTINGHAM; 'till the Dangers of 145
those Times increased to Extremity; and just Apprehensions arose for
the Safety of the Princess, our present Glorious Queen: then the Earl
of DORSET was thought the properest Guide of Her necessary Flight,

147–8 the Earl of] my Lord *1709*

and the Person under whose Courage and Direction the Nation might
most safely Trust a Charge so Precious and Important.   150

After the Establishment of Their late Majesties upon the Throne,
there was Room again at Court for Men of my Lord's Character. He
had a Part in the Councils of those Princes; a great Share in their
Friendship; and all the Marks of Distinction, with which a good
Government could reward a Patriot. He was made Chamberlain of their   155
Majesties Houshold; a Place which He so eminently Adorn'd, by the
Grace of His Person, the Fineness of His Breeding, and the Knowledge
and Practice of what was Decent and Magnificent: that He could only
be Rivalled in these Qualifications by one great Man, who has since
held the same Staff.   160

The last Honors He received from His Soveraign, (and indeed they
were the Greatest which a Subject could receive) were, that He was
made Knight of the Garter, and constituted One of the Regents of the
Kingdom, during His Majesty's Absence. But his Health, about that
time, sensibly Declining; and the Public Affairs not Threatned by any 165
Imminent Danger; He left the Business to Those who delighted more
in the State of it; and appeared only sometimes at Council, to show
his Respect to the Commission: giving as much Leisure as He could
to the Relief of those Pains, with which it pleased God to Afflict Him;
and Indulging the Reflexions of a Mind, that had looked thro' the   170
World with too piercing an Eye, and was grown weary of the Prospect.
Upon the whole; it may very justly be said of this Great Man, with
Regard to the Public, that thro' the Course of his Life, He Acted like
an able Pilot in a long Voyage; contented to sit Quiet in the Cabin,
when the Winds were allayed, and the Waters smooth; but Vigilant   175
and Ready to resume the Helm, when the Storm arose, and the Sea
grew Tumultuous.

I ask Your Pardon, My Lord, if I look yet a little more nearly into the
late Lord DORSET's Character: if I examine it not without some Intention of finding Fault; and (which is an odd way of making a Panegyric) 180
set his Blemishes and Imperfections in open View.

The Fire of His Youth carried Him to some Excesses: but they were
accompanied with a most lively Invention, and true Humour. The little
Violences and easie Mistakes of a Night too gayly spent, (and That too
in the Beginning of Life) were always set Right, the next Day, with   185
great Humanity, and ample Retribution. His Faults brought their

Excuse with them, and his very Failings had their Beauties. So much
Sweetness accompanied what He said, and so great Generosity what
He did; that People were always prepossess'd in his Favor: and it was in
Fact true, what the late Earl of ROCHESTER said, in Jest, to King 190
CHARLES; That He did not know how it was, but my Lord DORSET
might do any thing, yet was never to Blame.

He was naturally very subject to Passion; but the short Gust was
soon over, and served only to set off the Charms of his Temper, when
more Compos'd. That very Passion broke out with a Force of Wit, 195
which made even Anger agreeable: While it lasted, He said and forgot
a thousand Things, which other Men would have been glad to have
studied and wrote: but the Impetuosity was Corrected upon a Moment's Reflection; and the Measure altered with such Grace and Delicacy, that You could scarce perceive where the Key was Changed. 200

He was very Sharp in his Reflections; but never in the wrong Place.
His Darts were sure to Wound; but they were sure too to hit None but
those whose Follies gave Him very fair Aim. And when He allowed no
Quarter; He had certainly been provoked by more than common Error:
by Men's tedious and circumstantial Recitals of their Affairs; or by 205
their multiply'd Questions about his own: by extreme Ignorance and
Impertinence; or the mixture of these, an ill-judg'd and never-ceasing
Civility: or lastly, by the two Things which were his utter Aversion;
the Insinuation of a Flatterer, and the Whisper of a Tale-bearer.

If therefore, We set the Piece in it's worst Position; if it's Faults be 210
most exposed, the Shades will still appear very finely join'd with their
Lights; and every Imperfection will be diminished by the Lustre of
some Neighb'ring Virtue. But if We turn the great Drawings and
wonderful Colourings to their true Light; the Whole must appear
Beautiful, Noble, Admirable. 215

He possessed all those Virtues in the highest Degree, upon which the
Pleasure of Society, and the Happiness of Life depend: and He exercised
them with the greatest Decency, and best Manners. As good Nature is
said, by a great Author, to belong more particularly to the ENGLISH,
than any other Nation; it may again be said, that it belonged more 220
particularly to the late Earl of DORSET, than to any other ENGLISH
Man.

A kind Husband He was, without Fondness: and an indulgent
Father without Partiality. So extraordinary good a Master, that This

196 which] that *1709*   198 wrote:] writ; *1709*   203 Him] them *1709*   207 an]
1709 or *Copies of 1709 with uncancelled leaf*   208 which] that *1709*   224 This] that *1709*

Quality ought indeed to have been number'd among his Defects: for 225
He was often worse served than became his Station; from his Unwil-
lingness to assume an Authority too Severe. And, during those little
Transports of Passion, to which I just now said He was subject; I have
known his Servants get into his way, that They might make a Merit of
it immediately after: for He that had the good Fortune to be Chid, was 230
sure of being Rewarded for it.

His Table was one of the Last, that gave Us an Example of the Old
House-keeping of an ENGLISH Nobleman. A Freedom reigned at it,
which made every one of his Guests think Himself at Home: and an
Abundance, which shewed that the Master's Hospitality extended to 235
many More, than Those who had the Honor to sit at Table with Him.

In his Dealings with Others; his Care and Exactness, that every Man
should have his Due, was such, that You would think He had never
seen a Court: the Politeness and Civility with which this Justice was
administred, would convince You He never had lived out of One.   240

He was so strict an Observer of his Word, that no Consideration
whatever, could make him break it: yet so cautious, lest the Merit of
his Act should arise from that Obligation only; that He usually did the
greatest Favors, without making any previous Promise. So inviolable
was He in his Friendship; and so kind to the Character of Those, whom 245
He had once Honored with a more intimate Acquaintance; that nothing
less than a Demonstration of some Essential Fault, could make Him
break with Them: and then too, his good Nature did not consent to
it, without the greatest Reluctance and Difficulty. Let me give one
Instance of this amongst many. When, as Lord Chamberlain, He was 250
obliged to take the King's Pension from Mr. DRYDEN, who had long
before put Himself out of a Possibility of Receiving any Favor from the
Court: my Lord allowed Him an Equivalent, out of his own Estate.
However displeased with the Conduct of his old Acquaintance, He
relieved his Necessities; and while He gave Him his Assistance in 255
Private; in Public, He extenuated and pitied his Error.

The Foundation indeed of these Excellent Qualities, and the Perfection of my Lord DORSET's Character, was, That unbounded Charity
which ran through the whole Tenor of his Life; and sat as visibly Predominant over the other Faculties of his Soul; as She is said to do in 260
Heaven, above Her Sister Virtues.

Crouds of Poor daily thronged his Gates, expecting thence their

234 which] that *1709*   237 Others;] other Men, *1709*   Man] one *1709*   238 You]
one *1709*   240 You] one *1709*   One] it *1709*   256 and] or *1709*

Bread: and were still lessened by His sending the most proper Objects of his Bounty to Apprenticeships, or Hospitals. The Lazar and the Sick, as He accidentally saw them, were removed from the Street to the 265 Physician: and Many of Them not only restored to Health; but supplied with what might enable Them to resume their former Callings, and make their future Life happy. The Prisoner has often been released, by my Lord's paying the Debt; and the Condemned has been saved by his Intercession with the Sovereign; where He thought the Letter of 270 the Law too rigid. To Those whose Circumstances were such as made Them ashamed of their Poverty; He knew how to bestow his Munificence, without offending their Modesty: and under the Notion of frequent Presents, gave Them what amounted to a Subsistance. Many yet alive know This to be true, though He told it to None, nor ever was 275 more uneasy, than when any one mentioned it to Him.

We may find among the *Greeks* and *Latins*, TIBULLUS, and GALLUS; the Noblemen that writ Poetry: AUGUSTUS and MÆCENAS; the Protectors of Learning: ARISTIDES, the good Citizen; and ATTICUS, the well-bred Friend: and bring Them in, as Examples, of my Lord 280 DORSET's Wit; His Judgment; His Justice; and His Civility. But for His Charity, My Lord, We can scarce find a Parallel in History it self.

TITUS was not more the *Deliciæ Humani generis*, on this Account, than my Lord DORSET was. And, without any Exageration, that Prince did not do more good in Proportion out of the Revenue of the *Roman* 285 Empire, than Your Father out of the Income of a private Estate. Let this, my Lord, remain to You and Your Posterity a Possession for ever; to be Imitated, and if possible, to be Excelled.

As to my own Particular, I scarce knew what Life was, sooner than I found my self obliged to His Favor; nor have had Reason to feel any 290 Sorrow, so sensibly as That of His Death.

> *Ille dies——quem semper acerbum*
> *Semper honoratum (sic Dî voluistis) habebo.*

ÆNEAS could not reflect upon the loss of His own Father with greater Piety, My Lord, than I must recall the Memory of Yours: and when I 295 think whose Son I am writing to, the least I promise my self from Your Goodness is an uninterrupted Continuance of Favor, and a Friendship for Life. To which, that I may with some Justice Intitle my self, I send Your Lordship a Dedication, not filled with a long Detail of Your Praises, but with my sincerest Wishes that You may Deserve them. 300

263 proper] worthy *1709*   265 removed] sent *1709*

That You may Imploy those extraordinary Parts and Abilities with which Heaven has blessed You, to the Honor of Your Family, the Benefit of Your Friends, and the Good of Your Country; That all Your Actions may be Great, Open and Noble, such as may tell the World whose Son and whose Successor You are. 305

What I now offer to Your Lordship is a Collection of Poetry, a kind of Garland of Good Will. If any Verses of My Writing should appear in Print, under another Name and Patronage, than That of an Earl of DORSET, People might suspect them not to be Genuine. I have attained my present End, if these Poems prove the Diversion of some of Your 310 Youthful Hours, as they have been occasionally the Amusement of some of Mine; and I humbly hope, that as I may hereafter bind up my fuller Sheaf, and lay some Pieces of a very different Nature (the Product of my severer Studies) at Your Lordship's Feet, I shall engage Your more serious Reflection: Happy, if in all my Endeavors I may contribute 315 to Your Delight, or to Your Instruction. I am, with all Duty and Respect,

MY LORD,
Your Lordship's
most Obedient, and 320
most Humble Servant,
MAT. PRIOR.

An Ode.

I.

WHILE from our Looks, fair Nymph, You guess
The secret Passions of our Mind;
My heavy Eyes, You say, confess
A Heart to Love and Grief inclin'd.

II.

There needs, alas! but little Art, 5
To have this fatal Secret found:
With the same Ease You threw the Dart,
'Tis certain You may show the Wound.

III.

How can I see You, and not love;
　　While You as op'ning East are fair? 　　　　　10
While cold as Northern Blasts You prove;
　　How can I love, and not despair?

IV.

The Wretch in double Fetters bound
　　Your Potent Mercy may release:
Soon, if my Love but once were crown'd, 　　　　　15
　　Fair Prophetess, my Grief would cease.

Written in the Nouveaux Interests des Princes de l'Europe.

B LEST be the Princes, who have fought
　　For Pompous Names, or wide Dominion;
Since by Their Error We are taught,
　　That Happiness is but Opinion.

Seeing the Duke of Ormond's Picture, at Sir Godfrey Kneller's.

O UT from the injur'd Canvas, KNELLER, strike
These Lines too faint: the Picture is not like.
Exalt thy Thought, and try thy Toil again:
Dreadful in Arms, on LANDEN's glorious Plain
Place ORMOND's Duke: impendent in the Air 　　　5
Let His keen Sabre, Comet-like, appear,
Where-e'er it points, denouncing Death: below
Draw routed Squadrons, and the num'rous Foe
Falling beneath, or flying from His Blow:
'Till weak with Wounds, and cover'd o'er with Blood, 　10
Which from the Patriot's Breast in Torrents flow'd,

Written in the Nouveaux Interests. Title: the] the BOOK called *1709*

He faints: His Steed no longer hears the Rein;
But stumbles o'er the Heap, His Hand had slain.
And now exhausted, bleeding, pale He lyes;
Lovely, sad Object! in His half-clos'd Eyes   15
Stern Vengeance yet, and Hostile Terror stand:
His Front yet threatens; and His Frowns command:
The *Gallick* Chiefs their Troops around Him call;
Fear to approach Him, tho' they see Him fall.—

O KNELLER, could Thy Shades and Lights express   20
The perfect Hero in that glorious Dress;
Ages to come might ORMOND's Picture know;
And Palms for Thee beneath His Lawrels grow:
In spite of Time Thy Work might ever shine;
Nor HOMER's Colours last so long as Thine.   25

In Imitation of Anacreon.

LET 'em Censure: what care I?
    The Herd of Criticks I defie.
Let the Wretches know, I write
Regardless of their Grace, or Spight.
No, no: the Fair, the Gay, the Young   5
Govern the Numbers of my Song.
All that They approve is sweet:
And All is Sense, that They repeat.

Bid the warbling Nine retire:
VENUS, String thy Servant's Lyre: 10
Love shall be my endless Theme:
Pleasure shall triumph over Fame:
And when these Maxims I decline,
APOLLO, may Thy Fate be Mine:
May I grasp at empty Praise;   15
And lose the Nymph, to gain the Bays.

An Ode.

I.

THE Merchant, to secure his Treasure,
 Conveys it in a borrow'd Name:
EUPHELIA serves to grace my Measure;
 But CLOE is my real Flame.

II.

My softest Verse, my darling Lyre   5
 Upon EUPHELIA's Toylet lay;
When CLOE noted her Desire,
 That I should sing, that I should play.

III.

My Lyre I tune, my Voice I raise;
 But with my Numbers mix my Sighs: 10
And whilst I sing EUPHELIA's Praise,
 I fix my Soul on CLOE's Eyes.

IV.

Fair CLOE blush'd: EUPHELIA frown'd:
 I sung and gaz'd: I play'd and trembl'd:
And VENUS to the LOVES around   15
 Remark'd, how ill We all dissembl'd.

Paulo Purganti and His Wife:
An Honest, but a Simple Pair.

Est enim quiddam, idque intelligitur in omni Virtute, quod Deceat: quod Cogitatione
magis à Virtute potest quam Re separari.   Cic. de Officiis. Lib. 1.

BEYOND the fix'd and settl'd Rules
 Of Vice and Virtue in the Schools,
Beyond the Letter of the Law,
Which keeps our Men and Maids in Awe,
The better Sort should set before 'em   5
A Grace, a Manner, a Decorum;

Something, that gives their Acts a Light;
Makes 'em not only just, but bright;
And sets 'em in that open Fame,
Which witty Malice cannot blame.   10

For 'tis in Life, as 'tis in Painting:
Much may be Right, yet much be Wanting:
From Lines drawn true, our Eye may trace
A Foot, a Knee, a Hand, a Face:
May justly own the Picture wrought   15
Exact to Rule, exempt from Fault:
Yet if the Colouring be not there,
The TITIAN Stroke, the GUIDO Air;
To nicest Judgment show the Piece;
At best 'twill only not displease: 20
It would not gain on JERSEY's Eye:
BRADFORD would frown, and set it by.

Thus in the Picture of our Mind
The Action may be well design'd;
Guided by Law, and bound by Duty;   25
Yet want this *Je ne sçay quoy* of Beauty:
And tho' it's Error may be such,
As KNAGS and BURGESS cannot hit;
It yet may feel the nicer Touch
Of WICHERLEY's or CONGREVE's Wit.   30

What is this Talk? replies a Friend:
And where will this dry Moral end?
The Truth of what You here lay down
By some Example should be shown.—
With all my Heart,—for once;—read on.   35
An Honest, but a Simple Pair
(And Twenty other I forbear)
May serve to make this THESIS clear.

A Doctor of great Skill and Fame,
PAULO PURGANTI was his Name,   40
Had a good, comely, virtuous Wife:
No Woman led a better Life:

22 BRADFORD would frown] B—d—d would scold *1709*

She to Intrigues was ev'n hard-hearted:
She chuckl'd when a Bawd was carted:
And thought the Nation ne'er wou'd thrive,   45
'Till all the Whores were burnt alive.

On marry'd Men, that dare be bad,
She thought no Mercy should be had;
They should be hang'd, or starv'd, or flead,
Or serv'd like ROMISH Priests in SWEDE.—   50
In short, all Lewdness She defy'd:
And stiff was her Parochial Pride.

Yet in an honest Way, the Dame
Was a great Lover of That same;
And could from Scripture take her Cue,   55
That Husbands should give Wives their Due.

Her Prudence did so justly steer
Between the Gay and the Severe,
That if in some Regards She chose
To curb poor PAULO in too close;   60
In others She relax'd again,
And govern'd with a looser Rein.

Thus tho' She strictly did confine
The Doctor from Excess of Wine;
With Oysters, Eggs, and Vermicelli   65
She let Him almost burst his Belly:
Thus drying Coffee was deny'd;
But Chocolate that Loss supply'd:
And for Tobacco (who could bear it?)
Filthy Concomitant of Claret!   70
(Blest Revolution!) one might see
Eringo Roots, and Bohé Tea.

She often set the Doctor's Band,
And strok'd his Beard, and squeez'd his Hand:
Kindly complain'd, that after Noon   75
He went to pore on Books too soon:

She held it wholesomer by much,
To rest a little on the Couch:—
About his Waste in Bed a-nights
She clung so close—for fear of Sprites.   80

    The Doctor understood the Call;
But had not always wherewithal.

    The Lion's Skin too short, you know,
(As PLUTARCH's Morals finely show)
Was lengthen'd by the Fox's Tail: 85
And Art supplies, where Strength may fail.

    Unwilling then in Arms to meet
The Enemy, He could not beat;
He strove to lengthen the Campaign,
And save his Forces by Chicane.   90
FABIUS, the ROMAN Chief, who thus
By fair Retreat grew MAXIMUS,
Shows us, that all that Warrior can do
With Force inferior, is *Cunctando*.

    One Day then, as the Foe drew near,   95
With Love, and Joy, and Life, and Dear;
Our Don, who knew this Tittle Tattle
Did, sure as Trumpet, call to Battel;
Thought it extreamly *à propos*,
To ward against the coming Blow: 100
To ward: but how? Ay, there's the Question:
Fierce the Assault, unarm'd the Bastion.

    The Doctor feign'd a strange Surprise:
He felt her Pulse: he view'd her Eyes:
That beat too fast: These rowl'd too quick: 105
She was, He said, or would be Sick:
He judg'd it absolutely good,
That She should purge and cleanse her Blood.
SPAW Waters for that end were got:
If they past easily or not,   110

    93 all that] all, which *1709*   105 That] Those *1709*

What matters it? the Lady's Feaver
Continu'd violent as ever.

For a Distemper of this Kind,
(BLACKMORE and HANS are of my Mind)
If once it youthful Blood infects,   115
And chiefly of the Female Sex;
Is scarce remov'd by Pill or Potion;
What-e'er might be our Doctor's Notion.

One luckless Night then, as in Bed
The Doctor and the Dame were laid;   120
Again this cruel Feaver came,
High Pulse, short Breath, and Blood in Flame.
What Measures shall poor PAULO keep
With Madam, in this piteous taking?
She, like MACBETH, has murder'd Sleep,   125
And won't allow Him Rest, tho' waking.
Sad State of Matters! when We dare
Nor ask for Peace, nor offer War:
Nor LIVY nor COMINES have shown,
What in this Juncture may be done.   130
GROTIUS might own, that PAULO's Case is
Harder, than any which He places
Amongst his BELLI and his PACIS.

He strove, alas! but strove in vain,
By dint of Logic to maintain,   135
That all the Sex was born to grieve,
Down to her Ladyship from EVE.
He rang'd his Tropes, and preach'd up Patience;
Back'd his Opinion with Quotations,
Divines and Moralists; and run ye on   140
Quite thro' from SENECA to BUNYAN.
As much in vain He bid Her try
To fold her Arms, to close her Eye;
Telling Her, Rest would do Her Good;
If any thing in Nature cou'd: 145

137 Down to... from] Up from... to *1709*

So held the GREEKS quite down from GALEN,
Masters and Princes of the Calling:
So all our Modern Friends maintain
('Tho' no great GREEKS) in WARWICK-LANE.

Reduce, my Muse, the wand'ring Song: 150
A Tale should never be too long.

The more He talk'd, the more She burn'd,
And sigh'd, and tost, and groan'd, and turn'd:
At last, I wish, said She, my Dear—
(And whisper'd something in his Ear.)   155
You wish! wish on, the Doctor cries:
Lord! when will Womankind be wise?
What, in your Waters? are You mad?
Why Poyson is not half so bad.
I'll do it—But I give You Warning: 160
You'll die before To-morrow Morning.—
'Tis kind, my Dear, what You advise;
The Lady with a Sigh replies:
But Life, You know, at best is Pain:
And Death is what We should disdain.   165
So do it therefore, and Adieu:
For I will die for Love of You:—
Let wanton Wives by Death be scar'd:
But, to my Comfort, I'm prepar'd.

Written in the Beginning of Mezeray's History of France.

I.

WHATE'ER thy Countrymen have done
By Law and Wit, by Sword and Gun,
In Thee is faithfully recited:
And all the Living World, that view
Thy Work, give Thee the Praises due,   5
At once Instructed and Delighted.

Title: Written...of] READING *1709*

II.

Yet for the Fame of all these Deeds,
What Begger in the *Invalides*,
   With Lameness broke, with Blindness smitten,
Wish'd ever decently to die,   10
To have been either MEZERAY,
   Or any Monarch He has written?

III.

It strange, dear Author, yet it true is,
That down from PHARAMOND to LOÜIS,
   All covet Life, yet call it Pain: 15
All feel the Ill, yet shun the Cure:
Can Sense this Paradox endure?
   Resolve me, CAMBRAY, or FONTAINE.

IV.

The Man in graver Tragic known
(Tho' his best Part long since was done)   20
   Still on the Stage desires to tarry:
And He who play'd the *Harlequin*,
After the Jest still loads the Scene,
   Unwilling to retire, tho' Weary.

The First Hymn of Callimachus.

To Jupiter.

WHILE we to JOVE select the holy Victim;
   Whom apter shall we sing, than JOVE himself,
The God for ever Great, for ever King;
Who slew the Earth-born Race, and measures Right
To Heav'n's great Habitants? DICTÆAN hear'st Thou   5

7–10] *1709*

          Yet Let me Live, and I would Lye
          And growl, and whine, and scratch and cry
          On Dunghills Lowsy, and besh....n
          Rather than decently to dye,   *L 11*

12 written?] *1709* written. *L 11*
   3 King;] King? *1709*   5 Habitants?] Habitants; *1709*

More joyful, or LYCÆAN, long Dispute
And various Thought has trac'd. On IDA's Mount,
Or DICTE, studious of his Country's Praise,
The CRETAN boasts Thy Natal Place: but oft
He meets Reproof deserv'd: for He presumptuous   10
Has built a Tomb for Thee, who never know'st
To die, but liv'st the same To-day and Ever.
ARCADIAN therefore be Thy Birth: Great RHEA
Pregnant to high PARRHASIA's Cliffs retir'd,
And wild LYCÆUS, black with shading Pines: 15
Holy Retreat! Sithence no Female hither,
Conscious of Social Love and Nature's Rites,
Must dare approach, from the inferior Reptile
To Woman, Form Divine. There the blest Parent
Ungirt her spacious Bosom, and discharg'd   20
The pond'rous Birth: She sought a neighb'ring Spring,
To wash the recent Babe: In vain: ARCADIA,
(However streamy now) adust and dry,
Deny'd the Goddess Water: where deep MELAS,
And rocky CRATIS flow, the Chariot smoak'd,   25
Obscure with rising Dust: the thirsty Trav'ler
In vain requir'd the Current, then imprison'd
In subterranean Caverns: Forests grew
Upon the barren Hollows, high o'ershading
The Haunts of Savage Beasts, where now IAON,   30
And ERIMANTH incline their friendly Urns.

    Thou too, O Earth, great RHEA said, bring forth;
And short shall be thy Pangs: She said; and high
She rear'd her Arm, and with her Scepter struck
The yawning Cliff: from it's disparted Height   35
Adown the Mount the gushing Torrent ran,
And chear'd the Vallies: There the Heav'nly Mother
Bath'd, mighty King, Thy tender Limbs: She wrapt them
In purple Bands: She gave the precious Pledge
To prudent NEDA, charging her to guard Thee,   40
Careful and secret: NEDA of the Nymphs
That tended the great Birth, next PHILYRE
And STYX, the eldest. Smiling She receiv'd Thee,
And conscious of the Grace, absolv'd her Trust:

Not unrewarded; since the River bore   45
The Fav'rite Virgin's Name: fair NEDA rowls
By LEPRION's ancient Walls, a fruitful Stream.
Fast by her flow'ry Bank the Sons of ARCAS,
Fav'rites of Heav'n, with happy Care protect
Their fleecy Charge; and joyous drink her Wave.   50

Thee, God, to CNOSSUS NEDA brought: the Nymphs
And CORYBANTES Thee their sacred Charge
Receiv'd: ADRASTE rock'd Thy golden Cradle:
The Goat, now bright amidst her fellow-Stars,
Kind AMALTHEA, reach'd her Tett distent   55
With Milk, Thy early Food: the sedulous Bee
Distill'd her Honey on Thy purple Lips.

Around, the fierce CURETES (Order solemn
To thy foreknowing Mother!) trod tumultuous
Their Mystic Dance, and clang'd their sounding Arms;   60
Industrious with the warlike Din to quell
Thy Infant-Cries, and mock the Ear of SATURN.

Swift Growth and wond'rous Grace, O heav'nly JOVE,
Waited Thy blooming Years: Inventive Wit,
And perfect Judgment crown'd Thy youthful Act.   65
That SATURN's Sons receiv'd the three-fold Empire
Of Heav'n, of Ocean, and deep Hell beneath,
As the dark Urn and Chance of Lot determin'd,
Old Poets mention, fabling. Things of Moment
Well nigh equivalent and neighb'ring Value   70
By Lot are parted: But high Heav'n, Thy Share,
In equal Balance laid 'gainst Sea or Hell,
Flings up the adverse Scale, and shuns Proportion.
Wherefore not Chance, but Pow'r, above Thy Brethren
Exalted Thee, their King. When Thy great Will   75
Commands Thy Chariot forth; impetuous Strength,
And fiery Swiftness wing the rapid Wheels,
Incessant; high the Eagle flies before Thee.
And oh! as I and mine consult Thy Augur,
Grant the glad Omen; let Thy Fav'rite rise   80
Propitious, ever soaring from the Right.

Thou to the lesser Gods hast well assign'd
Their proper Shares of Pow'r; Thy own, great JOVE,
Boundless and universal. Those who labor
The sweaty Forge, who edge the crooked Scythe,   85
Bend stubborn Steel, and harden gleening Armor,
Acknowledge VULCAN's Aid. The early Hunter
Blesses DIANA's Hand, who leads Him safe
O'er hanging Cliffs; who spreads his Net successful,
And guides the Arrow through the Panther's Heart.   90
The Soldier from successful Camps returning,
With Laurel wreath'd, and rich with hostile Spoil,
Severs the Bull to MARS. The skilful Bard,
Striking the THRACIAN Harp, invokes APOLLO,
To make his Hero and Himself Immortal.   95
Those, mighty JOVE, mean time, Thy glorious Care,
Who model Nations, publish Laws, anounce
Or Life or Death, and found or change the Empire.
Man owns the Pow'r of Kings; and Kings of JOVE.

And as their Actions tend subordinate   100
To what Thy Will designs, Thou giv'st the Means
Proportion'd to the Work; Thou see'st impartial,
How They those Means imploy. Each Monarch rules
His different Realm, accountable to Thee,
Great Ruler of the World: These only have   105
To speak and be obey'd; to Those are giv'n
Assistant Days to ripen the Design;
To some whole Months; revolving Years to some:
Others, ill fated, are condemn'd to toil
Their tedious Life, and mourn their Purpose blasted   110
With fruitless Act, and Impotence of Council.

Hail! greatest Son of SATURN, wise Disposer
Of ev'ry Good: Thy Praise what Man yet born
Has sung? or who that may be born shall sing?
Again, and often hail! indulge our Prayer,   115
Great Father! grant us Virtue, grant us Wealth:
For without Virtue, Wealth to Man avails not;
And Virtue without Wealth exerts less Pow'r,
And less diffuses Good. Then grant us, Gracious,
Virtue, and Wealth; for both are of Thy Gift.   120

The Chameleon.

As the Chameleon, who is known
  To have no Colors of his own;
But borrows from his Neighbour's Hue
His White or Black, his Green or Blew;
And struts as much in ready Light,   5
Which Credit gives Him upon Sight;
As if the Rain-bow were in Tail
Settl'd on Him, and his Heirs Male:
So the young 'Squire, when first He comes
From Country Schole, to WILL's or TOM's;   10
And equally, in Truth, is fit
To be a Statesman, or a Wit;
Without one Notion of his own,
He Santers wildly up and down;
'Till some Acquaintance, good or bad,   15
Takes notice of a staring Lad;
Admits Him in among the Gang:
They jest, reply, dispute, harangue:
He acts and talks, as They befriend Him,
Smear'd with the Colors, which They lend Him.   20

    Thus merely, as his Fortune chances,
His Merit or his Vice advances.

    If happly He the Sect pursues,
That read and comment upon News;
He takes up Their mysterious Face: 25
He drinks his Coffee without Lace.
This Week his mimic-Tongue runs o'er
What They have said the Week before.
His Wisdom sets all Europe right;
And teaches MARLBRÔ when to Fight.   30

    Or if it be his Fate to meet
With Folks who have more Wealth than Wit;
He loves cheap *Port,* and double Bub;
And settles in the *Hum-Drum* Club.

11 equally, in Truth,] equally (G—d knows) *1709*   17 among] amongst *1709*

He learns how Stocks will Fall or Rise; 35
Holds Poverty the greatest Vice.
Thinks Wit the Bane of Conversation;
And says, that Learning spoils a Nation.

But if, at first, He minds his Hits,
And drinks *Champaine* among the Wits; 40
Five deep, He Toasts the tow'ring Lasses;
Repeats you Verses wrote on Glasses;
Is in the Chair; prescribes the Law;
And Lies with Those he never saw.

A Dutch Proverb.

FIRE, Water, Woman, are Man's Ruin;
Says wise Professor VANDER BRÜIN.
By Flames a House I hir'd was lost
Last Year: and I must pay the Cost.
This Spring the Rains o'erflow'd my Ground: 5
And my best Flanders Mare was drown'd.
A Slave I am to CLARA's Eyes:
The Gipsey knows her Pow'r, and flies.
Fire, Water, Woman, are My Ruin.
And great Thy Wisdom, VANDER BRÜIN. 10

To Cloe Weeping.

SEE, whilst Thou weep'st, fair CLOE, see
The World in Sympathy with Thee.
The chearful Birds no longer sing,
Each drops his Head, and hangs his Wing.
The Clouds have bent their Bosom lower, 5
And shed their Sorrows in a Show'r.
The Brooks beyond their Limits flow;
And louder Murmurs speak their Woe.

42 wrote] writ *1709*
  To Cloe Weeping. 4] But drop the Head, and hang the Wing. *1709*

The Nymphs and Swains adopt Thy Cares:
They heave Thy Sighs, and weep Thy Tears.   10
Fantastic Nymph! that Grief should move
Thy Heart, obdurate against Love.
Strange Tears! whose Pow'r can soften All,
But That dear Breast on which they fall.

Love Disarm'd.

BENEATH a Myrtle's verdant Shade
As CLOE half asleep was laid,
CUPID perch'd lightly on Her Breast,
And in That Heav'n desir'd to rest:
Over her Paps his Wings He spread: 5
Between He found a downy Bed,
And nestl'd in His little Head.

Still lay the God: The Nymph surpriz'd,
Yet Mistress of her self, devis'd,
How She the Vagrant might inthral,   10
And Captive Him, who Captives All.

Her Boddice half way She unlac'd:
About his Arms She slily cast
The silken Bond, and held Him fast.

The God awak'd; and thrice in vain   15
He strove to break the cruel Chain;
And thrice in vain He shook his Wing,
Incumber'd in the silken String.

Flutt'ring the God, and weeping said,
Pity poor CUPID, generous Maid,   20
Who happen'd, being Blind, to stray,
And on thy Bosom lost his Way:
Who stray'd, alas! but knew too well,
He never There must hope to dwell.
Set an unhappy Pris'ner free,   25
Who ne'er intended Harm to Thee.

12 Thy] The *1709*

To Me pertains not, She replies,
To know or care where CUPID flies;
What are his Haunts, or which his Way;
Where He would dwell, or whither stray: 30
Yet will I never set Thee free:
For Harm was meant, and Harm to Me.

Vain Fears that vex thy Virgin Heart!
I'll give Thee up my Bow and Dart:
Untangle but this cruel Chain,   35
And freely let Me fly again.

Agreed: Secure my Virgin Heart:
Instant give up thy Bow and Dart:
The Chain I'll in Return unty;
And freely Thou again shalt fly.   40

Thus She the Captive did deliver:
The Captive thus gave up his Quiver.

The God disarm'd, e'er since that Day
Passes his Life in harmless Play;
Flies round, or sits upon her Breast,   45
A little, flutt'ring, idle Guest.

E'er since that Day the beauteous Maid
Governs the World in CUPID's stead;
Directs his Arrow as She wills;
Gives Grief, or Pleasure; spares, or kills.   50

Cupid and Ganymede.

IN Heav'n, one Holy-day, You read
In wise *Anacreon*, GANYMEDE
Drew heedless CUPID in, to throw
A Main, to pass an Hour, or so.
The little Trojan, by the way,   5
By HERMES taught, play'd All the Play.

The God unhappily engag'd,
By Nature rash, by Play enrag'd,
Complain'd, and sigh'd, and cry'd, and fretted;
Lost ev'ry earthly thing He betted: 10
In ready Mony, all the Store
Pick'd up long since from DANAE's Show'r;
A Snush-Box, set with bleeding Hearts,
Rubies, all pierc'd with Diamond Darts;
His Nine-pins, made of Myrtle Wood;   15
(The Tree in IDA's Forest stood)
His Bowl pure Gold, the very same
Which PARIS gave the CYPRIAN Dame;
Two Table-Books in Shagreen Covers;
Fill'd with good Verse from real Lovers;   20
Merchandise rare! A Billet-doux,
It's Matter passionate, yet true:
Heaps of Hair Rings, and cypher'd Seals;
Rich Trifles; serious Bagatelles.

What sad Disorders Play begets!   25
Desp'rate and mad, at length He sets
Those Darts, whose Points make Gods adore
His Might, and deprecate his Pow'r:
Those Darts, whence all our Joy and Pain
Arise: those Darts—come, Seven's the Main,   30
Cries GANYMEDE: The usual Trick:
Seven, slur a Six; Eleven: A Nick.

Ill News goes fast: 'Twas quickly known,
That simple CUPID was undone.
Swifter than Lightning VENUS flew: 35
Too late She found the thing too true.
Guess how the Goddess greets her Son:
Come hither, Sirrah; no, begon;
And, hark Ye, is it so indeed?
A Comrade You for GANYMEDE?   40
An Imp as wicked, for his Age,
As any earthly Lady's Page;
A Scandal and a Scourge to TROY:
A Prince's Son? A Black-guard Boy:

A Sharper, that with Box and Dice   45
Draws in young Deities to Vice.
All Heav'n is by the Ears together,
Since first That little Rogue came hither:
JUNO her self has had no Peace:
And truly I've been favour'd less: 50
For JOVE, as FAME reports, (but FAME
Says things not fit for Me to name)
Has acted ill for such a God,
And taken Ways extreamly odd.

And Thou, unhappy Child, She said   55
(Her Anger by her Grief allay'd)
Unhappy Child, who thus hast lost
All the Estate We e'er could boast;
Whither, O whither wilt Thou run,
Thy Name despis'd, thy Weakness known?   60
Nor shall thy Shrine on Earth be crown'd:
Nor shall thy Pow'r in Heav'n be own'd;
When Thou, nor Man, nor God can'st wound.

Obedient CUPID kneeling cry'd,
Cease, dearest Mother, cease to chide: 65
GANY's a Cheat, and I'm a Bubble:
Yet why this great Excess of Trouble?
The Dice were false: the Darts are gone:
Yet how are You, or I undone?

The Loss of These I can supply   70
With keener Shafts from CLOE's Eye:
Fear not, We e'er can be disgrac'd,
While That bright Magazine shall last:
Your crowded Altars still shall smoke;
And Man your Friendly Aid invoke: 75
JOVE shall again revere your Pow'r,
And rise a Swan, or fall a Show'r.

71 Shafts] Darts *1709*

For the Plan of a Fountain,

on which is the Effigies of the Queen on a Triumphal Arch, the Figure of the Duke of Marlborough beneath, and the Chief Rivers of the World round the whole Work.

YE active Streams, where-e'er your Waters flow,
Let distant Climes and furthest Nations know,
What Ye from THAMES and DANUBE have been taught,
How ANNE Commanded, and how MARLBRÔ Fought.

Quacunque æterno properatis, Flumina, lapsu, 5
Divisis latè Terris, Populisque remotis
Dicite, nam vobis TAMISIS *narravit &* ISTER,
ANNA *quid Imperiis potuit, quid* MARLBURUS *Armis.*

To Mr. Howard: An Ode.

I.

DEAR HOWARD, from the soft Assaults of Love,
Poets and Painters never are Secure:
Can I untouch'd the Fair ones Passions move?
Or Thou draw Beauty, and not feel it's Pow'r?

II.

To Great APELLES when Young AMMON brought 5
The darling Idol of his Captive Heart;
And the pleas'd Nymph with kind Attention sat,
To have Her Charms recorded by His Art:

III.

The am'rous Master own'd Her potent Eyes;
Sigh'd when He look'd, and trembl'd as He drew: 10
Each flowing Line confirm'd his first Surprize;
And as the Piece advanc'd, the Passion grew.

IV.

While PHILIP's Son, while VENUS' Son was near,
  What different Tortures does his Bosom feel?
Great was the Rival, and the God severe: 15
  Nor could He hide his Flame, nor durst reveal.

V.

The Prince, renown'd in Bounty as in Arms,
  With Pity saw the ill-conceal'd Distress;
Quitted His Title to CAMPASPE's Charms,
  And gave the Fair one to the Friend's Embrace.   20

VI.

Thus the more beauteous CLOE sat to Thee,
  Good HOWARD, emu'lous of the GRÆCIAN Art:
But happy Thou, from CUPID's Arrow free,
  And Flames that pierc'd Thy Predecessor's Heart.

VII.

Had Thy poor Breast receiv'd an equal Pain;   25
  Had I been vested with the Monarch's Pow'r;
Thou must have sigh'd, unlucky Youth, in vain;
  Nor from My Bounty hadst Thou found a Cure.

VIII.

Tho' to convince Thee, that the Friend did feel
  A kind Concern for Thy ill-fated Care,   30
I would have sooth'd the Flame, I could not heal;
  Giv'n Thee the World; tho' I with-held the Fair.

Cupid Mistaken.

I.

As after Noon, one Summer's Day,
  VENUS stood bathing in a River;
CUPID a-shooting went that Way,
  New strung his Bow, new fill'd his Quiver.

22 Good] O *1709*   27 unlucky] unhappy *1709*   29 convince] evince *1709*

II.

With Skill He chose his sharpest Dart: 5
· With all his Might his Bow He drew:
Swift to His beauteous Parent's Heart
The too well-guided Arrow flew.

III.

I faint! I die! the Goddess cry'd:
O cruel, could'st Thou find none other,   10
To wreck thy Spleen on? Parricide!
Like NERO, Thou hast slain thy Mother.

IV.

Poor CUPID sobbing scarce could speak;
Indeed, Mamma, I did not know Ye:
Alas! how easie my Mistake?   15
I took You for your Likeness, CLOE.

Venus Mistaken.

I.

WHEN CLOE's Picture was to VENUS shown;
Surpriz'd, the Goddess took it for Her own.
And what, said She, does this bold Painter mean?
When was I Bathing thus, and Naked seen?

II.

Pleas'd CUPID heard, and check'd His Mother's Pride: 5
And who's blind now, Mamma? the Urchin cry'd.
'Tis CLOE's Eye, and Cheek, and Lip, and Breast:
Friend HOWARD's Genius fancy'd all the rest.

7 Swift to] Aim'd at *1709*   8 The too well-guided] With certain Speed the *1709*
15 Mistake?] Mistake! *1709*

Cloe Hunting.

BEHIND her Neck her comely Tresses ty'd,
Her Iv'ry Quiver graceful by her Side,
A-Hunting CLOE went: She lost her Way,
And thro' the Woods uncertain chanc'd to stray.
APOLLO passing by beheld the Maid;   5
And, Sister Dear, bright CYNTHIA turn, He said:
The hunted Hind lyes close in yonder Brake.
Loud CUPID laugh'd, to see the God's Mistake;
And laughing cry'd, Learn better, great Divine,
To know Thy Kindred, and to honour Mine.   10
Rightly advis'd, far hence Thy Sister seek,
Or on MEANDER's Bank, or LATMUS' Peak.
But in This Nymph, My Friend, My Sister know:
She draws My Arrows, and She bends My Bow:
Fair THAMES She haunts, and ev'ry neighb'ring Grove   15
Sacred to soft Recess, and gentle Love.
Go, with Thy CYNTHIA, hurl the pointed Spear
At the rough Boar; or chace the flying Deer:
I and My CLOE take a nobler Aim:
At human Hearts We fling, nor ever miss the Game.   20

Henry and Emma, a Poem, Upon the Model of The Nut-brown Maid.

To Cloe.

THOU, to whose Eyes I bend; at whose Command,
(Tho' low my Voice, tho' artless be my Hand)
I take the sprightly Reed, and sing, and play;
Careless of what the cens'ring World may say:
Bright CLOE, Object of my constant Vow,   5
Wilt thou awhile unbend thy serious Brow?
Wilt thou with Pleasure hear Thy Lover's Strains,
And with one Heav'nly Smile o'erpay His Pains?

12 Bank] Banks *1709*

No longer shall *the Nut-brown Maid* be old;
Tho' since her Youth three hundred Years have roll'd.   10
At Thy Desire, She shall again be rais'd;
And her reviving Charms in lasting Verse be prais'd.

   No longer Man of Woman shall complain,
That He may Love, and not be Lov'd again:
That We in vain the fickle Sex pursue,   15
Who change the Constant Lover for the New.
Whatever has been writ, whatever said
Of Female Passion feign'd, or Faith decay'd;
Henceforth shall in my Verse refuted stand,
Be said to Winds, or writ upon the Sand.   20
And while my Notes to future Times proclaim
Unconquer'd Love, and ever-during Flame;
O fairest of the Sex! be Thou my Muse:
Deign on my Work thy Influence to diffuse.
Let me partake the Blessings I rehearse;   25
And grant me Love, the just Reward of Verse.

   As Beauty's Potent Queen, with ev'ry Grace
That once was EMMA's, has adorn'd Thy Face;
And as Her Son has to My Bosom dealt
That constant Flame, which faithful HENRY felt: 30
O let the Story with Thy Life agree;
Let Men once more the bright Example see;
What EMMA was to Him, be Thou to Me.
Nor send Me by thy Frown from Her I love,
Distant and sad, a banish'd Man to rove.   35
But oh! with Pity long intreated Crown
My Pains and Hopes; and when thou say'st that One
Of all Mankind thou lov'st; Oh! think on Me alone.

W HERE beauteous ISIS and her Husband TAME
    With mingl'd Waves, for ever, flow the Same: 40
In Times of Yore, an antient Baron liv'd;
Great Gifts bestow'd, and great Respect receiv'd.

   When dreadful EDWARD, with successful Care,
Led his free BRITONS to the GALLIC War;

23 the] thy *1709*

This Lord had Headed his appointed Bands,   45
In firm Allegiance to his King's Commands.
And (all due Honors faithfully discharg'd)
Had brought back his Paternal Coat, inlarg'd
With a new Mark, the Witness of his Toil;
And no inglorious part of Foreign Spoil.   50

From the loud Camp retir'd, and noisy Court,
In Honorable Ease and Rural Sport,
The Remnant of his Days, He safely past;
Nor found they Lagg'd too slow, nor Flew too fast.
He made his Wish with his Estate comply;   55
Joyful to Live, yet not afraid to Dye.

One Child He had, a Daughter chast and fair;
His Age's Comfort, and his Fortune's Heir.
They call'd her EMMA; for the beauteous Dame
Who gave the Virgin Birth, had born the Name.   60
The Name th'indulgent Father doubly lov'd;
For in the Child the Mother's Charms improv'd.
Yet, as when little, round his Knees She plaid;
He call'd her oft, in Sport, His *Nut-brown Maid*:
The Friends and Tenants took the fondling Word;   65
(As still they please, who imitate their Lord)
Usage confirm'd what Fancy had begun:
The mutual Terms around the Lands were known;
And EMMA and *the Nut-brown Maid* were One.

As with her Stature, still her Charms encreas'd;   70
Thro' all the Isle her Beauty was confess'd.
Oh! what Perfections must that Virgin share,
Who Fairest is esteem'd, where all are Fair?
From distant Shires repair the noble Youth,
And find, Report, for once, had lessen'd Truth.   75
By Wonder first, and then by Passion mov'd,
They came; they saw; they marvell'd; and they lov'd.
By public Praises, and by secret Sighs,
Each own'd the gen'ral Pow'r of EMMA's Eyes.

In Tilts and Turnaments the Valiant strove,   80
By glorious Deeds, to purchase EMMA's Love.
In gentle Verse, the Witty told their Flame,
And grac'd their choicest Songs with EMMA's Name.
In vain they Combated, in vain they Writ:
Useless their Strength, and impotent their Wit.   85
Great VENUS only must direct the Dart,
Which else will never reach the Fair one's Heart;
Spight of th'Attempts of Force, and soft Effects of Art.
Great VENUS must prefer the happy One:
In HENRY's Cause Her Favour must be shown: 90
And EMMA, of Mankind, must Love but Him alone.

While These, in Public, to the Castle came,
And by their Grandeur justify'd their Flame:
More secret Ways the careful HENRY takes;
His Squires, his Arms, and Equipage forsakes.   95
In borrow'd Name, and false Attire, array'd,
Oft He finds Means to see the beauteous Maid.

When EMMA hunts, in Huntsman's Habit drest,
HENRY on Foot pursues the bounding Beast.
In his right Hand his beachen Pole he bears: 100
And graceful at his Side his Horn he wears.
Still to the Glade, where She has bent her Way,
With knowing Skill he drives the future Prey.
Bids her decline the Hill, and shun the Brake;
And shews the Path her Steed may safest take.   105
Directs her Spear to fix the glorious Wound;
Pleas'd, in his Toils, to have her Triumph Crown'd:
And blows her Praises in no common Sound.

A Falc'ner HENRY is, when EMMA Hawks:
With her of Tarsels, and of Lures he talks.   110
Upon his Wrist the tow'ring Merlin stands;
Practis'd to rise, and stoop, at her Commands.
And when Superior now the Bird has flown,
And headlong brought the tumbling Quarry down:
With humble Rev'rence he accosts the Fair;   115
And with the honor'd Feather decks her Hair.

Yet still, as from the sportive Field She goes,
His down-cast Eye reveals his inward Woes.
And by his Look and Sorrow is exprest,
A nobler Game pursu'd, than Bird or Beast.   120

A Shepherd now along the Plain he roves;
And, with his jolly Pipe, delights the Groves.
The neighb'ring Swains around the Stranger throng,
Or to admire, or emulate his Song:
While, with soft Sorrow, he renews his Lays,   125
Nor heedful of their Envy, nor their Praise.
But soon as EMMA's Eyes adorn the Plain,
His Notes he raises to a nobler Strain;
With dutiful Respect, and studious Fear,
Lest any careless Sound offend her Ear.   130

A frantick Gipsey, now the House He haunts,
And in wild Phrases, speaks dissembled Wants.
With the fond Maids in Palmistry he deals:
They Tell the Secret first, which he Reveals:
Says who shall Wed, and who shall be Beguil'd;   135
What Groom shall Get, and Squire maintain the Child.
But when bright EMMA wou'd her Fortune know;
A softer Look unbends his op'ning Brow.
With trembling Awe, he gazes on her Eye;
And in soft Accents, forms the kind Reply;   140
That She shall prove as Fortunate as Fair,
And HYMEN's choicest Gifts are All reserv'd for Her.

Now oft had HENRY chang'd his sly Disguise;
Unmark'd by all, but beauteous EMMA's Eyes.
Oft had found Means alone to see the Dame,   145
And at her Feet to breath his am'rous Flame;
And oft, the Pangs of Absence to remove
By Letters, soft Interpreters of Love:
'Till Time and Industry (the mighty Two
That bring our Wishes nearer to our View)   150
Made him perceive, that the inclining Fair
Receiv'd his Vows with no reluctant Ear;
That VENUS had confirm'd her equal Reign,
And dealt to EMMA's Heart a share of HENRY's Pain.

While CUPID smil'd, by kind Occasion bless'd,   155
And, with the Secret kept, the Love increas'd;
The am'rous Youth frequents the silent Groves;
And much He meditates; for much He loves.
He loves: 'tis true; and is belov'd again:
Great are his Joys: but will they long remain?   160
EMMA with Smiles receives his present Flame;
But smiling, will She ever be the same?
Beautiful Looks are rul'd by fickle Minds;
And Summer Seas are turn'd by sudden Winds.
Another Love may gain her easie Youth: 165
Time changes Thought; and Flatt'ry conquers Truth.

    O impotent Estate of human Life!
Where Hope and Fear maintain eternal Strife:
Where fleeting Joy does lasting Doubt inspire;
And most We Question, what We most Desire.   170
Amongst thy various Gifts, great Heav'n, bestow
Our Cup of Love unmix'd; forbear to throw
Bitter Ingredients in; nor pall the Draught
With nauseous Grief: for our ill-judging Thought
Hardly injoys the pleasurable Taste;   175
Or deems it not sincere; or fears it cannot last.

    With Wishes rais'd, with Jealousies opprest
(Alternate Tyrants of the Human Breast)
By one great Tryal He resolves to prove
The Faith of Woman, and the Force of Love.   180
If scanning EMMA's Virtues, He may find
That beauteous Frame inclose a steady Mind;
He'll fix his Hope, of future Joy secure;
And live a Slave to HYMEN's happy Pow'r.
But if the Fair one, as he fears, is frail;   185
If pois'd aright in Reason's equal Scale,
Light fly her Merits, and her Faults prevail;
His Mind He vows to free from am'rous Care,
The latent Mischief from his Heart to tear,
Resume his Azure Arms, and shine again in War.   190

    South of the Castle, in a verdant Glade,
A spreading Beach extends her friendly Shade:

Here oft the Nymph His breathing Vows had heard:
Here oft Her Silence had Her Heart declar'd.
As active Spring awak'd her Infant Buds;   195
And genial Life inform'd the verdant Woods;
HENRY, in Knots involving EMMA's Name,
Had half express'd, and half conceal'd his Flame
Upon This Tree: and as the tender Mark
Grew with the Year, and widen'd with the Bark: 200
VENUS had heard the Virgin's soft Address,
That, as the Wound, the Passion might increase.
As potent Nature shed her kindly Show'rs,
And deck'd the various Mead with op'ning Flow'rs;
Upon This Tree the Nymph's obliging Care   205
Had left a frequent Wreath for HENRY's Hair:
Which as with gay Delight the Lover found;
Pleas'd with his Conquest, with her Present crown'd,
Glorious thro' all the Plains He oft had gone,
And to each Swain the Mystic Honor shown;   210
The Gift still prais'd, the Giver still unknown.

His secret Note the troubled HENRY writes,
To the known Tree the Lovely Maid invites:
Imperfect Words and dubious Terms express,
That unforseen Mischance disturb'd his Peace;   215
That He must something to Her Ear commend,
On which Her Conduct, and His Life depend.

Soon as the Fair one had the Note receiv'd;
The remnant of the Day alone She griev'd:
For diff'rent This from ev'ry former Note,   220
Which VENUS dictated, and HENRY wrote;
Which told her all his future Hopes were laid
On the dear Bosom of *his Nut-brown Maid*;
Which always bless'd her Eyes, and own'd her Pow'r;
And bid her oft Adieu, yet added more.   225

Now Night advanc'd. The House in Sleep were laid,
The Nurse experienc'd, and the prying Maid;
And last That Sprite, which does incessant haunt
The Lover's Steps, the ancient Maiden Aunt.

228 Sprite...incessant] Spirit...closest *1709*

To her dear HENRY EMMA wings her Way,   230
With quicken'd Pace repairing forc'd Delay.
For Love, fantastic Pow'r, that is afraid
To stir abroad 'till Watchfulness be laid;
Undaunted then, o'er Cliffs and Valleys strays;
And leads his Vot'ries safe thro' pathless Ways.   235
Not ARGUS with his hundred Eyes shall find,
Where CUPID goes; tho' He poor Guide is blind.

   The Maiden first arriving, sent her Eye,
To ask, if yet it's Chief Delight were nigh:
With Fear, and with Desire, with Joy, and Pain   240
She sees, and runs to meet Him on the Plain.
But oh! his Steps proclaim no Lover's Haste:
On the low Ground his fix'd Regards are cast:
His artful Bosom heaves dissembl'd Sighs;
And Tears suborn'd fall copious from his Eyes.   245

   With Ease, alas! we Credit what we Love:
His painted Grief does real Sorrow move
In the afflicted Fair; Adown her Cheek
Trickling the genuine Tears their Current break.
Attentive stood the mournful Nymph: the Man   250
Broke Silence first: the Tale alternate ran.

HENRY.

SINCERE O tell me, hast thou felt a Pain,
  EMMA, beyond what Woman knows to feign?
Has Thy uncertain Bosom ever strove
With the first Tumults of a real Love?   255
Hast Thou now dreaded, and now blest his Sway;
By turns averse, and joyful to obey?
Thy Virgin Softness hast Thou e'er bewail'd,
As Reason yielded, and as Love prevail'd?
And wept the potent God's resistless Dart,   260
His killing Pleasure, his Ecstatic Smart,
And heav'nly Poison thrilling thro' thy Heart?
If so, with Pity view my wretched State;
At least deplore, and then forget my Fate:

To some more happy Knight reserve thy Charms,   265
By Fortune favor'd, and successful Arms:
And only, as the Sun's revolving Ray
Brings back each Year this melancholy Day;
Permit one Sigh, and set apart one Tear,
To an abandon'd Exile's endless Care.   270
For Me, alas! Out-cast of Human Race,
Love's Anger only waits, and dire Disgrace:
For lo! these Hands in Murther are imbru'd;
These trembling Feet by Justice are pursu'd:
Fate calls aloud, and hastens me away;   275
A shameful Death attends my longer Stay;
And I this Night must fly from Thee and Love,
Condemn'd in lonely Woods a banish'd Man to rove.

EMMA.

What is our Bliss, that changeth with the Moon;
And Day of Life, that darkens e'er 'tis Noon?   280
What is true Passion, if unblest it dies?
And where is EMMA's Joy, if HENRY flies?
If Love, alas! be Pain; the Pain I bear,
No Thought can figure, and no Tongue declare.
Ne'er faithful Woman felt, nor false one feign'd   285
The Flames, which long have in my Bosom reign'd:
The God of Love himself inhabits there,
With all his Rage, and Dread, and Grief, and Care,
His Complement of Stores, and total War.

O! cease then coldly to suspect my Love;   290
And let my Deed, at least, my Faith approve.
Alas! no Youth shall my Endearments share;
Nor Day nor Night shall interrupt my Care:
No future Story shall with Truth upbraid
The cold Indiff'rence of *the Nut-brown Maid*:   295
Nor to hard Banishment shall HENRY run;
While careless EMMA sleeps on Beds of Down.
View Me resolv'd, where-e'er Thou lead'st, to go,
Friend to thy Pain, and Partner of thy Woe:

298 View Me resolv'd] Behold me fix'd *1709*

For I attest fair VENUS, and her Son,   300
That I, of all Mankind, will love but Thee alone.

HENRY.

Let Prudence yet obstruct Thy vent'rous Way;
And take good heed, what Men will think and say;
That Beauteous EMMA vagrant Courses took;
Her Father's House and civil Life forsook;   305
That full of youthful Blood, and fond of Man,
She to the Wood-land with an Exile ran.
Reflect, that lessen'd Fame is ne'er regain'd;
And Virgin Honor once, is always stain'd:
Timely advis'd, the coming Evil shun: 310
Better not do the Deed, than weep it done.
No Penance can absolve our guilty Fame;
Nor Tears, that wash out Sin, can wash out Shame.
Then fly the sad Effects of desp'rate Love;
And leave a banish'd Man thro' lonely Woods to rove.   315

EMMA.

Let EMMA's hapless Case be falsely told
By the rash Young, or the ill-natur'd Old:
Let ev'ry Tongue it's various Censures chuse,
Absolve with Coldness, or with Spight accuse:
Fair Truth, at last, her radiant Beams will raise;   320
And Malice vanquish'd heightens Virtue's Praise.
Let then thy Favour but indulge my Flight;
O! let my Presence make thy Travels light;
And potent VENUS shall exalt my Name
Above the Rumors of censorious Fame: 325
Nor from that busie Demon's restless Pow'r
Will ever EMMA other Grace implore,
Than that this Truth should to the World be known,
That I, of all Mankind, have lov'd but Thee alone.

HENRY.

But canst Thou wield the Sword, and bend the Bow?   330
With active Force repel the sturdy Foe?

318 Censures] Censure *1709*

When the loud Tumult speaks the Battel nigh,
And winged Deaths in whistling Arrows fly;
Wilt Thou, tho' wounded, yet undaunted stay,
Perform thy Part, and share the dangerous Day?   335
Then, as thy Strength decays, thy Heart will fail;
Thy Limbs all trembling, and thy Cheeks all pale:
With fruitless Sorrow Thou, inglorious Maid,
Wilt weep thy Safety by thy Love betray'd:
Then to thy Friend, by Foes o'er-charg'd, deny   340
Thy little useless Aid, and Coward fly:
Then wilt thou curse the Chance that made Thee love
A banish'd Man, condemn'd in lonely Woods to rove.

EMMA.

With fatal Certainty THALESTRIS knew
To send the Arrow from the twanging Yew: 345
And great in Arms, and foremost in the War,
BONDUCA brandish'd high the BRITISH Spear.
Could Thirst of Vengeance, and Desire of Fame
Excite the Female Breast with Martial Flame?
And shall not Love's diviner Pow'r inspire   350
More hardy Virtue, and more gen'rous Fire?

Near Thee, mistrust not, constant I'll abide,
And fall, or vanquish, fighting by thy Side.
Tho' my Inferior Strength may not allow,
That I should bear, or draw the Warrior Bow;   355
With ready Hand I will the Shaft supply,
And joy to see thy Victor Arrows fly.
Touch'd in the Battel by the Hostile Reed,
Should'st Thou (but Heav'n avert it!) should'st Thou bleed;
To stop the Wounds my finest Lawn I'd tear;   360
Wash them with Tears, and wipe them with my Hair:
Blest, when my Dangers and my Toils have shown,
That I, of all Mankind, could love but Thee alone.

HENRY.

But canst Thou, tender Maid, canst Thou sustain
Afflictive Want, or Hunger's pressing Pain?   365

337 Cheeks] Cheek *1709*   357 Arrows] Arrow *1709*

Those Limbs, in Lawn and softest Silk array'd,
From Sun-beams guarded, and of Winds afraid;
Can they bear angry JOVE? Can they resist
The parching Dog-star, and the bleak North-East?
When chill'd by adverse Snows, and beating Rain,   370
We tread with weary Steps the longsome Plain;
When with hard Toil We seek our Ev'ning Food,
Berries and Acorns, from the neighb'ring Wood;
And find among the Cliffs no other House,
But the thin Covert of some gather'd Boughs;   375
Wilt Thou not then reluctant send thine Eye
Around the dreary Waste; and weeping try
(Tho' then, alas! that Tryal be too late)
To find thy Father's Hospitable Gate,
And Seats, where Ease and Plenty brooding sate?   380
Those Seats, whence long excluded Thou must mourn:
That Gate, for ever barr'd to thy Return:
Wilt Thou not then bewail ill-fated Love,
And hate a banish'd Man, condemn'd in Woods to rove?

EMMA.

Thy Rise of Fortune did I only wed,   385
From it's Decline determin'd to recede?
Did I but purpose to embark with Thee,
On the smooth Surface of a Summer's Sea;
While gentle ZEPHYRS play in prosp'rous Gales;
And Fortune's Favour fills the swelling Sails: 390
But would forsake the Ship, and make the Shoar,
When the Winds whistle, and the Tempests roar?
No, HENRY, no: One Sacred Oath has ty'd
Our Loves; One Destiny our Life shall guide;
Nor Wild, nor Deep our common Way divide.   395

When from the Cave Thou risest with the Day,
To beat the Woods, and rouse the bounding Prey;
The Cave with Moss and Branches I'll adorn,
And chearful sit, to wait my Lord's Return.
And when Thou frequent bring'st the smitten Deer;   400
(For seldom, Archers say, Thy Arrows err)

368 Can...Can] Will...will *1709*   374 among] amongst *1709*   399 to] and *1709*

I'll fetch quick Fewel from the neighb'ring Wood,
And strike the sparkling Flint, and dress the Food:
With humble Duty and officious Haste,
I'll cull the furthest Mead for Thy Repast: 405
The choicest Herbs I to Thy Board will bring;
And draw Thy Water from the freshest Spring:
And when at Night with weary Toil opprest,
Soft Slumbers Thou injoy'st, and wholesome Rest;
Watchful I'll guard Thee, and with Midnight Pray'r   410
Weary the Gods to keep Thee in their Care;
And joyous ask, at Morn's returning Ray,
If Thou hast Health, and I may bless the Day.
My Thought shall fix, my latest Wish depend
On Thee, Guide, Guardian, Kinsman, Father, Friend: 415
By all these sacred Names be HENRY known
To EMMA's Heart: and grateful let Him own,
That She, of all Mankind, could love but Him alone.

HENRY.

Vainly thou tell'st Me, what the Woman's Care
Shall in the Wildness of the Wood prepare: 420
Thou, e'er thou goest, unhapp'yest of thy Kind,
Must leave the Habit, and the Sex behind.
No longer shall thy comely Tresses break
In flowing Ringlets on thy snowy Neck;
Or sit behind thy Head, an ample Round,   425
In graceful Breeds with various Ribbon bound:
No longer shall the Boddice, aptly lac'd,
From thy full Bosome to thy slender Waste,
That Air and Harmony of Shape express,
Fine by Degrees, and beautifully less: 430
Nor shall thy lower Garments artful Pleat,
From thy fair Side dependent to thy Feet,
Arm their chaste Beauties with a modest Pride,
And double ev'ry Charm they seek to hide.
Th'Ambrosial Plenty of Thy shining Hair   435
Cropt off and lost, scarce lower than Thy Ear
Shall stand uncouth: a Horse-man's Coat shall hide
Thy taper Shape, and Comeliness of Side:

The short Trunk-Hose shall show Thy Foot and Knee
Licentious, and to common Eye-sight free: 440
And with a bolder Stride, and looser Air,
Mingl'd with Men, a Man Thou must appear.

Nor Solitude, nor gentle Peace of Mind,
Mistaken Maid, shalt Thou in Forests find:
'Tis long, since CYNTHIA and her Train were there;   445
Or Guardian Gods made Innocence their Care.
Vagrants and Out-laws shall offend Thy View;
For such must be my Friends; a hideous Crew,
By adverse Fortune mix'd in Social Ill,
Train'd to assault, and disciplin'd to kill: 450
Their common Loves, a lewd abandon'd Pack,
The Beadle's Lash still flagrant on their Back;
By Sloth corrupted, by Disorder fed,
Made bold by Want, and prostitute for Bread:
With such must EMMA hunt the tedious Day,   455
Assist their Violence, and divide their Prey:
With such She must return at setting Light,
Tho' not Partaker, Witness of their Night.
Thy Ear, inur'd to charitable Sounds,
And pitying Love, must feel the hateful Wounds   460
Of Jest obscene, and vulgar Ribaldry,
The ill-bred Question, and the lewd Reply;
Brought by long Habitude from Bad to Worse,
Must hear the frequent Oath, the direful Curse,
That latest Weapon of the Wretches War,   465
And Blasphemy, sad Comrade of Despair.

Now, EMMA, now the last Reflection make,
What Thou would'st follow, what Thou must forsake:
By our ill-omen'd Stars, and adverse Heav'n,
No middle Object to thy Choice is given.   470
Or yield thy Virtue, to attain thy Love;
Or leave a banish'd Man, condemn'd in Woods to rove.

EMMA.

O Grief of Heart! that our unhappy Fates
Force Thee to suffer what thy Honor hates:

Mix Thee amongst the Bad; or make Thee run   475
Too near the Paths, which Virtue bids Thee shun.
Yet with her HENRY still let EMMA go;
With Him abhor the Vice, but share the Woe:
And sure My little Heart can never err
Amidst the worst; if HENRY still be there.   480

    Our outward Act is prompted from within;
And from the Sinner's Mind proceeds the Sin:
By her own Choice free Virtue is approv'd;
Nor by the Force of outward Objects mov'd.
Who has assay'd no Danger, gains no Praise.   485
In a small Isle, amidst the widest Seas,
Triumphant Constancy has fix'd her Seat:
In vain the Syrens sing, the Tempests beat:
Their Flatt'ry She rejects, nor fears their Threat.

    For Thee alone these little Charms I drest;   490
Condemn'd them, or absolv'd them by thy Test.
In comely Figure rang'd, my Jewels shone,
Or negligently plac'd, for Thee alone:
For Thee again they shall be laid aside:
The Woman, HENRY, shall put off her Pride   495
For Thee: my Cloaths, my Sex exchang'd for Thee,
I'll mingle with the People's wretched Lee;
O Line extream of human Infamy!
Wanting the Scissors, with these Hands I'll tear
(If that obstructs my Flight) this load of Hair.   500
Black Soot, or yellow Walnut shall disgrace
This little Red and White of EMMA's Face.
These Nails with Scratches shall deform my Breast,
Lest by my Look, or Color be express'd
The Mark of ought High-born, or ever better dress'd.   505
Yet in this Commerce, under this Disguise,
Let Me be grateful still to HENRY's Eyes.
Lost to the World, let Me to Him be known:
My Fate I can absolve; if He shall own,
That leaving all Mankind, I love but Him alone.   510

    499 with these Hands I'll] and my Hands shall *1709*

HENRY.

O wildest Thought of an abandon'd Mind!
Name, Habit, Parents, Woman left behind,
Ev'n Honor dubious, Thou preferr'st to go
Wild to the Woods with Me: Said EMMA so?
Or did I dream what EMMA never said?   515
O guilty Error! and O wretched Maid!
Whose roving Fancy would resolve the same
With Him, who next should tempt her easie Fame;
And blow with empty Words the susceptible Flame.
Now why should doubtful Terms thy Mind perplex?   520
Confess thy Frailty, and avow the Sex:
No longer loose Desire for constant Love
Mistake; but say, 'tis Man, with whom Thou long'st to rove.

EMMA.

Are there not Poisons, Racks, and Flames, and Swords;
That EMMA thus must die by HENRY's Words?   525
Yet what could Swords or Poison, Racks or Flame,
But mangle and disjoint this brittle Frame?
More fatal HENRY's Words; they murder EMMA's Fame.

And fall these Sayings from that gentle Tongue,
Where civil Speech, and soft Persuasion hung;   530
Whose artful Sweetness and harmonious Strain,
Courting my Grace, yet courting it in vain,
Call'd Sighs, and Tears, and Wishes to it's Aid;
And, whilst it HENRY's glowing Flame convey'd,
Still blam'd the Coldness of *the Nut-brown Maid*?   535

Let envious Jealousie, and canker'd Spight
Produce my Action to severest Light,
And tax my open Day, or secret Night.
Did e'er my Tongue speak my unguarded Heart
The least inclin'd to play the Wanton's Part?   540
Did e'er my Eye One inward Thought reveal,
Which Angels might not hear, and Virgins tell?

520 doubtful] dubious *1709*   524, 526 Racks] Wracks *1709*   536 Let] Lest *1709*
538 Night.] Night? *1709*

And hast Thou, HENRY, in my Conduct known
One Fault, but That which I must ever own,
That I, of all Mankind, have lov'd but Thee alone?   } 545

HENRY.

Vainly thou talk'st of loving Me alone:
Each Man is Man; and all Our Sex is One.
False are our Words; and fickle is our Mind:
Nor in Love's Ritual can We ever find
Vows made to last, or Promises to bind.   } 550

By Nature prompted, and for Empire made,
Alike by Strength or Cunning We invade:
When arm'd with Rage We march against the Foe;
We lift the Battel-Ax, and draw the Bow:
When fir'd with Passion We attack the Fair;   555
Delusive Sighs and brittle Vows We bear;
Our Falshood and our Arms have equal Use;
As they our Conquest, or Delight produce.

The foolish Heart Thou gav'st, again receive,
The only Boon departing Love can give.   560
To be less Wretched, be no longer True:
What strives to fly Thee, why should'st Thou pursue?   }
Forget the Present Flame, indulge a New.
Single the loveliest of the am'rous Youth;
Ask for his Vow; but hope not for his Truth.   565
The next Man (and the next Thou shalt believe)
Will pawn his Gods, intending to deceive;   }
Will kneel, implore, persist, o'ercome, and leave.
Hence let Thy CUPID aim his Arrows right;
Be Wise and False, shun Trouble, seek Delight,   } 570
Change Thou the first, nor wait Thy Lover's Flight.

Why shouldst Thou weep? let Nature judge our Case:
I saw Thee Young, and Fair; pursu'd the Chase
Of Youth, and Beauty: I another saw
Fairer, and Younger: yielding to the Law   575

547 Our] the *1709*

Of our all-ruling Mother, I pursu'd
More Youth, more Beauty: Blest Vicissitude!
My active Heart still keeps it's pristine Flame;
The Object alter'd, the Desire the same.

This Younger Fairer pleads her rightful Charms: 580
With present Power compels me to her Arms.
And much I fear, from my subjected Mind
(If Beauty's Force to constant Love can bind)
That Years may roll, e'er in Her turn the Maid
Shall weep the Fury of my Love decay'd;   585
And weeping follow Me, as Thou dost now,
With idle Clamours of a broken Vow.

Nor can the wildness of thy Wishes err
So wide, to hope that Thou may'st live with Her.
Love, well Thou know'st, no Partnership allows: 590
CUPID averse rejects divided Vows.
Then from thy foolish Heart, vain Maid, remove
A useless Sorrow, and an ill-starr'd Love;
And leave me, with the Fair, at large in Woods to rove.

EMMA.

Are we in Life thro' one great Error led?   595
Is each Man perjur'd, and each Nymph betray'd?
Of the Superior Sex art Thou the worst?
Am I of Mine the most compleatly Curst?
Yet let me go with Thee; and going prove,
From what I will endure, how much I love.   600

This potent Beauty, this Triumphant Fair,
This happy Object of our diff'rent Care,
Her let me follow; Her let me attend,
A Servant: (She may scorn the Name of Friend.)
What She demands, incessant I'll prepare: 605
I'll weave Her Garlands; and I'll pleat Her Hair:
My busie Diligence shall deck Her Board;
(For there, at least, I may approach my Lord.)

593 A] An *1709*

And when Her HENRY's softer Hours advise
His Servant's Absence; with dejected Eyes   } 610
Far I'll recede, and Sighs forbid to rise.

Yet when encreasing Grief brings slow Disease;
And ebbing Life, on Terms severe as these,
Will have it's little Lamp no longer fed;
When HENRY's Mistress shows him EMMA dead;   615
Rescue my poor Remains from vile Neglect:
With Virgin Honors let my Herse be deckt,
And decent Emblem; and at least persuade
This happy Nymph, that EMMA may be laid,
Where Thou, dear Author of my Death, where She   620
With frequent Eye my Sepulchre may see.
The Nymph amidst her Joys may haply breath
One pious Sigh, reflecting on my Death,
And the sad Fate which She may one Day prove,
Who hopes from HENRY's Vows Eternal Love.   625
And Thou forsworn, Thou cruel, as Thou art,
If EMMA's Image ever touch'd thy Heart;
Thou sure must give one Thought, and drop one Tear
To Her, whom Love abandon'd to Despair;
To Her, who dying, on the wounded Stone   } 630
Bid it in lasting Characters be known,
That, of Mankind, She lov'd but Thee alone.

HENRY.

Hear, solemn JOVE; and, conscious VENUS, hear;
And Thou, bright Maid, believe Me, whilst I swear;
No Time, no Change, no future Flame shall move   635
The well-plac'd Basis of my lasting Love.
O Powerful Virtue! O Victorious Fair!   }
At least excuse a Tryal too severe:
Receive the Triumph, and forget the War.

No banish'd Man, condemn'd in Woods to rove,   640
Intreats thy Pardon, and implores thy Love:
No perjur'd Knight desires to quit thy Arms,
Fairest Collection of thy Sexe's Charms,

Crown of my Love, and Honor of my Youth:
HENRY, thy HENRY with Eternal Truth,   645
As Thou may'st wish, shall all his Life imploy,
And found his Glory in his EMMA's Joy.

In Me behold the Potent EDGAR's Heir,
Illustrious Earl: Him terrible in War
Let LOYRE confess; for She has felt His Sword,   650
And trembling fled before the BRITISH Lord.
Him great in Peace and Wealth fair DEVA knows;
For she amidst his spacious Meadows flows;
Inclines her Urn upon his fatten'd Lands;
And sees his num'rous Herd imprint her Sands.   655

And Thou, my Fair, my Dove, shalt raise thy Thought
To Greatness next to Empire; shalt be brought
With solemn Pomp to my Paternal Seat;
Where Peace and Plenty on Thy Word shall wait.
Music and Song shall wake the Marriage-Day: 660
And while the Priests accuse the Bride's Delay;
Myrtles and Roses shall obstruct Her Way.

Friendship shall still Thy Evening Feasts adorn;
And blooming Peace shall ever bless Thy Morn.
Succeeding Years their happy Race shall run;   665
And Age unheeded by Delight come on;
While yet Superior Love shall mock his Pow'r:
And when old Time shall turn the fated Hour,
Which only can our well-ty'd Knot unfold,
What rests of Both, One Sepulchre shall hold.   670

Hence then, for ever, from my EMMA's Breast
(That Heav'n of Softness, and that Seat of Rest)
Ye Doubts and Fears, and All that know to move
Tormenting Grief, and All that trouble Love,
Scatter'd by Winds recede, and wild in Forests rove.   675

EMMA.

O Day the fairest sure that ever rose!
Period and End of anxious EMMA's Woes!

655 Herd] Herds *1709*

Sire of her Joy, and Source of her Delight;
O! wing'd with Pleasure take thy happy Flight,
And give each future Morn a Tincture of thy White.   680
Yet tell thy Votary, potent Queen of Love,
HENRY, my HENRY, will He never rove?
Will He be ever Kind, and Just, and Good?
And is there yet no Mistress in the Wood?
None, none there is: The Thought was rash and vain;   685
A false Idea, and a fancy'd Pain.
Doubt shall for ever quit my strengthen'd Heart,
And anxious Jealousie's corroding Smart;
Nor other Inmate shall inhabit there,
But soft Belief, young Joy, and pleasing Care.   690

Hence let the Tides of Plenty ebb and flow,
And FORTUNE's various Gale unheeded blow.
If at my Feet the Suppliant Goddess stands,
And sheds her Treasure with unweary'd Hands;
Her present Favor cautious I'll embrace,   695
And not unthankful use the proffer'd Grace:
If She reclaims the Temporary Boon,
And tries her Pinions, flutt'ring to be gone;
Secure of Mind I'll obviate her Intent,
And unconcern'd return the Goods She lent.   700
Nor Happiness can I, nor Misery feel,
From any Turn of her Fantastic Wheel:
Friendship's great Laws, and Love's superior Pow'rs
Must mark the Colour of my future Hours.
From the Events which Thy Commands create   705
I must my Blessings or my Sorrows date;
And HENRY's Will must dictate EMMA's Fate.

Yet while with close Delight and inward Pride
(Which from the World my careful Soul shall hide)
I see Thee, Lord and End of my Desire,   710
Exalted high as Virtue can require;
With Pow'r invested, and with Pleasure chear'd;
Sought by the Good, by the Oppressor fear'd;
Loaded and blest with all the affluent Store,
Which human Vows at smoking Shrines implore;   715

694 Treasure] Treasures *1709*   703 Pow'rs] Pow'r, *1709*   704 Hours] Hour *1709*

Grateful and humble grant Me to employ
My Life, subservient only to thy Joy;
And at my Death to bless thy Kindness shown
To Her, who of Mankind could love but Thee alone.

WHILE thus the constant Pair alternate said,   720
    Joyful above them and around them play'd
Angels and sportive LOVES, a numerous Crowd;
Smiling They clapt their Wings, and low They bow'd:
They tumbled all their little Quivers o'er,
To chuse propitious Shafts; a precious Store: 725
That when their God should take his future Darts,
To strike (however rarely) constant Hearts,
His happy Skill might proper Arms imploy,
All tipt with Pleasure, and all wing'd with Joy:
And Those, They vow'd, whose Lives should imitate   730
These Lovers Constancy, should share their Fate.

    The Queen of Beauty stop'd her bridled Doves;
Approv'd the little Labour of the LOVES;
Was proud and pleas'd the mutual Vow to hear;
And to the Triumph call'd the God of War: }   735
Soon as She calls, the God is always near.

    Now MARS, she said, let FAME exalt her Voice;
Nor let thy Conquests only be her Choice:
But when She sings great EDWARD from the Field
Return'd, the Hostile Spear and Captive Shield   }   740
In CONCORD's Temple hung, and GALLIA taught to yield.
And when, as prudent SATURN shall compleat
The Years design'd to perfect BRITAIN's State,
The swift-wing'd Power shall take her Trump again,
To sing Her Fav'rite ANNA's wond'rous Reign;   745
To recollect unweary'd MARLBRÔ's Toils,
Old RUFUS' Hall unequal to his Spoils;
The BRITISH Soldier from his high Command
Glorious, and GAUL thrice Vanquish'd by his Hand:
Let Her at least perform what I desire;   750
With second Breath the Vocal Brass inspire;
And tell the Nations in no Vulgar Strain,
What Wars I manage, and what Wreaths I gain.

And when Thy Tumults and Thy Fights are past,
And when Thy Lawrels at my Feet are cast;   755
Faithful may'st Thou like *British* HENRY prove,
And EMMA-like let me return Thy Love.

Renown'd for Truth let all Thy Sons appear;
And constant Beauty shall reward their Care.

MARS smil'd, and bow'd; the CYPRIAN Deity   760
Turn'd to the glorious Ruler of the Sky:
And Thou, She smiling said, Great God of Days
And Verse, behold my Deed; and sing my Praise.
As on the *British* Earth, my Fav'rite Isle,
Thy gentle Rays and kindest Influence smile,   765
Thro' all her laughing Fields and verdant Groves,
Proclaim with Joy these memorable Loves.
From ev'ry annual Course let One great Day,
To celebrated Sports and Floral Play
Be set aside; and, in the softest Lays   770
Of Thy Poetic Sons, be solemn Praise,
And everlasting Marks of Honour paid,
To *the true Lover*, and *the Nut-brown Maid*.

Jinny the Just.

R ELEAS'D from the Noise of the Butcher and Baker,
Who, my old friends be thanked, did seldom forsake Her
And from the soft Duns of my Landlord the Quaker

From chiding the footmen and watching the lasses,
From Nel that burn't milk too, and Tom that brake glasses   5
(Sad mischeifs thrô which a good housekeeper passes!)

From some real Care but more fancied vexation
From a life party: colour'd half reason half passion
Here lyes after all the best Wench in the Nation.

Title: Supplied by Waller in 1907: *om.* L 29 (P), L 29 (D)   1 *See commentary for origina.*
opening   5 too] *del.* L 29 (D)   6 passes!) L 29 (D): passes! L 29 (P)   9 Nation.
edd.: Nation L 29 (P), L 29 (D)

From the Rhine to the Po, from the Thames to the Rhone   10
Joanna or Janneton, Jinny or Joan
Twas all one to Her by what name She was known

For the Idiom of words very little She heeded
Provided the Matter She drove at Succeeded,
She took and gave languages just as she needed: 15

So for Kitching and markett for bargain and Sale
She paid English or Dutch or French down on the Nail
But in telling a Story She Sometimes did fail

Then begging excuse as she happen'd to stammer
With respect to her betters but none to her Grammer   20
Her blush helpt Her out and her jargon became Her.

Her habit and mein she Endeavour'd to frame
To the different Gout of the place where she came,
Her outside still chang'd, but her Inside the Same:

At the Hague in her Slippers and hair as the mode is   25
At Paris all falbalow'd fine as a Goddess
And at censuring London in Smock sleeves and Bodice

She order'd affairs that few people could tell
In what part about Her that mixture did dwell
Of Vrough or Mistresse, or Mademoiselle.   30

For Her Sirname and race let the Heraults e'n answer,
Her own proper worth was enough to advance Her,
And He who lik'd Her little valu'd her Grandsire

But from what House soever her lineage may come
I wish my own Jinny but out of her tomb,   35
Thô all her relations were there in her Room.

Of such terrible beauty She never could boast
As with absolute sway oer all hearts rules the roast
When J—— bawls out to the Chair for a toast

17 French *edd.*: french *L 29 (P)*, *L 29 (D)*   22–48 *In L 29 (P)*, *the sheet with these verses precedes l. 1*   23 came, *edd.*: came *L 29 (P)*, *L 29 (D)*   24 Same: *edd.*: Same *L 29 (P)*, *L 29 (D)*   30 Of *L 29 (D)*: of *L 29 (P)*   Mademoiselle. *edd.*: Mademoiselle *L 29 (P)*, *L 29 (D)*   36 Room. *L 29 (D)*: rome *L 29 (P)*

But of good household features her Person was made   40
Nor by faction cry'd up nor of censure afraid
And her beauty was rather for use than Parade

Her blood so well mixt and flesh so well pasted
That tho her Youth faded her comliness lasted
The blue was worn off but the plum was well tasted.   45

Less smooth then her Skin and Less White then her breast
Was this polisht stone beneath which she lyes prest
Stop, reader and sigh while thou think'st on the rest.

With a just trim of virtue her Soul was endued
Not affectedly pious nor Secretly Lewd   50
She cutt even between the Coquette, and the Prude

And Her will with her duty so equally stood
That Seldom oppos'd she was commonly good
And did pretty well, doing just what She wou'd.

Declining all power She found means to persuade   55
Was then most regarded, when most she obey'd,
The Mistresse in truth when She seem'd but the Maid

Such care of her own proper actions she took
That on other folks lives She had no time to look
So Censure and Praise were struck out of her book   60

Her thought still confin'd to it's own little sphere
She minded not who did excell or did err
But just as the Matter related to Her

Then too when her private tribunal was rear'd
Her mercy so mixt with her judgement appear'd   65
That her foes were condemnd and her friend's always clear'd.

Her religion so well with her learning did suit
That in practice sincere, and in controverse mute
She show'd She knew better to live then dispute.

45 The *L 29* (*D*): the *L 29* (*P*)   worn] wore *L 29* (*D*)   69 dispute. *edd.*: dispute
L 29 (*P*), *L 29* (*D*)

Some parts of the Bible by heart she recited   70
And much in historical Chapters delighted
But in points about faith she was something short sighted

So Notions and modes she referr'd to the Scholes
And in matters of Conscience adher'd to two rules
To advise with no biggots and jeast with no fools   75

And Scrupling but little, enough She beleiv'd;
By Charity ample small sins she retriev'd
And when She had New Cloaths she always receiv'd

Thus still whilst her Morning unseen fled away
In ordering the Linnin and making the Tea   80
That She Scarce could have time for the Psalms of the Day

And while after Dinner the Night came so soon
That half she propos'd very seldom was done
With twenty God bless Me's how this day is gon

While she read and accounted and pay'd and abated   85
Eat and drank, play'd and work't, laught and cry'd, lov'd and hated
As answer'd the End of her being created

In the midst of her Age came a cruell desease
Which neither her broths nor recepts could appease
So down dropt her Clay, may her Soul be at Peace   90

Retire from this Sepulchre all the prophane
Ye that love for debauch or that marry for gain
Retire least Ye trouble the Manes of J——.

But Thou that know'st love above Interest or lust
Strew the Myrtle and rose on this once belov'd dust   95
And shed one pious tear upon Jinny the Just

Tread Soft on her grave, and do right to her honour
Lett neither rude hand nor Ill tongue light upon her
Do all the Small favours that now can be don her

---

76 beleiv'd; *edd.*: beleiv'd *L 29* (*P*), *L 29* (*D*)   84 Me's *L 29* (*D*): Mes *L 29* (*P*)
89 broths] Julips *L 29* (*D*)   92 Ye] You *L 29* (*D*)   97 do *L 29* (*D*): to. *L 29* (*P*)
97–102 *See commentary for variant text in original opening*

And when what Thou lik't Shall return to her Clay　　　100
For so Im persuaded She must do one day
What ever fantastic J—— Asgil may Say

When as I have don now thou shalt sett up a Stone
For Something however distinguisht or known
May Some pious friend the misfortune bemoan　　　105
And make thy Concern by reflexion his own.

Florimel.

CARELESS and Young, oh Florimel
　Thou little thinkst of whats to come:
Oh it would fright thee should I tell
What soon must be thy Countries doom.

Seneca, Troas, Act 2d. the Chorus Translated.

IS it a truth, or but a well told lye,
　That Souls have being, when their Bodyes dye.
When the Sad Wife, has closed her Husbands Eyes
And pierct the Ecchoing Vaults with Doleful Cryes,
Is not the Husbands life entirely fled,　　　5
His Soul extinguisht, as His Body dead;
Or does that other part of Him remain
Still chain'd to life, and Still condemn'd to pain?
No, No, before Our Friends officious Care,
Can light the Torch and Solemn rites prepare,　　　10
Our Breath is mixt, and lost, with common Air,

101, 104 For *L 29 (D)*: for *L 29 (P)*　　　106 own. *L 29 (D)*: own *L 29 (P)*
　Title: 'Contents' of *L 28* : om. *W, Text of L 28*　　　1 Florimel *L 28* : florimel *W*　　　2
come: *edd.*: come *W, L 28*　　　4 What *L 28* : what *W*
　4 pierct] pier'd *L 28*　　　6 His Body] the Body *L 28*　　　10 rites *edd.*: rights *W* :
Rites *L 28*

As far as East or West extended go,
As far as Sun beams Gild or Waters flow,
All beings have a Destin'd Space to run,
And All must Perish, as they all begun.   15
The Sun, the Moon, and every Sign above
Fixt by Strong Fate, in destind Courses move.
Like Us for certain Periods they endure,
Their life much longer, but their end as sure.
As Smoke which rises from the Kindling Fires   20
Is seen this moment, and the next Expires;
As Empty Clouds by rising Winds are tost,
Their fleeting forms Scarse sooner found, than lost,
So Vanishes Our State, so pas Our days,
So life but opens now and now decays   25
The Cradle and the Tomb alas! so nigh
To live is scarce distinguisht from to dye.
After Death nothing Is, and very Death,
It's self is nothing, 'tis but want of Breath;
The utmost Limit of a Narrow Span,   30
And End of motion which with life began.
Death Shows Us only what we know was near,
It cures the Misers Wish, and Checks the Cowards fear,
Where shalt thou be when thou art laid in Earth
Where wert thou Timorous thing, before thy Birth?   35
Disolv'd in Chaos, in the formless Mass,
Of what may be contending with what was,
Old Night and Death extend their Noxious Power,
O'er All the Man, the Body they Devour;
Nor spare the Soul, a Kingdom in the Dark   40
Furies that howl, three headed Dogs that bark,
Are empty Rumors formed in Childrens Schools
The Tales of Pedants, and the Dreams of Fools.

---

12 As far as East or...go,] *L 28 (137)* Far as the East or...goes *W (D)*: Far as the East and...goes, *L 28 (160)*   13] *L 28 (137)* Far as Light Glitters far as matter flows *W (D)*, *L 28 (160)*   14 Destin'd] *L 28 (137)* certain *W (D)*, *L 28 (160)*   25] *L 28* And that which Governs life with life decays. *Earlier reading in W*   So *L 28*: so *W* 26 The *L 28*: the *W*   so] too *L 28*   29 It's] It *L 28*   31 And] An *L 28* 33 It *L 28*: It's *W*   36 in the] on the *L 28*

Solomon on the Vanity of the World.

A Poem in Three Books.

'Ο Βίος γὰρ ὄνομ' ἔχει, πόνος δ' ἔργῳ πέλει.   Eurip.

Siquis Deus mihi largiatur, ut ex hac ætate repuerascam, & in cunis vagiam, valdè
recusem.   Cicero de Senect.

The bewailing of Man's Miseries hath been elegantly and copiously set forth by Many,
in the Writings as well of Philosophers, as Divines. And it is both a pleasant and
a profitable Contemplation.   Lord Bacon's Advancement of Learning.

THE PREFACE.

*I*T is hard for a Man to speak of himself with any tolerable Satisfaction or
Success: He can be no more pleased in blaming himself, than in reading a
Satyr made on him by another: and though He may justly desire, that a Friend
should praise him; yet if He makes his own Panegyric, He will get very Few to
read it. It is harder for him to speak of his own Writings. An Author is in the   5
Condition of a Culprit: the Public are his Judges: by allowing too much, and
condescending too far, He may injure his own Cause, and become a kind of Felo
de se; and by Pleading and Asserting too boldly, He may displease the Court that
sits upon him: His Apology may only heighten his Accusation. I would avoid
these Extremes: and though, I grant, it would not be very civil to trouble the   10
Reader with a long Preface, before he enters upon an indifferent Poem; I would
say something to perswade him to take it as it is, or to excuse it for not being better.

   The Noble Images and Reflections, the profound Reasonings upon Human
Actions, and excellent Precepts for the Government of Life, which are found in
the PROVERBS, ECCLESIASTES, and other Books commonly attributed to   15
SOLOMON, afford Subjects for finer Poems in every Kind, than have, I think,
as yet appeared in the GREEK, LATIN, or any Modern Language: How far
They were Verse in their Original, is a Dissertation not to be entred into at
present.

   Out of this great Treasure, which lies heaped up together, in a confused Mag-   20
nificence, above all Order, I had a Mind to collect and digest such Observations,
and Apophthegms, as most particularly tend to the Proof of that great Assertion,
laid down in the beginning of the ECCLESIASTES, ALL IS VANITY.

   Upon the Subject thus chosen, such various Images present themselves to a
Writer's Mind, that He must find it easier to judge, what should be rejected,   25
than what ought to be received. The Difficulty lies in drawing, and disposing; or
(as the Painters term it) in grouping such a Multitude of different Objects,

preserving still the Justice and Conformity of Style and Coloring, the Simplex
duntaxat & unum, *which* HORACE *prescribes, as requisite to make the whole
Picture beautiful and perfect.* 30

*As Precept, however true in Theory, or useful in Practice, would be but dry
and tedious in Verse, especially if the Recital be long; I found it necessary to form
some Story, and give a kind of Body to the Poem. Under what Species it may be
comprehended, whether* Didascalic, *or Heroic, I leave to the Judgment of the
Critics; desiring them to be favourable in their Censure; and not sollicitous what* 35
the Poem is called, provided it may be accepted.

The chief Personage or Character in the Epic, *is always proportioned to the
Design of the Work, to carry on the Narration, and the Moral.* HOMER *intended to shew us in his* Iliad, *that Dissentions amongst great Men obstruct the
Execution of the noblest Enterprizes, and tend to the Ruin of a State or Kingdom.* 40
His ACHILLES *therefore is haughty, and passionate, impatient of any Restraint
by Laws, and arrogant in Arms. In His* Odysses *the same Poet endeavours to
explain, that the hardest Difficulties may be overcome by Labor, and our Fortune
restored after the severest Afflictions.* ULYSSES *therefore is valiant, virtuous and
patient.* VIRGIL'*s Design was to tell us, how from a small Colony established by* 45
the TROJANS *in* ITALY, *the* ROMAN *Empire rose, and from what antient
Families* AUGUSTUS (*who was His Prince and Patron*) *descended. His Hero
therefore was to fight his Way to the Throne, still distinguish'd and protected by
the Favor of the Gods. The Poet to this End takes off from the Vices of* ACHILLES,
and adds to the Virtues of ULYSSES; *from both perfecting a Character proper for* 50
his Work in the Person of ÆNEAS.

As VIRGIL *copy'd after* HOMER, *other* Epic *Poets have copied after them
both.* TASSO'*s* Gierusalemme Liberata *is directly* Troy Town *Sacked; with
this Difference only, that the two chief Characters in* HOMER, *which the*
LATIN *Poet had joined in One, the* ITALIAN *has separated in his* GODFREY *and* 55
RINALDO: *but He makes them both carry on his Work with very great Success.*
RONSARD'*s* FRANCIADE, (*incomparably good as far as it goes*) *is again*
VIRGIL'*s* Æneis. *His Hero comes from a Foreign Country, settles a Colony, and
lays the Foundation of a future Empire. I instance in these, as the greatest*
ITALIAN *and* FRENCH *Poets in the* Epic. *In our Language* SPENSER *has not* 60
*contented himself with this submissive Manner of Imitation: He lanches out into
very flowery Paths, which still seem to conduct him into one great Road. His*
Fairy Queen (*had it been finished*) *must have ended in the Account, which every
Knight was to give of his Adventures, and in the accumulated Praises of his
Heroine* GLORIANA. *The Whole would have been an* Heroic *Poem, but in* 65
*another Cast and Figure, than any that had ever been written before. Yet it is
observable, that every Hero (as far as We can judge by the Books still remaining)*

*bears his distinguished Character, and represents some particular Virtue con-
ducive to the whole Design.*

To bring this to our present Subject: *The Pleasures of Life do not compensate* 70
*the Miseries: Age steals upon Us unawares; and Death, as the only Cure of our
Ills, ought to be expected, but not feared. This Instruction is to be illustrated by
the Action of some great Person. Who therefore more proper for the Business than*
SOLOMON *himself? And why may He not be supposed now to repeat what, We
take it for granted, He acted almost three thousand Years since? If in the fair* 75
*Situation where this Prince was placed, He was acquainted with Sorrow; If
endowed with the greatest Perfections of Nature, and possess'd of all the Advantages of external Condition, He could not find Happiness; the rest of Mankind may
safely take the Monarch's Word for the Truth of what He asserts. And the
Author who would perswade, that We should bear the Ills of Life patiently,* 80
meerly because SOLOMON *felt the same, has a better Argument, than* LUCRE-
TIUS *had, when in his imperious way, He at once convinces and commands, that
We ought to submit to Death without repining, because* EPICURUS *died.*

The whole Poem is a Soliloquy: SOLOMON *is the Person that speaks: He is at
once the Hero and the Author; but He tells Us very often what others say to Him.* 85
Those chiefly introduced are His Rabbies and Philosophers in the First Book, and
His Women and their Attendants in the Second: With These the Sacred History
mentions Him to have conversed; as likewise with the Angel brought down in the
Third Book, to help Him out of His Difficulties, or at least to teach Him how to
overcome them. 90

Nec Deus intersit nisi dignus vindice nodus.

*I presume this Poetical Liberty may be very justly allowed Me on so solemn an
Occasion.*

In my Description I have endeavored to keep to the Notions and Manners of the
JEWISH *Nation, at the time when* SOLOMON *lived: And where I allude to the* 95
Customs of the GREEKS, *I believe I may be justified by the strictest* Chronology;
though a Poet is not obliged to the Rules, that confine an Historian. VIRGIL *has
anticipated Two hundred Years; or the* TROJAN *Hero and* CARTHAGINIAN
Queen could not have been brought together: And without the same Anachron-
ism *several of the finest Parts of his* Æneis *must have been omitted. Our Country-* 100
man MILTON *goes yet further. He takes up many of his Material Images some
Thousands of Years after the Fall of Man: Nor could He otherwise have written,
or We read one of the sublimest Pieces of Invention that was ever yet produced.
This likewise takes off the Objection, that some Names of Countries, Terms of Art,
and Notions in Natural Philosophy are otherwise expressed, than can be warranted* 105

by the Geography *or* Astronomy *of* SOLOMON's *Time. Poets are allowed the same Liberty in their Descriptions and Comparisons, as Painters in their Draperies and Ornaments: Their Personages may be dress'd, not exactly in the same Habits which they wore, but in such as make them appear most graceful. In this case Probability must attone for the want of Truth. This Liberty has indeed been* 110 *abused by Eminent Masters in either Science.* RAPHAEL *and* TASSO *have shewed their Discretion, where* PAUL VERONESE *and* ARIOSTO *are to answer for their Extravagancies. It is the Excess, not the Thing it self, that is blameable.*

I would say one Word of the Measure, in which This, and most Poems of the Age are written. Heroic *with continued Rhime, as* DONNE *and his Con-* 115 *temporaries used it, carrying the Sense of one Verse most commonly into another, was found too dissolute and wild, and came very often too near Prose. As* DAVENANT *and* WALLER *corrected, and* DRYDEN *perfected it; It is too Confined: It cuts off the Sense at the end of every first Line, which must always rhime to the next following; and consequently produces too frequent an Identity in* 120 *the Sound, and brings every Couplet to the Point of an Epigram. It is indeed too broken and weak, to convey the Sentiments and represent the Images proper for* Epic. *And as it tires the Writer while he composes, it must do the same to the Reader while he repeats; especially in a Poem of any considerable length.*

If striking out into Blank Verse, *as* MILTON *did (and in this kind Mr.* 125 PHILIPPS, *had He lived, would have excelled) or running the Thought into* Alternate *and* Stanza, *which allows a greater Variety, and still preserves the Dignity of the Verse; as* SPENSER *and* FAIRFAX *have done; If either of these, I say, be a proper Remedy for my Poetical Complaint, or if any other may be found, I dare not determine: I am only enquiring, in order to be better informed;* 130 *without presuming to direct the Judgment of Others. And while I am speaking of the Verse it self, I give all just Praise to many of my Friends now living; who have in* Epic *carried the Harmony of their Numbers as far, as the Nature of this Measure will permit. But once more; He that writes in Rhimes, dances in Fetters: And as his Chain is more extended, he may certainly take larger Steps.* 135

I need make no Apology for the short Digressive Panegyric *upon* GREAT BRITAIN, *in the First Book: I am glad to have it observed, that there appears throughout all my Verses a Zeal for the Honor of my Country: and I had rather be thought a good* English-man, *than the best Poet, or greatest Scholar that ever wrote.* 140

And now, as to the publishing of this Piece, though I have in a literal Sense observed HORACE's Nonum prematur in Annum; *yet have I by no means obeyed our Poetical Lawgiver, according to the Spirit of the Precept. The Poem has indeed been written and laid aside much longer than the Term prescribed; but in the mean time I had little Leisure, and less Inclination to revise or print it. The* 145

*frequent Interruptions I have met with in my private Studies, and great Variety
of Public Life, in which I have been imployed; my Thoughts (such as they are)
having generally been expressed in Foreign Language, and even formed by a
Habitude very different from what the Beauty and Elegance of* English Poetry
requires: All These, and some other Circumstances, which we had as good pass by 150
*at present, do justly contribute to make my Excuse in this Behalf very plausible.
Far indeed from designing to print, I had locked up these Papers in my* Scritoire,
*there to lie in Peace, 'till my Executors might have taken Them out. What
altered this Design; or how my* Scritoire *came to be unlocked before my Coffin
was nailed; is the Question. The true Reason I take to be the best: Many of my* 155
*Friends of the first Quality, finest Learning, and greatest Understanding, have
wrested the Key from my Hands by a very kind and irresistible Violence: And
the Poem is published, not without my Consent indeed, but a little against my
Opinion; and with an implicite Submission to the Partiality of Their Judgment.
As I give up here the Fruits of many of my vacant Hours to Their Amusement* 160
*and Pleasure; I shall always think my self happy, if I may dedicate my most serious
Endeavors to Their Interest and Service. And I am proud to finish this Preface
by saying, that the Violence of many Enemies, whom I never justly offended, is
abundantly recompensed, by the Goodness of more Friends, whom I can never
sufficiently oblige. And if I here assume the Liberty of mentioning My Lord* 165
HARLEY *and Lord* BATHURST *as the Authors of this Amicable Confederacy,
among All Those, whose Names do me great Honor in the beginning of my Book:
These Two only ought to be angry with me; for I disobey their positive Order,
whilst I make even this small Acknowledgment of their particular Kindness.*

KNOWLEDGE;

THE FIRST BOOK.

The ARGUMENT.

SOLOMON *seeking Happiness from* Knowledge, *convenes the Learned Men
of His Kingdom; requires them to explain to Him the various Operations and
Effects of Nature; discourses of Vegetables, Animals, and Man; proposes some
Questions concerning the Origin, and Situation of the habitable Earth; proceeds
to examine the System of the visible Heaven; doubts if there may not be a
Plurality of Worlds; enquires into the Nature of Spirits and Angels; and wishes
to be more fully informed, as to the Attributes of the Supreme* Being. *He is
imperfectly answered by the* Rabbins, *and* Doctors; *blames His own Curiosity;
and concludes, that as to Human Science,* ALL IS VANITY.

Texts chiefly alluded to in this Book.

The Words of the Preacher, the Son of DAVID, King of JERUSALEM. ECCLESI-ASTES, Chap. I. Vers. 1.

Vanity of Vanities, saith the Preacher, Vanity of Vanities, all is Vanity. Vers. 2.

I communed with mine own Heart, saying, lo, I am come to great Estate, and have gotten more Wisdom, than all they that have been before me in JERUSALEM: Yea my Heart had great Experience of Wisdom and Knowledge. Vers. 16.

He spake of Trees, from the *Cedar*-tree that is in LEBANON, even unto the *Hyssop* that springeth out of the Wall: he spake also of Beasts, and of Fowl, and of creeping Things, and of Fishes. 1 KINGS, Chap. IV. Vers. 33.

I know, that whatsoever God doeth, it shall be for ever: nothing can be put to it, nor any thing taken from it: and God doeth it, that Men should fear before him. ECCLESIASTES, Chap. III. Vers. 14.

He hath made every *thing* beautiful in his time: Also he hath set the World in their Heart, so that no Man can find out the Work that God maketh from the beginning to the end. Vers. 11.

For in much Wisdom is much Grief: and He that increaseth Knowledge, increaseth Sorrow. Chap. I. Vers. 18.

And further, by these, my Son, be admonished: of making many Books there is no End; and much Study is a weariness of the Flesh. Chap. XII. Vers. 12.

KNOWLEDGE:

THE FIRST BOOK.

Y E Sons of Men, with just Regard attend,
  Observe the Preacher, and believe the Friend,
Whose serious MUSE inspires Him to explain,
That all we Act, and all we Think is Vain.
That in this Pilgrimage of Seventy Years,   5
O'er Rocks of Perils, and thro' Vales of Tears
Destin'd to march, our doubtful Steps we tend,
Tir'd with the Toil, yet fearful of it's End.
That from the Womb We take our fatal Shares
Of Follies, Passions, Labors, Tumults, Cares;   10
And at Approach of Death shall only know
The Truths, which from these pensive Numbers flow,
That We pursue false Joy, and suffer real Woe.

Happiness, Object of that waking Dream,
Which we call Life, mistaking; Fugitive Theme   15
Of my pursuing Verse, Ideal Shade,
Notional Good, by Fancy only made,
And by Tradition nurs'd, fallacious Fire,
Whose dancing Beams mis-lead our fond Desire,
Cause of our Care, and Error of our Mind: 20
O! had'st Thou ever been by Heav'n design'd
To ADAM, and his Mortal Race; the Boon
Entire, had been reserv'd for SOLOMON:
On Me the partial Lot had been bestow'd;
And in my Cup the golden Draught had flow'd.   25

But O! e'er yet Original Man was made;
E'er the Foundations of this Earth were laid;
It was, opponent to our Search, ordain'd,
That Joy, still sought, should never be attain'd.
This, sad Experience cites me to reveal;   30
And what I dictate, is from what I feel.

Born as I was, great DAVID's fav'rite Son,
Dear to my People, on the HEBREW Throne
Sublime, my Court with OPHIR's Treasures blest,
My Name extended to the farthest East,   35
My Body cloth'd with ev'ry outward Grace,
Strength in my Limbs, and Beauty in my Face,
My shining Thought with fruitful Notions crown'd,
Quick my Invention, and my Judgment sound.
Arise (I commun'd with my self) arise;   40
Think, to be Happy; to be Great, be Wise:
Content of Spirit must from Science flow;
For 'tis a Godlike Attribute, to Know.

I said; and sent my Edict thro' the Land:
Around my Throne the Letter'd *Rabbins* stand,   45
Historic Leaves revolve, long Volumes spread,
The Old discoursing, as the Younger read:
Attent I heard, propos'd my Doubts, and said;

The *Vegetable* World, each Plant, and Tree,
It's Seed, it's Name, it's Nature, it's Degree   50

I am allow'd, as FAME reports, to know,
From the fair *Cedar*, on the craggy Brow
Of LEBANON nodding supremely tall,
To creeping *Moss*, and *Hyssop* on the Wall:
Yet just and conscious to my self, I find   55
A thousand Doubts oppose the searching Mind.

    I know not why the *Beach* delights the Glade
With Boughs extended, and a rounder Shade;
Whilst tow'ring *Firrs* in *Conic* forms arise,
And with a pointed Spear divide the Skies: 60
Nor why again the changing *Oak* should shed
The Yearly Honour of his stately Head;
Whilst the distinguish'd *Yew* is ever seen,
Unchang'd his Branch, and permanent his Green.
Wanting the Sun why does the *Caltha* fade?   65
Why does the *Cypress* flourish in the Shade?
The *Fig* and *Date* why love they to remain
In middle Station, and an even Plain;
While in the lower Marsh the *Gourd* is found;
And while the Hill with *Olive*-shade is crown'd?   70
Why does one Climate, and one Soil endue
The blushing *Poppy* with a crimson Hue;
Yet leave the *Lilly* pale, and tinge the *Violet* blue?
Why does the fond *Carnation* love to shoot
A various Colour from one Parent Root;   75
While the fantastic *Tulip* strives to break
In two-fold Beauty, and a parted Streak?
The twining *Jasmine*, and the blushing *Rose*,
With lavish Grace their Morning Scents disclose:
The smelling *Tub'rose* and *Junquele* declare,   80
The stronger Impulse of an Evening Air.
Whence has the Tree (resolve me) or the Flow'r
A various Instinct, or a diff'rent Pow'r?
Why should one Earth, one Clime, one Stream, one Breath
Raise This to Strength, and sicken That to Death?   85

    Whence does it happen, that the Plant which well
We name the *Sensitive*, should move and feel?
Whence know her Leaves to answer her Command,
And with quick Horror fly the neighb'ring Hand?

Along the Sunny Bank, or wat'ry Mead,   90
Ten thousand Stalks their various Blossoms spread:
Peaceful and lowly in their native Soil,
They neither know to spin, nor care to toil;
Yet with confess'd Magnificence deride
Our vile Attire, and Impotence of Pride.   95
The *Cowslip* smiles, in brighter yellow dress'd,
Than That which veils the nubile Virgin's Breast.
A fairer Red stands blushing in the *Rose*,
Than That which on the Bridegroom's Vestment flows.
Take but the humblest *Lilly* of the Field;   100
And if our Pride will to our Reason yield,
It must by sure Comparison be shown,
That on the Regal Seat great DAVID's Son,
Aray'd in all his Robes, and Types of Pow'r,
Shines with less Glory, than that simple Flow'r.   105

Of Fishes next, my Friends, I would enquire,
How the mute Race engender, or respire;
From the small Fry that glide on JORDAN's Stream
Unmark'd, a Multitude without a Name,
To that *Leviathan*, who o'er the Seas   110
Immense rolls onward his impetuous Ways,
And mocks the Wind, and in the Tempest plays.
How They in warlike Bands march greatly forth
From freezing Waters, and the colder North,
To Southern Climes directing their Career,   115
Their Station changing with th'inverted Year.
How all with careful Knowledge are indu'd,
To chuse their proper Bed, and Wave, and Food:
To guard their Spawn, and educate their Brood.

Of Birds, how each according to her Kind   120
Proper Materials for her Nest can find;
And build a Frame, which deepest Thought in Man
Would or amend, or imitate in vain.
How in small Flights They know to try their Young,
And teach the callow Child her Parent's Song.   125
Why these frequent the Plain, and those the Wood.
Why ev'ry Land has her specific Brood.

Where the tall *Crane*, or winding *Swallow* goes,
Fearful of gathering Winds, and falling Snows:
If into Rocks, or hollow Trees they creep,   130
In temporary Death confin'd to Sleep;
Or conscious of the coming Evil, fly
To milder Regions, and a Southern Sky.

Of Beasts and creeping Insects shall we trace
The wond'rous Nature, and the various Race;   135
Or wild or tame, or Friend to Man or Foe,
Of Us what They, or what of Them We know?

Tell me, Ye studious, who pretend to see
Far into Nature's Bosom, whence the *Bee*
Was first inform'd her vent'rous Flight to steer   140
Thro' tractless Paths, and an Abyss of Air.
Whence She avoids the slimy Marsh, and knows
The fertile Hills, where sweeter Herbage grows,
And Hony-making Flow'rs their opening Buds disclose.
How from the thicken'd Mist, and setting Sun   145
Finds She the Labor of her Day is done?
Who taught Her against Winds and Rains to strive,
To bring her Burden to the certain Hive,
And thro' the liquid Fields again to pass
Dutious, and hark'ning to the sounding Brass?   150

And, O Thou Sluggard, tell me why the *Ant*
'Midst Summer's Plenty thinks of Winter's Want:
By constant Journeys careful to prepare
Her Stores; and bringing home the Corny Ear,
By what Instruction does She bite the Grain,   155
Lest hid in Earth, and taking Root again,
It might elude the Foresight of her Care?
Distinct in either Insect's Deed appear
The marks of Thought, Contrivance, Hope, and Fear.

Fix thy corporeal, and internal Eye   160
On the Young *Gnat*, or new-engender'd *Fly*;
On the vile *Worm*, that Yesterday began
To crawl; Thy Fellow-Creatures, abject Man!

Like Thee they breath, they move, they tast, they see,
They show their Passions by their Acts like Thee: 165
Darting their Stings, they previously declare
Design'd Revenge, and fierce intent of War:
Laying their Eggs, they evidently prove
The Genial Pow'r, and full Effect of Love.
Each then has Organs to digest his Food,   170
One to beget, and one receive the Brood:
Has Limbs and Sinews, Blood and Heart, and Brain,
Life, and her proper Functions to sustain;
Tho' the whole Fabric smaller than a Grain.
What more can our penurious Reason grant   175
To the large *Whale*, or Castled *Elephant*,
To those enormous Terrors of the NILE,
The crested *Snake*, and long-tail'd *Crocodile*,
Than that all differ but in Shape and Name,
Each destin'd to a less, or larger Frame?   180

For potent Nature loves a various Act,
Prone to enlarge, or studious to contract:
Now forms her Work too small, now too immense,
And scorns the Measures of our feeble Sense.
The Object spread too far, or rais'd too high,   185
Denies it's real Image to the Eye:
Too little, it eludes the dazl'd Sight;
Becomes mixt Blackness, or unparted Light.
Water and Air the varied Form confound;
The Strait looks crooked, and the Square grows round.   190

Thus while with fruitless Hope, and weary Pain,
We seek great Nature's Pow'r, but seek in vain;
Safe sits the Goddess in her dark Retreat;
Around Her, Myriads of *Ideas* wait,
And endless Shapes, which the Mysterious Queen   195
Can take or quit, can alter or retain:
As from our lost Pursuit She wills to hide
Her close Decrees, and chasten human Pride.

Untam'd and fierce the *Tiger* still remains:
He tires his Life in biting on his Chains: 200

For the kind Gifts of Water, and of Food,
Ungrateful, and returning Ill for Good,
He seeks his Keeper's Flesh, and thirsts his Blood:
While the strong *Camel*, and the gen'rous *Horse*,
Restrain'd and aw'd by Man's inferior Force,   205
Do to the Rider's Will their Rage submit,
And answer to the Spur, and own the Bit;
Stretch their glad Mouths to meet the Feeder's Hand,
Pleas'd with his Weight, and proud of his Command.

Again: the lonely *Fox* roams far abroad,   210
On secret Rapin bent, and Midnight Fraud;
Now haunts the Cliff, now traverses the Lawn;
And flies the hated Neighborhood of Man:
While the kind *Spaniel*, and the faithful *Hound*,
Likest that *Fox* in Shape and Species found,   215
Refuses thro' these Cliffs and Lawns to roam;
Pursues the noted Path, and covets home;
Does with kind Joy Domestic Faces meet;
Takes what the glutted Child denies to eat;
And dying, licks his long-lov'd Master's Feet.   220

By what immediate Cause They are inclin'd,
In many Acts, 'tis hard, I own, to find.
I see in others, or I think I see,
That strict their Principles, and our's agree.
Evil like Us they shun, and covet Good;   225
Abhor the Poison, and receive the Food.
Like Us they love or hate: like Us they know,
To joy the Friend, or grapple with the Foe.
With seeming Thought their Action they intend,
And use the Means proportion'd to the End.   230
Then vainly the Philosopher avers,
That Reason guides our Deed, and Instinct their's.
How can We justly diff'rent Causes frame,
When the Effects entirely are the same?
Instinct and Reason how can we divide?   235
'Tis the Fool's Ign'rance, and the Pedant's Pride.

With the same Folly sure, Man vaunts his Sway;
If the brute Beast refuses to Obey.

For tell me, when the empty Boaster's Word
Proclaims himself the Universal Lord;   240
Does He not tremble, lest the *Lion*'s Paw
Should join his Plea against the fancy'd Law?
Would not the Learned Coward leave the Chair;
If in the Schools or Porches should appear
The fierce *Hyæna*, or the foaming *Bear?*   245

The Combatant too late the Field declines;
When now the Sword is girded to his Loins.
When the swift Vessel flies before the Wind;
Too late the Sailor views the Land behind.
And 'tis too late now back again to bring   250
Enquiry, rais'd and tow'ring on the Wing;
Forward She strives, averse to be with-held
From nobler Objects, and a larger Field.

Consider with me this Ætherial Space,
Yielding to Earth and Sea the middle Place.   255
Anxious I ask Ye, how the Pensile Ball
Should never strive to rise, nor fear to fall.
When I reflect, how the revolving Sun
Does round our Globe his crooked Journies run;
I doubt of many Lands, if they contain   260
Or Herd of Beast, or Colony of Man:
If any Nations pass their destin'd Days
Beneath the neighb'ring Sun's directer Rays:
If any suffer on the Polar Coast,
The Rage of ARCTOS, and eternal Frost.   265

May not the Pleasure of Omnipotence
To each of These some secret Good dispense?
Those who amidst the Torrid Regions live,
May they not Gales unknown to us receive;
See daily Show'rs rejoice the thirsty Earth,   270
And bless the flow'ry Buds succeeding Birth?
May they not pity Us, condemn'd to bear
The various Heav'n of an obliquer Sphere;
While by fix'd Laws, and with a just Return,
They feel twelve Hours that shade, for twelve that burn; 275

And praise the neighb'ring Sun, whose constant Flame.
Enlightens them with Seasons still the same?
And may not Those, whose distant Lot is cast
North beyond TARTARY's extended Waste,
Where thro' the Plains of one continual Day,   280
Six shining Months pursue their even Way;
And Six succeeding urge their dusky Flight,
Obscur'd with Vapors and o'erwhelm'd in Night;
May not, I ask, the Natives of these Climes
(As Annals may inform succeeding Times)   285
To our Quotidian Change of Heav'n prefer
Their one Vicissitude, and equal Share
Of Day and Night, disparted thro' the Year?
May they not scorn our Sun's repeated Race,
To narrow bounds prescrib'd, and little space,   290
Hast'ning from Morn, and headlong driv'n from Noon,
Half of our Daily Toil yet scarcely done?
May they not justly to our Climes upbraid
Shortness of Night, and Penury of Shade;
That e'er our weary'd Limbs are justly blest   295
With wholesome Sleep, and necessary Rest;
Another Sun demands return of Care,
The remnant Toil of Yesterday to bear?
Whilst, when the Solar Beams salute their Sight,
Bold and secure in half a Year of Light,   300
Uninterrupted Voyages they take
To the remotest Wood, and farthest Lake;
Manage the Fishing, and pursue the Course
With more extended Nerves, and more continu'd Force.
And when declining Day forsakes their Sky;   305
When gath'ring Clouds speak gloomy Winter nigh;
With Plenty for the coming Season blest,
Six solid Months (an Age) they live, releas'd
From all the Labor, Process, Clamor, Woe,
Which our sad Scenes of daily Action know: 310
They light the shining Lamp, prepare the Feast,
And with full Mirth receive the welcome Guest;
Or tell their tender Loves (the only Care
Which now they suffer) to the list'ning Fair;

And rais'd in Pleasure, or repos'd in Ease   315
(Grateful Alternates of substantial Peace)
They bless the long Nocturnal Influence shed
On the crown'd Goblet, and the Genial Bed.

In foreign Isles which our Discov'rers find,
Far from this length of Continent disjoin'd,   320
The rugged *Bears*, or spotted *Lynx*'s brood;
Frighten the Vallies, and infest the Wood:
The hungry *Crocodile*, and hissing *Snake*
Lurk in the troubl'd Stream and fenny Brake:
And Man untaught, and rav'nous as the Beast,   325
Does Valley, Wood, and Brake, and Stream infest.
Deriv'd these Men and Animals their Birth
From Trunk of Oak, or pregnant Womb of Earth?
Whence then the Old Belief, that All began
In EDEN's Shade, and one created Man?   330
Or grant, this Progeny was wafted o'er
By coasting Boats from next adjacent Shoar:
Would Those, from whom We will suppose they spring,
Slaughter to harmless Lands, and Poyson bring?
Would they on Board or *Bears*, or *Lynxes* take,   335
Feed the She-*Adder*, and the brooding *Snake?*
Or could they think the new Discover'd Isle
Pleas'd to receive a pregnant *Crocodile?*

And since the Savage Lineage we must trace
From NOAH sav'd, and his distinguish'd Race;   340
How should their Fathers happen to forget
The Arts which NOAH taught, the Rules He set,
To sow the Glebe, to plant the gen'rous Vine,
And load with grateful Flames the Holy Shrine?
While the great Sire's unhappy Sons are found,   345
Unpress'd their Vintage, and untill'd their Ground,
Stragling o'er Dale and Hill in quest of Food,
And rude of Arts, of Virtue, and of God.

How shall We next o'er Earth and Seas pursue
The vary'd Forms of ev'ry thing we view;   350
That all is chang'd, tho' all is still the same,
Fluid the Parts, yet durable the Frame?

Of those Materials, which have been confess'd
The pristine Springs, and Parents of the rest,
Each becomes other. Water stop'd gives Birth   355
To Grass and Plants, and thickens into Earth:
Diffus'd it rises in a higher Sphere;
Dilates it's Drops, and softens into Air:
Those finer Parts of Air again aspire;
Move into Warmth, and brighten into Fire: 360
That Fire once more by thicker Air o'ercome,
And downward forc'd, in Earth's capacious Womb
Alters it's Particles; is Fire no more;
But lies resplendent Dust, and Shining Oar:
Or running thro' the mighty Mother's Veins,   365
Changes it's Shape; puts off it's old Remains;
With wat'ry Parts it's lessen'd Force divides;
Flows into Waves, and rises into Tides.

Disparted Streams shall from their Chanels fly,
And deep surcharg'd by sandy Mountains lye,   370
Obscurely sepulcher'd. By eating Rain,
And furious Wind, down to the distant Plain
The Hill, that hides his Head above the Skies,
Shall fall: The Plain by slow Degrees shall rise
Higher than er'st had stood the Summit-Hill: 375
For Time must Nature's great Behests fulfill.

Thus by a length of Years, and Change of Fate,
All Things are light or heavy, small or great:
Thus JORDAN's Waves shall future Clouds appear;
And EGYPT's *Pyramids* refine to Air.   380
Thus later Age shall ask for PISON's Flood;
And Travellers enquire, where BABEL stood.

Now where we see these Changes often fall,
Sedate we pass them by, as Natural:
Where to our Eye more rarely they appear,   385
The Pompous Name of Prodigy they bear:

383] Now frequent where We view these changes fall *W*   385 our] the *W*

Let active Thought these close *Mæanders* trace:
Let Human Wit their dubious Bound'ries place.
Are all Things Miracle; or nothing such?
And prove We not too little, or too much?   390

For that a Branch cut off, a wither'd Rod
Should at a Word pronounc'd revive and bud:
Is this more strange, than that the Mountain's Brow,
Strip'd by *December's* Frost, and white with Snow,
Should push, in Spring, ten thousand thousand Buds;   395
And boast returning Leaves, and blooming Woods?
That each successive Night from opening Heav'n
The Food of Angels should to Man be giv'n;
Is this more strange, than that with common Bread
Our fainting Bodies every Day are fed;   400
Than that each Grain and Seed consum'd in Earth,
Raises it's Store, and multiplies it's Birth;
And from the handful, which the Tiller sows,
The labour'd Fields rejoice, and future Harvest flows?

Then from whate'er We can to Sense produce   405
Common and plain, or wond'rous and abstruse,
From Nature's constant or Eccentric Laws,
The thoughtful Soul this gen'ral Influence draws,
That an Effect must presuppose a Cause.
And while She does her upward Flight sustain,   410
Touching each Link of the continu'd Chain,
At length she is oblig'd and forc'd to see
A First, a Source, a Life, a Deity;
What has for ever been, and must for ever be.

This great Existence thus by Reason found,   415
Blest by all Pow'r, with all Perfection crown'd;
How can we bind or limit His Decree,
By what our Ear has heard, or Eye may see?
Say then: Is all in Heaps of Water lost,
Beyond the Islands, and the Mid-land Coast?   420

387–90]
          Now say how far may curious reason go
          are all things miracle, or nothing so   *W*

Or has that God, who gave our World it's Birth,
Sever'd those Waters by some other Earth,
Countries by future Plow-shares to be torn,
And Cities rais'd by Nations yet unborn?
E'er the progressive Course of restless Age   425
Performs Three thousand times it's Annual Stage;
May not our Pow'r and Learning be supprest;
And Arts and Empire learn to travel West?

Where, by the Strength of this *Idea* charm'd,
Lighten'd with Glory, and with Rapture warm'd,   430
Ascends my Soul? what sees She White and Great
Amidst subjected Seas? An ISLE, the Seat
Of Pow'r and Plenty; Her Imperial Throne,
For Justice and for Mercy sought and known;
Virtues Sublime, great Attributes of Heav'n,   435
From thence to this distinguish'd Nation given.
Yet farther West the Western ISLE extends
Her happy Fame; her Armed Fleets She sends
To Climates folded yet from human Eye;
And Lands, which We imagine Wave and Sky.   440
From Pole to Pole She hears her Acts resound,
And rules an Empire by no Ocean bound;
Knows her Ships anchor'd, and her Sails unfurl'd
In other INDIES, and a second World.

Long shall BRITANNIA (That must be her Name)   445
Be first in Conquest, and preside in Fame:
Long shall her favor'd Monarchy engage
The Teeth of Envy, and the Force of Age:
Rever'd and Happy She shall long remain,
Of human Things least changeable, least vain.   450
Yet All must with the gen'ral Doom comply;
And this Great Glorious Pow'r, tho' last, must dye.

Now let us leave this Earth, and lift our Eye
To the large Convex of yon' Azure Sky:
Behold it like an ample Curtain spread,   455
Now streak'd and glowing with the Morning Red;
Anon at Noon in flaming Yellow bright,
And chusing Sable for the peaceful Night.

Ask Reason now, whence Light and Shade were giv'n,
And whence this great Variety of Heav'n: 460
Reason our Guide, what can She more reply,
Than that the Sun illuminates the Sky;
Than that Night rises from his absent Ray,
And his returning Lustre kindles Day?

But we expect the Morning Red in vain: 465
'Tis hid in Vapors, or obscur'd by Rain.
The Noontyde Yellow we in vain require:
'Tis black in Storm, or red in Light'ning Fire.
Pitchy and dark the Night sometimes appears,
Friend to our Woe, and Parent of our Fears: 470
Our Joy and Wonder sometimes She excites,
With Stars unnumber'd, and eternal Lights.
Send forth, Ye Wise, send forth your lab'ring Thought:
Let it return with empty Notions fraught,
Of airy Columns every Moment broke, 475
Of circling Whirlpools, and of Spheres of Smoke:
Yet this Solution but once more affords
New Change of Terms, and scaffolding of Words:
In other Garb my Question I receive;
And take the Doubt the very same I gave. 480

Lo! as a Giant strong the lusty Sun
Multiply'd Rounds in one great Round does run,
Twofold his Course, yet constant his Career,
Changing the Day, and finishing the Year.
Again when his descending Orb retires, 485
And Earth perceives the Absence of his Fires;
The Moon affords us Her alternate Ray,
And with kind Beams distributes fainter Day:
Yet keeps the Stages of her Monthly Race,
Various her Beams, and changeable her Face. 490
Each Planet shining in his proper Sphere,
Does with just Speed his radiant Voyage steer:
Each sees his Lamp with diff'rent Lustre crown'd:
Each knows his Course with diff'rent Periods bound;
And in his Passage thro' the liquid Space, 495
Nor hastens, nor retards his Neighbor's Race.

Now shine these Planets with substantial Rays?
Does innate Lustre gild their measur'd Days?
Or do they (as your Schemes, I think, have shown)
Dart furtive Beams, and Glory not their own,   500
All Servants to that Source of Light, the Sun?

    Again I see ten thousand thousand Stars,
Nor cast in Lines, in Circles, nor in Squares:
(Poor Rules, with which our bounded Mind is fill'd,
When We would plant, or cultivate, or build)   505
But shining with such vast, such various Light,
As speaks the Hand, that form'd them, Infinite:
How mean the Order and Perfection sought
In the best Product of the human Thought,
Compar'd to the great Harmony that reigns   510
In what the Spirit of the World ordains!

    Now if the Sun to Earth transmits his Ray,
Yet does not scorch us with too fierce a Day;
How small a Portion of his Pow'r is giv'n
To Orbs more distant, and remoter Heav'n?   515
And of those Stars, which our imperfect Eye
Has doom'd, and fix'd to one Eternal Sky,
Each by a native stock of Honor great,
May dart strong Influence, and diffuse kind Heat,
It self a Sun; and with transmissive Light   520
Enliven Worlds deny'd to human Sight:
Around the Circles of their ambient Skies
New Moons may grow or wane, may set or rise;
And other Stars may to those Suns be Earths;
Give their own Elements their proper Births;   525
Divide their Climes, or elevate their Pole;
See their Lands flourish, and their Oceans roll;
Yet these great Orbs thus radically bright,
Primitive Founts, and Origins of Light,
May each to other (as their diff'rent Sphere   530
Makes or their Distance, or their Height appear)
Be seen a nobler, or inferior Star;
And in that Space, which We call Air and Sky,
Myriads of Earths, and Moons, and Suns may lye
Unmeasur'd, and unknown by human Eye.   535

In vain We measure this amazing Sphere,
And find and fix it's Centre here or there;
Whilst it's Circumf'rence, scorning to be brought
Ev'n into fancy'd Space, illudes our vanquish'd Thought.

Where then are all the radiant *Monsters* driv'n,   540
With which your Guesses fill'd the frighten'd Heav'n?
Where will their fictious Images remain?
In paper Schemes, and the CHALDEAN's Brain.

This Problem yet, this Offspring of a Guess,
Let Us for once a Child of Truth confess;   545
That these fair Stars, these Objects of Delight,
And Terror, to our searching dazl'd Sight,
Are Worlds immense, unnumber'd, infinite.
But do these Worlds display their Beams, or guide
Their Orbs, to serve thy Use, to please thy Pride?   550
Thy self but Dust, thy Stature but a Span,
A Moment thy Duration; foolish Man!
As well may the minutest Emmet say,
That CAUCASUS was rais'd, to pave his Way:
The Snail, that LEBANON's extended Wood   555
Was destin'd only for his Walk, and Food:
The vilest Cockle, gaping on the Coast
That rounds the ample Seas, as well may boast,
The craggy Rock projects above the Sky,
That He in Safety at it's Foot may lye;   560
And the whole Ocean's confluent Waters swell,
Only to quench his Thirst, or move and blanch his Shell.

A higher Flight the vent'rous GODDESS tries,
Leaving material Worlds, and local Skies:
Enquires, what are the Beings, where the Space,   565
That form'd and held the ANGELS ancient Race.
For Rebel LUCIFER with MICHAEL fought:
(I offer only what Tradition taught:)
Embattl'd Cherub against Cherub rose;
Did Shield to Shield, and Pow'r to Pow'r oppose: 570
Heav'n rung with Triumph: Hell was fill'd with Woes.
What were these Forms, of which your Volumes tell,
How some fought great, and others recreant fell?

These bound to bear an everlasting Load,
Durance of Chain, and Banishment of God:　　　　575
By fatal Turns their wretched Strength to tire;
To swim in sulph'rous Lakes, or land on solid Fire:
While Those exalted to primæval Light,
Excess of Blessing, and Supreme Delight,
Only perceive some little Pause of Joys　　　　580
In those great Moments, when their God imploys
Their Ministry, to pour his threaten'd Hate
On the proud King, or the Rebellious State:
Or to reverse JEHOVAH's high Command,
And speak the Thunder falling from his Hand,　　　585
When to his Duty the proud King returns;
And the Rebellious State in Ashes mourns.
How can good Angels be in Heav'n confin'd;
Or view that Presence, which no Space can bind?
Is GOD above, beneath, or yon', or here?　　　　590
He who made all, is He not ev'ry where?
O how can wicked Angels find a Night
So dark, to hide 'em from that piercing Light,
Which form'd the Eye, and gave the Pow'r of Sight?

What mean I now of Angel, when I hear　　　　595
Firm Body, Spirit pure, or fluid Air?
Spirits to Action spiritual confin'd,
Friends to our Thought, and Kindred to our Mind,
Should only act and prompt us from within,
Nor by external Eye be ever seen.　　　　600
Was it not therefore to our Fathers known,
That these had Appetite, and Limb, and Bone?
Else how could ABRAM wash their weary'd Feet;
Or SARAH please their Taste with sav'ry Meat?
Whence should they fear? or why did LOT engage　　605
To save their Bodies from abusive Rage?
And how could JACOB, in a real Fight,
Feel or resist the wrestling Angel's Might?
How could a Form it's Strength with Matter try?
Or how a Spirit touch a Mortal's Thigh?　　　　610

Now are they Air condens'd, or gather'd Rays?
How guide they then our Pray'r, or keep our Ways,

By stronger Blasts still subject to be tost,
By Tempests scatter'd, and in Whirlwinds lost?

Have they again (as Sacred Song proclaims)   615
Substances real, and existing Frames?
How comes it, since with them we jointly share
The great Effect of one Creator's Care;
That whilst our Bodies sicken, and decay,
Their's are for ever healthy, young, and gay?   620
Why, whilst We struggle in this Vale beneath,
With Want and Sorrow, with Disease and Death;
Do They more bless'd perpetual Life employ
On Songs of Pleasure, and in Scenes of Joy?

Now when my Mind has all this World survey'd,   625
And found, that Nothing by it self was made;
When Thought has rais'd it self by just Degrees,
From Vallies crown'd with Flow'rs, and Hills with Trees;
From smoaking Min'rals, and from rising Streams;
From fatt'ning NILUS, or victorious THAMES;   630
From all the Living, that four-footed move
Along the Shoar, the Meadow, or the Grove;
From all that can with Finns, or Feathers fly
Thro' the Aërial, or the Wat'ry Sky;
From the poor Reptile with a reas'ning Soul,   635
That miserable Master of the Whole;
From this great Object of the Body's Eye,
This fair Half-round, this ample azure Sky,
Terribly large, and wonderfully bright
With Stars unnumber'd, and unmeasur'd Light;   640
From Essences unseen, Celestial Names,
Enlight'ning Spirits, and ministerial Flames,
Angels, Dominions, Potentates, and Thrones,
All that in each Degree the name of Creature owns:
Lift we our Reason to that Sov'reign Cause,   645
Who blest the whole with Life, and bounded it with Laws;
Who forth from Nothing call'd this comely Frame,
His Will and Act, His Word and Work the same;
To whom a thousand Years are but a Day;
Who bad the Light her genial Beams display;   650
And set the Moon, and taught the Sun his Way:

Who waking Time, his Creature, from the Source
Primæval, order'd his predestin'd Course:
Himself, as in the Hollow of His Hand,
Holding, obedient to His high Command,   655
The deep Abyss, the long continu'd Store,
Where Months, and Days, and Hours, and Minutes pour
Their floating Parts, and thenceforth are no more.
This ALPHA and OMEGA, First and Last,
Who like the Potter in a Mould has cast   660
The World's great Frame, commanding it to be
Such as the Eyes of Sense and Reason see;
Yet if He wills, may change or spoil the whole;
May take yon' beauteous, mystic, starry Roll,
And burn it, like an useless parchment Scroll: 665
May from it's *Basis* in one Moment pour
This melted Earth—
Like liquid Metal, and like burning Oar:
Who sole in Pow'r, at the Beginning said;
Let Sea, and Air, and Earth, and Heav'n be made: 670
And it was so—And when He shall ordain
In other Sort, has but to speak again,
And They shall be no more: Of this great Theme,
This Glorious, Hallow'd, Everlasting Name,
This GOD, I would discourse—   675

    The learned Elders sat appall'd, amaz'd;
And each with mutual Look on other gaz'd.
Nor Speech They meditate, nor Answer frame:
Too plain, alas! their Silence spake their Shame:
'Till One, in whom an outward Mien appear'd,   680
And Turn superior to the vulgar Herd,
Began; that Human Learning's furthest Reach
Was but to note the Doctrines I could teach;
That Mine to Speak, and Their's was to Obey:
For I in Knowledge more, than Pow'r did sway;   685
And the astonish'd World in Me beheld
MOSES eclips'd, and JESSE's Son excell'd.

---

682 Began; that Human] begun of Human's *W*   683 the Doctrines I] what Solomon
W   684–6] That I was born to make the learned yeild *W*

Humble a Second bow'd, and took the Word;
Foresaw my Name by future Age ador'd.
O Live, said He, Thou Wisest of the Wise!   690
As None has equall'd, None shall ever rise
Excelling Thee—

    Parent of wicked, Bane of honest Deeds,
Pernicious Flatt'ry! Thy malignant Seeds
In an ill Hour, and by a fatal Hand   695
Sadly diffus'd o'er Virtue's Gleby Land,
With rising Pride amidst the Corn appear,
And choak the Hopes and Harvest of the Year.

    And now the whole perplex'd ignoble Crowd
Mute to my Questions, in my Praises loud,   700
Echo'd the Word: whence Things arose, or how
They thus exist, the Aptest nothing know:
What yet is not, but is ordain'd to be,
All Veil of Doubt apart, the Dullest see.

    My Prophets, and my Sophists finish'd here   705
Their Civil Efforts of the Verbal War:
Not so my *Rabbins*, and Logicians yield:
Retiring still they combat: from the Field
Of open Arms unwilling they depart,
And sculk behind the Subterfuge of Art.   710
To speak one Thing mix'd Dialects they join;
Divide the Simple, and the Plain define;
Fix fancy'd Laws, and form imagin'd Rules,
Terms of their Art, and Jargon of their Schools,
Ill grounded Maxims by false Gloss enlarg'd,   715
And captious Science against Reason charg'd.

    Soon their crude Notions with each other fought:
The adverse Sect deny'd, what This had taught;
And He at length the amplest Triumph gain'd,
Who contradicted what the last maintain'd.   720

688 Humble] Humbly *W*   691–8]
          None ere has equalld and none ere shall rise
          that may excell: false flattery foolish prais
          That but destroys the mind it strives to raise. *W*

O wretched Impotence of human Mind!
We erring still Excuse for Error find;
And darkling grope, not knowing We are blind.

Vain Man! since first thy blushing Sire essay'd
His Folly with connected Leaves to shade;   725
How does the Crime of thy resembling Race
With like Attempt that pristine Error trace?
Too plain thy Nakedness of Soul espy'd,
Why dost Thou strive the conscious Shame to hide
By Masks of Eloquence, and Veils of Pride?   730

With outward Smiles their Flatt'ry I receiv'd;
Own'd my Sick Mind by their Discourse reliev'd;
But bent and inward to my Self again
Perplex'd, these Matters I revolv'd; in vain.
My Search still tir'd, my Labor still renew'd,   735
At length I Ignorance, and Knowledge view'd,
Impartial; Both in equal Balance laid:
Light flew the knowing Scale; the doubtful Heavy weigh'd.

Forc'd by reflective Reason I confess,
That human Science is uncertain Guess.   740
Alas! We grasp at Clouds, and beat the Air,
Vexing that Spirit We intend to clear.
Can Thought beyond the Bounds of Matter climb?
Or who shall tell Me, what is Space or Time?
In vain We lift up our presumptuous Eyes   745
To what our Maker to their Ken denies:
The Searcher follows fast; the Object faster flies.
The little which imperfectly We find,
Seduces only the bewilder'd Mind
To fruitless Search of Something yet behind.   750
Various Discussions tear our heated Brain:
Opinions often turn; still Doubts remain;
And who indulges Thought, increases Pain.

How narrow Limits were to Wisdom giv'n?
Earth She surveys: She thence would measure Heav'n: 755

754 How...were] Small the Content alass! *W*

Thro' Mists obscure, now wings her tedious Way;
Now wanders dazl'd with too bright a Day;
And from the Summit of a pathless Coast
Sees INFINITE, and in that Sight is lost.

Remember, that the curs'd Desire to know,   760
Off-spring of ADAM, was thy Source of Woe.
Why wilt Thou then renew the vain Pursuit,
And rashly catch at the forbidden Fruit?
With empty Labor and eluded Strife
Seeking, by Knowledge, to attain to Life;   765
For ever from that fatal Tree debarr'd,
Which flaming Swords and angry CHERUBS guard.

PLEASURE:

THE SECOND BOOK.

The ARGUMENT.

SOLOMON *again seeking Happiness, enquires if Wealth and Greatness can produce it: begins with the Magnificence of Gardens and Buildings, the Luxury of Music and Feasting; and proceeds to the Hopes and Desires of Love. In two Episodes are shewn the Follies and Troubles of that Passion.* SOLOMON *still disappointed, falls under the Temptations of Libertinism and Idolatry; recovers his Thought, reasons aright, and concludes, that as to the Pursuit of Pleasure, and sensual Delight,* ALL IS VANITY AND VEXATION OF SPIRIT.

Texts chiefly alluded to in this Book.

I said in my own Heart, go to now, I will prove thee with Mirth; therefore enjoy Pleasure. ECCLESIASTES, Chap. II. Vers. 1.

I made me great Works, I builded me Houses, I planted me Vineyards. Vers. 4.

I made me Gardens and Orchards; and I planted Trees in them of all kinds of Fruits. Vers. 5.

I made me Pools of Water, to water therewith the Wood that bringeth forth Trees. Vers. 6.

Then I looked on all the Works that my Hands had wrought, and on the

Labour that I had laboured to do: And behold, all was Vanity, and Vexation of Spirit; and there was no Profit under the Sun. Vers. 11.

I gat me Men-Singers and Women-Singers, and the Delights of the Sons of Men, as Musical Instruments, and that of all Sorts. Vers. 8.

I sought in mine Heart to give my self unto Wine (yet acquainting mine Heart with Wisdom) and to lay hold on Folly, 'till I might see what was that Good for the Sons of Men, which they should do under Heaven, all the Days of their Life. Vers. 3.

Then I said in my Heart, as it happeneth unto the Fool, so it happeneth even unto Me; and why was I then more Wise? Then I said in my Heart, that this also is Vanity. Vers. 15.

Therefore I hated Life, because the Work that is wrought under the Sun is grievous unto me. Chap. II. Vers. 17.

Dead Flies cause the Oyntment to send forth a stinking Savour: so doth the little Folly him that is in Reputation for Wisdom and Honour. Chap. X. Vers. 1.

The Memory of the Just is blessed, but the Memory of the Wicked shall rot. PROVERBS, Chap. X. Verse. 7.

PLEASURE:

THE SECOND BOOK.

TRY then, O Man, the Moments to deceive,
   That from the Womb attend Thee to the Grave:
For weary'd Nature find some apter Scheme:
Health be thy Hope; and Pleasure be thy Theme:
From the perplexing and unequal Ways,   5
Where Study brings Thee; from the endless Maze,
Which Doubt persuades to run, forewarn'd recede,
To the gay Field, and flow'ry Path, that lead
To jocund Mirth, soft Joy, and careless Ease:
Forsake what may instruct, for what may please: 10
Essay amusing Art, and proud Expence;
And make thy Reason subject to thy Sense.

   I commun'd thus: the Pow'r of Wealth I try'd,
And all the various Luxe of costly Pride.
Artists and Plans reliev'd my solemn Hours: 15
I founded Palaces, and planted Bow'rs.

Texts: Vers. 17 *edd.* : Vers. 27 *1718*

Birds, Fishes, Beasts of each Exotic Kind
I to the Limits of my Court confin'd.
To Trees transferr'd I gave a second Birth;
And bid a foreign Shade grace JUDAH's Earth.　　　20
Fish-ponds were made, where former Forrests grew;
And Hills were levell'd to extend the View.
Rivers diverted from their Native Course,
And bound with Chains of Artificial Force,
From large Cascades in pleasing Tumult roll'd;　　　25
Or rose thro' figur'd Stone, or breathing Gold.
From furthest AFRICA's tormented Womb
The Marble brought erects the spacious Dome;
Or forms the Pillars long-extended Rows,
On which the planted Grove, and pensile Garden grows.　　　30

The Workmen here obey the Master's Call,
To gild the Turret, and to paint the Wall;
To mark the Pavement there with various Stone;
And on the Jasper Steps to rear the Throne:
The spreading *Cedar*, that an Age had stood,　　　35
Supreme of Trees, and Mistress of the Wood,
Cut down and carv'd, my shining Roof adorns;
And LEBANON his ruin'd Honor mourns.

A thousand Artists shew their cunning Pow'r,
To raise the Wonders of the Iv'ry Tow'r.　　　40
A thousand Maidens ply the purple Loom,
To weave the Bed, and deck the Regal Room;
'Till TYRE confesses her exhausted Store,
That on her Coast the *Murex* is no more;
'Till from the PARIAN Isle, and LYBIA's Coast,　　　45
The Mountains grieve their hopes of Marble lost;
And INDIA's Woods return their just Complaint,
Their Brood decay'd, and want of *Elephant*.

My full Design with vast Expence atchiev'd,
I came, beheld, admir'd, reflected, griev'd.　　　50
I chid the Folly of my thoughtless Hast:
For, the Work perfected, the Joy was past.

To my new Courts sad Thought did still repair;
And round my gilded Roofs hung hov'ring Care.

In vain on silken Beds I sought Repose;   55
And restless oft' from purple Couches rose:
Vexatious Thought still found my flying Mind
Nor bound by Limits, nor to Place confin'd;
Haunted my Nights, and terrify'd my Days;
Stalk'd thro' my Gardens, and pursu'd my Ways,   60
Nor shut from artful Bow'r, nor lost in winding Maze.

     Yet take thy Bent, my Soul; another Sense
Indulge; add Music to Magnificence:
Essay, if Harmony may Grief controll;
Or Pow'r of Sound prevail upon the Soul.   65
Often our Seers and Poets have confest,
That Music's Force can tame the furious Beast;
Can make the Wolf, or foaming Boar restrain
His Rage; the Lion drop his crested Mane,
Attentive to the Song; the Lynx forget   70
His Wrath to Man, and lick the Minstrel's Feet.
Are we, alas! less savage yet than these?
Else Music sure may human Cares appease.

     I spake my Purpose; and the chearful Choir
Parted their shares of Harmony: the Lyre   75
Soften'd the Timbrel's Noise: the Trumpet's Sound
Provok'd the DORIAN Flute (both sweeter found
When mix'd:) the Fife the Viol's Notes refin'd;
And ev'ry Strength with ev'ry Grace was join'd.
Each Morn they wak'd Me with a sprightly Lay: 80
Of opening Heav'n they Sung, and gladsome Day.
Each Evening their repeated Skill express'd
Scenes of Repose, and Images of Rest:
Yet still in vain: for Music gather'd Thought:
But how unequal the Effects it brought?   85
The soft *Ideas* of the chearful Note,
Lightly receiv'd, were easily forgot.
The solemn Violence of the graver Sound
Knew to strike deep, and leave a lasting Wound.

     And now reflecting, I with Grief descry   90
The sickly Lust of the fantastic Eye;

How the weak Organ is with Seeing cloy'd,
Flying e'er Night what it at Noon enjoy'd.
And now (unhappy Search of Thought!) I found
The fickle Ear soon glutted with the Sound,   95
Condemn'd eternal Changes to pursue,
Tir'd with the last, and eager of the New.

I bad the Virgins and the Youth advance,
To temper Music with the sprightly Dance.
In Vain! too low the Mimic-Motions seem: 100
What takes our Heart, must merit our Esteem.
Nature, I thought, perform'd too mean a Part,
Forming her Movements to the Rules of Art;
And vex'd I found, that the Musician's Hand
Had o'er the Dancer's Mind too great Command.   105

I drank; I lik'd it not: 'twas Rage; 'twas Noise;
An airy Scene of transitory Joys.
In vain I trusted, that the flowing Bowl
Would banish Sorrow, and enlarge the Soul.
To the late Revel, and protracted Feast   110
Wild Dreams succeeded, and disorder'd Rest;
And as at Dawn of Morn fair Reason's Light
Broke thro' the Fumes and Phantoms of the Night;
What had been said, I ask'd my Soul, what done;
How flow'd our Mirth, and whence the Source begun?   115
Perhaps the Jest that charm'd the sprightly Croud,
And made the Jovial Table laugh so loud,
To some false Notion ow'd it's poor Pretence,
To an ambiguous Word's perverted Sense,
To a wild Sonnet, or a wanton Air,   120
Offence and Torture to the sober Ear.
Perhaps, alas! the pleasing Stream was brought
From this Man's Error, from another's Fault;
From Topics which Good-nature would forget,
And Prudence mention with the last Regret.   125

Add yet unnumber'd Ills, that lye unseen
In the pernicious Draught; the Word obscene,
Or harsh, which once elanc'd must ever fly
Irrevocable; the too prompt Reply,

Seed of severe Distrust, and fierce Debate;   130
What We should shun, and what We ought to hate.

Add too the Blood impoverish'd, and the Course
Of Health suppress'd, by Wine's continu'd Force.

Unhappy Man! whom Sorrow thus and Rage
To diff'rent Ills alternately engage.   135
Who drinks, alas! but to forget; nor sees,
That melancholy Sloath, severe Disease,
Mem'ry confus'd, and interrupted Thought,
Death's Harbingers, lye latent in the Draught:
And in the Flow'rs that wreath the sparkling Bowl,   140
Fell Adders hiss, and poys'nous Serpents roll.

Remains there Ought untry'd, that may remove
Sickness of Mind, and heal the Bosom?—Love,
Love yet remains: Indulge his genial Fire,
Cherish fair Hope, solicit young Desire,   145
And boldly bid thy anxious Soul explore
This last great Remedy's Mysterious Pow'r.

Why therefore hesitates my doubtful Breast?
Why ceases it one Moment to be blest?
Fly swift, my Friends; my Servants, fly; imploy   150
Your instant Pains to bring your Master Joy.
Let all my Wives and Concubines be dress'd:
Let them to Night attend the Royal Feast;
All ISRAEL's Beauty, all the foreign Fair,
The Gifts of Princes, or the Spoils of War.   155
Before their Monarch They shall singly pass;
And the most Worthy shall obtain the Grace.

I said: the Feast was serv'd: the Bowl was crown'd;
To the King's Pleasure went the mirthful Round:
The Women came: as Custom wills, they past: 160
On One (O that distinguish'd One!) I cast
The fav'rite Glance: O! yet my Mind retains
That fond Beginning of my infant Pains.
Mature the Virgin was of EGYPT's Race:
Grace shap'd her Limbs; and Beauty deck'd her Face: 165

Easy her Motion seem'd, serene her Air:
Full, tho' unzon'd, her Bosom rose: her Hair
Unty'd, and ignorant of artful Aid,
Adown her Shoulders loosely lay display'd;
And in the Jetty Curls ten thousand CUPIDS play'd. } 170

    Fix'd on her Charms, and pleas'd that I could love,
Aid me my Friends, contribute to improve
Your Monarch's Bliss, I said; fresh Roses bring
To strow my Bed; 'till the impov'rish'd Spring
Confess her Want; around my am'rous Head   175
Be dropping Myrrhe, and liquid Amber shed,
'Till ARAB has no more. From the soft Lyre,
Sweet Flute, and ten-string'd Instrument, require
Sounds of Delight: and Thou, fair Nymph, draw nigh;
Thou, in whose graceful Form, and potent Eye   180
Thy Master's Joy long sought at length is found;
And as thy Brow, let my Desires be crown'd;
O fav'rite Virgin, that hast warm'd the Breast,
Whose sov'reign Dictates subjugate the East!

    I said; and sudden from the golden Throne   185
With a submissive Step I hasted down.
The glowing Garland from my Hair I took,
Love in my Heart, Obedience in my Look;
Prepar'd to place it on her comely Head:
O fav'rite Virgin! (yet again I said)   190
Receive the Honors destin'd to thy Brow;
And O above thy Fellows happy Thou!
Their Duty must thy sov'reign Word obey.
Rise up, my Love; my fair One, come away.

    What Pang, alas! what Ecstasy of Smart   195
Tore up my Senses, and transfix'd my Heart;
When She with modest Scorn the Wreath return'd,
Reclin'd her beauteous Neck, and inward mourn'd?

    Forc'd by my Pride, I my Concern suppress'd
Pretended Drowsiness, and Wish of Rest; } 200
And sullen I forsook th'Imperfect Feast:

Ordering the Eunuchs, to whose proper Care
Our Eastern Grandeur gives th'imprison'd Fair,
To lead Her forth to a distinguish'd Bow'r,
And bid her dress the Bed, and wait the Hour.   205

Restless I follow'd this obdurate Maid;
(Swift are the Steps that Love and Anger tread:)
Approach'd her Person, courted her Embrace,
Renew'd my Flame, repeated my Disgrace:
By Turns put on the Suppliant and the Lord;   210
Threaten'd this Moment, and the next implor'd;
Offer'd again the unaccepted Wreath,
And Choice of happy Love, or instant Death.

Averse to all her am'rous King desir'd,
Far as She might, She decently retir'd;   215
And darting Scorn, and Sorrow from her Eyes,
What means, said She, King SOLOMON the Wise?

This wretched Body trembles at your Pow'r:
Thus far could Fortune: but She can no more.
Free to her Self my potent Mind remains;   220
Nor fears the Victor's Rage, nor feels his Chains.

'Tis said, that Thou can'st plausibly dispute,
Supreme of Seers, of Angel, Man, and Brute;
Can'st plead, with subtil Wit and fair Discourse,
Of Passion's Folly, and of Reason's Force.   225
That to the Tribes attentive Thou can'st show,
Whence their Misfortunes, or their Blessings flow.
That Thou in Science, as in Pow'r art great;
And Truth and Honor on Thy Edicts wait.
Where is that Knowledge now, that regal Thought,   230
With just Advice, and timely Counsel fraught?
Where now, O Judge of ISRAEL, does it rove?
What in one Moment dost Thou offer? Love—
Love? why 'tis Joy or Sorrow, Peace or Strife:
'Tis all the Color of remaining Life: 235
And Human Mis'ry must begin or end,
As He becomes a Tyrant, or a Friend.

Would DAVID's Son, religious, just, and grave,
To the first Bride-bed of the World receive
A Foreigner, a Heathen, and a Slave? 240
Or grant, Thy Passion has these Names destroy'd;
That Love, like Death, makes all Distinction void;
Yet in his Empire o'er Thy abject Breast,
His Flames and Torments only are exprest:
His Rage can in my Smiles alone relent; 245
And all his Joys solicit my Consent.

Soft Love, spontaneous Tree, it's parted Root
Must from two Hearts with equal Vigour shoot:
Whilst each delighted, and delighting, gives
The pleasing Ecstasy, which each receives: 250
Cherish'd with Hope, and fed with Joy it grows:
It's chearful Buds their opening Bloom disclose;
And round the happy Soil diffusive Odor flows.
If angry Fate that mutual Care denies;
The fading Plant bewails it's due Supplies: 255
Wild with Despair, or sick with Grief, it dies.

By Force Beasts act, and are by Force restrain'd:
The Human Mind by gentle Means is gain'd.
Thy useless Strength, mistaken King, employ:
Sated with Rage, and ignorant of Joy, 260
Thou shalt not gain what I deny to yield;
Nor reap the Harvest, tho' Thou spoil'st the Field.
Know, SOLOMON, Thy poor Extent of Sway;
Contract thy Brow, and ISRAEL shall obey:
But wilful Love Thou must with Smiles appease; 265
Approach his awful Throne by just Degrees;
And if Thou would'st be Happy, learn to please.

Not that those Arts can here successful prove:
For I am destin'd to another's Love.
Beyond the cruel Bounds of Thy Command, 270
To my dear Equal, in my Native Land,
My plighted Vow I gave: I His receiv'd:
Each swore with Truth: with Pleasure each believ'd.
The mutual Contract was to Heav'n convey'd:
In equal Scales the busy Angels weigh'd 275

It's solemn Force, and clap'd their Wings, and spread
The lasting Roll, recording what We said.

Now in my Heart behold Thy Poynard stain'd:
Take the sad Life which I have long disdain'd:
End, in a dying Virgin's wretched Fate,   280
Thy ill-starr'd Passion, and My steadfast Hate.
For long as Blood informs these circling Veins;
Or fleeting Breath it's latest Pow'r retains;
Hear Me to EGYPT's vengeful Gods declare,
Hate is My Part: be Thine, O King, Despair.   285

Now strike, She said, and open'd bare her Breast:
Stand it in JUDAH's Chronicles confest,
That DAVID's Son, by impious Passion mov'd,
Smote a She-Slave, and murder'd what He lov'd.

Asham'd, confus'd I started from the Bed;   290
And to my Soul yet uncollected said:
Into Thy self, fond SOLOMON, return;
Reflect again, and Thou again shalt mourn.
When I through number'd Years have Pleasure sought;
And in vain Hope the wanton Phantom caught;   295
To mock my Sense, and mortify my Pride,
'Tis in another's Pow'r, and is deny'd.
Am I a King, great Heav'n! does Life or Death
Hang on the Wrath, or Mercy of My Breath;
While kneeling I My Servant's Smiles implore;   300
And One mad Dam'sel dares dispute My Pow'r?

To Ravish Her? That Thought was soon suppress'd,
Which must debase the Monarch to the Beast.
To send Her back? O whither, and to whom?
To Lands where SOLOMON must never come;   305
To that Insulting Rival's happy Arms,
For whom, disdaining Me, She keeps her Charms.

Fantastic Tyrant of the am'rous Heart;
How hard Thy Yoke! how cruel is Thy Dart!
Those 'scape Thy Anger, who refuse Thy Sway;   310
And those are punish'd most, who most Obey.

See JUDAH's King revere thy greater Pow'r:
What can'st Thou covet, or how triumph more?
Why then, O LOVE, with an obdurate Ear
Does this proud Nymph reject a Monarch's Pray'r?   315
Why to some simple Shepherd does She run,
From the fond Arms of DAVID's Fav'rite Son?
Why flies She from the Glories of a Court,
Where Wealth and Pleasure may Thy Reign support,
To some poor Cottage on the Mountain's Brow,   320
Now bleak with Winds, and cover'd now with Snow,
Where pinching Want must curb her warm Desires,
And Household Cares suppress Thy Genial Fires?

Too aptly the afflicted HEATHEN prove
The Force, while they erect the Shrines of LOVE.   325
His Mystic Form the Artizans of GREECE
In wounded Stone, or molten Gold express:
And CYPRUS to his Godhead pays her Vow:
Fast in his Hand the Idol holds his Bow;
A Quiver by his Side sustains a Store   330
Of pointed Darts; sad Emblems of his Pow'r;
A pair of Wings He has, which He extends
Now to be gone; which now again He bends
Prone to return, as best may serve his wanton Ends.
Entirely thus I find the Fiend pourtray'd,   335
Since first, alas! I saw the beauteous Maid:
I felt Him strike; and now I see Him fly:
Curs'd Dæmon! O! for ever broken lye
Those fatal Shafts, by which I inward bleed!
O! can my Wishes yet o'ertake thy Speed!   340
Tir'd may'st Thou pant, and hang thy flagging Wing;
Except Thou turn'st Thy Course, resolv'd to bring
The Dam'sel back, and save the Love-sick King.

My Soul thus strugling in the fatal Net,
Unable to enjoy, or to forget;   345
I reason'd much, alas! but more I lov'd;
Sent and recall'd, ordain'd and disapprov'd:
'Till hopeless plung'd in an Abyss of Grief,
I from Necessity receiv'd Relief:

Time gently aided to asswage my Pain;   350
And Wisdom took once more the slacken'd Rein.

But O how short My Interval of Woe!
Our Griefs how swift; our Remedies how slow!
Another Nymph (for so did Heav'n ordain,
To change the Manner, but renew the Pain)   355
Another Nymph, amongst the many Fair,
That made My softer Hours their solemn Care,
Before the rest affected still to stand;
And watch'd My Eye, preventing My Command.
ABRA, She so was call'd, did soonest hast   360
To grace my Presence: ABRA went the last:
ABRA was ready e'er I call'd her Name;
And tho' I call'd another, ABRA came.

Her Equals first observ'd her growing Zeal;
And laughing gloss'd, that ABRA serv'd so well.   365
To Me her Actions did unheeded dye,
Or were remark'd but with a common Eye;
'Till more appris'd of what the Rumor said,
More I observ'd peculiar in the Maid.

The Sun declin'd had shot his Western Ray;   370
When tir'd with Bus'ness of the solemn Day,
I purpos'd to unbend the Evening Hours,
And banquet private in the Women's Bow'rs.
I call'd, before I sat, to wash My Hands:
For so the Precept of the Law commands.   375
LOVE had ordain'd, that it was ABRA's Turn
To mix the Sweets, and minister the Urn.

With awful Homage, and submissive Dread
The Maid approach'd, on my declining Head
To pour the Oyls: She trembled as She pour'd;   380
With an unguarded Look She now devour'd
My nearer Face: and now recall'd her Eye,
And heav'd, and strove to hide a sudden Sigh.
And whence, said I, canst Thou have Dread, or Pain?
What can thy Imag'ry of Sorrow mean?   385

Secluded from the World, and all it's Care,
Hast Thou to grieve or joy, to hope or fear?
For sure, I added, sure thy little Heart
Ne'er felt LOVE's Anger, or receiv'd his Dart.

Abash'd She blush'd, and with Disorder spoke: 390
Her rising Shame adorn'd the Words it broke.

If the great Master will descend to hear
The humble Series of His Hand-maid's Care;
O! while She tells it, let him not put on
The Look, that awes the Nations from the Throne: 395
O! let not Death severe in Glory lye
In the King's Frown, and Terror of his Eye.

Mine to obey; Thy Part is to ordain:
And tho' to mention, be to suffer Pain;
If the King smiles, whilst I my Woe recite;   400
If weeping I find Favour in His Sight;
Flow fast my Tears, full rising his Delight.

O! Witness Earth beneath, and Heav'n above;
For can I hide it? I am sick of Love:
If Madness may the Name of Passion bear;   405
Or Love be call'd, what is indeed Despair.

Thou Sov'reign Pow'r, whose secret Will controlls
The inward Bent and Motion of our Souls!
Why hast Thou plac'd such infinite Degrees
Between the Cause and Cure of my Disease?   410
The mighty Object of that raging Fire,
In which unpity'd ABRA must expire,
Had He been born some simple Shepherd's Heir,
The lowing Herd, or fleecy Sheep his Care;
At Morn with him I o'er the Hills had run,   415
Scornful of Winter's Frost, and Summer's Sun,
Still asking, where He made his Flock to rest at Noon.
For him at Night, the dear expected Guest,
I had with hasty Joy prepar'd the Feast;
And from the Cottage, o'er the distant Plain,   420
Sent forth my longing Eye to meet the Swain;

Wav'ring, impatient, toss'd by Hope and Fear;
Till He and Joy together should appear;
And the lov'd Dog declare his Master near.
On my declining Neck, and open Breast,   425
I should have lull'd the lovely Youth to Rest;
And from beneath his Head, at dawning Day,
With softest Care have stol'n my Arm away;
To rise, and from the Fold release the Sheep,
Fond of his Flock, indulgent to his Sleep.   430

Or if kind Heav'n propitious to my Flame
(For sure from Heav'n the faithful Ardor came)
Had blest my Life, and deck'd my natal Hour
With Height of Title, and Extent of Pow'r:
Without a Crime my Passion had aspir'd,   435
Found the lov'd Prince, and told what I desir'd.

Then I had come, preventing SHEBA's Queen,
To see the comeliest of the Sons of Men;
To hear the charming Poet's am'rous Song,
And gather Honey falling from his Tongue;   440
To take the fragrant Kisses of his Mouth,
Sweeter than Breezes of her native South;
Likening his Grace, his Person, and his Mien
To all that Great or Beauteous I had seen.
Serene and bright his Eyes, as solar Beams   445
Reflecting temper'd Light from Crystal Streams;
Ruddy as Gold his Cheek; his Bosom fair
As Silver; the curl'd Ringlets of his Hair
Black as the Raven's Wing; his Lip more red,
Than Eastern Coral, or the scarlet Thread;   450
Even his Teeth, and white, like a young Flock
Coeval, newly shorn, from the clear Brook
Recent, and blanching on the Sunny Rock.
Iv'ry with Saphirs interspers'd, explains
How white his Hands, how blue the Manly Veins.   455
Columns of polish'd Marble firmly set
On golden Bases, are his Legs, and Feet.
His Stature all Majestic, all Divine,
Strait as the Palmtree, strong as is the Pine.

Saffron and Myrrhe are on his Garments shed:
And everlasting Sweets bloom round his Head.
What utter I? where am I? wretched Maid!
Dye, ABRA, dye: too plainly hast Thou said
Thy Soul's Desire to meet His high Embrace,
And Blessings stamp'd upon thy future Race;   465
To bid attentive Nations bless thy Womb,
With unborn Monarchs charg'd, and SOLOMONS to come.

   Here o'er her Speech her flowing Eyes prevail.
O foolish Maid! and O unhappy Tale!
My suff'ring Heart for ever shall defy   470
New Wounds, and Danger from a future Eye.
O! yet my tortur'd Senses deep retain
The wretched Mem'ry of my former Pain,
The dire Affront, and my EGYPTIAN Chain.

   As Time, I said, may happily efface   475
That cruel Image of the King's Disgrace;
Imperial Reason shall resume her Seat;
And SOLOMON once fall'n, again be great.
Betray'd by Passion, as subdu'd in War,
We wisely should exert a double Care,   480
Nor ever ought a second time to Err.

   This ABRA then—
I saw Her; 'twas Humanity: it gave
Some Respite to the Sorrows of my Slave.
Her fond Excess proclaim'd her Passion true;   485
And generous Pity to that Truth was due.
Well I intreated Her, who well deserv'd;
I call'd Her often; for She always serv'd.
Use made her Person easy to my Sight;
And Ease insensibly produc'd Delight.   490

   Whene'er I revell'd in the Women's Bow'rs;
(For first I sought Her but at looser Hours:)
The Apples She had gather'd smelt most sweet:
The Cake She kneaded was the sav'ry Meat:

477 Imperial] Again fair *W*   478 And...again] Sublime, again shal Solomon *W*

But Fruits their Odor lost, and Meats their Taste;   495
If gentle ABRA had not deck'd the Feast.
Dishonor'd did the sparkling Goblet stand,
Unless receiv'd from gentle ABRA's Hand:
And when the Virgins form'd the Evening Choir,
Raising their Voices to the Master-Lyre;   500
Too flat I thought This Voice, and That too shrill;
One show'd too much, and one too little Skill:
Nor could my Soul approve the Music's Tone;
'Till all was hush'd, and ABRA Sung alone.
Fairer She seem'd, distinguish'd from the rest;   505
And better Mein disclos'd, as better drest.
A bright *Tiara* round her Forehead ty'd,
To juster Bounds confin'd it's rising Pride:
The blushing Ruby on her snowy Breast,
Render'd it's panting Whiteness more confess'd: 510
Bracelets of Pearl gave Roundness to her Arm;
And ev'ry Gem augmented ev'ry Charm.
Her Senses pleas'd, her Beauty still improv'd;
And She more lovely grew, as more belov'd.

And now I could behold, avow, and blame   515
The several Follies of my former Flame;
Willing my Heart for Recompence to prove
The certain Joys that lye in prosp'rous Love.
For what, said I, from ABRA can I fear,
Too humble to insult, too soft to be severe?   520
The Dam'sel's sole Ambition is to please:
With Freedom I may like, and quit with Ease:
She sooths, but never can enthrall my Mind:
Why may not Peace and Love for once be join'd?

Great Heav'n! how frail thy Creature Man is made!   525
How by Himself insensibly betray'd!
In our own Strength unhappily secure,
Too little cautious of the adverse Pow'r;
And by the Blast of Self-opinion mov'd,
We wish to charm, and seek to be belov'd.   530
On Pleasure's flowing Brink We idly stray,
Masters as yet of our returning Way:

Seeing no Danger, We disarm our Mind;
And give our Conduct to the Waves and Wind:
Then in the flow'ry Mead, or verdant Shade   535
To wanton Dalliance negligently laid,
We weave the Chaplet, and We crown the Bowl;
And smiling see the nearer Waters roll;
'Till the strong Gusts of raging Passion rise;
'Till the dire Tempest mingles Earth and Skies;   540
And swift into the boundless Ocean born,
Our foolish Confidence too late We mourn:
Round our devoted Heads the Billows beat;
And from our troubl'd View the lessen'd Lands retreat.

O mighty Love! from thy unbounded Pow'r   545
How shall the human Bosom rest secure?
How shall our Thought avoid the various Snare?
Or Wisdom to our caution'd Soul declare
The diff'rent Shapes, Thou pleasest to imploy,
When bent to hurt, and certain to destroy?   550

The haughty Nymph in open Beauty drest,
To-Day encounters our unguarded Breast:
She looks with Majesty, and moves with State:
Unbent her Soul, and in Misfortune great,
She scorns the World, and dares the Rage of Fate. } 555

Here whilst we take stern Manhood for our Guide,
And guard our Conduct with becoming Pride;
Charm'd with the Courage in her Action shown,
We praise her Mind, the Image of our own.
She that can please, is certain to perswade: 560
To-day belov'd, To-morrow is obey'd.
We think we see thro' Reason's Optics right;
Nor find, how Beauty's Rays elude our Sight:
Struck with her Eye whilst We applaud her Mind;
And when We speak Her great, We wish Her kind.   565

To-morrow, cruel Pow'r, Thou arm'st the Fair
With flowing Sorrow, and dishevel'd Hair:

561] *W* and lov'd one day the next she [is] obeyd: *Earlier reading in W*

Sad her Complaint, and humble is her Tale,
Her Sighs explaining where her Accents fail.
Here gen'rous Softness warms the honest Breast: 570
We raise the sad, and succour the distress'd:
And whilst our Wish prepares the kind Relief;
Whilst Pity mitigates her rising Grief:
We sicken soon from her contagious Care;
Grieve for her Sorrows, groan for her Despair;   575
And against Love too late those Bosoms arm,
Which Tears can soften, and which Sighs can warm.

Against this nearest cruelest of Foes,
What shall Wit meditate, or Force oppose?
Whence, feeble Nature, shall We summon Aid;   580
If by our Pity, and our Pride betray'd?
External Remedy shall We hope to find,
When the close Fiend has gain'd our treach'rous Mind;
Insulting there does Reason's Pow'r deride;
And blind Himself, conducts the dazl'd Guide?   585

My Conqueror now, my Lovely ABRA held
My Freedom in her Chains: my Heart was fill'd
With Her, with Her alone: in Her alone
It sought it's Peace and Joy: while She was gone,
It sigh'd, and griev'd, impatient of her Stay: 590
Return'd, She chas'd those Sighs, that Grief away:
Her Absence made the Night: her Presence brought the Day.

The Ball, the Play, the Mask by Turns succeed.
For Her I make the Song: the Dance with Her I lead.
I court Her various in each Shape and Dress,   595
That Luxury may form, or Thought express.

To-day beneath the Palm-tree on the Plains
In DEBORAH's Arms and Habit ABRA reigns:
The Wreath denoting Conquest guides her Brow:
And low, like BARAK, at her Feet I bow.   600
The Mimic Chorus sings her prosp'rous Hand;
As She had slain the Foe, and sav'd the Land.

576 And...too late] We...in vain *L 13*

To-morrow She approves a softer Air;
Forsakes the Pomp and Pageantry of War;
The Form of peaceful ABIGAIL assumes;   605
And from the Village with the Present comes:
The Youthful Band depose their glitt'ring Arms;
Receive her Bounties, and recite her Charms;
Whilst I assume my Father's Step and Mein,
To meet with due Regard my future Queen.   610

If hap'ly ABRA's Will be now inclin'd
To range the Woods, or chace the flying Hind;
Soon as the Sun awakes, the sprightly Court
Leave their Repose, and hasten to the Sport.
In lessen'd Royalty, and humble State,   615
Thy King, JERUSALEM, descends to wait,
'Till ABRA comes. She comes: a Milk-white Steed,
Mixture of PERSIA's, and ARABIA's Breed,
Sustains the Nymph: her Garments flying loose
(As the SYDONIAN Maids, or THRACIAN use)   620
And half her Knee, and half her Breast appear,
By Art, like Negligence, disclos'd, and bare.
Her left Hand guides the hunting Courser's Flight:
A Silver Bow She carries in her Right:
And from the golden Quiver at her Side,   625
Rustles the Ebon Arrow's feather'd Pride.
Saphirs and Diamonds on her Front display
An artificial Moon's increasing Ray.
DIANA, Huntress, Mistress of the Groves,
The fav'rite ABRA speaks, and looks, and moves.   630
Her, as the present Goddess, I obey:
Beneath her Feet the captive Game I lay.
The mingl'd Chorus sings DIANA's Fame:
Clarions and Horns in louder Peals proclaim
Her Mystic Praise: the vocal Triumphs bound   635
Against the Hills: the Hills reflect the Sound.

If tir'd this Evening with the hunted Woods,
To the large Fish-pools, or the glassy Floods
Her Mind To-morrow points; a thousand Hands
To-night employ'd, obey the King's Commands.   640

Upon the wat'ry Beach an artful Pile
Of Planks is join'd, and forms a moving Isle.
A golden Chariot in the Midst is set;
And silver Cygnets seem to feel it's Weight.
ABRA, bright Queen, ascends her gaudy Throne,   645
In semblance of the GRÆCIAN VENUS known:
TRITONS and Sea-green NAIADS round Her move;
And sing in moving Strains the Force of Love:
Whilst as th'approaching Pageant does appear;
And echoing Crouds speak mighty VENUS near;   650
I, her Adorer, too devoutly stand
Fast on the utmost Margin of the Land,
With Arms and Hopes extended, to receive
The fancy'd Goddess rising from the Wave.

    O subject Reason! O imperious Love!   655
Whither yet further would My Folly rove?
Is it enough, that ABRA should be great
In the wall'd Palace, or the Rural Seat?
That masking Habits, and a borrow'd Name
Contrive to hide my Plenitude of Shame?   660
No, no: JERUSALEM combin'd must see
My open Fault, and Regal Infamy.
Solemn a Month is destin'd for the Feast:
ABRA Invites: the Nation is the Guest.
To have the Honor of each Day sustain'd,   665
The Woods are travers'd; and the Lakes are drain'd:
ARABIA's Wilds, and EGYPT's are explor'd:
The Edible Creation decks the Board:
Hardly the *Phœnix* 'scapes—
The Men their Lyres, the Maids their Voices raise,   670
To sing my Happiness, and ABRA's Praise.
And slavish Bards our mutual Loves rehearse
In lying Strains, and ignominious Verse:
While from the Banquet leading forth the Bride,
Whom prudent Love from public Eyes should hide;   675
I show Her to the World, confess'd and known
Queen of my Heart, and Part'ner of my Throne.

    And now her Friends and Flatt'rers fill the Court:
From DAN, and from BEERSHEBA They resort:

They barter Places, and dispose of Grants, 680
Whole Provinces unequal to their Wants.
They teach Her to recede, or to debate;
With Toys of Love to mix Affairs of State;
By practis'd Rules her Empire to secure;
And in my Pleasure make my Ruin sure. 685
They gave, and She transferr'd the curs'd Advice,
That Monarchs should their inward Soul disguise,
Dissemble, and command; be false, and wise;
By ignominious Arts for servile Ends
Should compliment their Foes, and shun their Friends. 690
And now I leave the true and just Supports
Of Legal Princes, and of honest Courts,
BARZILLAI's, and the fierce BENAIAH's Heirs;
Whose Sires, Great Part'ners in my Father's Cares,
Saluted their young King at HEBRON crown'd, 695
Great by their Toil, and glorious by their Wound.
And now, unhappy Council, I prefer
Those whom my Follies only made me fear,
Old CORAH's Brood, and taunting SHIMEI's Race;
Miscreants who ow'd their Lives to DAVID's Grace; 700
Tho' they had spurn'd his Rule, and curs'd Him to his Face.

Still ABRA's Pow'r, my Scandal still increas'd;
Justice submitted to what ABRA pleas'd:
Her Will alone could settle or revoke;
And Law was fix'd by what She latest spoke. 705

ISRAEL neglected, ABRA was my Care:
I only acted, thought, and liv'd for Her.
I durst not reason with my wounded Heart.
ABRA possess'd; She was it's better Part.
O! had I now review'd the famous Cause, 710
Which gave my righteous Youth so just Applause;
In vain on the dissembl'd Mother's Tongue
Had cunning Art, and sly Perswasion hung;
And real Care in vain, and native Love
In the true Parent's panting Breast had strove; 715
While both deceiv'd had seen the destin'd Child
Or slain, or sav'd, as ABRA frown'd or smil'd.

Unknowing to command, proud to obey,
A life-less King, a Royal Shade I lay.
Unhear'd the injur'd Orphans now complain: 720
The Widow's Cries address the Throne in vain.
Causes unjudg'd disgrace the loaded File;
And sleeping Laws the King's Neglect revile.
No more the Elders throng'd around my Throne,
To hear My Maxims, and reform their own.   725
No more the Young Nobility were taught,
How MOSES govern'd, and how DAVID fought.
Loose and undisciplin'd the Soldier lay;
Or lost in Drink, and Game, the solid Day:
Porches and Scholes, design'd for public Good,   730
Uncover'd, and with Scaffolds cumber'd stood,
Or nodded, threat'ning Ruin—
Half Pillars wanted their expected Height;
And Roofs imperfect prejudic'd the Sight.
The Artists grieve; the lab'ring People droop: 735
My Father's Legacy, my Country's Hope,
God's Temple lies unfinish'd—

The Wise and Grave deplor'd their Monarch's Fate,
And future Mischiefs of a sinking State.
Is this, the Serious said, is this the Man,   740
Whose active Soul thro' every Science ran?
Who by just Rule and elevated Skill
Prescrib'd the dubious Bounds of Good and Ill?
Whose Golden Sayings, and Immortal Wit,
On large *Phylacteries* expressive writ,   745
Were to the Forehead of the *Rabbins* ty'd,
Our Youth's Instruction, and our Age's Pride?
Could not the Wise his wild Desires restrain?
Then was our Hearing, and his Preaching vain:
What from his Life and Letters were we taught,   750
But that his Knowledge aggravates his Fault?

In lighter Mood the Humorous and the Gay,
As crown'd with Roses at their Feasts they lay;
Sent the full Goblet, charg'd with ABRA's Name,
And Charms superior to their Master's Fame: 755

Laughing some praise the King, who let 'em see,
How aptly Luxe and Empire might agree:
Some gloss'd, how Love and Wisdom were at Strife;
And brought my Proverbs to confront my Life.
However, Friend, here's to the King, one cries: 760
To Him who was the King, the Friend replies.
The King, for JUDAH's, and for Wisdom's Curse,
To ABRA yields: could I, or Thou do worse?
Our looser Lives let Chance or Folly steer;
If thus the Prudent and Determin'd err.   765
Let DINAH bind with Flowers her flowing Hair;
And touch the Lute, and sound the wanton Air:
Let Us the Bliss without the Sting receive,
Free, as We will, or to injoy, or leave.
Pleasures on Levity's smooth Surface flow: 770
Thought brings the Weight, that sinks the Soul to Woe.
Now be this Maxim to the King convey'd,
And added to the Thousand He has made.

Sadly, O Reason, is thy Pow'r express'd,
Thou gloomy Tyrant of the frighted Breast!   775
And harsh the Rules, which We from Thee receive;
If for our Wisdom We our Pleasure give;
And more to think be only more to grieve.
If JUDAH's King at thy Tribunal try'd,
Forsakes his Joy to vindicate his Pride;   780
And changing Sorrows, I am only found
Loos'd from the Chains of Love, in Thine more strictly bound.

But do I call Thee Tyrant, or complain,
How hard thy Laws, how absolute thy Reign?
While Thou, alas! art but an empty Name,   785
To no Two Men, who e'er discours'd, the same;
The idle Product of a troubled Thought,
In borrow'd Shapes, and airy Colors wrought;
A fancy'd Line, and a reflected Shade;
A Chain which Man to fetter Man has made,   790
By Artifice impos'd, by Fear obey'd.

Yet, wretched Name, or Arbitrary Thing,
Whence ever I thy cruel Essence bring,
I own thy Influence; for I feel thy Sting.

Reluctant I perceive thee in my Soul,   795
Form'd to command, and destin'd to control.
Yes; thy insulting Dictates shall be heard:
Virtue for once shall be Her own Reward.
Yes; Rebel ISRAEL, this unhappy Maid
Shall be dismiss'd: the Crowd shall be obey'd: 800
The King his Passion, and his Rule shall leave,
No longer ABRA's, but the People's Slave.
My Coward Soul shall bear it's wayward Fate:
I will, alas! be wretched, to be great;
And sigh in Royalty, and grieve in State.   805

   I said: resolv'd to plunge into my Grief
At once so far, as to expect Relief
From my Despair alone—
I chose to write the Thing I durst not speak,
To Her I lov'd; to Her I must forsake.   810
The harsh Epistle labour'd much to prove,
How inconsistent Majesty, and Love.
I always should, It said, esteem Her well;
But never see her more: It bid Her feel
No future Pain for Me; but instant wed   815
A Lover more proportion'd to her Bed;
And quiet dedicate her remnant Life
To the just Duties of an humble Wife.

   She read; and forth to Me She wildly ran,
To Me, the Ease of all her former Pain.   820
She kneel'd intreated, struggl'd, threaten'd, cry'd;
And with alternate Passion liv'd, and dy'd:
'Till now deny'd the Liberty to mourn,
And by rude Fury from my Presence torn,
This only Object of my real Care,   825
Cut off from Hope, abandon'd to Despair,
In some few posting fatal Hours is hurl'd
From Wealth, from Pow'r, from Love, and from the World.

   Here tell Me, if Thou dar'st, my conscious Soul,
What diff'rent Sorrows did within Thee roll: 830
What Pangs, what Fires, what Racks didst Thou sustain,
What sad Vicissitudes of smarting Pain?

How oft from Pomp and State did I remove,
To feed Despair, and cherish hopeless Love?
How oft, all Day, recall'd I ABRA's Charms,   835
Her Beauties press'd, and panting in my Arms?
How oft, with Sighs, view'd every Female Face,
Where mimic Fancy might her Likeness trace?
How oft desir'd to fly from ISRAEL's Throne,
And live in Shades with Her and Love alone?   840
How oft, all Night, pursu'd Her in my Dreams,
O'er flow'ry Vallies, and thro' Crystal Streams;
And waking, view'd with Grief the rising Sun,
And fondly mourn'd the dear Delusion gone?

　　When thus the gather'd Storms of wretched Love   845
In my swoln Bosom, with long War had strove;
At length they broke their Bounds: at length their Force
Bore down whatever met it's stronger Course:
Lay'd all the Civil Bonds of Manhood waste;
And scatter'd Ruin as the Torrent past.   850

　　So from the Hills, whose hollow Caves contain
The congregated Snow, and swelling Rain;
'Till the full Stores their antient Bounds disdain;
Precipitate the furious Torrent flows:
In vain would Speed avoid, or Strength oppose: 855
Towns, Forests, Herds, and Men promiscuous drown'd,
With one great Death deform the dreary Ground;
The echo'd Woes from distant Rocks resound.

　　And now what impious Ways my Wishes took;
How they the Monarch, and the Man forsook;   860
And how I follow'd an abandon'd Will,
Thro' crooked Paths, and sad Retreats of Ill;
How JUDAH's Daughters now, now foreign Slaves,
By turns my prostituted Bed receives.
Thro' Tribes of Women how I loosely rang'd   865
Impatient; lik'd To-night, To-morrow chang'd;
And by the Instinct of capricious Lust,
Enjoy'd, disdain'd, was grateful, or unjust:
O, be these Scenes from human Eyes conceal'd,
In Clouds of decent Silence justly veil'd!   870

O, be the wanton Images convey'd
To black Oblivion, and eternal Shade!
Or let their sad *Epitome* alone,
And outward Lines to future Age be known,
Enough to propagate the sure Belief,   875
That Vice engenders Shame; and Folly broods o'er Grief.

Bury'd in Sloth, and lost in Ease I lay:
The Night I revell'd; and I slept the Day.
New Heaps of Fewel damp'd my kindling Fires;
And daily Change extinguish'd young Desires.   880
By it's own Force destroy'd, Fruition ceas'd;
And always weary'd, I was never pleas'd.
No longer now does my neglected Mind
It's wonted Stores, and old *Ideas* find.
Fix'd Judgment there no longer does abide,   885
To take the True, or set the False aside.
No longer does swift Mem'ry trace the Cells,
Where springing Wit, or young Invention dwells.
Frequent Debauch to Habitude prevails:
Patience of Toil, and Love of Virtue fails.   890
By sad Degrees impair'd my Vigor dyes;
Till I Command no longer ev'n in Vice.

The Women on my Dotage build their Sway:
They ask; I grant: They threaten; I obey.
In Regal Garments now I gravely stride,   895
Aw'd by the PERSIAN Dam'sel's haughty Pride.
Now with the looser SYRIAN dance, and sing,
In Robes tuck'd up, opprobrious to the King.

Charm'd by their Eyes, their Manners I acquire;
And shape my Foolishness to their Desire.   900
Seduc'd and aw'd by the PHILISTINE Dame,
At DAGON's Shrine I kindle impious Flame.
With the CHALDEAN's Charms her Rites prevail;
And curling Frankincense ascends to BAAL.
To each new Harlot I new Altars dress;   905
And serve Her God, whose Person I caress.

Where, my deluded Sense, was Reason flown?
Where the high Majesty of DAVID's Throne?

Where all the Maxims of Eternal Truth,
With which the Living GOD inform'd my Youth?   910
When with the lewd EGYPTIAN I adore
Vain Idols, Deities that ne'er before
In ISRAEL's Land had fix'd their dire Abodes,
Beastly Divinities, and Droves of Gods:
OSIRIS, APIS, Pow'rs that chew the Cud,   915
And Dog ANUBIS, Flatt'rer for his Food:
When in the Woody Hill's forbidden Shade
I carv'd the Marble, and invok'd it's Aid:
When in the Fens to Snakes and Flies, with Zeal
Unworthy human Thought, I prostrate fell;   920
To Shrubs and Plants my vile Devotion paid;
And set the bearded Leek, to which I pray'd:
When to all Beings Sacred Rites were giv'n;
Forgot the Arbiter of Earth and Heav'n.

Thro' these sad Shades, this *Chaos* in my Soul,   925
Some Seeds of Light at length began to roll.
The rising Motion of an Infant Ray
Shot glimm'ring thro' the Cloud, and promis'd Day.
And now one Moment able to reflect,
I found the King abandon'd to Neglect,   930
Seen without Awe, and serv'd without Respect.
I found my Subjects amicably joyn,
To lessen their Defects, by citing Mine.
The Priest with Pity pray'd for DAVID's Race;
And left his Text, to dwell on my Disgrace.   935
The Father, whilst he warn'd his erring Son,
The sad Examples which He ought to shun,
Describ'd, and only nam'd not, SOLOMON.
Each Bard, each Sire did to his Pupil sing,
A Wise Child better than a Foolish King.   940

Into My self my Reason's Eye I turn'd;
And as I much reflected, much I mourn'd.
A Mighty King I am, an Earthly God:
Nations obey my Word, and wait my Nod.
I raise or sink, imprison or set free;   945
And Life or Death depends on My Decree.

Fond the *Idea*, and the Thought is vain:
O'er JUDAH's King ten thousand Tyrants reign.
Legions of Lust, and various Pow'rs of Ill
Insult the Master's Tributary Will: 950
And He, from whom the Nations should receive
Justice, and Freedom, lyes Himself a Slave,
Tortur'd by cruel Change of wild Desires,
Lash'd by mad Rage, and scorch'd by brutal Fires.

O Reason! once again to Thee I call: 955
Accept my Sorrow, and retrieve my Fall.
Wisdom, Thou say'st, from Heav'n receiv'd her Birth;
Her Beams transmitted to the subject Earth.
Yet this great Empress of the human Soul
Does only with imagin'd Pow'r controul;   960
If restless Passion by Rebellious Sway
Compells the weak Usurper to obey.

O troubled, weak, and Coward, as thou art!
Without thy poor Advice the lab'ring Heart
To worse Extremes with swifter Steps would run,   965
Not sav'd by Virtue, yet by Vice undone.

Oft have I said, the Praise of doing well
Is to the Ear, as Oyntment to the Smell.
Now if some Flies perchance, however small,
Into the Alabaster Urn should fall;   970
The Odors of the Sweets inclos'd would dye;
And Stench corrupt (sad Change!) their Place supply.
So the least Faults, if mix'd with fairest Deed,
Of future Ill become the fatal Seed:
Into the Balm of purest Virtue cast,   975
Annoy all Life with one contagious Blast.

Lost SOLOMON! pursue this Thought no more:
Of thy past Errors recollect the Store:
And silent weep, that while the Deathless Muse
Shall sing the Just; shall o'er their Head diffuse   980
Perfumes with lavish Hand; She shall proclaim
Thy Crimes alone; and to Thy evil Fame
Impartial, scatter Damps, and Poysons on thy Name.

Awaking therefore, as who long had dream'd,
Much of my Women, and their Gods asham'd, 985
From this Abyss of exemplary Vice
Resolv'd, as Time might aid my Thought, to rise;
Again I bid the mournful Goddess write
The fond Pursuit of fugitive Delight:
Bid her exalt her melancholy Wing, 990
And rais'd from Earth, and sav'd from Passion, sing
Of human Hope by cross Event destroy'd,
Of useless Wealth, and Greatness unenjoy'd,
Of Lust and Love, with their fantastic Train,
Their Wishes, Smiles, and Looks deceitful all, and vain. 995

POWER;

THE THIRD BOOK.

The ARGUMENT.

SOLOMON *considers Man through the several Stages and Conditions of Life; and concludes in general, that We are all Miserable. He reflects more particularly upon the Trouble and Uncertainty of Greatness and Power; gives some Instances thereof from* ADAM *down to Himself; and still concludes that* ALL *is* VANITY. *He reasons again upon Life, Death, and a future Being; finds Human Wisdom too imperfect to resolve his Doubts; has Recourse to Religion; is informed by an Angel, what shall happen to Himself, his Family, and his Kingdom, 'till the Redemption of* ISRAEL: *and, upon the whole, resolves to submit his Enquiries and Anxieties to the Will of his Creator.*

Texts chiefly alluded to in this Book.

Or ever the Silver Cord be loosed, or the golden Bowl be broken, or the Pitcher be broken at the Fountain, or the Wheel broken at the Cistern. ECCLESIASTES, Chap. XII. Vers. 6.

The Sun ariseth, and the Sun goeth down, and hasteth to his Place where He arose. ECCLESIASTES, Chap. I. Vers. 5.

The Wind goeth towards the South, and turneth about unto the North. It whirleth about continually; and the Wind returneth again according to his Circuit. Vers. 6.

All the Rivers run into the Sea: yet the Sea is not full. Unto the Place from whence the Rivers come, thither they return again. Vers. 7.

Then shall the Dust return to the Earth, as it was: and the Spirit shall return unto God who gave it. ECCLESIASTES, Chap. XII. Vers. 7.

Now when SOLOMON had made an End of Praying, the Fire came down from Heaven, and consumed the Burnt-offering, and the Sacrifices; and the Glory of the Lord filled the House. II CHRONICLES, Chap. VII. Vers. 1.

By the Rivers of BABYLON, there We sat down; Yea We wept, when We remembred Sion &c. PSALM CXXXVII. Vers. 1.

I said of Laughter, it is mad; and of Mirth, what doeth it? ECCLESIASTES, Chap. II. Vers. 2.

—No Man can find out the Work that God maketh, from the Beginning to the End. ECCLESIASTES, Chap. III. Vers. 11.

Whatsoever God doeth, it shall be for ever: nothing can be put to it, nor any thing taken from it: and God doeth it, that Men should fear before Him. Vers. 14.

Let us hear the Conclusion of the whole Matter; Fear God, and keep his Commandments; for this is the whole Duty of Man. ECCLESIASTES, Chap. XII. Verse. 13.

POWER;

THE THIRD BOOK.

COME then, my Soul: I call Thee by that Name,
Thou busie Thing, from whence I know I am:
For knowing that I am, I know Thou art;
Since That must needs exist, which can impart.
But how cam'st Thou to be, or whence Thy Spring? 5
For various of Thee Priests and Poets sing.

Hear'st Thou submissive, but a lowly Birth,
Some sep'rate Particles of finer Earth,
A plain Effect, which Nature must beget,
As Motion orders, and as Atoms meet; 10
Companion of the Body's Good or Ill,
From Force of Instinct more than Choice of Will;
Conscious of Fear or Valor, Joy or Pain,
As the wild Courses of the Blood ordain;

5 cam'st Thou ... Spring? *edd.*: Thou cam'st ... Spring: *1718*

Who as Degrees of Heat and Cold prevail, 15
In Youth dost flourish, and with Age shalt fail;
'Till mingl'd with thy Part'ner's latest Breath
Thou fly'st, dissolv'd in Air, and lost in Death.

Or if Thy great Existence would aspire
To Causes more sublime; of Heav'nly Fire 20
Wer't Thou a Spark struck off, a sep'rate Ray,
Ordain'd to mingle with Terrestrial Clay;
With it condemn'd for certain Years to dwell,
To grieve it's Frailties, and it's Pains to feel;
To teach it Good and Ill, Disgrace or Fame; 25
Pale it with Rage, or redden it with Shame:
To guide it's Actions with informing Care,
In Peace to Judge, to Conquer in the War;
Render it Agile, Witty, Valiant, Sage,
As fits the various Course of human Age; 30
Till as the Earthly Part decays and falls,
The Captive breaks Her Prison's mould'ring Walls;
Hovers a-while upon the sad Remains,
Which now the Pile, or Sepulchre contains;
And thence with Liberty unbounded flies, 35
Impatient to regain Her native Skies.

Whate'er Thou art, where-e'er ordain'd to go:
(Points which We rather may dispute, than know)
Come on, Thou little Inmate of this Breast,
Which for Thy Sake from Passions I divest: 40
For these, Thou say'st, raise all the stormy Strife,
Which hinder Thy Repose, and trouble Life.
Be the fair Level of Thy Actions laid,
As Temp'rance wills, and Prudence may perswade;
Be Thy Affections undisturb'd and clear, 45
Guided to what may Great or Good appear;
And try if Life be worth the Liver's Care.

Amass'd in Man there justly is beheld
What thro' the whole Creation has excell'd:
The Life and Growth of Plants, of Beasts the Sense, 50
The Angel's Forecast and Intelligence:

Say from these glorious Seeds what Harvest flows;
Recount our Blessings, and compare our Woes.
In it's true Light let clearest Reason see
The Man dragg'd out to Act, and forc'd to Be;   55
Helpless and Naked on a Woman's Knees
To be expos'd or rear'd as She may please;
Feel her Neglect, and pine from her Disease.
His tender Eye by too direct a Ray
Wounded, and flying from unpractis'd Day;   60
His Heart assaulted by invading Air,
And beating fervent to the vital War;
To his Young Sense how various Forms appear;
That strike his Wonder, and excite his Fear?
By his Distortions he reveals his Pains;   65
He by his Tears, and by his Sighs complains;
'Till Time and Use assist the Infant Wretch,
By broken Words, and Rudiments of Speech,
His Wants in plainer Characters to show,
And paint more perfect Figures of his Woe.   70
Condemn'd to sacrifice his childish Years
To babling Ign'rance, and to empty Fears;
To pass the riper Period of his Age,
Acting his Part upon a crowded Stage;
To lasting Toils expos'd, and endless Cares,   75
To open Dangers, and to secret Snares;
To Malice which the vengeful Foe intends,
And the more dangerous Love of seeming Friends.
His Deeds examin'd by the People's Will,
Prone to forget the Good, and blame the Ill: 80
Or sadly censur'd in their curs'd Debate,
Who in the Scorner's, or the Judge's Seat
Dare to condemn the Virtue which They hate.
Or would he rather leave this frantic Scene;
And Trees and Beasts prefer to Courts and Men?   85
In the remotest Wood and lonely Grott
Certain to meet that worst of Evils, Thought;
Diff'rent IDEAS to his Mem'ry brought:
Some intricate, as are the pathless Woods;
Impetuous some, as the descending Floods: 90

With anxious Doubts, with raging Passions torn,
No sweet Companion near with whom to mourn;
He hears the Echoing Rock return his Sighs;
And from himself the frighted Hermit flies.

Thus, thro' what Path soe'er of Life We rove,   95
Rage companies our Hate, and Grief our Love:
Vex'd with the present Moment's heavy Gloom,
Why seek We Brightness from the Years to come?
Disturb'd and broken like a sick Man's Sleep,
Our troubl'd Thoughts to distant Prospects leap;   100
Desirous still what flies us to o'ertake:
For Hope is but the Dream of Those that wake:
But looking back, We see the dreadful Train
Of Woes, a-new which were We to sustain,
We should refuse to tread the Path again.   105
Still adding Grief, still counting from the first;
Judging the latest Evils still the worst;
And sadly finding each progressive Hour
Heighten their Number, and augment their Pow'r;
Till by one countless Sum of Woes opprest,   110
Hoary with Cares, and Ignorant of Rest,
We find the vital Springs relax'd and worn:
Compell'd our common Impotence to mourn,
Thus, thro' the Round of Age, to Childhood We return;
Reflecting find, that naked from the Womb   115
We yesterday came forth; that in the Tomb
Naked again We must To-morrow lye,
Born to lament, to labor, and to dye.

Pass We the Ills, which each Man feels or dreads,
The Weight or fall'n, or hanging o'er our Heads;   120
The Bear, The Lyon, Terrors of the Plain,
The Sheepfold scatter'd, and the Shepherd slain;
The frequent Errors of the pathless Wood,
The giddy Precipice, and the dang'rous Flood:
The noisom Pest'lence, that in open War   125
Terrible, marches thro' the Mid-day Air,
And scatters Death; the Arrow that by Night
Cuts the dank Mist, and fatal wings it's Flight;

The billowing Snow, and Violence of the Show'r,
That from the Hills disperse their dreadful Store,   130
And o'er the Vales collected Ruin pour;
The Worm that gnaws the ripening Fruit, sad Guest,
Canker or Locust hurtful to infest
The Blade; while Husks elude the Tiller's Care,
And Eminence of Want distinguishes the Year.   135

Pass we the slow Disease, and subtil Pain,
Which our weak Frame is destin'd to sustain;
The cruel Stone, with congregated War
Tearing his bloody Way; the cold Catarrh,
With frequent Impulse, and continu'd Strife,   140
Weak'ning the wasted Seats of irksom Life;
The Gout's fierce Rack, the burning Feaver's Rage,
The sad Experience of Decay; and Age,
Her self the soarest Ill; while Death, and Ease,
Oft and in vain invok'd, or to appease,   145
Or end the Grief, with hasty Wings receed
From the vext Patient, and the sickly Bed.

Nought shall it profit, that the charming Fair,
Angelic, softest Work of Heav'n, draws near
To the cold shaking paralytic Hand,   150
Senseless of Beauty's Touch, or Love's Command,
Nor longer apt, or able to fulfill
The Dictates of it's feeble Master's Will.

Nought shall the Psaltry, and the Harp avail,
The pleasing Song, or well repeated Tale,   155
When the quick Spirits their warm March forbear;
And numbing Coldness has unbrac'd the Ear.

The verdant Rising of the flow'ry Hill,
The Vale enamell'd, and the Crystal Rill,
The Ocean rolling, and the shelly Shoar,   160
Beautiful Objects, shall delight no more;
When the lax'd Sinews of the weaken'd Eye
In wat'ry Damps, or dim Suffusion lye.
Day follows Night; the Clouds return again
After the falling of the later Rain: 165

But to the Aged-blind shall ne'er return
Grateful Vicissitude: He still must mourn
The Sun, and Moon, and ev'ry Starry Light
Eclips'd to Him, and lost in everlasting Night.

Behold where Age's wretched Victim lies: 170
See his Head trembling, and his half-clos'd Eyes:
Frequent for Breath his panting Bosom heaves:
To broken Sleeps his remnant Sense He gives;
And only by his Pains, awaking finds He Lives.

Loos'd by devouring Time the Silver Cord   175
Dissever'd lies: unhonor'd from the Board
The Crystal Urn, when broken, is thrown by;
And apter Utensils their Place supply.
These Things and Thou must share One equal Lot;
Dye and be lost, corrupt and be forgot;   180
While still another, and another Race
Shall now supply, and now give up the Place.
From Earth all came, to Earth must all return;
Frail as the Cord, and brittle as the Urn.

But be the Terror of these Ills suppress'd: 185
And view We Man with Health and Vigor blest.
Home He returns with the declining Sun,
His destin'd Task of Labor hardly done;
Goes forth again with the ascending Ray,
Again his Travel for his Bread to pay,   190
And find the Ill sufficient to the Day.
Hap'ly at Night He does with Horror shun
A widow'd Daughter, or a dying Son:
His Neighbor's Off-spring He To-morrow sees;
And doubly feels his Want in their Increase: 195
The next Day, and the next he must attend
His Foe triumphant, or his buried Friend.
In ev'ry Act and Turn of Life he feels
Public Calamities, or Household Ills:
The due Reward to just Desert refus'd: 200
The Trust betray'd, the Nuptial Bed abus'd:
The Judge corrupt, the long depending Cause,
And doubtful Issue of misconstru'd Laws:

The crafty Turns of a dishonest State,
And violent Will of the wrong-doing Great: 205
The Venom'd Tongue injurious to his Fame,
Which nor can Wisdom shun, nor fair Advice reclaim.

Esteem We these, my Friends, Event and Chance,
Produc'd as Atoms form their flutt'ring Dance?
Or higher yet their Essence may We draw   210
From destin'd Order, and Eternal Law?
Again, my Muse, the cruel Doubt repeat:
Spring they, I say, from Accident, or Fate?
Yet such, We find, they are, as can controll
The servile Actions of our wav'ring Soul;   215
Can fright, can alter, or can chain the Will;
Their Ills all built on Life, that fundamental Ill.

O fatal Search! in which the lab'ring Mind,
Still press'd with Weight of Woe, still hopes to find
A Shadow of Delight, a Dream of Peace,   220
From Years of Pain, one Moment of Release;
Hoping at least She may Her self deceive,
Against Experience willing to believe,
Desirous to rejoice, condemn'd to grieve.

Happy the Mortal Man, who now at last   225
Has thro' this doleful Vale of Mis'ry past;
Who to his destin'd Stage has carry'd on
The tedious Load, and laid his Burden down;
Whom the cut Brass, or wounded Marble shows
Victor o'er Life, and all Her Train of Woes.   230
He happyer yet, who privileg'd by Fate
To shorter Labor, and a lighter Weight,
Receiv'd but Yesterday the Gift of Breath,
Order'd To-morrow to return to Death.
But O! beyond Description happyest He,   235
Who ne'er must roll on Life's tumultuous Sea;
Who with bless'd Freedom from the gen'ral Doom
Exempt, must never force the teeming Womb,
Nor see the Sun, nor sink into the Tomb.

Who breaths, must suffer; and who thinks, must mourn;   240
And He alone is bless'd, who ne'er was born.

"Yet in thy turn, Thou frowning Preacher, hear:
"Are not these general Maxims too severe?
"Say: cannot Pow'r secure it's Owner's Bliss?
"And is not Wealth the potent Sire of Peace?   } 245
"Are Victors bless'd with Fame, or Kings with Ease?

    I tell Thee, Life is but one common Care;
And Man was born to suffer, and to fear.

    "But is no Rank, no Station, no Degree
"From this contagious Taint of Sorrow free?   250

    None, Mortal, None: Yet in a bolder Strain
Let Me this melancholy Truth maintain:
But hence, Ye Worldly, and Prophane, retire:
For I adapt my Voice, and raise my Lyre
To Notions not by Vulgar Ear receiv'd: 255
Ye still must covet Life, and be deceiv'd:
Your very Fear of Death shall make Ye try
To catch the Shade of Immortality;
Wishing on Earth to linger, and to save
Part of it's Prey from the devouring Grave;   260
To those who may survive Ye, to bequeath
Something entire, in spight of Time, and Death;
A fancy'd Kind of Being to retrieve,
And in a Book, or from a Building live.
False Hope! vain Labor! let some Ages fly: 265
The Dome shall moulder, and the Volume dye:
Wretches, still taught, still will Ye think it strange,
That all the Parts of this great Fabric change;
Quit their old Station, and Primæval Frame;
And lose their Shape, their Essence, and their Name?   270

    Reduce the Song: our Hopes, our Joys are vain:
Our Lot is Sorrow; and Our Portion Pain.

    What Pause from Woe, what Hopes of Comfort bring
The Name of Wise or Great, of Judge or King?
What is a King? A Man condemn'd to bear   275
The public Burden of the Nation's Care;
Now crown'd some angry Faction to appease;
Now falls a Victim to the People's Ease:

From the first blooming of his ill-taught Youth,
Nourish'd in Flatt'ry, and estrang'd from Truth: 280
At Home surrounded by a servile Crowd,
Prompt to abuse, and in Detraction loud:
Abroad begirt with Men, and Swords, and Spears;
His very State acknowledging his Fears:
Marching amidst a thousand Guards, He shows   285
His secret Terror of a thousand Foes;
In War however Prudent, Great, or Brave,
To blind Events, and fickle Chance a Slave:
Seeking to settle what for ever flies;
Sure of the Toil, uncertain of the Prize.   290

But He returns with Conquest on his Brow;
Brings up the Triumph, and absolves the Vow:
The Captive Generals to his Carr are ty'd:
The Joyful Citizens tumultuous Tyde
Echoing his Glory, gratify his Pride.   295
What is this Triumph? Madness, Shouts, and Noise,
One great Collection of the People's Voice.
The Wretches he brings back, in Chains relate,
What may To-morrow be the Victor's Fate.
The Spoils and Trophies born before Him, show   300
National Loss, and Epidemic Woe,
Various Distress, which He and His may know.
Does He not mourn the valiant Thousands slain;
The Heroes, once the Glory of the Plain,
Left in the Conflict of the Fatal Day,   305
Or the Wolve's Portion, or the Vulture's Prey?
Does He not weep the Lawrel, which he wears,
Wet with the Soldier's Blood, and Widow's Tears?

See, where He comes, the Darling of the War!
See Millions crowding round the gilded Car!   310
In the vast Joys of this Ecstatic Hour,
And full Fruition of successful Pow'r,
One Moment and one Thought might let Him scan
The various Turns of Life, and fickle State of Man.

Are the dire Images of sad Distrust,   315
And Popular Change, obscur'd a-mid the Dust,

That rises from the Victor's rapid Wheel?
Can the loud Clarion, or shrill Fife repel
The inward Cries of Care? can Nature's Voice
Plaintive be drown'd, or lessen'd in the Noise; 320
Tho' Shouts as Thunder loud afflict the Air;
Stun the Birds now releas'd, and shake the Iv'ry Chair?

   Yon' Crowd (He might reflect) yon' joyful Crowd,
Pleas'd with my Honors, in my Praises loud,
(Should fleeting Vict'ry to the Vanquish'd go; 325
Should She depress my Arms, and raise the Foe;)
Would for That Foe with equal Ardor wait
At the high Palace, or the crowded Gate;
With restless Rage would pull my Statues down;
And cast the Brass a-new to His Renown. 330

   O impotent Desire of Worldly Sway!
That I, who make the Triumph of To-day,
May of To-morrow's Pomp one Part appear,
Ghastly with Wounds, and lifeless on the Bier!
Then (Vileness of Mankind!) then of all These, 335
Whom my dilated Eye with Labor sees,
Would one, alas! repeat Me Good, or Great?
Wash my pale Body, or bewail my Fate?
Or, march'd I chain'd behind the Hostile Carr,
The Victor's Pastime, and the Sport of War; 340
Would One, would One his pitying Sorrow lend,
Or be so poor, to own He was my Friend?

   Avails it then, O Reason, to be Wise?
To see this cruel Scene with quicker Eyes?
To know with more Distinction to complain, 345
And have superior Sense in feeling Pain?

   Let us revolve that Roll with strictest Eye,
Where safe from Time distinguish'd Actions lye;
And judge if Greatness be exempt from Pain,
Or Pleasure ever may with Pow'r remain. 350

   ADAM, great *Type*, for whom the World was made,
The fairest Blessing to his Arms convey'd,

A charming Wife; and Air, and Sea, and Land,
And all that move therein, to his Command
Render'd obedient: say, my Pensive Muse, 355
What did these golden Promises produce?
Scarce tasting Life, He was of Joy bereav'd:
One Day, I think, in PARADISE He liv'd;
Destin'd the next His Journey to pursue,
Where wounding Thorns, and cursed Thistles grew. 360
E'er yet He earns his Bread, a-down his Brow,
Inclin'd to Earth, his lab'ring Sweat must flow:
His Limbs must ake, with daily Toils oppress'd;
E'er long-wish'd Night brings necessary Rest:
Still viewing with Regret his Darling EVE, 365
He for Her Follies, and His own must grieve.
Bewailing still a-fresh their hapless Choice;
His Ear oft frighted with the imag'd Voice
Of Heav'n, when first it thunder'd; oft his View
A-ghast, as when the Infant Light'ning flew; 370
And the stern CHERUB stop'd the fatal Road,
Arm'd with the Flames of an Avenging GOD.
His Younger Son on the polluted Ground,
First Fruit of Death, lies Plaintif of a Wound
Giv'n by a Brother's Hand: His Eldest Birth 375
Flies, mark'd by Heav'n, a Fugitive o'er Earth.
Yet why these Sorrows heap'd upon the Sire,
Becomes nor Man, nor Angel to enquire.

Each Age sinn'd on; and Guilt advanc'd with Time:
The Son still added to the Father's Crime; 380
'Till GOD arose, and great in Anger said:
Lo! it repenteth Me, that Man was made.
Withdraw thy Light, Thou Sun! be dark, Ye Skies!
And from your deep Abyss, Ye Waters, rise!

The frighted Angels heard th'Almighty Lord; 385
And o'er the Earth from wrathful Viols pour'd
Tempests and Storm, obedient to His Word.
Mean time, His Providence to NOAH gave
The Guard of All, that He design'd to save.
Exempt from general Doom the Patriarch stood; 390
Contemn'd the Waves, and triumph'd o'er the Flood.

The Winds fall silent; and the Waves decrease:
The Dove brings Quiet, and the Olive Peace:
Yet still His Heart does inward Sorrow feel,
Which Faith alone forbids Him to reveal.　　　　　　395
If on the backward World his Views are cast;
'Tis Death diffus'd, and universal Waste.
Present (sad Prospect!) can He Ought descry,
But (what affects his melancholy Eye)
The Beauties of the Antient Fabric lost,　　　　　　400
In Chains of craggy Hill, or Lengths of dreary Coast?
While to high Heav'n his pious Breathings turn'd,
Weeping He hop'd, and Sacrificing mourn'd;
When of GOD's Image only Eight He found
Snatch'd from the Wat'ry Grave, and sav'd from Nations drown'd;　405
And of three Sons, the future Hopes of Earth,
The Seed, whence Empires must receive their Birth,
One He foresees excluded Heav'nly Grace,
And mark'd with Curses, fatal to his Race.

ABRAHAM, Potent Prince, the Friend of GOD,　　　　410
Of Human Ills must bear the destin'd Load;
By Blood and Battles must his Pow'r maintain,
And slay the Monarchs, e'er He rules the Plain;
Must deal just Portions of a servile Life
To a proud Handmaid, and a peevish Wife;　　　　415
Must with the Mother leave the weeping Son,
In Want to wander, and in Wilds to groan;
Must take his other Child, his Age's Hope
To trembling MORIAM's melancholy Top,
Order'd to drench his Knife in filial Blood;　　　　420
Destroy his Heir, or disobey his GOD.

MOSES beheld that GOD; but how beheld?
The Deity in radiant Beams conceal'd,
And clouded in a deep Abyss of Light;
While present, too severe for Human Sight,　　　　425
Nor staying longer than one swift-wing'd Night.
The following Days, and Months, and Years decreed
To fierce Encounter, and to toilsome Deed.
His Youth with Wants and Hardships must engage:
Plots and Rebellions must disturb his Age.　　　　430

Some CORAH still arose, some Rebel Slave,
Prompter to sink the State, than He to save:
And ISRAEL did his Rage so far provoke,
That what the God-head wrote, the Prophet broke.
His Voice scarce heard, his Dictates scarce believ'd,   435
In Camps, in Arms, in Pilgrimage, He liv'd;
And dy'd obedient to severest Law,
Forbid to tread the promis'd Land, He saw.

My Father's Life was one long Line of Care,
A Scene of Danger, and a State of War.   440
Alarm'd, expos'd, his Childhood must engage
The Bear's rough Gripe, and foaming Lion's Rage.
By various Turns his threaten'd Youth must fear
GOLIAH's lifted Sword, and SAUL's emitted Spear.
Forlorn He must, and persecuted fly;   445
Climb the steep Mountain, in the Cavern lye;
And often ask, and be refus'd to dye.

For ever, from His manly Toils, are known
The Weight of Pow'r, and Anguish of a Crown.
What Tongue can speak the restless Monarch's Woes;   450
When GOD, and NATHAN were declar'd his Foes?
When ev'ry Object his Offence revil'd,
The Husband murder'd, and the Wife defil'd,
The Parent's Sins impress'd upon the dying Child?
What Heart can think the Grief which He sustain'd;   455
When the King's Crime brought Vengeance on the Land;
And the inexorable Prophet's Voice
Gave Famine, Plague, or War; and bid Him fix his Choice?

He dy'd; and Oh! may no Reflection shed
It's poys'nous Venom on the Royal Dead: 460
Yet the unwilling Truth must be express'd;
Which long has labor'd in this pensive Breast:
Dying He added to my Weight of Care:
He made Me to his Crimes undoubted Heir:
Left his unfinish'd Murder to his Son,   465
And JOAB's Blood intail'd on JUDAH's Crown.

Young as I was, I hasted to fulfill
The cruel Dictates of My Parent's Will.

Of his fair Deeds a distant View I took;
But turn'd the Tube upon his Faults to look;   470
Forgot his Youth, spent in his Country's Cause,
His Care of Right, his Rev'rence to the Laws:
But could with Joy his Years of Folly trace,
Broken and old in BATHSHEBA's Embrace;
Could follow Him, where e'er He stray'd from Good,   } 475
And cite his sad Example; whilst I trod
Paths open to Deceit, and track'd with Blood.
Soon docile to the secret Acts of Ill,
With Smiles I could betray, with Temper kill:
Soon in a Brother could a Rival view;   480
Watch all his Acts, and all his Ways pursue.
In vain for Life He to the Altar fled:
Ambition and Revenge have certain Speed.
Ev'n there, My Soul, ev'n there He should have fell;
But that my Interest did my Rage conceal.   485
Doubling my Crime, I promise, and deceive;
Purpose to slay, whilst swearing to forgive.
Treaties, Perswasions, Sighs, and Tears are vain:
With a mean Lie curs'd Vengeance I sustain;
Joyn Fraud to Force, and Policy to Pow'r;   490
'Till of the destin'd Fugitive secure,
In solemn State to Parricide I rise;
And, as GOD lives, this Day my Brother dies.

  Be Witness to my Tears, Celestial Muse!
In vain I would forget, in vain excuse   495
Fraternal Blood by my Direction spilt;
In vain on JOAB's Head transfer the Guilt:
The Deed was acted by the Subject's Hand;
The Sword was pointed by the King's Command.
Mine was the Murder: it was Mine alone;   500
Years of Contrition must the Crime attone:
Nor can my guilty Soul expect Relief,
But from a long Sincerity of Grief.

With an imperfect Hand, and trembling Heart,
Her Love of Truth superior to her Art,   505
Already the reflecting Muse has trac'd
The mournful Figures of my Action past.

The pensive Goddess has already taught,
How vain is Hope, and how vexatious Thought;
From growing Childhood to declining Age,   510
How tedious ev'ry Step, how gloomy ev'ry Stage.
This Course of Vanity almost compleat,
Tir'd in the Field of Life, I hope Retreat
In the still Shades of Death: for Dread and Pain,
And Grief will find their Shafts elanc'd in vain,   515
And their Points broke, retorted from the Head,
Safe in the Grave, and free among the Dead.

    Yet tell Me, frighted Reason! what is Death?
Blood only stopp'd, and interrupted Breath?
The utmost Limit of a narrow Span,   520
And End of Motion which with Life began?
As Smoke that rises from the kindling Fires
Is seen this Moment, and the next expires:
As empty Clouds by rising Winds are tost,
Their fleeting Forms scarce sooner found than lost: 525
So vanishes our State: so pass our Days:
So Life but opens now, and now decays:
The Cradle and the Tomb, alas! so nigh;
To live is scarce distinguish'd from to dye.

    Cure of the Miser's Wish, and Coward's Fear,   530
Death only shews Us, what We knew was near.
With Courage therefore view the pointed Hour;
Dread not Death's Anger; but expect his Pow'r;
Nor Nature's Law with fruitless Sorrow mourn;
But dye, O Mortal Man! for Thou wast born.   535

    Cautious thro' Doubt; by Want of Courage, Wise,
To such Advice, the Reas'ner still replies.

    Yet measuring all the long continu'd Space,
Ev'ry successive Day's repeated Race,
Since Time first started from his pristin Goal,   540
'Till He had reach'd that Hour, wherein my Soul
Joyn'd to my Body swell'd the Womb; I was,
(At least I think so) Nothing: must I pass

513 Tir'd in…I hope] I fly…and seek *W*   517 among] amongst *W*

Again to Nothing, when this vital Breath
Ceasing, consigns Me o'er to Rest, and Death?   545
Must the whole Man, amazing Thought! return
To the cold Marble, or contracted Urn?
And never shall those Particles agree,
That were in Life this Individual He?
But sever'd, must They join the general Mass,   550
Thro' other Forms, and Shapes ordain'd to pass;
Nor Thought nor Image kept of what He was?
Does the great Word that gave him Sense, ordain,
That Life shall never wake that Sense again?
And will no Pow'r his sinking Spirits save   555
From the dark Caves of Death, and Chambers of the Grave?

Each Evening I behold the setting Sun
With down-ward Speed into the Ocean run:
Yet the same Light (pass but some fleeting Hours)
Exerts his Vigor, and renews his Pow'rs;   560
Starts the bright Race again: His constant Flame
Rises and sets, returning still the Same.
I mark the various Fury of the Winds:
These neither Seasons guide, nor Order binds:
They now dilate, and now contract their Force: 565
Various their Speed, but endless is their Course.
From his first Fountain and beginning Ouze,
Down to the Sea each Brook, and Torrent flows:
Tho' sundry Drops or leave, or swell the Stream;
The Whole still runs, with equal Pace, the Same.   570
Still other Waves supply the rising Urns;
And the eternal Floud no Want of Water mourns.

Why then must Man obey the sad Decree,
Which subjects neither Sun, nor Wind, nor Sea?

A Flow'r, that does with opening Morn arise,   575
And flourishing the Day, at Evening dyes;
A Winged Eastern Blast, just skimming o'er
The Ocean's Brow, and sinking on the Shore;
A Fire, whose Flames thro' crackling Stubble fly;
A Meteor shooting from the Summer Sky;   580

A Bowl a-down the bending Mountain roll'd;
A Bubble breaking, and a Fable told;
A Noon-tide Shadow, and a Mid-night Dream;
Are Emblems, which with Semblance apt proclaim
Our Earthly Course: But, O my Soul! so fast   585
Must Life run off; and Death for ever last?

  This dark Opinion, sure, is too confin'd:
Else whence this Hope, and Terror of the Mind?
Does Something still, and Somewhere yet remain,
Reward or Punishment, Delight or Pain?   590
Say: shall our Relicks second Birth receive?
Sleep We to wake, and only dye to live?
When the sad Wife has clos'd her Husband's Eyes,
And pierc'd the Echoing Vault with doleful Cries;
Lyes the pale Corps not yet entirely Dead?   595
The Spirit only from the Body fled,
The grosser Part of Heat and Motion void,
To be by Fire, or Worm, or Time destroy'd;
The Soul, immortal Substance, to remain,
Conscious of Joy, and capable of Pain?   600
And if Her Acts have been directed well,
While with her friendly Clay She deign'd to dwell;
Shall She with Safety reach her pristine Seat?
Find her Rest endless, and her Bliss compleat?
And while the buried Man We idly mourn;   605
Do Angels joy to see His better Half return?
But if She has deform'd this Earthly Life
With murd'rous Rapine, and seditious Strife;
Amaz'd, repuls'd, and by those Angels driv'n
From the Ætherial Seat, and blissful Heav'n,   610
In everlasting Darkness must She lye,
Still more unhappy, that She cannot dye?

  Amid Two Seas on One small Point of Land
Weary'd, uncertain, and amaz'd We stand:
On either Side our Thoughts incessant turn: 615
Forward We dread; and looking back We mourn.
Losing the Present in this dubious Hast;
And lost Our selves betwixt the Future, and the Past.

These cruel Doubts contending in my Breast,
My Reason stagg'ring, and my Hopes oppress'd,   620
Once more I said: once more I will enquire,
What is this little, agile, pervious Fire,
This flutt'ring Motion, which We call the Mind?
How does She act? and where is She confin'd?
Have We the Pow'r to guide Her, as We please?   625
Whence then those Evils, that obstruct our Ease?
We Happiness pursue; We fly from Pain;
Yet the Pursuit, and yet the Flight is vain:
And, while poor Nature labors to be blest,
By Day with Pleasure, and by Night with Rest;   630
Some stronger Pow'r eludes our sickly Will;
Dashes our rising Hope with certain Ill;
And makes Us with reflective Trouble see,
That all is destin'd, which We fancy free.

That Pow'r superior then, which rules our Mind,   635
Is His high Will by Human Pray'r inclin'd?
Will He for Sacrifice our Sorrows ease?
And can our Tears reverse His firm Decrees?
Then let Religion aid, where Reason fails:
Throw Loads of Incense in, to turn the Scales;   640
And let the silent Sanctuary show,
What from the babling Scholes We may not know,
How Man may shun, or bear his destin'd Part of Woe.

What shall amend, or what absolve our Fate?
Anxious We hover in a mediate State,   645
Betwixt Infinity and Nothing; Bounds,
Or boundless Terms, whose doubtful Sense confounds
Unequal Thought; whilst All We apprehend,
Is, that our Hopes must rise, our Sorrows end;
As our Creator deigns to be our Friend.   650

I said;—and instant bad the Priests prepare
The ritual Sacrifice, and solemn Pray'r.
Select from vulgar Herds, with Garlands gay,
A hundred Bulls ascend the Sacred Way.
The artful Youth proceed to form the Choir;   655
They breath the Flute, or strike the vocal Wire.

636 inclin'd? *edd.*: inclin'd. *1718*

The Maids in comely Order next advance;
They beat the Tymbrel, and instruct the Dance.
Follows the chosen Tribe from LEVI sprung,
Chanting by just Return the Holy Song.   660
Along the Choir in Solemn State they past.
—The Anxious King came last.
The Sacred Hymn perform'd, my promis'd Vow
I paid; and bowing at the Altar low,

    Father of Heav'n! I said, and Judge of Earth!   665
Whose Word call'd out this Universe to Birth;
By whose kind Pow'r and influencing Care
The various Creatures move, and live, and are;
But, ceasing once that Care; withdrawn that Pow'r;
They move (alas!) and live, and are no more: 670
Omni-scient Master, Omni-present King,
To Thee, to Thee, my last Distress I bring.

    Thou, that can'st Still the Raging of the Seas,
Chain up the Winds, and bid the Tempests cease;
Redeem my ship-wreck'd Soul from raging Gusts   675
Of cruel Passion, and deceitful Lusts:
From Storms of Rage, and dang'rous Rocks of Pride,
Let Thy strong Hand this little Vessel guide
(It was Thy Hand that made it) thro' the Tide
Impetuous of this Life: let Thy Command   680
Direct my Course, and bring me safe to Land.

    If, while this weary'd Flesh draws fleeting Breath,
Not satisfy'd with Life, afraid of Death,
It hap'ly be Thy Will, that I should know
Glimpse of Delight, or Pause from anxious Woe;   685
From *Now*, from instant *Now*, great Sire, dispell
The Clouds that press my Soul; from *Now* reveal
A gracious Beam of Light; from *Now* inspire
My Tongue to sing, my Hand to touch the Lyre:
My open'd Thought to joyous Prospects raise;   690
And, for Thy Mercy, let me sing Thy Praise.
Or, if Thy Will ordains, I still shall wait
Some New *Here-after*, and a future State;

Permit me Strength, my Weight of Woe to bear;
And raise my Mind superior to my Care. 695
Let Me, howe'er unable to explain
The secret Lab'rynths of Thy Ways to Man,
With humble Zeal confess Thy awful Pow'r;
Still weeping Hope, and wond'ring still Adore.
So in my Conquest be Thy Might declar'd: 700
And, for Thy Justice, be Thy Name rever'd.

My Pray'r scarce ended, a stupendous Gloom
Darkens the Air; loud Thunder shakes the Dome:
To the beginning Miracle succeed
An awful Silence, and religious Dread. 705
Sudden breaks forth a more than common Day:
The sacred Wood, which on the Altar lay,
Untouch'd, unlighted glows—
Ambrosial Odor, such as never flows
From ARAB's Gum, or the SABÆAN Rose, 710
Does round the Air evolving Scents diffuse:
The holy Ground is wet with Heav'nly Dews:
Celestial Music (such JESSIDES' Lyre,
Such MIRIAM's Timbrel would in vain require)
Strikes to my Thought thro' my admiring Ear, 715
With Ecstasy too fine, and Pleasure hard to bear.
And lo! what sees my ravish'd Eye? what feels
My wond'ring Soul? an opening Cloud reveals
An Heav'nly Form embody'd and array'd
With Robes of Light. I heard: the Angel said: 720

Cease, Man of Woman born, to hope Relief
From daily Trouble, and continu'd Grief.
Thy Hope of Joy deliver to the Wind:
Suppress thy Passions; and prepare thy Mind.
Free and familiar with Misfortune grow: 725
Be us'd to Sorrow, and inur'd to Woe.
By weak'ning Toil, and hoary Age o'ercome,
See thy Decrease; and hasten to thy Tomb.
Leave to thy Children Tumult, Strife, and War,
Portions of Toil, and Legacies of Care. 730
Send the Successive Ills thro' Ages down;
And let each weeping Father tell his Son,

That deeper struck, and more distinctly griev'd,
He must augment the Sorrows He receiv'd.

    The Child to whose Success thy Hope is bound,   735
E'er thou art scarce Interr'd, or he is Crown'd;
To Lust of Arbitrary Sway inclin'd,
(That cursed Poyson to the Prince's Mind!)
Shall from thy Dictates and his Duty rove,
And lose his great Defence, his People's Love.   740
Ill Counsell'd, Vanquish'd, Fugitive, Disgrac'd,
Shall mourn the Fame of JACOB's Strength effac'd.
Shall sigh, the King diminish'd, and the Crown
With lessen'd Rays descending to his Son.
Shall see the Wreaths, His Grandsire knew to reap   745
By active Toil, and Military Sweat,
Pining incline their sickly Leaves, and shed
Their falling Honors from His giddy Head.
By Arms, or Pray'r unable to asswage
Domestic Horror, and intestine Rage,   750
Shall from the Victor, and the Vanquish'd fear,
From ISRAEL's Arrow, and from JUDAH's Spear:
Shall cast his weary'd Limbs on JORDAN's Floud,
By Brother's Arms disturb'd, and stain'd with Kindred-Blood.

    Hence lab'ring Years shall weep their destin'd Race   755
Charg'd with ill Omens; sully'd with Disgrace.
Time by Necessity compell'd, shall go
Thro' Scenes of War, and Epocha's of Woe.
The Empire lessen'd in a parted Stream,
Shall lose it's Course—   760
Indulge thy Tears: the Heathen shall blaspheme:
JUDAH shall fall, oppress'd by Grief and Shame;
And Men shall from her Ruins know her Fame.

    New ÆGYPTS yet, and second Bonds remain,
A harsher PHARAOH, and a heavyer Chain.   765
Again obedient to a dire Command,
Thy Captive Sons shall leave the promis'd Land.
Their Name more low, their Servitude more vile,
Shall, on EUPHRATES' Bank, renew the Grief of NILE.

These pointed Spires that wound the ambient Sky   770
Inglorious Change! shall in Destruction lye
Low, levell'd with the Dust; their Heights unknown,
Or measur'd by their Ruin. Yonder Throne,
For lasting Glory built, design'd the Seat
Of Kings for ever blest, for ever great,   775
Remov'd by the Invader's barb'rous Hand,
Shall grace his Triumph in a foreign Land.
The Tyrant shall demand yon' sacred Load
Of Gold and Vessels set a-part to GOD,
Then by vile Hands to common Use debas'd;   780
Shall send them flowing round his drunken Feast,
With sacrilegious Taunt, and impious Jest.

Twice fourteen Ages shall their Way complete:
Empires by various Turns shall rise and set;
While Thy abandon'd Tribes shall only know   785
A diff'rent Master, and a Change of Woe:
With down-cast Eye-lids, and with Looks a-ghast,
Shall dread the Future, or bewail the Past.

Afflicted ISRAEL shall sit weeping down,
Fast by the Streams, where BABEL's Waters run;   790
Their Harps upon the neighb'ring Willows hung,
Nor joyous Hymn encouraging their Tongue,
Nor chearful Dance their Feet; with Toil oppress'd,
Their weary'd Limbs aspiring but to Rest.
In the reflective Stream the sighing Bride,   795
Viewing her Charms impair'd, abash'd shall hide
Her pensive Head; and in her languid Face
The Bridegroom shall fore-see his sickly Race:
While pond'rous Fetters vex their close Embrace.
With irksome Anguish then your Priests shall mourn   800
Their long-neglected Feasts despair'd Return,
And sad Oblivion of their solemn Days.
Thenceforth their Voices They shall only raise,
Louder to weep. By Day your frighted Seers
Shall call for Fountains to express their Tears;   805
And wish their Eyes were Flouds: by Night from Dreams
Of opening Gulphs, black Storms, and raging Flames,

787 With down-cast...and] While with cast...or *W*   788 Shall] We *W*

Starting amaz'd, shall to the People show
Emblems of Heav'nly Wrath, and Mystic Types of Woe.

The Captives, as their Tyrant shall require,   810
That They should breath the Song, and touch the Lyre,
Shall say: can JACOB's servile Race rejoice,
Untun'd the Music, and disus'd the Voice?
What can We play? (They shall discourse) how sing
In foreign Lands, and to a Barb'rous King?   815
We and our Fathers from our Childhood bred
To watch the cruel Victor's Eye, to dread
The arbitrary Lash, to bend, to grieve;
(Out-cast of Mortal Race!) can We conceive
Image of ought delightful, soft, or gay?   820
Alas! when We have toyl'd the longsome Day;
The fullest Bliss our Hearts aspire to know,
Is but some Interval from active Woe;
In broken Rest, and startling Sleep to mourn;
'Till Morn, the Tyrant, and the Scourge return.   825
Bred up in Grief, can Pleasure be our Theme?
Our endless Anguish does not Nature claim?
Reason, and Sorrow are to Us the Same.
Alas! with wild Amazement We require,
If Idle Folly was not Pleasure's Sire: 830
Madness, We fancy, gave an Ill-tim'd Birth
To grinning Laughter, and to frantic Mirth.

This is the Series of perpetual Woe,
Which Thou, alas! and Thine are born to know.
Illustrious Wretch, repine not, nor reply: 835
View not, what Heav'n ordains, with Reason's Eye;
Too bright the Object is: the Distance is too high.
The Man who would resolve the Work of Fate,
May limit Number, and make Crooked Strait:
Stop Thy Enquiry then; and curb Thy Sense;   840
Nor let Dust argue with Omnipotence.
'Tis GOD who must dispose, and Man sustain,
Born to endure, forbidden to complain.
Thy Sum of Life must His Decrees fulfill:
What derogates from His Command, is Ill;   845
And that alone is Good, which centers in His Will.

Yet that thy Lab'ring Senses may not droop,
Lost to Delight, and destitute of Hope;
Remark what I, GOD's Messenger, aver
From Him, who neither can deceive, nor err.   850
The Land at length redeem'd, shall cease to mourn;
Shall from her sad Captivity return.
SION shall raise her long-dejected Head;
And in her Courts the Law again be read.
Again the glorious Temple shall arise,   855
And with new Lustre pierce the neighb'ring Skies.
The promis'd Seat of Empire shall again
Cover the Mountain, and command the Plain,
And from Thy Race distinguish'd, ONE shall spring,
Greater in Act than Victor, more than King   860
In Dignity and Pow'r, sent down from Heav'n,
To succour Earth. To HIM, to HIM 'tis giv'n,
Passion, and Care, and Anguish to destroy.
Thro' HIM soft Peace, and Plenitude of Joy
Perpetual o'er the World redeem'd shall flow.   865
No more may Man inquire, nor Angel know.

Now, SOLOMON, rememb'ring Who thou art,
Act thro' thy remnant Life the decent Part.
Go forth: Be strong: With Patience, and with Care
Perform, and Suffer: To Thy self severe,   870
Gracious to Others, Thy Desires suppress'd,
Diffus'd Thy Virtues, First of Men, be Best.
Thy Sum of Duty let Two Words contain;
O may they graven in thy Heart remain!
Be Humble, and be Just. The Angel said: 875
With upward Speed His agile Wings He spread;
Whilst on the holy Ground I prostrate lay,
By various Doubts impell'd, or to obey,
Or to object: at length (my mournful Look
Heav'n-ward erect) determin'd, thus I spoke: 880

Supreme, Allwise, Eternal Potentate!
Sole Author, Sole Disposer of our Fate!
Enthron'd in Light, and Immortality,
Whom no Man fully sees, and none can see!

Original of Beings! Pow'r Divine!   885
Since that I Live, and that I Think, is Thine;
Benign Creator, let Thy plastic Hand
Dispose it's own Effect. Let Thy Command
Restore, Great Father, Thy Instructed Son;
And in My Act may THY great WILL BE DONE.   890

1709

To Isaac Bickerstaff commonly called the Tatler.

SIR

I cannot say positively that I am in love with Your Cousin *Jinny Distaff*, but I think I like her well enough to make her my Wife, and that is all which You as her Kinsman ought to require; For provided a Family can but get rid of a Female upon Honorable Terms, they seldom care three Straws what becomes of her after. This premised, I fancy 5 there will be no great difficulty in making our Alliance; For allowing all to be true that your Kinsman, at the Heralds Office says concerning the Antiquity of the *Bickerstaffs* I do not find much mention of their Lands & Tenements, So I presume *Jinny* has no great portion, Nor would I enter very nicely into that matter, for fear, she should be too 10 curious on the other side in Enquiries about Settlement and Jointure, Thô her Family may be very good, I can assure You, I do not much covet her upon that account, for however you may branch your Genealogy there remains stil in it that hard Original Monosyllable *Staff*, which you know is a thing that one would not have belong 15 properly to ones Wife, if one could with any Decency avoid it. But, Dear Sir, Her having been bred up by You, and her being useful to You in composing those Excellent Pieces the Tatlers are the real motives of my Inclinations to her; for I would have a Wife exempt from the crying Sin of the Ladys of this Age, You will easily guess I mean Taciturnity; 20 I beg leave therefore, Sir, to address to Mrs: *Jinny Distaff* in the following Verses, in which I tell her she is very cruel to me, thô I never spoke to her in my Life; and in a Poetical but I think a fine Manner, I desire her to hold out a little, for in truth if she yielded too soon My second Stanza would have come off very wretchedly, and my first would have 25 been downright Nonsense. I have chosen my own Birth Day for the

Title] Letter to Isaac...Tatler. *'Index'* to M

Subject, which you see I place about the middle of May, thô among Friends, I was born in December; but between this and then you know many odd things may happen, *Jinny* may be otherwise disposed of (or which is worse) my verses may not be printed. *Multa cadunt inter* 30 *Calicem*——.

Furthermore, *Mr Bickerstaff*, as to my Birth Day, I must beg your indulgence and favor; for since you have proved beyond all Question that *Partridge* is dead, whatever he may idly fancy to the Contrary, I am a little apprehensive that You may have Logic enough to Demon- 35 strate that I never was born, thô I positively assert the Fact, and should produce the Register of the Parish.

And now Cousen *Isaac*, as I may call you upon a supposition that the Match goes on, as to the Name which you Know is a great deal in a Song, *Jinny* is too light, therefore I had pitched upon *Cloe*, which You, 40 who are a great Critic, may find to be of an equal length, or potestas, Vizt: Two Syllables, *Joanna* on the contrary I found too Solemn, so I thought of *Clarissa*, which just Occupies the same Space, these being the fashionable Names of Two very fine Persons, whose charms as you very accurately observe, a good Friend and Fellow Virtuoso of ours had 45 rendered Immortal by putting Straw hatts upon their Heads, to the End they may appear rather pritty than beautiful, to the great admira- tion of all those who prefer the Gusto of *Honthurst* and *Houseman* to that of *Titian* or *Coreggio*. Now it is evident I could have taken *Clarissa* or *Cloe*, for my Verses are some longer & others shorter by a Syllable, as I 50 please to allow myself a *Licentia Poetica*. I hope some modern Critics will bite (as we elegantly express it) at this disproportion, since that would give me an opportunity which I have long wished for, of shewing my great Learning, and producing unquestionable Authority for the Liberty I take, as well from the Ancients, who would not scan their own 55 Verses, as from some Moderns who cannot.

Rejecting therefore both these Names, as likewise *Dictinna*, *Pastorella* and a hundred more, at last it came into my head, that the ancient *Clotho* was exactly *Jinny Distaff* of the Moderns, i e, A Young Woman very inexorable, with the Flax and Reel in her hand; what sprung from 60 this thought immediately but *Clotilda*? good, said I, I like that Name, it is much in Voge, and modestly speaking, I am something better qualified for Clotilda's acquaintance in the World than either of those

34 is dead *edd.*: is is dead *M*   37 Parish. *edd.*: Parish *M*   39 on, *edd.*: on *M*
42 on...found] I found on the contrary *Deleted reading in M*   49 Now *edd.*: now *M*
52 disproportion *edd.*: dispropotion *M*   57 Dictinna, *edd.*: Dictinna *M*

Gentlemen are that warble love to her upon the Stage, but now, Dear
Cousen, I'll tell you what confirmed me in the Choice of this Name, for 65
I know you would have found it out by the Stars thô I had endeavoured
never so strenuosly to have conceal'd it from you, —Clotilda therefore
is really *Distaff* according to *Menage, Furetiere* and the best Etymo-
logists. *Clotilda* says the Latin from the Greek Clotho (as I observed
before) then comes the Goth who pronouncing D instead of Cl calls 70
it *Dotilda*, The Germans make it *Dotildaff Ditildaff Distildaff*, the Saxon
Dialect has it more particularly *Distidaff* or *Distitaff* whence the English
by contraction *Distaff*.

I am very happy you must know, in these sorts of Derivations and
Conjectures, and as you have a particular regard to the Antiquity of 75
the Blood of the *Bickerstaffs*, so if I have apply'd my knowledge to the
Honor of some of my own Relations—*Exempli gratiâ*, My Uncle Ned,
who is a Person of a haughty and morose Temper I have brought from
Nebuchadnezzar & little Couz Molly, who grows a little fattish, I derive
from *Amalthea*, Our Sir Name you see I prudently reserve for the bottom 80
of my Letter: I have some very curious Desertations by me concerning
its Original, that Jinny may see she neither is to marry an Ignorant
Person nor an Upstart.

I beleive, Cousen *Isaac*, I shal be able to give the world a great deal
more of this kind of Learning when I publish my Notes upon *Horace*, 85
and some other Classic Writers, who have lain very little understood
these Seventeen hundred Years for want of some Genius eminent in
this kind of Learning. And now, Sir, I humbly beg your Pardon for
having kept you too Long from my Excellent Verses, which if you like
half so well as I do I shal be infinitely happy; do me the Justice to beleive 90
that I love you very heartily, and If you'l honer me with a Letter, you
need not fear a Bite. I lodge at Mr Mark Hagglehair a Barbers, at the
Sign of the Hand and Razor in smal Scizars Alley, near Shear Lane. In
the mean time pray, Sir, take no Notice of me if you should see me att
the St *Jame's* Coffee House, at *Wills* or at the *Smyrna*, for I would not 95
have it known that I am acquainted with You till my Affair with *Jinny*
is consummated, I am

Dear Cousen,
Your Most Affectionate Friend
and humble Servant, 100
Walter Wou'd have Wit.

MY BIRTH DAY

I my Dear, was born to Day:
So all my Jolly Comrades say.
They bring me Music, Wreaths, and Mirth,   105
And ask to celebrate my Birth.
Little alas, my Comrades know
That I was born to Pain and Woe:
To thy Denyal to Thy Scorn:
Better I had n'er been born!   110
I wish to Dye, ev'n whilst I say
I, my Dear, was born to Day.

I, my Dear, was born to Day:
Shal I salute the rising ray?
Welspring of all my Joy or Woe,   115
Clotilda, Thou alone dost know.
Shal the Wreath surround my Hair?
Or shal the Music please my Ear?
Shal I my Comrades Mirth receive,
And bless my Birth, and wish to live?   120
Then let me see great *Venus* chace
Imperious anger from thy Face,
Then let me hear thee smiling say
Thou, my Dear, wer't born to day.

1710

A Fable.

Personam Tragicam forte Vulpes viderat,
O quanta species, inquit, cerebrum non habet!   Phædr.

THE Fox an Actor's *Vizard* found,
    And peer'd and felt, and turn'd it round;
Then threw it, in Contempt, away;
And thus old Phædrus *heard him say:*
What noble Part canst thou sustain,   5
Thou Specious Head, without a Brain?

102] *L 27* ON MY BIRTH-DAY. *1740*   115 or] *L 27* and *1740*
    Title: 1740 : om. 1710

The Examiner. Numb. 6.

From Thursday, August 31. to Thursday, September 7. 1710.

Nec prave factis decorari versibus opto,
Ne rubeam pingui donatus munere. Hor.

THE *Collective* Body of the Whigs have already engross'd our
Riches; and their *Representative* the *Kit cat*, have pretended to make
a Monopoly of our Sense. Thus it happens, that Mr. *P——r*, by being
expell'd the Club, ceases to be a *Poet*; and Sir *Harry F——e* becomes one,
by being admitted into it. 'Tis here that Wit and Beauty are decided 5
by plurality of Voices: The *Child*'s Judgment shall make *H——y* pass
for a Fool; and *Jacob*'s Indulgence shall preserve Lady *H——t* from the
Tallow-Candle.

'Tis the Misfortune of our *Athens*, like that of ancient *Greece*, to be
govern'd by a set number of Tyrants: The Works of Learned Men are 10
weigh'd here by the unerring Balance of Party; and he is sure to be most
Ingenious in his Writings, who is, in their Phrase, most *thorough-pac'd*
in his Politicks. *Trelooby* kept the general Applause for a whole Winter;
while poor *Phædra* cou'd scarce get into the Theatre, 'till she had thrown
her self at the Feet of one of these *Reguli*. 'Twas in this Mint, that a 15
curious Piece of Poetical Workmanship was lately wrought, and, by the
Masters of the Company, allow'd as current and authentick Coin. Notwithstanding which Stamp of Authority, a Critick, unknown to me,
has presum'd to make some Observations upon this Performance; both
which, I hope Dr. *Bent——y* will excuse me for Publishing, since this is 20
such Poetry, as he has never found among the *Greek* or *Latin* Writers.

To the E. of G——n.

WHILST *weeping Europe bends beneath her Ills,*
  And where the Sword destroys not, Famine kills;
Our Isle enjoys by your successful Care, 25
The Pomp of Peace amidst the Woes of War.
So much the Publick to your Prudence owes,
You think no Labours long for our Repose.
Such Conduct, such Integrity are shown,
There are no Coffers empty, but your own. 30
From mean Dependance Merit you retrieve,
Unaskt you offer, and unseen you give.

Your Favour like the Nile *increase bestows,*
And yet conceals the Source from whence it flows,
So poiz'd your Passions are, we find no Frown,   35
If Funds opprest not, and if Commerce run.
Taxes DIMINISHT, Liberty entire,
Those are the Grants your Services require.
Thus far the State-Machine wants no repair,
But moves in Matchless Order by your Care.   40
Free from Confusion, settl'd and serene,
And, like the Universe, by Springs unseen.
But now some Star, sinister to our Prayers,
Contrives new Schemes, and calls you from Affairs.
No Anguish in your Looks, nor Cares appear,   45
But how to teach the unpractis'd Crew to steer.
Thus, like some Victim, no Constraint you need,
To expiate their Offence, by whom you bleed.

Ingratitude's a Weed in every Clime,
It thrives too fast at first, but fades in Time.   50
The God of Day, and your own Lot's the same,
The Vapours you have rais'd, obscure your Flame.
But tho' you suffer, and a while retreat,
Your Globe of Light looks larger as you set.

A Letter to the EXAMINER.   55

'I SEND you these Verses enclos'd, which I have read with great
'Attention; and from the Character of the Patron, as well as of the
'Poet, with no ordinary Inclination to be pleas'd. But so dull am I, that
'there does not appear to my Apprehension, either Poetry, Grammar,
'or Design in the Composition. The whole seems to be, as the *Sixth* 60
'Editor of the *Dispensary* happily expresses it,

A strong unlabour'd Impotence of Thought!

'If we examin it by the New *Test* of good Poetry, which the Dr. himself
'has establish'd, *Pleasing at first Blush*, has this Piece the least Title even
'to that? Or, if we compare it with the only Pattern, as he thinks, of 65
'just Writing in this kind, *Ovid*, is there any thing in *De Tristibus* so
'wild, so childish, or so flat?
    'What can the Ingenious Dr. mean? Or at what time could he write
'these Verses? Half of the Poem is a Panegyrick on a Lord Treasurer in

'being; and the rest a Complement of Condolance to an Earl that has 70
'lost the Staff.

'In thirty Lines his Patron is a *River*, the *Primum Mobile*, a *Pilot*, a
'*Victim*, the *Sun*, any Thing and Nothing. He *bestows Increase, conceals*
'*his Source, makes the Machine move, teaches to Steer, expiates our Offences,*
'*raises Vapours,* and *looks larger as he sets.*   75

'Nor is the Choice of his *Expressions* less exquisite, than that of his
'Similes. For *Commerce* to *run*, *Passions* to be *poiz'd*, *Merit* to be *retriev'd*
'from *Dependance*, and a *Machine* to be *Serene*, is perfectly New: The
'Doctor has a happy Talent at Invention; and has had the Glory of
'inriching our Language by his Phrases, as much as he has improv'd 80
'*Medicine* by his *Bills*.

'But to be more particular—

And where the Sword destroys not (says our Panegyrist.) *Famine kills.*

'I could wish the Verse would have allow'd of the Word *Plague*, or
'*Pestilence*; for I suppose that's what the Author means. I have heard of 85
'the Plague at *Dantzick*; but what part of *Europe* Famine rages in, I
'know not. Why won't *Physick* stand here? 'Tis better Sense, and runs
'as well. What the *Pomp of Peace* is, I as little comprehend, as how it can
'be enjoy'd *amidst the Woes of War.*

Such Conduct, such Integrity are shown,   90
There are no Coffers empty, but your own.

'Since there is so little *Poetry* in this Couplet, I wish there were more
'Truth in it. Some *Coffers*, I have heard were *empty* three Weeks ago; and
'if they are not so still, the Nation is more oblig'd to the Doctor's *Un-*
'*practis'd Crew*, than to the Experienc'd *Pilot.*   95

Unask'd you offer.—

'A great Discovery! I always thought till now, he that was ask'd,
'might be said to *give*; but not properly to *offer*. The Malicious Part of
'the World will, I doubt, be apt to observe, That this Sentence, as it
'stands here, is as true in Fact, as 'tis exact in Language.   100

Your Favour, like the Nile, *Increase bestows.*

'If the Beauty of the Simile is to be judg'd of by the frequent Use
'which the Poets of all Ages have made of it, scarce any can come in
'Competition with the Doctor's *River*. The *Nile* on these Occasions is
'as Trite, as the Stories of *Icarus* and *Phaethon*. I remember I us'd it, when 105

82 But *edd.*: But *1710* (*where it is not indented*)

'I was about Twelve, in a *New-Years-Gift* to my Uncle, and was heartily
'asham'd of it a Year after. A School-Boy can no more miss the *Nile*,
'than a *French* Author, when he Dedicates to the *Grand Monarch*, can
'live without the *Sun*, that other Simile in which the Doctor rejoyces.

> —*Some Star sinister to our Prayers*,   110
> *Contrives new Schemes.*

'Alii legunt *Five Stars*; which makes this Passage Intelligible. I have
'often heard *Astrologers* talk of a sort of Influence, that Stars have upon
'Human Affairs; but I know of no Stars, but those in Mr. *Bickerstaff*'s
'Constellation, that ever contriv'd *Schemes*, and those too were erected 115
'under no very benign *Aspect*.

'My Lord's Care, he tells us, is to teach the *Unpractis'd Crew to Steer*.
'By *Crew*, we are to understand the *Lords of the Treasury*. A very civil
'Expression! But as to the Sense of it: What Affinity is there between
'*Crew* and *Steering*? Is *Steering* the Business of the whole Ship's Crew? 120
'This is a true Image of the *Whig Scheme*, where every Man is his own
'*Pilot*.

'If we read the next two Lines, we shall find these People have
'wounded him, and yet like the best-natur'd *Victim* imaginable, he
'*needs no Constraint to expiate their Offence*. All this is what the *French* call 125
'*Gallimatias*, and what the *English* Cricks term *Nonsense*. But what fol-
'lows? *For whom you Bleed. Bleed!* What, is the Devil in the *Doctor*, to
'mention such a Word, and give so unlucky a Hint. I hop'd that this
'Point had been so well guarded, that there could be no farther need of
'an *Act of Security*.   130

> *The God of Day, and your own Lot's the same;*

'A hundred Pound for a *Genitive* Case, as Old *Busby* us'd to cry out upon
'such an Occasion.

'But to go on, from *Grammar* to *Decency*. Of this Happiness of *Great*
'*Britain*, is any part ascrib'd to the Queen? To this *Machine*, which 135
'moves so like the *Universe*, does the Royal Hand give any Turn? Me-
'thinks he might at least allow Her Majesty, as much as his Friends did
'in the Coronation-Medal.

> *VICEM GERIT ILLA.*

'But as the Poet observes,   140

> *Ingratitude's a Weed of every Clime.*

'He will give me leave, in my own Turn, to observe, That in *Don*
'*Sebastian* it is,

Ingratitude's the GROWTH of every Clime.

'What occasion was there of altering a Verse he thought fit to steal? 145
'This is being a meer *Banditti* in Poetry, to *Rob* and *Murder* too. But who
'is to be charg'd with this Ingratitude? The whole Body of the Nation
'did indeed wish the T——r out; but 'twas Her Majesty only that
'could displace him. Such are the Complements which the Crown
'receives from this *Antimonarchical* Academy. Excellent Poets, dutiful 150
'Subjects!

'I could give you many more Observations upon the Beauties of this
'sublime *Panegyrick*, if I had my *Longinus* by me. It has been *Corrected*,
'I find, *twice* or *thrice* already, and if the Author *Corrects* it *once* more, I
'am so well acquainted with his lucky Performances that way, that I 155
'don't doubt, but I shall be tempted to write to you again upon the
'same Subject. He will not be like himself, if he does not *shift* his *Patron*
'as well as his *Phrases*; and it won't surprize me at all, if in the next
'*Edition* the Poem should come out Inscrib'd to the late T——r of
'*Ireland*.   160

'But I believe by this time the Town is tir'd with the Verses, and you
'with the Criticisms of

Your most Humble Servant,

Philodingle.

My unknown Friend Mr. *Philodingle* has taken my Province from me; 165
however, I am oblig'd to him for his Essay. The best Return which can
be made to an Ingenious Man, is to afford him fresh Matter to employ
his Thoughts, and more Opportunities of shewing his Sagacity. For
this Reason I present my Brother *Examiner* with a *Riddle*, which was
sent me by a Sage, studious of *Egyptian* Knowledge, and much addicted 170
to the *Hieroglyphicks*.

The RIDDLE.

SPHINX was a Monster, that wou'd eat
Whatever Stranger she cou'd get;
Unless his ready Wit disclos'd</i>   175
The subtle Riddle she propos'd.
Oedipus was resolv'd to go,
And try what strength of Parts cou'd do.

172] TWO RIDDLES. 1710. *1740*   178 *cou'd*] would *1740*

Says Sphinx, *On this depends your Fate;*
Tell me what Animal is that,   180
Which has four Feet at Morning bright;
Has two at Noon, and three at Night?
'Tis Man, said he, *who weak by Nature,*
At first creeps like his fellow-Creature,
Upon all four: as Years accrue,   185
With sturdy Steps he walks on two:
In Age, at length, grown weak and sick,
For his third Leg adopts his Stick.
Now in your turn, 'tis just, methinks,
You shou'd resolve me, Madam Sphinx,   190
What stranger Creature yet is he,
Who has four Legs, then two, then three;
Then loses one; then gets two more;
And runs away, at last, on four.

Horace Lib. I. Epist. IX.

Septimius, Claudi, nimirum intelligit unus, Quanti me facias:
&c. Imitated. To the Right Honorable Mr. Harley.

DEAR DICK, how e'er it comes into his Head,
Believes, as firmly as He does his Creed,
That You and I, SIR, are extremely great;
Tho' I plain MAT, You *Minister of State.*
One Word from Me, without all doubt, He says,   5
Wou'd fix his Fortune in some little Place.
Thus better than My self, it seems, He knows,
How far my Interest with my Patron goes;
And answering all Objections I can make,
Still plunges deeper in his dear Mistake.   10

188 *his Stick*] the stick *1740*   191 *stranger Creature*] greater stranger *1740*
    Title: Lib. I. Epist. IX.] Lib. I. Epistle the Ninth. *1711*: Lib. I. Ep. 9 *Lpo 11*: Epistle the
9th: Lib: the 1st: *W*: Epistle the 9th: Lib: Ist: *Lansd*   *Septimius...&c.*] *1711*, *Lpo 11*
om. *W*, *Lansd*   *Imitated.*] addressed *Lansd*: om. *1711*, *Lpo 11*, *W*   *To...Mr. Harley.*]
To...Robert Harley, Esq: *Lpo 11*: To...R—— H——, Esq; *1711*: To Mr: Harley Ch: of
the Exchequer by Mr: Prior 1710. *Lansd*: om. *W*   1 DEAR] *1711*, *Lpo 11* Friend *W*,
Lansd

From this wild Fancy, SIR, there may proceed
One wilder yet, which I foresee, and dread;
That I, in Fact, a real Interest have,
Which to my own Advantage I wou'd save,
And, with the usual Courtier's Trick, intend   15
To serve My self, forgetful of my Friend.

To shun this Censure, I all Shame lay by;
And make my Reason with his Will comply;
Hoping, for my Excuse, 'twill be confest,
That of two Evils I have chose the least.   20
So, SIR, with this Epistolary Scroll,
Receive the Partner of my inmost Soul:
Him you will find in Letters, and in Laws
Not unexpert, firm to his Country's Cause,
Warm in the Glorious Interest You pursue,   25
And, in one Word, a Good Man and a True.

To the Lady Elizabeth Harley, Since Marchioness of Carmarthen, On a Column of Her Drawing.

WHEN future Ages shall with Wonder view
These glorious Lines, which HARLEY's Daughter drew;
They shall confess, that BRITAIN could not raise
A fairer Column to the Father's Praise.

---

13 have] *1711, W, Lansd* heave *Lpo 11*   18 And make] *1711, Lpo 11* Against *W, Lansd*
19 Hoping] *1711, Lpo 11* And hope *W, Lansd*
Title] Written under a Piller Drawn by the Lady ELIZABETH HARLEY. Since Marchiness of
Carmarthen. *Lpo 11*: Written under a Column drawn by a Pen: by the Honble Mrs Eliz:
Harley since Marchioness of Carmarthen *W*: On a Pillar drawn by Mrs: Elizabeth Harley
1710 *Lansd*: om. *L 29*   3 BRITAIN] *L 29, Lansd* BRITON *Lpo 11*   4 the] *L 29, Lansd*
Her *Lpo 11*

Gualterus Danistonus *Ad Amicos.*
Imitated.

STUDIOUS the busie Moments to deceive,
  That fleet between the Cradle and the Grave,
I credit what the GREECIAN Dictates say,
And SAMIAN Sounds o'er SCOTIA's Hills convey.
When mortal Man resigns his transient Breath;   5
The Body only I give o'er to Death.
The Parts dissolv'd, and broken Frame I mourn:
What came from Earth, I see to Earth return.
The Immaterial Part, th'Æthereal Soul,
Nor can Change vanquish, nor can Death controul.   10
Glad I release it from it's Partner's Cares;
And bid good Angels waft it to the Stars.
Then in the flowing Bowl I drown those Sighs,
Which, Spight of Wisdom, from our Weakness rise.
The Draught to the Dead's Mem'ry I commend,   15
And offer to the now immortal Friend.
But if oppos'd to what my Thoughts approve,
Nor PLUTO's Rage there be, nor Pow'r of JOVE;
On it's dark Side if Thou the Prospect take;
Grant all forgot beyond black LETHE's Lake: 20
In total Death suppose the Mortal lye,
No new Hereafter, nor a future Sky:
Yet bear thy Lot content; yet cease to grieve:
Why, e'er Death comes, dost Thou forbear to live?
The little Time Thou hast, 'twixt Instant Now   25
And Fate's Approach, is All the Gods allow:
And of this little hast Thou ought to spare
To sad Reflection, and corroding Care?
The Moments past, if Thou art wise, retrieve
With pleasant Mem'ry of the Bliss they gave.
The present Hours in present Mirth imploy;   30
And bribe the Future with the Hopes of Joy.

Title: *Gualterus...Amicos*] Walter Danniston, ad Amicos *Lansd, N.D., 1712m: ARCHI-*
BALDI PITCARNII SCOTI. Carmen. Anno Aetatis suae LX. *1712*   24 comes]
Lansd, N.D., 1712m come *1712*   25 hast] *N.D., 1712m* has *1712* : say'st *Lansd*   26
Fate's] *N.D., 1712m* Deaths *Lansd, 1712*

The Future (few or more, how e'er they be)
Were destin'd e'rst; nor can by Fate's Decree
Be now cut off, betwixt the Grave and Thee. } 35

To a Person who wrote Ill, and spake Worse against Me.

LYE, PHILO, untouch'd on my peaceable Shelf;
  Nor take it amiss, that so little I heed Thee;
I've no Envy to Thee, and some Love to my Self:
  Then why shou'd I answer; since first I must read Thee?

Drunk with HELICON's Waters and double-brew'd Bub,   5
  Be a Linguist, a Poet, a Critic, a Wag;
To the solid Delight of thy Well-judging Club,
  To the Damage alone of thy Bookseller BRAG.

Pursue me with Satyr: what Harm is there in't?
  But from all *vivâ voce* Reflection forbear: 10
There can be no Danger from what Thou shalt Print:
  There may be a little from what Thou may'st swear.

On the Same Person.

WHILE faster than his costive Brain indites,
  PHILO's quick Hand in flowing Letters writes;
His Case appears to Me like honest TEAGUE's,
When he was run away with, by his Legs.
PHOEBUS, give PHILO o'er Himself Command;   5
Quicken his Senses, or restrain His Hand.
Let Him be kept from Paper, Pen, and Ink:
So may He cease to Write, and learn to Think.

1711

To Mr. Harley.

Wounded by Guiscard. 1711.

—ab ipso
Ducit opes animumque ferro. Hor.

I.

IN one great *Now*, Superior to an Age,
The full Extremes of Nature's Force We find:
How Heav'nly Virtue can exalt; or Rage
Infernal, how degrade the Human Mind.

II.

While the fierce Monk does at his Tryal stand;   5
He chews Revenge, abjuring his Offence:
Guile in his Tongue, and Murther in his Hand,
He stabs his Judge, to prove his Innocence.

III.

The guilty Stroke and Torture of the Steel
Infix'd, our dauntless BRITON scarce perceives: 10
The Wounds His Countrey from His Death must feel,
The PATRIOT views; for those alone He grieves.

IV.

The barb'rous Rage that durst attempt Thy Life,
HARLEY, great Counsellor, extends Thy Fame:
And the sharp Point of cruel GUISCARD's Knife,   15
In Brass and Marble carves Thy deathless Name.

V.

Faithful Assertor of Thy Country's Cause,
BRITAIN with Tears shall bath Thy glorious Wound:
She for thy Safety shall enlarge Her Laws;
And in Her Statutes shall Thy Worth be found.   20

Title: To Mr....Guiscard. 1711.] To the Right Honourable Mr....*Guiscard. 1711, Lpo 11,*
Lpo 17, Lansd   2 full] *Lpo 17* great *1711, Lpo 11, Lansd*   3 Heav'nly] *Lpo 17*
high calm *1711, Lpo 11, Lansd*   4 Infernal, how] *Lpo 17* Furious, how low *1711,*
Lpo 11, Lansd   5 While] Whilst *1711, Lpo 11, Lpo 17, Lansd*   18 bath] *1711,*
Lpo 11, Lansd bathe *Lpo 17*

VI.

Yet 'midst Her Sighs She Triumphs, on the Hand
  Reflecting, that diffus'd the Publick Woe;
A Stranger to her Altars, and her Land:
  No Son of Her's could meditate this Blow.

VII.

Mean Time Thy Pain is gracious ANNA's Care: 25
  Our Queen, our Saint, with sacrificing Breath
Softens Thy Anguish: In Her pow'rful Pray'r
  She pleads Thy Service, and forbids Thy Death.

VIII.

Great as Thou art, Thou canst demand no more,
  O Breast bewail'd by Earth, preserv'd by Heav'n!   30
No higher can aspiring Virtue soar:
  Enough to Thee of Grief, and Fame is giv'n.

1712

An Extempore Invitation to the Earl of Oxford, Lord High Treasurer. 1712.

My LORD,

OUR Weekly Friends To-morrow meet
  At MATTHEW's Palace, in *Duke-street*;
To try for once, if They can Dine
On Bacon-Ham, and Mutton-chine:
If weary'd with the great Affairs,   5
Which BRITAIN trusts to HARLEY's Cares,
Thou, humble Statesman, may'st descend,
Thy Mind one Moment to unbend;

---

23 Altars] *1711, Lpo 11, Lpo 17,* Altar *Lansd*   28 Service] *1711, Lpo 11,* **Lansd**
Sorrows *Lpo 17*   31 No] Nor *1711, Lpo 11, Lpo 17, Lansd*
  Title] To the Right Honourable the Earl of Oxford. *Lpo 11*: Mr: Priors Invitation to My
Ld: Treasurer Wednesday 16⁰ April 1712 *Lansd*   2 MATTHEW's] PRIOR's *Lpo 11,*
Lansd   6 Which BRITAIN] *Lansd* That BRITON *Lpo 11*

To see Thy Servant from his Soul
Crown with Thy Health the sprightly Bowl: 10
Among the Guests, which e'er my House
Receiv'd, it never can produce
Of Honor a more glorious Proof—
Tho' DORSET us'd to bless the Roof.

An Imitation of Chaucer.

FAIR SUSAN did her Wif-hede well menteine,
  Algates assaulted sore by Letchours tweine:
Now, and I read aright that Auncient Song,
Olde were the Paramours, the Dame full yong.

Had thilke same Tale in other Guise been tolde;   5
Had They been Yong (pardie) and She been Olde;
That, by S^t KIT, had wrought much sorer Tryal;
Full merveillous, I wote, were swilk Denyal.

Erle Robert's Mice.

In Chaucer's Stile.

TWAY Mice, full Blythe and Amicable,
  Batten beside Erle ROBERT's Table.
Lies there ne Trap their Necks to catch,
Ne old black Cat their Steps to watch.
Their Fill they eat of Fowl and Fish;   5
Feast-lyche as Heart of Mouse mote wish.

As Guests sat Jovial at the Board,
Forth leap'd our Mice: Eftsoons the Lord
Of BOLING, whilome JOHN the SAINT,
Who maketh oft Propos full queint,   10
Laugh'd jocund, and aloud He cry'd,
To MATTHEW seated on t'oth' side;

10 sprightly] moderate *Lpo 11, Lansd*   11 Among...which] Amongs't...that *Lpo 11*:
Amongst...which *Lansd*
  Title: 1712m: *In the same Style. 1718 (where it follows 'Erle Robert's Mice. In Chaucer's Stile')*
3 and] an' *1712m*   4] The Paramours were Olde, the Dame was Yong, *1712m*   7
That...wrought] Sweet Jesu! that had been *1712m*   8 swilk] such *1712m*
  Title: In Chaucer's Stile.] A TALE, IN Imitation of *CHAUCER*, &c. *1712m*: om. *Lansd*
2 beside] *1712m* besydes *Lansd*

To Thee, lean Bard, it doth partain
To understand these Creatures Tweine.
Come frame Us now some clean Device,　　　　　15
Or playsant Rhime on yonder Mice:
They seem, God shield Me, MAT. and CHARLES.

　　Bad as Sir TOPAZ, or 'Squire QUARLES
(MATTHEW did for the nonce reply)
At Emblem, or Device am I:　　　　　　　20
But could I Chaunt, or Rhyme, pardie,
Clear as *Dan* CHAUCER, or as Thee;
Ne Verse from Me (so God me shrive)
On Mouse, or other Beast alive.
Certes, I have these many Days　　　　　25
Sent myne Poetic Herd to graze.
Ne Armed Knight ydrad in War
With Lyon fierce will I compare:
Ne Judge unjust, with furred Fox,
Harming in Secret Guise the Flocks:　　　　30
Ne Priest unworth of Goddes Coat,
To Swine ydrunk, or filthy Stoat.
Elk Similè farwell for aye,
From Elephant, I trow, to Flea.

　　Reply'd the friendlike Peer, I weene,　　　35
MATTHEW is angred on the Spleen.
Ne so, quoth MAT. ne shall be e'er,
With Wit that falleth all so fair:
Eftsoons, well weet Ye, mine Intent
Boweth to your Commaundement.　　　　40
If by these Creatures Ye have seen,
Pourtrayed CHARLES and MATTHEW been;
Behoveth neet to wreck my Brain,
The rest in Order to explain.

　　That Cup-board, where the Mice disport,　　45
I liken to St. STEPHEN's Court:
Therein is Space enough, I trow,
For elke Comrade to come and goe:

And therein eke may Both be fed
With Shiver of the Wheaten Bread.   5'
And when, as these mine Eyen survey,
They cease to skip, and squeak, and play;
Return they may to different Cells,
AUDITING One, whilst t'other TELLS.

     Dear ROBERT, quoth the SAINT, whose Mind   55
In Bounteous Deed no Mean can bind;
Now as I hope to grow devout,
I deem this Matter well made out.
Laugh I, whilst thus I serious Pray?
Let that be wrought which MAT. doth say: } 60
Yea, quoth the ERLE; but not to Day.

1713

Written in Montaigne's Essays,

Given to the Duke of Shrewsbury in France, after the Peace,
1713.

DICTATE, O mighty Judge, what Thou hast seen
    Of Cities, and of Courts, of Books, and Men;
And deign to let Thy Servant hold the Pen.

     Thro' Ages thus I may presume to live;
And from the Transcript of Thy Prose receive,   5
What my own short-liv'd Verse can never give.

     Thus shall fair BRITAIN with a gracious Smile
Accept the Work; and the instructed Isle,
For more than Treaties made, shall bless my Toil.

     Nor longer hence the GALLIC Style preferr'd,   10
Wisdom in ENGLISH *Idiom* shall be heard;
While TALBOT tells the World, where MONTAIGNE err'd.

51 when, as] *Lansd* whenas *1712m*   59 Pray?] Pray, *Lansd, 1712m*
   Title] To his Grace the Duke of Shrewsbury. *Ltr*   7 shall] should *Ltr*   8 Accept...and the instructed] Receive...the venerable *Ltr*   9, 11 shall] should *Ltr*
12 TALBOT tells] Shrewsbury told *Ltr*

Doctors Differ. An Epigram.

WHEN WILLIS of Ephraim heard ROCHESTER preach,
Thus BENTLY said to him, I pr'ythee, dear brother,
How lik'st Thou this Sermon? 'tis out of My reach.
His is One way, said WILLIS, and Ours is Another.
I care not for carping, but this I can tell,   5
We preach very sadly, if he preaches well.

Beauty.

PURSU'D by time the power of beauty flyes
Arises, flourishes, decays and dyes;
In its mid-empire darts precarious rays
By distance bounded and confin'd to place:

Thô joyfull health and blooming youth combine   5
To lay the gift on Cythereas Shrine:
Far as the Nymph can look she only reigns
The Youth must see her charms to own her Chains.

Sickness can spoyle and absence can remove
The fond Ideas that arise from Love.   10

Title] Dialogue between Dr Bentley & Dr Willis when Dr Sprat Bp of Rochester was preaching before the Queen at St. James. *Clarke*: *om. Lpo 11*   1 WHEN] *Clarke* As *Lpo 11*   2 Thus...dear] *Lpo 11* Sower...good *Clarke*   3 this] *Clarke* the *Lpo 11* 4 said] *Clarke* says *Lpo 11*   5 I...but] *Lpo 11* But tho' I'me no Critick, yet *Clarke*
        Title: 'Contents' *of L 28* : *om. W, Text of L 28*   1–8 *Cancelled (by Pope?) in L 28*   1–2]
        How'er confest, oh queen of love thy power
        It acts precarious to the coming hour
        and as with certain Wings old Saturn flyes
        It bloossoms, flourishes decays and dyes   *Earlier reading in W, L 28*
2 dyes; *edd.*: dyes *W, L 28*   3–4]
        Whilst yet it flourishes with fullest Grace
        Tis bound by distance and confind to Place   *Earlier reading in W, L 28*
4 By *L 28*: by *W*   5 Thô *edd.*: thô *W*: Tho *L 28*   6 lay...Cythereas] bring the sacred flame to Cupids *Earlier reading in W, L 28*   7 Far *L 28*: far *W*   8 The *L 28*: the *W*   own] sigh *Alt. reading in W, L 28 (D)*: feel *L 28 (Pope)*   Chains. *L 28* : Chains *W*   10 Love. *edd.*: Love *W, L 28*

1714

Frederic &ca: From Boccace.

WHAT Bocace with superior Genius Cloath'd
    In Tuscan Dress and ludicrous Fontaine
(Modern Anacreon) well has imitated
In Gallic Style, Himself inimitable:
How'er unequal to the Glorious task   5
Yet of the Noblest heights, and best Examples
Ambitious, I in English Verse Attempt
But not as heretofore, the line prescrib'd
To equal cadence, and with Semblant Sounds
Pointed (so modern Harmony Advises)   10
But in the ancient guise, free, uncontroll'd,
The Verse: Compress'd the Period or dilated
As close discourse requires or fine Discription.
Such Homer wrote; such Milton imitated;
And Shrewsbury candid Judge of Verse approves: 15
What Shrewsbury may approve, to whom pertains it
But to Thee Lady, loving Shrewsbury best,
And best by Him beloved? To Thee fair Matron
The warm Debate I bring and soft Recital
Of constant Passion and rewarded Friendship: 20
Weak the performance haply, yet the work
Beneath Thy feet I lay, and bless'd in this
As Thou good Princess, in each part of Life:
That I but Act what Thy great Lord Commands.

*We cite W (D & P) only when necessary to distinguish it from W (D). Some of the punctuation
in L 28 is in another hand (Pope's?)*
    Title: L 28, 'Contents' of L 28 (D) : Prelude to a Tale from Boccace in blank Verse. To the
Ds. of Shrewsbury *'Contents' of L 28 (Pope)*, M : *om.* W   3 (Modern Anacreon) *L 28, M* :
Modern Anacreon *W*   4 inimitable: *L 28* : inimitable *W, M*   10 (so ... Advises)
edd. : so ... Advises *W* : (so ... advises) *L 28, M*   13 or *W (D & P), L 28 (corrected
from* of), *M* : of *W (D)*   Discription. *edd.* : Discription *W* : description. *L 28* : description
M   14 wrote; ... imitated; *L 28* : wrote ... imitated *W, M*   15, 16, 17 Shrewsbury *W (D & P)* : S—— *W (D)* : Shrewsb'ury *L 28, M*   15 approves: *W (D & P)* :
approves *W (D), M* : approves. *L 28*   16 approve, *W (D & P), L 28, M* : approve
W (D)   17 Thee] the *L 28, M*   18 beloved? *edd.* : beloved, *W* : belov'd? *L 28, M*
21 haply, *L 28* : haply *W, M*   23 Life: *L 28* : Life *W, M*

As Dorset's Smile benign and fair Example   25
In pleasing Rhime indulg'd my Infant Years
(O be his Mem'ry ever wept and Honor'd!)
May Shrewsburys will prescribe my Elder Muse
A diff'rent course, great bounteous Adelida
Be Thou my Friend my gentle Intercessor   30
That Thy great Lord with his Illustrious Name
May Sheild the Goddess from the Darts of Censure
Unwounded, and assure her future flight
With equal favor and Successive goodness
Continuing what his Noble Friend began.   35

How e'er again reflecting, She must blame
Her own Ambition that with vain Attempt
Wou'd bring Thee ought from Paris or from Rome
Transfer'd and Habited in English Dress
When Thou great Mistress in Italian Sounds   40
Canst breath thy Thought, not Petrarchs Laura Sweeter:
When thou in Gallic Style can well indite
So well that famous Scuderys learned Sister
Or Fabers Daughter might Attentive learn.
Yet thou hast right fair Dame to claim the Song   45
In British Sounds; amongst her best Lov'd daughters
Britannia Numbers Thee, by Twofold Title
To her endear'd: Partner of Talbots bed
And right Descended from the race of Dudley.
And well hast Thou with Correspondent Grace   50
Answer'd thy gentle Mothers Love indeavouring
To form her Accents and to speak her Language.
In Womanhood industrious to Reclaim
By Study and by Art the legal Portion
Which Fortune to thy Infancy deny'd.   55
And well hast Thou Achiev'd the Task: thy care

27 (O...Honor'd!) *L 28*: O...Honor'd *W*: (O...honor'd) *M*   28 Shrewsburys *W*
(*D & P*): S——s *W* (*D*): Shrewsb'ury's *L 28*: Shrewsbury's *M*   31 Thy great Lord]
L 28, M He may daign *W* (*D & P*)   32 May...the] *L 28, M* To Sheild my Muse
from pointed *W* (*D & P*)   35] *om. L 28, M*   36 reflecting, *L 28*: reflecting *W, M*
37 Her *L 28, M*: her *W*   41 Sweeter: *L 28*: Sweeter *W, M*   43 that *W* (*D & P*):
the *W* (*D*), *L 28, M*   Scuderys] *L 28* Scudery *M*   44 learn. *L 28*: learn *W, M*
46 Sounds; *edd.*: Sounds *W*: sounds; *L 28*: sounds. *M*   47 Thee, *L 28, M*: Thee *W*
48 endear'd: *L 28*: endear'd *W*: endear'd; *M*   49 Dudley. *W* (*D & P*), *L 28*: Dudly
W (*D*): Dudley *M*   51 indeavouring *W* (*D & P*): endearing *W* (*D*), *L 28, M*   56
Task: *L 28, M*: Task *W*

By Subtil Mem'ry Aided and Thy Lessons
Practised with Wit and perfected by Judgment.
But Love, fair Dame (and Thou with Pride mayst own
The grateful impulse) constant o'er Thy Toyl   60
Presided, Well we learn when he is Master.

Not harsh, I hope fair Judge thou wilt avow
The British Tongue tho sometimes chargd with words
Saxon and Danish, when the Manly Sounds
Break from the Potent Lips of Finch or Harcourt.   65
Our Language semblant to our native Streams
O'er little Flints, and scatter'd Pebbles rolling
Its curled wave, unequal not unpleasing
The Surface. But O Mercury! O Venus!
(For I attest You Both) when the fair Sex,   70
When Buckingham or Grafton (kind Comperes
And faithful Friends to that Illustrious Dame
Who claims my Song) when They (or beauteous Cloe
My Hope my Joy) emit their Natal Sound
Softer than Down from Venus fav'rite Birds   75
Or flakes of Feather'd Snow the Accents fall.
Exalt Thy Thought my Muse. When Our great Sov'raign
Disparts Her comly Lips, August pronouncing
The Speech, 'tis Sweet as Morning fumes which rise
From Sharons Rose; grateful as Arab Gums   80
By Cædar fir'd and curling from the Altar:
Our Dread at once and our Delight. She guides
And charms the Senate, from her Silver voice
Pouring Her fierce forefathers diction temper'd
With Heav'nly Mildness and Angelic grace.   85
We then disdainful of our Modern Rivals
Provoke the Latian or the Greek resigning
But to the Sacred Hebrew. Agripina

57 Mem'ry *W* (*D & P*): Mem'ory *W* (*D*), *L 28*, *M*   58 Judgment. *L 28*: Judgment
W, *M*   59 Love,...(and *L 28*: Love...and *W*: Love...(and *M*   60 impulse)
edd.: impulse *W*: Impulse) *L 28*, *M*   62–63] *L 28*, *M* Not harsh the British Tongue
tho charg'd with words *Earlier version in W*   65 Harcourt. *L 28*, *M*: Harcourt *W*
69 Mercury! O Venus! *L 28*: Mercury O Venus *W*, *M*   70 (For...Both) *L 28*, *M*:
For...Both *W*   Sex, *L 28*: Sex *W*, *M*   71 (kind *L 28*: kind *W*, *M*   73 Song)
L 28, *M*: Song *W*   77 When *edd.*: when *W*, *L 28*, *M*   80 Rose; *L 28*, *M*:
Rose *W*   Arab] Arabs *L 28*, *M*   81 Altar: *L 28*: Altar *W*, *M*   84 Pouring *M*:
Pou'ring *W*, *L 28*   85 grace. *edd.*: grace *W*: Grace. *L 28*: Grace *M*   88 Hebrew.
L 28: Hebrew *W*: Hebrew, *M*

Or great Andromache by Homer aided
Speaks with less height and Majesty of Style 90
Then British ANNA. With resembling prevalence
Pleads Hester and Victorious Deborah Sings.
Around the Throne the Nations to their Queen
Obedient Stand and bid Her Live for ever.

Illustrious Patroness excuse the Prelude 95
And Thou Calliope begin the Song.

IN FLORENCE heretofore, who knows not Florence
Beautiful Soverein of Etrurias Cities,
Liv'd Frederic, from a Noble Race descended
With fair Revenues blest, and large Estate 100
His Years were just arriv'd to perfect Manhood
Well limb'd his Body and his person comely
His Mind with all those open Virtues bright
Which an Indulgent Mothers Previous hope
Can figure for her best lov'd Infants Age. 105
Unmarried yet, his Marriage is my Story.
On Frederic therefore every Eye was cast
What e'er he did was talkt. He went or came
The public Care: The P—— the G . . .:
Illustrious houses courted his Alliance 110
And every Noble Virgin Sighing Wish'd
Her Father might Succeed, but Oh in vain
Propose the Parents, or the Daughters hope:
Clitia, so Venus destins, must alone
Gain Frederic's Love, and love must rule his fortune. 115
Rich, young She was a Widow, of One Son
The Mother, and the Tutoress: Frederic courts Her
Courts Her but how, with Presents, with Expense
Surpassing all his Rivals, of that sort
How many gather, where the prevalent Charms 120
At once of Beauty and of Wealth Attract

---

91 ANNA. With *L 28 (Pope?)*: ANNA with *W*: ANNA, With *M*   92 Sings. *L 28, M*:
Sings *W*   93 their] *L 28* the *M*   96 *After this line in L 28, Pope inserted*: ****
Imperfect.   97–134 *Marked for deletion, by Pope, in L 28*: *om. M*   98 Cities,
edd.: Cities *W, L 28*   105 Age. *W (D & P)*: Age *W (D), L 28*   106 yet, *W*
(D & P): yet *W (D), L 28*   Story. *W (D & P)*: Story *W (D), L 28*   108 talkt. He
edd.: talkt he *W*: Talk'd he *L 28*   112 Her *W (D & P), L 28*: her *W (D)*   115
fortune. *W (D & P)*: fortune *W (D)*: Fortune *L 28*   121 At] Of *L 28*

From Homers Time to Ours stand fair recorded.
The Tilt and Tournament, so Gallantry
Ancient allow'd and Frederic well excell'd
In feats of Arms and Manly Exercises   125
Took up the day delightful: Clitia Seated
Sublime, commands the Sports. Clitia's Device
Portray'd on Frederic's Shield declares her Champion.
Music the splendid Ball and costly banquet
First fruits to hopeful Love by all his Zealots   130
Offer'd employ the softer hours of Night,
Queen of the Feast reigns Clitia, Clitias Name
Adorns the Song, and at her health alone
Breaths the Shrill Hautboy, and the Clarion Sounds.

An Epistle, Desiring the Queen's Picture.

Written at Paris, 1714. But left unfinish'd, by the sudden News of Her Majesty's Death.

THE Train of Equipage and Pomp of State,
The shining Side-board, and the burnish'd Plate
Let other Ministers, Great ANNE, require;
And partial fall Thy Gift to their Desire.
To the fair Portrait of my Sov'reign Dame,   5
To That alone, eternal be my Claim.

My bright Defender, and my dread Delight,
If ever I found Favor in Thy Sight;
If all the Pains that for Thy BRITAIN's Sake
My past has took, or future Life may take,   10
Be grateful to my QUEEN; permit my Pray'r,
And with This Gift reward my total Care.

Will Thy indulgent Hand, fair Saint, allow
The Boon? and will Thy Ear accept the Vow?

---

124 Frederic *L 28* : Frederick *W*   126 day *W (D & P)* : Dance *W (D)*, *L 28*   128
Portray'd] *L 28* Impressed *Earlier reading in W*   Frederic's *W (D & P)*, *L 28* : Fredericks
W (D)   129 costly *L 28* : costly, *W*   banquet] *L 28* bouquet *Earlier reading in W*
131 Night, *L 28* : Night *W*   134 Sounds. *edd.*: Sounds *W* : sounds. *L 28*

That in despight of Age, of impious Flame,   15
And eating Time, Thy Picture like Thy Fame
Entire may last; that as their Eyes survey
The semblant Shade, Men yet unborn may say;
Thus Great, thus Gracious look'd BRITANNIA's Queen;
Her Brow thus smooth, Her Look was thus serene;   20
When to a Low, but to a Loyal Hand
The mighty Empress gave Her high Command,
That He to Hostile Camps, and Kings shou'd haste,
To speak Her Vengeance as Their Danger past;
To say, She Wills detested Wars to cease;   } 25
She checks Her Conquest, for Her Subjects Ease;
And bids the World attend Her Terms of Peace.

     Thee, Gracious ANNE, Thee present I adore,
Thee, QUEEN of PEACE—If Time and Fate have Pow'r
Higher to raise the Glories of thy Reign;   30
In Words sublimer, and a nobler Strain,
May future Bards the mighty Theme rehearse.
Here, STATOR JOVE, and PHOEBUS King of Verse,
The Votive Tablet I suspend * * * *

For His own Epitaph.

A s Doctors give Physic by way of prevention,
    MATT alive and in health of his Tomb-stone took care;
For delays are unsafe, and his Pious Intention
     May haply be never fulfill'd by his Heir.

Then take MATTs word for it, the Sculptor is paid,   5
     That the Figure is fine pray believe Your own Eye,
Yet credit but lightly what more may be said,
     For we flatter our Selves, and teach Marble to lye.

Yet counting as far as to Fifty his Years,
     His Virtues and Vices were as other Mens are,   10
High Hopes he conceiv'd, and he smother'd great fears,
     In a Life party-colour'd, half Pleasure half care.

17 may] my *Copies of 1718 with reset sheet*
    Title: edd.: Mr: Prior for His own Epitaph *L 27*: FOR My own MONUMENT. *1740*
5 it, *1740* : it *L 27*   10 are, *1740* : are *L 27*   12 party-colour'd, *1740* : party colour'd
L 27

Nor to Buisness a Drudge, nor to Faction a Slave,
    He strove to make Intrest and freedom agree.
In public Employments industrious and grave,   15
    And alone with his Friends, Lord, how merry was He.

Now in Equipage Stately, now humbly on foot,
    Both Fortunes he Try'd but to neither wou'd Trust,
And whirl'd in the round, as the Wheel turn'd about
    He found Riches had wings, and knew Man was but Dust.   20

This Verse little polish'd thô mighty sincere
    Sets neither his Titles nor Merit to view,
It says that his Relicks collected lye here,
    And no Mortal yet knows too if this may be true.

Fierce Robbers there are that infest the Highway   25
    So MATT may be kill'd and his Bones never found;
False Witness at Court, and fierce Tempests at Sea,
    So MATT may yet chance to be Hang'd, or be Drown'd.

If his Bones lye in Earth, roll in Sea, fly in Air
    To Fate We must yeild, and the things are the same,   30
And if passing Thou giv'st Him a Smile, or a Tear
    He cares not—Yet prythee be kind to his Fame.

The Remedy, Worse than the Disease.

I.

I SENT for RADCLIFFE, was so ill,
    That other Doctors gave me over,
He felt my Pulse, prescribed his *Pill*
    And I was likely to recover.

II.

But when the *Wit* began to wheeze,   5
    And Wine had warmed the *Politician*,
Cur'd yesterday of my Disease,
    I died last night of my *Physician*.

True Statesmen.

TRUE Statesmen only Love or hate
What Lessens 'em or makes 'em Great.
With wondrous kindness each ascends
Supported by his Should'ring Friends
And fleering Criticks sometimes Note   5
His dirt imprinted on his Coat.

Some Lords like Wife and Husband squable
For this fine thing or that blew bauble
But soon the present folly ends
And common Int'rest makes 'em Friends.   10
Whilst yet Erinnis rages high
And paper Darts in Pamphlets fly
He whose hot Head wou'd interpose
Is sure to have his share of blows
But in the reconciling Feast   15
When all the Bustle proves a Jest
Where matters are adjusted fairly
And —— sweetly Kisses ——
The little Agents of the Plott
The understrappers are forgot.   20
And if the Doctor Uninvited
Afraid to fancy he was Slighted
Comes in, his Labours he may Spy
Fixt to the Bottom of a Pye
Or find how those reward his trouble   25
That light their Pipes with Dear T. D.

Be not the Bully of the Nation
Nor foam at mouth for Moderation.
Take not thy Sentiments on trust
Nor be by others Notions just.   30

Title: L 28 (*Pope*), M: *om.* W, L 28 (D)   2 Great. *edd.*: Great W: great. L 28:
grate M   5–6] L 28, M
And one Mans dirty feet, beholders
Find often mark't on tothers Shoulders   *Alt. reading in* W
8 or] for L 28, M   10 Friends. L 28: Friends W, M   11 Erinnis L 28
(*Pope*), M: Erenis W, L 28 (D)   18 Kisses ——] kisses [*blank*] L 28 (D): kisses
H——y L 28 (*Pope*), M   30 just. *edd.*: just W, L 28, M

To Church and Queen and Laws be hearty
But hate a Trick and scorn a Party
And if Thou ever hast a Voice
Thô it be only in the Choice
Of Vestry Men or Grey Coat Boys   35
Vote Right thô certain to be blam'd
And rather Starve than be asham'd.
This method I shou'd fancy best
You may think otherwise, I rest.

Thos: Britton, Small-Coal-Man.

*T*HO' *doom'd to Small Coal, yet, to Arts ally'd,*
    Rich without Wealth and Famous without Pride,
Musick's Best Patron, Judge of Books and Men,
Belov'd and Honour'd by Apollo's Train;
In Greece or Rome, sure never did appear   5
So Bright a Genius, in so dark a Sphere;
More of the Man had artfully been Sav'd,
Had Kneller painted and had Vertue Grav'd.

1715

To a Lady given with a Nosegay.

*S*OUVIENS Toy, Cloe, du destin
    De ces fleurs si fraiches si belles
        Elles ne durent qu'un matin
Comme Elles vous brillez, vous passerez comme Elles.

37 asham'd. *edd.*: asham'd *W*, *L 28*, *M*   39 rest. *L 28*: rest *W*: rest; *M*

To the Horse of Henry the Fourth of France.

PETIT Cheval, gentil Cheval
Propre à monter, propre à descendre
Tu n'es pas grand comme Bucephale
Tu porte plus que l'Alexandre.

Fragment.

FOR K . . . . . t call'd White and Burnet Gil— show
That Doctors may Change as preferment may go
And Twenty Year hence for ought You and I know
T'will be Hoadly the High and Sachevril the Low.

Who knows how each Author may Alter their mind 5
As they on the Text other Comments may find.

Daphne and Apollo.

Faithfully translated from Ovids Metamorp.
Book 1st: Nympha, Precor, Penei, mane: &ca.

A.   ABATE fair Fugitive, abate thy Speed
Dismiss thy fears, and turn thy beauteous head,
With kind regard a Panting Lover view
Less Swiftly fly, less swiftly I'll pursue.

Title] Lansd On Seeing the King of France on a very Little horse, the following Lines were
made Extempore by Monsieur Malherbe. Harv   3 grand comme] Lansd tant que Harv
4 porte plus que l'] Lansd portes un plus grand qu' Harv
   Title: L 28 (Pope) : om. W, L 28 (D): Epigram 'Contents' of L 28 (D)   1 K.....t
...Burnet] K..... ...B.....L 28 (D): K-n-tt...Bu...t L 28 (Pope?)   3 Year] Years
L 28   4 Hoadly...Sachevril] H...... ...S........L 28 (D): Hoadly...Sacheverel
L 28 (Pope?)   Low. L 28: Low W   5–6 Cancelled in L 28 (by Pope?)   5 their]
his L 28   6 on edd.: or W, L 28   find. edd.: find W, L 28
   Title: Daphne...Book 1st:] L 28, M DAPHNE and APOLLO. IMITATED 1740: om.
W (P)   Nympha...mane: &ca.] L 28, M Nympha...mane.——OVID. Met. Lib. I.
1740: om. W (P)   In W (D & P), the speakers are indicated by initials or by abbreviations; these are here normalized to italicized initials, those within the line being bracketed. In
W (P), the speakers are not identified. In all other texts, the full name is centred on the line before
each speech   1 Fugitive, edd.: Fugitive W (D & P), L 28, M: fugitive, W (P), 1740
2 fears, W (P), 1740: fears W (D & P), L 28, M   head, 1740: head W (P), W (D & P)
L 28, M   4 fly, W (P), 1740: fly W (D & P), L 28, M   less] W (P), L 28, 1740
lest M   pursue. W (P): pursue W (D & P), L 28, M: pursue; 1740

Pathless alas and rugged is the ground   5
Some Stone may hurt thee or some thorn may wound.

D. This care is for himself, as sure as Death
One mile has put the Fellow out of Breath
He'll never do, I'll lead him t'other round
Washy he is, perhaps not over Sound.   10

A. You fly alas not knowing whom you fly
Nor ill bred Swain, nor rusty Clown am I
I Claros Isle and Tenedos command—

D. Thank you, I would not leave my Native Land.

A. What is to come by certain Art I know.   15

D. Pish Partridge has as fair pretence as Thou.

A. Behold the Beauties of my locks— [*D.*] a Fig,
That may be counterfeit a Spanish Wigg.
Who cares for all that Bush of curling hair
Whilst your Smooth Chin is so extreamly bare.   20

A. I sing— [*D.*] that never shal be Daphnes choice.
Syphacio had an Admirable Voice.

A. Of ev'ry Herb I tell the Mystic pow'r.
To certain Health the patient I restore,
Sent for, Carres't, — [*D.*] ours is a wholsom Air   25
You'd better go to Town and practice there:
For me I've no obstructions to remove
I'm pritty well I thank your Father Jove,
And Physic is a weak Ally to Love.

6 or] *L 28, M, 1740* and *W (P)*   wound. *W (P), L 28, 1740*: wound *W (D & P), M*
In *W (P)* followed by: o turn thy head o Stop——as sure as   7–16 *om. W (P)*   10
is, *M, 1740*: is *W (D & P), L 28*   Sound. *L 28*: Sound *W (D & P)*: sound. *M, 1740*
11 whom] who *L 28, M, 1740*   12 rusty] *L 28 (D), 1740* rustic *L 28 (Pope), M*   14
you] *L 28, M* ye *1740*   15 Art] Arts *L 28, M, 1740*   16 Thou] *L 28, M* you *1740*
17 Beauties] *W (P), 1740* Beauty *L 28, M*   Fig, *edd.*: Fig *W (D & P), L 28, M*:
figg, *W (P)*: fig— *1740*   18 Spanish] *L 28, M, 1740* Natural *W (P)*   Wigg. *W (P)*:
Wigg *W (D & P), L 28, M*: Wig; *1740*   20 bare. *W (P), 1740*: bare *W (D & P),*
L 28, M   21–22 *om. W (P)*   22 Voice. *L 28, 1740*: Voice *W (D & P), M*
24 restore, *W (P), 1740*: restore *W (D & P), L 28, M*   25 Sent for, Carres't, —]
L 28, M, 1740 Courted rever'd. *W (P)*   26 there: *1740*: there *W (P), W (D & P),*
L 28, M   28 Jove, *W (P), 1740*: Jove *W (D & P), L 28, M*   29 Love. *W*
(P), 1740: Love *W (D & P), L 28, M*

A. For Learning Fam'd fine Verses I compose.   30

D. So do your Brother Quacks and Brother Beaux
Memorials only and Reviews write Prose.

A. From the Bent Eugh I send the pointed Reed
Sure of it's Aim and fatal in its Speed—

D. Then leaving me whom sure you wou'dn't kill   35
In yonder Thicket exercise your skill
Shoot there at Beasts but for the Human Heart
Your Couzen Cupid has the only Dart.

A. Yet turn Oh beauteous Maid yet deign to hear
A Love sick Deities impetuous pray'r   40
Oh let me woo thee as thou wou'd'st be woo'd.

D. First therefore don't be so extreamly rude
Don't tear the Hedges down and tread the Clover
Like a Hobgoblin rather than a Lover
Next to my Fathers Grotto sometimes come.   45
At ebbing Tyde He always is at home.
Read the Courant with him and let him know
A little Politicks how matters go
Upon his Brother Rivers Rhine and Po.
As any Maid or Footman comes or goes   50
Pull off your Hatt and ask how Daphne does:
These sort of Folks will to each other tell
That you respect me, That you know looks well.
Then if you are as you pretend the God
That rules the Day and much upon the Road   55
You'l find a hundred Trifles in your way
That you may bring one home from Africa

30–32 *om. W (P)*   30 compose. *edd.*: compose *W (D & P), L 28, M*: compose, *1740*
32 Memorials *M, 1740*: Mem:ˡˡˢ *W (D & P)*: *Memorials L 28*   33–34] *W (P), L 28,*
M, 1740
                 With certain Speed I know
       to Send the arrow from the twanging bow, *Alt. reading in W (P)*
35 whom] *L 28, M, 1740* who *W (P)*   37 for the ... Heart] *L 28, M, 1740* oh for
... hearts *W (P)*   38 Dart. *edd.*: Dart *W (D & P), M*: dart. *L 28, 1740* darts.
W (P)   39–44 *om. W (P)*   41 woo'd. *edd.*: woo'd *W (D & P), L 28*: wood.
M: woo'd, *1740*   43 tear] *L 28, 1740* tread *M*   45 Next] *L 28, M, 1740* then
W (P)   46 He always] *L 28, M, 1740* he is always *W (P)*   47–48] *L 28, M,*
1740 and let him know how matters go *W (P)*   49 and *W (P), L 28, M*: or *W*
(D & P), 1740   50 As any] *L 28, M, 1740* and as a *W (P)*   52 Folks] *L 28, M, 1740*
folk *W (P)*   other] *L 28, M, 1740 om. W (P)*   53 well. *W (P)*: well *W (D & P),*
L 28, M: well: *1740*   54–57 *om. W (P)*

Some little Rarity some Bird or Beast
And now and then a Jewel from the East
A Lacquer'd Cabinet some China Ware　　　　　　　　　　60
You have them mighty cheap at Pekin fair.
Next *Nota Bene* you shal never rove
Nor take example by your Father Jove.
Last for the ease and Comfort of my life
Make me Your—Lord what Startles you—your wife.　　　　65
I'm now they say Sixteen or something more.
We Mortals Seldom live above fourscore.
Fourscore—you're good at Numbers—let us See
Seventeen Suppose remaining Sixty three,
Ay in that Span of Time you'l bury me.　　　　　　　　70
Mean time if you have Tumult Noise and Strife
(Things not abhorrent to a marri'd life)
They'l quickly end you See; what Signify
A Few odd years to you that never Dye?
And after all you're half your time away　　　　　　　75
You know your business takes you up all day
And coming late to Bed you need not fear
What ever Noise I make you'l sleep my Dear
Or if a Winter Evening Shou'd be long
E'en read your Physick Book or make a Song.　　　　　80
Your Steeds, your Wife, Diaculum, and Rhime
May take up any Honest Godheads time.
Thus as you like it you may love again
And let another Daphne have her Reign,

58 little] *L 28, M, 1740* om. *W (P)*　　　Bird] *L 28, M, 1740* birds *W (P)*　　　60–63
om. *W (P)*　　　63 Jove. *edd.*: Jove *W (D & P), L 28, M*: JOVE. *1740*　　　64 Comfort]
L 28, M, 1740 credit *W (P)*　　　65 wife. *W (P)*: wife *W (D & P), L 28, M*: wife; *1740*
68–76 om. *W (P)*　　　68 Fourscore—...Numbers— *L 28, M*: Fourscore...Numbers *W*
D & P): Fourscore,...numbers, *1740*　　　you're] Y'are *L 28, 1740*: Y're *M*　　　69 three,
L 28, 1740: three *W (D & P), M*　　　70 Span] *1740* space *L 28, M*　　me. *L 28, 1740*:
me *W (D & P), M*　　　71 and] *L 28, 1740* or *M*　　　72 (Things...life) *edd.*:
Things...life *W (D & P)*: Things...life, *1740*: (Things...Life) *L 28, M*　　　73 See;
edd.: See *W (D & P)*: see; *L 28*: see, *M, 1740*　　　74 Dye? *edd.*: Dye *W (D & P)*,
M: dye? *L 28*: die; *1740*　　　75 you're] Y'are *L 28, M, 1740*: you're *W (D & P)*
1740: you're *W (D & P)*　　　77] *L 28, M, 1740* Returning wett and weary home, ne'r
fear *W (P)*　　　78 What...make] *L 28, M, 1740* And by your own wifes Side, *W (P)*
79] *L 28, M, 1740* or at the worst when winter nights are long *W (P)*　　　80 E'en]
L 28, M, 1740 You'l *W (P)*　　　your] *W (P), L 28, M* you *1740*　　　Song. *W (P)*: song.
1740: Song *W (D & P), L 28, M*　　　81–84 om. *W (P)*　　　81 Your Steeds,...Wife,
Diaculum, *L 28, M*: Your steeds, ... wife, diachalon, *1740*: You're Steeds...Wife
Diaculum *W (D & P)*　　　84 Reign, *edd.*: Reign *W (D & P), L 28, M*: reign, *1740*

Now Love or leave, my Dear, retreat or follow.   85
I Daphne, this premis'd, take Thee Apollo,
And may I split into ten thousand Trees
If I give up on other Terms than these.

She said, but what the Am'rous God reply'd
So Fate ordains is to Our search Deny'd: 90
By Ratts alas the Manuscript is eat
O Cruel Banquet which we all regret;
Bavius Thy Labours must this work restore
May thy good Will be equal to thy Pow'r!

Observations on Homer. A Letter.

I KNOW you and the Learned are ever partial to Father Homer, I have
run over his Iliad not in Greek dont mistake me but in French and
Latin; recurring to the Original as well as my long Disuse of the Clasic
Writers gave me leave, and venture to Send you my Diary upon it.

The Conection between the Books is too just to give room for any   5
Man to think they were only distinct Songs, or Pieces, Rapsodies Collected and bound together by any Critic after Homers Death. The
same Story, and generally the same Spirit goes thrô the whole, and if
Homer as our Friend Horace confesses Does sometimes Sleep, he makes
a very glorious Noise wherever he is thorowly awake. I cannot however   10
think it a perfect Epic Poem, At least if he intended to Sing the Destruction of Troy, for thô it is very easy to imagine that the Town must be
Destroyed after Hectors Death, Yet *Priam* and *Hecuba*, *Anchises* and
Æneas, and even *Helena* her self, the very cause and begining of the War,
are not disposed of, nor does the Poet give you occasion to imagine   15
what can possibly become of them. Those who say that the Chief Subject of the *Iliad* was only to Show how destructive the Disentions of

85–86 *Order of lines reversed in* W (P)   85 Love] *L 28*, *M*, *1740 like* W (P)   leave,
my Dear,...follow. W (P): leave, my Dear,...follow M: leave, my dear:...follow, *1740*:
leave my Dear...follow W (D & P), *L 28*   86 Daphne,...premis'd,...Apollo, W (P),
1740: Daphne...premis'd...Apollo W (D & P), *L 28*: Daphne,...premis'd,...Apollo M
89–94] *In L 28, marked for deletion (by Pope?): om.* M   89 said, *L 28*, *1740*: said W
(P), W (D & P)   90 ordains] W (P) Ordain'd *L 28*, *1740*   Deny'd: *edd.*: Deny'd
W (D & P), *L 28*: denyed: W (P): deny'd, *1740*   92 regret; *1740*: regret W (P), W
(D & P), *L 28*   93 Bavius...this] *L 28*, *1740* Till B——s labour shall the W (P)
94 May thy good...thy] *L 28*, *1740* Oh may his...his W (P)
    Title: Homer. *L 28*: Homer W   *A Letter*] Letter To..........with Observations on
Homer. A Letter To—— *L 28*   1 ever] even *L 28*   15 of *L 28*: off W

the Great are to the Public, and that *Homer* only meant to tell Us the retardment which the Quarrel of *Achilles* and *Agamemnon* brought to the Trojan Expedition, and the Success with which it was carryed on 20 after the reconcilliation of these two Princes, make *Homers* work more Perfect, but his Design not so great.

The whole Quarrel is concerning three harlots. *Paris* runs away with *Menelaus*'s Wife *Helena*, all *Greece* are in Arms upon this Occasion, and while they lye before the Seige of *Troy*, *Agamemnon* will not give up his 25 Lass the Priests Daughter to her Father and her Temple, or at least when he is forced to give her up, he Seizes Achilles's Mistriss, and from hence arises the whole Scene of Anger, which occasions the Iliad.

The Person of neither of these Ladys is enough known to raise your Concern for 'em, You only know that they have fair cheeks, Imbroider 30 well, or make a Bed soft.

Lib: 1st: Do not these Occasions seem too trivial for the work that is made of 'em? does not *Agamemnon* make a very frank Confession when he says he Loves *Chryseis* as well as his own Wife *Clytemnestra*? And dos not Achilles make a foolish Figure, when he tells his Mother, with Tears in 35 his Eyes, that they have taken away his Damsel from him?

Achilles and *Agamemnon* are very free with one another; A great many say for Homers Heros in this Case that thô it is not Civil egad it is Heroick, Others excuse it upon the impoliteness of the times in which the Poet writ: In all Cases Drunken Sot, Dogs face, and Coward, is very 40 odd Language for the Sons and Grandsons of Gods and Goddesses.

Lib: 1st: *Apollo* gives the Trojans a Wind, this seems to be out of his Sphere; *Virgil* is much more just who makes ev'n *Juno* who might be supposed to have Some influence in the Air to fly her Self to *Æolus* when She had a mind to have a Tempest raised.   45

Ibid 2d: *Jupiter* sends a lying Dream to *Agamemnon*; The Lord sent out a lying Spirit to Seduce *Ahab*. In these cases how can Heroic Virtue know how it is deceiv'd.

Ibid 3d: *Scaliger*'s Criticism upon Homer is certainly right, that his Heroes make long Speeches in the heat of their Battles, They some times tell 50 Stories, and reckon up Genealogies, To this I wou'd add, that he who is like to have the worst of it is always taken away by his Patron God

or Goddess either in a Cloud or a Mist, and so you hear no more of
them for that time, These Gods and Goddesses always appear in other
Peoples Shapes. This takes all merit and blame from human Action and 55
is in a less degree the fault of all Epic Writers from Virgil to Sir R: Bl——

Jupiter upon whom all human Affairs depend, and who bestows Lib: 4th:
Victory where he pleases &ca. is finely expressed and so is the pow'r
of Jupiter who makes the Wall tumble as he pleases. *Ajax*'s Body of Lib: 9th:
Foot that moves on like a black cloud and covers the Earth is fine, So Lib: 4th:
is Agamemnons Compliment to *Nestor* upon his age, and Nestors 61
Answer. But how do you like Agamemnons Civility to *Idomeneus* that
he always gave him the liberty to fill himself Bumpers at his Feasts,
or his Saying to Ulysses a little after that he let him drink as much as
he pleased. When he commends Ulysses for his Moderation he says 65
Diomedes knows only to talk, which is not so well bred, as the Clang
of Diomedes's Arms which frighted the Soldiers is not so very Sublime.
Discord at first weak erecting her head to Heav'n is very good.

Venus wounded by Diomedes and the account of her bleeding, and Lib: 5th:
Mars wounded by the same Hero, and crying as loud as ten thousand 70
Men, both of 'em roaring and crying to their Father Jupiter. All this is
very childish.

Glaucus to Diomedes of the shortness of Life is well. The Account of Lib: 6th:
his Family in the midst of the fight is insupportable; Glaucus changing
his Arms which were Gold and worth a hundred Oxen for those of 75
Diomedes, which were only Steel and worth but nine is yet worse.

Hecuba asks Hector returning from the Fight if he'll have a Cup of Ibid
Wine, and Hector tells her he is hot and it may do him harm. In the
next book Hector looks pale and trembles when Ajax is to fight him. Lib: 7th:

Achilles says finely that he dos not hate the Gates of Hell more then Lib: 9th:
the Man who dares not say what he thinks, but he spoils all presently 81
after by his Wise observation, that when a Man has lost his Life he
cannot have it again.

Phœnix tells Achilles that the Gods are mov'd by Pray'r; very well; Lib: 9th:
Throughout the whole Iliad Achilles has no other Virtue but that of 85
Courage.

56 Epic *L 28*: *Missing from W*   60 Lib: 4th: *edd.*: *om. W*, *L 28*   66 bred, *edd.*:
bred *W*, *L 28*   69, 73, 76 Diomedes] Diomede *L 28*   71 All *L 28*: all *W*
77 asks] asked *L 28*   79 him. *L 28*: him *W*   82 Man *L 28*: *Partially illeg.*
in W   84 Lib: 9th: *edd.*: Liber 9th *W*: *om. L 28*

Lib: 2d: In the Ardor of the Combat he takes all Amphimachus's Gold from him, here notwithstanding his Love to Briseis when he retains
Ibid 9th: Phœnix in his Tents, he has a Lesbian Wench to lye with him, and *Patroclus* his Friend retires civily with Iphis whom Achilles had given 90
Lib: 22d: to him. So much for his Continence. He afterwards drags Hectors body after his Carr, let's all the Soldiers kick and insult it, This is no great mark of his generosity, particularly Hector having told him that in case he overcame he would give his Body Sepulchre; He after sells Hectors Body to Priam, which sordid Coveteousness compleats the 95 Character of a Person very far from Heroick Virtue. All these Defects Virgil has most Judiciously corrected in his Æneas.

Nestors Character shou'd be Wisdom but I see no very great marks of it, he tells Agamemnon that he wou'd give him Council, such as the greatest and Wisest Man never gave before, yet all this terminates in 100 his advising him to appease Achilles and oblige him to return to the Army. Phœnix likewise thô he is charged with a very important Commission from the Greeks, tells Storys of his own Adventures, and things done in the Nursery, that Achilles and every Man else must laugh at. This dos not Answer Horace's Character of Homer.   105

Lib: 10th: The Gods prove Men by difficultys, Our safety or our Death depend upon the point of our Sword, very well.

The guards that were awake and alert against the Trojans compared to the Dogs that watch lest the Lyon comes out of the Forrest upon the
Lib: 11th: Sheep. The Rainbow the mark of Jupiters might and Anger, all this is 110
10th: very well. But Diomedes having a mind to take Rhesus Chariot off
11th: upon his back. Agamemnon feeling pains from his wound like those of a Woman in Labour. Diomedes shot by Paris thro' the foot so that he is nail'd down to the Ground.

14th: Neptune crying as loud as ten thousand Men; Jupiter making Love 115
15th: very baudily to Juno, and then changing that Love with very great ill manners: are incidents very rediculous.

16th: From Agamemnons taking away Briseis, 'till this time, we hear
9th: nothing of her. Achilles has but Agamemnons bare word that She has

87 Lib: 2d:] *om. L 28*   89 Ibid 9th: *edd.*: ibid. 9. *L 28*: *om. W*   91 He *L 28*: he *W* 93 that in *L 28*: *Partially illeg. in W*   106 difficultys, *edd.*: difficultys *W*: Difficulties, *L 28*   108 and *L 28*: *Missing from W*   compared *L 28*: *Partially illeg. in W* 110 Sheep. *L 28*: Sheep *W*   111, 113 Diomedes] Diomede *L 28*   112 back. *L 28*: back *W*   114 Ground. *edd.*: Ground *W*, *L 28*   117 manners: *edd.*: manners. *W*: Manners *L 28*   rediculous. *L 28*: rediculous *W*

not been false to her Heroes bed, or if she had, the matter had not been 120 very great, for as I have observ'd Achilles did not lye alone in her absence.

Menelaus with Patroclus's body upon his back, must needs be a 17th: pleasant sight.

Achilles's reflection that Hercules did, and he must Dye, is very fine. 18th. So likewise is what Hector says to Polydamus that Mars favours one 126 as well as another and that the Victory is not always given to him who thought himself most sure of it. The Simile of the fire round Achilles's head like a thousand Flambeaux is horrible. Achilles deploring Patroclus like a Lyon robb'd of his Whelp, is fine. The Statues of Gold that fol- 130 low'd Vulcan and talk'd when Thetis came to see him, are very rediculous. The Discription of Achilles's Shield is very various, but silly. Virgil has made Sence of it.

Achilles is mightily in Pain about the flys that might light upon 19th: Patroclus's Body, and Thetis rubs it with Ambrosia to keep it a year 135 from corruption. This Idea of having our bodyes preserved after Death is very ancient.

Achilles, and afterwards Agamemnon lay the fault upon Jupiter, and fate, and the Furies, that they quarrell'd which gives no very just Idea of those powers. Ulysses' Wisdom terminates in persuading Achilles to 140 go to breakfast before he goes to Battel.

Achilles's Horse speaks to his Master, So did Balaams Ass and the Prophet and the Hero answer much alike.

Æneas to Achilles talks Nonsense when they shou'd fight, about the 20th swiftness of Ericthonious's Horses.   145

Hector runs thrice round Troy and Achilles after him.   22d:

Antilochus makes a long Speech to his Horses, and tells 'em that his 23d: Father shal sell 'em, or he'll cut their Throats if they dont do their Duty.

Priam comes out only accompanied by his Charioteer in the dark to 24th: go with his Presents to Achilles and the Grecian Camp, and is afraid 151

123 upon] on *L 28*   124 sight. *L 28* : *Missing from W*   125 did] Dyed *L 28*
136 This *L 28* : this *W*   137 ancient. *edd.* : ancient *W* : Ancient. *L 28*   139 fate,]
Fates *L 28*   141 Battel. *edd.* : Battel, *W* : Battle. *L 28*   142 Master, *L 28* :
Master *W*   143 alike. *L 28* : alike *W*   144 fight, *L 28* : fight *W*   146 runs]
un *L 28*   149 Duty. *L 28* : Duty *W*

of every thing he meets. This is far from the Dignity and Character of so great a King: And in the way he holds a foolish Discourse with Mercury, not knowing him, and asking him who he is.

The two great Basons at the Gate of Heav'n, One fill'd with pleasures 155 and Blessings, the t'other with ills and Sorrows that Jupiter never puts his hand into the first, without adding something of the second But very often takes out of the Second without adding any thing from the first, is as fine as any thing in Homer.

Throughout the whole Iliad, the Gods and Goddesses falling out, 160 calling Names, and Cuffing is extreamly rediculous. Homer ought very often to remember what he makes Apollo say very finely to Neptune 20th: that the Gods should not be concerned about Men, who are short liv'd as flowers.

I observed at the begining of my Letter that the whole Iliad 165 terminated with the Funeral of Hector, and the Greeks are just where they were as to the War at the begining of the book. Not to repeat that there is a great deal, which must happen between Hectors Death and the burning of the Town upon a Suppossition that Homer intended the Ruin of Troy for the Subject of the Iliad, And consequently that the 170 Poem is imperfect. On the other side, if you take it for granted that the Poet intended to omit these Incidents and finish with the great Stroak which is the Death of Hector, he should have ended in the 22d Iliad. The 23d contains only the Game celebrated upon Patroclus's Death, which Episode Virgil imitating has plac't more artfully in the middle 175 of his Æneis, And the 24th Iliad gives you Compassion for Hector upon the Trojans bewailing him, which you may very well suppose they did, but should have omitted the Discription of it, for it takes off from the grandeur of Homers Hero Achilles by giving you a concern for the Man he kill'd, and without the Death of whom it was impossible that 180 Troy should be Taken.

The length of the Iliad seems to be Comprehended in the Space of a Year, but I do not see very great art in that contrivance for, from Achilles reconcilliation with Agamemnon, and returning to Action till the Death of Hector, the whole might have been comprehended in a 185 Week.

---

153 Discourse *L 28*: *Missing from W*   164 flowers. *edd.*: flowers *W*: Flowers. *L 28*
170 Troy *L 28*: *Missing from W*

The Viceroy. A Ballad.

To the Tune of The Lady Isabella's Tragedy: Or: The Step-Mother's Cruelty.

I.

OF NERO, tyrant, petty king,
　　Who hertofore did reign
In fam'd Hibernia, I will sing,
　　And in a ditty plain.

II.

He hated was by rich and poor,　　　　　　5
　　For reasons you shall hear,
So ill he exercis'd his pow'r,
　　That he himself did fear.

III.

Full proud and arrogant was he,
　　And covetous withal,　　　　　　10
The guilty he would still set free,
　　But guiltless men enthral.

IV.

He with a haughty impious nod
　　Would curse and dogmatize,
Not fearing either man or God,　　　　　　15
　　Gold he did idolize.

V.

A patriot of high degree,
　　Who could no longer bear
This upstart Viceroy's tyranny,
　　Against him did declare.　　　　　　20

VI.

And arm'd with truth impeach'd the Don,
　　Of his enormous crimes,
Which I'll unfold to you anon,
　　In low, but faithful rimes.

VII.

The articles recorded stand,   25
   Against this peerless peer,
Search but the archives of the land,
   You'll find them written there.

VIII.

Attend, and justly I'll recite
   His treasons to you all,   30
The heads set in their native light,
   (And sigh poor GAPHNY's fall.)

IX.

That trait'rously he did abuse
   The pow'r in him repos'd,
And wickedly the same did use,   35
   On all mankind impos'd.

X.

That he, contrary to all law,
   An oath did frame and make,
Compelling the militia,
   Th' illegal oath to take.   40

XI.

Free-quarters for the army too,
   He did exact and force,
On Protestants, his love to show,
   Than Papists us'd them worse.

XII.

On all provisions destin'd for   45
   The camp at Limerick,
He laid a tax full hard and sore,
   Tho' many men were sick.

XIII.

The suttlers too he did ordain
   For licences should pay,   50
Which they refus'd with just disdain,
   And fled the camp away.

XIV.

By which provisions were so scant,
  That hundreds there did die,
The soldiers food and drink did want,   55
  Nor famine cou'd they fly.

XV.

He so much lov'd his private gain,
  He could nor hear or see,
They might, or die, or might complain,
  Without relief pardie.   60

XVI.

That above and against all right,
  By word of mouth did he,
In council sitting, hellish spite,
  The farmer's fate decree.

XVII.

That he, O! Ciel, without trial,   65
  Straitway shou'd hanged be,
Tho' then the courts were open all,
  Yet NERO judge wou'd be.

XVIII.

No sooner said, but it was done,
  The Borreau did his worst,   70
GAPHNY alas! is dead and gone,
  And left his judge accurst.

XIX.

In this concise, despotic way,
  Unhappy GAPHNY fell,
Which did all honest men affray,   75
  As truly it might well.

XX.

Full two good hundred pounds a year,
  This poor man's real estate,
He set'led on his fav'rite dear,
  And CULLIFORD can say't.   80

XXI.

Besides, he gave five hundred pound
  To FIELDING his own scribe,
Who was his bail, one friend he found,
  He ow'd him to the bribe.

XXII.

But for this horrid murder vile,   85
  None did him prosecute,
His old friend helpt him o'er the stile,
  With SATAN who'd dispute?

XXIII.

With France, fair England's mortal foe,
  A trade he carry'd on,   90
Had any other done't, I trow,
  To Tripos he had gone.

XXIV.

That he did likewise trait'rously,
  To bring his ends to bear,
Enrich himself most knavishly,   95
  O thief without compare.

XXV.

Vast quantities of stores did he
  Embezzel and purloin,
Of the King's stores he kept a key,
  Converting them to coin.   100

XXVI.

The forfeited estates also,
  Both real and personal,
Did with the stores together go,
  Fierce Cerb'rus swallow'd all.

XXVII.

Mean while the soldiers sigh'd and sobb'd,   105
  For not one souse had they,
His EXCELLENCE had each man fobb'd,
  For He had sunk their pay.

91 done't *edd.*: don't *1740*   107 EXCELLENCE *edd.*: EXCELLENCE' *1740*

XXVIII.

NERO, without the least disguise,
   The Papists at all times   110
Still favour'd, and their robberies
   Look'd on as trivial crimes.

XXIX.

The Protestants whom they did rob,
   During his government,
Were forc'd with patience, like good JOB,   115
   To rest themselves content.

XXX.

For he did basely them refuse
   All legal remedy,
The Romans he still well did use,
   Still screen'd their roguery.   120

XXXI.

Succinctly thus to you I've told,
   How this VICEROY did reign,
And other truths I shall unfold,
   For truth is always plain.

XXXII.

The best of QUEENS he hath revil'd,   125
   Before, and since her death,
He, cruel and ungrateful, smil'd
   When she resign'd her breath.

XXXIII.

Forgetful of the favours kind,
   She had on him bestow'd,   130
Like LUCIFER, his ranc'rous mind,
   He lov'd nor Her nor GOD.

XXXIV.

But listen NERO, lend thy ears,
   As still thou hast them on;
Hear what BRITANNIA says with tears,   135
   Of ANNA, dead and gone.

125 QUEENS *edd.*: QUEEN'S *1740*

XXXV.

"O! sacred be Her memory,
 "For ever dear Her name,
"There never was, or e'er can be,
 "A brighter, juster, DAME.   140

XXXVI.

"Blest be My SONS, and eke all those,
 "Who on Her praises dwell,
"She conquer'd Britain's fiercest foes,
 "She did all Queens excel.

XXXVII.

"All Princes, Kings, and Potentates,   145
 "Ambassadors did send,
"All nations, provinces, and states,
 "Sought ANNA for their friend.

XXXVIII.

"In ANNA They did all confide,
 "For ANNA They could trust,   150
"Her royal faith they all had try'd,
 "For ANNA still was just.

XXXIX.

"Truth, Mercy, Justice, did surround
 "Her awful judgment-seat,
"In Her the GRACES all were found,   155
 "In ANNA all compleat.

XL.

"She held the sword and ballance right,
 "And sought Her people's good,
"In clemency she did delight;
 "Her reign not stain'd with blood.   160

XLI.

"Her gracious goodness, piety
 "In all her deeds did shine,
"And bounteous was her charity,
 "All attributes divine.

XLII.

"Consummate wisdom, meekness all,   165
    "Adorn'd the words she spoke,
"When they from Her fair lips did fall,
    "And sweet her lovely look.

XLIII.

"Ten thousand glorious deeds to crown,
    "She caus'd dire war to cease,   170
"A greater Empress ne'er was known,
    "She fix'd the world in peace.

XLIV.

"This last and Godlike-act atchiev'd,
    "To Heav'n She wing'd Her flight,
"Her loss with tears all Europe griev'd,   175
    "Their strength, and dear delight.

XLV.

"Leave we in bliss this heav'nly SAINT,
    "Revere, ye just, Her urn,
"Her virtues high and excellent,
    "ASTREA gone we mourn.   180

XLVI.

"Commemorate my SONS the day,
    "Which gave great ANNA birth,
"Keep it for ever, and for aye,
    "And annual be your mirth."

XLVII.

Illustrious GEORGE now fills the throne,   185
    Our wise, benign, good king,
Who can his wond'rous deeds make known?
    Or his bright actions sing?

XLVIII.

Thee, fav'rite NERO, he has deign'd,
    To raise to high degree,   190
Well Thou thy honours hast sustain'd,
    Well voucht Thy ancestry.

178 Revere, ye just, *edd.*: Revere ye just *1740*

XLIX.

But pass—These honours on Thee laid,
  Can they e'er make thee white,
Don't GAPHNY's blood, which thou hast shed,   195
  Thy guilty soul affright?

L.

O! is there not, grim mortal tell,
  Places of bliss and wo?
O! is there not a Heav'n, a Hell?
  But whither wilt Thou go?   200

LI.

Can nought change thy obdurate mind?
  Wilt Thou for ever rail?
The prophet on Thee well refin'd,
  And set thy wit to sale.

LII.

How Thou art lost to sense and shame,   205
  Three countries witness be,
Thy conduct all just men do blame,
  Lib'ra nos Domine.

LIII.

Dame Justice waits Thee well I ween,
  Her sword is brandish'd high,   210
Nought can thee from Her vengeance screen,
  Nor can'st Thou from Her fly.

LIV.

Heavy Her ire will fall on THEE,
  The glitt'ring steel is sure,
Sooner or later, all agree,   215
  She cuts off the impure.

LV.

To Her I leave Thee, gloomy PEER,
  Think on Thy crimes committed,
Repent, and be for once sincere,
  Thou ne'er wilt be DE-WITTED.   220

1716

Cantata. Set by Monsieur Galliard.

RECIT.

Beneath a verdant Lawrel's ample Shade,
His Lyre to mournful Numbers strung,
Horace, immortal Bard, supinely laid,
To Venus thus address'd the Song:
    Ten thousand little Loves around   5
    List'ning, dwelt on ev'ry Sound.

ARIET.

Potent Venus, bid Thy Son
    Sound no more His dire Alarms.
Youth on silent Wings is flown:
    Graver Years come rolling on.   10
Spare my Age, unfit for Arms:
    Safe and Humble let Me rest,
    From all Am'rous Care releas'd.
Potent Venus, bid Thy Son
    Sound no more His dire Alarms.   15

RECIT.

Yet, Venus, why do I each Morn prepare
The fragrant Wreath for Cloe's Hair?
Why, why do I all Day lament, and sigh,
Unless the beauteous Maid be nigh?
And why all Night pursue Her in my Dreams,   20
Thro' Flow'ry Meads, and Crystal Streams?

RECIT.

Thus sung the Bard; and thus the Goddess spoke:
Submissive bow to Love's imperious Yoke.
    Ev'ry State, and ev'ry Age
    Shall own My Rule, and fear My Rage: 25

4 the] *his 1716*   7 *ARIET.*] Aria. *1716*   11 my Age,] *me now 1716*   16
Venus, why] *Why alass 1716*   17 Wreath] *Wreaths 1716*   18 all] *Each 1716*
22 *RECIT.*] *om. 1716*   25 and] *or 1716*

Compell'd by Me Thy Muse shall prove,
That all the World was born to love.

ARIET.

Bid Thy destin'd Lyre discover
   Soft Desire, and gentle Pain:
Often praise, and always love Her: 30
   Thro' her Ear her Heart obtain.
Verse shall please, and Sighs shall move Her:
   CUPID does with PHOEBUS reign.

Epigram.

WHILST I in Prison on a Court look down,
   Nor beg Thy Favor, nor deserve Thy frown;
In vain, malicious FORTUNE, hast Thou try'd
By taking from my State, to quell my Pride:
Insulting Girle, Thy present rage abate;   5
To keep Me humble, Thou must make me great.

1717

The Dove.

—Tantæne animis cælestibus Iræ ? Virg.

I.

IN VIRGIL'S Sacred Verse we find,
   That Passion can depress or raise
The Heav'nly, as the Human Mind:
   Who dare deny what VIRGIL says?

II.

But if They shou'd; what our Great Master   5
   Has thus laid down, my Tale shall prove.
Fair VENUS wept the sad Disaster
   Of having lost her Fav'rite DOVE.

28 *ARIET.*] Aria *1716*   31 Ear] *Ears 1716*
   Title: edd.: om. L *14*: TO FORTUNE. ANOTHER [EPIGRAM]. *1740*   6 To...
must] And would'st thou have me humble, *1740*
   Title] THE DOVE. A POEM. *1717*   *Motto:* Iræ?] Iræ. *1717*   4 dare] dares *1717*

III.

In Complaisance poor CUPID mourn'd;
 His Grief reliev'd his Mother's Pain;   10
He vow'd he'd leave no Stone unturn'd,
 But She shou'd have her DOVE again.

IV.

Tho' None, said He, shall yet be nam'd,
 I know the Felon well enough:
But be She not, Mamma, condemn'd   15
 Without a fair and legal Proof.

V.

With that, his longest Dart he took,
 As Constable wou'd take his Staff:
That Gods desire like Men to look,
 Wou'd make ev'n HERACLITUS laugh.   20

VI.

LOVES Subaltern, a Duteous Band,
 Like Watchmen round their Chief appear:
Each had his Lanthorn in his Hand:
 And VENUS mask'd brought up the Rear.

VII.

Accouter'd thus, their eager Step   25
 To CLOE's Lodging They directed:
(At once I write, alas! and weep,
 That CLOE is of Theft suspected.)

VIII.

Late They set out, had far to go:
 St. DUNSTAN's, as They pass'd, struck One.   30
CLOE, for Reasons good, You know,
 Lives at the sober End o'th' Town.

IX.

With one great Peal They rap the Door,
 Like Footmen on a Visiting-Day.
Folks at Her House at such an Hour!   35
 Lord! what will all the Neighbours say?

21 LOVES Subaltern] Subaltern Loves *1717*

X.

The Door is open'd: up They run:
　　Nor Prayers, nor Threats divert their Speed:
Thieves, Thieves! cries SUSAN; We're undone;
　　They'll kill my Mistress in her Bed.   40

XI.

In Bed indeed the Nymph had been
　　Three Hours: for all Historians say,
She commonly went up at Ten,
　　Unless *Picquet* was in the Way.

XII.

She wak'd, be sure, with strange Surprize.   45
　　O CUPID, is this Right or Law,
Thus to disturb the brightest Eyes,
　　That ever slept, or ever saw?

XIII.

Have You observ'd a sitting Hare,
　　List'ning, and fearful of the Storm   50
Of Horns and Hounds, clap back her Ear,
　　Afraid to keep, or leave her Form?

XIV.

Or have You mark'd a Partridge quake,
　　Viewing the tow'ring Faulcon nigh?
She cuddles low behind the Brake: 55
　　Nor wou'd she stay: nor dares she fly.

XV.

Then have You seen the Beauteous Maid;
　　When gazing on her Midnight Foes,
She turn'd each Way her frighted Head,
　　Then sunk it deap beneath the Cloaths.   60

XVI.

VENUS this while was in the Chamber
　　Incognito: for SUSAN said,
It smelt so strong of Myrrh and Amber—
　　And SUSAN is no lying Maid.

39 We're] w'are *1717*

XVII.

But since We have no present Need   65
    Of Venus for an Episode;
With Cupid let us e'en proceed;
    And thus to Cloe spoke the God:

XVIII.

Hold up your Head: hold up your Hand:
    Wou'd it were not my Lot to show ye   70
This cruel *Writ*, wherein you stand
    Indicted by the Name of Cloe:

XIX.

For that by secret Malice stirr'd,
    Or by an emulous Pride invited,
You have purloin'd the fav'rite Bird,   75
    In which my Mother most delighted.

XX.

Her blushing Face the lovely Maid
    Rais'd just above the milk-white Sheet.
A Rose-Tree in a Lilly Bed,
    Nor glows so red, nor breathes so sweet.   80

XXI.

Are You not He whom Virgins fear,
    And Widows court? Is not your Name
Cupid? If so, pray come not near—
    Fair Maiden, I'm the very same.

XXII.

Then what have I, good Sir, to say,   85
    Or do with Her, You call your Mother?
If I shou'd meet Her in my Way,
    We hardly court'sy to each other.

XXIII.

Diana Chaste, and Hebe Sweet,
    Witness that what I speak is true: 90
I wou'd not give my Paroquet
    For all the Doves that ever flew.

XXIV.

Yet, to compose this Midnight Noise,
     Go freely search where-e'er you please:
(The Rage that rais'd, adorn'd Her Voice)   95
     Upon yon' Toilet lie my Keys.

XXV.

Her Keys He takes; her Doors unlocks;
     Thro' Wardrobe, and thro' Closet bounces;
Peeps into ev'ry Chest and Box;
     Turns all her Furbeloes and Flounces.   100

XXVI.

But DOVE, depend on't, finds He none;
     So to the Bed returns again:
And now the Maiden, bolder grown,
     Begins to treat Him with Disdain.

XXVII.

I marvel much, She smiling said,   105
     Your Poultry cannot yet be found:
Lies he in yonder Slipper dead,
     Or, may be, in the Tea-pot drown'd?

XXVIII.

No, Traytor, angry Love replies,
     He's hid somewhere about Your Breast;   110
A Place, nor God, nor Man denies,
     For VENUS' DOVE the proper Nest.

XXIX.

Search then, She said, put in your Hand,
     And CYNTHIA, dear Protectress, guard Me:
As guilty I, or free may stand,   115
     Do Thou, or punish, or reward Me.

XXX.

But ah! what Maid to Love can trust?
     He scorns, and breaks all Legal Power:
Into her Breast his Hand He thrust;
     And in a Moment forc'd it lower.   120

117 ah!] O, *1717*

XXXI.

O, whither do those Fingers rove,
    Cries CLOE, treacherous Urchin, whither?
O VENUS! I shall find thy DOVE,
    Says He; for sure I touch his Feather.

Epistles.

I PRAY, good Lord Harley, let Jonathan know
    How long you intend to live Incognito
                Your humble Servant
            ELKINAH SETTLE.

I pray Lady Harriett, the time to assigne   5
When She shall receive a Turkey and Chine
That a Body may come to St James's to Dine.
                    Idem.

Epilogue to Lucius.

Spoken by Mrs. Horton.

THE Female Author who recites to Day,
    Trusts to her Sex the Merit of her Play.
Like Father BAYES securely She sits down:
Pitt, Box and Gallery, Gad! All's our Own.
In antient GREECE, She says, when SAPPHO writ,   5
By their Applause the Critics show'd their Wit.
They tun'd their Voices to her LYRIC String;
Tho' they cou'd All do something more, than Sing.
But one Exception to this Fact we find;
That Booby PHAON only was unkind,   10
An ill-bred Boat-man, rough as Waves and Wind.
From SAPPHO down thro' all succeeding Ages,
And now on FRENCH, or on ITALIAN Stages,

124 for...his] I'm...the *1717*
   Title: edd.: om. Harl
   Title: to Lucius] om. 1717

Rough Satyrs, sly Remarks, ill-natur'd Speeches,
Are always aim'd at Poets, that wear Breeches.   15
Arm'd with LONGINUS, or with RAPIN, No Man
Drew a sharp Pen upon a Naked Woman.
The blust'ring Bully in our neighb'ring Streets,
Scorns to attack the Female that He meets:
Fearless the Petticoat contemns his Frowns: 20
The Hoop secures, whatever it surrounds.
The many-color'd Gentry there above,
By turns are rul'd by Tumult, and by Love:
And while their Sweet-hearts their Attention fix,
Suspend the Din of their damn'd clatt'ring Sticks.   25
Now Sirs—
To You our Author makes Her soft Request,
Who speak the kindest, and who write the best.
Your *Sympathetic* Hearts She hopes to move,
From tender Friendship, and endearing Love.   30
If PETRARCH's Muse did LAURA's Wit rehearse,
And COWLEY flatter'd dear ORINDA's Verse;
She hopes from You—Pox take her Hopes and Fears;
I plead her Sexe's Claim: what matters Hers?
By Our full Pow'r of Beauty We think fit,   35
To damn this *Salique* Law impos'd on Wit:
We'll try the Empire You so long have boasted;
And if We are not Prais'd, We'll not be Toasted.
Approve what One of us presents to Night;
Or ev'ry Mortal Woman here shall write: 40
Rural, Pathetic, Narrative, Sublime,   ⎫
We'll write to You, and make You write in Rhime: ⎬
Female Remarks shall take up all Your Time.   ⎭
Your Time, poor Souls! we'll take your very Money;
Female Third Days shall come so thick upon Ye.   45
As long as We have Eyes, or Hands, or Breath,
We'll Look, or Write, or Talk You All to Death.
Unless Ye yield for Better and for Worse: ⎫
Then the She-PEGASUS shall gain the Course;   ⎬
And the Grey Mare will prove the better Horse.   ⎭ 50

            24 while] whilst *1717*   45 Ye] you *1717*

To my Lord.

PEN, Ink and Wax and paper send
   To the kind Wife, the lovely Friend.
Smiling bid Her freely write
What Her happy Thoughts indite
Of Virtue, Goodness, Peace and Love,   5
Thoughts which Angells may approve.

Engraven on a Column in the Church of Halstead in Essex.

Samuel Fiske
By descent a Gentleman
By profession an Apothecary
In his practice
Honest, knowing, successfull.   5
In his life
Just, pious, charitable.
The Riches he acquired He used
Only as the means of doing Good.
A friend to the public, a father to   10
the poor, a great benefactor to this Town
of Halstead.
More particularly
The Spire of this Church burnt down
by lightning He rebuilt   15
at His own Expence
Anno. 1717.

VIEW not this Spire by Measure giv'n
   To Buildings rais'd by common Hands:
That Fabric rises high as Heav'n,   20
   Whose *Basis* on Devotion stands.

Title] *Lpo 18, Harl* To My Lord Harley Extempore, *An Epigram. L 27*: To My Lord
Harley Ex Tempore. *Wel, L 28, 1740*   2 Friend. *L 28*: Friend *L 29, Wel, Lpo 18, Harl*:
Friend, *L 27*: FRIEND; *1740*   6 *In 1740, this is followed by:* M.P.
   Title: Engraven...Essex. edd.: Engraven...ESSEX, *1718: om. L 29, Mem*   1–17 *Re-
placed in 1718 by this sub-title: The Spire of which, burnt down by Lightning, was rebuilt at the
Expense of Mr.* SAMUEL FISKE, *1717.*   5 Honest, *Mem*: Honest *L 29*   7] Pious,
just and charitable *Mem*   9 Only] *om. Mem*

While yet We draw this vital Breath,
  We can our FAITH and HOPE declare:
But CHARITY beyond our Death,
  Will ever in our Works appear.   25

Best be He call'd among good Men,
  Who to his GOD this Column rais'd:
Tho' Lightning strike the Dome again;
  The Man, who built it, shall be prais'd.

Yet Spires and Towers in Dust shall lye,   30
  The weak Efforts of Human Pains:
And FAITH, and HOPE themselves shall dye;
  While Deathless CHARITY remains.

1718

Postscript.

I MUST *help my Preface by a Postscript, to tell the Reader, that there is Ten Years Distance between my writing the One and the Other; and that (whatever I thought then, and have somewhere said, that I would publish no more Poetry) He will find several Copies of Verses scattered through this Edition, which were not printed in the First. Those relating to the Publick stand in the* 5 *Order They did before, and according to the several Years, in which They were written; however the Disposition of our National Affairs, the Actions, or the Fortunes of some Men, and the Opinions of others may have changed. Prose, and other Human Things may take what Turn they can; but Poetry, which pretends to have something of Divinity in it, is to be more permanent. Odes once printed* 10 *cannot well be altered, when the Author has already said, that He expects His Works should Live for Ever. And it had been very foolish in my Friend* HORACE, *if some Years after His* Exegi Monumentum, *He should have desired to see his Building taken down again.*

  The Dedication *likewise is Reprinted to the Earl of* DORSET, *in the fore-* 15 *going Leaves, without any Alteration; though I had the fairest Opportunity, and the strongest Inclination to have added a great deal to it. The blooming Hopes, which I said the World expected from my then very Young Patron, have been confirmed by most Noble and distinguished First-Fruits; and His Life is going on*

22–25] *Mem   del. L 29*   30 Yet] *Mem* But *L 29*   31 Efforts] *Mem* effects *L 29*

towards a plentiful Harvest of all accumulated Virtues. He has, in Fact, ex- 20
ceeded whatever the Fondness of my Wishes could invent in His Favor: His equally
Good and Beautiful Lady enjoys in Him an Indulgent and Obliging Husband;
His Children, a Kind and Careful Father; and His Acquaintance, a Faithful,
Generous, and Polite Friend. His Fellow-Peers have attended to the Perswasion
of His Eloquence; and have been convinced by the Solidity of His Reasoning. He 25
has, long since, deserved and attained the Honor of the Garter. He has managed
some of the greatest Charges of the Kingdom with known Ability; and laid them
down with entire Disinteressment. And as He continues the Exercises of these
eminent Virtues (which that He may do to a very old Age, shall be my perpetual
Wish) He may be One of the Greatest Men that our Age, or possibly our Nation 30
has bred; and leave Materials for a Panegyric, not unworthy the Pen of some
future PLINY.

From so Noble a Subject as the Earl of DORSET, *to so mean a one as my self,*
is (I confess) a very Pindaric Transition. I shall only say one Word, and trouble
the Reader no further. I published my Poems formerly, as Monsieur JOURDAIN 35
sold his Silk: He would not be thought a Tradesman; but ordered some Pieces to
be measured out to his particular Friends. Now I give up my Shop, and dispose of
all my Poetical Goods at once: I must therefore desire, that the Public would
please to take them in the Gross; and that every Body would turn over what He
does not like. 40

A Lover's Anger.

As CLOE came into the Room t'other Day,
I peevish began; Where so long cou'd You stay?
In your Life-time You never regarded your Hour:
You promis'd at Two; and (pray look Child) 'tis Four.
A Lady's Watch needs neither Figures nor Wheels: 5
'Tis enough, that 'tis loaded with Baubles and Seals.
A Temper so heedless no Mortal can bear—
Thus far I went on with a resolute Air.
Lord bless Me! said She; let a Body but speak:
Here's an ugly hard Rose-Bud fall'n into my Neck: 10
It has hurt Me, and vext Me to such a Degree—
See here; for You never believe Me; pray see,
On the left Side my Breast what a Mark it has made.
So saying, her Bosom She careless display'd.
That Seat of Delight I with Wonder survey'd; 15
And forgot ev'ry Word I design'd to have said.

Mercury and Cupid.

IN sullen Humour one Day JOVE
Sent HERMES down to IDA's Grove,
Commanding CUPID to deliver
His Store of Darts, his total Quiver;
That HERMES shou'd the Weapons break,   5
Or throw 'em into LETHE's Lake.

HERMES, You know, must do his Errand:
He found his Man, produc'd his Warrant:
CUPID, your Darts—this very Hour—
There's no contending against Power.   10

How sullen JUPITER, just now
I think I said: and You'll allow,
That CUPID was as bad as He:
Hear but the Youngster's Repartée.

Come Kinsman (said the little God)   15
Put off your Wings; lay by your Rod;
Retire with Me to yonder Bower;
And rest your self for half an Hour:
'Tis far indeed from hence to Heav'n:
And You fly fast: and 'tis but Seven.   20
We'll take one cooling Cup of Nectar;
And drink to this Celestial Hector—

He break my Darts, or hurt my Pow'r!
He, LEDA's Swan, and DANAE's Show'r!
Go, bid him his Wife's Tongue restrain;   25
And mind his Thunder, and his Rain.—
My Darts? O certainly I'll give 'em:
From CLOE's Eyes He shall receive 'em.
There's One, the Best in all my Quiver,
Twang! thro' his very Heart and Liver.   30
He then shall Pine, and Sigh, and Rave:
Good Lord! what Bustle shall We have!
NEPTUNE must straight be sent to Sea;
And FLORA summon'd twice a-day:

6 LETHE's edd.: LETHE' 1718: LETHE Reset sheet in 1718

One must find Shells, and t'other Flow'rs,   35
For cooling Grotts, and fragrant Bow'rs,
That CLOE may be serv'd in State:
The HOURS must at Her Toilet wait:
Whilst all the reasoning Fools below,
Wonder their Watches go too slow.   40
LYBS must fly South, and EURUS East,
For Jewels for Her Hair and Breast:
No Matter tho' their cruel Haste
Sink Cities, and lay Forrests waste.
No Matter tho' This Fleet be lost;   45
Or That lie wind-bound on the Coast.
What whis'pring in my Mother's Ear!
What Care, that JUNO shou'd not hear!
What Work among You Scholar Gods!
PHOEBUS must write Him am'rous Odes: 50
And Thou, poor Cousin, must compose
His Letters in submissive Prose:
Whilst haughty CLOE, to sustain
The Honour of My mystic Reign,
Shall all his Gifts and Vows disdain;   55
And laugh at your Old Bully's Pain.

    Dear Couz, said HERMES in a Fright,
For Heav'n sake keep Your Darts: Good Night.

Her Right Name.

As NANCY at Her Toylet sat,
Admiring This, and blaming That;
Tell Me, She said; but tell Me true;
The Nymph who cou'd your Heart subdue,
What Sort of Charms does She possess?   5
Absolve Me Fair One: I'll confess;
With Pleasure I reply'd. Her Hair,
In Ringlets rather dark than fair,
Does down her Iv'ry Bosom roll,
And hiding Half, adorns the Whole.   10
In her high Forehead's fair half-round
LOVE sits in open Triumph crown'd:

He in the Dimple of her Chin,
In private State by Friends is seen.
Her Eyes are neither black, nor grey;   15
Nor fierce, nor feeble is their Ray:
Their dubious Lustre seems to show
Something that speaks nor Yes, nor No.
Her Lips no living Bard, I weet,
May say, how Red, how Round, how Sweet: 20
Old HOMER only cou'd indite
Their vagrant Grace, and soft Delight:
They stand Recorded in his Book,
When HELEN smil'd, and HEBE spoke—
The Gipsy turning to her Glass,   25
Too plainly show'd, She knew the Face:
And which am I most like, She said,
Your CLOE, or Your *Nut-brown Maid*?

On Beauty.
A Riddle.

RESOLVE Me, CLOE, what is THIS:
Or forfeit me One precious Kiss.
'Tis the first Off-spring of the Graces;
Bears diff'rent Forms in diff'rent Places;
Acknowledg'd fine, where-e'er beheld;   5
Yet fancy'd finer, when conceal'd.
'Twas FLORA's Wealth, and CIRCE's Charm;
PANDORA's Box of Good and Harm:
'Twas MARS's Wish, ENDYMION's Dream;
APELLES' Draught, and OVID's Theme.   10
THIS guided THESEUS thro' the Maze;
And sent Him home with Life and Praise.
But THIS undid the PHRYGIAN Boy;
And blew the Flames that ruin'd TROY.
THIS shew'd great Kindness to old GREECE,   15
And help'd rich JASON to the FLEECE.
THIS thro' the East just Vengeance hurl'd,
And lost poor ANTHONY the World.

Injur'd, tho' LUCRECE found her Doom;
THIS banish'd Tyranny from ROME.   20
Appeas'd, tho' LAIS gain'd her Hire;
THIS set PERSEPOLIS on Fire.
For THIS ALCIDES learn'd to Spin;
His Club laid down, and Lion's Skin.
For THIS APOLLO deign'd to keep,   25
With servile Care, a Mortal's Sheep.
For THIS the Father of the Gods,
Content to leave His high Abodes,
In borrow'd Figures loosely ran,
EUROPA's Bull, and LEDA's Swan.   30
For THIS He reassumes the Nod;
(While SEMELE commands the God)
Launces the Bolt, and shakes the Poles;
Tho' MOMUS laughs, and JUNO scolds.

    Here list'ning CLOE smil'd, and said;   35
Your Riddle is not hard to read:
I Guess it—Fair one, if You do;
Need I, alas! the Theme pursue?
For THIS, Thou see'st, for THIS I leave,
Whate'er the World thinks Wise or Grave,   40
Ambition, Business, Friendship, News,
My useful Books, and serious Muse.
For THIS I willingly decline
The Mirth of Feasts, and Joys of Wine;
And chuse to sit and talk with Thee,   45
(As Thy great Orders may decree)
Of Cocks and Bulls, of Flutes and Fiddles,
Of Idle Tales, and foolish Riddles.

The Question, to Lisetta.

WHAT Nymph shou'd I admire, or trust,
    But CLOE Beauteous, CLOE Just?
What Nymph shou'd I desire to see,
But Her who leaves the Plain for Me?
To Whom shou'd I compose the Lay,
But Her who listens, when I play?

To Whom in Song repeat my Cares,
But Her who in my Sorrow shares?
For Whom shou'd I the Garland make,
But Her who joys the Gift to take,   10
And boasts She wears it for My Sake?
In Love am I not fully blest?
LISETTA, pr'ythee tell the rest.

Lisetta's Reply.

SURE CLOE Just, and CLOE Fair
   Deserves to be Your only Care:
But when You and She to Day
Far into the Wood did stray,
And I happen'd to pass by;   5
Which way did You cast your Eye?
But when your Cares to Her You sing,
Yet dare not tell Her whence they spring;
Does it not more afflict your Heart,
That in those Cares She bears a Part?   10
When You the Flow'rs for CLOE twine,
Why do You to Her Garland join
The meanest Bud that falls from Mine?
Simplest of Swains! the World may see,
Whom CLOE loves, and Who loves Me.   15

The Garland.

I.

THE Pride of ev'ry Grove I chose,
   The Violet sweet, and Lilly fair,
The dappl'd Pink, and blushing Rose,
   To deck my charming CLOE's Hair.

II.

At Morn the Nymph vouchsaft to place   5
   Upon her Brow the various Wreath;
The Flow'rs less blooming than Her Face,
   The Scent less fragrant than Her Breath.

III.

The Flow'rs She wore along the Day:
   And ev'ry Nymph and Shepherd said,   10
That in her Hair they lookt more gay,
   Than glowing in their Native Bed.

IV.

Undrest at Evening, when She found
   Their Odours lost, their Colours past;
She chang'd her Look, and on the Ground   15
   Her Garland and her Eye She cast.

V.

That Eye dropt Sense distinct and clear,
   As any MUSE's Tongue cou'd speak;
When from it's Lid a pearly Tear
   Ran trickling down her beauteous Cheek.   20

VI.

Dissembling, what I knew too well,
   My Love, my Life, said I, explain
This Change of Humour: pr'ythee tell:
   That falling Tear—What does it mean?

VII.

She sigh'd; She smil'd: and to the Flow'rs   25
   Pointing, the Lovely Moralist said:
See! Friend, in some few fleeting Hours,
   See yonder, what a Change is made.

VIII.

Ah Me! the blooming Pride of MAY,
   And That of Beauty are but One: 30
At Morn Both flourish bright and gay,
   Both fade at Evening, pale, and gone.

IX.

At Dawn poor STELLA danc'd and sung;
   The am'rous Youth around Her bow'd:
At Night her fatal Knell was rung;   35
   I saw, and kiss'd Her in her Shrowd.

X.

Such as She is, who dy'd to Day;
    Such I, alas! may be to Morrow:
Go, DAMON, bid Thy Muse display
    The Justice of thy CLOE's Sorrow.   40

The Lady who offers her Looking-Glass to Venus.

VENUS, take my Votive Glass:
    Since I am not what I was;
What from this Day I shall be,
VENUS, let Me never see.

Cloe Jealous.

I.

FORBEAR to ask Me, why I weep;
    Vext CLOE to her Shepherd said:
'Tis for my Two poor stragling Sheep
    Perhaps, or for my Squirrel dead.

II.

For mind I what You late have writ?   5
    Your subtle Questions, and Replies;
Emblems, to teach a Female Wit
    The Ways, where changing CUPID flies.

III.

Your Riddle, purpos'd to rehearse
    The general Pow'r that Beauty has: 10
But why did no peculiar Verse
    Describe one Charm of CLOE's Face?

IV.

The Glass, which was at VENUS' Shrine,
    With such Mysterious Sorrow laid:
The Garland (and You call it Mine)   15
    Which show'd how Youth and Beauty fade.

V.

Ten thousand Trifles light as These
  Nor can my Rage, nor Anger move:
She shou'd be humble, who wou'd please:
  And She must suffer, who can love.   20

VI.

When in My Glass I chanc'd to look;
  Of VENUS what did I implore?
That ev'ry Grace which thence I took,
  Shou'd know to charm my DAMON more.

VII.

Reading Thy Verse; who heeds, said I,   25
  If here or there his Glances flew?
O free for ever be His Eye,
  Whose Heart to Me is always true.

VIII.

My Bloom indeed, my little Flow'r
  Of Beauty quickly lost it's Pride: 30
For sever'd from it's Native Bow'r,
  It on Thy glowing Bosom dy'd.

IX.

Yet car'd I not, what might presage
  Or withering Wreath, or fleeting Youth:
Love I esteem'd more strong than Age,   35
  And Time less permanent than Truth.

X.

Why then I weep, forbear to know:
  Fall uncontroll'd my Tears, and free:
O DAMON, 'tis the only Woe,
  I ever yet conceal'd from Thee.   40

XI.

The secret Wound with which I bleed
  Shall lie wrapt up, ev'n in my Herse:
But on my Tomb-stone Thou shalt read
  My Answer to Thy dubious Verse.

41 XI. *Reset sheet in 1718* : XII. *1718*

Answer to Cloe Jealous, in the same Stile.
The Author sick.

I.

YES, fairest Proof of Beauty's Pow'r,
  Dear Idol of My panting Heart,
Nature points This my fatal Hour:
  And I have liv'd; and We must part.

II.

While now I take my last Adieu,
  Heave Thou no Sigh, nor shed a Tear;
Lest yet my half-clos'd Eye may view
  On Earth an Object worth it's Care.

III.

From Jealousy's tormenting Strife
  For ever be Thy Bosom free'd:
That nothing may disturb Thy Life,
  Content I hasten to the Dead.

IV.

Yet when some better-fated Youth
  Shall with his am'rous Parly move Thee;
Reflect One Moment on His Truth,
  Who dying Thus, persists to love Thee.

A Better Answer.

I.

DEAR CLOE, how blubber'd is that pretty Face?
  Thy Cheek all on Fire, and Thy Hair all uncurl'd:
Pr'ythee quit this Caprice; and (as Old FALSTAF says)
  Let Us e'en talk a little like Folks of This World.

II.

How can'st Thou presume, Thou hast leave to destroy
  The Beauties, which VENUS but lent to Thy keeping?
Those Looks were design'd to inspire Love and Joy:
  More ord'nary Eyes may serve People for weeping.

III.

To be vext at a Trifle or two that I writ,
  Your Judgment at once, and my Passion You wrong: 10
You take that for Fact, which will scarce be found Wit:
  Od's Life! must One swear to the Truth of a Song?

IV.

What I speak, my fair CLOE, and what I write, shews
  The Diff'rence there is betwixt Nature and Art:
I court others in Verse; but I love Thee in Prose: 15
  And They have my Whimsies; but Thou hast my Heart.

V.

The God of us Verse-men (You know Child) the SUN,
  How after his Journeys He sets up his Rest:
If at Morning o'er Earth 'tis his Fancy to run;
  At Night he reclines on his THETIS's Breast.   20

VI.

So when I am weary'd with wand'ring all Day;
  To Thee my Delight in the Evening I come:
No Matter what Beauties I saw in my Way:
  They were but my Visits; but Thou art my Home.

VII.

Then finish, Dear CLOE, this Pastoral War;   25
  And let us like HORACE and LYDIA agree:
For Thou art a Girl as much brighter than Her,
  As He was a Poet sublimer than Me.

A Passage in the Moriæ Encomium of Erasmus Imitated.

IN awful Pomp, and Melancholy State,
See settl'd REASON on the Judgment Seat:
Around Her croud DISTRUST, and DOUBT, and FEAR,
And thoughtful FORESIGHT, and tormenting CARE:
Far from the Throne, the trembling PLEASURES stand,   5
Chain'd up, or Exil'd by her stern Command.

Wretched her Subjects, gloomy sits the Queen;
'Till happy CHANCE reverts the cruel Scene:
And apish FOLLY with her wild Resort
Of Wit and Jest disturbs the solemn Court.   10

   See the fantastic Minstrelsy advance,
To breathe the Song, and animate the Dance.
Blest the Usurper! happy the Surprize!
Her Mimic Postures catch our eager Eyes:
Her Jingling Bells affect our captive Ear: 15
And in the Sights We see, and Sounds We hear,
Against our Judgment She our Sense employs:
The Laws of troubl'd REASON She destroys:
And in Their Place rejoyces to indite
Wild Schemes of Mirth, and Plans of loose Delight.   20

Merry Andrew.

S LY MERRY ANDREW, the last *Southwark* Fair
  (At *Barthol'mew* He did not much appear;
So peevish was the Edict of the May'r.)
At *Southwark*, therefore, as his Tricks He show'd,
To please our Masters, and his Friends, the Croud;   5
A huge Neats-Tongue He in his Right Hand held:
His Left was with a good Black-Pudding fill'd.
With a grave Look, in this odd Equipage,
The clownish Mimic traverses the Stage:
Why how now, ANDREW! cries his Brother Droll,   10
To Day's Conceit, methinks, is something dull:
Come on, Sir, to our worthy Friends explain,
What does Your Emblematic Worship mean?
Quoth ANDREW; Honest English let Us speak:
Your Emble— (what d'ye call't?) is Heathen Greek.   15
To Tongue or Pudding, Thou hast no Pretence:
Learning Thy Talent is; but Mine is Sense.
That busie Fool I was, which Thou art now;
Desirous to Correct, not knowing how;
With very good Design, but little Wit,   20
Blaming or Praising Things, as I thought fit.

I for this Conduct had what I deserv'd;
And dealing honestly, was almost starv'd.
But Thanks to my indulgent Stars, I Eat;
Since I have found the Secret to be Great.   25
O dearest ANDREW, says the humble Droll,
Henceforth may I Obey, and Thou Controll;
Provided Thou impart Thy useful Skill.
Bow then, says ANDREW; and, for once, I will.
Be of your Patron's Mind, whate'er He says;   30
Sleep very much; Think little; and Talk less:
Mind neither Good nor Bad, nor Right nor Wrong;
But Eat your Pudding, Slave; and Hold your Tongue.

     A Rev'rend Prelate stopt his Coach and Six,
To laugh a little at our ANDREW's Tricks.   35
But when He heard him give this Golden Rule;
Drive on; (He cry'd,) This Fellow is no Fool.

The Flies.

SAY, Sire of Insects, mighty SOL,
  (A Fly upon the Chariot-Pole
Cries out:) what Blew-Bottle alive
Did ever with such Fury drive?
Tell, BELZEBUB, Great Father, tell,   5
(Says t'other, perch'd upon the Wheel:)
Did ever any Mortal Fly
Raise such a Cloud of Dust, as I?

     My Judgement Turn'd the whole Debate:
My Valor Sav'd the sinking State.   10
So talk two Idle buzzing Things;
Toss up their Heads, and stretch their Wings.
But let the Truth to Light be brought:
This neither Spoke, nor t'other Fought:
No Merit in their own Behav'or: 15
Both rais'd, but by their Party's Favor.

From the Greek.

GREAT BACCHUS, born in Thunder and in Fire,
By Native Heat asserts His dreadful Sire.
Nourish'd near shady Rills and cooling Streams,
He to the Nymphs avows his Am'rous Flames.
To all the Breth'ren at the *Bell* and *Vine*,   5
The Moral says; Mix Water with your Wine.

Epigram.

FRANK Carves very ill, yet will palm all the Meats:
He Eats more than Six; and Drinks more than he Eats.
Four Pipes after Dinner he constantly smokes;
And seasons his Whifs with impertinent Jokes.
Yet sighing, he says, We must certainly break;   5
And my cruel Unkindness compells him to speak:
For of late I invite Him—but Four Times a Week.

Another.

TO JOHN I ow'd great Obligation;
But JOHN, unhappily, thought fit
To publish it to all the Nation:
Sure JOHN and I are more than Quit.

Another.

YES, every Poet is a Fool:
By Demonstration NED can show it:
Happy, cou'd NED's inverted Rule
Prove every Fool to be a Poet.

Another.

THY Naggs (the leanest Things alive)
So very hard Thou lov'st to drive;
I heard thy anxious Coach-man say,
It costs Thee more in Whips, than Hay.

Quid sit futurum Cras fuge quærere.

FOR what To-morrow shall disclose,
 May spoil what You To-night propose:
ENGLAND may change; or CLOE stray:
Love and Life are for To-day.

Written in an Ovid.

OVID is the surest Guide,
 You can name, to show the Way
To any Woman, Maid, or Bride,
 Who resolves to go astray.

A True Maid.

NO, no; for my Virginity,
 When I lose that, says ROSE, I'll dye:
Behind the Elmes, last Night, cry'd DICK,
ROSE, were You not extreamly Sick?

Another.

TEN Months after FLORIMEL happen'd to wed,
 And was brought in a laudable Manner to Bed;
She warbl'd Her Groans with so charming a Voice,
That one half of the Parish was stun'd with the Noise.
But when FLORIMEL deign'd to lie privately in,   5
Ten Months before She and her Spouse were a-kin;
She chose with such Prudence her Pangs to conceal,
That her Nurse, nay her Midwife, scarce heard her once squeal.
Learn, Husbands, from hence, for the Peace of your Lives,
That Maids make not half such a Tumult, as Wives.   10

Written in an Ovid. 4 Who] That *W*
A True Maid. Title] om. *W*

A Reasonable Affliction.

ON His Death-Bed poor LUBIN lies:
  His Spouse is in Despair:
With frequent Sobs, and mutual Cries,
  They Both express their Care.

A diff'rent Cause, says Parson SLY,
  The same Effect may give:
Poor LUBIN fears, that He shall Die;
  His Wife, that He may Live.

5

Another Reasonable Affliction.

FROM her own Native FRANCE as old ALISON past,
  She reproach'd *English* NELL with Neglect or with Malice,
That the Slattern had left, in the Hurry and Hast,
Her Lady's Complexion, and Eye-brows at CALAIS.

Another.

HER Eye-brow-Box one Morning lost,
  (The best of Folks are oft'nest crost)
Sad HELEN thus to JENNY said,
Her careless but afflicted Maid;
Put me to Bed then, wretched JANE:
Alas! when shall I rise again?
I can behold no Mortal now:
For what's an Eye without a Brow?

5

On the same Subject.

IN a dark Corner of the House,
  Poor HELEN sits, and sobs and cries:
She will not see her Loving Spouse,
  Nor her more dear *Picquet*-Allies:
    Unless She finds her Eye-brows,
    She'll e'en weep out her Eyes.

5

On the Same.

HELEN was just slipt into Bed:
　　Her Eye-brows on the Toilet lay:
　　Away the Kitten with them fled,
As Fees belonging to her Prey.

For this Misfortune careless JANE,　　　　5
Assure your self, was loudly rated:
　　And Madam getting up again,
With her own Hand the Mouse-Trap baited.

On little Things, as Sages write,
Depends our Human Joy, or Sorrow:　　　10
　　If We don't catch a Mouse To-night,
Alas! no Eye-brows for To-morrow.

Phyllis's Age.

HOW old may PHYLLIS be, You ask,
　　Whose Beauty thus all Hearts engages?
To Answer is no easie Task;
　　For She has really two Ages.

Stiff in Brocard, and pinch'd in Stays,　　5
　　Her Patches, Paint, and Jewels on;
All Day let Envy view her Face;
　　And PHYLLIS is but Twenty-one.

Paint, Patches, Jewels laid aside,
　　At Night Astronomers agree,　　　　10
The Evening has the Day bely'd;
　　And PHYLLIS is some Forty-three.

Forma Bonum Fragile.

WHAT a frail Thing is Beauty, says Baron LE CRAS,
Perceiving his Mistress had one Eye of Glass:
And scarcely had He spoke it;
When She more confus'd, as more angry She grew,
By a negligent Rage prov'd the Maxim too true: 5
She dropt the Eye, and broke it.

A Critical Moment.

HOW capricious were Nature and Art to poor NELL?
She was painting her Cheeks at the time her Nose fell.

An Epigram.

Written to the Duke de Noailles.

VAIN the Concern which You express,
That uncall'd ALARD will possess
Your House and Coach, both Day and Night;
And that MACKBETH was haunted less
By BANQUO's restless Spright.   5

With Fifteen Thousand Pound a Year,
Do You complain, You cannot bear
An Ill, You may so soon retrieve?
Good ALARD, faith, is modester
By much, than You believe.   10

Lend Him but fifty *Louis' d'or*;
And You shall never see Him more:
Take the Advice; *Probatum est.*
Why do the Gods indulge our Store,
But to secure our Rest?   15

The Thief and the Cordelier, a Ballad.

To the Tune of King John, and the Abbot of Canterbury.

WHO has e'er been at PARIS, must needs know the *Greve*,
 The fatal Retreat of th'unfortunate Brave;
Where Honor and Justice most odly contribute,
To ease Hero's Pains by a Halter and Gibbet.
 Derry down, down, hey derry down.   5

There Death breaks the Shackles, which Force had put on;
And the Hangman compleats, what the Judge but begun:
There the 'Squire of the Pad, and the Knight of the Post,
Find their Pains no more balk'd, and their Hopes no more crost.
 Derry down, &c.   10

Great Claims are there made, and great Secrets are known;
And the King, and the Law, and the Thief has His own:
But my Hearers cry out; What a duce dost Thou ayl?
Cut off thy Reflections; and give Us thy Tale.
 Derry down, &c.   15

'Twas there, then, in civil Respect to harsh Laws,
And for want of false Witness, to back a bad Cause,
A NORMAN, tho' late, was oblig'd to appear:
And Who to assist, but a grave CORDELIER?
 Derry down, &c.   20

The 'Squire, whose good Grace was to open the Scene,
Seem'd not in great Haste, that the Show shou'd begin:
Now fitted the Halter, now travers'd the Cart;
And often took Leave; but was loath to Depart.
 Derry down, &c.   25

What frightens You thus, my good Son? says the Priest:
You Murther'd, are Sorry, and have been Confest.
O Father! My Sorrow will scarce save my Bacon:
For 'twas not that I Murther'd, but that I was Taken.
 Derry down, &c.   30

Title: King...Canterbury.] the King and the Abbot Derry down &c. *W*   2 The]
That *W*   5] Derry down &c *W*   6 which] that *W*   10, 15, 20, 25, 30, 35, 40]
Derry &c *W*   29 was] am *W*

Pough! pr'ythee ne'er trouble thy Head with such Fancies:
Rely on the Aid You shall have from Saint FRANCIS:
If the Money You promis'd be brought to the Chest;
You have only to Dye: let the Church do the rest.
  Derry down, &c.   35

And what will Folks say, if they see You afraid?
It reflects upon Me; as I knew not my Trade:
Courage, Friend; To-day is your Period of Sorrow;
And Things will go better, believe Me, To-morrow.
  Derry down, &c.   40

To-morrow? our Hero reply'd in a Fright:
He that's hang'd before Noon, ought to think of To-night.
Tell your Beads, quoth the Priest, and be fairly truss'd up:
For You surely To-night shall in PARADISE Sup.
  Derry down, &c.   45

Alas! quoth the 'Squire, howe'er sumptuous the Treat,
Parblew, I shall have little Stomach to Eat:
I should therefore esteem it great Favor, and Grace;
Wou'd You be so kind, as to go in my Place.
  Derry down, &c.   50

That I wou'd, quoth the Father, and thank you to boot;
But our Actions, You know, with our Duty must suit.
The Feast, I propos'd to You, I cannot taste:
For this Night, by our Order, is mark'd for a Fast.
  Derry down, &c.   55

Then turning about to the Hangman, He said;
Dispatch me, I pr'ythee, this troublesome Blade:
For Thy Cord, and My Cord both equally tie;
And We Live by the Gold, for which other Men Dye.
  Derry down, &c.   60

43 Tell . . . be] If you tell your beads quick and are *W*   44 For You surely] Quoth the
Preist you *W*   45, 50, 55] *om. W*   60 &c.] *om. W*

An Epitaph.

Stet quicunque volet potens
Aulæ culmine lubrico, &c.   Senec.

INTERR'D beneath this Marble Stone,
Lie Saunt'ring JACK, and Idle JOAN.
While rolling Threescore Years and One
Did round this Globe their Courses run;
If Human Things went Ill or Well;   5
If changing Empires rose or fell;
The Morning past, the Evening came,
And found this Couple still the same.
They Walk'd and Eat, good Folks: What then?
Why then They Walk'd and Eat again: 10
They soundly slept the Night away:
They did just Nothing all the Day:
And having bury'd Children Four,
Wou'd not take Pains to try for more.
Nor Sister either had, nor Brother: 15
They seem'd just Tally'd for each other.

   Their Moral and Oeconomy
Most perfectly They made agree:
Each Virtue kept it's proper Bound,
Nor Trespass'd on the other's Ground.   20
Nor Fame, nor Censure They regarded:
They neither Punish'd, nor Rewarded.
He car'd not what the Footmen did:
Her Maids She neither prais'd, nor chid:
So ev'ry Servant took his Course;   25
And bad at First, They all grew worse.
Slothful Disorder fill'd His Stable;
And sluttish Plenty deck'd Her Table.
Their Beer was strong; Their Wine was *Port*;
Their Meal was large; Their Grace was short.   30
They gave the Poor the Remnant-meat,
Just when it grew not fit to eat.

   They paid the Church and Parish-Rate;
And took, but read not the Receit:

For which They claim'd their *Sunday*'s Due, 35
Of slumb'ring in an upper Pew.

No Man's Defects sought They to know;
So never made Themselves a Foe.
No Man's good Deeds did They commend;
So never rais'd Themselves a Friend. 40
Nor cherish'd They Relations poor:
That might decrease Their present Store:
Nor Barn nor House did they repair:
That might oblige Their future Heir.

They neither Added, nor Confounded: 45
They neither Wanted, nor Abounded.
Each *Christmas* They Accompts did clear;
And wound their Bottom round the Year.
Nor Tear, nor Smile did They imploy
At News of Public Grief, or Joy. 50
When Bells were Rung, and Bonfires made;
If ask'd, They ne'er deny'd their Aid:
Their Jugg was to the Ringers carry'd;
Who ever either Dy'd, or Marry'd.
Their Billet at the Fire was found; 55
Who ever was Depos'd, or Crown'd.

Nor Good, nor Bad, nor Fools, nor Wise;
They wou'd not learn, nor cou'd advise:
Without Love, Hatred, Joy, or Fear,
They led—a kind of—as it were: 60
Nor Wish'd, nor Car'd, nor Laugh'd, nor Cry'd:
And so They liv'd; and so They dy'd.

In Chaucer's Stile.

FULL oft doth MAT. with TOPAZ dine,
Eateth bak'd Meats, drinketh Greek Wine:
But TOPAZ his own Werke rehearseth;
And MAT. mote praise what TOPAZ verseth.
Now sure as Priest did e'er shrive Sinner, 5
Full hardly earneth MAT. his Dinner.

Title: Supplied from 'Erle Robert's Mice', which preceded in 1718: In the same Style. 1718

Protogenes and Apelles.

WHEN Poets wrote, and Painters drew,
   As Nature pointed out the View:
E'er GOTHIC Forms were known in GREECE,
To spoil the well-proportion'd Piece:
And in our Verse e'er Monkish Rhimes   5
Had jangl'd their fantastic Chimes:
E'er on the flow'ry Lands of RHODES
Those Knights had fix'd their dull Abodes,
Who knew not much to paint or write,
Nor car'd to pray, nor dar'd to fight: 10
PROTOGENES, Historians note,
Liv'd there, a Burgess Scot and Lot;
And, as old PLINY's Writings show,
APELLES did the same at Co.
Agreed these Points of Time, and Place,   15
Proceed We in the present Case.

Picqu'd by PROTOGENES's Fame,
From CO to RHODES, APELLES came;
To see a Rival and a Friend,
Prepar'd to Censure, or Commend,   20
Here to absolve, and there object,
As Art with Candor might direct.
He sails, He lands, He comes, He rings:
His Servants follow with the Things:
Appears the Governante of th'House: 25
(For such in GREECE were much in use.)
If Young or Handsom, Yea or No,
Concerns not Me, or Thee to know.

Does 'Squire PROTOGENES live here?
Yes, Sir, says She with gracious Air,   30
And Curt'sey low; but just call'd out
By Lords peculiarly devout;
Who came on purpose, Sir, to borrow
Our VENUS, for the Feast To-morrow,
To grace the Church: 'tis VENUS' Day: 35
I hope, Sir, You intend to stay,

To see our VENUS: 'tis the Piece
The most renown'd throughout all GREECE,
So like th'Original, they say:
But I have no great Skill that Way.   40
But, Sir, at Six ('tis now past Three)
DROMO must make my Master's Tea:
At Six, Sir, if You please to come,
You'll find my Master, Sir, at Home.

Tea, says a Critic big with Laughter,   45
Was found some twenty Ages after:
Authors, before they write, shou'd read:
'Tis very true; but We'll proceed.

And, Sir, at present wou'd you please
To leave your Name—Fair Maiden, yes: 50
Reach me that Board. No sooner spoke
But done. With one judicious Stroke,
On the plain Ground APELLES drew
A Circle regularly true:
And will you please, Sweet-heart, said He,   55
To shew your Master this from Me?
By it He presently will know,
How Painters write their Names at Co.

He gave the Pannel to the Maid.
Smiling and Curt'sing, Sir, She said,   60
I shall not fail to tell my Master:
And, Sir, for fear of all Disaster,
I'll keep it my own self: Safe bind,
Says the old Proverb, and Safe find.
So, Sir, as sure as Key or Lock—   65
Your Servant Sir—at Six a Clock.

Again at Six APELLES came;
Found the same prating civil Dame.
Sir, that my Master has been here,
Will by the Board it self appear.   70
If from the perfect Line He found,
He has presum'd to swell the Round,
Or Colors on the Draught to lay;
'Tis thus (He order'd me to say)

Thus write the Painters of this Isle: 75
Let those of Co remark the Style.

She said; and to his Hand restor'd
The rival Pledge, the Missive Board.
Upon the happy Line were laid
Such obvious Light, and easie Shade;   80
That PARIS' Apple stood confest,
Or LEDA's Egg, or CLOE's Breast.

APELLES view'd the finish'd Piece;
And Live, said He, the Arts of GREECE!
Howe'er PROTOGENES and I   85
May in our Rival Talents vie;
Howe'er our Works may have express'd,
Who truest drew, or color'd best;
When He beheld my flowing Line;
He found at least I cou'd design: 90
And from his artful Round, I grant,
That He with perfect Skill can paint.

The dullest GENIUS cannot fail
To find the Moral of my Tale:
That the distinguish'd Part of Men,   95
With Compass, Pencil, Sword, or Pen,
Shou'd in Life's Visit leave their Name,
In Characters, which may proclaim
That They with Ardor strove to raise
At once their Arts, and Countrey's Praise: 100
And in their Working took great Care,
That all was Full, and Round, and Fair.

Democritus and Heraclitus.

DEMOCRITUS, dear Droll, revisit Earth,
And with our Follies glut Thy heighten'd Mirth:
Sad HERACLITUS, serious Wretch, return,
In louder Grief our greater Crimes to mourn.
Between You both I unconcern'd stand by: 5
Hurt, can I laugh? and Honest, need I cry?

For my own Tomb-stone.

To Me 'twas giv'n to die: to Thee 'tis giv'n
   To live: Alas! one Moment sets us ev'n.
Mark! how impartial is the Will of Heav'n?

The Second Hymn of Callimachus.

To Apollo.

HAH! how the Laurel, great APOLLO's Tree,
   And all the Cavern shakes! far off, far off,
The Man that is unhallow'd: for the God,
The God approaches. Hark! He knocks: the Gates
Feel the glad Impulse: and the sever'd Bars   5
Submissive clink against their brazen Portals.
Why do the DELIAN Palms incline their Boughs,
Self-mov'd: and hov'ring Swans, their Throats releas'd
From native Silence, carol Sounds harmonious?

Begin, young Men, the Hymn: let all your Harps   10
Break their inglorious Silence; and the Dance,
In mystic Numbers trod, explain the Music.
But first by ardent Pray'r, and clear Lustration
Purge the contagious Spots of Human Weakness:
Impure no Mortal can behold APOLLO.   15
So may Ye flourish, favor'd by the God,
In Youth with happy Nuptials, and in Age
With silver Hairs, and fair Descent of Children;
So lay Foundations for aspiring Cities,
And bless your spreading Colonies Encrease.   20

Pay sacred Rev'rence to APOLLO's Song;
Lest wrathful the far-shooting God emitt
His fatal Arrows. Silent Nature stands;
And Seas subside, obedient to the Sound
Of Io, Io PEAN! nor dares THETIS   25
Longer bewail Her lov'd ACHILLES' Death:

For PHOEBUS was his Foe. Nor must sad NIOBE
In fruitless Sorrow persevere, or weep
Ev'n thro' the PHRYGIAN Marble. Hapless Mother!
Whose Fondness cou'd compare her Mortal Off-spring   30
To those which fair LATONA bore to JOVE.
Io! again repeat Ye, Io PEAN!

    Against the Deity 'tis hard to strive.
He that resists the Power of PTOLEMY,
Resists the Pow'r of Heav'n: for Pow'r from Heav'n   35
Derives; and Monarchs rule by Gods appointed.

    Recite APOLLO's Praise, 'till Night draws on,
The Ditty still unfinish'd; and the Day
Unequal to the Godhead's Attributes
Various, and Matter copious of your Songs.   40

    Sublime at JOVE's right Hand APOLLO sits,
And thence distributes Honor, gracious King,
And Theme of Verse perpetual. From his Robe
Flows Light ineffable: his Harp, his Quiver,
And LICTIAN Bow are Gold: with golden Sandals   45
His Feet are shod; how rich! how beautiful!
Beneath his Steps the yellow Min'ral rises;
And Earth reveals her Treasures. Youth and Beauty
Eternal deck his Cheek: from his fair Head
Perfumes distill their Sweets; and chearful HEALTH,   50
His dutious Handmaid, thro' the Air improv'd,
With lavish Hand diffuses Scents Ambrosial.

    The Spear-man's Arm by Thee, great God, directed,
Sends forth a certain Wound. The Laurel'd Bard,
Inspir'd by Thee, composes Verse Immortal.   55
Taught by thy Art Divine, the sage Physician
Eludes the Urn; and chains, or exiles Death.

    Thee NOMIAN We adore; for that from Heav'n
Descending, Thou on fair AMPHRYSUS' Banks
Did'st guard ADMETUS' Herds. Sithence the Cow   60
Produc'd an ampler Store of Milk; the She-Goat

Not without Pain dragg'd her distended Udder;
And Ewes, that erst brought forth but single Lambs,
Now drop'd their Two-fold Burdens. Blest the Cattle,
On which APOLLO cast his fav'ring Eye!   65

But, PHOEBUS, Thou to Man beneficent,
Delight'st in building Cities. Bright DIANA,
Kind Sister to thy infant-Deity
New-wean'd, and just arising from the Cradle,
Brought hunted wild Goats-Heads, and branching Antlers   70
Of Stags, The Fruit and Honor of her Toil.
These with discerning Hand Thou knew'st to range,
(Young as Thou wast) and in the well-fram'd Models,
With Emblematic Skill, and mystic Order,
Thou shew'dst, where Towers, or Battlements should rise;   75
Where Gates should open; or where Walls should compass:
While from thy childish Pastime Man receiv'd
The future Strength, and Ornament of Nations.

BATTUS, our great Progenitor, now touch'd
The LYBIAN Strand; when the fore-boding Crow   80
Flew on the Right before the People, marking
The Country destin'd the auspicious Seat
Of future Kings, and Favor of the God,
Whose Oath is sure, and Promise stands Eternal.

Or BOEDROMIAN hear'st Thou pleas'd, or CLARIAN,   85
PHOEBUS, great King? for diff'rent are Thy Names,
As Thy kind Hand has founded many Cities,
Or dealt benign Thy various Gifts to Man.
CARNEAN let Me call Thee; for my Country
Calls Thee CARNEAN: the fair Colony   90
Thrice by Thy gracious Guidance was transported,
E'er settl'd in CYRENE; there W'appointed
Thy annual Feasts, kind God, and bless thy Altars
Smoaking with Hecatombs of slaughter'd Bulls;
As CARNUS, thy High-Priest, and favor'd Friend,   95
Had er'st ordain'd; and with mysterious Rites,
Our great Forefathers taught their Sons to worship.
Io CARNEAN PHOEBUS! Io PEAN!

The yellow *Crocus* there, and fair *Narcissus*
Reserve the Honors of their Winter-Store, 100
To deck Thy Temple; 'till returning Spring
Diffuses Nature's various Pride; and Flow'rs
Innumerable, by the soft South-west
Open'd, and gather'd by Religious Hands,
Rebound their Sweets from th'odorif'rous Pavement. 105
Perpetual Fires shine hallow'd on Thy Altars.
When Annual the CARNEAN Feast is held,
The warlike LIBYANS clad in Armor, lead
The Dance, with clanging Swords and Shields They beat
The dreadful Measure: in the Chorus join 110
Their Women, Brown but Beautiful: such Rites
To Thee well-pleasing. Nor had yet Thy Votaries,
From GREECE transplanted, touch'd CYRENE's Banks,
And Lands determin'd for their last Abodes;
But wander'd thro' AZILIS' horrid Forrest 115
Dispers'd; when from MYRTUSA's craggy Brow,
Fond of the Maid, auspicious to the City,
Which must hereafter bear her favor'd Name,
Thou Gracious deign'st to let the Fair One view
Her *Typic* People; Thou with Pleasure taught'st Her 120
To draw the Bow, to slay the shaggy Lyon,
And stop the spreading Ruin of the Plains.
Happy the Nymph, who honor'd by Thy Passion,
Was aided by thy Pow'r! The monstrous PYTHON
Durst tempt Thy Wrath in vain: for dead He fell, 125
To thy great Strength, and golden Arms unequal.

Io! while Thy unerring Hand elanc'd
Another, and another Dart; The People
Joyful repeated, Io! Io PEAN!
Elance the Dart, APOLLO: for the Safety, 130
And Health of Man, gracious Thy Mother bore Thee.

ENVY Thy latest Foe suggested thus:
Like Thee I am a Pow'r Immortal; therefore
To Thee dare speak. How can'st Thou favor partial
Those Poets who write little? Vast and Great 135
Is what I Love: The far extended Ocean

To a small Riv'let I prefer. APOLLO
Spurn'd ENVY with His Foot; and thus the God:
DÆMON, the head-long Current of EUPHRATES,
ASSYRIAN River, copious runs, but Muddy;   140
And carries forward with his stupid Force
Polluting Dirt; His Torrent still augmenting,
His Wave still more defil'd: mean while the Nymphs
MELISSAN, Sacred and Recluse to CERES,
Studious to have their Off'rings well receiv'd,   145
And fit for Heav'nly Use, from little Urns
Pour Streams select, and Purity of Waters.

    Io! APOLLO, mighty King, let ENVY
Ill-judging and Verbose, from LETHE's Lake
Draw Tons unmeasurable; while Thy Favor   150
Administers to my ambitious Thirst
The wholesome Draught from AGANIPPE's Spring
Genuine, and with soft Murmurs gently rilling
Adown the Mountains, where Thy Daughters haunt.

Alma: or, The Progress of the Mind.

In Three Cantos.

Πάντα γέλως, καὶ πάντα κόνις, καὶ πάντα τὸ μηδέν·
Πάντα γὰρ ἐξ ἀλόγων ἐστὶ τὰ γιγνόμενα.   Incert. ap. Stobœum.

THE FIRST CANTO.

MATTHEW met RICHARD; when or where
From Story is not mighty clear:
Of many knotty Points They spoke;
And *Pro* and *Con* by turns They took.
Ratts half the Manuscript have eat: 5
Dire Hunger! which We still regret:
O! may they ne'er again digest
The Horrors of so sad a Feast.
Yet less our Grief, if what remains,
Dear JACOB, by thy Care and Pains   10

Motto] om. L 30

Shall be to future Times convey'd.
It thus begins:
   *   *   *   *   Here MATTHEW said:

ALMA in Verse; in Prose, the MIND,
By ARISTOTLE's Pen defin'd,   15
Throughout the Body squat or tall,
Is, *bonâ fide*, All in All.
And yet, slap dash, is All again
In every Sinew, Nerve, and Vein.
Runs here and there, like HAMLET's Ghost;   20
While every where She rules the roast.

    This *System*, RICHARD, We are told,
The Men of OXFORD firmly hold.
The CAMBRIDGE Wits, You know, deny
With *Ipse dixit* to comply.   25
They say (for in good truth They speak
With small Respect of that old GREEK)
That, putting all his Words together,
'Tis Three blew Beans in One blew Bladder.

    ALMA, They strenuously maintain,   30
Sits Cock-horse on Her Throne, the Brain;
And from that Seat of Thought dispenses
Her Sov'reign Pleasure to the Senses.
Two *Optic* Nerves, They say, She tyes,
Like Spectacles, a-cross the Eyes;   35
By which the Spirits bring her Word,
Whene'er the Balls are fix'd, or stirr'd;
How quick at Park and Play they strike;
The Duke they court; the Toast they like;
And at Sᵀ JAMES's turn their Grace   40
From former Friends, now out of Place.

    Without these Aids, to be more serious,
Her Pow'r, They hold, had been precarious:
The Eyes might have conspir'd her Ruin;
And She not known, what They were doing.   45
Foolish it had been, and unkind,
That They shou'd see, and She be blind.

Wise Nature likewise, They suppose,
Has drawn two Conduits down our Nose:
Cou'd ALMA else with Judgment tell,   50
When *Cabbage* stinks, or *Roses* smell?
Or who wou'd ask for her Opinion
Between an *Oyster*, and an *Onion*?
For from most Bodies, DICK, You know,
Some little Bits ask Leave to flow;   55
And, as thro' these Canals They roll,
Bring up a Sample of the Whole.
Like Footmen running before Coaches,
To tell the Inn, what Lord approaches.

By Nerves about our Palate plac'd,   60
She likewise judges of the Taste.
Else (dismal Thought!) our Warlike Men
Might drink thick *Port* for fine *Champagne*;
And our ill-judging Wives and Daughters
Mistake Small-beer for *Citron*-Waters.   65

Hence too, that She might better hear,
She sets a Drum at either Ear;
And Loud or Gentle, Harsh or Sweet,
Are but th'*Alarums* which They beat.

Last, to enjoy her Sense of Feeling   70
(A thing She much delights to deal in)
A thousand little Nerves She sends
Quite to our Toes, and Fingers Ends;
And These in Gratitude again
Return their Spirits to the Brain;   75
In which their Figure being printed
(As just before, I think, I hinted)
ALMA inform'd can try the Case,
As She had been upon the Place.

Thus, while the Judge gives diff'rent Journeys   80
To Country Counsel, and Attornies;
He on the Bench in quiet sits,
Deciding, as They bring the Writs.

The POPE thus prays and sleeps at ROME,
And very seldom stirs from Home: 85
Yet sending forth his Holy Spies,
And having heard what They advise,
He rules the Church's blest Dominions;
And sets Men's Faith by His Opinions.

The Scholars of the STAGYRITE, 90
Who for the Old Opinion fight,
Would make their Modern Friends confess,
The diff'rence but from More to Less.
The MIND, say They, while You sustain
To hold her Station in the Brain; 95
You grant, at least, She is extended:
Ergo the whole Dispute is ended.
For, 'till To-morrow shou'd You plead
From Form and Structure of the Head;
The MIND as visibly is seen 100
Extended thro' the whole *Machine*.
Why shou'd all Honor then be ta'en
From Lower Parts to load the Brain;
When other Limbs we plainly see,
Each in his way, as brisk as He? 105
For Music, grant the Head receives it;
It is the Artist's Hand that gives it.
And tho' the Scull may wear the Laurel;
The Soldier's Arm sustains the Quarrel.
Besides, the Nostrils, Ears, and Eyes 110
Are not his Parts, but his Allies.
Ev'n what You hear the Tongue proclaim,
Comes *ab Origine* from them.
What could the Head perform Alone,
If all Their friendly Aids were gone? 115
A foolish figure He must make;
Do nothing else, but sleep and ake.

Nor matters it, that You can show,
How to the Head the Spirits go.
Those Spirits started from some Goal, 120
Before they thro' the Veins cou'd roll.

Now We shou'd hold Them much to blame,
If They went back, before They came.

If therefore, as We must suppose,
They came from Fingers, and from Toes;   125
Or Toes, or Fingers, in this Case,
Of *Num-scull*'s Self shou'd take the Place.
Disputing fair, You grant thus much,
That all Sensation is but Touch.
Dip but your Toes into cold Water;   130
Their Correspondent Teeth will chatter:
And strike the Bottom of your Feet;
You set your Head into a Heat.
The Bully beat, and happy Lover
Confess, that Feeling lies all over.   135

Note here, LUCRETIUS dares to teach
(As all our Youth may learn from CREECH)
That Eyes were made, but cou'd not view;
Nor Hands embrace, nor Feet pursue:
But heedless Nature did produce   140
The Members first, and then the Use.
What Each must act, was yet unknown,
'Till All is mov'd by Chance alone.

A Man first builds a Country Seat;
Then finds the Walls not good to eat.   145
Another plants, and wond'ring sees
Nor Books, nor Medals on his Trees.
Yet Poet and Philosopher
Was He, who durst such Whims aver.
Blest, for his Sake, be human Reason,   150
That came at all, tho' late, in Season.

But no Man sure e'er left his House,
And saddl'd *Ball*, with Thoughts so wild,
To bring a Midwife to his Spouse,
Before He knew She was with Child.   155

130 Dip but your] *L 30* Sett his *W*   131 Their] *L 30* His *W*   132, 133 your]
L 30 his *W*   132–3]
                    to set his head into a heat
                    Strike but the Soles of a man's feet   *Alt. reading in W*

And no Man ever reapt his Corn,
Or from the Oven drew his Bread,
E'er Hinds and Bakers yet were born,
That taught him both to Sow, and Knead.
Before They're ask'd, can Maids refuse?   160
Can—Pray, says DICK, hold in your Muse.
While You *Pindaric* Truths rehearse;
She hobbles in *Alternate* Verse.
Verse? MAT. reply'd: is that my Care?
Go on, quoth RICHARD, soft and fair.   165

    This looks, friend DICK, as Nature had
But exercis'd the *Salesman*'s Trade:
As if She haply had sat down,
And cut out Cloaths for all the Town;
Then sent them out to *Monmouth*-Street,   170
To try, what Persons they wou'd fit.
But ev'ry Free and Licenc'd Taylor
Would in this *Thesis* find a Failure.
Should Whims like these his Head perplex,
How could he work for either Sex?   175
His Cloaths, as Atomes might prevail,
Might fit a Pismire, or a Whale.
No, no: He views with studious Pleasure
Your Shape, before He takes your Measure.
For real KATE He made the Boddice,   180
And not for an *Ideal* Goddess.
No Error near his Shop-board lurk'd:
He knew the Folks for whom He work'd.
Still to Their Size He aim'd his Skill:
Else, pr'ythee, who wou'd pay his Bill?   185

    Next, DICK, if Chance her self shou'd vary;
Observe, how Matters would miscarry:
Across your Eyes, Friend, place your Shoes;
Your Spectacles upon your Toes:
Then You and MEMMIUS shall agree,   190
How nicely Men would walk, or see.

    But Wisdom, peevish and cross-grain'd,
Must be oppos'd, to be sustain'd.

And still your Knowledge will increase,
As You make other People's less.   195
In Arms and Science 'tis the same:
Our Rival's Hurts create our Fame.
At FAUBERT's if Disputes arise
Among the Champions for the Prize;
To prove, who gave the fairer Butt,   200
JOHN shows the Chalk on ROBERT's Coat.
So, for the Honor of your Book,
It tells, where other Folks mistook:
And, as their Notions You confound,
Those You invent get farther Ground.   205

The Commentators on old ARI-
STOTLE ('tis urg'd) in Judgment vary:
They to their own Conceits have brought
The Image of his general Thought.
Just as the Melancholic Eye   210
Sees Fleets and Armies in the Sky;
And to the poor Apprentice Ear
The Bells sound *Whittington* Lord May'r.
The Conj'rer thus explains his *Scheme*
Thus Spirits walk, and Prophets dream: 215
NORTH BRITONS thus have *Second Sight*;
And GERMANS free from Gunshot fight.

THEODORET, and ORIGEN,
And fifty other Learned Men
Attest, that if their Comments find   220
The Traces of their Master's Mind;
ALMA can ne'er decay nor dye:
This flatly t'other Sect deny,
SIMPLICIUS, THEOPHRAST, DURAND;
Great Names, but hard in Verse to stand.   225
They wonder Men should have mistook
The *Tenets* of their Master's Book;
And hold, that ALMA yields her Breath,
O'ercome by Age, and seiz'd by Death.
Now which were Wise? and which were Fools?   230
Poor ALMA sits between two Stools:

The more She reads, the more perplext;
The Comment ruining the Text:
Now fears, now hopes her doubtful Fate:
But, RICHARD, let her look to That—   235
Whilst We our own Affairs pursue.

These diff'rent *Systems*, Old or New,
A Man with half an Eye may see,
Were only form'd to disagree.
Now to bring Things to fair Conclusion,   240
And save much Christian Ink's Effusion;
Let me propose an Healing *Scheme*,
And sail along the Middle Stream:
For, DICK, if We could reconcile
    Old ARISTOTLE with GASSENDUS;   245
How many would admire our Toil;
    And yet how few would comprehend us?

Here, RICHARD, let my *Scheme* commence.
Oh! may my Words be lost in Sense;
While pleas'd THALIA deigns to write   250
The Slips and Bounds of ALMA's Flight.

My simple *System* shall suppose,
That ALMA enters at the Toes;
That then She mounts by just Degrees
Up to the Ancles, Legs, and Knees: 255
Next, as the Sap of Life does rise,
She lends her Vigor to the Thighs:
And, all these under-Regions past,
She nestles somewhere near the Waste:
Gives Pain or Pleasure, Grief or Laughter;   260
As We shall show at large hereafter.
Mature, if not improv'd, by Time
Up to the Heart She loves to climb:
From thence, compell'd by Craft and Age,
She makes the Head her latest Stage.   265

From the Feet upward to the Head;
Pithy, and short, says DICK: proceed.

DICK, this is not an idle Notion:
Observe the Progress of the Motion.
First I demonstratively prove,　　　　　　　270
That Feet were only made to move;
And Legs desire to come and go:
For they have nothing else to do.

Hence, long before the Child can crawl,
He learns to kick, and wince, and sprawl:　　　275
To hinder which, your Midwife knows
To bind Those Parts extremely close;
Lest ALMA newly enter'd in,
And stunn'd at her own Christ'ning's Din,
Fearful of future Grief and Pain,　　　　　280
Should silently sneak out again.
Full piteous seems young ALMA's Case:
As in a luckless Gamester's Place,
She would not play, yet must not pass.

Again as She grows something stronger,　　　285
And Master's Feet are swath'd no longer,
If in the Night too oft He kicks,
Or shows his *Loco-motive* Tricks;
These first Assaults fat KATE repays Him,
When half asleep She overlays Him.　　　　290

Now mark, Dear RICHARD, from the Age
That Children tread this Worldly Stage,
Broom-staff or Poaker they bestride,
And round the Parlor love to ride;
'Till thoughtful Father's pious Care　　　　295
Provides his Brood, next *Smithfield* Fair,
With Supplemental Hobby-Horses:
And happy be their Infant Courses!

Hence for some Years they ne'er stand still:
Their Legs, You see, direct their Will.
From opening Morn 'till setting Sun,　　　　300
A-round the Fields and Woods They run:

270 First] *L* 30 Now *W*　　　271 Feet] *L* 30 Legs *W*

They frisk, and dance, and leap, and play;
Nor heed, what FRIEND or SNAPE can say.

To Her next Stage as ALMA flies,   305
And likes, as I have said, the Thighs:
With *Sympathetic* Pow'r She warms,
Their good Allies and Friends, the Arms.
While BETTY dances on the Green;
And SUSAN is at Stool-ball seen: 310
While JOHN for Nine-pins does declare;
And ROGER loves to pitch the Bar;
Both Legs and Arms spontaneous move:
Which was the Thing I meant to prove.

Another Motion now She makes: 315
O need I name the Seat She takes?
His Thought quite chang'd the Stripling finds;
The Sport and Race no more He minds:
Neglected *Tray* and *Pointer* lye;
And Covies unmolested fly.   320
Sudden the jocund Plain He leaves;
And for the Nymph in Secret grieves.
In dying Accents He complains
Of cruel Fires, and raging Pains.
The Nymph too longs to be alone;   325
Leaves all the Swains; and sighs for One.
The Nymph is warm'd with young Desire;
And feels, and dies to quench His Fire.
They meet each Evening in the Grove:
Their Parley but augments their Love.   330
So to the Priest their Case They tell:
He ties the Knot; and all goes well.

But, O my MUSE, just Distance keep:
Thou art a Maid, and must not peep.
In nine Months Time the Boddice loose,   335
And Petticoats too short, disclose,
That at This Age the active Mind
About the Waste lies most confin'd;
And that young Life, and quick'ning Sense
Spring from His Influence darted thence.   340

So from the Middle of the World
The SUN's prolifick Rays are hurl'd:
'Tis from That Seat He darts those Beams,
Which quicken Earth with genial Flames.

 DICK, who thus long had passive sat,   345
Here stroak'd his Chin, and cock'd his Hat;
Then slapp'd his Hand upon the Board;
And thus the Youth put in his Word.
Love's Advocates, sweet Sir, would find Him
A higher Place, than You assign'd Him.   350
Love's Advocates, DICK, who are those?—
The Poets, You may well suppose.
I'm sorry, Sir, You have discarded
The Men, with whom 'till now You herded.
Prose-Men alone, for private Ends,   355
I thought, forsook their ancient Friends.
In cor stillavit, crys LUCRETIUS;
If He may be allow'd to teach Us.
The self-same Thing soft OVID says
(A proper Judge in such a Case.)   360
HORACE his Phrase is *torret Jecur*;
And happy was that curious Speaker.
Here VIRGIL too has plac'd this Passion:
What signifies too long Quotation?
In *Ode* and *Epic* plain the Case is,   365
That Love holds One of these Two Places.

 DICK, without Passion or Reflection,
I'll strait demolish this Objection.

 First Poets, all the World agrees,
Write half to profit, half to please.   370
Matter and Figure They produce;
For Garnish This, and That for Use;
And, in the Structure of their Feasts,
They seek to feed, and please their Guests:

369 all...agrees,] *L 30* as themselves confess *W* 370 half...half] *L 30* or...or *W*
371 Matter and Figure] *L 30* Matters and figures *W* 372 For...That] *L 30* these
for amusement those *W* 373–4] *L 30*
   and like Guildhall's Parnassus feasts
   at once delight and feed the guests. *W*:
   at Tempes as at Guild Hall feasts
   With food and show you please your Guests *Alt. reading in W*

But One may balk this good Intent,   375
And take Things otherwise than meant.
Thus, if You Dine with my Lord May'r,
Roast-Beef, and Ven'son is your Fare;
Thence You proceed to Swan, and Bustard,
And persevere in Tart, and Custard: 380
But *Tulip-leaves*, and *Limon-peel*
Help only to adorn the Meal;
And painted Flags, superb and neat,
Proclaim You welcome to the Treat.
The Man of Sense his Meat devours;   385
But only smells the Peel, and Flow'rs:
And He must be an idle Dreamer,
Who leaves the Pie, and gnaws the Streamer.

    That CUPID goes with Bow and Arrows,
And VENUS keeps her Coach and Sparrows,   390
Is all but Emblem, to acquaint One,
The Son is sharp, the Mother wanton.
Such Images have sometimes shown
A *Mystic* Sense, but oft'ner None.
For who conceives, what Bards devise,   395
That Heav'n is plac'd in CELIA's Eyes?
Or where's the Sense, direct or moral,
That Teeth are Pearl, or Lips are Coral?

    Your HORACE owns, He various writ,
As wild, or sober Maggots bit: 400
And, where too much the Poet ranted,
The Sage Philosopher recanted.
His grave *Epistles* may disprove
The wanton *Odes* He made to LOVE.

    LUCRETIUS keeps a mighty Pother   405
With CUPID, and his fancy'd Mother:
Calls her great Queen of Earth and Air;
Declares, that Winds and Seas obey Her;

377 Thus,] *L 30* Now *W*   378 Roast-Beef...is] *L 30* Venison and beef is first *W*
379] *L 30* You Second fall upon Swan or bustard *W*   380] *L 30* So cast your heart
[on] pye and Custard *W*   383–4] *L 30*
                 And like your Citt your Poet treats
                 Sticks Gilded flaggs round wholsom meats *W*

And, while Her Honor he rehearses,
Implores Her to inspire his Verses.　　　　　　　　　410

　　Yet, free from this Poetic Madness;
Next Page, He says in sober Sadness,
That She and all her fellow-Gods
Sit idling in their high Abodes,
Regardless of this World below,　　　　　　　　　415
Our Health or Hanging, Weal or Woe;
Nor once disturb their Heav'nly Spirits
With SCAPIN's Cheats, or CÆSAR's Merits.

　　Nor e'er can LATIN Poets prove,
Where lies the real Seat of Love.　　　　　　　　420
Jecur they burn, and *Cor* they pierce,
As either best supplies their Verse:
And, if Folks ask the Reason for't,
Say, one was long, and t'other short.
Thus, I presume, the BRITISH Muse,　　　　　　　425
May take the Freedom Strangers use.
In Prose our Property is greater:
Why should it then be less in Metre?
If CUPID throws a single Dart;
We make him wound the Lover's *Heart*:　　　　　430
But if He takes his Bow, and Quiver;
'Tis sure, He must transfix the *Liver*:
For Rhime with Reason may dispense;
And Sound has Right to govern Sense.

　　But let your Friends in Verse suppose,　　　　435
What ne'er shall be allow'd in Prose:
Anatomists can make it clear,
The *Liver* minds his own Affair:
Kindly supplies our publick Uses;
And parts, and strains the Vital Juices:　　　　　440
Still lays some useful Bile aside,
To tinge the Chyle's insipid Tide:

421] *L 30* Thus heart or Liver you may pierce *W*　　　　422] *L 30* Victim in a latin
Verse *W*　　　423 the] *L 30* a *W*　　424 was] *L 30* is *W*　　425 Thus...the] *L 30*
thus youl grant it to *W*: Nor in this case is *Alt. reading in W*　　426 May...Freedom]
L 30 all privilege that *W*: Denyd the license *Alt. reading in W*　　428 Why...then]
L 30 then why should it *W*　　　433 may] *L 30* must *W*

Else We should want both Gibe and Satyr;
And all be burst with pure Good-nature.
Now Gall is bitter with a Witness;   445
And Love is all Delight and Sweetness.
My *Logic* then has lost it's Aim,
If Sweet and Bitter be the same:
And He, methinks, is no great Scholar,
Who can mistake Desire for Choler.   450

   The like may of the *Heart* be said:
Courage and Terror there are bred.
All those, whose *Hearts* are loose and low,
Start, if they hear but the *Tattoo*:
And mighty Physical their Fear is: 455
For, soon as Noise of Combat near is,
Their Heart, descending to their Breeches,
Must give their Stomach cruel twitches.
But Heroes who o'ercome or dye,
Have their Hearts hung extremely high;   460
The Strings of which, in Battel's Heat,
Against their very *Corslets* beat;
Keep Time with their own Trumpet's Measure;
And yield 'em most excessive Pleasure.

   Now if 'tis chiefly in the Heart,   465
That Courage does it self exert;
'Twill be prodigious hard to prove,
That This is eke the Throne of Love.
Would Nature make One Place the Seat
Of fond Desire, and fell Debate?   470
Must People only take Delight in
Those Hours, when They are tir'd with Fighting?
And has no Man, but who has kill'd
A Father, right to get a Child?
These Notions then I think but idle: 475
And Love shall still possess the Middle.

   This Truth more plainly to discover,
Suppose your Hero were a Lover.
Tho' He before had Gall and Rage,
Which Death, or Conquest must asswage;   480

He grows dispirited and low:
He hates the Fight, and shuns the Foe.

In scornful Sloth ACHILLES slept;
And for his Wench, like TALL-BOY, wept:
Nor would return to War and Slaughter;   485
'Till They brought back the Parson's Daughter.

ANTONIUS fled from ACTIUM's Coast,
AUGUSTUS pressing, ASIA lost:
His Sails by CUPID's Hand unfurl'd,
To keep the Fair, he gave the World.   490

EDWARD our Fourth, rever'd and crown'd,
Vig'rous in Youth, in Arms renown'd;
While ENGLAND's Voice, and WARWICK's Care
Design'd him GALLIA's beauteous Heir;
Chang'd Peace and Pow'r for Rage and Wars,   495
Only to dry One Widow's Tears.

FRANCE's fourth HENRY we may see,
A Servant to the fair D'ESTREE;
When quitting COUTRAS prosp'rous Field,
And Fortune taught at length to yield,   500
He from his Guards and Mid-night Tent,
Disguis'd o'er Hills and Vallies went,
To wanton with the sprightly Dame;
And in his Pleasure lost his Fame.

Bold is the Critic, who dares prove,   505
These Heroes were no Friends to Love;
And bolder He, who dares aver,
That they were Enemies to War.
Yet, when their Thought should, now or never,
Have rais'd their *Heart*, or fir'd their *Liver*;   510
Fond ALMA to those Parts was gone,
Which LOVE more justly calls his own.

Examples I could cite You more;
But be contented with these Four:
For when One's Proofs are aptly chosen;   515
Four are as valid as four Dozen.

One came from GREECE, and one from ROME;
The other Two grew nearer Home.
For some in Antient Books delight:
Others prefer what Moderns write: 520
Now I should be extremely loath,
Not to be thought expert in Both.

THE SECOND CANTO.

B UT shall we take the MUSE abroad,
To drop her idly on the Road?
And leave our Subject in the middle;
As BUTLER did his Bear and Fiddle?
Yet He, consummate Master, knew   5
When to recede, and where pursue:
His noble Negligences teach,
What Others Toils despair to reach.
He, perfect Dancer, climbs the Rope,
And balances your Fear and Hope: 10
If after some distinguish'd Leap,
He drops his Pole, and seems to slip;
Straight gath'ring all his active Strength,
He rises higher half his Length.
With Wonder You approve his Slight;   15
And owe your Pleasure to your Fright.
But, like poor ANDREW, I advance,
False *Mimic* of my Master's Dance:
A-round the Cord a while I sprawl;
And thence, tho' low, in earnest fall.   20

My Preface tells You, I digress'd:
He's half absolv'd who has confess'd.

I like, quoth DICK, your *Simile*:
And in Return, take Two from Me.
As Masters in the *Clare-obscure*,   25
With various Light your Eyes allure:
A flaming Yellow here They spread;
Draw off in Blew, or charge in Red:
Yet from these Colors odly mix'd,
Your Sight upon the Whole is fix'd.   30

Or as, again, your Courtly Dames,
(Whose Cloaths returning Birth-Day claims,)
By Arts improve the Stuffs they vary;
And Things are best, as most contrary.
The Gown with stiff Embroid'ry shining,   35
Looks charming with a slighter Lining:
The Out-, if INDIAN Figures stain;
The In-side must be rich and plain.
So You, great Authors, have thought fit,
To make Digression temper Wit: 40
When Arguments too fiercely glare;
You calm 'em with a milder Air:
To break their Points, You turn their Force;
And *Furbelow* the plain Discourse.

RICHARD, quoth MAT, these Words of Thine,   45
Speak something sly, and something fine:
But I shall e'en resume my *Theme*;
However Thou may'st praise, or blame.

As People marry now, and settle;
Fierce Love abates his usual Mettle: 50
Worldly Desires, and Household Cares
Disturb the Godhead's soft Affairs:
So now, as Health or Temper changes,
In larger Compass ALMA ranges,
This Day below, the next above;   55
As light, or solid Whimsies move.
So Merchant has his House in Town,
And Country-Seat near BANSTED Down:
From One he dates his Foreign Letters,
Sends out his Goods, and duns his Debtors: 60
In t'other, at his Hours of Leisure,
He smokes his Pipe, and takes his Pleasure.

And now your Matrimonial CUPID,
Lash'd on by Time, grows tir'd and stupid.
For Story and Experience tell Us,   65
That Man grows cold, and Woman jealous.

63] *L 30* At length your Matrimonial Cupid *W*: In tract of time your married Cupid *Alt. reading in W*   64] *L 30* Rid down betime grows mighty Stupid *W*   65 For] *L 30* And *W*   66] *L 30* That Men are Cold and Wives are Jealous *W*

Both would their little Ends secure:
He sighs for Freedom, She for Pow'r.
His Wishes tend abroad to roam;
And Her's, to domineer at Home.   70
Thus Passion flags by slow Degrees;
And ruffl'd more, delighted less,
The busy Mind does seldom go
To those once charming Seats below:
But, in the Breast incamp'd, prepares   75
For well-bred Feints, and future Wars.
The Man suspects his Lady's crying
(When he last Autumn lay a-dying)
Was but to gain him to appoint Her
By Codicil a larger Jointure.   80
The Woman finds it all a Trick,
That He could swoon, when She was sick;
And knows, that in That Grief he reckon'd
On black-ey'd SUSAN for his Second.

     Thus having strove some tedious Years   85
With feign'd Desires, and real Fears;
And tir'd with Answers, and Replies,
Of JOHN affirms, and MARTHA lies;
Leaving this endless Altercation,
The Mind affects a higher Station.   90

     POLTIS, that gen'rous King of THRACE,
I think, was in this very Case.
All ASIA now was by the Ears:
And Gods beat up for Voluntiers
To GREECE, and TROY; while POLTIS sat   95
In Quiet, governing his State.
And whence, said the Pacific King,
Does all this Noise, and Discord spring?
Why, PARIS took ATRIDES' Wife—
With Ease I could compose this Strife: 100
The injur'd Hero should not lose,
Nor the young Lover want a Spouse:

71] *L 30* Thus Love at last dos wholly Cease *W*   78 Autumn] *L 30* August *W*
80] *L 30* A Codicile beyond her Jointer *W*

But HELEN chang'd her first Condition,
Without her Husband's just Permission.
What from the Dame can PARIS hope? 105
She may as well from Him elope.
Again, how can her old Good-man
With Honor take Her back again?
From hence I logically gather,
The Woman cannot live with Either. 110
Now I have Two right honest Wives,
For whose Possession No Man strives:
One to ATRIDES I will send;
And t'other to my TROJAN Friend.
Each Prince shall thus with Honor have, 115
What Both so warmly seem to crave:
The Wrath of Gods and Man shall cease;
And POLTIS live and die in Peace.

DICK, if this Story pleaseth Thee,
Pray thank DAN POPE, who told it Me. 120

Howe'er swift ALMA's Flight may vary;
(Take this by way of *Corollary:*)
Some Limbs She finds the very same,
In Place, and Dignity, and Name:
These dwell at such convenient Distance, 125
That each may give his Friend Assistance.
Thus He who runs or dances, begs
The equal Vigor of Two Legs:
So much to both does ALMA trust,
She ne'er regards, which goes the first. 130
TEAGUE could make neither of them stay,
When with Himself he ran away.
The Man who struggles in the Fight,
Fatigues left Arm, as well as right:
For whilst one Hand exalts the Blow, 135
And on the Earth extends the Foe;
T'other would take it wond'rous ill,
If in your Pocket He lay still.

125 These dwell] *L 30* and plact *W*   126 give] *L 30* yeild *W*   128 equal Vigor]
L 30 Kind assistance *W*   133 The...struggles] *L 30* And those who struggle *W*
134 Fatigues left Arm,] *L 30* fatigue left Arms *W*

And when you shoot, and shut one Eye,
You cannot think, He would deny   140
To lend the t'other friendly Aid,
Or wink, as Coward, and affraid.
No, Sir; whilst He withdraws his Flame,
His Comrade takes the surer Aim.
One Moment if his Beams recede;   145
As soon as e'er the Bird is dead,
Opening again, He lays his Claim,
To half the Profit, half the Fame,
And helps to Pocket up the Game.
'Tis thus, One Tradesman slips away,   150
To give his Part'ner fairer Play.

    Some Limbs again in Bulk or Stature
Unlike, and not a-kin by Nature,
In Concert act, like modern Friends;
Because one serves the t'other's Ends.   155
The Arm thus waits upon the Heart,
So quick to take the Bully's Part,
That one, tho' warm, decides more slow,
Than t'other executes the Blow.
A Stander-by may chance to have it,   160
E'er HACK himself perceives, He gave it.

    The am'rous Eyes thus always go
A-stroling for their Friends below:
For long before the 'Squire and Dame
Have *tête à tête* reliev'd their Flame;   165
E'er Visits yet are brought about,
The Eye by Sympathy looks out;
Knows FLORIMEL, and longs to meet Her;
And, if He sees, is sure to greet Her,
Tho' at Sash-Window, on the Stairs,   170
At Court, nay (Authors say) at Pray'rs.—

    The Funeral of some valiant Knight
May give this Thing it's proper Light.
View his Two Gantlets: these declare,
That Both his Hands were us'd to War.   175

And from his Two gilt Spurs 'tis learn'd,
His Feet were equally concern'd.
But have You not with Thought beheld
The Sword hang dangling o'er the Shield?
Which shows the Breast, That Plate was us'd to,   180
Had an Ally right Arm to trust to.
And by the Peep-holes in his Crest,
Is it not virtually confest,
That there his Eye took distant Aim,
And glanc'd Respect to that bright Dame,   185
In whose Delight his Hope was center'd,
And for whose Glove his Life he ventur'd?

Objections to my general *System*
May 'rise, perhaps, and I have mist them:
But I can call to my Assistance   190
Proximity (mark that!) and Distance:
Can prove, that all Things, on Occasion,
Love Union, and desire Adhesion;
That ALMA merely is a Scale;
And Motives, like the Weights, prevail.   195
If neither Side turn down or up,
With Loss or Gain, with Fear or Hope;
The Balance always would hang ev'n,
Like MAH'MET's Tomb, 'twixt Earth and Heav'n.

This, RICHARD, is a curious Case: 200
Suppose your Eyes sent equal Rays
Upon two distant Pots of Ale,
Not knowing, which was Mild or Stale:
In this sad State your doubtful Choice
Would never have the casting Voice: 205
Which Best, or Worst, You could not think;
And die You must, for want of Drink:
Unless some Chance inclines your Sight,
Setting one Pot in fairer Light;
Then You prefer or A, or B,   210
As Lines and Angles best agree:
Your Sense resolv'd impells your Will;
She guides your Hand,—So drink your Fill.

Have you not seen a Baker's Maid
Between two equal Panniers sway'd? 215
Her Tallies useless lie, and idle,
If plac'd exactly in the Middle:
But forc'd from this unactive State,
By virtue of some casual Weight;
On either Side You hear 'em clatter, 220
And judge of right and left-hand Matter.

Now, RICHARD, this coercive Force,
Without your Choice, must take it's Course.
Great Kings to Wars are pointed forth,
Like loaded Needles to the North. 225
And Thou and I, by Pow'r unseen,
Are barely Passive, and suck'd in
To HENAULT's Vaults, or CELIA's Chamber,
As Straw and Paper are by Amber.
If we sit down to play or set 230
(Suppose at *Ombre* or *Basset*)
Let People call us Cheats, or Fools;
Our Cards and We are equal Tools.
We sure in vain the Cards condemn:
Our selves both cut and shuffl'd them. 235
In vain on Fortune's Aid rely:
She only is a Stander-by.
Poor Men! poor Papers! We and They
Do some impulsive Force obey;
And are but play'd with:—Do not play. ⎬ 240
But Space and Matter we should blame:
They palm'd the Trick that lost the Game.

Thus to save further Contradiction,
Against what You may think but Fiction;
I for Attraction, DICK, declare: 245
Deny it those bold Men that dare.
As well your Motion, as your Thought
Is all by hidden Impulse wrought:
Ev'n saying, that You Think or Walk,
How like a Country 'Squire you talk? 250

Mark then;—Where Fancy or Desire
Collects the Beams of Vital Fire;
Into that Limb fair ALMA slides,
And there, *pro tempore*, resides.
She dwells in NICHOLINI's Tongue,   255
When PYRRHUS chants the Heav'nly Song.
When PEDRO does the Lute command,
She guides the cunning Artist's Hand.
Thro' MACER's Gullet she runs down,
When the vile Glutton dines alone.   260
And void of Modesty and Thought,
She follows BIBO's endless Draught.
Thro' the soft Sex again She ranges;
As Youth, Caprice, or Fashion changes.
Fair ALMA careless and serene,   265
In FANNY's sprightly Eyes is seen;
While they diffuse their Infant Beams,
Themselves not conscious of their Flames.
Again fair ALMA sits confest,
On FLORIMEL's experter Breast;   270
When She the rising Sigh constrains,
And by concealing speaks her Pains.
In CYNTHIA's Neck fair ALMA glows;
When the vain Thing her Jewels shows:
When JENNY's Stays are newly lac'd,   275
Fair ALMA plays about her Waste;
And when the swelling Hoop sustains
The rich Brocard, fair ALMA deigns
Into that lower Space to enter,
Of the large Round, Her self the Center.   280

    Again: That Single Limb or Feature
(Such is the cogent Force of Nature)
Which most did ALMA's Passion move,
In the first Object of her Love,
For ever will be found confest,   285
And printed on the am'rous Breast.

    O ABELARD, ill-fated Youth,
Thy Tale will justify this Truth:

But well I weet, thy cruel Wrong
Adorns a nobler Poet's Song.   290
Dan POPE for thy Misfortune griev'd,
With kind Concern, and Skill has weav'd
A silken Web; and ne'er shall fade
It's Colors: gently has He laid
The Mantle o'er thy sad Distress: 295
And VENUS shall the Texture bless.
He o'er the weeping Nun has drawn,
Such artful Folds of Sacred Lawn,
That LOVE with equal Grief and Pride,
Shall see the Crime, He strives to hide: 300
And softly drawing back the Veil,
The God shall to his Vot'ries tell
Each conscious Tear, each blushing Grace,
That deck'd Dear ELOISA's Face.

    Happy the Poet, blest the Lays,   305
Which BUCKINGHAM has deign'd to praise.

    Next, DICK, as Youth and Habit sways,
A hundred Gambols ALMA plays.
If, whilst a Boy, JACK run from Schole,
Fond of his Hunting-horn, and Pole;   310
Tho' Gout and Age his Speed detain,
Old JOHN halloo's his Hounds again.
By his Fire-side he starts the Hare;
And turns Her in his Wicker-Chair:
His Feet, however lame, You find,   315
Have got the better of his Mind.

    If while the Mind was in her Leg,
The Dance affected nimble PEG;
Old MADGE, bewitch'd at Sixty one,
Calls for *Green Sleeves*, and *Jumping Joan*.   320
In public Mask, or private Ball,
From *Lincoln's Inn*, to *Goldsmith's Hall*,
All Christmas long away She trudges;
Trips it with Prentices and Judges:
In vain her Children urge her Stay;   325
And Age or Palsey bar the Way.

But if those Images prevail,
Which whilom did affect the Tail;
She still reviews the ancient Scene;
Forgets the forty Years between: 330
Awkardly gay, and odly merry,
Her Scarf pale Pink, her Head-Knot Cherry;
O'er heated with *Ideal* Rage,
She cheats her Son, to wed her Page.

If ALMA, whilst the Man was young,   335
Slip'd up too soon into his Tongue:
Pleas'd with his own fantastic Skill,
He lets that Weapon ne'er lie still.
On any Point if You dispute;
Depend upon it, He'll confute: 340
Change Sides; and You increase your Pain:
For He'll confute You back again.
For One may speak with TULLY's Tongue;
Yet all the while be in the wrong.
And 'tis remarkable, that They   345
Talk most, who have the least to say.
Your dainty Speakers have the Curse,
To plead bad Causes down to worse:
As Dames, who Native Beauty want,
Still uglier look, the more They paint.   350

Again: If in the Female Sex
ALMA should on this Member fix;
(A cruel and a desp'rate Case,
From which Heav'n shield my lovely Lass!)
For evermore all Care is vain,   355
That would bring ALMA down again.
As in habitual Gout, or Stone,
The only Thing that can be done,
Is to correct your Drink and Diet,
And keep the inward Foe in Quiet: 360
So, if for any Sins of Our's,
Or our Forefathers, Higher Pow'rs,
Severe tho' just, afflict our Life
With that Prime Ill, a talking Wife;

'Till Death shall bring the kind Relief,   365
We must be Patient, or be Deaf.

You know, a certain Lady, DICK,
Who saw Me, when I last was sick:
She kindly talk'd, at least three Hours,
Of *Plastic* Forms, and *Mental* Pow'rs: 370
Describ'd our pre-existing Station,
Before this vile Terrene Creation:
And lest I should be weary'd, Madam,
To cut Things short, came down to ADAM;
From whence, as fast as She was able,   375
She drowns the World, and builds up BABEL;
Thro' SYRIA, PERSIA, GREECE She goes;
And takes the ROMANS in the Close.

But We'll descant on gen'ral Nature:
This is a *System*, not a Satyr.   380

Turn We this Globe; and let Us see,
How diff'rent Nations disagree,
In what We wear, or eat and drink;
Nay, DICK, perhaps in what We think.
In Water as You smell and tast   385
The Soyls, thro' which it rose and past:
In ALMA's Manners You may read
The Place, where She was born and bred.

One People from their swadling Bands
Releas'd their Infants Feet and Hands: 390
Here ALMA to these Limbs was brought;
And SPARTA's Offspring kick'd and fought.

Another taught their Babes to talk,
E'er they could yet in Goe-carts walk:
There ALMA settl'd in the Tongue;   395
And Orators from ATHENS sprung.

Observe but in these Neighb'ring Lands,
The diff'rent Use of Mouths and Hands:
As Men repos'd their various Hopes,
In Battles These, and Those in Tropes.   400

383 eat and] eat, or *L 30*

In BRITAIN's Isles, as HEYLYN notes,
The Ladies trip in Petticoats;
Which, for the Honor of their Nation,
They quit but on some great Occasion.
Men there in Breeches clad You view: 405
They claim that Garment, as their due.
In TURKEY the Reverse appears;
Long Coats the haughty Husband wears,
And greets His Wife with angry Speeches;
If She be seen without her Breeches.   410

In our Fantastic *Climes* the Fair
With cleanly Powder dry their Hair:
And round their lovely Breast and Head
Fresh Flow'rs their mingl'd Odors shed.
Your nicer HOTTENTOTES think meet   415
With Guts and Tripe to deck their Feet:
With down-cast Looks on TOTTA's Legs,
The ogling Youth most humbly begs,
She would not from his Hopes remove
At once his Breakfast, and his Love: 420
And if the skittish Nymph should fly;
He in a double Sense must die.

We simple *Toasters* take Delight
To see our Women's Teeth look white.
And ev'ry saucy ill-bred Fellow   425
Sneers at a Mouth profoundly yellow.
In CHINA none hold Women sweet,
Except their Snags are black as Jett.
King CHIHU put Nine Queens to Death,
Convict on Statute, *Iv'ry Teeth*.   430

At TONQUIN if a Prince should die;
(As Jesuits write, who never lye)
The Wife, and Counsellor, and Priest,
Who serv'd Him most, and lov'd Him best;
Prepare, and light his Fun'ral Fire,   435
And chearful on the Pile expire.
In EUROPE 'twould be hard to find
In each Degree One half so kind.

Now turn We to the farthest East,
And there observe the Gentry Drest. 440
Prince GIOLO, and his Royal Sisters,
Scarr'd with ten thousand comely Blisters;
The Marks remaining on the Skin,
To tell the Quality within.
Distinguish'd Slashes deck the Great: 445
As each excells in Birth, or State;
His Oylet-holes are more, and ampler:
The King's own Body was a Samplar.
Happy the Climate, where the *Beau*
Wears the same Suit for Use, and Show: 450
And at a small Expence your Wife,
If once well pink'd, is cloth'd for Life.

Westward again the INDIAN Fair,
Is nicely smear'd with Fat of Bear.
Before You see, You smell your Toast, 455
And sweetest She, who stinks the most.
The finest Sparks, and cleanest *Beaux*
Drip from the Shoulders to the Toes.
How sleek their Skins! their Joints how easy!
There Slovens only are not greasy. 460

I mention'd diff'rent Ways of Breeding:
Begin We in our Children's Reading.
To Master JOHN the ENGLISH Maid
A Horn-book gives of Ginger-bread:
And that the Child may learn the better, 465
As He can name, He eats the Letter:
Proceeding thus with vast Delight,
He spells, and gnaws, from Left to Right.
But shew a HEBREW's hopeful Son,
Where We suppose the Book begun; 470
The Child would thank You for your Kindness,
And read quite backward from our *Finis*:
Devour He Learning ne'er so fast;
Great A would be reserv'd the last.

An equal Instance of this Matter, 475
Is in the Manners of a Daughter.

In EUROPE, if a harmless Maid,
By Nature and by Love betray'd,
Should e'er a Wife become a Nurse;
Her Friends would look on Her the Worse.   480
In CHINA, DAMPIER's Travels tell Ye;
(Look in his Index for PAGELLI:)
Soon as the BRITISH Ships unmoore,
And jolly Long-boat rows to Shore;
Down come the Nobles of the Land: 485
Each brings his Daughter in his Hand,
Beseeching the Imperious Tar
To make Her but One Hour his Care.
The tender Mother stands affrighted,
Lest her dear Daughter should be slighted: 490
And poor Miss YAYA dreads the Shame
Of going back the Maid She came.

Observe how Custom, DICK, compells
The Lady that in EUROPE dwells:
After her Tea She slips away;   495
And what to do, One need not say.
Now see how great POMONQUE's Queen
Behav'd Herself amongst the Men:
Pleas'd with her Punch, the Gallant Soul
First drank, then water'd in the Bowl;   500
And sprinkl'd in the Captain's Face
The Marks of Her Peculiar Grace—

To close this Point, We need not roam
For Instances so far from Home.
What parts gay FRANCE from sober SPAIN?   505
A little rising Rocky Chain.
Of Men born South or North o'th' Hill,
Those seldom move; These ne'er stand still.
DICK, You love Maps, and may perceive
ROME not far distant from GENEVE.   510
If the good POPE remains at Home,
He's the First Prince in CHRISTENDOME.
Choose then, good POPE, at Home to stay;
Nor Westward curious take Thy Way.

501 sprinkl'd] scatter'd *L 30*

Thy Way unhappy should'st Thou take   515
From TIBER's Bank to LEMAN-Lake;
Thou art an Aged Priest no more,
But a Young flaring Painted Whore:
Thy Sex is lost: Thy Town is gone,
No longer ROME, but BABYLON.   520
That some few Leagues should make this Change,
To Men unlearn'd seems mighty strange.

But need We, Friend, insist on This?
Since in the very CANTONS SWISS,
All Your Philosophers agree,   525
And prove it plain, that One may be
A Heretic, or True Believer,
On this, or t'other Side a River.

Here with an artful Smile, quoth DICK,
Your Proofs come mighty full, and thick—   530

The Bard on this extensive Chapter,
Wound up into Poetic Rapture,
Continu'd: RICHARD, cast your Eye
By Night upon a Winter-Sky:
Cast it by Day-light on the Strand,   535
Which compasses fair ALBION's Land:
If You can count the Stars that glow
Above, or Sands that lie below;
Into those Common-places look,
Which from great Authors I have took;   540
And count the Proofs I have collected,
To have my Writings well protected.
These I lay by for Time of Need;
And Thou may'st at thy Leisure read.
For standing every Critic's Rage,   545
I safely will to future Age
My *System*, as a Gift, bequeath,
Victorious over Spight, and Death.

THE THIRD CANTO.

RICHARD, who now was half a-sleep,
  Rous'd; nor would longer Silence keep:
And Sense like this, in vocal Breath
Broke from his twofold Hedge of Teeth.
Now if this Phrase too harsh be thought;   5
POPE, tell the World, 'tis not my Fault.
Old HOMER taught us thus to speak:
If 'tis not Sense; at least 'tis GREEK.

  As Folks, quoth RICHARD, prone to Leasing,
Say Things at first because they're pleasing;   10
Then prove what they have once asserted,
Nor care to have their Lie deserted;
'Till their own Dreams at length deceive 'em;
And oft repeating, they believe 'em.
Or as again those am'rous Blades,   15
Who trifle with their Mother's Maids;
Tho' at the first their wild Desire,
Was but to quench a present Fire;
Yet if the object of their Love
Chance by LUCINA's Aid to prove;   20
They seldom let the Bantling roar
In Basket, at a Neighbour's Door:
But by the flatt'ring Glass of Nature,
Viewing themselves in *Cake-bread*'s Feature;
With serious Thought and Care support,   25
What only was begun in Sport.

  Just so with You, my Friend, it fares,
Who deal in Philosophic Wares:
Atoms You cut; and Forms You measure,
To gratifie your private Pleasure;   30
'Till airy Seeds of casual Wit
Do some fantastic Birth beget:
And pleas'd to find your *System* mended,
Beyond what You at first intended,
The happy Whimsey You pursue;   35
'Till You at length believe it true.

Caught by your own delusive Art,
You fancy first, and then assert.

   Quoth MATTHEW: Friend, as far as I
Thro' Art or Nature cast my Eye,
This *Axiom* clearly I discern,   40
That One must Teach, and t'Other Learn.
No Fool PYTHAGORAS was thought:
Whilst He his weighty Doctrines taught;
He made his list'ning Scholars stand,
Their Mouth still cover'd with their Hand: 45
Else, may be, some odd-thinking Youth,
Less Friend to Doctrine than to Truth,
Might have refus'd to let his Ears
Attend the Musick of the Spheres;
Deny'd all *transmigrating* Scenes,   50
And introduc'd the Use of Beans.
From great LUCRETIUS take His Void;
And all the World is quite destroy'd.
Deny DES-CART His subtil Matter;
You leave Him neither Fire, nor Water.   55
How odly would Sir ISAAC look,
If You, in Answer to his Book,
Say in the Front of your Discourse,
That Things have no *Elastic* Force?
How could our *Chymic* Friends go on,   60
To find the *Philosophic* Stone;
If You more pow'rful Reasons bring,
To prove, that there is no such Thing?

   Your Chiefs in Sciences and Arts,
Have great Contempt of ALMA's Parts.   65
They find, She giddy is, or dull;
She doubts, if Things are void, or full:
And who should be presum'd to tell,
What She Her self should see, or feel?
She doubts, if two and two make four;   70
Tho' She has told them ten times o'er.
It can't—it may be—and it must:
To which of these must ALMA trust?

    39 Quoth *L* 30: Quoth, *1718*

Nay, further yet They make Her go,   75
In doubting, if She doubts, or no.
Can *Syllogysm* set Things right?
No: *Majors* soon with *Minors* fight:
Or, Both in friendly Consort join'd;
The *Consequence* limps false behind.   80
So to some Cunning-Man She goes,
And asks of Him, how much She knows.
With Patience grave He hears Her speak;
And from his short Notes, gives Her back
What from her Tale He comprehended: 85
Thus the Dispute is wisely ended.

From the Account the Loser brings,
The Conj'ror knows, who stole the Things.

'Squire (interrupted DICK) since when
Were You amongst these Cunning-Men?   90

Dear DICK, quoth MAT, let not Thy Force
Of Eloquence spoil my Discourse.
I tell Thee, this is ALMA's Case,
Still asking, what some Wise-man says,
Who does his Mind in Words reveal,   95
Which All must grant; tho' Few can spell.
You tell Your Doctor, that Y'are ill:
And what does He, but write a Bill,
Of which You need not read one Letter?
The worse the Scrawl, the Dose the better.   100
For if You knew but what You take;
Tho' You recover, He must break.

Ideas, Forms, and *Intellects,*
Have furnish'd out three diff'rent Sects.
Substance, or *Accident* divides   105
All EUROPE into adverse Sides.

Now, as engag'd in Arms or Laws,
You must have Friends to back your Cause:
In *Philosophic* Matters so
Your Judgment must with others go.   110

For as in Senates, so in Scholes,
Majority of Voices rules.

Poor ALMA, like a lonely Deer,
O'er Hills and Dales does doubtful err:
With panting Haste, and quick Surprise,   115
From ev'ry Leaf that stirs, She flies;
'Till mingl'd with the neighb'ring Herd,
She slights what erst She singly fear'd:
And now, exempt from Doubt and Dread,
She dares pursue; if They dare lead: 120
As Their Example still prevails;
She tempts the Stream, or leaps the Pales.

He then, quoth DICK, who by Your Rule
Thinks for Himself, becomes a Fool.
As Party-Man who leaves the rest,   125
Is call'd but *Whimsical* at Best.
Now, by Your Favour, Master MAT,
Like RALPHO, here I smell a Rat.
I must be listed in Your Sect;
Who, tho' They teach not, can protect.   130
Right, RICHARD, MAT. in Triumph cri'd;
So put off all Mistrust and Pride.
And while My Principles I beg;
Pray answer only with Your Leg.
Believe what friendly I advise: 135
Be first secure; and then be wise.
The Man within the Coach that sits,
And to another's Skill submits,
Is safer much (whate'er arrives)
And warmer too, than He that drives.   140

So, DICK *Adept*, tuck back Thy Hair;
And I will pour into Thy Ear
Remarks, which None did e'er disclose,
In smooth-pac'd Verse, or hobling Prose.
Attend, Dear DICK; but don't reply: 145
And Thou may'st prove as Wise as I.

When ALMA now in diff'rent Ages,
Has finish'd Her ascending Stages;

Into the Head at length She gets,
And There in Public Grandeur sits,
To judge of Things, and censure Wits.   } 150

   Here, RICHARD, how could I explain,
The various Lab'rinths of the Brain?
Surprise My Readers, whilst I tell 'em
Of *Cerebrum*, and *Cerebellum*?   155
How could I play the Commentator
On *Dura*, and on *Pia Mater*?
Where Hot and Cold, and Dry and Wet,
Strive each the t'other's Place to get;
And with incessant Toil and Strife,   160
Would keep Possession during Life.
I could demonstrate every Pore,
Where Mem'ry lays up all her Store;
And to an Inch compute the Station,
'Twixt Judgment, and Imagination.   165
O Friend! I could display much Learning,
At least to Men of small Discerning.
The Brain contains ten thousand Cells:
In each some active Fancy dwells;
Which always is at Work, and framing   170
The several Follies I was naming.
As in a Hive's vimineous Dome,
Ten thousand Bees enjoy their Home;
Each does her studious Action vary,
To go and come, to fetch and carry: 175
Each still renews her little Labor;
Nor justles her assiduous Neighbour:
Each—whilst this *Thesis* I maintain;
I fancy, DICK, I know thy Brain.
O with the mighty *Theme* affected,   180
Could I but see thy Head dissected!

   My Head, quoth DICK, to serve your Whim?
Spare That, and take some other Limb.
Sir, in your nice Affairs of *System*,
Wise Men propose; but Fools assist 'em.   185

Says MATTHEW: RICHARD, keep thy Head,
And hold thy Peace; and I'll proceed.

Proceed? quoth DICK: Sir, I aver,
You have already gone too far.
When People once are in the Wrong;   190
Each Line they add, is much too long.
Who fastest walks, but walks astray,
Is only furthest from his Way.
Bless your Conceits! must I believe,
Howe'er absurd, what You conceive;   195
And, for your Friendship, live and dye
A Papist in Philosophy?
I say, whatever You maintain
Of ALMA in the Heart, or Brain;
The plainest Man alive may tell Ye,   200
Her Seat of Empire is the Belly:
From hence She sends out those Supplies,
Which make Us either stout, or wise:
The Strength of ev'ry other Member,
Is founded on your Belly-Timber: 205
The Qualms or Raptures of your Blood
Rise in Proportion to your Food:
And if you would improve your Thought;
You must be fed, as well as taught.
Your Stomach makes your Fabric roll;   210
Just as the Biass rules the Bowl.
That great ACHILLES might imploy
The Strength, design'd to ruin TROY;
He Din'd on Lion's Marrow, spread
On Toasts of Ammunition-Bread: 215
But by His Mother sent away,
Amongst the THRACIAN Girls to play,
Effeminate He sat, and quiet:
Strange Product of a Cheese-cake Diet!
Now give my Argument fair Play;   220
And take the Thing the t'other Way:

192-3] L 30

and whilst with nimble steps you stray
You still are further from your Way *W*

The Youngster, who at Nine and Three
Drinks with his Sisters Milk and Tea,
From Break-fast reads, 'till twelve a Clock,
BURNET and HEYLYN, HOBBES and LOCK: 225
He pays due Visits after Noon
To Cousin ALICE, and Uncle JOHN:
At Ten from Coffee-House or Play
Returning, finishes the Day.
But give him Port, and potent Sack;   230
From *Milk-sop* He starts up *Mohack*:
Holds that the Happy know no Hours;
So thro' the Street at Midnight scow'rs:
Breaks Watch-men's Heads, and Chair-men's Glasses;
And thence proceeds to nicking Sashes: 235
Till by some tougher Hand o'ercome,
And first knock'd down, and then led Home;
He damns the Foot-man, strikes the Maid,
And decently reels up to Bed.

Observe the various Operations   240
Of Food, and Drink in several Nations.
Was ever TARTAR fierce or cruel,
Upon the Strength of Water-Gruel?
But who shall stand His Rage and Force;
If first he rides, then eats his Horse?   245
Sallads, and Eggs, and lighter Fare
Tune the ITALIAN Spark's Guitar.
And, if I take *Dan* CONGREVE right;
Pudding and Beef make BRITONS fight.
TOKAY and COFFEE cause this Work,   250
Between the GERMAN and the TURK:
And Both, as They Provisions want,
Chicane, avoid, retire, and faint.

Hunger and Thirst, or Guns and Swords,
Give the same Death in diff'rent Words.   255
To push this Argument no further;
To starve a Man, in Law, is Murther.

As in a WATCHE's fine Machine,
Tho' many artful Springs are seen;

The added Movements, which declare,   260
How full the Moon, how old the Year,
Derive their secondary Pow'r
From that, which simply points the Hour.
For, tho' these Gim-cracks were away;
(QUARE would not swear; but QUARE would say)   265
However more reduc'd and plain,
The Watch would still a Watch remain:
But if the *Horal* Orbite ceases;
The whole stands still, or breaks to pieces;
Is now no longer what it was;   270
And You may e'en go sell the Case.
So if unprejudic'd you scan
The Goings of this Clock-work, Man;
You find a hundred Movements made
By fine Devices in his Head: 275
But 'tis the Stomach's solid Stroke,
That tells his Being, what's a Clock.
If You take off his *Rhet'ric*-Trigger;
He talks no more in Mood and Figure:
Or clog his *Mathematic*-Wheel;   280
His Buildings fall; his Ship stands still.
Or lastly, break his *Politic*-Weight;
His Voice no longer rules the State.
Yet if these finer Whims were gone;
Your Clock, tho' plain, would still go on: 285
But spoil the Engine of Digestion;
And You entirely change the Question.
ALMA's Affairs no Pow'r can mend;
The Jest, alas! is at an End:
Soon ceases all this worldly Bustle;   290
And you consign the Corps to RUSSEL.

     Now make your ALMA come or go,
From Leg to Hand, from Top to Toe;
Your *System*, without My Addition,
Is in a very sad Condition.   295
So HARLEQUIN extoll'd his Horse,
Fit for the War, or Road, or Course;

His Mouth was soft; his Eye was good;
His Foot was sure as ever trod:
One Fault he had, a Fault indeed;   300
And what was that? The Horse was Dead.

DICK, from these Instances and Fetches,
Thou mak'st of Horses, Clocks, and Watches,
Quoth MAT, to Me thou seem'st to mean,
That ALMA is a mere *Machine*;   305
That telling others what's a Clock,
She knows not what Her self has struck;
But leaves to Standers-by the Tryal,
Of what is mark'd upon her Dial.

Here hold a Blow, good Friend, quoth DICK,   310
And rais'd his Voice exceeding quick:
Fight fair, Sir: what I never meant
Don't You infer. In Argument,
Similies are like Songs in Love:
They much describe; they nothing prove.   315

MAT, who was here a little gravel'd,
Tost up his Nose, and would have cavil'd:
But calling HERMES to his Aid,
Half pleas'd, half angry, thus He said:

Where mind ('tis for the Author's Fame)   320
That MATTHEW call'd, and HERMES came.
In Danger Heroes, and in Doubt
Poets find Gods to help 'em out.

Friend RICHARD, I begin to see,
That You and I shall scarce agree.   325
Observe how odly you behave:
The more I grant, the more You crave.
But, Comrade, as I said just now,
I should affirm, and You allow.
We *System*-makers can sustain   330
The *Thesis*, which, You grant, was plain;

---

320 Where] *L 30* Here *W*   321 and HERMES] *L 30* and Pallas *W*: Minerva *Earlier*
reading in W   322] *L 30* Heroes in peril and in doubt *W*

And with Remarks and Comments teaze Ye;
In case the Thing before was easy.
But in a Point obscure and dark,
We fight as LEIBNITS did with CLARK;   335
And when no Reason we can show,
Why Matters This or That Way go;
The shortest Way the Thing We try,
And what We know not, We deny:
True to our own o'erbearing Pride,   340
And false to all the World beside.

    That old Philosopher grew cross,
Who could not tell what Motion was:
Because He walk'd against his Will;
He fac'd Men down, that He stood still.   345
And He who reading on the Heart,
(When all his *Quodlibets* of Art
Could not expound it's Pulse and Heat)
Swore, He had never felt it beat.
CHRYSIPPUS, foil'd by EPICURUS,   350
Makes bold (JOVE bless Him!) to assure Us,
That all things, which our Mind can view,
May be at once both false, and true.
And MALBRANCH has an odd Conceit,
As ever enter'd FRENCHMAN's Pate: 355
Says He, so little can our Mind
Of Matter, or of Spirit find,
That We by Guess, at least, may gather
Something, which may be Both, or Neither.
Faith, DICK, I must confess, 'tis true   360
(But this is only *Entre Nous*)
That many knotty Points there are,
Which All discuss, but Few can clear:
As Nature slily had thought fit,
For some by-Ends, to cross-bite Wit.   365
Circles to square, and Cubes to double,
Would give a Man excessive Trouble:

366 square, and] *L 30* round or *W*   367 Would give a Man] *L 30* One give one's
thought *W*

The Longitude uncertain roams,
In spight of WH——N and his Bombs.
What *System*, DICK, has right averr'd   370
The Cause, why Woman has no Beard;
Or why, as Years our Frame attack,
Our Hair grows white, our Teeth grow black?
In Points like These We must agree,
Our Barber knows as much as We.   375
Yet still unable to explain,
We must persist the best We can;
With Care our *Systems* still renew,
And prove Things likely, tho' not true.

I could, Thou see'st, in quaint Dispute,   380
By dint of *Logic* strike Thee mute;
With learned Skill, now push, now parry,
From *Darii* to *Bocardo* vary,
And never yield, or what is worst,
Never conclude the Point discours'd.   385
Yet, that You *hic & nunc* may know,
How much You to my Candor owe;
I'll from the Disputant descend,
To show Thee, I assume the Friend:
I'll take Thy Notion for my own—   390
(So most Philosophers have done)
It makes my *System* more complete:
DICK, can it have a Nobler Fate?
Take what Thou wilt, said DICK, Dear Friend;
But bring thy Matters to an End.   395

I find, quoth MAT, Reproof is vain:
Who first offend will first complain.
Thou wishest, I should make to Shoar;
Yet still put'st in Thy thwarting Oar.
What I have told Thee fifty times   400
In Prose, receive for once in Rhimes:
A huge fat Man in Countrey-Fair,
Or City-Church, (no matter where)
Labor'd and push'd amidst the Croud,
Still bauling out extremely loud;   405

373 Our...our] *L* 30 Your...your *W*

Lord save Us! why do People press?
Another marking his Distress,
Friendly reply'd; Plump Gentleman,
Get out as fast as e'er You can:
Or cease to push, or to exclaim: 410
You make the very Croud You blame.

 Says DICK, your Moral does not need
The least Return; So e'en proceed:
Your Tale, howe'er apply'd, was short:
So far, at least, I thank You for't.   415

 MAT. took his Thanks, and in a Tone
More Magisterial, thus went on.

 Now ALMA settles in the Head;
As has before been sung, or said:
And here begins this Farce of Life;   420
Enter Revenge, Ambition, Strife:
Behold on both Sides Men advance,
To form in Earnest BAYS's Dance.
L'AVARE not using Half his Store,
Still grumbles, that He has no more;   425
Strikes not the present Tun, for fear
The Vintage should be bad next Year:
And eats To-day with inward Sorrow,
And Dread of fancy'd Want To-morrow.
Abroad if the *Sour-tout* You wear,   430
Repells the Rigor of the Air;
Would You be warmer, if at Home
You had the Fabric, and the Loom?
And if two Boots keep out the Weather;
What need You have two Hides of Leather?   435
Could PEDRO, think You, make no Tryal
Of a *Sonata* on his Viol,
Unless he had the total Gut,
Whence every String at first was cut?

 When RARUS shows You his Carton;   440
He always tells You, with a Groan,
Where two of that same Hand were torn,
Long before You, or He were born.

Poor VENTO's Mind so much is crost,
For Part of His PETRONIUS lost;   445
That He can never take the Pains
To understand what yet remains.

What Toil did honest CURIO take?
What strict Enquiries did He make,
To get one Medal wanting yet,   450
And perfect all his ROMAN Sett?
'Tis found: and O his happy Lot!
'Tis bought, lock'd up, and lies forgot:
Of These no more You hear Him speak:
He now begins upon the GREEK.   455
These rang'd and show'd, shall in their Turns
Remain obscure, as in their Urns.
My Copper-Lamps at any Rate, ⎫
For being True Antique, I bought; ⎪
Yet wisely melted down my Plate, ⎬   460
On Modern Models to be wrought: ⎪
And Trifles I alike pursue; ⎭
Because They're Old; because They're New.

DICK, I have seen You with Delight,
For GEORGY make a Paper-Kite.   465
And simple Odes too many show Ye,
My servile Complaisance to CLOE.
Parents and Lovers are decreed
By Nature Fools—That's brave indeed!
Quoth DICK: such Truths are worth receiving: 470
Yet still DICK look'd, as not believing.

Now, ALMA, to Divines and Prose
I leave Thy Frauds, and Crimes, and Woes:
Nor think To-night of Thy Ill-Nature,
But of Thy Follies, Idle Creature,   475
The turns of Thy uncertain Wing,
And not the Malice of Thy Sting:
Thy Pride of being great and wise,
I do but mention, to despise.

467 to] for *L 30*   479 do but mention,] mention not but *L 30*

I view with Anger and Disdain,   480
How little gives Thee Joy, or Pain:
A Print, a *Bronze*, a Flow'r, a Root,
A Shell, a Butter-fly can do't.
Ev'n a Romance, a Tune, a Rhime
Help Thee to pass the tedious Time,   485
Which else would on thy Hand remain:
Tho' flown, it ne'er looks back again.
And Cards are dealt, and Chess-boards brought,
To ease the Pain of Coward-Thought.
Happy Result of Human Wit!   490
That ALMA may Her self forget.

    DICK, thus We act; and thus We are,
Or toss'd by Hope, or sunk by Care.
With endless Pain This Man pursues
What, if he gain'd, He could not use: 495
And T'other fondly Hopes to see
What never was, nor e'er shall be.
We err by Use, go wrong by Rules;
In Gesture grave, in Action Fools:
We join Hypocrisie to Pride,   500
Doubling the Faults, We strive to hide.
Or grant, that with extreme Surprize,
We find our selves at Sixty wise;
And twenty pretty Things are known,
Of which we can't accomplish One;   505
Whilst, as my *System* says, the Mind
Is to these upper Rooms confin'd:
Should I, my Friend, at large repeat
Her borrow'd Sense, her fond Conceit;
The Bede-roll of her vicious Tricks;   510
My Poem would be too prolix.
For could I my Remarks sustain,
Like SOCRATES, or MILES MONTAIGNE;
Who in these Times would read my Books,
But TOM O' STILES, or JOHN O' NOKES?   515

    As BRENTFORD Kings discrete and wise,
After long Thought and grave Advice,

Into LARDELLA's Coffin peeping,
Saw nought to cause their Mirth or Weeping:
So ALMA now to Joy or Grief   520
Superior, finds her late Relief:
Weary'd of being High, or Great,
And nodding in her Chair of State;
Stun'd and worn out with endless Chat,
Of WILL did this, and NAN said that;   525
She finds, poor Thing, some little Crack,
Which Nature, forc'd by Time, must make;
Thro' which She wings her destin'd Way:
Upward She soars; and down drops Clay:
While some surviving Friend supplies   530
Hic jacet, and a hundred Lies.

O RICHARD, 'till that Day appears,
Which must decide our Hopes and Fears:
Would FORTUNE calm her present Rage,
And give us Play-things for our Age: 535
Would CLOTHO wash her Hands in Milk,
And twist our Thread with Gold and Silk:
Would She in Friendship, Peace, and Plenty,
Spin out our Years to four times Twenty:
And should We both in this Condition,   540
Have conquer'd Love, and worse Ambition;
(Else those two Passions, by the way,
May chance to show us scurvy Play:)
Then RICHARD, then should We sit down,
Far from the Tumult of this Town: 545
I fond of my well-chosen Seat,
My Pictures, Medals, Books compleat:
Or should We mix our friendly Talk,
O'er-shaded in that Fav'rite Walk,
Which Thy own Hand had whilom planted,   550
Both pleas'd with all we thought We wanted:

526–7] *L 30*

    In Short this little Bird at last
    Up all its perches having past
    Finds at the Summerry Cage
    Some crany made by time and Age   *W*

528 wings . . . Way:] *L 30* struggling gets away *W*   529 Upward She] *L 30* She
upward *W*

Yet then, ev'n then one cross Reflection
Would spoil Thy Grove, and My Collection:
Thy Son and his, e'er that, may die;
And Time some uncouth Heir supply;   555
Who shall for nothing else be known,
But spoiling All, that Thou hast done.
Who set the Twigs, shall He remember,
That is in Hast to sell the Timber?
And what shall of thy Woods remain,   560
Except the Box that threw the Main?

   Nay may not Time and Death remove
The near Relations, whom I love?
And my Coz TOM, or his Coz MARY
(Who hold the Plough, or skim the Dairy)   565
My Fav'rite Books and Pictures sell
To SMART, or DOILEY by the Ell?
Kindly throw in a little Figure,
And set their Price upon the bigger?
Those who could never read their Grammar;   570
When my dear Volumes touch the Hammer;
May think Books best, as richest bound.
My Copper Medals by the Pound
May be with learned Justice weigh'd:
To turn the Ballance, OTHO's Head   575
May be thrown in; And for the Mettle,
The Coin may mend a Tinker's Kettle—

   Tir'd with these Thoughts—Less tir'd than I,
Quoth DICK, with Your Philosophy—
That People live and dye, I knew   580
An hour ago, as well as You.
And if Fate spins Us longer Years,
Or is in haste to take the Shears;
I know, We must Both Fortunes try,
And bear our Evils, wet or dry.   585
Yet let the Goddess smile, or frown;
Bread We shall eat, or white, or brown:
And in a Cottage, or a Court,
Drink fine *Champaigne*, or muddl'd *Port*.

What need of Books these Truths to tell,   590
Which Folks perceive, who cannot spell?
And must We Spectacles apply,
To view, what hurts our naked Eye?

Sir, if it be Your Wisdom's Aim,
To make Me merrier than I am;   595
I'll be all Night at Your Devotion—
Come on, Friend; broach the pleasing Notion:
But if You would depress my Thought;
Your *System* is not worth a Groat—

For PLATO's Fancies what care I?   600
I hope You would not have me die,
Like simple CATO in the Play,
For any Thing that He can say?
E'en let Him of *Ideas* speak
To Heathens in his Native GREEK.   605
If to be sad is to be wise;
I do most heartily despise
Whatever SOCRATES has said,
Or TULLY writ, or WANLEY read.

Dear DRIFT, to set our Matters right,   610
Remove these Papers from my Sight;
Burn MAT's DES-CART', and ARISTOTLE:
Here, JONATHAN, Your Master's Bottle.

Song.

Now how shall I do with my love and my pride?
    Dear Dick Give me Councill if friendship has any.
Prithee purge or lett blood, surly Richard replyed
And forget the Coquet in the Arms of your N——.

Title: L 28 (Pope), M: om. *W, L 28 (D)*: Epigram '*Contents*' *of L 28*: A CASE STATED.
1740   1 Now *L 28, M*: now *W*: NOW *1740*   pride? *edd.*: pride *W*: Pride? *L 28*:
Pride *M*: pride, *1740*   2 Dear *L 28, M, 1740*: Dr *W*   3 Richard *L 28, M*:
Rich^d *W*: RICHARD *1740*   4 N——. *add.*: N. *W*: Nanny. *L 28, M, 1740*

While I pleaded with passion how much I deservd   5
For the pains and the torments of more than a year
She lookt in an almanack, whence She observd,
That it wanted a fortnight to B—— fair.

My Cowley and Waller how vainly I quote
While my Negligent Judge only hears with her Eye?   10
In a long flaxen Wigg, and Embroiderd new Coat
Thom Spark saying nothing talks better than I.

Answer to the Female Phaeton.

As Almoner in Holy Week
    Dealing Good George's Cloth and Bread
Sends forth His Officers to Seek
    The People who stand most in Need

So Thou Director Great of Wit   5
    Amongst Us Authors Rule'st the Roast
Distributing as Thou think'st fit
    To those that seem to want the most.

Thou did'st to Me a Bard half Starv'd
    A Plenteous Dole of Fame Provide   10
And gav'st Me what I n'er Deserv'd
    Something of Phaeton and Hyde.

Respect and Mem'ry O look back
    Recall the Beauteous Mothers Youth
Curl Thou has't put Me on the Wrack   15
    And now believe I tell Thee Truth.

---

5 While *L 28, M, 1740*: wile *W*   pleaded *L 28, M, 1740*: pleased (?) *W*   6 For *L 28, M, 1740*: for *W*   of] for *L 28, M, 1740*   7 She *L 28, M, 1740*: she *W* an *L 28, M, 1740*: om. *W*   8 That *L 28, M, 1740*: that *W*   B——] Bartholmew *L 28, M, 1740*   fair. *edd.*: fair *W*: Fair. *L 28, M*: FAIR. *1740*   9 My *L 28, M, 1740*: my *W*   10 Eye? *L 28*: Eye *W, M*: Eye, *1740*   11 Wigg *L 28, M*: Whigg *W*: wig *1740*   12 Thom] Her *L 28, M, 1740*   I. *L 28, M, 1740*: I *W*
    Title: '*Contents*' *of L 28: om. W, L 28*   5 of] in *L 28*   8 most. *edd.*: most *W, L 28*   13 Respect *L 28*: *Partially torn out in W*   Mem'ry *edd.*: Mem'ory *W*: Memory *L 28*   14 Recall *L 28*: *Partially torn out in W*

That Bright, Great, Good Nymph such I found
　　Such! How? dur'st I? cou'd Kneller Tell:
How many Years Hid I the Wound
　　Which forc'd by Curl I now Reveal!　　　　　　20

The Mothers Beauties as I Lov'd,
　　And thought She Rul'd by Right Divine
I saw the Daughters Charms improv'd
　　I Courted—in the Legal Line.

When I saw J—— what can They mean　　　　　25
　　Said I, that e'er can think of Kitty?
As Kathrine grew and pleas'd my View
　　Poor Charlotte I beheld with Pitty.

Charlotte came last, the Race march't on
　　Like Banco's Offspring in Mackbeth　　　　　30
All to the Rebells of their Throne,
　　Denouncing Anger Wrath and Death.

If beauteous Hyde can thus supply
　　Her everlasting Store of Darts
Come on I cry'd We all must Dye　　　　　　　35
　　Thô Every Man had twenty Hearts.

What'er may to my Charge be laid
　　In Publick prints or Secrett whispers
I'l tell thee all I ever said
　　Of Jinny or her beauteous Sisters.　　　　　40

In these I haild the Graces Three
　　All Beautiful, All like Their Mother,
And each the Reigning Toast shall be
　　Why? because each is likest t' Other.

21–24] *L 28 Incomplete version in W and L 28 reads:*
　　　　　Having the Mother's Charms confest
　　　　　I to the daughters next addrest
26 Said I, *edd.*: Said, I *W*: Said I *L 28*　　Kitty? *edd.*: Kitty *W, L 28*　　28 Charlotte
L 28: *Partially illeg. in W*　　Pitty. *edd.*: Pitty *W*: pitty *L 28*　　29] Next Charlotte
comes and on They run *L 28, Alt. reading in W*　　32 Death. *edd.*: Death *W, L 28*
33 beauteous Hyde *L 28*: *A misplaced caret in W would make it* Hyde beauteous　　36
Hearts. *edd.*: Hearts *W, L 28*　　37 What'er *edd.*: What er *W*: What e'er *L 28*
39 tell thee *L 28*: tell tell thee *W*　　ever *L 28*: *Partially illeg. in W*　　40 Of *L 28*:
of *W*　　Sisters. *L 28*: *Missing in W*　　41 haild *Uncertain reading in W*: Blank in *L 28*
44 likest *L 28*: likes't *W*

If You Three Sister Roses View   45
  From that which is the fullest blown
The Beauties of the other Two
  Without much forecast may be known.

Soft April, blooming May, bright June
  Do each in diff'rent Charms appear   50
Yet with Succeeding Pleasures Crown
  The Joys and Honours of the Year

But *Phaeton*'s or *Kittys* Act
  Has set our Am'rous World on fire
If Sim'les are not quite Exact   55
  Why must They needs be made by Prior.

By adding to my fame
  Dear Curl, thou hast undone Me.
Making me richer than I am
  Thou drawst My Creditors upon Me.   60

From Blanket and from Physic free
  Thou long shal't Live and We'll be freinds,
Put out my Name and We'll agree
  Make me at least this smal Amends.

Then Curl for Mine and for Truths sake   65
  Thy Righteous Printing Press employ,
To prove I never did Mistake
  A Lady for a Boy.

---

45 If *L 28*: *Illeg. in W*   49 June] Jane *L 28*   53 *Phaeton*'s] Phaeton *L 28*
54 Am'rous World] *L 28* Polite Orb *Earlier reading in W*   55 Sim'les *edd.*: Simi'les *W*:
Similes *L 28*   57 By *L 28 (D)*: by *W*: Alas By *L 28 (Pope)*   58 Dear] *L 28 (D)*
Oh gentle *L 28 (Pope)*   60 Creditors *L 28*: Cred^rs *W*   Me. *edd.*: Me *W, L 28*
61 from Physic] *L 28 (D)* Purgation *L 28 (Pope)*   62 freinds, *edd.*: freind *W*: friends,
L 28   65 Then *L 28*: Than *W*

1719

A Prologue intended to the Play of Chit Chat, but never finished.

THE ugly Beau too partial to his Glass,
    As more he looks, and better likes his face,
In every place is certain to appear
Abroad I mean—but there are None such here.
'Tis much the same with those who trade in verse   5
Fondly they write, then saucily rehearse,
By frequent Repetition bolder grown
First tire their Friends and after plague the Town.
This from Our Author I am bid to say
As some Excuse for his First coup d'Essay   10
When next he dares his Cens'ring Pen to draw
E'en leave him to the Letter of the Law:
With gentle Stripes Correct the young beginner,
And hang him if he proves a Harden'd Sinner.
What he attempts to paint is Human life,   15
A good Man injur'd by a Modern wife;
While neither Sense or kindness have the Charms
To keep the Cocquet from the Coxcombs arms.
Had the wrong'd Husband been deseas'd and Old
Or to her play deny'd the needful gold,   20
The Lady might have done as She thought fit,
And these loose Scenes perhaps had n'er been writ.
But in the flower and vigour of His Age
To Cuckold him, creates so just a rage
It is a very Scandal—to the Stage.   } 25

Now à propos to what we nam'd, these Scenes:
Some will be asking what the Author means.
Loose and irregular they are 'tis true,
But pray reflect it is your Lives he drew.

---

8 Town. *edd.*: Town *L 28, M*   11 Cens'ring *edd.*: Cens'uring *L 28*: censuring *M*
18 arms. *edd.*: arms *L 28, M*   22 loose *M*: lose *L 28*   25 Stage. *edd.*: Stage
L 28, M

A well laid Plot, close order, clear design   30
Shou'd all conspire to make the Dramma Shine
His Plot he hopes will pardon every fault
'Tis what wou'd puzzle Machiavels own thought
'Tis such—pray find it out—
As Alberoni to his Pupil taught.   35
Follow these Steps, ye learn'd in State Intreagues!
Who deal in Politicks and Powder'd Wiggs.
E'er yet quite form'd, your Schemes are all reveal'd,
But here————
The action's done, but yet the Plot conceal'd.   40
For the design, 'tis twenty several facts,
First dropt in Scenes, then shuffl'd into Acts.
He builds his Schemes in the Lucretian way;
Atoms their motions into forms convey:
And Chance may rule in wit, as well as play.   45
One thing he bids me beg in his Defence,
That none may Praise or blame that have not Sense.
Take not poor Culprits just request amiss;
It reaches None of You—pray freely Clap or Hiss.

Verses Spoke to the Lady Henrietta-Cavendish Holles Harley,

in the Library of St. John's College, Cambridge, November the 9th. An. 1719.

MADAM,

SINCE ANNA visited the Muses Seat,
(Around Her Tomb let weeping Angels wait)
Hail THOU, the Brightest of thy Sex, and Best,
Most gracious Neighbour, and most welcome Guest.
Not HARLEY's Self to *Cam* and *Isis* dear,   5
In Virtues and in Arts great OXFORD's Heir,
Not HE such present Honors shall receive,
As to his CONSORT We aspire to give.

49 freely] *om. M*
    Title] L 27, 1720 *om.* L 29

Writings of Men our Thought to Day neglects,
To pay due Homage to the Softer Sex: 10
Plato and *Tully* We forbear to read,
And their great Followers whom this House has bred,
To study Lessons from Thy Morals given,
And shining Characters, impress'd by Heaven.
Science in Books no longer We pursue,   15
Minerva's Self in HARRIET's Face We view;
For when with Beauty we can Virtue join,
We paint the Semblance of a Form Divine.

Their pious Incense let our Neighbours bring,
To the kind Mem'ry of some bounteous King,   20
With grateful Hand, due Altars let Them raise
To some good Knight's, or holy Prelate's Praise;
We tune our Voices to a nobler Theme,
Your Eyes We bless, your Praises We proclaim,
S^t. *John's* was Founded in a Woman's Name: 25
Enjoin'd by Statute, to the Fair We bow;
In Spight of Time, We keep our antient Vow;
What MARGARET TUDOR was, is HARRIET HARLEY now.

Engraved on Three Sides of an Antique Lamp given by me to the Right Honorable the Lord Harley.

ANTIQUAM hanc Lampadem
é Museo *Colbertino* allatam,
Domino *Harleo* inter Κειμήλια sua
reponendam D D: *Matthæus Prior.*

This Lamp which *Prior* to his *Harley* gave,   5
    Brought from the Altar of the *Cyprian* Dame,
Indulgent *Time*, thrô future Ages save,
    Before the *Muse* to burn with purer flame.

9 Thought] *L 29, 1720* Thoughts *L 27*   12 whom] *L 27, 1720* which *L 29*
    Title: *Engraved...Harley. M:* Engraven...Harley. *M.P. 1740: om. L 29, 1720, Ped*
3 Κειμήλια *1720, 1740, Ped, Marginal correction in L 29:* Κεινηλία Text in *L 29:* Κεμηλι
& M

Sperne dilectum *Veneris* sacellum,
Sanctius, Lampas, tibi munus orno,
I fove casto vigil *Harleanas*
　　　Igne *Camœnas*.

10

1720

The Conversation. A Tale.

IT always has been thought discreet,
To know the Company You meet;
And sure there may be secret Danger,
In talking much before a Stranger.
Agreed: What then? Then drink your Ale:　　5
I'll pledge You, and repeat my Tale.

No Matter where the Scene is fixt:
The Persons were but odly mixt;
When Sober DAMON thus began:
(And DAMON is a clever Man)　　　10
I now grow Old; but still, from Youth,
Have held for Modesty and Truth:
The Men who by these Sea-marks steer,
In Life's great Voyage never Err:
Upon this Point I dare defy　　　15
The World: I pause for a Reply.

Sir, Either is a good Assistant:
Said One who sat a little distant:
Truth decks our Speeches and our Books;
And Modesty adorns our Looks:　　　20
But farther Progress We must take,
Not only born to Look and Speak:

10 Sanctius] *1720, 1740, Ped* Sanctus *M*　　　11 casto] *M, 1720, 1740, Ped* puro *Deleted reading in L 29*
　　Title: *A Tale.*] *L 27 om. L 29*　　　3 And] *L 27, L 29* For *W*　　　8 Persons were but]
L 27, L 29 company was *W*　　　9 Sober] *L 27, L 29* heedles *W*　　　11–12] *L 27, L 29*
　　　　　　　　　　I hold for Modesty and Truth
　　　　　　　　　　As Lessons to our British Youth　*W*
13 Men] *L 27, L 29* Man *W*　　these] *W, L 27* those *L 29*　　steer] *L 27, L 29* Stears *W*
14 Err] *L 27, L 29* errs *W*　　18 Said] *L 27, L 29* Says *W*　　21 farther] *L 29* further *L 27*

The Man must Act. The STAGYRITE
Says thus, and says extremely right:
Strict Justice is the Sov'raign Guide,   25
That o'er our Action shou'd preside:
This Queen of Virtues is confest,
To regulate and bind the rest.
Thrice Happy, if You once can find
Her equal Balance poize your Mind: 30
All different Graces soon will enter,
Like Lines concurrent to their Center.

'Twas thus, in short, these Two went on,
With Yea and Nay, and Pro and Con,
Thro' many Points divinely dark,   35
And WATERLAND assaulting CLARK;
'Till, in Theology half lost,
DAMON took up the Evening Post;
Confounded SPAIN, compos'd the NORTH,
And deep in Politics held forth.   40

Methinks We're in the like Condition,
As at the TREATY of PARTITION:
That Stroke, for All King WILLIAM's Care,
Begat another Tedious War:
MATTHEW, who knew the whole Intrigue,   45
Ne'er much approv'd That Mystic League.
In the vile UTRECHT TREATY too,
Poor Man, He found enough to do:
Sometimes to Me He did apply;
But down-right Dunstable was I,   50
And told Him, where They were mistaken;
And counsell'd Him to save his Bacon:
But (pass His Politics and Prose)
I never herded with his Foes;
Nay, in his Verses, as a Friend,   55
I still found Something to commend:
Sir, I excus'd his NUT-BROWN MAID;
Whate'er severer Critics said:

---

35 Thro' many] *L 27, L 29* Thus on to *W*   36 And] *W, L 27, L 29* As *MS. emend.*
(by Pope) in L 28 copy of 1720   40] *L 29 om. L 27*

Too far, I own, the Girl was try'd:
The Women All were on my Side.   60
For ALMA I return'd Him Thanks:
I lik'd Her with her little Pranks:
Indeed poor SOLOMON in Rhime
Was much too grave to be Sublime.

PINDAR and DAMON scorn Transition: 65
So on He ran a new Division;
'Till out of Breath he turn'd to spit:
(Chance often helps Us more than Wit)
T'other that lucky Moment took,
Just nick'd the Time, broke in, and spoke.   70

Of all the Gifts the Gods afford,
(If we may take old TULLY's Word)
The greatest is a Friend; whose Love
Knows how to praise, and when reprove:
From such a Treasure never part,   75
But hang the Jewel on your Heart:
And, pray, Sir (it delights Me) tell;
You know this Author mighty well—
Know Him! d'ye question it? Ods-fish!
Sir, does a Beggar know his Dish?   80
I lov'd Him, as I told You, I
Advis'd Him—Here a Stander-by
Twitch'd DAMON gently by the Cloak,
And thus unwilling Silence broke:
DAMON, 'tis Time We shou'd retire: 85
The Man You talk with is MAT. PRIOR.

PATRON thro' Life, and from Thy Birth my Friend,
DORSET, to Thee this Fable let Me send:
With DAMON's Lightness weigh Thy solid Worth;
The Foil is known to set the Diamond forth: 90
Let the feign'd Tale this real Moral give,
How many DAMONS, how few DORSETS Live.

Prologue to The Orphan.

Represented by some of the Westminster-Scholars at Hickford's Dancing-Room, the 2d of February, 1720. Spoken by the Lord Duplin, Who acted Cordelio.

WHAT wou'd my humble Comrades have Me say?
 Gentle Spectators, pray excuse the Play?
Such Work by hireling Actors shou'd be done,
Whom You may Clap or Hiss, for half a Crown:
Our generous Scenes for Friendship We repeat;   5
And if We don't delight, at least We treat.
Ours is the Damage, if We chance to blunder;
We may be ask'd, whose Patent We act under.

 How shall We gain You? *A-la-mode de France?*
We hir'd this Room; but none of Us can dance: 10
In cutting Capers We shall never please:
Our Learning does not lye below our Knees.

 Shall We procure You Symphony and Sound?
Then You must Each subscribe Two hundred Pound.
There We shou'd fail too, as to Point of Voice: 15
Mistake Us not; We're no ITALIAN Boys:
True BRITONS born from WESTMINSTER We come;
And only speak the Style of ancient ROME.
We wou'd deserve, not poorly beg Applause;
And stand or fall by FREIND's and BUSBY's Laws.   20

 For the Distress'd Your Pity We implore:
If once refus'd, We trouble You no more,
But leave Our ORPHAN squawling at your Door.

A Letter to the Honorable Lady Mrs: Margaret Candish Harley.

MY noble, lovely, little Peggy,
  Lett this my first Epistle beg Ye
At dawn of Morn and close of Even,
To lift Your Heart and Hands to Heaven:
In double Beauty say Your Prayer,   5
Our Father first, then Nôtre Pere.
And, Dearest Child, along the Day,
In every thing You do or say
Obey and please my Lord and Lady,
So God shall love, and Angels aid Ye.   10

If to these precepts You attend,
No second letter need I send:
And so I rest, Your constant Friend

          Matthew Prior.

Wimple March 29.   15
    1720

'Fame counting Thy books'

FAME counting Thy books, my dear Harley, shall tell
  No Man had so many, who knew them so well.

Title: L 27, Harl: *om.* L 1: A... LADY *Miss* Margaret-Cavendish-Holles-Harley.
1740   5 Prayer, *edd.*: Prayer *L 1*, L 27, Harl: pray'r, *1740*   14] M.P. *1740*:
om. L 27, Harl   15–16] *om.* L 27, Harl, *1740*
   Title: edd.: *om.* Wh, *1863*: Verses written in Lord Harleys Library 1720 '*Index*' *to* M
2 many, who] many and *1863*   *In 1863, followed by:*
          "*Written in the Library*, Dec. 2, 1720.
             "M.P."

Epitaph for Sir Thomas Powys.

M.S.

Here Lyeth Interr'd
Sr Thomas Powys Knt
Second Son of Thomas Powys of Henley in the
County of Salop, Serjeant at Law and of Anne Daughter   5
of Sr. Adam Littleton of Stoke Milburgh in the said
County, Bart.
By his first Wife Sarah, Daughter of Ambrose Holbech
of Mollington in the County of Warwick, Esqr.
He had three Sons, Thomas, Edward, and Ambrose,   10
And three Daughters, Sarah, Anne, and Jane.
By his Second, Elizabeth daughter of Sr Phillip Meadows Knt,
He had two Sons, Both Named Phillip.
He was appointed Solicitor General, Anno 1686,
Attorney General, 1687, Premier Serjeant at Law 1702.   15
One of the Judges of the Queen's Bench 1713.
He Dyed the 4th of April 1719. Aged 70.
As to His Profession,
In Accusing Cautious, in Defending Vehement;
In all His Pleadings Sedate, Clear, Strong,   20
In all His Decisions Unprejudic'd, and Equitable.
He Studied, Practised, and Govern'd the Law
In such a Manner, that
Nothing equal'd His Knowledge,
Except His Eloquence;   25
Nothing Excell'd Both,
Except His Justice:
And Whether He was Greater,
As an Advocate, or a Judge,
Is the only Cause He left Undecided.   30
As to His Life,
He Possessed by a natural Happyness
All those Civil Virtues, which form the perfect Gentleman;
And to those by Divine Goodness were added
That fervent Zeal, and extensive Charity   35
Which distinguish the perfect Christian.

Title: Supplied from first pub., 1732

THE TREE IS KNOWN BY HIS FRUIT,
He was a loving Husband, and an indulgent Father,
A Constant Friend, and a Charitable Patron,
Frequenting the Devotions of the Church,   40
Pleading the Cause, and Relieving the Necessities of the Poor.
What by His Example He Taught throughout His Life
At His Death He Recommended to His Family, and His Friends,
To Fear God, and Live Uprightly.
Let Whosoever reads this Stone   45
Be Wise, and be Instructed.

Virgils Georgic 4 Verse 511

Qualis...to implet Translated.

So Philomel beneath the Poplar shade
Mournful bewails her Brood whom the rough hind
Finding has taken Callow from the Nest.
All night she weeps and sitting on the branch
Often repeats her Melancholly song   5
And fills the Country with her sad complaint.

Ronsard's Franciade.

Book the IVth: Folio 465. Translated.

ON yonder guilty Plain, long Seasons hence
Perhaps a thousand Years, Helmets and Shields,
And plated harnois shal be found, sad marks
Of memorable War, with sudden wonder
Appal'd the Villager lab'ring the Glebe   5
Shal hear his Plow-Share crash on buried Armour,
And throw up bones of Heroes slain in Battle.

The Turtle and the Sparrow.

BEHIND an unfrequented Glade,
Where Eugh and Myrtle mix their Shade,
A Widow TURTLE pensive sat,
And wept her Murder'd Lover's fate.

Title] Virgil Georgic 4th: *L 7: om. Lpo 18*   3 Nest. *Lpo 18*: Nest *L 7, L 28*
Title: Sparrow.] SPARROW. MDCCXX. *L 27*: SPARROW. A POEM. *1723*

The SPARROW chanc'd that way to walk,   5
(A Bird that loves to chirp and talk)
Be sure he did the TURTLE greet,
She answer'd him as She thought meet.
SPARROWS and TURTLES, by the by,
Can think as well as You or I: 10
But how did They their thoughts express?
The Margin shows by T and S.

T.   My hopes are lost, my Joys are fled,
Alas! I weep COLUMBO dead:
Come all Yee winged Lovers, come,   15
Drop Pinks and Daisys on his Tomb:
Sing, Philomel, his Funeral Verse,
Yee pious Redbreasts, deck his Herse:
Fair Swans extend Your dying throats,
COLUMBO's death requires Your Notes: 20
For him, my Friends, for him I moan,
My dear COLUMBO dead and gone.

Stretch'd on the Bier COLUMBO lies,
Pale are his Cheeks, and clos'd his Eyes;
Those Cheeks, where Beauty smiling lay;   25
Those Eyes, where Love was us'd to play:
Ah cruel Fate alas! how soon
That Beauty and those Joys are flown!

COLUMBO is no more, Yee Flouds,
Bear the sad sound to distant Woods;   30
The sound let ECHO's voice restore;
And say, COLUMBO is no more.
Yee Flouds, Yee Woods, Yee Echo's moan
My dear COLUMBO dead and gone.

The DRYADS all forsook the Wood,   35
And mournful NAYIDS round me stood;
The tripping FAUNES and FAIRIES came,
All conscious of our mutual flame;
To Sigh for him, with me to moan
My dear COLUMBO dead and gone.   40

19 Swans] *L 27, 1723 errata* Swains *1723 text*   37 FAUNES] *L 27* Fawns *1723*

VENUS disdain'd not to appear
To lend my grief a friendly ear;
But what avails Her kindness now?
She n'er shal hear my Second vow:
The Loves that round their Mother flew   45
Did in her face her Sorrows view.
Their drooping Wings They pensive hung,
Their Arrows broke, their bows unstrung;
They heard attentive what I said,
And wept with me COLUMBO dead: 50
For him I sigh, for him I moan,
My dear COLUMBO, dead and gone.

   'Tis ours to weep, great VENUS said,
'Tis JOVE's alone to be Obey'd:
Nor Birds nor Goddesses can move   55
The just behests of fatal JOVE;
I saw thy Mate with sad regret,
And curst the Fowlers cruel Nett:
Ah dear COLUMBO how he fell
Whom TURTURELLA lov'd so well!   60
I saw him bleeding on the ground,
The sight tore up my Ancient wound;
And whilst You wept, alas, I cry'd,
COLUMBO and ADONIS dy'd.

   Weep all Yee Streams yee Mountains groan   65
I mourn COLUMBO dead and gone;
Stil let my tender grief complain,
Nor day nor Night That grief restrain,
I said, and VENUS stil reply'd,
COLUMBO and ADONIS dy'd.   70

S.   Poor TURTURELLA, hard thy case
   And just thy Tears, alas, alas!

T.   And hast Thou lov'd and can'st Thou hear
   With piteous heart a Lover's care?
   Come then, with me thy Sorrows join,   75
   And ease my Woes by telling Thine:

42 ear] Ear *1723*: tear *L 27*

For thou, poor Bird, perhaps may'st moan
Some PASSERELLA dead and gone.

S.   Dame TURTLE, this runs soft in Rhime
But neither Suits the Place nor time.   80
That Fowlers hand, whose cruel Care,
For Dear COLUMBO set the Snare,
The Snare again for Thee may set;
Two Birds may perish in one Nett:
Thou shou'dst avoid this cruel field,   85
And sorrow shou'd to prudence yield.
'Tis sad to dye.   T. It may be so,
'Tis sadder yet to Live in Woe.

S.   When Widdows use this Canting strain
They seem Resolv'd to wedd again.   90

T.   When Widdowers wou'd this Truth disprove
They never tasted real Love.

S.   Love is soft Joy and gentle Strife,
His Efforts all depend on life:
When He has thrown two golden darts   95
And struck the Lovers mutual hearts
Of his black Shafts let death send One
Alas! the pleasing Game is done,
Ill is the poor Survivor Sped,
A Corps feels mighty cold in Bed.   100
VENUS said Right, nor Tears can move
Nor plaints revoke the Will of JOVE,
ALL must obey the general Doom,
Down from ALCIDES to TOM THUMB,
Grim PLUTO will not be withstood   105
By force or Craft, tall ROBINHOOD
As well as little JOHN is dead
(You see how deeply I am read).
With FATES lean Tipstaff none can dodge,
He'l find You out where e'er You lodge.   110

---

78 gone] *L 27, 1723 errata* done *1723 text*   81 whose] *L 27 whole 1723*   82 Snare,
1723: Snare *W, L 27*   99 Sped, *edd.*: Sped *W*: sped *L 27*: sped, *1723*   101 Right,
edd.: Right *W*: right *L 27*: right, *1723*

AJAX to shun his general pow'r
In vain absconded in a Flow'r.
An idle Scene TYTHONUS acted,
When to a Grasshopper contracted:
Death struck them in those Shapes again   115
As once he did when They were Men.
For Reptils perish, Plants decay,
Flesh is but Grass, Grass turns to Hay,
And Hay to Dung, and Dung to Clay.
Thus heads extremely nice discover   120
That Folks may dye some ten times over;
But oft by too refin'd a touch
To prove things plain, they prove too much.
What e'er PYTHAGORAS may say,
(For each You know will have his way,)   125
With great Submission I pronounce
That People dye no more than once:
But once is sure and Death is common
To Bird and Man, including Woman.
From the Spread Eagle to the Wren   130
Alas! no Mortal Fowle knows when,
All that wear Feathers, first or last,
Must one day perch on CHARON's Mast;
Must lye beneath the Cypress Shade,
Where STRADA's Nightengale was laid.   135
Those Fowle who seem alive to sit
Assembl'd by DAN CHAUCER's Witt
In Prose have Slept Three hundred Years
Exempt from Worldly hopes and fears;
And laid in State upon their Herse   140
Are truly but Embalm'd in Verse.
As sure as LESBIA's Sparrow, I,
Thou sure as PRIOR's Dove must Dye:
And n'er again from LETHE's Streams
Return to ADIGE or to THAMES.   145

T.   I therefore weep COLUMBO dead,
My hopes bereav'd, my pleasures fled;
I therefore must for ever Moan
My dear COLUMBO dead and gone.

S.   COLUMBO never sees Your Tears,   150
Your crys COLUMBO never hears;
A Wall of Brass and one of Lead
Divide the Living from the Dead.
Repell'd by This, the gather'd Rain
Of Tears beats back to Earth again;   155
In t'other the Collected sound
Of Groans, when once receiv'd, is drown'd.
'Tis therefore vain one hour to grieve
What Time it self can n'er retrieve.
By Nature soft, I know, a Dove   160
Can never live without her Love;
Then quit this flame and light another;
Dame, I advise You like a Brother.

T.   What, I to make a Second choice?
In other Nuptials to rejoice?   165

S.   Why not my Bird?   T. No, SPARROW, No,
Let me indulge my pleasing Woe:
Thus Sighing, Coeing, ease my pain;
But never wish nor Love again:
Distress'd for ever let me moan   170
My Dear COLUMBO dead and gone.

S.   Our winged Friends thrô all the Grove
Contemn Thy Mad excess of Love:
I tell thee, Dame, the t'other day
I met a Parrot and a Jay,   175
Who mock'd Thee in their Mimic Tone
And wept COLUMBO, dead and gone.

T.   What e'er the Jay or Parrot said,
My hopes are lost, my Joys are fled;
And I for ever must deplore   180
COLUMBO dead and gone—   S. Encore!
For shame forsake this BION-style
Wee'l talk an hour, and walk a Mile.

151 hears; *1723*: hears *W*, *L 27*   154 This, *edd.*: This *W*: this *L 27, 1723*   159
retrieve. *1723*: retrieve *W*, *L 27*   164 What, *1723*: What *W*, *L 27*   181 Encore
edd.: encore *W*, *L 27*: Encore *1723*

Does it with Sense or health agree
To sit thus moping on a Tree?   185
To throw away a Widow's life
When You again may be a Wife?

Come on, I'll tell You my Amours:
Who knows but they may influence Yours?
Example draws where Precept fails,   190
And Sermons are less read than Tales.

T.   SPARROW, I take Thee for my Friend,
As such will hear thee, I descend;
Hop on and talk, but honest Bird
Take care that no immodest word   195
May venture to offend my Ear—

S.   Too Saint-like TURTLE never fear—
By Method things are best discourst,
Begin We then with Wife the First:
A handsome, senseless, aukward Fool   200
Who wou'd not yield, and cou'd not rule:
Her Actions did her Charms disgrace,
And stil her Tongue talkt off her face:
Count me the leaves on yonder Tree,
So many diffrent Wills had She,   205
And like the leaves, as chance inclin'd,
Those Wills were chang'd with ev'ry wind:
She courted the Beaumonde to-Night
L'Assemblée her Supreme delight.
The next She Sat immur'd, unseen,   210
And in full health injoy'd the Spleen.
She censur'd That, She alter'd This,
And with great care set all amiss;
She now cou'd chide, now laugh, now cry,
Now Sing, now pout, all God knows why.   215
Short was her reign, She Cough'd and dy'd,
Proceed we to my Second Bride,
Well born she was, gentily bred,
And bucksom both at Board and bed,

1 92 SPARROW *L 27* : Sparrow *W* : *Sparrow 1723*   208 Beaumonde *L 27* : Baumonde *W* :
Beau Monde 1723

Glad to oblige, and pleas'd to please,   220
And as TOM SOUTHERN wisely says
"No other Fault had She in life
"But only that She was my Wife:"
O Widow TURTLE, ev'ry She
(So Natures pleasure does decree)   225
Appears a Goddess 'till enjoy'd,
But Birds, and Men, and Gods are cloy'd.
Was HERCULES one Woman's Man?
Or JOVE for ever LEDA's Swan?
Ah, Madam, cease to be mistaken,   230
Few Marry'd Fowl peck DUNMOW Bacon.
Variety alone gives Joy,
The sweetest Meats the soonest cloy:
What Sparrow, Dame, what Dove alive
Tho VENUS shou'd the Chariot drive   235
But wou'd accuse the Harness weight
If always coupl'd to one Mate;
And often wish the Fetter broke?
Tis freedom but to change the Yoke.

T.   Impious to wish to Wed again,   240
      E'er Death dissolv'd the former Chain.

S.   Spare your remark, and hear the rest,
      She brought me Sons, but JOVE be blest,
      She Dy'd in Child-bed on the Nest.
      Well, rest her Bones, quoth I, she's gone: 245
      But must I therefore lye alone?
      What, am I to her Memory ty'd?
      Must I not live, because She dy'd?
      And thus I Logically said,
      ('Tis good to have a Reas'ning head)   250
      Is this my Wife, *probatur*, Not;
      For Death dissolv'd the Mariage Knot:

223 my] *L 27, 1723 errata* a *1723 text*   224 TURTLE *L 27*: Turtle *W*: Turtle *1723*
232 alone gives] *L 27, 1723* produces *W* (*P*)   234 Sparrow, Dame, *W* (*P*), *L 27*:
Sparow Dame *W* (*D & P*): *Sparrow-Dame, 1723*   235 VENUS *L 27*: Venus *W*: *Venus*
1723   238 Fetter] *L 27, 1723* Harness *W* (*P*)   *Additional lines in W* (*P*):
                              Difference of Pain does greif appeas
                              and change of Bondage gives some Ease
244 in] *L 27* on *1723*

She was, *Concedo*, during life;
But is a piece of Clay a Wife?
Again, if not a Wife, D'y see,   255
Why then no Kin at all to me:
And he who general tears can shed
For folks, that happen to be dead,
May e'en with equal Justice mourn,
For those who never yet were born.   260

T.   Those Points indeed you quaintly prove
But Logic is no friend to Love.

S.   My Children then were just Pen feather'd;
Some little Corn for them I gather'd,
And sent them to my Spouses Mother,   265
So left that Brood to get another.
And as old HARRY whilome said
Reflecting on ANNE BULLEN dead
"Cocksbones I now again do Stand
"The Jollyest Batchelor i'th' Land."   270

T.   Ah me! my Joys, my hopes are fled;
My first, my only Love is Dead.
With endless grief let me bemoan
COLUMBO's loss. S. Let me go on.
As yet my Fortune was but narrow   275
I woo'd my Cousen PHILLY SPARROW,
O'th elder House of CHIRPING-END,
Whence we the Younger branch descend;
Well Seated, in a Field of Pease,
She liv'd extremely at her ease: 280
But when the Honey-moon was past
The following Nights were soon o'ercast,
She kept her own, could plead the Law,
And quarrel for a Barley straw;
Both, you may judge, became less kind,   285
As more we knew each others mind:
She soon grew Sullen, I hard hearted,
We Scolded, hated, fought, and parted.

270 Land." *edd.*: Land. *W, L 27, 1723*   278 we] *L 27 om. 1723*: all *MS. insertion (by Pope?) in L 28 copy of 1723*   285 less] *L 27* the less *1723*

To LONDON, blessed Town, I went,
She boarded at a Farm in KENT: 290
A Magpye from the Country fled,
And kindly told me She was dead:
I prun'd my Feathers, cock't my Tail,
And set my heart again to Sale.

My Fourth a meer Coquet, or such   295
I thought her, nor avails it much
If true or false, our troubles spring
More from the fancy than the thing.
Two staring Horns, I often said,
But ill become a SPARROWS Head   300
But then, to set that Ballance ev'n,
Your Cuckold SPARROW goes to Heav'n.
The Thing you fear, suppose it done,
If you enquire you make it known:
Whilst at the root your horns are sore,   305
The more you scratch, they ach the more.
But turn the Tables and reflect
All may not be which you suspect:
By the Mind's Eye, the Horns we mean
Are only in Ideas seen;   310
'Tis from the inside of the head
Their branches Shoot, their Antlers spread;
Fruitful Suspicions often bear 'em,
You feel 'em from the time you fear 'em.
Cuckoo! Cuckoo! that Echo'd word   315
Offends the Ear of Vulgar Bird;
But those of finer Tast have found
There's nothing in't beside the sound.
Preferment always waits on Horns;
And Household peace the gift adorns: 320
This way or That let Factions tend,
The Spark is stil his Cuckolds friend;
This way or That let Madam roam,
Well pleas'd and quiet She comes home.

289 LONDON *L 27: London W: LONDON 1723*   290 KENT *edd.*: Kent *W, L 27*:
Kent *1723*   301 ev'n *L 27*: ev'en *W*: even *1723*   308 which] *L 27* that *1723*
312 spread; *1723*: spread *W, L 27*   313 'em] *L 27* them *1723*   322 his] *L 27* the
1723   323 roam, *1723*: roam *W, L 27*

Now weigh the Pleasure with the pain,   325
The *plus* and *minus*, Loss and gain,
And what LAFONTAINE laughing says
Is serious truth, in such a case
Who slights the Evil feals it least,
And who does nothing does the best.   330
These Notions oft did I recite,
She drank them in with vast delight.
At Home with equal freedom blest
We acted Both as each thought best;
I never strove to rule the roast;   335
She n'er refus'd to pledge my Toast:
In Visits, if we chanc'd to meet,
I seem'd Obliging, She discreet;
We neither much Caress'd nor strove,
But good dissembling past for Love.   340

T.   What e'er of light our eye may know
'Tis only light it self can show:
What e'er of love our heart can feel
Tis mutual Love alone can tell.

S.   My pritty, Am'rous, foolish bird,   345
A moments patience, in one word
The Three kind Sisters broke this chain,
She dy'd, I mourn'd, and woo'd again.

T.   Let me with juster grief deplore
My Dear COLUMBO, now no more.   350
Lett me with constant Tears bewail—

S.   Your Sorrow does but spoil my Tale.
My Fifth, She prov'd a Jealous Wife,
Lord shield us all from such a Life!
'Twas doubt, complaint, Reply, chit-chat,   355
'Twas This to-day, to Morrow That.
Sometimes forsooth, upon the brook
I kept a Miss; An honest Rook

327 LAFONTAINE *L 27*: Lafontaine *W*: *Lafontaine 1723*   329 feals] *L 27* finds *1723*
331–4] *L 27 om. 1723*   345 Am'rous *edd.*: Am'orous *W*, *L 27*: amorous *1723*   347
this] *L 27* the *1723*

Told it a Snipe, who told a Stear,
Who told it Those who told it Her.   360
One day a Linnet and a Lark
Had met me strolling in the dark;
The next, a Wood-cock and an Owle
Quick sighted, grave and sober fowle,
Wou'd on their Corp'ral Oath alledge   365
I kiss'd a Hen behind the Hedge.
Well, Madam TURTLE, to be brief
(Repeating but renews our grief)
As once She watch'd me, from a rail,
Poor Soul! her footing chanc'd to fail,   370
And down she fell, and broke her hip,
The Fever came, and then the Pip:
Death did the only cure apply;
She was at quiet, So was I.

T.   Cou'd Love, unmov'd these Changes view?   375
     His Sorrows, as his Joys, are true.

S.   My Dearest Dove, One Wise-Man says,
     Alluding to our present Case,
     We're here to-day, and gone to-morrow:
     Then what avails Superfluous Sorrow?   380
     Another, full as Wise as he
     Adds, that a Marry'd Man may see
     Two happy hours, and which are They?
     The First and Last, perhaps you'l say;
     Tis true, when blith she goes to bed: ⎫   385
     And when She peaceably lies dead,   ⎮
     Women twixt Sheets *are best, 'tis said,*   ⎬
     Be they of Holland *or of* Lead.   ⎭

     Now cur'd of HYMENS hopes and fears,
     And sliding down the Vale of Years,   390
     I hop'd to fix my future rest,
     And took a Widow to my Nest.
     Ah TURTLE! had she been like Thee,
     Sober, yet Gentle; Wise, yet free;

365 Corp'ral *edd.:* Corp'oral *W, 1723:* Corporal *L 27*   383 They? *edd.:* They *W,*
L 27: they? *1723*

But She was peevish, noisy, bold,   395
A Witch engrafted on a Scold:
JOVE in PANDORA's Box confin'd
A hundred Ills to vex Mankind;
To vex one Bird in Her bandore
He hid at least a hundred more: 400
And as that Veil She backward drew
And show'd Her opener Face to View
The Plagues o'er all the Parish flew;
Her Stock of Borrow'd Tears grew dry
And native Tempests arm'd her Eye,   405
Black clouds around her forehead hung,
And Thunder rattl'd on her Tongue.
We, Young or Old, or Cock or Hen,
All liv'd in ÆOLUS's Den;
The nearest her the more Accurst,   410
Ill far'd her Friends, her Husband worst.
But JOVE amidst his Anger spares,
Remarks our faults, but hears our Pray'rs.
In short She Dy'd, Why then She's dead
Quoth I, and Once again I'll Wed.   415
Wou'd Heav'n this Mourning year were past,
One may have better luck at last.
Matters at worst are sure to mend,
The DEVILLS Wife was but a FIEND.

T.   Thy Tale has rais'd a TURTLES Spleen,   420
Uxorious Inmate, Bird obscene,
Dar'st thou defile these Sacred Groves,
These Silent Seats of Faithful Loves?
Begon, with flagging Wings sit down
On some Old Pent-house near the Town;   425
In Brewers-Stables Peck thy grain,
Then wash it down with Pudl'd rain:
And hear thy dirty Offspring Squawle,
From Bottles, on a Suburb Wall.

401–2] *L 27* And soon as Time that Veil withdrew *1723: del. in W*   407 Tongue.
L 27, 1723: Tongue *W*   410 nearest] *L 27, 1723* nearer *MS. emend. (by Pope?) in L 28
copy of 1723*   412 spares, *1723*: spares *W, L 27*   416 were] *L 27* was *1723*
424 sit] *L 27* set *1723*

Where thou hast been return again: 430
Vile Bird, thou hast Converst with Men;
Notions like these from Men were giv'n,
Those vilest Creatures under Heav'n:
To Cities and to Courts repair,
Flatt'ry and Falshood flourish there: 435
There all thy wretched Arts employ,
Where Riches triumph over Joy.
Where Passion does with Int'rest Barter;
And HYMEN holds by MAMMON's Charter;
Where Truth by point of Law is Parry'd;   440
And Knaves and Prudes are Six times Marry'd.

O DEAREST Daughter of Two dearest Friends
    To Thee my Muse this little Tale commends;
Loving and Lov'd regard Thy future Mate
Long love His Person thô deplore His Fate   445
Seem Young when Old in Thy Dear Husbands Arms
For constant Virtue has Immortal Charms.
And when I lye low Sepulch'red in Earth
And the glad Year returns Thy day of Birth
Vouchsafe to say, E'er I cou'd write or Spell   450
The Bard who from my Cradle wish'd me well
Told me I shou'd the Prating SPARROW blame
And bid me Imitate the TURTLES Fame.

Epigram.

H ER time with equal prudence Celia shares,
    First writes her billet doux then says her prayrs
Her Mass and Toylet, Vespres and the Play;
Thus God and Astorath divide the day:

432 were] *L 27* are *1723*   438 Passion] *L 27* Passions *1723*   442–53] *om. W,
1723*; *in 1740, these lines were printed separately with the title:* APPLICATION OF THE
TURTLE *and* SPARROW.   443 commends; *1740:* commends *L 29, L 27, L 28, Lpo 18*
445 thô...Fate] *L 27, L 28, 1740 om. Lpo 18*   446–7] *L 27, L 28, Lpo 18, 1740*
> Grow Ancient in a worthy Husbands Arms
> Enamour'd by Thy Virtues deathless charms
>   *Alt. reading in L 29, L 27, L 28*
450 say, E'er *edd.:* say e'er *L 29, L 27, L 28, Lpo 18, 1740*
        Title: L 27, L 28: ANOTHER. [EPIGRAM.] *1740: om. W*   1 Celia] Cælia *L 28:*
SILVIA *L 27, 1740*   shares, *1740:* shares *W, L 27, L 28*   2 First *L 27, L 28, 1740:*
first *W*   3 Her] *L 27, 1740* For *L 28*   4 day: *1740:* day *W, L 28:* Day. *L 27*

Constant she keeps her Ember week and Lent 5
At Easter calls all Israel to her tent:
Loose without bound, and pious without zeal
She still repeats the Sins she would conceal;
Envy her Self from Celias life must grant
An artfull Woman makes a modern Saint. 10

The Lame and the Blind disputing the right to an Oyster found;
The Lawyer decides the controversy.

B LIND Plaintif, Lame Defendent share
The Friendly Laws impartial Care,
A Shel for Him a Shell for Thee
The Middle is the Lawyers Fee.

Truth and Falshood. A Tale.

O NCE on a time, in sun-shine weather,
FALSHOOD and TRUTH walk'd out together,
The neighb'ring woods and lawns to view,
As opposites will sometimes do.
Thro' many a blooming mead They past, 5
And at a brook arriv'd at last.
The purling stream, the margin green,
With flowers bedeck'd, a vernal scene,
Invited each itin'rant maid
To rest a while beneath the shade; 10
Under a spreading beach They sat,
And pass'd the time with female chat;
Whilst each her character maintain'd;
ONE spoke her thoughts; the OTHER feign'd.

6 tent: *1740*: tent *W*: Tent. *L 27*: Tent *L 28*   7 bound] *L 27, L 28* band *1740*
8 conceal; *1740*: conceal *W, L 28*: conceal. *L 27*   9 Celias] Cælias *L 28*: SILVIA'S
L 27, 1740   10 Saint. *L 27, L 28*: Saint *W*: saint. *1740*
     Title] *M* The Lawyers Decision '*Index*' to *M*: TWO BEGGARS Disputing their RIGHT
to an OYSTER they had Found; a LAWYER thus decides the CAUSE. *1740*: *om. N.D.*
     Title: Tale] Fable *1729*

At length, quoth FALSHOOD, Sister TRUTH,   15
For so She call'd Her from Her youth,
What if to shun yon sult'ry beam,
We bathe in this delightful stream;
The bottom smooth, the water clear,
And there's no prying shepherd near?—   20
With all my heart, the NYMPH reply'd,
And threw Her snowy robes aside,
Stript her self naked to the skin,
And with a spring leapt headlong in.
FALSHOOD more leisurely undrest,   25
And laying by Her tawdry vest,
Trick'd her self out in TRUTH's array,
And cross the meadows tript away.

From this curst hour, the FRAUDFUL DAME,
Of sacred TRUTH usurps the name,   30
And with a vile, perfidious mind,
Roams far and near to cheat mankind;
False sighs suborns, and artful tears,
And starts with vain, pretended fears;
In visits, still appears most wise,   35
And rolls at church Her saint-like-eyes.
Talks very much, plays idle tricks,
While rising-stock Her conscience pricks,
When being, poor thing, extremely gravell'd,
She secrets ope'd, and all unravell'd.   40
But on She will, and secrets tell
Of JOHN and JOAN, and NED and NELL,
Reviling ev'ry One She knows,
As fancy leads, beneath the rose.
Her tongue so voluble and kind,   45
It always runs before Her mind;
As times do serve She slily pleads,
And copious tears still shew Her needs,
With promises as thick as weeds.—
Speaks *pro* and *con*, is wond'rous civil,   50
To-day a SAINT, to-morrow DEVIL.

35–57 *See commentary*

Poor TRUTH She stript, as has been said,
And naked left the lovely MAID,
Who scorning from Her cause to wince,
Has gone stark-naked ever since; 55
And ever NAKED will appear,
Belov'd by ALL who TRUTH revere.

1721

Colin's Mistakes.

Written in Imitation of Spenser's Style.

*Me ludit Amabilis
Insania.* Hor.

I.

FAST by the Banks of *Cam* was *Colin* bred:
Ye *Nymphs*, for ever guard That sacred Stream!
To *Wimpole*'s woody Shade his Way He sped:
Flourish those Woods, the *Muses* endless Theme!
As whilom *Colin* ancient Books had read, 5
Lays *Greek* and *Roman* wou'd he oft rehearse;
And much he lov'd, and much by heart he said
What Father *Spenser* sung in *British* Verse.
Who reads that Bard desires like Him to write,
Still fearful of Success, still tempted by Delight. 10

II.

Soon as *Aurora* had unbarr'd the Morn,
And Light discover'd Nature's chearful Face;
The sounding Clarion, and the sprightly Horn
Call'd the blyth Huntsmen to the distant Chace.

Title] *L 27* Colin's Mistakes, *at Wimpole. In* Spencer's *Style. L 29* 8] *L 27* His
great Forefather SPENCER's native Verse. *L 29* 10] *L 27* So tempting is the bait, so
poys'nous the delight. *L 29* 14 blyth] *L 27* brisk *L 29*

Eftsoons They issue forth, a goodly Band;   15
The deep-mouth'd Hounds with Thunder rend the Air;
The fiery Coursers strike the rising Sand;
Far thro' the Thicket flies the frighted Deer;
Harley the Honor of the Day supports;
His Presence glads the Wood; His Orders guide the Sports.   20

III.

On a fair Palfrey well equip't did sit
An Amazonian Dame; a scarlet Vest
For active Horsemanship adaptly fit
Enclos'd her dainty Limbs; a plumed Crest
Wav'd o'er her Head; obedient by her Side   25
Her Friends and Servants rode; with artful Hand
Full well knew She the Steed to turn and guide:
The willing Steed receiv'd her soft Command:
Courage and Sweetness in her Face were seated;
On Her all Eyes were bent, and all good Wishes waited.   30

IV.

This seeing, *Colin* thus his *Muse* bespake:
For alltydes was the *Muse* to *Colin* nigh,
Ah me too nigh! Or, *Clio*, I mistake;
Or that bright Form that pleaseth so mine Eye,
Is *Jove*'s fair Daughter *Pallas*, gracious Queen   35
Of liberal Arts; with Wonder and Delight
In *Homer*'s Verse we read Her; well I ween,
That emu'lous of his *Grecian* Master's Flight,
Dan *Spenser* makes the fav'rite Goddess known;
When in her graceful Look fair *Britomart* is shown.   40

V.

At Noon as *Colin* to the Castle came,
Ope'd were the Gates, and right prepar'd the Feast:
Appears at Table rich yclad a Dame,
The Lord's Delight, and Wonder of the Guest.

---

17 fiery Coursers strike] *L 27* madding Coursers spurn *L 29*   18 flies] *L 29* fly *L 27*
23 active] *L 27* use of *L 29*   25 Wav'd o'er] *L 27* Rounded *L 29*   28] *L 27* The
Steed receiv'd and own'd the Dames command: *L 29*   33 *Clio*] *L 27* Goddess *L 29*
34 bright Form] *L 27* fair shape *L 29*   35 fair] *L 27* bright *L 29*   37 In...Her;]
L 27 HOMER describes Her charms, and *L 29*   42 right prepar'd] *L 27* ready was *L 29*

With Pearl and Jewels was She sumptuous deckt,   45
As well became her Dignity and Place;
But the Beholders mought her Gems neglect,
To fix their Eyes on her more lovely Face,
Serene with Glory, and with Softness bright:
O Beauty sent from Heav'n, to cheer the mortal Sight!   50

VI.

Liberal *Munificence* behind Her stood;
And decent *State* obey'd her high Command;
And *Charity* diffuse of native Good
At once portrayes her Mind, and guides her Hand.
As to each Guest some Fruits She deign'd to lift,   55
And Silence with obliging Parley broke;
How gracious seem'd to each th'imparted Gift?
But how more gracious what the Giver spoke?
Such Ease, such Freedom did her Deed attend,
That every Guest rejoic'd, exalted to a Friend.   60

VII.

Quoth *Colin*; *Clio*, if my feeble Sense
Can well distinguish Yon illustrious Dame,
Who nobly doth such gentle Gifts dispense;
In *Latian* Numbers *Juno* is her Name,
Great Goddess who with Peace and Plenty crown'd,   65
To all that under Sky breath vital Air
Diffuseth Bliss, and thro' the World around
Pours wealthy Ease, and scatters joyous Chear;
Certes of Her in semblant Guise I read;
Where *Spenser* decks his Lays with *Gloriana*'s Deed.   70

VIII.

As *Colin* mus'd at Evening near the Wood;
A Nymph undress'd, beseemeth, by Him past:
Down to her Feet her silken Garment flow'd:
A Ribbon bound and shap'd her slender Waste:

---

48 on her more] *L 27* upon her *L 29*   54] *L 27* Portray'd her Mind while She imploy'd
her hand. *L 29*   57 th'imparted] *L 27* the various *L 29*   70 Where...with] *L 27*
When SPENCER deckt his Rhime in *L 29*   74 shap'd] *L 27* show'd *L 29*

A Veil dependent from her comely Head, 75
And beauteous Plenty of ambrosial Hair,
O'er her fair Breast and lovely Shoulders spread,
Behind fell loose, and wanton'd with the Air.
The smiling *Zephyrs* call'd their am'rous Brothers:
They kiss'd the waving Lawn, and wafted it to Others. 80

IX.

Daisies and Violets rose, where She had trod;
As *Flora* kind her Roots and Buds had sorted:
And led by *Hymen*, Wedlock's mystic God,
Ten thousand *Loves* around the Nymph disported.
Quoth *Colin*; now I ken the Goddess bright, 85
Whom Poets sing: All human Hearts enthrall'd
Obey her Pow'r; her Kindness the Delight
Of Gods and Men; great *Venus* She is call'd,
When *Mantuan Virgil* doth her Charms rehearse;
Belphebé is her Name, in gentle *Edmund*'s Verse. 90

X.

Heard this the *Muse*, and with a Smile reply'd,
Which show'd soft Anger mixt with friendly Love:
Twin Sisters still were Ignorance and Pride;
Can we know Right, 'till Error we remove?
But *Colin*, well I wist, will never learn: 95
Who slights his Guide shall deviate from his Way.
Me to have ask'd what Thou coud'st not discern,
To Thee pertain'd; to Me, the Thing to say.
What Heavenly Will from human Eye conceals,
How can the Bard aread, unless the *Muse* reveals? 100

XI.

Nor *Pallas* thou, nor *Britomart* hast seen;
When soon at Morn the flying Deer was chac't:
Nor *Jove*'s great Wife, nor *Spenser*'s Fairy Queen
At Noon-tyde dealt the Honors of the Feast:

79 The...*Zephyrs*...their...Brothers:] *L* 27 Each...ZEPHYR...his...brother, *L* 29
80 They...Others] *L* 27 And...Other *L* 29 89 Charms] *L* 27 praise *L* 29 90
gentle *Edmund*'s] *L* 27 EDMUNDS British *L* 29 92 Which] *L* 27 That *L* 29 93
Sisters] *L* 27 Breth'ren *L* 29 94] *L* 27 And right to know is Error to remove. *L* 29

Nor *Venus*, nor *Belphebé* did'st Thou spy, 105
The Evening's Glory, and the Grove's Delight.
Henceforth, if ask'd, instructed right, reply,
That all the Day to knowing Mortals Sight
Bright *Ca'ndish-Holles-Harley* stood confest,
As various Hour advis'd, in various Habit drest. 110

Epitaph.

MEEK Franco lyes here, Friend, without stop or stay
As You value your Peace; make the best of your way.
Thô arrested at present by Deaths catif claw
If He stirs, He may yet have recourse to the Law:
And in the Kings Bench shou'd a Verdict be found 5
That by Livery and Seisin his Grave is his ground;
He may claim to himself what is strictly his due,
And an Action of Trespass will straitway ensue,
That You without right on His premisses tread,
On a single Surmise that the Owner is dead. 10

The Epitaph upon Gilbert Glanvill Bishop of Rochester, as written in Rochester Cathedral. Translated.

GILBERTUS GLANVIL whose heart was as hard as an Anvil
Always litigious when he should have been highly religious,
Still charg'd with Law suits he to that Court aptly descended
Where quiet appears not and quarrells never are ended.

108 all] *L 27* 'long *L 29* 110 various Habit] *L 27* different Habit *L 29*
Title] Epitaph on father Francis *B.M.*: om. *1751* 1 Franco] *B.M.* Francis *1751*
2 As...Peace] *1751* if...life *B.M.* 3 arrested at present] *B.M.* at present arrested
1751 catif] *1751* satifatica *B.M.* 4 yet] still *1751*: om. *B.M.* 5 in] *1751*
att *B.M.* 6 by Livery and Seisin] *1751* by force of Lirie & seisions *B.M.* 7 He
may] He will *1751*: hele: *B.M.* strictly] *1751* justly *B.M.* 8 straitway] *1751*
surely *B.M.* 10 single] *B.M.* simple *1751* Surmise that the Owner is] *1751* surmise the owner was *B.M.*
Title: The] om. *L 29* *as written*] *L 29* now *Earlier reading in W* 2 Always]
L 29 Mighty *Alt. reading in W* when he] who *L 29* religious, *edd.*: religious *W*,
L 29 3 Still charg'd] Full fraught *L 29* 4 ended. *L 29*: ended *W*

Epigram.

MY Lord there's a Christ'ning the Officer said,
The Gossips are ready, the Cushions are laid:
What, without my leave ask'd? said the Prelate inflam'd
Go lock up My Font, let the Infant be damn'd.

On Bishop Atterbury's Burying the Duke of Buckingham.

I *HAVE no Hopes*, the *Duke* he says, and Dies;
In sure and certain Hopes—the *Prelate* cries:
Of These Two learned *Peers*, I prithee say, Man,
Who is the *lying Knave*, the *Priest* or *Layman*?
The *Duke* he stands an Infidel Confest,   5
He's our dear Brother, quoth the Lordly Priest.
The *Duke*, tho' *Knave*, Still *Brother dear* he cries,
And, who can say, the Rev'rend *Prelate* lies?

Down-Hall; A Ballad.

To the Tune of King John and the Abbot of Canterbury.

STANZA.

I.

I SING not old JASON, who travell'd thrô GREECE,
To kiss the fair Maids, and possess the rich Fleece;
Nor sing I ÆNEAS, who, led by his Mother,
Got rid of one Wife, and went far for another.
            Derry DOWN, DOWN, hey derry DOWN.   5

Epigram. Title] *L 29 (all texts)* Liberty to D: F: to christian his children in the abbye *B.M.*
1] *L 29 (all texts)* the officer went to the bishop and said *B.M.*   3 without...said] *L 29*
(all texts) my leave not askd quoth *B.M.*

II.

Nor him who thrô ASIA and EUROPE did roam,
ULYSSES by Name, who n'er cry'd to go Home;
But rather desir'd to see Cities, and Men,
Than return to his Farms, and converse with old PEN.

III.

Hang HOMER and VIRGIL, their Meaning to seek,   10
A Man must go poke in the LATIN and GREEK;
They who love their own Tongue, we have reason to hope,
Have read them translated by DRYDEN and POPE.

IV.

But I sing of Exploits that have lately been done
By two BRITISH Heroes, call'd MATTHEW and JOHN;   15
And how they rid friendly from fair LONDON Town,
Fair ESSEX to see, and a Place they call DOWN.

V.

Now e'er they went out you may rightly suppose
How much they discours'd, both in Prudence and Prose;
For before this great Journey was throughly concerted,   20
Full often they met, and as often they Parted.

VI.

And thus MATTHEW said, Look You here my friend JOHN,
I fairly have travell'd Years thirty and one;
And thô I stil carry'd my Sovereign's Warrants,
I only have gone upon other Folks Errands.   25

VII.

And now in this Journey of Life I wou'd have
A Place where to bait, 'twixt the Court and the Grave;
Where joyful to Live, not unwilling to Dye.
Gadzooks, I have just such a Place in my Eye.

11 poke] *1723* pore *MS. emend.* (*by Pope*) *in L* 28 *copy of 1723*   29 Eye. *1723:*
Eye *L 27*

VIII.

There are Gardens so stately, and Arbors so thick,   30
A Portal of Stone, and a Fabric of Brick;
The matter next Week shal be all in your Pow'r,
But the Money, Gadzooks, must be paid to an Hour.

IX.

For things of this World must by Law be made certain,
We both must repair to OLIVER MARTIN;   35
For He is a Lawyer of worthy Renown;
I'll bring You to See, He must fix you at DOWN.

X.

Quoth MATTHEW, I know that from BERWICK to DOVER,
You have Sold all your Premisses over and over;
And now if Your Buyers and Sellers agree,   40
You may throw all our Acres into the SOUTH-SEA.

XI.

But a word to the Purpose, to Morrow, dear Friend;
We'll see what to Night you so highly commend;
And if with a Garden and House I am blest,
Let the Devil, and CON . . . . BY go with the rest.   45

XII.

Then answer'd Friend MORLEY, pray get a Calash,
That in Summer may burn, and in Winter may Splash;
I love Dirt and Dust, and 'tis always my pleasure,
To take with me much of the Soil which I measure.

XIII.

But MATTHEW thought better, for MATTHEW thought right,   50
And Hir'd a Chariot so trim and so tight,
That Extremes both of Winter and Summer might pass;
For one Window was Canvas, the other was glass.

35 repair to] *1723* repair up to *MS. emend. (by Pope) in L 28 copy of 1723* MARTIN]
M———n 1723   45 Devil] *D———l 1723*   46 MORLEY] *M———y 1723*   49 which]
that *1723*

XIV.

Draw up, quoth Friend MATTHEW, Pull down, quoth Friend JOHN,
We shal be both hotter and colder anon.   55
Thus talking and scolding, they forward did speed;
And RALPHO pac'd by, under NEWMAN the SWEED.

XV.

Into an old Inn did this Equipage roll,
At a Town they call HODSDON, the Sign of the Bull;
Near a Nymph with an Urn divides the high way,   60
And into a Puddle throws Mother of Tea.

XVI.

Come here my sweet Landlady, pray how do you do?
Where is SISLEY so cleanly, and PRUDENCE, and SUE?
And where is the Widow, that liv'd here below?
And the Hostler that Sung about Eight Years ago?   65

XVII.

And where is your Sister so mild and so Dear
Whose voice to her Maids like a Trumpet was clear?
By my troth, She replies, you grow Younger, I think:
And pray, Sir, what Wine does the Gentleman drink?

XVIII.

Why now let me Die, Sir, or live upon Trust,   70
If I know to which Question to answer you first;
Why Things since I saw you most strangely have vari'd;
The Hostler is hang'd, and the Widow is marry'd.

XIX.

And PRUE left a Child for the Parish to Nurse,
And SISLEY went off with a Gentlemans Purse;   75
And as to my Sister, so mild, and so Dear,
She has lain in the Church-yard full many a Year.

---

54 down, *1723*: down *L 27*   60 Near] *1723* Where *MS. emend. (by Pope) in L 28 copy
of 1723*   67 clear? *edd.*: clear. *L 27, 1723*   72 have] are *1723*

XX.

Well, Peace to her Ashes; What signifies grief?
She roasted red Veal, and She powder'd lean Beef;
Full nicely She knew to cook up a fine dish,   80
For tough were her Pullets, and tender her Fish.

XXI.

For that matter, Sir, be Ye Squire, Knight, or Lord,
I'll give You whate'er a good Inn can afford.
I shou'd look on my self as unhappily sped,
Did I yeild to a Sister, or living or Dead.   85

XXII.

Of Mutton a delicate Neck and a Breast,
Shal Swim in the Water in which they were drest;
And because you great Folks are with Rarities taken,
Addle Eggs shal be next Course, tost up with rank Bacon.

XXIII.

The Supper was Serv'd, and the Sheets they were laid,   90
And MORLEY most lovingly whisper'd the Maid:
The Maid—was she handsom? why, truly, so, so,
But what MORLEY whisper'd we never shal know.

XXIV.

Then up rose these Heroes, as brisk as the Sun,
And their Horses like his were prepared to run.   95
Now when in the Morning MATT ask'd for the Score;
JOHN kindly had paid it the Evening before.

XXV.

Their Breakfast so warm, to be sure they did eat;
(A Custom in Travellers mighty discreet)
And thus with great Friendship, and Glee, they went on,   100
To find out the Place you shal hear of anon
             Call'd DOWN, DOWN, hey derry DOWN.

82 Ye] *MS. insertion (by Drift) in L 28 copy of 1723: om. 1723*   83 whate'er *1723*:
whate'ver *L 27*   91, 93 MORLEY] *M——y 1723*   102 Call'd Down] *MS. emend.*
(by Drift) in L 28 copy of 1723: Called hey *1723*

XXVI.

But what did they talk of from Morning 'till Noon?
Why of Spots in the Sun, and the Man in the Moon;
Of the CZAR's gentle Temper, and the Stocks in the City;   105
Of the wise Men of GREECE, and the Secret Committee.

XXVII.

So to HARLOW they came, and—Hey, where are ye All?
Show us into the Parlour, and mind when I call;
Why your Maids have no Motion, your Men have no Life.
Well, Master, I hear you have bury'd your Wife.   110

XXVIII.

Come this very Instant take Care to provide
Tea, Sugar, and Toast, and a Horse, and a Guide.
Are the HARRISONS here, both the old and the Young?
And where stands fair DOWN?—The delight of my Song.

XXIX.

Oh! Sir, to the Grief of my heart I may say,   115
I have bury'd Two Wives since you travell'd this way;
And the HARRISONS both may be presently here;
And DOWN stands, I think, where it stood the last Year.

XXX.

Then JOAN brought the Tea-Pot, and CALEB the Toast,
And the Wine was froth'd out by the hand of our Host;   120
But we clear'd our *extempore* Banquet so fast,
That the HARRISONS both were forgot in the Haste.

XXXI.

Now hey for DOWN-HALL, for the Guide he was got,
The Chariot was mounted, the Horses did trot;
The Guide he did bring Us a Dozen Mile round;   125
But oh! all in vain for no DOWN cou'd be found.

105 and] *1723 Deleted (by Pope?) in L 28 copy of 1723*   106 Secret Committee. *1723*:
Scret Committee *L 27*   114 DOWN? *edd.*: DOWN *L 27*: *Down? 1723*

XXXII.

Oh thou Popish Guide, thou hast led us astray.
Says he, How the Devil shou'd I know the way?
I never yet travell'd this Road in my Life;
Down lies on the left, I was told by my Wife.   130

XXXIII.

Thy Wife, answer'd Matthew, when She went abroad,
Ne'er told thee of half the By-Ways she had trod;
Perhaps she met Friends, and brought Pence to thy House;
But thou shalt go Home without ever a Souse.

XXXIV.

What is this Thing, Morley? and how can you mean it?   135
We have lost our Estate before we have seen it.
Have Patience, soft Morley in Anger reply'd,
To find out our way, let us send off our Guide.

XXXV.

Oh! here I spy Down, cast your Eye to the West,
Where a Wind-Mill so stately stands plainly confess'd.   140
On the West, reply'd Matthew, no Wind-Mill I find
As well thou may'st tell me I see the West Wind.

XXXVI.

Now pardon me, Morley, the Wind-Mill I spy;
But faithful Achates no House is there nigh.
Look again says mild Morley, Gadzooks you are blind;   145
The Mill stands before, and the House lies behind.

XXXVII.

Oh! now a low, ruin'd, white Shed I discern,
Until'd, and unglaz'd, I believe 'tis a Barn.
A Barn!—Why you rave—'Tis a House for a Squire,
A Justice of Peace, or a Knight of our Shire.   150

131 Wife, *1723*: Wife *L 27*   135 Thing, *1723*: Thing *L 27*   135, 137 Morley]
M——y *1723*   136 Estate before] Estate here before *1723*   143, 145 Morley]
M——y *1723*   144 there *1723*: their *L 27*

XXXVIII.

A House shou'd be built, or with Brick, or with Stone.
Why 'tis Plaister, and Lath, and I think that's all one;
And such as it is, it has stood with great Fame,
Been call'd a Hall, and has given its Name
        To DOWN, DOWN, hey derry DOWN.   155

XXXIX.

Oh! MORLEY, Oh! MORLEY, if that be a Hall,
The Fame with the Building will suddenly fall.
With your Friend JEMMY GIBBS about Building agree;
My Business is Land, and it matters not Me.

XL.

I wish you cou'd tell what a Duce your head ails;   160
I show'd you DOWN-HALL, did you look for VERSAILLES?
Then take House and Farm, as JOHN BALLOTT will let Ye,
For better for worse, as I took my Dame BETTY.

XLI.

And now, Sir, a Word to the wise is enough,
You'll make very little of all your old Stuff;   165
And to build at your Age, by my Troth you grow simple;
Are you Young and Rich, like the MASTER of WIMPLE?
        With your DOWN, DOWN, hey derry DOWN.

XLII.

If you have these Whims of Apartments and Gardens,
From twice Fifty Acres You'l n'er see Five Farthings.   170
And in Yours I shal find the true Gentlemans Fate,
E'er you finish your House, you'l have spent your Estate.

XLIII.

Now let us touch Thumbs, and be Friends e'er we part,
Here JOHN is my Thumb—And here MATT is my Heart.
To HALSTED I speed, and you go back to Town.   175
Thus ends the First Part of the Ballad of DOWN.

151 Stone. *edd.*: Stone, *L 27, 1723*   156 MORLEY, Oh! MORLEY] *M*——*y*, Oh! *M*——*y*
1723   158 GIBBS] *G*——*bs 1723*   162 BALLOTT] *B*——*tt 1723*   163 BETTY]
B——*tty 1723*   167 WIMPLE? *edd.*: WIMPLE. *L 27*: *Wimple. 1723*   168] *MS.*
insertion (by Drift) in L 28 copy of 1723: om. 1723   170 twice *1723*: 'twice *L 27*

Translated from the Original French.

WHILE soft She Parly'd, with becoming Grace,
    And courteous Smiles adorn'd her lovely face;
Who heard her speak Himself might soon deceive;
And fondly hope She felt the wound She gave:
But, Oh! great Love, Thy Vot'ries must take care   5
To serve Thee well, but trust Thee not too far.

The Old Gentry.

THAT all from Adam first begun
    None but ungodly Wh——— doubts,
And that his Son, and his Son's Son
Were all but Plowmen, Clowns, and Louts:

Each when his rustic pains begun   5
To merit pleaded equal right;
'Twas only who left off at Noon
Or who went on to work till Night.

Kenoul, Eight hundred Years have rowld
Since thy forefathers held the plow;   10
When this shall be in Story told
Add, that my Kindred do so now.

The Man who by his labor getts
His bread, in independent State,

                                                           15
Himself can fix or change his fate.

---

5 Vot'ries *edd.*: Vota'ries *L 29 (D & P), L 29 (D)*: Votarie's *L 28*
    Title: L 28 (Pope), 1740: *om. W, L 28 (D)*   1–4 *L 28 (Pope), 1740*: *om. W, L 28*
(D)   1 *begun L 28*: began *1740*   2 *Wh——— L 28*: WOOLSTON *1740*   5 begun]
began, *L 28, 1740*   6 right; *L 28 (Pope?)*: right *W*: right, *1740*   8 Night. *L 28,*
1740: Night *W*   *Earlier draft in W includes here this fragmentary stanza:*
                    to the (?) books We cast
                    Our Eye We must allow
                    That those are happiest who last
                    Took their hand from the plow.
9 *Preceded in L 28 and 1740 by the present ll. 17–20*   Kenoul] K ..... *L 28*: KINGSALE
1740   Eight *L 28, 1740*: 8 *W*: three   *Earlier reading in W*   10 plow; *edd.*: plow
W: Plough *L 28*: plow, *1740*   12 now. *L 28, 1740*: now *W*   15] and Eats
L 28 (D): Who never beggs, and [*blank*] Eats *L 28 (Pope)*: Who never begs, and seldom eats
1740   16 fate. *1740*: fate *W*: Fate. *L 28*

But Coronetts we owe to crowns
And favors to a Courts affection;
By Nature We are Adams Sons
And Sons of Anstis by Election.   20

Epigram.

STIL craving yet stil Roger cry'd
I'll live to-Morrow but to-Night he dy'd.
Strange the delusion of his hopes and fears
While that he Starv'd Himself to cram his Heirs.

Predestination, A Poem.

APOSTLES teach, and Holy books declare,
That 'tis in God we move, and live, and are:
In him we all begin, continue, end,
And all our Actions on his help depend.
I therefore must eternally have laid   5
In Nothings bosom, and Oblivions shade,
Among existing Beings not confest,
(For nothing by no words can be exprest)
Unless obedient to his high command,
Call'd by his word, and Plastor'd by his Hand,   10
And from his breath receiving Vital flame,
I had begun to be the thing I am.

Then the same pow'rfull, constant, heav'nly Aid
Must stil preserve the Creature it had made.
For shou'd that Aid one Moment be deny'd;   15
Dissolv'd and lost, I shou'd again subside
Into the sad Negation where I lay,
Before I swell'd the Womb, or saw the Day.

17–20 *In L 28 and 1740, these precede the present l. 9*   17 crowns *edd.*: crown *W*:
Crowns, *L 28, 1740*   18 favors] Favor *L 28, 1740*   affection; *L 28 (Pope?)*: affection
W: affection, *1740*   20 Election. *L 28*: Election *W*: election. *1740*
    Title: 'Contents' *of L 28: om. Text of L 28*   2 dy'd. *edd.*: dy'd *L 28*
    Predestination. Much of the punctuation in L 28 is in another hand (Pope's?)

Form'd by his Will, assisted by his Powr,
From the great period of my Native hour   20
Forward I hasten thro this path of life,
Nor with false pleasure smooth no violent Strife
Wh   was   then of my guide bereft?
And why to errour and amazement left?
Collected to my self I sadly find   25
Ten thousand doubts divide my anxious mind.
The potent biass of my crooked will
I found averse to good, and prone to ill;
Whence rises this depravity of thought
Was it from mine or my forefathers fault?   30
Shal I descend and say that Death and Sin
Did from ill judging Adams crime begin
Or tracing them from springs perhaps too high
To good and Ill give Coeternity?

Say did the Godhead infinitely wise   35
Create all good? then whence did ill arise?
Do two great Pow'rs their adverse strength employ
This to preserve, and t'other to Destroy?

Wou'd God set free what Dæmon cou'd enslave?
Cou'd Sin annoy what Sanctity wou'd save?   40
Of this no further Mortal man can know,
Than as from Scripture God has deign'd to show.
Here too we find the mighty Probleme laid
In Mystic darkness, and Prophetic shade:
Pen'd by the Poets rage and breast enlarg'd,   45
Adorn'd with Emblems, and with figures charg'd;
Form'd to the Lyre, and fitted to be Sung
To proper measures of the Hebrew Tongue;
By time corrupt, at first however pure;
And by Translation render'd more obscure;   50
By Sects eluded, and by Scholes perplext,
Till in the Comment we involve the Text.

E'er Time was bid his measures to begin,
E'er Angels knew to praise, or man to sin,

22–23 *A hand drawn in the margin indicates that these lines are imperfect*   23 L 28 (D):
Why was I then of my sole guide bereft? L 28 (Pope)

(Says Austin's words transfer'd to Calvins school,)   55
God fix'd one firm, unalterable rule.
The word was fated which the Almighty spoke,
Nor can his future Will that will revoke.
All things determin'd by this Solemn Doom,
And settled in the order they must come.   60
Select to pleasures, or condemn'd to pains;
Man only Executes what God ordains.
Is God subservient to his own Decree?
Is that Omnipotent which is not free?
Providence then in her continual course   65
Must stil be stopt by some superior force:
Then upon strict enquiry will be found,
That God himself by his own Act is bound;
That in a like dependence, He and Man
Must own a Pow'r which neither can restrain?   70
Then those Elect by this eternal doom
Must have been Sav'd, thô it had never come;
And the reprov'd in vain for Mercy call
To Him who came to free and save us All.
Vain therefore prudent thought, and previous care   75
Useless our Alms, and foolish is our Pray'r:
And with superfluous babling we have said,
"Give us this day our Father! dayly bread;"
If what We ask by fixt decree of Heav'n
Was giv'n before, or never can be giv'n.   80

   Now what is Man? a reasonable Machine,
A puppet danc'd upon this Earthly Scene,
An instrument in Gods o'erbearing hand,
Mov'd by his Pow'r, and forc'd by his command.
Cou'd destin'd Judas long before he fell   85
Avoid the terrors of a future Hell?
Cou'd Paul deny, resist, or not embrace
Obtruded Heav'n, and efficacious Grace?

   Yet is the great Apostle heard to say,
"Does not the Potters hand dispose the Clay?   90

55 Says *L 28 (D)*: Say *L 28 (Pope?)* *There is a hand in the margin opposite this line* 57
the *L 28 (D)*: th' *L 28 (Pope?)*   60 come. *edd.*: come, *L 28*   78 bread;" *edd.*:
bread; *L 28*   81 reasonable *L 28 (D)*: reas'nable *L 28 (Pope?)*

"And shal the Vase his makers Art upbraid,
"If or to Honor or Destruction made?"
'Tis true; but view we then the different State
Of beings living and inanimate:
Incapable of Sense and void of mind,   95
The passive Vessel cou'd no pleasure find,
Thô plac'd above where Saints and Angels reign;
And damn'd to Hell beneath, cou'd feel no Pain.

   Nor in his action is that Agent free
Who must fulfill immutable decree.   100
Allow we freedom to the whirling Stone,
Which in the Battel from the Sling is thrown?
Allow we freedom to the flying reed,
From the drawn Bow elanc'd with vi'lent speed?
If these attain, or if they lose their Aim,   105
Their rectitude or Error is the same:
Who blames their Fault, or celebrates their Fame?
Now Scale our Deeds and let the Plummet fall
Betwixt the senseless and the rational.
If Both alike by primitive decree   110
Are bound to act, and if what is must be;
For Slain Goliah to young Davids Praise
Can we in justice greater triumph raise,
Than to the chosen Pebble, which he took
Among the thousand from the Neighb'ring brook?   115
Or greater Crime impute to Furious Saul,
Than to his Jav'lin struck against the wall?

   Far other sure with Human mind it fares,
Now rais'd to pleasures, now deprest with Cares.

   Possess we not free liberty of Will   120
How are our Acts imbu'd with good or ill
Allow Gods Promises and threatnings made
E'er the Foundations of the world were laid;
They were contingent, and conditional;
From Adams Choice proceeded Adams fall.   125

92 made?" *edd.*: made? *L 28*   104 vi'lent *edd.*: vi'olent *L 28*   117 Jav'lin *edd.*:
Jav'elin *L 28*   118 Far *L 28 (Pope?)*: For *L 28 (D)*

By Cains free action Abells blood was spilt,
His Punishment must presuppose his Guilt.
And Abra'ms faith on Isaac doom'd to dye
Was founded on the Patriarchs Piety.
When Judah breaks Jehovahs great command,   130
He turns his wrathful Viols on the land:
When of her Sins in Ashes she repents,
The weeping Priest attones and God relents.
Our Deed is form'd and guided by our thought,
And equal to our Duty or our Fault.   135
By means However hid from Human Eyes
Gods future threatnings and his Mercy rise.

While yet we reconcile free Will to Fate,
To solve this doubt we greater doubts create:
That God regards the Simple Act alone,   140
Making Omnipotence by Prescience known;
And leaves to Us by Impulse from within,
To Cloath that Act with Duty, or with Sin.

But does he then his previous Will suspend,
And does his Science on our Deed attend?   145
If this way acting, we the sequel draw,
We act as God permitted and foresaw:
But if our Act be otherways employ'd,
Is his Permission and prevision voyd?
Has He, as human means may change the Scene,   150
In other guise permitted or foreseen;
And left the Slacken'd Reins of Providence
To the mad guidance of our feeble Sense?

Say rather, that he Will'd what he Foresaw;
That his volition is His Creatures law: 155
For God (excuse the saying) cou'd not see
Contingences which never were to be.
And if they were to be, that very Sight
Brought them from Nothing into Future light:
Permitting their Existence, fix'd their fate;   160
And to forsee, was to Predestinate.

That with spontaneous Liberty we move
In vain the adverse Sect desires to prove

From inward Power and Nature of the Soul
Which Natures God can alter or controll.   165

    By time and Age its Notions are disrang'd
By passions short and by distemper chang'd
Nor let us vaunting fancy we are Free
That we can mend or alter Heavn's decree
Or with our little Arms go up to fight   170
With Omnipresence and with Infinite
Our Operations by his Will were wrought
And when he gave he Fixt the Pow'r of thought.

    All matters particles, all Motions laws,
Cou'd not produce so great a Second cause.   175
Attoms, how ever separate or combin'd,
Cou'd not compose or animate the mind.
Earth cou'd not form it, then from Heav'n it came,
A part it self of the Celestial flame.
Let Christians Sanctify the Heathen chain   180
And that Prometheus which their Poets feign
Was Gods great Spirit enlight'ning Passive Earth
And kindling Human action into birth.
If then its vigor does from Heav'n proceed
By Heav'n its force and measure is decreed   185
That First who did this Second Cause produce
Proportions it to each Recipients use
'Tis Sisyphus' Stone returning stil
If God who gave the freedom Form'd the Will
To form it and incline it was the same   190
You grant the thing while You dispute the Name.

    Well then Man Wills and from that Will proceed
The stains and Colours of his sinfull deed
The Son whom he destroy'd he might have Sav'd
And freed the Captive whom his Hand enslav'd.   195

    So rolling down the Rocks the waters bring
The tast and hue of their original spring;

176 separate *L 28* (*D*): sep'rate *L 28* (*Pope?*)   179 flame. *edd.*: flame *L 28*   183
birth. *edd.*: birth *L 28*   188 Sisyphus' *edd.*: Sisyphu's *L 28*   192–5] *Marked for
deletion* (*by Pope*)   196 So *L 28* (*D*): As *L 28* (*Pope*)

So from our Will, that Fontain of our Deed,
The stains and Colours of our Acts proceed.

Pursue this Search to its Original:　　　　　200
Allowing Heav'ns Decree and Adams fall
A new Alliance and firm Covenant made
By God to be requir'd by Man Obey'd
Faith and Repentance on the Mortal side
The two great Knots by which the Bond is ty'd　　　　　205
And on the part of God the Human race
Assisting Mercy and preventing Grace
Yet how can we believe or how repent
Unless the influence first from Heav'n is sent
Strong the Condition to our bounded view　　　　　210
Contracted seemingly and Sign'd by Two
To perfect which unable one attends
While t'other furnishes the Total means.

Again whilst Grace is Gods immediate Gift
To Heav'n in vain my Voice and heart I lift　　　　　215
To ask th' Almighty's Tutelary Care
Except his Grace prevents my very Prayer
Now of this Gift if once I stand posses't
Yee Angels am I not for ever blest?
Tell me can Satan take what God has giv'n　　　　　220
Or all Hells darkness quench the light of Heav'n?
What after this do I implore or Crave
And need I ask what I already have?
What light of Comment can these Clouds remove
Backward and forward I uncertain rove　　　　　225
Thrô Labyrinths wander and in Circles prove.
If the Creator call'd me forth to birth
Wou'd he, I ask, his helpless Creature leave
Thus wand'ring dark, thus groveling low on Earth
That I might Sin, he Punish or Forgive.　　　　　230

The deep decrees the Fatalist replyes
Of an eternal God supremely Wise
As firmly fixt are permanently sure
Thro endless chains of Ages shal endure

213 means. *edd.*: means *L 28*　　　　226 prove. *edd.*: prove *L 28*

Made before Heav'n and Earth the word shal last   235
Unchangeable when Heav'n and Earth are past.
Allow free will that Sentence is destroy'd
A Covenant Seal'd which after Acts may void
A Casual Fabric built upon the sand
Which can nor winds nor falling rains withstand   240
But yields inflex'd and sapp'd by Human Pray'rs
Blown down with Sighs and wash'd away by tears.

Or trace your Steps thro the determin'd way
Or from the Christian Principles You stray
The Godhead thô with all perfection crown'd   245
Inclin'd to Mercy is by justice bound
Else whence the wond'rous kind necessity
That to Absolve poor Adam Christ must Dye
Whence the old stains imprest on Human race
The Heav'nly means that must those stains efface   ⎫
And Nature lost redeem'd by saving Grace.   ⎬ 250
                                                    ⎭

Hence the long Series of Events to come
And four Monarchic Empires stated doom
Else future Knowledge of Three thousand Years
The Psalmists raptures and the Prophets tears   255
The unveil'd Mysteries to a world restor'd
Forseen by Angels and by Men ador'd
Hence the great Object of our Future hope
And blessings flowing in that bitter Cup
Which God incarnate loving and belov'd   260
How'ever yielding beg'd might be remov'd
When prest with Agonies the suffering Son
Said Father not my will but Thine be done.

Almighty Lord the way, the door, the light,   ⎫
O let me stil Find Favor in thy sight   ⎬ 265
Excuse my going wrong or set me right.   ⎭

O Soveraign! great Three One! O God and Man!
Who set those Measures which I dare not Scan;
If I have leave to chuse, I beg that choice
Guided at least by thy Assistant Voice.   270

236 past. *edd.*: past *L 28*   242 tears. *edd.*: tears *L 28*   266 right. *edd.*: right *L 28*

If I must pursue a Destin'd way
Direct my Footsteps for thou can'st not stray.
From dangerous doubts my wandring Soul retrieve
I cannot Argue, grant me to believe!
Lifeless I lay, Thou wak'st me into Sense;   275
Frailty is mine, and Thine Omnipotence.

Argument of Ladislaus.

V INCESSLAUS King of Poland had two Sons, Ladislaus violent
and Passionate, generous and brave, Alexander more sedate and
Courtly, the one had all the Virtues fitting for a Camp, the other was
endowed with those Excellencies which adorn a Court, He had likewise one Daughter, Theodora, a Lady Religious and of strict honour. 5
   Frederic Earl of Coningsberg had long made Warr with Vincesslaus,
and having been driven out of his Dominions by his Rebell Subjects
had So much confidence in the Virtue of his old Enemy that thô he
had formerly two Sons Slain in the Wars against Poland, he retired to
Ladislaus Court, with one Daughter an Infant, the only remaining part 10
of his Family, was received Hospitably, and Dyed there, leaving his
Young Daughter Cassandra to be bred up with Vincesslaus Children,
Vincesslaus promising this unhappy Earl on his Death Bed, to restore
his Daughter to her Dominions. Cassandra is bred up with the Princess
Theodora between whom there grows a strict and intire Friendship. 15
   The King growing Old confides in the Courage and prudence of his
Favorite Conon whom he has made Duke of Courland, and Loaded with
great Riches. The eldest Prince Ladislaus unable to bear the power of
the Favorite, often Shocks him, the favorite becoming most a Friend
to the Younger Prince Alexander. Ladislaus behaves himself insolently 20
to his Brother and quarrels with him, The Authority and Command of
the Father interposes, and the Younger Brother behaves himself so
civilly to his Elder by the Advice of the Favorite that the reconcilliation
seems perfectly made to the old King, However imperfectly assented
to by the haughty carriage of the Prince.   25
   Ladislaus falls in Love with Cassandra, but as his humor was impetuous and violent, he makes brutal Love to her, and finding an

272 stray. *edd.*: stray *L 28*   273 dangerous *L 28 (D)*: dang'rous *L 28 (Pope?)*
   1 King *L 28*: K *W*   9 retired *edd.*: retires *W, L 28*   14 her] his *L 28*
   15 there *L 28*: their *W*   20 Alexander. *L 28*: Alexandr: *W*

opportunity was offering once to Ravish her. This She conceals from all the World except her Friend Theodora. With a respectfull and honourable Passion Alexander is all this while secretly in Love with Cassandra, He tells his flame to the Favorite, and his Suspitions that his elder Brother is likewise in Love with her. The favorite is in Love with the Princess Theodora, but dos not yet tell this Secret to Prince Alexander, Prince Alexander easily prevails with him to carry on a seeming Courtship to Cassandra in his own Name, But in effect to make Love for him. And he rather performs this piece of Friendship to Alexander, hoping that he would use his Interest afterwards with his Sister Theodora in his behalf, and help to appease the Kings Anger for the Ambition of his Choice. The King now seeing his Sons reconciled grows fonder of his Favorite, and in a Festival on his birth Day gives him a Ring, telling him that his former Services had So far merited that when ever he produced that Ring he should obtain what request so ever he made, upon this assurance his hopes of obtaining the Princess Theodora being confirmed he desires public Audience of the King, Says that he Loves and requires the Kings consent to his marriage, But at the Minute that he is giving the Ring to the King, and naming the Person, Prince Ladislaus imagining as the rest of the Court did that it was Cassandra, he steps up snatches the Ring from the favorites hand, reproaches the Weakness and age of his Father, reproaches the Duke as having got his Fathers favour from him, and as being now desirous to supplant him in his Love, and leaves the place with great rage and Disorder.

Alexander who as was said is Secretly in Love with Cassandra asks his Sister Theodora if She thinks that Cassandra will ever be brought to Love his elder Brother Ladislaus. She assures him that Cassandra never will, he then desires her good Offices to Cassandra in favour of the Duke his Friend, having as was Said before engaged the Duke to make love seemingly in his own name but really in Alexanders to Cassandra So to Screen him from the Violence of his elder Brother and the resentments which the King might have upon that marriage which after it was accomplished Time and Submission must reconcile.

While the Prince is in this Fury and Disorder Octavius Governor of Warsaw having an Affair with Leonora woman to Cassandra, tells the Prince that he had heard from Leonora that a Man disguised and a Priest were to be ready at Midnight in Cassandras appartment.

28 offering once] once offering *L 28*   29 Theodora *edd.*: Theodosia *W*, *L 28* With *L 28*: with *W*   47 it *L 28*: is *W*   51 Disorder. *L 28*: Disorder *W*   52 asks *edd.*: askt *W*, *L 28*   56 Friend, *L 28*: Friend. *W*   60 reconcile. *L 28*: reconcile *W*

Ladislaus thinks this appointment made to the Duke, gets privately 65
into Cassandras House by Octavius's means, finds his Brother Alexander there disguised and waiting for Cassandra who had promised so to
marry him, draws forth a Poinyard and kills his Brother, his Brother in
the Scuffle and in the Dark wrests the Ponyard out of his hand and
wounds him, endeavoring to escape and having lost much blood he is 70
found by Octavius and brought as to the nearest place, and where its
probable he would not be look't for, to a Chappell adjacent to his
Sister Theodoras Lodging, and where She was then performing a very
early Devotion to Some particular Saint. The King rises restless and
uneasy, complains of the inconveniences and distempers of Age and 75
the troubles of Empire that hinder him from Sleep, Says he has had
horrid Dreams and Fancies and Seeing the light in the Chappel commends his Daughters Piety and calmness of mind, Says that from her
Discourse he always receives his Joy, but coming in finds Prince
Ladislaus lying wounded and bloody upon a Couch and Theodora 80
weeping by him. The King asks the reason of this cruel Scene, the
Prince Says that being mad and in Love hating in the Duke both the
Favorite and the Rival he had stabbed him; The Princess Theodora
laments this misfortune, and just as the Story is told, and the Prince
is fainting a Messenger tells the King that the Duke desires to be 85
admitted into his prescence. He enters to the Supprise of the Prince the
Princess and the King who thought him Dead. But says he comes to
prepare them for the saddest Spectacle that ever was Seen, and Cas-
sandra enters with her Hair deshevelled and her Robes torn followed
by the Body of Prince Alexander upon a Bier. She shows the King his 90
Son murdered, demands Justice upon the Prince his Murtherer, the
Prince desires to Dye Since Cassandra accuses him, the King Says
Justice Shal be done and orders the Prince to be kept Prisoner in the
Chappel, retires with the melancholly consideration that he had Slain
in Battle two of Cassandras Brothers, who now had occasioned the 95
Death of his two Sons.

The Princess Theodora in Tears sends a Letter to the Duke, to come
to her, in this conference upbraids him, for having lent his Name to
help her Brother Alexander to carry on his Love to Cassandra, Since
that disguize was the Cause of his Death. He tells her the reason of it, 100
that Alexander had mutually promised him, to assist him in a passion

66 means, *L 28*: means *W*   68 him, *L 28*: him *W*   69 wrests *L 28*: wrest *W*
72 for, *edd.*: for *W*, *L 28*   74 Saint. *L 28*: St:, *W*   81 Scene, *L 28*: Scene *W*
86 prescence. He *edd.*: prescence he *W*: Presence. he *L 28*   90 Alexander *L 28*:
Alexandr: *W*   93 orders the *L 28*: *Illeg. in W*   98 her, *L 28*: her *W*

which otherwise he never durst aspire to, She replys hastily that any Fortune in Poland, Her Fathers Freindship to him might have got for him, asked therefore hastily who could be the object of this passion, he pulls out her Letter, and Shows her at the Bottom of it her own 105 Name Theodora. By Degrees She receives his Love, charges him to Show his Fidelity by interceeding with her to her father for her Brothers Life, He indeavors it, renews his Services, and the Cruelty of the Act, Theodora joins her Tears, Cassandra Sees the violence of the Princes passion to her, who since his wound talks to her, desires to Dye 110 that he may satisfy her just revenge to her former Lover, the King continues inexorable, sees the Prince, imbraces him, forgives him, gives him his Blessing, and commands him to Dye upon the Scaffold, with all the resolution that becomes his Eldest and now only Son. The Prince is brought to the Scaffold, and all things are prepared for his 115 Death, Octavius Governor of the Town excites the People to Mutiny, They break down the Scaffold, besiege the King in the Regal Castle, and threaten to make him perish with hunger except he Pardons the Prince. The People seize upon Theodora as She was taking the last leave of her Brother. The fav'rite Duke however desirous to obey 120 Theodora's Commands and save the Prince continues besieged in the Castle with the King, and says he'l Dye with the King. Theodora appears below with the People, and vows to become a Nun the moment her Brother Dyes. The King in these Straits demands a parley with the People, He comes down, brings the Regal Ensigns of Honour with him, 125 explains how he has distributed Justice forty Year to every Man, and that the Laws shal never be Violated while he Reigns, So gives up the Crown and Scepter which the Duke carrys over to the People having done that he immediately Sides with the People against the King, Says he's no longer his Prince, consequently owes him no Allegiance, and 130 says that the Surest way to save the Prince is to set him above the Law, upon which the People immediately unbind the Prince and proclaim him King. His Father instructs him to lay aside the Violence of his Passion, and rule well, recommends Cassandra to him, for a Wife, which She accepts, the Princess Theodora is advised by the young King to 135 marry the Duke as the Man to whom he owes his Life, The King full of Years retires to his Religion and Rural pleasures and Ladislaus reigns King of Poland.

104 this] his *L 28*   106 Theodora. *L 28* : Theodora *W*   110 her, desires *L 28* : her desires *W*   111 that he... satisfy *L 28* : *Illeg. in W*   119 Prince. The *L 28* : Prince the *W* 120 Brother. *L 28* : Brother *W*   122 and says... King] *om. L 28*   126 Year] Years *L 28*   127 So *L 28* : *Illeg. in W*

Britanicus and Junia.

Minutes for a Tragedy.

I.

Pallas, Agrippina

Agrippina.   Tis true
That Nature had her part in that affection
That bent my fond desires towards Nero's greatness,
The Easy Mother pointed to her Son
That throne where Seated he might be her Master.   5
But tenderness and friendship but begun,
Ambition perfected the glorious work
And while with Easy manners, and wise precept
By just degrees I temper'd his rough Nature,
'Twas that his Soul inur'd to smooth obedience   10
Should own the Power that Agrippina lent him.
             Nor shall Nero govern Earth
Unless I govern Nero.

Pallas.   Your commands
Madam—

Agrippina.   Shall be obey'd, reply not Pallas.
The Man should bear the Weaker Womans frailties,   15
The Son should thank the Kindness of a Mother.
The Prince should hear the conseil of a friend.
Let Rome attest if ever I was thought
The weaker of my Sex, the worst of friends
Or most unkind of Mothers, yet great Heav'n,   20
Lost Agrippina Sinks for Nero frowns:
Rhea, great Mother, rule my Son like Jove.

Pallas.   Help Me Close Artifice, conceal'd design and deep dissimulation, arts which this Woman knows and practices and with which I only can confound her cruell Malice.   25

See commentary   Title: *L 28*: Fragment of a Tragedy '*Contents*' *of L 28*: om. *W* (*At the bottom of W, 157, D wrote*: Brouillon of a Tradegy)   1 Agrippina. *edd.*: om. *W*, *L 28*   2 that] the *L 28*   5 That] and that *L 28*   6 But tenderness] But Pallas while tenderness *L 28*   begun, *edd.*: begun *W*: began *L 28*   8 Easy] early *L 28* wise] om. *L 28*   10 that] then *L 28*   11] his awful gratitude proven by | his ductile thought relying on *Earlier readings in W, L 28*   that] om. *L 28*   him. *edd.*: him *W*, *L 28*   14 Madam— *edd.*: Madam, *W, L 28*   21 for] om. *L 28*   22 In *W and L 28, the intended position of this line is uncertain*   like] he: *L 28*   23 Pallas. *edd.*: om. *W, L 28*   24 this Woman ... practices] shal ... Practiced *L 28*

2.

Nero, Burrhus

Burrhus.   Agrippina Sent Pallas to inform Me that soon as You arose
    she purposed to visit You.

Nero.   Is She a Goddess or a Mortal speak,
    If like Egeria when she counsell'd Numa
    She comes from Heav'n, all Space is pervious to Her   30
    But if she be a Mortal I see her not
    Nor any of the Sex except,
    Oh whither am I roving, Junia.

Burrhus.   Mortal or Woman, her I mention'd Sir
    Is Nero's mother.   35

Nero.   Be She Joves mother, Sir I see her not
    Till I have Seen Narcissus, on your Duty
    Lett None else enter, to your post, inform her
    This is my will my Souldier.

Burrhus.   Well my Emperor
    That will shall be obey'd.

Nero.   Go to, thou knowest   40
    I like thy rugged honesty.

3.

Agrippina, Burrhus

Agrippina.   Ha! dream'st thou Burrhus. Say can Agrippina
    By any power imprest on words, be severed
    From Nero's presence: say recite thy order;
    Perhaps, that whilst his Music entertains him   45
    One hour, He would suspend the public Court
    Nor think of News from Senates and from armies
    That Such as Burrhus might too rudely offer
    With blundering Duty and ill tim'd obedience.
    Perhaps that having revel'd late the Night   50
    He would Indulge a longer rest this morning.

Burrhus.   Tis of a Subject, madam to obey
    And of a Woman to resent, the Emperor

---

28 speak, *edd.*: speak *W*, *L 28*   32 any *L 28*: *Partially illeg. in W*   34 Burrhus
edd.: Borrhus *L 28*: *om. W*   36 Nero. *L 28*: *om. W*   39 Burrhus. *edd.*: Borrhus *L 28*:
om. W   40 Nero. *L 28*: *om. W*   42 Agrippina. *L 28*: *om. W*   43 on] in *L 28*
46 suspend...Court] *L 28* not be disturb'd by news *Earlier reading in W and L 28*

Can best explain the orders I deliverd.
Madam: I own the grosness of my mind　　　　　　55
My military roughness, my great Ignorance
And my severe contempt of Courtly arts.
　　　　　　But never shall forgett
With due respect to treat—

Agrippina.　　　　　　　　　　　Ha; due respect,
And is it come to that, and from thy mouth,　　　60
Say Burrhus dost thou Know me, speak who am I.

Burrhus.　　The Neice descended from Augustus Cæsar,
As he your poets tell you from Enneas,
The wife to brave Domitius Ænobarbus
My fellow Souldier and my friend in Arms,　　　65
The wife again of my old master Claudius
And last the mother of Imperial Nero,
In the whole world the Second of your Sex
For while Octavia shares the regal bed
She must be held the first.

Agrippina.　　　　　　　　　Peace, Dotard Schreech owl　70
Canst thou prescribe me Place, then Agrippina
Is fall'n indeed, but thou below my anger
I fear art warranted too far, and Nero
Shall answer and shall punish thy offence
But see He comes, the disobedient Son　　　　　75
The growing Politician, the young tyrant
He comes.

4.

Nero, Agrippina

Nero.　　Good morrow and long health to Agrippina.
Agrippina.　My thanks are owing to those filial wishes.
Son I would commune with you, I have something　　80
That loads my breast and you alone can Ease it.
Nero.　　Madam the publick business of the Empire
Claims my Immediate presence, the first hour

54 deliverd. *edd.*: del erd *W*: delivered *L 28*　　55 Madam: *edd.*: M: *W om. L 28*　　59:
Agrippina. *L 28*: *om. W*　　62 Burrhus. *edd.*: Borrhus *L 28*: *om. W*　　63 Enneas,
edd.: Enneas *W*: Eneas *L 28*　　67 last the] *om. L 28*　　70 Agrippina *L 28*: *om. W*
73 art] th'art *L 28*　　79 Agrippina. *L 28*: *om. W*　　owing *L 28*: owning *W*

That may be Mine, I'l gladly dedicate
To what may please my ever gracious Mother. 85
Lead lictors to the Senate.

5.

Agrippina, Britanicus, Narcissus

Agrippina.   What do you seek?

Britanicus.   My life, my love, my treasure: Junia, taken away by
Souldiers &c Both banish'd from Empire. What did we desire but
to mingle Sorrows, cruel Agrippina? 90

Agrippina.   I resent your Injuries, will help you to revenge them, hope,
where Agrippina takes part, your goodness perhaps your very
sufferings have engaged Me. [Exit]

Britanicus to Narcissus.   Is not this that cruell mother in law, that has
given the Empire from me, that Poisoned my father? 95

Narcissus.   What then, common Interest unites you, when she raised
Nero she Expected to be Empress of the world. She may give it to
You.

Britanicus.   Ah Narcissus thou raisest a thought, but I am watched, my
great Youth, I see some that like Thee with silent sorrow only 100
own my sufferings. You my confident, go see how our friends are
assembled, and keep up the anger of Agrippina. [Exit]

Narcissus.   Who wou'd prevail o'er Men must first observe
Their Darling Passion of their hearts and thence
Govern their ductile Reason, in Britanicus 105
The power of Love prevails the dazled Lover.

6.

Nero, Narcissus

Nero.   Every thing thou sayst comforts Me, thy conseils ease my
apprehensions with which I am besett, a brother yet Strong by
those whom Claudius raised, a mother imperious &c yet I see light
thrô all this, and may reign in Safety, and recompence thee, but 110
I shall bring Thee farther than ever thou didst intend.

---

85 Mother. *edd.*: Mother *W*, *L 28*   90 Sorrows] Sorrow *L 28*   94 that has
L 28: *Partially illeg. in W*   95 Poisoned *edd.*: Poison *W*: Poysoned *L 28*   96
then, *edd.*: then *W*, *L 28*   97 She *L 28*: she *W*   100 some] none *L 28*   Thee with
edd.: Thee that with *W*, *L 28*   101 own] owns *L 28*   104 thence *L 28*:
Partially illeg. in W   108 apprehensions] apprehension *L 28*   brother *edd.*: Brother
L 28: *Partially illeg. in W*   109 Claudius *L 28*: claudius *W*

Narcissus. Is there a thought that I would not Serve the Emperor in,
    speak it and if it be in my power be sure you shall obtain it.

Nero.   Narcissus, Nero is in love—

Narcissus. With Junia speak it.   115

Nero.   Is there another far as Rome extends
        Her ample power, whose charms could captivate
        The guarded heart of Nero, oh! I love her
        Love Her Said I tis little, I adore Her,
                   That Night   120
        When by my order she was brought to Rome
               her flowing garments
        Amidst the gleaming Armor of the Souldiers,
        Who bated of their strutting pace
        To ease her labring steps, and turn'd their heads   125
        To look with sullen sweetness on her Greif.
        At the portico in the colonade
        That opens the new court, unseen I saw her
        O beauteous, fatal sight.
        The vail that half conceald her breast   130
        But only added Modesty to Beauty
        While Sorrow shone thrô both: her face now gloing
        Now pale, by turns declar'd her anxious Mind
        Now Seiz'd with doubt now combated with fear
        And ever and anon a trickling tear   135
        Dropt from her Eyes restor'd their native brightness:
        Why was not I that colonel of the Legion
        That led her on, that toucht her hand Narcissus.
        Oh Junia Junia.

Narcissus. Is to be wedded to Britanicus   140
        So Agrippina wills.

Nero.   Narcissus hear Me:
        Before that Will shall meet its wish'd effect
        All law shall be dissolv'd all Senates banish'd.

---

113 speak it] speak *L 28*   114 Narcissus, *L 28*: Narcissus *W*   116 Nero. *edd.*:
om. W: *In L 28, placed with last half of l.* 118   far...extends] so, as None exceeds
her *L 28*   121 by] to *L 28*   Rome *edd.*: rome *W, L 28*   122 garments]
Garment *L 28*   123 Souldiers, *edd.*: Souldier. *W*: Soldier *L 28*   127 At the
portico] *om. L 28*   128 the new] th' inner *L 28*   130 conceald *edd.*: conceals *W*,
L 28   132 Sorrow] horror *L 28*   137 colonel *edd.*: coll̄ *W*: Cott: *L 28*   138
her on, *edd.*: her, on, *W*: her on *L 28*   141 Nero. *L 28*: *om. W*   hear] leave *L 28*
142 wish'd *L 28*: *Illeg. in W*   143 dissolv'd *edd.*: dissol'd *W*: Dissolv'd *L 28*
all] and *L 28*

The Roman Empire basis shall be shaken
And Nero perish in the mighty ruine.   145
Bring the bright Maiden to these willing arms
And from the Influence of that happy hour
Narcissus, share my friendship and my power.

7.

Nero, Agrippina

Agrippina. Why was this Womb not blest with barrenness
         Ere yet it brought Thee forth: why do I cease   150
         To beat and tear these breasts that gave Thee Suck?
Nero.   Romulus, founder of the Roman Empire
         Was nurst by a Shee wolf—
Agrippina.   Ha: durst thou Nero
         Afflict thy Mother with upbraiding speech?
Nero.   Oh Madam would you have Me mollified   155
         By female tears teach Junia how to weep.
Agrippina. Domitius I am come to chide You.
Nero.   Sett back the Chair, yet further, sett it well
         Madam, the court the Senate and the Empire
         Shall know with what Submission Nero heard   160
         When Agrippina chid him.
Agrippina.   Less respect
         And greater gratitude to her whose pangs
         Gave Thee to see the world, to Her whose Kindness
         Has guided Thee Till Thou art Master of it.

8.

Nero, Narcissus

Narcissus. I contemn it, if I have not friendship, I'l poyson my Self.   165
Nero.   Augustus reign'd with Clemency, and ever forgave his foes.
Narcissus. Yes, when he first had cemented the Empire In blood.
Nero.   Tis hard Narcissus.
Narcissus. Tis Said that Either you or Britanicus must dye: Empire
         and Love admit no partnership.   170

145 ruine. *edd.*: ruine *W*: ruins *L 28*   147 that] the *L 28*   149 this Womb not]
not this Womb *L 28*   153 Agrippina. *L 28: om. W*   155 Nero. *L 28: om. W*
157 I am come *edd.*: I am I come *W*: I—I come *L 28*   166, 168 Nero. *L 28: om. W*
169–70 *In L 28, this is part of Nero's speech beginning l. 168*   169 Narcissus. *edd.*:
om. W, L 28   Said *edd.*: Sd: *W*: hard *L 28*

Nero.   But what is vertue?

Narcissus. Tis a dream, all alow tis nothing in itself, yet all: tis that
    whose Influence governs the world, it is the Tyrant of the mind.
    It is a weapon, whose point you should always offer against your
    Enemies breast, but never turn it to your own, tis What preists 175
    should teach the people that Kings may reign in safety.

Nero.   And didst thou teach Britanicus these Notions?

Narcissus. I reserv'd them for his Master, while in aw and slavery I
    bred him for a Subject.

>   Change conditions with him, let him know   180
>   The real Maxim that should govern Rome:
>   And be Emperor, while You read Seneca
>   While You read Cæsars Gallic warrs explained by Burrhus.

    Already Britanicus at large Triumphs. The Army shout for his
    being released, Agrippina boasts her Empire over your Mind re- 185
    gained, that as Soon as she saw you You asked terms of accomoda-
    tion, happy to be reconciled to her.

    Content your self to drive a Chariot or recite verses in the
    Theatre, returning to court sitt down contented to be the Empress
    Agrippina's Son   190

>   And pale Octavia's husband.

Nero.   Cease to torment.

Narcissus. Times are changed, Since Remus stained the walls and all
    the Empire knew it, things are Softer, are there no more Mustroms
    since Claudius death? And, pardon Me for the same Zeal that
    recommends Me to your Service, thô mother &c stood in the way 195
    would still go on, is it not better that Britanicus should dye than
    You, it shall be Sayd that Nero with good parts was govern'd a
    pupill by his mother, was Scard by Seneca, who practiced none of
    those virtues he taught and having preach't against Covetousness
    had hoarded Millions, that Nero could not be divorced from 200
    Octavia because he fear'd Britanicus her brother and durst not

---

171–6 *Both MSS. have this as one speech; W gives it to Nero, L 28 to Narcissus*   172
all alow] all a Dream *L 28*   173 mind. *edd.*: Mind. *L 28*: mind *W*   179 Subject.
edd.: Subject *W, L 28*   183 Gallic *L 28*: gallic *W*   184 The *L 28*: the *W*
shout for] shouts Sir *L 28*   185 released,] rewarded. *L 28*   185–6 regained,
edd.: regained *W*: regained. *L 28*   187–8 her. Content *L 28*: her, content *W*   188
Chariot *edd.*: Char. *W, L 28*   in] on *L 28*   191 torment *L 28*: *om. W*   192
stained] slain *L 28*   walls] *om. L 28*   193 Mustroms] Nursetrees *L 28*   194 death?
And *edd.*: death and *W*: Death and *L 28*   same] sure *L 28*   195 Me] Narcissus
L 28   196 that *L 28*: *Illeg. in W*   198 Scard] scorned *L 28*   201 Britanicus]
om. L 28

make love to Junia, least Britanicus should be found to have more
Power than He.

Nero.   Thou hast waked Something vishous in my breast.

Narcissus. Something that never should have Slept and there is 205
Something an ugly Something that torments that breast Which
ought sleep for ever.

Nero.   Oh Narcissus,
          Faithfull Physician thou with skillfull hand
          Hast probd the wound, but hast thou healing balsam   210
          To Cure it?

Narcissus.   Gracious Emperor when Phœbus
          Godhead of Medicin with kind lenitives
          No longer can assist the rebell patient,
          He draws his arrows forth, confounds the rebel
          And by rough methods vindicates his power.   215

Nero.   Cruel and adventrous Counsellor
          Too well I understand Thee
          Do what thou wilt,
     Show me my rival Dead, and Junia weeping that death yet hast-
ing to my arms.   220

Heads for a Treatise upon Learning.

WHAT we commonly call Schole learning is so necessary that he
who has it not in some degree can hardly be accounted a Man;
The several parts of it are to the Mind what our different Limbs are
to the Body, as we cannot see without Eyes, or walk without Feet, so
neither can we Judge rightly of what we have seen, or tell exactly how 5
or where we have walk'd without the Assistance of Arethmetic and
Geometry: We cannot build or Enclose, we cannot attain or improve
many other conveniences and blessings of life without some knowledge
in these parts of the Mathematicks, we can neither rightly understand
our Own or learn any other Modern language without a Previous 10
insight into the Latin and the Greek. The Good and Excellence of

204 hast *L 28*: has *W*   vishous in] within *L 28*   208 Nero. *L 28*: *om. W*
211 Narcissus. *L 28*: *om. W*   219–20 hasting] *om. L 28*   220 arms. *edd.*:
harms, *W*: Harms *L 28*
     Title] *L 26* An Essay upon Learning. *Extra title in L 26*   2 accounted] counted
L 26   6 walk'd *edd.*: walk'ed *L 25*: walked *L 26*   9 the] *om. L 26*   11
Greek. The *edd.*: Greek the *L 25*: Greek The *L 26*

Learning has been the Theme of the greatest Writers for above three thousand Years, the Inconveniences and Ills it may produce if not well regulated, is the Subject of my Present Letter.

As in general, Reading improves the Judgement of a Man of Sense, 15 it only renders the Caprice of a Coxcomb more visible. It has been truly said that he who is Master of Three or four Languages may be reckened three or four Men, understanding and being understood in as many Countries; but If he utters Impertinences, he is only the same fool so many times multiplyed, If he had been bred by his Friends at home, to 20 what an honest Farmer would call reading and writing, he could have been ridiculous only from the Isles of Orkney to the Cliff of Dover, but being sent to one of our Universities first, and thence to a foreign Academy, his Sphere of Activity is enlarged and he has the Privilege to be laughed at at Paris or Madrid, at Rome or Constantinople. 25 Languages in the Mouth of a Fool are like Weapons in the hand of a Madman, the more he has of them, the more harm he may do to himself as well as to every Body within his reach.

Too great an Application to any one sort of Study may spoil a Man of good Natural Parts, either as to his being agreable in Conversation 30 or Useful to the Public; being too far involved in Mathematicks and abstracted Science, he may become neither heedful enough to mind or Able enough to answer what is said in Company And from reading of History and Travel, he may be at Last a meer Story teller, rather able to recite a matter of Fact than to apply it to a right Purpose. As to that 35 Study indeed, which a Man makes his Profession there is an Exception, for Life is so Short and the Avocations of it so various that without a peculiar application to one kind of Learning he cannot attain to a very Eminent Perfection in it, Thus Divines Lawyers and Physitians are esteemed great Scholars if they understand and Discourse well of what 40 belongs to their own Profession, and Allowances are made in other Parts of general Learning, in which they may not be so perfectly versed, It is therefore incumbent on these Gentlemen to gain this point as well for their Reputation as their Profit. History in general is pleasurable, and as it depends upon the Memory is to be acquired while we are 45 Young. The History of our own Country from the Conquest and of the other Nations of Europe for about three hundred Years past is most diligently to be studied especialy by Persons of Quality and such as are to make any Figure in the State or design for any Public Employ-ment: I have heard some quote Alexander and Cæsar, who knew very 50 little of Gustavus Adolphus or William of Orange, and were acquainted rather with Thomyris and Zenobia than with Katherine of Medicis or Queen Elizabeth, They can dispute if there were four Gordions in Rome without being very well assured there were as many Henrys in France. As to Ancient History it may be remarked that You find 55 Letters and Orations not Genuine, which tell you not what the Persons spake or wrote but what the Historian Fancys they should have done. The Politicians Soldiers, and Women in Tacitus make observations and turn Sentences alike, and all Livys Heroes harangue in the same Style, Julius Cæsar commonly esteemed so happy in that he had a Pen able to 60 grave in neat Language what his Sword had first more roughly cut out if rightly examined may be censured on this head, for he who for the Credit of his own Witt makes the most barbarous People speak in a Style much better than they could possibly have, may for the Honor of his Conquests make them fight in an other manner than they really 65 did. But in Modern History it is otherwise. These sort of Memoires are proved to be authentic and give you the very Picture of their Minds in whose name they were published, or at least such an Idea as you may conceive to be just, whoever reads the Apology of William the first of Orange, whom I just now quoted, will find a Patriot determined Valiant 70 and Great, whoever peruses the Conferences and Declarations of King Charles the First will presently acknowledge A Prince just and Pious, Tenacious of his own Right but with great regard to the good and safety of his People, Pieces of this kind give you as infallibly an Idea of the Situation of the Mind and Circumstance of Fortune of the Person 75 you read of, as an Original Drawing will show you the hand of any Painter, it can hardly be counterfeited thô by a better hand, nay even as to Minors, and weak Princes, thô it cannot be supposed that they write their own Letters there may be found a likeness of their thought from the better Draught that their Ministers have given of it.   80

Again the Customes and Maximes of the Greeks and Romans are so different from those of the present Nations and times that thô we may be thought more learned we are not in proportion so fully instructed from these as from more modern Authors, and they are only useful as

---

55 France. *L 26*: France, *L 25*   66 But *L 26*: but *L 25*   These *L 26*: these *L 25*
67 Picture] Pictures *L 26*   69 William *L 26*: Wm: *L 25*   72 Pious, *edd.*: Pious
L 25, L 26   74 an *L 26*: *om. L 25*   75 the Mind] Mind *L 26*   76 will
L 26: will will *L 25*

compared to what is nearer us, and as to quoting History the greatest 85
care Imaginable is to be taken that the Story be proper to the Subject
upon which it was introduced, In this some have a peculiar happyness,
and others often miscarry, therefore every Man is to consult his own
Talent avoiding Long Stories and especially Tautology.

Of History in general Chronology is the very life and Quintiscence; 90
the rest without it is but a Rope of Sand, a Tale of a Tub: where any
Writer has failed in it, his whole Book has been condemn'd; and where
any Speaker is not guided by it, his Discourse will not be minded.
Medals are again a help to Chronology, but the Scarcity and expence
of good Ones make it difficult for any Man less than a Prince to possess 95
such a Series of them as shal be of real use to him; for here I make the
greatest Difference imaginable between Study and Curiosity, since one
is to profit the Mind, the t'other to please the Eye; The Gentleman
who likes Medals very well, will always be desirous to possess the best
of them; and the Antiquary or Virtuoso will be sure to top false ones 100
upon him; besides that too much Money may be spent in the Acquisition, too much time may be spent in the Contemplation of them.
Medals as to reading are what Counters are to Cards, you may Contemplate The Figures upon them while you neglect going on with
your Game, Monsieur Spanheim one of the Greatest Antiquarys and 105
Scholars of the last Centuary, had no other Medals but those printed
in Series and Books; but I stil restrain this Curiosity rather than
condemn it.

The Ancient Poets are more looked into, and oftner quoted than the
Historians; the Mythology of their Religion, and the Morality as well 110
as the Beauty of their Ideas continuing always the same. Our Judgement as well as our Fancy is engaged in favor of Poets; we are taught
it very Young, and finding when we come into the World that it meets
with universal Approbation, as we have learned it from our Fathers,
We study it our Selves, and deliver it to our Children by a kind of 115
Tradition, but here we must take special care, for it is easier to play
the Pedant by way of Quotation in Poetry than in Prose; there are a
hundred Scraps of Verses which for above twice as many Years People
have successively quoted; and by often hearing them, every Body are
tired of, these are absolutely to be rejected, as are likewise All common 120
Place Jests or Observations in Prose; they ought never to be us'd except

92 condemn'd; *edd.*: condemn'ed; *L 25*: Condemned, *L 26*   98 Mind, *edd.*: Mind
L 25, L 26   108 it. *L 26*: it *L 25*   111 as the *L 26*: as their *L 25*   121 us'd
edd.: us'ed *L 25*: used *L 26*

they give a greater force to the Argument you would maintain, or a new Turn to the Thought you would express: Then indeed the Commoness of the Quotation is so far from taking off that it adds to the Lustre of the Discourse. 125

The Italian and Spanish Writers have quoted with great success; but where they have made bold with Passages in holy Scripture, which indeed is too frequently, they are not to be Imitated. The French and the English in the Choice of their Texts, as well as in the Body of their Sermons and discourses, have done Justice to the Writers of the Bible, 130 who besides the Truth and loftiness of their thought have really more witt than any People who have liv'd since. Amongst the French the Jesuits have excelled in this, and amongst our English Writers the Author of the whole Duty of Man, and of those Books that pass under his Name, Some now Living as Dr Atterbury, Smaldridge, Gastrel have 135 placed Texts of Scripture as advantagiously, as Expert Jewellers would set precious Stones. Without degrading from Others, I think this Nicety of Judgement particularly eminent in those bred at Westminster Schole, and gained probably from their being used very Young to what Dr Sprat calls *the Genius of that Place*, which is to Verses made Extempore, 140 and Declamations composed in very few hours, in which sort of Exercises when Children they take from whence so ever they can, which when Men they repay with great Interest from the abundance of their own thought thus exercised improved and dilated.

As I have said you must be sure to quote with Justness or you will be 145 insipid; You may quote with freedom in Matters of Panygeric, but with great reserve in those of Satyr. Your saying is an Inscription engraven round an Insense pot, but a bloody Letter if bound to an Arrow; In the first case your *bon mot* will be praised for the Present, and in some Time Forgot; but in the Latter the Ill Nature of Men will help their Memory 150 and the Reflection being conveyed in Sentence already known, the Sarcasm may happen to remain much longer than either He on whom it was spoken, or he who spake it may Desire.

What ever you read you must so observe and digest, as to form from it in speaking especially in your own Language a Stile close, distinct 155 and Familiar; and in your Writing easy and Civil, How many do I know, who have read a great deal, and can Scarce finish one Intelligble Sentence. Many have talked to me of Demosthenes Orations and Tullys

123 Then *L 26*: Than *L 25*   135 Atterbury, Smaldridge, *L 26*: Atterbury Smaldridge *L 25*   138 in *edd.*: *om. L 25, L 26*   150 Latter] *om. L 26*   151 Reflection *edd.*: Rflection *L 25*: reflection *L 26*   in Sentence] in the Sentence *L 26*   156 Familiar; *edd.*: Familar; *L 25*: familiar, *L 26*   158 Many *edd.*: many *L 25, L 26*

Epistles, who tell you but very sadly in the beginning of their Letter
that they are in health, or at the End of it that they are your humble 160
Servant, The first of the First and second of the Second, namely Thirdly
and lastly &ca: of the Divines; and the under favor and with sub-
mission to better Judgements, and pray spare me one word &ca: of the
Lawyers; in short all cant of Words of any Profession must be avoided.
Artis est celare artem is in this Case a true Maxim; your hiding your 165
Method gives the greatest Beauty to it. A plain free Polite Gentile
Style, must with the greatest Industry be acquired and fixed, for every
Man is obliged to speak and write prose; as to Poetry I mean the
writing of Verses, it is another thing, I would advise no Man to attempt
it except he cannot help it, and if he cannot it is in vain to disswade 170
him from it. This Genius is perceived so soon even in our Childhood,
and increases so strongly in our Youth, that he who has it will never be
brought from it, do what you will; Cowley felt it at ten Years Old, and
Waller could not get rid of it at Sixty—*Poeta Morietur* may be said as
truly as *Poeta nascitur.* The greatest care Imaginable must be taken of 175
those who have this particular bent of thought, they must begin soon
and continue long in the Course of some severer Studies. As to my own
Part I found this Impulse very soon, and shall continue to feel it as long
as I can Think; I remember nothing further in life than that I made
Verses, I chose Guy of Warwick for my first Hero and killed Colborn 180
the Gyant before I was big enough for Westminster Schole. But I had
two Accidents in Youth which hindred me from being quite possest
with the Muse: I was bred in a Colledge where prose was more in
fashion than Verse, and as soon as I had taken my First Degree was sent
the Kings Secretary to the Hague, there I had enough to do in studying 185
French and Dutch and altering my Terentian and Virgilian Style into
that of Articles Conventions and Memorials, So that Poetry which by
the bent of my Mind might have become the business of my Life, was
by the happyness of my Education only the Amusement of it, and in
this too, having the Prospect of some little Fortune to be made, and 190
Friendship to be cultivated with the great Men, I did not launch much
out into Satyr; which however agreable for the present to the Writers
or Incouragers of it does in time do neither of them good, considering
the uncertainty of Fortune, and the various change of Ministry, where
every Man as he resents may punish in his turn of Greatness; and that 195

175 The *edd.*: the *L 25, L 26*   177 long *L 26*: *om. L 25*   own *L 26*: *om. L 25*
180 Verses, *L 26*: Verses *L 25*   181 But *L 26*: but *L 25*   183 where *L 26*: were
L 25   187 Conventions *L 26*: Convention *L 25*

in England a Man is less safe as to Politics, than he is in a Bark upon the Coast in regard to the Change of the Wind, and the Danger of Shipwreck.

Wit in Conversation, which is easier perceived when one hears it then explain'd by any diffinition depends upon the Support of great Stock 200 and plentiful variety of reading, without which what ever a Mans humour may be, his thought will not be sufficiently various and plentiful, his catching in discourse upon a Subject, which he understands, will be too easily perceived, and one shal almost know what he would say before he begins to speak; his Jest will be, If I may so express 205 it, too Identical, he will endeavour to turn every thing into his own way, as those who have not a sufficient Plenty of Water bring every Brook to their own Canal; Villiers Duke of Buckingham was too much enclined to Burlesque, Sir Fleetwood Shephard ran too much into Romance and Improbability, and the late Earl of Ranelagh into Quibble 210 and Banter, Yet each of these three had a great deal of Witt, and if they had had more Study than generaly a Court Life allows, as their Ideas would have been more Numerous their Witt would have been more Perfect. The Late Earl of Dorset was indeed a great Exception to this Rule for he had thoughts which no Book could lend him, and a way of 215 expressing them which no Man ever knew to prescribe; One general Rule is, that Wit what ever share a Man has Naturally of it, or however he may have fortifyed it by reading, it should be used as a shield rather than a Sword to defend yourself but not to wound another, however this sort of warfare has sometimes been necessary, as the World is at 220 present ordered, especially in public Assemblies, in our Parliaments and even amongst our Divines in Convocation; when a Man sees a blow a coming he is actually obliged to prevent it by strikeing first, for if he defered the stroke, it will be too late to strike at all; In this case no rule is to be given to your Eloquence more than to your Valour in 225 the field, You must ward as cautiously and strike boldly, and as Poet Bays said of his Rant, if it is not civil egad it must be sublime; but in ordinary Conversation it is a very low Character to be as witty as you can, many like the thing but few esteem the Person, and if a Man is thought to have so much Wit, that his good Nature begins to be called 230 in Question, in my Opinion he has made but a sad bargain by the

198 Shipwreck. *L 26* : Shipwreck *L 25*   200 explain'd *edd.* : explain'ed *L 25* : explained *L 26*   depends *edd.* : depend *L 25, L 26*   206 too *L 26* : to *L 25*   210 Ranelagh *L 26* : Renelagh *L 25*   into] in *L 26*   211 Banter *L 26* : Bantor *L 25* 223 a coming] coming *L 26*   226 as cautiously] Cautiously *L 26*   231 bargain *edd.* : bergain *L 25* : Bargain *L 26*

Exchange. I knew one Man, and never but one who had this Talent of Railary in so particular a manner that while he said things severe enough, he rather surprised than hurt the Person, he assailed and brought himself always off so with the Mention of some greater Merit 235 to compensate the Foible he attacked in the same Person, that by a Turn imperceptible his Satyrs slid into Panygeric, which appeared the finer as it seemed less meant; but this is a perfection so hard to attain, and a thing so clumsey if a Man aimes at and misses it, that it is safer and better not to attempt it.   240

Besides the serious Study which is to be the general Exercise and Employment of your Life and without being Master of which You can never make any great Figure in the World, you should be pretty well versed in some more pleasing, and if I may so express it, some Secundary Science.   245

This you will find convenient, it will take idle Hours from your Hand when alone, and have a proper Use in company, a double one if you are in any public Station; for it will hinder the Curious pressing upon You as to more Solemn matter, and enable you without appearing Ignorant or ill bred, to turn the Discourse to what may at once conceal 250 your secret, and entertain your Company.

Amongst these Arts of a Mechanical consideration, I reckon Architecture, Sculpture, Painting Gardening &ca.

The choice of these must be determined by the bent of every Mans own mind, and without such an Inclination or what we call a Genius, 255 he will make a very little progress in these or any of those Sciences, which thô supported and improved by Judgement, are founded upon Imagination, These Arts I say, at once Instruct and amuse, help Men that have estates to Employ them agreably, and to oblige those who have not, and may yet participate of an other Mans pleasure, and add 260 at the same time to it; for there is no man that does any thing of this Kind, but is pleased to show it, and no Man that understands it but is obliged to him for the Communication. Besides the Company which the Exercise of these Arts bring a Man into is as well honorable as agreable, Their Studies are mixt with other Arts, and the conversation 265 they must have met with before they can have arrived to any Perfection in their own Art must needs have rendered them in a great Measure Scholars and Gentlemen.

To these I add Music, but with these Cautions that it takes up too

232 knew *L 26*: know *L 25*   236 same *L 26*: sam *L 25*   237 imperceptible *L 26*: inperceptable *L 25*

much of our Time and does not furnish us with the best Company, 270 Those who are obliged to get their Livelyhood by it have addicted so much of their Life to the Study of it that they have very little knowledge in any other Science. I wish the Art were more incouraged, and that Musicians were not forced even to practice so much that they have not time to study their own Science, much less any other; but so it is 275 —now a Gentleman musically given cannot blow his Flute or strike his Violin alone; and as to Conversation he is insensibly in a Chorus instead of a Company, and thô when he came into the Opera he thought he took his place in the Box or the pit before the Entertainment is half done he finds himself in the middle of the Orchestre.   280

Opinion.

SINCE OPINION is said to be the Queen of the World, and our Actions must Depend a good deal upon the Sentiments which others conceive of them it may be worth our while to Enquire a little what this Opinion is, How it is commonly formed, upon what it subsists, and in what manner it is Altered.   5

OPINION is in one Word the Estimate, which every Man makes of every Thing he sees, the Product of what he calls common Sence, and takes it very ill if he is not allowed to be the Master of it; Many cannot Read, more cannot write, but all can and will Discourse and Determine: They have Eyes they Say, and consequently can See; They have Ears 10 and must be allowed to Hear, So all visible and Audible Objects are properly within their Connoissance, as to any Thing Shown or proposed to them, they can tell if it Delights or Displeases Them, and the greatest Judges can do no more. Then again the General Opinion will be found to be only a Collection of the Sentiments of particular Per- 15 sons, or to use a Modern Phrase a majority of Voices.

LET us Consider then First the different Sentiments which Men have of Things, These Sentiments guided by difference of Age, Appetite and Inclination as well as by the Degrees of Natural Sence or Acquired Knowledge of which the Person Judging is possessed, and 20 then let us observe the greater difference in Opinion which must flow from the Sentiment of each Society, Province and Kingdom, in

280 of the L 26: of L 25

Title] L 25 (D), L 26 An Essay upon Opinion *Extra title in L 26*   18 These] L 25 (D) those L 26

which relation must be had to their Utility, their Pleasure, their Manners and Customes.

I DONT pretend to Examine the Nature and Essence of this Mind of Ours, This *Divinæ particula auræ* as a Divine or a Philosopher, but as a Stander by to take a little Notice of some of its Motions, the feats of Activity it plays, and the Sudden Escapes and Changes it often makes.

MAN is to himself so great a Stranger that *Nosce Te ipsum* is quoted as One of the Wisest Sayings that ever was pronounced: Our frame is Such as may be Compared to a River, the Solid part are no more than Banks and Dykes, which keep the Current within its natural Course, the fluid are in perpetual motion, in Eternal Flux and Reflux: As in our Body, so is there a continued Motion in our Mind; How far one may have an Influence or Operation upon the other, I shal not at present Enquire, But certain it is that the Same Man at different times alters his Opinion of the same Things.

HE that in the opening of Manhood Delights in Dogs and Horses, Hunting and Exercise (as Horace finely describes it) in the middle of Life turns his Thoughts to the Acquisition of Wealth and search of Honour, and towards the End of it, He insures his Ease, Counts his Riches, and prattles over the Scenes of his Youth to Younger People, who all the while are weary of Hearing Him. Terence founds his finest Comedies upon the Observation of this Change of our Manners with our Ages, and the concessions that Human Nature ought to make to it.

I HAVE read somewhere a pritty Spanish Conceit, that, as we are Born our Mind comes in at our Toes, so goes upward thrô our Leggs to our Middle, thence to our Heart and Breast, Lodges at last in Our Head and from thence flies away; The meaning of which is that Childish Sports and Youthful Wrestlings, and Tryals of Strength, Amorous Desires, Couragious and Manly Designs, Council and Policy succeed each other in the Course of our Lives till the whole terminates in Death; The consequence of it is Obvious, Our Passions change with our Ages, and our Opinion with our Passions.

LET Us next Observe the different Passions by which People of the same Age are moved, and observe what Power either Choler or Flegme, a Sanguine or a Melancholly Complexion have in the motions or Operations of Our Mind. And here I might bring in all BURTONS Melancholly, Anger is a Short Frenzy, and Fear the worst of Counsellors, we are

hardly Thought reasonable Men, or Responsible for our Actions whilst 60
we Continue possessed with the Violence of either of these Passions.
The Cautious Man Suspects every thing, The Bold fears Nothing, a
harsh and close Temper shal Spend half his Estate in a Law Suit, while
one more free and Open would not give three pence for the most Compleat Revenge imaginable of this kind. The Lover Retrenches from the 65
necessarys of Life that the object of his Passion may Shine in Velvet,
and Brocard, The Miser that sees her thus Dressed had rather have her
Pettycoat than her Person. Every Man on this head may as actually be
Tryed as Achilles when shut up with Licomedes Daughters, in the
Chest amongst the Ribbons Ear Rings and Necklaces, You will pre- 70
sently observe him find the Sword: The Predominant Passion will
appear thrô all the Disguise of Artifice and Hypocrisy.

THE Two great Passions which Triumph over our Judgement and
Consequently Subjugate our Opinion are Ambition and Love, The
first makes us think too well, and the latter too meanly of our Selves. 75
Ambition calls in all our Friends to our Assistance, and sends us into
Camps and Cities, Noise, and Popularity; Love retires us into Solitude,
Subjects Us to one Person, and makes Us like nothing but what She
does, nor Desire any Place but where She is; And indeed She alone. I
speak of these as the Frailtys of the greatest Minds; JULIUS lost all the 80
Praises that could be given to a Successfull General, and all the Blessings
that could be heaped upon an Honest Patriot only because He would
be the first Man in the World, And MARK ANTHONY forgetting the
pursuit of his Vengeance and Honour fled into a corner of Egypt, con-
tenting Himself only to possess that Beauty which the Same JULIUS 85
had some Years before enjoyed and Abandoned. Add to this that JULIUS
hazarded his Estate, gave up his Quiet, and lost his Life for what in
truth could do him no good; And ANTHONY did the same for what
must do him Mischief. Our EDWARD the fourth had like to have lost
England for his Passion to his beautiful Widdow, and HARRY the fourth 90
of France was as near losing that Crown for leaving his Army to pay
a Visit to LA BELLE GABRIELLE. Yet in some Years so avowedly indifferent were these Princes to the Objects of their Passion that both
of them had other Mistresses, and Lived only with common Civility
towards those Persons, to whom they would sometime before have 95
Sacrifiz'd their Fortunes, and their Lives, So hard is it for the best and
greatest of Men to form a just Opinion of Things contributing to their
own Interest, and to be decided by their own Election.

72 the] *L 25 (D) om. L 26*

THIS Love, and this Ambition it may be Objected were the Same Passions, the Objects were only Changed, and indeed it is hard to con- 100 ceive any Opinion but what is founded on or Sustained by One passion or other, But now let Us think how often the Passion it Self does change in the Same Person: Did not DIOCLESIAN quit the Empire of Rome to Cultivate a Garden? and CHARLES the fifth Abdicate the Government of half Europe to tell his Beeds in a Monestery? How many Examples 105 may be given of One Passion yeilding to another directly contrary but more prevalent. CORNARO is Jealous of his Wife so far as to draw a line in the middle of her Chamber, beyond which She is not to Approach towards the Window, yet worked up by Mosca and Avarice, he Consents to putt her to Bed to another Man, This Instance for the Poets 110 honour however fictitious explains a thousand real Ones of the same kind, which every Man who Consults BAUDIUS's ANTHOLOGIA, MORERI's Dictionary may think himself Entituled to Quote.

LET us now see how our Passions vary as guided by Our Judgement and understanding: in minds most worthy to be distinguished there 115 is a Natural Fire or Impulse.

Est Deus in nobis agitante calescimus illo

a tendency to Know, Practice and Esteem, some things, some matters, some Objects preferably to others, and this Desire increases with the Knowledge which the Person has of the Thing desired. Hence arise 120 those particular applications and Studys which form what we call a Genius, hence Poets, Painters, Orators, Mathematicians, and these Subdivided again into twenty other Classes, and hence it comes to pass that the Man who has Spent all his time in One Science and Consequently neglected the rest may talk finely upon some few Subjects and 125 like a Child upon all others. Not only so but the further Some of these Genius's go in the pursuit of their beloved Study the more persevere They in some New Sentiment. PTOLOMY had for many Ages fixed the Earth, 'till COPERNICUS was pleased to Bowl it off again from its Basis, and EPICURUS had enjoyed his Attoms for about Two thousand Year 130 with the greatest Satisfaction imaginable till DESCARTES thought good to contest with him the Subtility and Indivisibility of matter. Half a Century has past in the Agitation of this Question, and I am glad now to hear that some Ingenious Gentlemen are like to Silence them both, by proving beyond all Contradiction that there is no such thing as 135 Matter, the very Subject of their Dispute, nor ever was nor ever can be.

127 the pursuit] *L 25 (D)* pursuit *L 26*

THE Various Estimate we make as to the value of things cannot be better Illustrated then by the wants we find in the pursuit of our Studies, every Man adding to his heap, and desirous to Compleat his Collection; Books, Pictures, Medals, nay Dryed Flowers, Insects, 140 Cockleshels, any thing will do, but then the Cruel Losses which we some times Sustain, The late Monarch and Court of France were all Disturbed, and CHARLES PATIN, was Banished the Kingdom because it was Suspected by some that the Otho which he Sold the King was not Genuine, perhaps a little Boy yesterday at Canterbury tore that 145 Butterfly in Pieces, or at Dover threw the very Shell into the Sea, The Species of which were the only Ones now missing in SIR HANS SLOANS Cabinet, and an Oyleman on Fish street Hill did actually wrap up his Anchovies in the first Horace that was ever Printed, whilst FRAZER has with useless Pains been looking for the Book this Two and Twenty 150 Years. How many better Editions have been since Published, or why the worst is the most Valuable I refer to an other Opportunity.

THIS difference of Genius produces the most indifferent Effect imaginable upon divers Persons, as to the same Object, while one Man is admiring the Beauties of a Picture another Shal observe indeed that 155 the frame is very fine. As I showed a Friend of mine, who is really a Man of Great parts and Learning, a Flower piece of BIMBI finely Painted, he observed that the Butter Fly at the Corner was the prettiest thing he ever Saw, and upon the view of a little Closet, where are some good Originals, he contented himself by taking Notice that the Green hang- 160 ings edged with Gold looked exceeding handsom. One of the greatest Men of this Age hates Tragedy, I have heard him say, he only goes to a Play to Laugh, another thô he is far from being a Cruel Man in his Temper likes to see the Butcher of the West really wounded at the Bear Garden, not content with the Sham Red that glows upon the 165 Shirt of BANCO's Ghost. A Country Gentleman I have heard of, who had seen SHAKESPEARS HARRY THE EIGHT, forgetting unhappily the fall of BUCKINGHAM, or the Policy of WOOLSEY, remarked to his Friend, a Man of the Town, who carried him to the Play, that the Bishop of WINCHESTER, who sat at the Tryal of Queen KATHERINE, 170 was the same Man that Snuft the Candles between the Acts with a greater Dexterity than could be conceiv'd in human Fingers. To this I would add, that the common Herd of Mankind (and I am afraid the

142 some times L 25 (D): sometime L 25 (D & P): sometimes L 26   151 have] L 25 (D) has L 26   152 Opportunity. L 26: Oportunity L 25 (D & P), L 25 (D)   166 Shirt] L 25 (D) Skirt L 26   169 Play, L 25 (D), L 26: Play L 25 (D & P)

Majority is on their Side) have really no Opinion, or, they seem to be
in the same case in relation to that which they think they have as 175
BARTHOLMEW COAKS was as to his Purse, They scarse know if they
lost it before they had it, or after; How different so ever their Inclinations may be, They Consent in this at least, that They are always
Changing: It is impossible for any rational being to Please them, because
it is impossible to Oblige them long: Tis hard for them to continue in 180
a Mind, which was determined by no Previous Consideration, not being
in any wise capable of Judging what was Right, they generally think
most Things Wrong: They know just enough to find their own want,
and from that Knowledge fancy that every Body finds it as well as
themselves; having no Opinion of their own, They do as an Old Roman 185
would, who had no Child; They adopt that of the first Man they like,
and from a Debate in Parliament or a new Play, go to the next Coffee
House to be informed of their own Sentiments. If You trace this Man
thrô Life (For One and a hundred of them are the Same) You will find
him always Uncertain. A Husband or a Lover He's Jealous or Anxious, 190
an Unequal Parent and a froward Master. As he never thinks he has
Friendship or respect enough from those about him, His Opinion of
their Service and Duty is always various; He whispers with One, Chides
t'other, Embroils himself from the Stories of both, and hearkning
to Lies finds his Servants, as SOLOMON expresses it, always Wicked. 195
Does his Whim run to Building, and has he seen any House within
Twenty Miles of his own, the New Appartment he made last Year
must as certainly down as the Old Parlour did the Year before, to give
it Place; And for Gardening meerly upon the observation that his
Neighbours Gravel Walk is too narrow or too large, his own shal be 200
altered twice in a Year, and his Terras shal be Raised or Depressed by
the same Rule, he giving You only for Reason that he likes it so: for
fear You should think he was Governed by any Body. If he comes to
Town as he sees more Objects, he finds more Distraction, Loads of ill
Pictures, and worse Books are sent to the Carryers 'till the end of the 205
Session, but lye Unpacked and unthought of when they come into the
Country, and if he gives into what the French call *la Quinquaillieré* (as
it is ten to one but he does,) QUARE does not sett his Watch more
Actually than MATHAR does his understanding: He Buys a Pocket
Book, but Dislikes it before he has set down one word in it, Can he rest 210

174 really] *L 25 (D) om. L 26*   185 themselves; ... own, *edd.*: themselves, ... own;
L 25 (D & P), L 25 (D), L 26   202 Rule, *edd.*: Rule *L 25 (D & P), L 25 (D), L 26*
for Reason] *L 25 (D)* the reason *L 26*   210 Dislikes it] *L 25 (D)* dislikes *L 26*

when he has seen a Cane better Clouded then his own, and disliking the Hinge of his Snuff Box, must not the Dinner stay whilst he immediately drives to Temple Bar to give five Guineas more to Exchange it for a Worse.

LET Us leave him and return to the human Mind in general upon 215 which So many external Objects have an influence, regularity of Dyet, Intemperence or Abstinence as to Wine, the continuance or Interuption of Health, The too frequent Excitation or Disuse of any Passion from the Neighbourhood, or abcence of its Object, The Favour of Fortune or the hand of Adversity, A word thrown Casually into a Discourse, 220 The reading of a Book, the Sight of a Picture or Statue, an Emblem, a Motto, a Seal, every thing intelligible in Art, nay every thing visible in Nature may form new Impressions in our mind, and alter those Already formed there. We Judge of things according to the Humour we are in, and that very Humour is Subject to infinite Variety; If Six 225 Bells as JOHN KEIL tells me can make more than a thousand Millions of Changes, what must be the result of the Jangling of ten or twelve Passions sustained by an infinite variety of Objects in minds upon which every thing can operate; The Dawning of Light excites us into Chearfulness, The approach of Night depresses us into Melancholly; 230 A different weight of Air raises or Depresses our Spirits, a Trumpet alarms Us to an Ardour and Action of War, and a Flute softens us again into Thoughts of Love and Delight. An Herb, a Flower, can render us either pleased or Grave as we consider the Beauty of its Colours or the Shortness of its Duration, and the very Accident that makes Us Angry, 235 makes us Laugh at the same time if any little Redicule accompanies the Action, So many Things seem I say to Contribute to the forming our Opinion the least of which has Power in a great Measure to make us change it, So that no Man is so different from another as the Same man is from himself. 240

AMONGST the External Causes which as I say have an Influence upon our Minds I have thought One very Comical, that is, the Opinion which other Men conceive of our Opinion, We desire not only to be Justifyed but applauded, and our Pride has a great Share in the Confirmation of Our choice; It's a pritty thought that SEMELE was not 245 content to be Beloved by Jupiter except the World knew She was kept by the King of the Gods, else Thunder and Lightning are but odd Furniture or Ornaments to a Ladys Bed-chamber, and that CANDAULES

226 Millions] *L 26* Million *L 25 (D)*   233 An *L 25 (D)*, *L 26*: an *L 25 (D & P)*
236 Laugh *L 25 (D)*, *L 26*: Laugh, *L 25 (D & P)*   241 have] has *L 25 (D)*, *L 26*

was not sufficiently happy in the enjoyment of a Beautiful Wife 'till
he had Showed her Naked to his Friend; Perillous Tryals, but natural 250
enough. A Man in the Reign of NERO or COMMODUS would have past
his time ill if he had not given it for Granted that the first of these
Emperors was the best Musician and the other the most Skilful
Gladiator then alive. I cite these as the most extravagant Actions that
Men of their great Quality were ever guilty of, and yet You see their 255
Pleasure depended upon the sentiments which other People had of
them. EPICTETUS thô a Stoic Confesses truly enough that it is not the
thing but the Opinion conceived of the thing that vexes. HARRY the
Second of France built a Palace, which is yet standing for his favorite
Dutchesse de VALENTINOIS in the form of a Crescent, the Architraves 260
and Windows are adorned with Horns, Netts and Hunting Spears; and
all this meerly upon the Conceit of her Name being DIANA, and our
HARRY the Eight, about the same time brought MRS. BULLEN a
private Gentlewoman from the Tower to Westminster in the first open
Calesch, which had been then seen in England, that all the City by 265
viewing his Mistresse might approve his Passion. What a Mortification
had it been to either of these warm Spirits if they had heard any Body
Whisper the least thing about the House or the Calesche, as declaring
too publickly the Weakness of these Princes. But if the same Person had
said, that LA VALENTINOIS had been Mistresse many Years to the 270
Kings Father, that She was much Older than his Majesty, and had
a Grand Daughter Mariagable, or that MRS. BULLEN, was a raw Girle,
knew no more then her Lute or her Sarabrand and was just returned
from being a waiting Woman to the Kings Sister, unequal to him in all
Degrees of Quality, Conversation and Age, Good Lord what must have 275
ensued: *Bella horrida Bella,* The Person had been Disaffected, a Hugonot
or a Traitor in his Heart.

ALFRANK who had set his Mind upon his Roan one of the finest
Horses in England, yet never could be brought to ride him after the
E: of G: had said freely he could not be of the Same Opinion: And 280
PYSO did not care to Show a Beautiful Picture of which before he was
very fond after the D: of B: had told him he thought it was not an
Original: What was the matter? The Picture and the Horse were the
same the Day after as they were the Day before these dreadful Accidents
arrived. Happy is it for Us have I often said, that every Man can find 285

250 Showed] *L 26* Shewn *L 25 (D)*   276 ensued: *edd.*: ensued *L 25 (D & P)*, *L 25*
(D), *L 26*   Disaffected, *edd.*: Disaffected *L 25 (D & P)*, *L 25 (D)*, *L 26*   282 him
he] *L 26* him that he *L 25 (D)*   284 as they *L 25 (D)*, *L 26*: as the they *L 25 (D & P)*
285 it] *L 25 (D) om. L 26*

his own amusement, and that we do not all like the same thing; That the Man who Gardens or Builds follows his own Plans, and is Satisfyed with the Execution of them; That one hundred Men in Love, each viewing his Mistresse at the same time (suppose in a Theater or other public Place) wonders that the other Ninety Nine, should see so wrong 290 as not to admit his particular Woman to be (what he would certainly call it) take her altogether the most agreable. But how short alas is this happyness if the Gravel Walk must be Altered from our Neighbours thinking it too Narrow or too broad, and the Wall raised or depressed from the Person who endeavoring to look over it being Taller or shorter 295 was pleased to Exercise a different Criticism upon it. Your observation comes too late, Sir, Roan is Sold, and the Picture is sent into Wales. Is this enough, pough! The very Mistresse Selected from the rest of Womankind shal be thought to change as to her Beauty or her Merit, as a Male Friend to the Lover, a Female Friend to the Lady, and per- 300 haps both Rivals to one or t'other shal describe her; from a hint of this kind She shal be thought first too round Shoulder'd, too fatt, or not bred enough in the World, and in a little time after She is down Right crump backed, a Boss, and knows not how to Live: Ten thousand Instances of this kind Show us that the Opinion of One Man is altered 305 by the Sentiment of an other in relation to the same Object. So plain is it that we do not See with our own Eyes, nor Judge by our own understanding.

BUT let us Suppose our Mind to be a little more consonant to it self than I have described it. Our Opinion for all what EPICTETUS says must 310 be directed by something without us, for Opinion it self is really nothing else but the effect of that impression, which an External or Intellectual object makes upon our Thoughts: I leave here the diclination between imagination and Judgment as a Speculation upon which we may Dispute, and that is all. But true in Fact it is that we cannot 315 but chuse what we think best: best not as the thing is in it self and singly considered, but with relation, to the Circumstances with which we find it accompanied: Our Mind like a Looking-glass reflects only the Beauty or deformity of the Images placed before it, and as these Images vary So varies likewise our opinion. This in plainer English is 320 before we judge of things we are already determined to shun what we

294 depressed] *L 25 (D)*, *L 26* levelled *Emend. (by unknown hand) in L 25*   304 crump]
L 25 (D) Crumpt *L 26*   306 Sentiment] Sentiments *L 25 (D)*, *L 26*   309 BUT
L 25 (D), *L 26* : But *L 25 (D & P) From this point, sm. caps. are supplied in accordance with*
L 26   315 But *edd.* : but *L 25 (D & P)*, *L 25 (D)*, *L 26*   316 chuse *L 25 (D)*,
L 26 : chose *L 25 (D & P)*

think hurtful, and to embrace what we esteem Good, so that under the Denomination of profit or pleasure we always pursue our Interest, or gratify our Vanity, and this single thought thrown into different forms gives us all that ROCHFOCAULT ever writ.   325

UPON the natural frailties of our minds falls yet another Incumbrance very hard to be removed, I mean the prejudice of Education and Custom. Against this our Tutors and Parents find themselves obliged to oppose reading, Conversation, Travell and Experience, all which are commonly of too little force to Efface the first Notions Engraven upon 330 Our Minds, whilst yet they were Young and soft enough to receive those Impressions, and which as they grow harder stil retain the same marks. The Concern which every Man has first for his Family, and so on to his Parish, his Province, his Country is such as from a Prevention Erects it self by Degrees into a Principle. Every Man is partial to the 335 House from whence he Descended, finds it filled with famous Warriors, or great Scholars, or at least Supplies that Defect by the force of his own fancy. Every Man in Warwick-Shire has part of the Prowess of GUY Earl of Warwick, and every Woman in Coventry has part of the Chastity of the Queen, who rode Naked through that City, which of 340 the Two Universities are most Ancient or flourishing is the lasting Contest of People bred at either. Every English Man however he Disagrees with his Country-Men at home: Let him Travel from Calais to Rome, and from Rome to Ispahan, will venture his life any hour he hears the least Reflection made upon his Nation. The Swiss are re- 345 marked to have a Distemper, which they call the Heimvie, a desire of going home; And where ever They are in Service they get leave to return to their Canton at least once in some Years, and certainly desire to Dye there. I have heard King WILLIAM confess the same longing as to his going to Holland; and I am sure when I was there I found 350 the effects of the same Distemper in my Desire to return to England. I remember a Story which the same great Man was used to tell, since it comes not *mal a propos*, to what I am saying; A Polander who rode in the Dutch Guards desired him, then Prince of Orange, to give him leave to go to Warsaw, the Crown being then Vacant, alledging that 355 being a Gentleman he might be Chosen King: The Prince gave him leave, and when the Man, some Months after, returned to his Post, His HIGHNESS asked him jestingly if he was Chosen? No, Sir, replyed the

328 Against *L 25 (D)*, *L 26* : against *L 25 (D & P)*   332 grow] *L 25 (D)* grew *L 26*
344 Ispahan] Isaphaen *L 25 (D)*, *L 26*   358 jestingly *L 26* : jestinly *L 25 (D & P)* :
Jestingly *L 25 (D)*

Man, in a very grave and composed manner, I am not Chosen King this time, but I return with the Satisfaction of Knowing that the Election 360 was free. Upon this very imagination the greatness of the Roman Empire was founded, and the safety of every Common-wealth, or State in the World does in a great measure depend. Whether these Idea's were implanted in our minds by Nature at our Birth, or arrive from the Impressions made by the first Objects we behold, We will refer at 365 present to the Metaphysicians. This is certain, that they hardly leave us 'till our Death. ST: PAUL does not scruple to give this habitude the Name of Nature. As abroad I have sometimes talked with Carthusians or Franciscans, Men seemingly forsaking the World, and lost to it, One has looked intently upon my Hatt, t'other felt my Coat, and asked if 370 it was English Cloth; a Third more Politely enquired about our Noble familys of England. Now, as to these People before they took their Habits; The first had been a Hatter, the Second a Draper, and the third a Man of Quality; And the Instance infered from this, is, that those Primitive Colors, which our Understanding First imbibed Stick 375 upon it for ever, nor can be altered by any Tincture, which another sort of life, and a different way of thinking can cast over them. It may be here considered that our Mind is Such a buisy thing that it will never Stand Neutre, but is medling and Interesting it self upon all Occasions. If we see a Stranger come into a Room we are imediately possessed in 380 his favor, or prejudiced against him before he speaks one word: And here comliness of Person and gracefulness of Mien do very often put a Manifest cheat upon our Judgment, which a more thorow Knowledge of the Person may happen to Redress. We cannot see two People play but we take part with One, and wish the other Should lose, this without 385 any previous reason or consideration: But alas! the Bowl takes a stronger Bias, as we more know the Person: If we Love him his Defects are diminished, if we hate him, his faults are Exagerated. We look upon the different objects without finding that we have insensibly turned the Tube. And here those enormous Judgments may be taken notice of, 390 which the greatest Men in several Stations and professions have pronounced upon the Abilities and Performances of their Contemporaries. The difference is commonly begot by the Pride of the Persons concerned, and nourished by the ill nature of the Standers by. Our own internal Pride is a Jaunice of the mind, and makes us see things in a bad 395 Color, but the ill nature of others intervening is a sort of whirlwind

365–6 refer at present] *L 26* at present refer *L 25 (D)*   375 Stick] *L 25 (D)* sticks *L 26*
393 is] *L 26* it *L 25 (D)*

that raises Such a Dust as hinders us from seeing the thing even in its true dimensions. Hence the extravagant Censure and Eternal war between Persons of the same age and Profession. From CÆSAR and POMPEY, to CHARLES the Fifth and HARRY the Eighth, and so on to 400 LOUIS the Fourteenth, and WILLIAM the Third. From PROTOGENES and APELLES to PAOLO VERONEZE and PONTORMO. From JAMES the first and SCHIOPPIUS to BAYLE and JURIEU, for I think it not civil to give any Living Instances while I am telling People they are in the Wrong. Hence it happens that North or West shal insensibly engage 405 the Spirits at the Wrestling ring or BODMIN or TRURO shal break more Bones at a whirling in Cornwal than the ablest Surgeon in London shal be able to Set. WILLIAM Earl of Pembroke in the Reign of HARRY the Eighth, lost his Estate and remained several Years Banished upon a Quarrel merely at some Tryals of Skill between the County of Somerset 410 and the Town of Bristol. Am not I rediculous to cite History upon this head, when no Man can go into a Coffee House without being insulted upon the Account of Whig or Tory. A Party-Man indeed, and such most of us are, or must be, is an Animal that no Commentator upon human nature can sufficiently explain. He has not his Opinion, how 415 sorry a world so ever it may be, in his own keeping. *Quo ad hoc* he is mad, must Speak without believing what he understands, without inquiring He acts as implicitely according to the word of Command given out by the heads of his Faction as a Carthusian or a Jesuit does to the Will of his Superior. The Lye of the Day is the Rule of his Life, 420 and as his Judgment depends upon that of other Men, he must justify every thing that his party Acts with the greatest Injustice, 'till from the degrees of warm and Violent, he comes up to Furious and Wicked, *Fænum habet incornu*, and every Body is obliged to yield to or run from him. 425

IT may here be Noted that however our Vanities or Desires are un-confined our Abilities have only a certain Sphere of Activity, and every Man is a Wit or a Hero somewhere. In most Families You have a Droll Servant, each Club has it's President, that gives rules to it, And each Parish has an invincible Butcher or Tyler, a Witty Cobbler, or a grave 430 Assistant to the Clerk in raising the Psalme, the genius of these, and of the greatest Men recorded in History is Stimulated by the Same Ambition, and the honor of both hath bounds as certain thô not as extensive, there being no such thing as universal Esteem, however

---

401 WILLIAM *L 25 (D)*, *L 26* : Wm: *L 25 (D & P)*   417 understands, *L 25 (D)*, *L 26* : understands *L 25 (D & P)*   424 yield to] *L 25 (D)* yield *L 26*

prettily fame and her flight thrô the World would be Described and 435
magnifyed by the Poets. In prose She will be cramped and limited. To
take her in her greatest Extent, the Man who may be praised thrô
Europe is not heard of in Asia, or Africa, and again how very few are
renowned beyond the bounds of their own Country, so great a hin-
drance to Knowledge is the Diversity of Languages, and so prevalent is 440
Custom to the Esteem we put upon things. Had SIR FRANCIS BACON
or SIR PHILIP SYDNEY been taken by a Tripolin or Sally Pyrat, the
footman of either of them would have been Sold for as much more than
his Master as he was Stronger. The same in all probability would
happen to SIR ISAAC NEWTON in relation to the Water-man in 445
Southwark, who makes Almanacks. Suppose the like case to happen to
the best Poet now Living, and to the Zany of a Mountebank upon
Tower hil, The first would be left on Board the Gallies stript and unregarded, condemned to Row there during life, whilst the other would
have his Harlequins Coat restored to him, and be taken up to the 450
Castle, to divert the Governor.

THUS, I say, other People may not be just enough to Us, and we may
be too partial to our Selves, and not to our Selves only, but to those
who most resemble us. Thus one Mans vice if Examined by another
Man equally inclined to it, is either diminished or Christen'd by the 455
name of some resembling Virtue: Sordidness of life by the Covetous
Man is called Frugality, and Intemperance is called good Fellowship
by the Bon Vivant, The loosest pleasures of the Amorous are but
Gallantries, and the Caprice or Revenge of the Wrathful, lyes Covered
under the Shield of his honor. *Defendit Numerus*, Who ever heard of such 460
a thing as Usury in Lombard Street, or Perjury at the Custom House.
Now what a jumble must this make in the difference of our Censures,
To carry the Thought a little further, the bounds of Virtue and Vice

Quos ultra citraque nequit consistere rectum

are in many cases pretty difficult to find; How nicely must one dis- 465
tinguish between Patience, and Pusillanimity, between Courage and
foolhardiness, and so of the rest. Add to this that as to Opinion Success
qualifies the Action: if FABIUS MAXIMUS had not gained his point by
avoiding Battle, he had past for a Coward, and if ALEXANDER had Lost
the Day at Arbella, he had been Consigned by History for a Madman. 470

441 Had *L 25 (D)*, *L 26*: had *L 25 (D & P)*   452 THUS *L 26*: Thus *L 25 (D & P)*:
THIS *L 25 (D)*   460 *Defendit Numerus L 26*: Defendit Numerus *L 25 (D & P)*: *Defendit
numerus L 25 (D)*   463 Vice *L 25 (D)*: Vice. *L 25 (D & P)*, *L 26*   464 *Italics
supplied as in L 25 (D)*, *L 26*   rectum *L 26*: rectum. *L 25 (D & P)*: *rectum. L 25 (D)*

WE need not go from our own Country, or our own Memory for Instances of this Kind; The DUKE OF MONMOUTH came to England with Liberty and Property, and the Protestant Religion on his Standard: He was beaten and Beheaded, his Honors were taken from his Family. The Prince of Orange does the same thing, he is Successfull, is Crowned 475 King of England, transmits an Imortal Memory to Posterity; Gives us a new Epoche of Time, and a different Sett of Principles from the Revolution.

A Dialogue between Charles the Emperor and Clenard the Grammarian.

Charles. Burgundy with Brabant and Flanders, Castile, Arragon, Germany Possessed: Italy, France, Africa, Greece Attempted.
Clenard. Noun Substantive and Adjective, Pronoun, Verb, Participle Declined: Adverb, Conjonction, preposition Interjection un-declined.   5
Charles. Into this Model I had cast Europe, how Glorious was the Design?
Clenard. How happy was the Division I made of all Greece into five Dialects.
Charles. Thou art pretty bold, Friend, not only to hearken to what 10 I say, but to dare to Mimick it, stand farther off I command Thee.
Clenard. Aye, there it is, that Imparative Mood, that Style of Kings founded on the reasonable Maxim of *tel est nôtre Plaisir*.
Charles. Why how should I speak but like my Self. I am Charles the Emperor.   15
Clenard. Then don't be offended If I answer like my Self, I am Clenard the Schole-Master.
Charles. A Discovery of great importance truly, what can the Man mean by it?
Clenard. That each of Us should give a fair and just Account of him- 20 self as a Man; and then—
Charles. And what then?
Clenard. Why then, if You would divest your self of that Princely way of thinking, and argue a little cooler, You would not find so much difference between us Two as You imagine.   25

Title: *A Dialogue between* L 26 : Dialogue. L 25 (63) : *om.* L 25 (84)

Charles. Difference? Why I was by Birth Monarch of Nations, by Acquisition and Power Emperor of the West, and by Stratagem and refinement one of the most Cunning Politicians and most renowned Warriors of my time.

Clenard. And I was the best Grammarian of Mine, very Virtuous as 30 to my Morals, well versed in the *Belles Lettres*, and of an agreable Wit in Conversation.

Charles. Why Thou dost not intend I should submit to so Comical a Comparison.

Clenard. Comical! Egad I am very serious while I tell You I think my 35 Self as Great as Wise, and certainly as happy a Man as your Self.

Charles. Why Learning has made Thee Mad Clenard. Thou hast crouded thy Head with Notions, and forgot Plain Facts. Refresh thy Memory a little. Hast thou not seen me at Franckfort and Aix la Chapelle with the Imperial Diadem on my Head, presiding 40 in the Three Colleges of Electors Princes and Imperial Towns, Served in all the State, and vested in all the Types and Ornaments that human greatness is capable of Receiving. The King of Bohemia my Cup-bearer, the three first Potentates of Germany Waiting on me as Menial Officers. The greatest Ecclesiasticks 45 acknowledging themselves my Chancellors, and all the Nobility of the Empire either my Soldiers or my Servants.

Clenard. O rarey Show, pretty Show! and have You not heard of me at Lovain and Nurembourg, Presiding over the Hebrew, Greek and Latin Scholes. Had I not my Formes and Classes as You your 50 Squadrons and Regiments. Had not I equally my Captains, and Subaltern Officers, And did not I distribute Rewards and Punishments as I thought good as well as You? What were Your Ancestors Fasces but a bundle of Rods, what Your Scepter but my Ferula? could not I exert as Imperial Power as absolutely as any Emperor 55 alive if I had pleased *Naì μὰ τόδε σκῆπτρον*; but Greek is lost upon You.

Charles. Rediculous! while I commanded at the head of An hundred thousand Men by Land and Sea, Embarked half of them One Campaign to Affrica, Marched them the next thrô Italy, You 60 Ruled only Two or Three hundred Boyes, Sauntering leisurely

---

28 most Cunning] *L 26* Cunningest *L 25 (63)* 29 Warriors *L 25 (63)*: Warrior *L 25 (84)*, *L 26* 34 Comparison. *L 25 (63)*, *L 26*: Comparison *L 25 (84)* 39 Hast] *L 26* Why hast *L 25 (63)* 43 greatness] *L 26* Grandeur *L 25 (63)* 45 The greatest] *L 26* The Three greatest *L 25 (63)* 55 as absolutely] *L 26 om. L 25 (63)* 56 *Naì ... σκῆπτρον*] *L 25 (63) om. L 26* 58 An] *L 26* One *L 25 (63)*

after them from the Schole to the Cathederal, from thence to the
Hall, and so returning—

Clenard. Hold, good Charles, let us fairly State our Matters, for I love
Method extremly. The first part of the Question is which of Us 65
Two had most Power. Now of the Hundred thousand Men, with
whom You went Dub a Dub, and Tantara rara thrô the World
Nineteen parts in Twenty were only Machines, meer Instruments
of War, made use of to fill Trenches, or stop Breaches, played off
by whole Battallions, Food for Powder, as Sir John Falstaff calls 70
it, in the English Play. The Sensible and animated part of Your
Army were only useful to You as they had been Instructed by me
or some other of my Profession. Could they have Marched thrô
different Countries without having the Languages, Could they
have taken Towns or Attacked Fortifications without some 75
Previous Knowledge in Geometry, nay, could they have Mustered
their own Soldiers or Calculated their Pay without Arethmetic?
In effect I formed Your Officers thô You imployed them. Without
my Instructions, and the practice of that Discipline which They
learned at Schole, You had better have Commanded Hoards of Tar- 80
tars or Nations of Wild Indians. And who Governed your Towns
all this while, and Administred your Laws for You but those People
whom I had Educated. When ever it was otherwise, You see all
Your constitutions Institutes and Diplomata trampled upon. A
John of Leyden in our very time, A Cromwell, nay a Massaniello 85
a little since have made the greatest Kings of You all tremble. Now
see what You owe to Us Scholars, who tame the World and make
it Subordinate to your power. For my Self in particular how many
good Commanders and descreet Governors have I bred up for You?

Charles.   Well; but were You not payd for Your Pains? did not I take 90
care that the Towns where You Taught should allow you honorable Stipends, and that the Parents of Your Scholars should add to
your Income?

Clenard. Right Charles, *Quod erat demonstrandum*. Did not You therefore raise Contributions for me, nay pay them your Self? What 95
plainer Acknowledgment could You make of my being really the
greater Man of the Two. Prythee what does any Vassal in the
Empire do more to his Lord?

Charles.   Pough, this is mere Sophistry.

72 only] *L 26 om. L 25 (63)*   80 Hoards] *L 25 (63)* Herds *L 26*   90 not I] *L 25 (63)*
I not *L 26*   94 Did *L 26*: did *L 25 (63) & (84)*

Clenard. Real Truth, *bonâ fide*, but pray go on in your own way.   100

Charles. Why, I tell You, the Eyes of the whole World were upon Me, every Body enquiring into my Designs, and Solicitous to be Informed of my Measures.

Clenard. And every Body wishing you were a Thousand Mile off when ever you left your Kingdomes, which you might have Governed 105 quietly; and every body praying heartily for your Exit out of that World, which You harrassed and tormented.

Charles. You break in upon me too soon. What Two glorious Days were those in which I put the Armies of Solyman and Barbarossa to flight. How Compleat was the Victory at Pavie when I took 110 Francis the First Prisoner, and how memorable the Saccage of Rome when I got the Pope into my Clutches. The Jest pleases me stil, when I think on't. That I detained *Il beatissimo padre Clemente* close Prisoner, when I put my Self into Mourning for my Victory, and Ordered public Processions to be made for his Deliverance.   115

Clenard. To Crown your Happyness, pray think of some other of your great Days, That, for Instance when You returned from Africa soundly Beaten, by the same Barbarossa You just now Quoted. That Day when you were driven from before Marseilles over the Alps, with the loss of above thirty thousand Men, or 120 That, when you were forced to raise the Seige of Metz, when the Wits of the Age were so merry with You as to give You for Devise a Sea-Crab and your own *Plus ultra* turned into *plus citra* for the Motto, when They Painted your Eagle chained to Your Hercules's Pillars with *Non ultra Metas* at the bottom, and not to trouble You 125 too much, (for I could put many days of Mortification into Your Calendar) What think You of that Distinguished One when You gave yourself up to the bonne foy of your Old Antagonist Francis, and in the middle of a seeming Triumph was in Bodily fear least He Should use You as Scurvily as you had done the Pope. And 130 now after all Your Wars carryed on in Germany for your Pretended Catholicism You were forced to Conclude a Peace in favor of the Protestants, and after all the Designs against France you were not able to recover even what that Crown had gained upon You.

Charles. Aye, now Thou talkest like a Philosopher indeed; Must we 135 not all bear our Crosses and disappointments in Life?

110 at] L 25 (63) of L 26   114 into] L 26 om. L 25 (63)   115 public] L 26 om. L 25 (63)   Deliverance. L 26 : Deliverance L 25 (84) : deliverance. L 25 (63)   136 in Life] L 26 in this life L 25 (63)

Clenard. Yes, but there is the greatest difference in the World between bearing and Creating them, the first arises from the Malice of Fortune, the latter from the Effects of our own Folly, for one we ought to be Pittyed, for the other blamed.   140

Charles. In every State of life, Friend Clenard, a Man is subject to mistake, and as the Attempt is higher the blunder is more visible, but error excepted, If we cast up our Accounts there is no Comparison between the greatness of my Fortune and the obscurity of Yours.   145

> —my share
> In equal Ballance laid————
> Flings up the Adverse Scale and scorns proportion

as Prior says in a Hymn of Callimachus.

Clenard. Prior may say what he will in Verse, that Hymn was all 150 Enthusiasm. All Heros, Stars, and Gods. In Prose I am sure he is of another Opinion. But what does His Master Horace say, and no Body can say it better?

> *Est modus in rebus, sunt certi denique fines*
> *Quos ultrà—nequit consistere rectum.*   155

For once I'l Translate it for You, because possibly You have forgot the little Latin You had.

> One equal bound there is, one Stated line,
> Which shou'd the Justice of our Act confine:
> There Right resides, what goes beyond is Wrong: 160
> Grows idly vast, and trails absurdly long.

Now You Heros never mind this rule, You always overshoot the Mark, or to express it more properly you do not see the Object you aim at. Yee are so intent upon conquering that You have no time to govern. Reason should Direct your view, but Ambition 165 dazles it, So you never attain your Desires, because you never sufficiently consider what will satisfy them. This is the Cause of all those troubles which You bring upon Your selves and the rest of the World. There is something in what is called Heroic Virtue, which exceeding the measure of Nature from Sublime turns to 170 Ridiculous. When You were a Boy You used to run your Sword against Cæsar or Sertorius in Your Mothers Tapistry; Hopeful

---

139 latter] *L 26* later *L 25 (63)*   143 error excepted, *edd.*: error excepted. *L 25 (84)*: Errors excepted, *L 25 (63)*: (Error excepted) *L 26*   157 the] *L 25 (63)* your *L 26* 164 at. *L 26*: at *L 25 (63) & (84)*   164-5 Yee ... govern.] *L 26 om. L 25 (63)*

Symptoms indeed! And when you grew bigger you attack'd People, who had done you no more harm than those figures in the Hangings. In short you Heros are too forward Children to stop 175 at being Sensible Men; And while you abuse the Trust which Providence reposed in You in setting You to preside over the rest of your Species for their Safety and Benefit, You debase Your Selves beneath the lowest Rank of your fellow Creatures. By Jupiter Ammon, your Great Predecessor, a Drunken Cobler that 180 gets Ten Children is a more useful Member of the Commonwealth than a hott headed Prince, who, without any other cause than that of his own Pride leads as many hundred to have their Brains knocked out.

As to the common excuse of Enlarging your Dominions, while 185 you are doing it, you ruin your Subjects: I have some Verses for you upon that occasion.

> Recruits and Arms abroad cause Home-bred wants,
> The Monarch Triumphs, but the Nation faints.
> His hungry Fame that Cormorant Bird devours   190
> The Harvest destin'd to the Public Stores.
> New gather'd Laurels load the Victors brow,
> But Senates aw'd with lower Homage bow.
> With Iös while they Swell the general voice,
> Watch'd they are Loyal, and constrain'd Rejoice: 195
> Their Secret Sighs belye their loud Address;
> They Speak their Masters Fame, but wish it less:
> Ty'd to his Chariot-wheels at once he draws
> His En'mies Ensigns, and his Peoples Laws.
> His own Success the Soldier last bewails,   200
> Above his Pride his Countries Love prevails;
> He dreads the Pow'r he did too long Sustain,
> And sees the Sword he drops new forg'd into a Chain.

Charles.   Why this is a meer Libel, Clenard, down right Sedition every
    word of it. If I was Serious with You I would tell You, You are 205
    a dangerous Person, and ought to be laid in a gentle Confinement
    for the good of the Public.

173 attack'd *edd.*: attack'ed *L 25 (84)*: Attacked *L 25 (63), L 26*   174 those figures]
L 26 the Heroes *L 25 (63)*   181–2 Commonwealth than] *L 26* Common Wealth *Quo
ad hoc* than *L 25 (63)*   185 Dominions, *L 26*: Dominions *L 25 (63) & (84)*   187
upon] *L 25 (63)* on *L 26*   199 En'mies *edd.*: En'emies *L 25 (63) & (84), L 26*   207
Public. *L 26*: Public *L 25 (63) & (84)*

Clenard. Ha, ha, ha, You really make me laugh, dont You imagin that we think such as You dangerous Persons, only that for our private Safety we dare not say so. Am I to be laid up because You cant bear 210 truth? I tell You, that for the good of the Public You should all have your Swords taken from You as if You were actual Lunaticks, and not be suffered to go a Madding with this rattle of a Globe to play with. Believe me You grope thrô the World with Your Scepters like blind Beggars with their Staves, and are moved and 215 Directed by the Neighing of a Steed, and the Sound of a Trumpet as those by the Barking of a Dog and the tinckling of a Bell. What a Changling was Cyrus when he left a fine Country where he might have Governed quietly and ran over Hill and Dale into a worse Climate to attack a Woman who had never injured him? 220 And what a figure did he make when one of Thomyris's Chamber-Maids shewed his grim Phyz in a bloody Bason? How ridiculous was Alexander when he blubbered for another World to Conquer, and what did Hanibal get by vexing half Europe but to be made the subject of a Declamation for my Boys. To talk once more of 225 your own Extravagancies, Dear Emperor, when You had given your self Such incredible troubles, and made that Universal Bustle in Italy, what did You bring home but your own Name of *Charles le Quint* corrupted by the Venetian pronounciation into *Harlequin,* a little restless Fellow with a black Muzzle, a patch-work coat on 230 his back, and a Lath Sword in his hand, Assaulting All he met, leaping thrô every Mans Windowes, and disturbing the Business of his House. And have You not been represented under this foolish Character in all the Fairs throughout Europe, That, of Franckfort not excepted, where You valued your self just now for 235 having been Crowned: In one word Human Nature is a very poor thing, Neighbor Charles, Despotic pow'r never ought to be Trusted with it, Considering what sad effects Ignorance, Self will and Flattery may Produce. I am astonished that, an Absolute Monarch does not Degenerate into a meer Driveller.   240

Charles. Well, I will not show my Anger against this Word-Man.

O brave Clenard, why this is all

Hydrops, Nycticorax, Thorax et mascula vervex.

Clenard. Upon my word good Emperor I am glad to find you

219 ran] *L 25 (63)* run *L 26*   228 Italy, *L 26*: Italy. *L 25 (84)*: Italy *L 25 (63)*   230
Muzzle *L 25 (63)*: Mussle *L 25 (84)*: Muzle *L 26*   231 All] *L 26* every Body *L 25 (63)*
234 Europe] *L 26* Christendom *L 25 (63)*   of] *L 25 (63) om. L 26*

understand your Grammer so well, for I shall be with you upon 245
that subject too presently, But first of the First, as I have heard Your
Story pray give me leave to tell You mine, It shal be very short.
You said the Eyes of all the World were upon You; Now, I had my
Eyes upon all the World: When I was known for a very famous
Schole-Master, I Travelled thrô Flanders, Germany and Spain as 250
well as You. I passed into Africa, not indeed with half so much
Noise and Tumult but with more Satisfaction and Safety. In short
I contented my self to Visit those Countries in which You were
never quiet, because You had not Conquered them.

Charles.   I must Confess that jogging on in a Passage-Boat or a Stage- 255
Coach with Three or Four Friends is but an odd way of Travelling,
a Fleet and an Army are Delicious Attendants.

Clenard.   Aye Charles, but what other Company had You? Fear that
the Bread-Waggons should not come up in due time, Doubts lest
the Magazines might be Surprised, Restlessness and want of Sleep 260
lest Your Design should either be Revealed or Prevented, Besides
Your Two Intestine Comrades the Stone and the Gout.

Charles.   There is too much truth in what this pert Philosopher says,
but I must bear up to Him for the sake of my Honor, that Dear
Honor which makes us too often Commit a Second mistake in 265
defence of the first—Well, friend Clenard You are stil harping at
a Comparison between your way of Living and mine, Would you
infer from all this, that every man in an Inferior Station has an
equal Share of Happyness and Glory with those who hold the first
Seats in the World?   270

Clenard.   Every Wise Man has, Charles, for as to Happyness he must
form it himself, and this is soon done, when the necessarys of Life
very few and easy to come at, almost within every Mans reach are
once acquired. As for Fame which You all run mad after, It is not
in any Mans own Power to Purchace it, It depends upon the good 275
Will and free Gift of other People, and is only got by a Mans
behaving himself so as to Oblige the World to speak well of him,
so let the Emperor and the Schole Master do what they will One
will be called a Tyrant the other a Pedant unless they really
Deserve the contrary. But prythee let me go on. I read Books, 280
promoted Knowledge, I was kindly received by my Friends where

247 pray] *L 26 om. L 25 (63)*   248 said the] *L 25 (63)* said that the *L 26*   249 very]
L 26 om. L 25 (63)   259 come *L 25 (63), L 26* : cone *L 25 (84)*   262 the Gout.]
L 26 Gout *L 25 (63)*   269 of] *L 25 (63), L 26* and *Earlier reading in L 25 (84)*   271
Wise] *L 25 (63)* om. *L 26*   273 to come *L 25 (63), L 26* : to to come *L 25 (84)*

ever I came, I was invited into Portugal, past, as I tell You, into
Africa in quest of Oriental Manuscripts, brought Mahometan
Servants back with me, gave them their Liberty, taught them
Latin, made them Christians, nay got some of them advanced to 285
the Dignity of Priesthood—an Honor to which You with all your
Interest aspired in vain, while your Tutor Adrian a Brother
Grammarian of mine obtained it and became more a Master to
You when You were now grown up a Man and an Emperor then
when You was simply Charles of Gaunt and a little Boy under his 290
Ferula.

Charles.   Egad that last was a Home thrust I must not let him Perceive
I feel it so Sensibly. Once more, I tell Thee, there is as much
Difference between Our Actions as between our Stations and
Qualities. Facts, Clenard, real visible Facts are on my side. Thy 295
Glory is only Speculative, Meer imagination. To alter the Con-
stitution of Provinces, to raise or Depose Princes, to give War or
Peace as I pleased. This has laid the foundation of a lasting renown
for me and a Monument upon which Fame must sit for ever.

Clenard.   You are little in the Clouds, Charles, something upon the 300
Phoebus as the French call it, but I shal fetch You down imme-
diately, a very easy way of Reasoning may set our Actions in the
Right light. Suppose I should walk my Children over other Mens
Gardens, let 'em pull down the Hedges, root up the Melons, and
Rob the Orchard, what would People say, but that I was a Sense- 305
less Creature, and a Drunken Sott. But yet when one of You
Princes take a Fancy to Burn whole Towns, and lay the Provinces
round them Desolate You seem Satisfyed when You Answer it was
for your Glory. This my Predecessors have preached to Yours
for two thousand Years past, and very few of You ever mended 310
upon it. Thô when You are near Death, when the Clouds of
Prejudice and Ambition are Dispersed, and, as my Master Plato
says, the Soul sees things with a quicker and clearer Eye, some of
You have been forced to Acknowledge the Truth of these Maximes.

Charles.   But this is meer Preaching Domine Clenard.   315

Clenard.   No matter if it be so, as long as I keep to my Text. As to
Your Facts therefore, all Errors Excepted, as you just now desired,

299 ever. *edd.*: ever L 25 (63) & (84): Ever. L 26   305 Orchard] L 25 (63)
Orchards L 26   306 But L 25 (63): but L 25 (84), L 26   307 take] L 25 (63)
takes L 26   308 Answer] L 26 have Answered L 25 (63)   309 for your] L 26 for
Your Interest or your L 25 (63)   317 desired, L 25 (63): desired L 25 (84): desired)
L 26

the best would Dye almost stil born without my Midwifry, Take
this as a Maxim Facts depend upon Words, The greatest Monarch
and most Fortunate Captain, allowing his Cause to be strictly 320
just, and the Event equally Fortunate is obliged for the Recital to
a dealer either in Syntax or Prosodia. The out lines and drawings
are only seen in the bare Action of the Hero, But 'tis the Scholar
that adds the heightnings and Colorings that gives the Beauty,
nay faith, in great measure the very life and Substance to the 325
Picture. So that this lasting Monument of which You seem so fond
is founded upon the Pleasure of us Gramarians and your Fame
might sit there long enough cooling her heels, Silent and dispirited
except we find Ideas to move her Vigor and put sounds into her
Trumpet. Did you never mind a large Ship going out of Port, 330
Charles, with her Sails all spread, and her Streamers flying? How
insensibly yet how soon her Bulk diminishes to the Eye of those
that stand upon the Shoar 'till as the distance increases She
becomes quite lost: After this if you would know the Intrinsic
Value of the Goods She carryed out You must apply your Selves 335
to the Surintendents and Customers that Keep the Register.

Charles.   Well what then?

Clenard.   Why then One of You great Men is just that Stately Vessel,
and You go out of the World as She does out of Harbor. You are
launched into the Ocean of Eternity with all your Scutchons and 340
Bandirolls about your Hearse, and probably you may have Four
Marble Virtues to Support the Monument you were Speaking of
just now. But alas, the Funeral Pomp is soon diminishd worn out
and forgotten: Age and Accident deface the Tomb, And, it is only
one of Us Scholars that must take an Account of Your true Worth, 345
and transmit it safe to succeeding Generations. Not to go to
Old Stories of how many of You Heros Dyed unknown before
Agamemnon because none of their Contemporaries writ their
Story, or how Alexander wept for fear he should not be as advan-
tageously treated as Achilles was before him, what Could Elizabeth 350
of England or Henry le grand of France have done without the
Assistance of a Camden or a Perefix, yet these were Grammarians,

318 best would] *L 26* best of them would *L 25 (63)*   320 be strictly] *L 25 (63)* be most
strictly *L 26*   324 Colorings] *L 25 (63)* Colouring *L 26*   325 to] *L 25 (63)* of *L 26*
330 Trumpet. *L 26* : Trumpet *L 25 (84)* : Trumpet, *L 25 (63)*   330–46 Did … Generations.] *om. L 25 (63)*   331 flying? How *edd.* : flying how *L 25 (84)* : flying? how *L 26*
333 that] who *L 26*   339 does] goes *L 26*   of Harbor] of the Harbour *L 26*
346 Generations. *L 26* : Generations *L 25 (84)*   347 of how] *L 25 (63)* how *L 26*
352 were Grammarians] *L 26* were mere Gramarians *L 25 (63)*

Charles, meer Traders in Gerunds and retailers of Supines: What need any more Examples, the thing is Meridiano Sole Clarior, as we say in our Declamations. Cæsar indeed could describe what he 355 saw, and Antoninus could tell how he Thought. On my Conscience I think there are not above three or four more of You that are Exceptions to my general rule.

Charles. Spoke in the Style of a Gramarian, but prythee Man—what Signifyes telling and describing in comparison to Acting and 360 governing. Words are your Province, Deeds are ours. For under favor, Sir, all this while you live upon us, You only write what we perform, Your Chapters and Tomes are Divided by our Wars and Treaties; The First Book ends where one of Us Dye, and the next begins with his Successors Coronation.   365

Clenard. We live upon You! quite otherwise, We could live better without You. It is upon your Account that we Suffer that we are accused so often of Flattery and partiality; when we have conversed with Clasicks that leave the Noblest Dictates of Morality upon our own Minds and have Inculcated Virtue and honor into 370 our Youth, We could give the rest of our Time to the Contemplation of Nature and Study of Philosophy. We can live and be encouraged any where, nay have a part of the Power in all mixt Governments and Republics, Places let me tell You where One of You would meet but a very cold Reception, and make but a very 375 foolish Figure; just the Reverse of what You say is true, (to Speak it in as Civil terms as I can) the Obligation is from You to Us; For your own part thô you did not take your Latin very kindly, You owe it to the care of Your Tutor Adrian that You can spell, and if You'l believe him as to the point in Question, he had one greater 380 Vexation than that of teaching a dull Boy, for he had it engraved on his Tomb-Stone that he knew nothing more grievous in Life than to Reign. Wolsey a down right Schole-Master at Oxford Governed his Harry the Eighth as absolutely as ever I did my Boys, and even shared the Regal Dignity with his Soveraign; thô 385 Harry was of the Heroic Strain too of a temper not unlike your

355 Declamations. *L 25 (63), L 26* : Declamations *L 25 (84)*   355–8 Cæsar . . . rule.]
on my Conscience I think there are but two very great Exceptions to my General Rule. Julius
Cæsar and Antoninus who could either tell what they did or how they thought. *L 25 (63)*
356 Antoninus] Antonius *L 26*   359 Spoke . . . Man] *L 26 om. L 25 (63)*   360–1
and describing . . . governing.] *L 26 om. L 25 (63)*   363 perform] *L 26* Act *L 25 (63)*   364
where] *L 26* when *L 25 (63)*   372 Philosophy. *L 26* : Philosophy *L 25 (84)* : Philosophy,
L 25 (63)   373 of] *L 25 (63)* in *L 26*   386 of the *L 25 (63), L 26* : of of the
L 25 (84)

917.27   R r

own. And another of my Profession upon the like Occasion has
done pretty well with one of your Successors in Spain. So that You
see a Schole-Master can Instruct nay Personate a King, but *Vice*
versâ, It is very seldom observed that a King makes a good Schole 390
Master, Pray take notice that when any Man eminent in my profession Dies, it is pretty hard to get his place supplyed. But as to
Principality, if it is Hereditary Your Son be he good or bad,
a Youth without any Experience, or a Child in a Cradle Succeeds
You. Nay, in most places, your Daughter, who probably never yet 395
Stirred out of her Nursery, and in an Elective Government when
ever a Vacancy happens you find twenty People ready to fill it. A
broken General, a younger Brother of a Princely Family, A Nobleman that has Estate enough to Buy it, any body in Short: So true
is it that every Man thinks he can Govern, and few know that they 400
can Teach. I'll go a little further with your Majesty, since I have
you upon this point. Your very Titles, Your Serenissimus and
Augustissimus are Superlatives created by the Power of us Grammarians. Rex Germaniæ, Hispaniarum, Hungariæ, Bohemiæ &ca:
then on to Archidux Austriæ, Dux Burgundiæ, Brabantiæ &ca: 405
then to Princeps Sueviæ, and Marchio Sacri Imperij, Burgaviæ,
Moraviæ, and so away with it 'till one is out of Breath. Now what
is all this but so many words fitted Civily to their respective genitive Cases, of which if one be wanting or misplaced You can neither
Eat Your Dinner, nor sleep quietly in Your Bed, 'till You have 410
raised New Imposts and Waged New Wars to obtain Satisfaction
for so considerable an Affront; And after all that You can do in
these great Affairs, You are forced to Address your Selves to
Grammarians and Heralds, Your Recorders of Words and Sentences that they may be pleased to set you right again, and when 415
ever You have Fought and Conquered with Your Ruyters and
Swashbucklers are you not obliged to call us in again to draw up
Your Concordates, your Pacta and Diplomata. How simply would
you look even upon Your own Money if Your Titles round it were
wrong Spelt, and is not a piece of false Grammer in any Article 420
Sufficient to Spoil a whole Treaty? Quo ad hunc sets one Man upon
the Throne, and sends another into Exile. Quo ad hanc makes all

---

391–401 Pray . . . Teach.] *om. L 25 (63)*   395 Nay *L 26*: nay *L 25 (84)*   406
to] *L 26* till *L 25 (63)*   408 their] *L 26* the *L 25 (63)*   410 sleep] *L 25 (63)*
sup *L 26*   416 Fought] *L 25 (63)* Thought *L 26*   421 Treaty? *L 26*: Treaty
L 25 (63) & *(84)*   421–4 sets . . . out] hanc and hoc have been the different
Causes of Mariages and Divorces that have separated whole Kingdoms and made *L 25 (63)*

the Mariages and Divorces upon which the Succession of your Kingdoms depend, and for Quo ad hoc it has cut out more bloody work than either the Trojan or Carthaginian Wars. We have had an Account from the other World within this twenty Year that even the Spirit and word of an Agreement made between one of Your Successors and his Contemporary Princes made and broke the Partition of all your Dominions. Two Latin prepositions *Trans* and *Cum* joined with *Substantiation* a word invented by us Schole-men were the Cause of all your troubles in Germany, and the same Contention is stil on foot thô it is now one hundred and fifty Years Since we were discharged from having any part in it, and I am credibly informed by an English Divine who is just come down hither that there is at this very time a Schissm in that Kingdom concerning the Doxology. There is *Et* and *Et* on one Side and *Per* and *in* on t'other side, and happy is it for that whimsical Nation if their Two Universities may be able to compose the Difference. To cut the Discourse Short; Great Charles of Austria, Swords Conquer some, but words Subdue all Men. Since as You say You love Facts my Dear Emperor, before we leave this Subject let me instance one Fact to You, which neither You nor I can ever forget: When the Misfortunes of the Landgrave Philip of Hess had made him consent to Sign a Treaty with You, grievous enough for him in the best Sense, for by it he was obliged to Submit to a Confine-ment, from which he thought Your Generosity would release him as soon as Your Vanity was gratifyed in his Personal Submission; to perform his Treaty, he presented himself to Your Majesty, The Princes of the Empire by whose perswasion he had done this, and he himself imagining, as I say, that the Confinement was required only, *pro formâ*, that it would be very Short, nay but for a Night, and that too spent in Feasting and Play, but the next Morning your Chancellor, whom they expected to bring the order of Release for this unhappy Prince, declared in your Name that they were all mistaken in the matter, and that the Confinement was understood to be perpetual. As the matter was looked into this difference was found to arise from an Equivoque in Two German words: EINIG

424 Kingdoms] Kingdom *L 26*   426 other] *L 26* tother *L 25 (63)*   437 it] *L 25 (63) om. L 26*   438–9 Difference. To *edd.*: Difference to *L 25 (63) & (84)*: difference. To *L 26*   439 Short; *edd.*: Short. *L 25 (84)*: short *L 25 (63)*: short; *L 26* 440–1 Since … Emperor] *L 25 (63), L 26* Nay since You love Facts, Charles *Earlier reading in L 25 (63)*   441 Emperor, *L 26*: Empr: *L 25 (63) & (84)*   457 in *L 25 (63)*, *L 26*: *om. L 25 (84)*   words: *L 26* : words *L 25 (63) & (84)*

Some, was agreed to in the Article and EUIG *perpetual* was inserted
in the Transcribing it. Now Charles for the Power of an *n* and
a *u* here is the Grandson of Maximilian of Austria, and Mary of 460
Burgundy, the Man in whose Blood the Spanish and German
Monarchies are United, playing a Trick for which a public Notary
in the smallest Imperial District would be Censured, and to say
no worse of the matter, The Emperor both as to his Sense and
honor depending wholly upon the Grammarian.   465

Charles. This Fellow presses me hard, and I grow weary of his
Company. I'l e'en draw down my main Argument, my great Batter-
ing Piece upon him, and Strike him Dead at once. Well, Clenard
what ever there may be of Solid or Fickle, Pleasurable or Painful in
Power: He that having Exerted it can lay it down is a great Man. 470
Now this You know I did. I abdicated all my Dominions, retired
to a Monastery, and contented my Self with a Pension of two
hundred thousand Crowns a year.

Clenard. A Physitian, who cures himself of a Dropsey has great Skill,
but a Man who never had the Distemper has Sounder health. Well, 475
Sir, at first view this Abdication of Yours has the appearance of a
great Action, but if it was Wisdom it came very late, Disappointments Diseases and Vexations Preceded it, and the rising Fortune
of Harry the Second helped it on mightily, *Qui sta bene non se move*
You know: Your Resolution of quitting the World Showed very 480
plainly you were uneasy in it, Nay Your self Confessed in the
Harangue You made to the States at Bruxelles, when you took
your last Farewell of them that the greatest prosperity you had
in the World had been mix't with so much greater Adversity
that You could not say that You ever had enjoyed any real Satis- 485
faction in it. Besides there are pretty Odd Stories about that
matter, as if You resolved upon Your Retreat too rashly, and
Repented it at leasure. Do You Remember what Your Son Philip
Answered to Cardinal Grainville when the Cardinal said to him,
It is now a Year, Sir, since your Father Abdicated. It is a Year then 490
said Philip that he was first Sorry for so Doing. Do You remember
the Young Monck at St: Just, where you were retired, and when
you waked him too soon in a Morning, What, said he, after You

467 Company. *L 26* : Compa: *L 25 (84)* : Company, *L 25 (63)*   470 Power: *edd.* : Power.
L 25 (84) : Power *L 25 (63)* : power. *L 26*   479 *move*] *L 25 (63) more L 26*   482
at] *L 25 (63)* of *L 26*   489 him, *L 26* : him. *L 25 (84)* : him *L 25 (63)*   492 at]
L 25 (63) of *L 26*   492–3 when you] *L 25 (63) om. L 26*   493 What *L 26* : what
L 25 (63) & *(84)*

have disturbed the rest of Mankind are you come to Plague us in
our Cloyster, Can nothing be quiet where You are? So that You 495
found the Same reflection returned particularly upon You after
Your Abdication that had generally been made before, and that—

Charles. Why thou art not well full nor fasting. Wouldest Thou neither
have me in the World nor out of it?

Clenard. Nay, since You were so much in the World that You made 500
your Self and every Body else weary of it, I think You were in the
Right to get out of it as fast as You could. One would not Advise
a Fellow to Climb to the top of a Spire, whence he is every Moment
in danger of falling only that he may have the Chance of Saving his
life by leaping down upon a feather Bed, But now Your Abdication 505
at best Showed either that You could not stand longer upon the
Pinacle, or were tyred with standing there so long; So your head
turned, Your hand Slipt and down came You. Prythee, Charles,
remember these Two Verses.

> None Climb so high or fall so low 510
> As those who know not where they go.

Charles. Whither in Gods Name art Thou running on?

Clenard. Only to finish my Story and my Comparison. I had my Eyes
in my head, I looked before I leaped, I never endeavored to Climb
too high, So I was never constrained to fall too low. I always 515
walked like a Man Erect upon my Feet, and as I took not too much
upon my Self, So I never relinquished what I had once taken. I
had my Share of Credit in the World, because I proportioned my
Action to the end Desired, and as that end was always Lawful,
when it was obtained it became Laudable, I never went so far to 520
Sea, but I had stil my Eye upon the Shoar, nor loaded my Ship so
deep that I was forced to throw my goods over Board in the
Tempest. I did not Divide my Estate in my Life time between a
Brother and a Son, who had both from that Moment the Power
in their hands of using me ill for so doing. I prudently kept what 525
I had till I Dyed; And my Goods were not Scuffled for before
my Will was Opened; And as in life I had not been Guilty of
Oppression or Injury towards Mankind I had no Occasion for
a Discipline of Knots and Wiers to quicken my Repentance and

498 Wouldest *edd.*: wouldest *L 25 (84)*: Wouldst *L 25 (63)*: would *L 26*   499 it? *L 26*:
it. *L 25 (63) & (84)*   502 get] *L 25 (63)* go *L 26*   503 whence] *L 25 (63)*
where *L 26*   505 But] *L 26 om. L 25 (63)*   511 go. *L 25 (63), L 26*: go *L 25 (84)*
512 Whither] *L 26* Whether *L 25 (63)*   523 my Life] *L 26* my own life *L 25 (63)*

prepare me for Death. Now, which of Us Two was the Happyest 530
Man?

Charles.   Go to, You are a prating Fellow.

Clenard.   I am so, and You are a Silly Combatant, to Fight me at my
own Weapon. Every Man to his Trade, Charles, You should have
Challenged me at long Pike or broad Sword: In a Tilt or Tourna- 535
ment you might probably have had the better of Me, But at
Syllogism or Paradox—

Charles.   Confound Your Jargon.

Clenard.   Calm your Passion, I have no Design to offend You, But You
Hero's never rightly know Your Friends from Your Enemies.   540

> Sir Egledemore that Valiant Knight
> He put on his Sword, and he wou'd go fight

not three pence matter against who. In one word good Emperor
We will fairly refer our Dispute to Dionysius, if we can find him
yonder upon the Greek walk; He that was both a Prince and 545
a Schole Master may very properly decide it, As in the Ancient
Poets I remember a Curious Question of another kind: who had
most pleasure the Man or the Woman was refered to Cæneus as
a Person whose immediate Experience ought to be Relyed on

> *It comes et juvenis quondam nunc fœmina Cæneus.*   550

I'l translate that for You too for I am in a mighty good Humor.

> Ambiguous Cæneus has both Sexes try'd
> Let him or her the doubtful Point decide.

Charles.   I'll yeild to no Decision I tell You I am tyred with your
Pedantry. I was always Subject only to my own Will, and can be 555
tryed by nothing else.

Clenard.   So that we end just where We begun.

> Making the Circle of their Reign Compleat
> These Suns of Empire where they rise they Set.

But however, Charles, if Princes are Governed only by their own 560
Will, You must Confess at least it was a Mad World that We
Lived in.

Charles.   Adieu, Messire Clenard.

Clenard.   Adieu, Monseigneur Charles.

---

542 fight *L 25 (63)*: fight. *L 25 (84)*, *L 26*   543 who] *L 25 (63)* whom *L 26*   550
Cæneus. *L 26* : Cæneus *L 25 (63)* & *(84)*   557 begun] *L 25 (63)* began *L 26*

Charles. But hark You, one word more, Pray dont take the least 565
Notice to any of my Fellow Princes of the Discourse we have had.

Clenard. After all I confess that Injunction is pretty hard, but however
I'l Obey it, Provided You remember what I have said, I'l endeavor
to forget it.

A Dialogue between Mr: John Lock and Seigneur de Montaigne.

Lock. Is it not wonderfull that after what Plato and Aristotle, Descartes and Malbranch have written of Human understanding, it
should be reserved to Me to give the most clear, and Distinct
Account of it?

Montaigne. Plato and Aristotle are great Names, but as you disclaim 5
Authority You have no right to Quote them, thô a great deal may
be said even upon their Subject, if the ambiguity of many Greek
words, and the Prejudice we have in favor of Antiquity were
removed. But as for Descartes, Malbranch and your self, is it not
more wonderful that any of You should be Satisfyed with your own 10
Writings, or have found Readers to Admire them? To deal plainly
with You, this single Reflection upon human Understanding
charges it with a Weakness that all your Books do not sufficiently
account for.

Lock. Short and pithy in good faith! by that sprightly way of think- 15
ing, as wildly as your imagination can suggest, and by your
expressing that thought as flowingly as your Tongue can throw it
off, I should judge You to be Michael Montaigne.

Montaigne. Seigneur de Montaigne, if you please, Knight of the
Order of St: Michael, and some time Mayor of Bourdeaux.   20

Lock. Yes, Sir, I know your Person by your Insisting So much upon
your Titles, and I find the same Strain run with a most voluble
impetuosity almost thrô every Chapter of your Book; as you see
the Simplicity of my Mind in my very Title Page, where I only
call my Self John Lock. Gent: 25

565 You] L 26 Ye L 25 (63)
    Title: A] L 26 om. L 25 (154)   John] L 26 om. L 25 (154)   de L 26: om. L 25 (117)
& (154)   6 great] L 26 good L 25 (154)   17 throw L 25 (154), L 26: thrô L 25
(117)   19 de] L 26 om. L 25 (154)   25 Gent:] Gentleman. L 25 (154), L 26

Montaigne.   Diogenes when he trod upon Plato's Robe, (whom you named just now) and was asked what he meant by it, said he contemned the Pride of Plato; a stander by Answered, that there was more Pride in trampling upon the Purple than in wearing of it. Honor you know is my Idol, so I tell You who I am, and where I 30 live, what I possess, and how I act, because I think our Vanities may be so managed as to Sustain our Virtues. Now, you divest the Mind from these human Trappings, and strip off her Cloths to shew her stark Naked. The perfection therefore of your Humility would have appeared in your giving us a Book without any Name 35 at all. If You had come out like the whole Duty of Man in your Language I would have said something to You. But so it is with us, we would be humble and we are Proud, we fall into contrary Excesses, and are guilty of one Vice by a mistaken Design of avoiding another. There is some Crany, some winding Meandre 40 in every Mans brain, which he himself is the last that finds out.

Lock.   It is for that very reason, good Seigneur de Montaigne, that I searched my own head, and desected my Understanding, with so great Diligence and Accuracy, that I cannot but think the Study of many Years very usefully bestowed on that Subject. I will give 45 you some Account of it: First, I found out, and explained that an Idea is the Object of the Human understanding, That You may call it Idea, Phantasm, Notion or Species.

Montaigne.   Which is, that any Man may Speak either Greek or Latin, as he pleases, then Sir you proceed.   50

Lock.   O, most happily, in proving that we have no Innate Speculative or Practical Principles; That Complex proceed from Simple Idea's, that Idea's of Reflection come later than those of Sensation, that uncompounded Appearances—

Montaigne.   O, Sir, I know all that as well as if I had been one of your 55 Disciples. Two Simple Idea's are the least that can possibly be allowed to make one Complex, many more may chance to be thrown into the bargain, and a whole set of them may be resolved again into their Native Simplicity to the Tune of

Ex plico fit plicui Solvo, Solvique Solutumque   60

But Jerné, Lock, what can'st thou mean, if these words expressed any real things, or subsisted any where but in the writers brain

32 Virtues] *L 26* Virtue *L 25 (154)*   36–37 the . . . Language] *L 26* Your whole Duty of Man *L 25 (154)*

(and faith I can't tell what impression they can make there neither)
but if they are, I say, any thing, or can signify any thing, what
matters it three pence if all you have said be true or no. 65

Lock.   If you could correct that Gascon fire of Yours, I would tell you
that I use these terms as Instruments and means to attain to Truth.
You know the Ancient Philosophers said Truth lay at the bottom
of a Well.

Montaigne.   It may be so, but foy de Gentilhomme, You will never 70
draw her out except your Tools are more accomodated to Your
Work, in short, Sir, call 'em what You will, or tumble them where
ever you please, they are but words: bring them together again
they will no more make things Solid and useful than grains of
Sand will make a Rope. 75

Lock.   Before we go any further, tell me truly have You read my Book
quite thrô, and with Care?

Montaigne.   Yes in good truth I have read it, and just as I read other
Books, with care where they instruct me, with pleasure where they
amuse me and half asleep where they tire me. To convince you of 80
the Truth of what I say, I will give you some of your own Axioms
almost in the order in which they lye.

Lock.   With candor I beseech You.

Montaigne.   Oh trust Me as to that upon my Honor. Colors come in
only by the Eyes, all kind of Noises by the Ears, Tastes and Smels 85
by the Nose and Palat; touching from every Member (thô some
indeed more Sensible than others) by the jonction of Two Bodies.
Red is not blew, a Sucking Bottle is not a Rod, A Child certainly
knows that the Nurse that feeds it is neither the Catt it plays with,
nor the Blackmore it is afraid of; Wormseed and Mustard are not 90
Apples and Sugar, and there is an Essential Difference between
a Sillybub and a Bromestaff.

Lock.   This I tell You is only my Substratum, the very Rubbige upon
which I build.

Montaigne.   A House of Cards is a stronger foundation. 95

Lock.   Hear me a little; from these plain Propositions I go on to greater
Discoveries, that an Infant in the Cradle cannot make a Syllogism
half so well as a Sophister in the Schols, and that a Hottentote is

68 said Truth] *L 26* said that Truth *L 25 (154)*   78 have] *L 26* did *L 25 (154)*   79
me, *L 25 (154)*, *L 26* : me *L 25 (117)*   80 you] *L 26 om. L 25 (154)*   83–84 With...
Honor.] *om. L 25 (154)*   83 With *L 26* : with *L 25 (117)* :   84 Oh *edd.* : oh *L 25 (117)* :
O, *L 26*   86 touching] *L 26* and touching *L 25 (154)*   thô] *L 26* thrô *L 25 (154)*
90 of; *edd.* : off, *L 25 (117)* : *L 25 (154)* : of. *L 26*

not so learned in the Bay of Sardaignia as he would have been if
his Friends had Educated him at Oxford, or Cambridge.   100
Montaigne. Who the Devil did not know all these undoubted truths
before you set Pen to Paper, and who ever questioned them since?
There are a hundred things plain in themselves that are only made
Ambiguous by your Comment upon them. I hold a Stone in my
hand, and ask you what it is, You tell me 'tis a body, I ask you 105
what is a Body, you reply it is a Substance; I am troublesome
enough once more to ask You what is a Substance, you look graver
imediately, and inform me that it is something whose Essence consists in Extension in such a manner as to be capable of receiving
it, in Longitude, Latitude, and Profundity; The Devil is in it if I 110
am not Answered. I may Sooner pave the Road between London
and York than have a thorow Knowledge of the least Pebble in
the way except I take this Jargon in full of all Accounts. Socrates,
I have some where told you asked Memnon what was Virtue?
There is replyed Memnon the virtue of a Man and of a Woman, 115
of a Child, and of an aged Person, of a Majestrate and of a Private
Citizen, and as he was going on Socrates interrupting him, said, I
am mightily obliged to your Generosity: I asked concerning one
Virtue, and You have already given me half a Dozen. Now, Mr
Lock, I apprehend clearer what is meant by understanding than 120
I do by your Definition of it, *the Power of thinking*, and I know better
what the Will is then when I hear you call it *the Power of Volition*.
A Plough Boy, says to his Father, Ay Ay, I understand that as well
as You; and to his Mother, I wont do it because you bid me. Yet
he knows not, all this while, that he hath exercised the two great 125
and Principal Actions of his Mind, as You call them, or if that mind
had two Actions, or two and Twenty.

You have heard of the Citizen turned Gentleman, Mr: Lock,
who had a mind to be a Scholar, and was dabbling in Grammer.
He discoursed a long time to his Wife of Regimen and Syntax, and 130
at last asked her, Sweetheart, what is it I am talking now? On my
Conscience, quoth She, Husband, I think 'tis Nonsense. That may
be he replyed, you simple Woman, But did not you know all this
time that it was not Verse but prose? Now the good Woman could

99 so learned] *L 25 (154)* so well Learned *L 26*   102 who] *L 25 (154) om. L 26*
107 a] *L 25 (154) om. L 26*   109 a] *L 25 (154) om. L 26*   118 asked] *L 26* ask
L 25 (154)   125 hath] *L 26* has *L 25 (154)*   131 now? *L 25 (154), L 26*: now.
L 25 (117)   132 Nonsense. That *L 26*: Nonsense, that *L 25 (117)*: Nonsense, That
L 25 (154)   134 prose? *edd.*: prose. *L 25 (117) & (154)*: Prose? *L 26*

not be more obliged to her Husband for this Piece of Learning than 135
your young Sectators are to You for the Discovery of Some of those
incomparable Axioms, which you just now quoted, when they find
them amidst a heap of Metaphysical terms. How grateful are they
to the Doctor, and in return for your Civility in giving them Six
or eight words together of which they can make common Sense, 140
how joyfully do they let themselves be Bambouzled thrô as many
Chapters. For among the variety of Errors, to which weak Minds
are Subject, there is one very Conspicuous: that they are most
prone to admire what they do not perfectly understand, and are
very apt to judge of the Depth of anothers thoughts by the 145
Obscurity of his Expression. Aristotle, I have heard, valued himself upon having a Tallent of concealing part of his meaning, or
rendring the whole Ambiguous, for which damned affectation I
most heartily hate Aristotle, and all his Imitators in this Kind. I do
not say, Mr Lock, that you affect this Obscurity, but I beg your 150
pardon, while I take the Liberty to tell You, that You often fall
into it: while you are Sowing words too Plentifully You do not
always forsee what Crop they will bear.

Lock.   This is a pretty large Accusation, I hope You can make it good.

Montaigne.   Why, You confess in your very Preface, that, when You 155
first put Pen to Paper, you thought that all you should have to say
on the matter would have been contained in One Sheet of Paper,
and yet, you see, you have Swelled it into a Volume. How imperfectly therefore did you Judge either of the Extent of what was
to be Written, or of the Method in which it should be Digested. 160
But as we say in France, the Appetite comes in Eating, So in
writing you stil found more to write. From Ideas most un-
expectedly sprung Solidity, Perception, Extension, duration, Number and Infinity, and from these again mixed Modes, Complex and
Collective Ideas of Substances, Identity, Diversity, and fifty other 165
glorious Tresor-trouves, to which You the Master of the Soyle have
the only Right and Property, and are intitled to Dispose of them
ex mero motu and *Purâ gratiâ*, to all Your Sectators and Disciples *in
Secula Seculorum*. Now, by the same way of working, you might have

143 Conspicuous: *edd.* : Conspicuous *L 25 (117)*: conspicuous *L 25 (154)* : conspicuous; *L 26*
144 prone *L 25 (154), L 26*: pron *L 25 (117)*   148 rendring *L 25 (154), L 26* : rending
L 25 (117)   153 what Crop] *L 25 (154)* what a Crop *L 26*   157 of Paper]
Underlined in L 25 (117) & (154), perhaps for deletion   159 Extent] *L 25 (154)* Extant
L 26   164 Modes, *L 26*: Modes *L 25 (117) & (154)*   165 Collective] *L 25 (154)*
Collected *L 26*   167 them] *L 26 om. L 25 (154)*

left them Ten Volumes as well as one, nay, every Chapter might [170]
have been beaten out into a whole Book, and after Potentiallity, per-
ceptivity, Mobility and Motivity, (which by the by you should have
added to your Chapter of the abuse of Words) You might have
found out Ten thousand other -Alitys and -Ivitys, that would
have looked equally well to the Eye in a handsom Print, and con- [175]
veyed just as much Knowledge to the Mind. Why, Mr: Lock, your
very definition of Liberty is, that it is something, which You your
Self must feel, what signifies it therefore to Define it at all? Can
any words out of another Mans Mouth make me understand if I
feel a thing or No? Believe me, Mr: Lock, You Metaphysicians [180]
define your Object as some Naturalists divide it, *in infinitum*, but,
while You are doing so, the parts become so far Separated from
each other, that you lose the Sight of the thing it Self. Another
happyness arises from all this, that when ever the Writer of this
Sort of Mysterious Demonstration, and his Reader Disagree, as [185]
happened between You and Stillingfleet, and in a Case not unlike
Yours between South and Sherlock, Both are in the Right, and
both are in the Wrong, While no Man else can well Judge what
either of them meant. So the Dispute only terminates as it grows
forgot, and as the property of the Bookseller in the unsold Sheets [190]
that contained it, is transfer'd to his next door Neighbors, the
Groser and the Pastry Cook.

Lock.   So that You, the loosest of Writers, have no great respect for
my close way of Reasoning.

Montaigne.   Really, Mr: Lock, I should flatter You, if I said I had. One [195]
may read your Book over as the Irish Man eat Whipt Cream, and
when they asked him what he had been doing, he said he had been
tasting a great Nothing. All the while you wrote you were only
thinking that You thought; You, and Your understanding are the
Personæ Dramatis, and the whole amounts to no more than a Dia- [200]
logue between John and Lock.

> As I walked by my Self
> I talked to my Self,
> And my Self said unto me.

You seem, in my poor apprehension, to go to and fro upon a [205]
Philosophical Swing like a Child upon a wooden Horse always in

---

189 them] *L 26* You *L 25 (154)*   192 Pastry Cook] *L 26* Fishmonger *L 25 (154)*
193 loosest *L 25 (154), L 26* : losest *L 25 (117)*

motion but without any Progress, and to Act as if a Man instead of Practising his Trade should spend all his Life in Naming his Tools.

Lock. *Pian Piano*, good Seigneur, one must be able to Name one's 210 Tools before one Learns the use of them, But, if a Man does not leap Hedge and Ditch, in your Opinion, he stands stock stil. I begin, continue, and always keep close to my Subject, the Human Understanding.

Montaigne. That's the very thing I object to, I think you keep so 215 close to your Subject, that You have spoilt your Book. When You have set your Self in your Metaphysical Goe-cart, in order to step sure, You walk too Slow to rid any Ground; and as soon as you are out of it, you commonly mistake Your way. The least things must be Demonstrated to You where No Body could doubt of them, and 220 when ever (which is indeed most commonly) such Proof is want-ing, You take the whole upon Trust, without the previous Examination, which any other reasonable Man would make. You strain, as the Proverb says, at a Gnat, and Swallow a Camel, not giving a Just allowance to Probability, You sink between two 225 Extreams, and when You are not Supported by Evident Demon-stration You fall into the greatest Credulity imaginable. The Identity of the same Man consists in a participation of the same continued life by constantly fleeting particles of Matter in Suc-cession Vitally United to the same Organized Body. So that an 230 Embryo is not a Person of One and Twenty. Ismael is not Socrates, Pilate is not St Austin. Who Questions any thing of this, good Mr Lock, yet, by the way, Cæsar who led to Battle many thousand of these Organized Bodies, Cicero who could appease or Excite them in the Senate, Bartholin, who could tell You how these 235 Particles lay in relation to each other, and from thence what Remedies were to be applyed to the several Deseases and Violences they Suffered, Spencer, who could describe 'em all in Mythological words, and Raphael who could imitate them in Animated Colors: All these I say, neither Thought or Acted in Virtue of Your 240 Definition, and if they did would not have performed any thing better in their Several Arts and Sciences. So again the Chess-men standing upon those Squares of the Board where we placed them,

220 could doubt] *L 25 (154)* could have doubt *L 26*   231 One and Twenty] *L 26 21 L 25 (154)*   232 Austin. Who *L 26* : Austin, who *L 25 (117) & (154)*   240 Your *edd.* : You *L 25 (117)* : your *L 25 (154), L 26*   243 those] *L 26* the same *L 25 (154)*

thô the Chess board be carryed out of one Room into another are Stil Said to Remain in the same place, and the Chess board is Stil said to be in the same place it was, If it remains in the same part of the Cabin, thô perhaps the Ship it is in, Sails all the while, and the Ship is stil in the same place, supposing it kept the same Distance with the parts of the Neighboring Land, thô perhaps the Earth has turned round, and So both Chess Men and Board and Ship have every one changed place in respect of remoter Bodies, which have kept the same Distance one with another, and So on to the end of the Chapter. Who ever Denyed one word of all this? And do You think now that You have explaind what motion and repose is, so as to do any good to Mankind. Archimedes found out the Burning-glass, Jacob Metius the Tellescope, Sanctorius the Thermometre, and Flavio Goia the Compass, without Consulting or being guided by any sort of Verbiage like this, and I dare Swear neither Christopher Colombo nor Francis Drake ever reasoned one half hour if their Chess Board was in Motion in relation to their Cabin, or their Cabin in regard to the Ship, all the while they were Sailing round the World and adding a fourth part to what was known of it before.

Lock.   But when in the Name of Patience shal I have Liberty to Reply?

Montaigne.   Immediately, as soon as I have waked Your Ideas into a remembrance that You tell Us upon the Orginazation of the Body, That Prince Maurice had an Old Parot in Brazil who Spoke and Asked and Answered Questions like a reasonable Creature, who told the Prince he knew him to be a General, that he himself belonged to a Portuguese, that he came from Marinnan, and that his imployment was to keep the Chickens. Now who ever believed this but Sir William Temple and your Self? And then again upon the rules of Motion, That a Young Gentleman who had learned to Dance, in great perfection in the Garret, where an Old Trunk Stood, could never as much as cut one Caper, rightly in any other room, unless that Trunk or another exceeding like it, was set in the same position, So that the Man rather Danced to the Trunk than to the Violin. Parbleu, Squire Lock, I appeal to all Mankind,

244–5 thô . . . place,] L 26 are said to be in the same place thô the board it self be carryed out of one Rome into another L 25 (154)   246 said to be] L 26 om. L 25 (154) remains] L 25 (154) remain L 26   249 parts] L 25 (154)part L 26   257 Flavio edd.: Flavi L 25 (117): Flavia L 26: Last letter blotted in L 25 (154)   261 were] L 26 and L 25 (154)   262 fourth L 26: forth L 25 (117) & (154)   267 who] L 26 that L 25 (154)   268 Creature L 25 (154), L 26: Cretaure L 25 (117)   who] L 26 that L 25 (154)   275 could] L 26 but could L 25 (154)

if I ever said any thing so extravagant as this in my Chapter of the
force of Imagination in Man and Beasts. 280

Lock. How this Gascon runs away with things, I do not say I have the
exact *Criterion veritatis*, but I Search it. I dont pretend to Infallibility, but as much as I can I endeavor to avoid Error, and since it
is only by my understanding that I can judge of other things, It is
proper in order to that end that I make that understanding first 285
Judge of it self.

Montaigne. There is a Je ne-scay quoy in those words that affords me
but little Satisfaction. But you Metaphysicians think with too
much Subtilty to be pleased with what is natural.

Lock. Natural, why is any thing plainer then what I said? I Studied 290
to know my Self, *Nosce Te ipsum*. You love Authority, and I might
quote it as the saying of one of the Wise Men of Greece.

Montaigne. I understand You now, Mr Lock, but I no more respect
it (as much as You think I love Authority) for being meerly the
saying of One of the wise Men of Greece than if it had been of One 295
of the Seven Wise Masters of Rome, or the Seven Champions of
Christendom: The Truth of the saying must Justify the Author.

Lock. But according to Your own way, has the Maxim weight with
it, without any regard to Authority? Should not a Man know
himself? Answer Directly. 300

Montaigne. I will, Sir, and in the Saying of another wise Man, of
what Country not three Straws matter, he that does not talk with
a Wiser Man than himself may happen to Dye Ignorant. Really
who ever writes in Folio should convince people that he knows
something besides himself, else few would read his Book, except 305
his very particular Friends.

Lock. I will give You up as many as you please of those particular
Friends, provided the few, be they my Friends or no, that can
think consequentially, and reason justly upon Premises, approve
my Writings; in one word I do not write to the Vulgar. 310

Montaigne. And they are the only People that should be writ to.
Not write to the Vulgar quoth Thou, Egad the Vulgar are the
only Scholars, If they had not taught us we had been Stupid. The
Observations made by Shephards in Egypt and Chaldea gave Birth

---

279 I ever] *L 25 (154)* ever I *L 26*　　　285 that end *L 25 (154)*: that, and *L 25 (117)*: that,
L 26　　　290 said? *L 26*: said, *L 25 (117)*: said *L 25 (154)*　　　291 *ipsum. L 26*: *ipsum*
L 25 (117) & *(154)*　　　293 I no] *L 25 (154)* I do no *L 26*　　　295 One of the wise]
L 25 (154) the Wise *L 26*　　　297 Author. *L 25 (154)*, *L 26*: Author *L 25 (117)*
300 Directly *L 25 (154)*, *L 26*: Dircetly *L 25 (117)*

to Geometry and Astronomy. The variety of sound from the 315
Hammers of Smiths striking on their Anvil was the Original of the
Scale of Music, and some traces made on the Sand by a poor Cow-
herd gave the first Idea of Painting. Homer and Virgil will scarse
be exempted from the Company of the Vulgar, if One went a
begging thrô all Greece and composed his Iliads for his Bread, and 320
'tother, the Son of a Potter at Mantua, came on foot to Rome, to
Solicite the favor of Augustus. Was not Gun powder Invented by
a Poor Monk at Nuremberg, and Printing by an Inferior Tradesman at Haerlem? Look thrô your Microscopes and know, that
Lewinhoeck that brought them to such Perfection was a Glasier, 325
and when You next Set Your Watch remember that Tompion was
a farrier, and began his great Knowledge in the Equation of time
by Regulating the Wheels of a common Jack, to roast meat. Nay
faith, the Vulgar are the only Criticks too, for what is praise but
the Universal Collection of their Consent, and whence can that 330
consent be Derived but from their understanding our Writings.
Esop and Epictetus had more Sense than their Masters. Sophocles
shewed his Tragedies to his Maid. Since our time Racine, said, he
doubted of the Success of his Phædra till his Coachman told him
he liked the Character of Hypolitus, and Boileau, addresses one of 335
his Epistles to Antoine his Fav'rite Gardiner. In short I am one of
those Vulgar for whom You say You do not write, and in the Name
of our whole Community, I take leave to tell You I think You have
wronged both Us and Your Subject.

Lock.   You are not Serious when You say this?   340

Montaigne.   As ever I was in my life, and so I go on, Mr: Lock, Your
Mind was given You for the Conduct of your Life, not meerly for
Your own Speculation; nor should it be imployed only upon it self,
but upon other things. I think we Should take our Understanding
as Providence hath given it to us, upon Content, As we would do 345
a handsom Summ of Money, sent us by a good Friend; and spend
our time rather in making use of it than in counting it. A Man
should live with his *Alma* (as Friend Prior calls her) as he would
do with his Wife, having taken her for Better and for Worse. He
should be civil to her, keep her in good humor, but not cut her 350

315 Geometry and] *L 26 om. L 25 (154)*   316–17 the Scale] *L 25 (154)* their Scale *L 26*
317 made] *L 25 (154) om. L 26*   324 Microscopes *L 25 (154), L 26 :* Miscroscopes
L 25 (117)   329 for *L 25 (154), L 26 :* but *L 25 (117)*   333 Tragedies *L 25 (154),*
L 26 : Trgedies *L 25 (117)*   337 You say] *L 26 om. L 25 (154)*   344 Understanding]
L 26 Understandings *L 25 (154)*   345 would] *L 25 (154)* could *L 26*

up like an Anatomy to show the Situation of her parts, and read
Lectures upon the Soundness or Defects of her Intrails. If You are
always tugging at Your Purse Strings, you may chance to break
them, and if you turn and tumble the Purse it self, At last You will
drop Your Money out of it. What occasion have you for a Tongue 355
if you are to talk for ever to your Self. If you were always poking
your Fingers into your Eyes, You would hardly See the Clearer,
and if again your Eyes were continually endeavoring to look one
upon Another, you would only get a habit of Squinting. If you be
stil trying to See your own back, you might one time or other 360
break your Neck. Don't be angry with me, Lock, if in my odd
way of Imaging things I have often thought that a Metaphysician
running in a Circle after his own understanding, is like a Dog
turning round and endeavoring to catch his own Taile:, if he cannot take hold of it he grows giddy, and when ever he does, he bites 365
it, and it hurts him, and so he lets it go again.

Lock.   That last Simile indeed was a little Ludicrous.

Montaigne.   I will give You another more Serious, while I repeat to
You that Your own Mind (in the manner You consider it) is too
near You. It is like some uncouth Figures and Colors laid together 370
unparted and unformed, If you look upon the whole too closely;
but if You view it in a due Medium thrô the Cylinder opposed
to it, the rays rise up to their just Dimension, and Shew You something plain and Intelligible.

Lock.   Simile upon Simile, no Consequential Proof, right Montaigne 375
by my Troth. Why, Sir, you catch at Similes as a Swallow does at
Flies.

Montaigne.   And You make Similes while You blame them. But be
that as it will, Mr Lock, arguing by Simile is not so absurd as some
of You dry Reasoners would make People believe. If Your Simile 380
be proper and good, it is at once a full proof, and a lively Illustra-
tion of Your matter, and where it does not hold, the very disproportion gives You Occasion to reconsider it, and You set it in
all it's lights, if it be only to find at least how unlike it is. Egad
Simile is the very Algebra of Discourse.   385

361 Don't *L 25 (154)*: dont *L 25 (117)*: Dont *L 26*   364 Taile] *L 25 (154)* Tailes *L 26*
366 again. *L 25 (154)*, *L 26*: again *L 25 (117)*   368 Montaigne *L 26*: Mont *L 25 (117)*
& *(154) From this point* Montaigne *is spelled out in accordance with L 26 whenever L 25
(117) abbreviates*   370-1 together unparted] *L 26* together seemingly unparted *L 25
(154)*   372 in . . . thrô] *L 26* through . . . in *L 25 (154)*   374 Intelligible.
L 26: Intelligible *L 25 (117)* & *(154)*   376 a Swallow] *L 25 (154)* Swallows *L 26*
378 But *edd.*: but *L 25 (117)* & *(154)*, *L 26*

Lock.   Let me therefore Answer You in your own way, and give You
back your Cylinder, while I take the Liberty to tell you that the
Glass I looked into, was a fair true Mirour, and rightly placed.

Montaigne.   Let the Glass be of what Figure You please, if You presented nothing before it but Your own Dear Person, what could 390
you See but what flattered the Foppery of Youth, and at last
Shewed only the Decays and wrinkles of Age.

Lock.   And ¡pray, Sir, inform us a little into what Glass did You
look?

Montaigne.   Into the great Miror of the World, where I saw the Uni- 395
versal face of Nature, and the Images of all Objects that the Eye
can possibly take in. I pursued the human Mind thrô all her lurking holes, and Retreats, the Prevention of Education, the Mimickry
of Habitudes, and the power of Custom, I represented Ignorance
and folly in their Native Colors, I gave just encouragement thrô 400
all my Writings to plain Honesty and to open Honor. Showed very
often, as I said just now, how our Vanity might contribute to our
Virtue. I endeavored to find the Medium between the Aversion to
Pain and love of Pleasure, to mingle our hopes and fears So in their
just temperature of what we will at present call Prudence, that if 405
my thought could not enjoy full Satisfaction, it might at least find
the Evils of Life Diminished. I drew together the Reflections,
which Courts, Camps, Cities and Nations presented unto me.
Gave You fairly my Opinion of Emperors and Law Givers, Soldiers
and Philosophers. I contemplated the Situation of Earths and Seas, 410
The Revolutions of the Sun, the different Motions and Operations
of the Stars, and from the works of Nature, and my Observations
upon them, I deduced the Being, and forced my Reader to own the
Power of a Diety. Yet, all this while, I durst not pretend to fix the
bounds of Truth and Error, at least I thought that could not be 415
done by a set of words. It must rather depend, as I concluded, upon
Experience or at least Probability. I gave the World my Writings,
as the effects only of my own Meditation, Rather what I my self
thought than what other Men should think, and was always So
far from setting up for an Instructor, that (as I have often said) I 420
was ready to alter my Opinion as I might be better Instructed by

392 Decays] *L 25 (154)* decay *L 26*   398 Mimickry] *L 25 (154)* Mimicking *L 26*
399 Habitudes] *L 25 (154)* habitude *L 26*   401 and to] *L 26* and *L 25 (154)*   402
often, . . . now, how *L 26* : often . . . now how *L 25 (117)* : often how *L 25 (154)*   403
the Aversion] *L 26* aversion *L 25 (154)*   407 Evils] *L 25 (154)* Evil *L 26*   408 unto]
L 26 to *L 25 (154)*   418 Meditation,] *L 25 (154)* Meditations; *L 26*

the Discourses or Writings of any of my Friends. This was my
manner of thinking. Now, Sir, as at the beginning of our Discourse
we had some of Your Axiomes, will You let Me here give You half
a Dozen of mine?   425

Lock. As You please, Sir, I have Patience, and You love talking.

Montaigne. As to our Selves first, Opinion and Custom do every thing,
Divide us into Sects, make Laws and Govern our Lives. Our Wishes
contemn what is easy and near, and aspire to what is forbid or hard
to come at, and whilst we desire what is not in our Possession we   430
less enjoy that which is. Our chief Business in life is to learn to bear
the ills of it. He that fears to Suffer, suffers already what he fears,
or would you have it in other words, He that dreads Punishment
already Suffers it, and he that merits it, must always dread it.
Again we are always beyond our selves, fear, Desire, hope, throw   435
us forward into futurity, and take away our Sense of what is to
amuse us, with what shal be, and that too possibly when we cannot
perceive it. We should neither fly nor follow Pleasures, but take
them as they come. There is no pleasure so just and Lawfull but
is blamable if used in Intemperance or Excess. Have You composed   440
Your own Manners, and lived as You ought to do with Your
Neighbors? You have done more than he who has written Volumes
or taken Cities. To be honest is the end and Design of our Life. To
heap up, to Build, to Conquer, to Reign are things only Accidental
and Secondary. A Lie is below the Dignity of Human Nature. As   445
we are distinguishd from other Creatures by Speech, the very bond
of our Society is tyed by the Truth of our Words. If Falshood, like
Truth, had but one face, how happy should we be. We should take
that for certain, which was directly contrary to what the Liar
(if we thought him such) said. But, alas! Error has fifty Deviating 450
Paths, whereas there is but one Road directly Right. Of Valor
now; who could say better than this, Valor has its Limits as well
as other Virtues, and foolhardiness is as great a Vice as Cowardise.
Of Civility; The greatest Civility is sometimes Shown in being
less Ceremonius. I have seen People impertinent by too much   455
good Manners, and troublesome with the greatest Decorum. As to
Government; the Notion of Liberty in a Common Wealth hath the
same effect upon a Man born under that Rule, As the Glory of the

431 Our *L 25 (154), L 26*: our *L 25 (117)*   437 with] *L 26* to *L 25 (154)*   441
lived] *L 26* Live *L 25 (154)*   442 Neighbors? You have] Neighbors. You have *L 25*
(154): Neighbor? have you [have *crossed through*] *L 26*   443 our] *L 26* your *L 25 (154)*
458 Rule, *edd.*: Rule. *L 25 (117)*: rule, *L 25 (154), L 26*

King has upon one born in an Absolute Monarchy; and every Man
Loves and speaks well of the Country where he was born, and 460
sucked in his first Notions, be it France or Tartary. Hence it is that
after all our Travells thrô the World we Desire to come and Dye
at home. As to Science; Plants may be Killed with too plentifull
Nourishment, and Lamps Extinguisht by too great a supply of
Oyle; We may have so much Science that it may confound our 465
Judgment. It is not enough to Know the Theory of things without
being able to put them in Practice. In the Commerce of Life instead
of Desiring to learn from others we are only seeking to make our
Selves known, and are more in Pain to put off our Old Merchandise
than to endeavor to acquire any New. Of Solitude; It is in vain that 470
we retire from the World if we carry our faults with Us, Our Vanity
and our Avarice may follow us where ever we go. No Retreat, no
Cloyster, no Desert can exclude them: To enable us to live in true
Solitude we must make our Satisfaction depend upon our Selves:
We should do well sometimes to fancy we had no Family, no 475
Wealth, no Relations, no Servants, that if any of those Losses
happen to Us, they may not appear new. What think you of my
Contemplations upon Death? Things sometimes appear greater
to Us as they are farther off. In health I have apprehended the
thoughts of Sickness with more horror than I have felt it; go out 480
of the World as you came into it, without Passion and without fear.
Your Death is one part of the Universal Order of Nature, and every
Day You have lived was only to bring you nearer to that in which
You must Dye. Can you think You must never arrive at that place
towards which You are always going. Comfort Your self, You have 485
good Company in the way. A thousand Men and ten thousand
Animals Dye in the very same moment with You. Now for two or
three things I have Said of Princes, the Advantages of the great
are mostly imaginary, the Inconveniences and hindrances of Life,
which they must Suffer are reall; while every Man naturally hates 490
to be watched and Spyed, They are the only People that must yield
to this Subjection. Every Subject thinks he has a right to observe
even the Countenance and thoughts of his Prince, and the Master

---

463 plentifull] *L 26* much *L 25 (154)*.   465 confound] *L 26* destroy *L 25 (154)*   470
New. Of] *L 26* new. And another observation Nothing is so firmly believed as that of which
we know the least. Of *L 25 (154)*   476 Losses *L 25 (154), L 26 :* Loses *L 25 (117)*
477 happen ... may] *L 26* should happen ... should *L 25 (154)*   485 going.] *L 25 (154)*
a going? *L 26*   486 way. *L 26 :* way *L 25 (117) & (154)*   489 Inconveniences]
L 26 Inconveniencies *L 25 (154)*   493 thoughts] *L 26* thought *L 25 (154)*

dares not blame but must thank him for his Care. If Princes would begin to retrench from Luxury, and live with Sobriety and Mode- 495 ration there would be no Occasion for Sumptuary Laws: In a Month the Court would imitate the King, and the People in a Year would imitate the Court: Virtue would soon be Practised as it became fashionable. We owe our Submission and Obedience to Kings whether They be good or Bad. This regards their Dignity 500 and Office, But we give them our Esteem and Affection in proportion only to their Merit and Virtue. The Lives of Princes are subject to be Examined after their Death, The Justice which cannot be obtained against their Persons is with great Reason Executed upon their Reputation. Would You have any more, Mr Lock, 505 Mort de ma Vie, Why You are fast asleep! Man.

Lock.   I might continue so 'till to morrow Morning, and when I wake I might find You stil walking up Stairs in Buskins. Ay, Sir, and all this, and fifty times more of fifty sorts, all jumbled all Pindaric, All Lucrecius' his World. One Chapter is of Friendship; the next 510 of Nine and Twenty Songs of Boetius; One of Moderation; the next of Canibals. From the use of Clothing away we Scud to a Character of Cato Junior, and from remarks upon Virgil to a Dissertation concerning Coaches. This leaf is upon Experience, turn it but over, you are upon Phisionomy and among lame People. 515 Here is the Resemblance that Children have to their Fathers, and there a Defence of Seneca and Plutarch; In short no Man ever dreamt so wildly as You have writ, without the least regard to Method. This, Chanet, very justly charges you with in his Treatise of the Operations of the understanding, When he tells 520 you, that, whereas every Judicious Man Studys Order, there is nothing but Confusion in your whole Book. Pere Malbranch I think strikes you home, and Scaliger—

Montaigne.   Scaliger, was a Pedant that thought himself a Prince. Chanet and Malbranch were People of your own Trade, meer 525 Mataphysicians, Yet disagreeing in their Notions; The Priest condemns me but to shew his judgment: it is with Seneca and Tertullian, good Company however: t'other accuses me only for want of Method, the thing in which I glory. I have observed that there

499 owe] *L 26 om. L 25 (154)*   510 All Lucrecius' his] *L 25 (154)* all like Lucretius *L 26* 512 Scud] *L 26* Skip *L 25 (154), Alt. reading in L 25 (117)*   515 upon] *L 26* in *L 25 (154)* among] *L 26 om. L 25 (154)*   518 so *L 25 (154), L 26 :* to *L 25 (117)*   523 Scaliger *L 26 :* Scalinger *L 25 (117) :* Schalinger *L 25 (154)*   527 judgment: *edd. :* judgment *L 25* *(117) :* Jugemt *L 25 (154) :* Judgment: *L 26*

is Abcedarian Ignorance that precedes Knowledge, and a Doctoral 530
Ignorance that comes after it. A Man that writes freely, as I do, as
he is in danger to be persecuted by them both, ought to have the
courage to Dispise them both. Method! our Life is too short for it.
The general rules even of Morality are commonly too long and
tedious. How many young Scholars have been Debauched before 535
they have gone thrô Aristotles Precepts upon Temperance; And
how many more might have fallen into the worst Excess imaginable before they had quite read o'er Plato's Dialogues between
Socrates and his Pupil Alcibiades. Method in the Sense you mean
it, is the thing I contemn; Tis poor 'tis little: I put my thoughts 540
down, just as they occurred to me. Could I have better Method
than that which the course of my life gave me, and the order of
things as they presented themselves to my view. How would You
have had me range them. Is it not the variety it self that pleases
while it instructs: If the Black, the White, the Red and the green 545
were laid upon distinct parts of the Canvas where would be the
Harmony of Coloring, or the *tout ensemble* of the Picture. You may
See the Painters Method upon his Palette, but he contemns it when
he would Shew his Science. If all your Lillies were Collected together in one bed next your House, then all your Roses in an other, 550
and all your Sun flowers in a Third, Who would admire the Beauty
of your Garden? However your Picture and your Garden are stil
the effects of Art, and art her self is gross and poor where her ways
of Working are seen, She appears most Lovely where She most
Imitates her Mistress Nature: but Contemplate the great Goddess 555
her Self *Ipsa suis pollens opibus*: Hills, Cities, Woods, Rivers so Situate
that the irregularity makes the beauty of the Prospect, and at
Night consider the Copes of Heaven glorious with Myriads of
Stars, not set in Ranks, spread into Squares or Circled in rounds,
but all Shining in a Beautiful Superiority to Number and Order. 560

Lock.   O! brave Seigneur of Gascony, why this was a most noble rant;
        thô, by the by, the last part of it was Stolen from my Lord Bacon.

Montaigne.   It may be so, and he perhaps took it from Petrarch, and
        Petrarch borrowed it from Cicero, and Cicero again might have it
        from Socrates, and Socrates from David. If I am in the Possession 565
        of a Medal or a Jewel, what care I if it came out of the Arundel

530 is Abcedarian] *L 25 (154)* is an Abcidarian *L 26*   536 Aristotles *L 25 (154)*, *L 26* :
Aristoles *L 25 (117)*   537 worst *L 26* : worse *L 25 (117)* & *(154)*   550 then
L 25 (154), *L 26* : than *L 25 (117)*   556 opibus: *L 26* : opibus *L 25 (117)* : opibus.
L 25 (154)

Collection, was taken by the Duke of Bourbon in the plunder of
the Vatican, If Irene wore it in her Bulla, or even if Memmius
brought it to Rome from Corinth. Truth and reason lye in common
to all the World like Air and Water.   570

Lock.   Hola, good Seigneur, I remember You have sayd, and indeed
I liked the saying till I find you now contradict it, that we Praise
no Creature besides our Selves except for his Natural qualities and
endowments. We commend a Horse for being Vigorous and handsom, not for the fineness of His Harness or Caparisons, a Grey- 575
hound for his Swiftness, not for the Richness of his Collar, and
a Hawk for his Wing, not for his Gesses or his Bells. But we dont,
say You, do the same in regard to Man. He has a Magnificent
Palace, rich Equipage or fine Cloaths, alas! these are things about
him, but not in him. Now apply this to your way of Writing (the 580
point to which with much ado I have brought You). Montaign
has noble Ideas, but they are taken from Plato, fine Stories but
from Plutarch, great Expression but from Tully and Seneca, and
right Quotation but from Horace and Virgil, now do any of these
Excellencies any more belong to You, than the Harness to Your 585
Horse, the Collar to Your Greyhound, or the Gesses to Your
Hawk? and would it not follow that if Plato, Plutarch, Cicero,
Seneca, Horace and Virgil should each reclaim his own, Montaign
hath writ no Book, Speak, Sir, Answer me Logically, You are not
used to Pause for a Reply.   590

Montaigne.   Faith I think he has me a little upon the hipp, with
his Logic, where one cannot perfectly Excuse, all one can do is
to recriminate. You know, Sir, I never was a great admirer of
Logic, no friend to Your Ergoismes. I have told the World more
than once that I had rather be a good Horseman, than a Subtile 595
Logician. You begin, as I said to You, just now, with propositions
which no Body Denies, and go on to prove Paradoxes, which
no body will admit. A Man is not a flitch of Bacon, Concedo.
Montaign did not write his own Book, Nego, without the least
regard to Bocardo or Baralipton. Can I answer your Objection 600

567 was] *L 25 (154)* or was *L 26*   568 Vatican, *L 25 (154)*: Vatican *L 25 (117)*: Vatican. *L 26*   571 have sayd] *L 26* say *L 25 (154)*   572 find you now] *L 25 (154)*
now find you *L 26*   573 no Creature] *L 26* no other Creature *L 25 (154)*   577
Gesses] *L 26* Tassels *L 25 (154)*   580 (the *L 26*: (, the *L 25 (117)*: the *L 25 (154)*
581 You). *edd.*: You.) *L 25 (117)*: You. *L 25 (154)*: You] *L 26*   584 now] *L 26* but
L 25 (154)   586 Gesses] *L 26* Tassels *L 25 (154)*   589 hath] *L 26* has *L 25 (154)*
594 have] *L 26 om. L 25 (154)*   599 Nego, *L 26*: Nego. *L 25 (117) & (154)*
600 Can *L 26*: can *L 25 (117) & (154)*   Objection] *L 25 (154)* Question *L 26*

fairer than by returning Your Question, who did write Mr: Locks Book?

Lock.   Why, Mr: Lock himself, I tell my Readers almost at the Beginning of it, that I spin my Work out of my own thoughts.

Montaigne.   Spin! so does a Spider out of her own Bowels; and yet a ⁶⁰⁵ Cobweb is good for Nothing else that I know of but to catch flies, and Stanch cut Thumbs. I am so far from concealing what you seem to call Thefts that I glory in them. I have made other Mens thoughts my own, and given them to the World in greater Beauty than I received them from their Authors. Let me be Compared to ⁶¹⁰ a Bee, who takes Something from every Flower and Shrub, and by that various Labour collects one of the greatest Ingredients of Human health, and the very Emblem of Plenty. But to come nearer to You, Mr: Lock, You like many other Writers, Deceive your Self in this Point, and as much a Spider as you fancy your Self, You ⁶¹⁵ very often cast your Webb upon other Mens Textures.

Lock.   What then? I make the work my own, by not knowing it was Theirs. What ever may have been Written by others, if I have not read their Books, what I write is as much my own Invention as if no Man had thought the Same thing before me. But you, Sir, have ⁶²⁰ only to go to Your common place Book, find out some Excerpta, and—

Montaigne.   Why the best One can do is but to compose, I hope you do not pretend to Create.

Lock.   I tell You what I write is my own, Yours is at best but compila- ⁶²⁵ tion.

Montaigne.   Why there is another Mistake now, a trick which your own Understanding puts upon You. Your Ideas, as you call them, however you have endeavored to set them right, were so mixed and Blended, long before You began to write, in the great Variety ⁶³⁰ of things that fall under their Cognizance that it was impossible for You to Distinguish what you Invented from what You Remembered. Plato says that all Knowledge is only reminiscence, and a Wiser Man than he, that there was nothing new under the Sun: Besides this, my good Mr: Lock, Self Love, natural Vanity, and ⁶³⁵ desire of Acquisition help us extremly in these Sorts of Thefts. In the Bounding our Estates, or at least in the fixing our Wishes in

608 seem to] *L 25 (154) om. L 26*   621 Book, *L 25 (154)* : Book. *L 25 (117)* : book, *L 26*
631 fall] *L 25 (154)* fell *L 26*   636 Sorts] *L 25 (154)* sort *L 26*   637 In *L 26* : in
L 25 (117) & (154)   637–8 or ... Estates,] *L 25 (154) om. L 26*

regard to those Estates, we are Pretty partial to our selves. Our Neighbors Acre on the left hand, if taken in, would make our Garden on that Side, Square; And if the Wood on the right could 640 be added to our Grove, that Improvement would give it perfect Symetry and Beauty. Thô here the Civil power has already determined what is ours and what is not. But as to the Extent of our Knowledge, where neither Nature nor Law has made any Prescription, and human Curiosity is stil pressing forward, we take all that 645 comes fairly in our way, and either think it Originally our own, or at least not trouble our Selves whose it was before it came into our Possession. Descartes in the middle of the Joy he felt when he was certain he doubted of every thing and only knew his own Ignorance, was just in the same piteous estate where Pyrrho found 650 himself two thousand Year before; And when he gave Us his Subtil matter he only new Christened Aristotle's Materia Prima. Gassendi and Rohault are but Epicurus and Lucretius revived. As to your Self, Mr: Lock, You have either Copied Pritty Servilly from your Predecessors, or happened not only upon their thoughts 655 but their Method, (of which you are so fond). You seem to me to have worked in the Same frame with Dun Scotus, Swarez and Baronius, nay faith honest Smiglesius and even Burgerdicius may come in for a Snack with my Landlord. But these petty Larcenarys you System makers confess the last of any Men, 'till you are con- 660 tradicted the Book is all your own, and one continued Scheme. But when you are pressed You call Freinds of all kinds to your Assistance: while Malbranch writes against the force of Imagination, and the impression which things too lively Painted may make upon our Judgment, his Discourse is filled with that very Imagery and 665 Painting, from which he Deswades us, and the Strength of his Argument consists in the beauty of his Figures; and when you Seem to have least regard to Orators and Poets you have recourse to both for your very turn of Style and manner of Expression. Parblew Mr. Lock, when You had writ half your Book in favor of 670 your own Dear Understanding You quote Cicero to prove the very Existence of a God.

649 certain he] *L 26* certain that He *L 25 (154)*   649–50 and . . . Ignorance,] *L 26 om.* *L 25 (154)*   650 where] *L 25 (154) om. L 26*   651 Year] *L 25 (154)* Years *L 26* 662 Freinds of all kinds] *L 26* in as many as you can of your Brother Philosophers *L 25 (154)* 663–8 while . . . regard to] *L 26* Nay sometimes when You are talking against *L 25 (154)* 669 turn . . . manner of] *L 26* Figure and *L 25 (154)*   670 Parblew Mr. Lock,] *L 26 om. L 25 (154)*   671 quote Cicero] *L 26 Blotted in L 25 (154)*

Lock.   I am not to Answer for Malbranch but for my Self I make use
of Authors only as they come into my Subject, but I never go out
of my way to bring them in.   675
Montaigne.   I wont dispute that, but in my Opinion You write best
when You Steal most. When You contradict the Ancients You fall
into the very Error you blame. When You ask what more exquisite
Jargon could the Wit of Man invent than this Definition 'the Act
of being in Power as far forth as in power' within ten Pages you 680
give us as many Definitions less Intelligible, and what miserable
work do you make of it while you are Puzling Tully with the
Dutch mans telling what *Beweeging* was when Mynheer explains
it to him in Latin Actus entis in Potentiâ quatenus in Potentiâ?
Lock.   Well and is not it Nonsense?   685
Montaigne.   And is not it nonsense of your own Producing?
Lock.   I cite it only to prove the Absurdity of the Definition.
Montaigne.   And when ever I cite an Author it is to Show his Excellence: There is one Essential Difference now in our Two ways of
Writing.   690
Lock.   And faith to do you Justice what ever you write or find Written
by any Body else, you put it off with a most noble assurance. I
cannot but think it must have been a pleasant Scene enough to see
you come strutting by thrô the great Hall of your own Chateau in
the Perigord, while one of your Servants or Tenants Sons were 695
reading your Works with an Audible voice to the Country, who
came in to hear the Wisdom of the Seigneur de Montaigne Baylif
of Bordeaux. How truly they Spelt and pronounced the Names
Demetrius Poliorcetes, Publius Sulpitius Galba, and Albuquerque
Viceroy of Emanuel King of Portugal. All brought together as if 700
they had lived at the same time, and were as well acquainted as
the Three Kings of Cologn. How often the Reader Stopt and the
Audience Admired while you were pleased to Expound to them
your Quotations of Greek and Latin Sentences, Shreds of Ancient
Orations, and pieces of Broken Verses, The effect of a good Fathers 705
care, who taught you the Languages by Rote, and of a lively
Memory that retained a million of Idea's, and (as I said just now)
gave them out again with very little Jugement, Confused and

673 I . . . Self] *L 26 om. L 25 (154)*   679–80 'the . . . power' *edd.*: the . . . power.
L 25 (117): the . . . Power *L 25 (154)*: *the . . . Power*; *L 26*   694 by thrô] *L 25 (154)*
thro by *L 26*   699 Sulpitius *L 25 (154), L 26*: Sulpitius, *L 25 (117)*   702–3 the
Audience *L 25 (154)*: *om. L 25 (117), L 26*   706 Languages] *L 25 (154)* Language
L 26

promiscuous. True French by the way, and good Grammer some-
times wanting. Confess Seigneur that it must have been very 710
Theatrical; Your Dear self all the while the Hero of the Play. The
Descent of Your Family, Your Coat of Arms, the high Tower in
which you Lodged, the Page that waited on You, all faithfully
Represented, and your Dialogue with your Cat So recited that if
Laughter were not the incommunicable property of Man, Pus 715
might be really allowed to Smile upon so fantastic a Subject.

Montaigne. Why, faith, Mr: Lock, if You would have me, you must
take me altogether, Gallant or Debonnaire, Serious or Comical just
in the Humor I happened to be when I wrote; Too confident perhaps in the Strength of my own Natural parts, and too partial to 720
my own Vanities, yet free enough in Confessing my Defects, and
Submitting my Judgment to the Censure of my Friends. I dont
dislike what I heard one of your Countrymen said of me that by
the Style of many Authors he could imagine at least something
of their temper, and Guess at their Inclinations or Virtues, but 725
when he read Me he fancyed he knew my Person, and that he had
seen and converst with me in France thô I dyed above one hundred
Year before he was born. My Ideas as you observe are Confused
and promiscuous, but stil describing or Painting something, producing the Picture of my Self and a Thousand People more. But 730
Mr: Lock, your work is mere Grotesque, half Images of Centaures
and Sphinxes trailing into flowers and Branches, Satyrs and Masks
interlaced into Knotts with Cupids; all imperfect, and only so
joined that the Chain of the work is Stil continued: But however
since You are pleased to give the Comedy out of my Writings, I 735
am sure You will not take it ill if I furnish the Farce, the Petite
Piece, as we call it, out of Yours.

Suppose, Mr: Lock, You returned to your own Chamber from
the Business, the Visits, and pleasures of the Day. Your Night
gown on, Your Books before You. John, say you to Your Man, You 740
may go down and Sup, Shut the Door. John, who at his liesure
hours has been dabling in your Book, and consequently Admired
the Wisdom of it, reasons thus upon the matter. The Senses first
let in particular Ideas into the Sensorium, the Brain, or as my

---

709 True L 25 (154): true L 25 (117), L 26   713 the Page . . . faithfully] L 26 Your
Page all L 25 (154)   715 Pus] L 26 the Cat L 25 (154)   722–8 I dont . . . born.]
om. L 25 (154)   725 or] and L 26   728 Year] Years L 26   730 Thousand]
L 26 hundred L 25 (154)   738 Suppose, Mr: Lock,] L 26 Mr: Lock Suppose L 25 (154)
742 has] L 25 (154) had L 26

Master admirably expresses it to the Drawing Room, which are 745
from thence conveyed to the heitherto empty Cabinet of the
Mind, right! The vibration of the Air and it's Undulation Strike
the Tympanum of my Ear, and these Modifications being thus
Conveyed to my Sensorium, certain words in the English Language, (for no other do I understand) produce a determined Con- 750
ception. John You may go down and Sup; Shut the door. Now
John has been a common Appellative to Millions of Men, thrô
many Ages, from Apostles, Emperors, Doctors and Philosophers,
down to Butlers and Valets de Chambre and Persons of my
Quality; some of whom however Christened John, are commonly 755
called Jack, but pass for that; Now to none of these could my
Master Speak, for they are either Dead or Absent; it must therefore be to me; doubtful again: for my Masters own Name is John,
and being a Whimsical Person, he may probably talk to himself.
No, that cant be neither, for if he had Commanded himself, why 760
did he not obey himself: If he would go down why does he sit stil
in the Elbow-chair, 'twas certainly therefore meant to me *John*,
not to him *John*. Well then, go down and Sup, go down. Whither?
To the Centre of the Earth, there I may Sup with Fiends upon
Brimstone broth, to the bottom of the Thames, there I may Sup 765
with Cod and Mackerell, and as Hamlet says not Eat but be Eaten, To
the Coal hole or the Woodhouse, there indeed I may find what will
dress a Supper, but nothing else to the present purpose of my own
Supping. It must therefore be to the Kitching, and in this determined Sense I will receive my Masters kind Admonition. Now 770
again, you may go down, and Sup, why if I may, then I may not
go down, the liberty of my Volition being undetermined, and the
Action of going down quatenus going down being in it self indifferent to me. Ay! but you may go down and Sup, the Proposi-
tion seems Conjunctive, I cannot sup without going down, and 775
thô going down was indifferent, yet Supping is far from being So,
for I am really and Sensibly and feelingly hungry; Besides, you may
go down and Sup is not a bare permission but a Civiler command,
and thô I may chuse whether I will Sup or no when I am down,
yet I ought to go down when my Master enjoyns it in so obliging 780

745 it to] into *L 25 (154), L 26*   752 thrô] *L 25 (154)* these *L 26*   755 are *L 25
(154)*: and *L 25 (117), L 26*   762 the] *L 26* his *L 25 (154)*   764 upon] *L 25 (154)*
on *L 26*   765 Thames, *edd.*: Thames *L 25 (117) & (154)*: Thames? *L 26*   767 the
Woodhouse] *L 25 (154)* woodhouse *L 26*   777 and Sensibly] *L 26* sensibly *L 25 (154)*
hungry] *L 25 (154)* a Hungry *L 26*

a Manner; But now comes an Essential difficulty, which however
by right ratiotination I hope to overcome. John, you may go down,
and sup, Shut the Door, the Door I take to be a combination of
Planks in an Oblong Figure artfully compacted by the Skill of a
Carpenter, and set upon Compages, Hooks or Hinges of Iron or 785
Brass by the aditional Science and Labor of the Smith with a Lock
Aplicable to the Action which my Master enjoynes me of Shutting
it. This Action is to be determined by my Eye to find out this
Lock, and by my hand to touch it. But now again am I, as the
order in which the words are placed may import, first to go down 790
and Sup, and then to Shut the Door, no surely for in the mean time
there may come such a wind from the Stair head that my Master
may catch his Death before I have filled my Belly; there is certainly therefore an Anacronism or at least an unguarded trans-
position, in these words, the regular Conception of them must be 795
thus taken, not John go down and Sup, shut the Door, but John shut
the Door go down and Sup; well, so far I think I am right, but now
as to shutting the Door there is a Lock on the inside, there is a bolt
on the outside, which implys Two Modus's of performing this
Action: If I lock the Door on this side how the Devil can I go down 800
except I was a fairy and could creep thrô the Keyhole, If I bolt it
on the other side, I shut my Master in, which sure he could never
intend. Two Modus's I said there were, yet neither of these are
proper to the present purpose; there must therefore be a Third,
which I believe by a happy concurrence of Idea's I have found out, 805
that is, neither to Lock the Door on this side, nor to bolt it on the
t'other but to apply it as close as may be to the Doorcase, and to
leave it in that position, which I take to be Equivalent to what my
Master meant by the expression of Shutting the Door.

Lock.　Well, Sir, have you done with my Man?　　　　　　810

Montaigne.　Not quite, Mr Lock, I am bringing him to a Conference
　　with your Maid. Let us now imagine the Door Shut, and John
　　safely arrived in the Kitching, Margaret the Cook Maid sets the
　　cold Beef before Him, Robin the Butler gives Him a Bottle of
　　Strong Beer, and they proceed Amicably to the News of the Day, 815
　　If the Regent is at Madrid, or the King of Spain upon the Coast

---

786 and] *L 25 (154)* or *L 26*　　　788 This *L 26*: this *L 25 (117)* & *(154)*　　　789 am
L 26: am, *L 25 (117)* & *(154)*　　　　　　　798 on *L 25 (154)*: in *L 25 (117)*, *L 26*
inside, there] *L 25 (154)* inside, and there *L 26*　　　801 could] *L 25 (154)* would *L 26*
804 proper . . . purpose] *L 26* practicable *L 25 (154)*　　　806 nor] *L 25 (154)* or *L 26*
809 the Door. *L 26*: the Door *L 25 (117)*: *om. L 25 (154)*

of Scotland. If Digwell the Gardiner Stole two of Sir Thomas's Spoones, or the Match holds between my Lord Truemadams Coachman and Prue the Dairy maid. All this goes on the best in the World from point to point till John Stroking Trip, the Grehound, 820 says, to Margaret, do You think, Child, that a Dog, thô he can retain several Combinations of simple Ideas, can ever compound enlarge or make complex Idea's? Truly John, says Margrett I neither Know nor care. John Proceeds, and Margaret thô you have Stewed many a Barrel or quart of Oysters, You never 825 examined if an Oyster was capable of thinking, and tho you have seen many a hundred Old Men, You never found out that an Old Man who has lost his Senses is exceedingly like an Oyster, As like as he is to a rotten Apple says the Butler. John pittying the Butlers Ignorance continues his Discourse to the Maid, Do you believe 830 Margaret that there are any Original Characters impressed upon a Child in the Womb? Prethey John, replyes She, let us talk of our own Concerns, what have You or I to do with Children in the Womb? Stil John goes on; I would fain make you perceive Margaret, that my Body is a Solid Substance endued with an Extension of 835 parts, and that You have in your Body a Power of communicating Motion by impulse, that motion will produce an intense heat, and then again that heat—Look You John, says Margaret, I have often told You of this: When ever you get half Drunk you run on in this filthy baudy manner. Faith says the Butler, who was a little 840 envious at Johns Learning, thats e'en too true, John always was and will be a pragmatical Puppey. Puppy says John, in what Predicament do you place the human Species. Sirrah, Robin Answers in great Anger I scorn your words, I am neither Predicament nor Species any more than your Self; But I wont Stand by 845 and see my fellow Servant affronted. Here, Mr: Lock, you find, Bella plus quam Civilia. John and Margaret form their different Aliances, the whole Family is set into a flame by three leaves of Your own Book, and you may knock Your heart out for Your Boyled Chicken, and Your Roasted Apples.   850

818 Truemadams] Trulmadams *L 25 (154)*: True Madams *L 26*   823 Idea's? Truly *L 26*: Ideas's, truly *L 25 (117)*: Ideas, Truly *L 25 (154)*   824 Margaret] *L 25 (154)* *om. L 26*   825 or] *L 25 (154)* and *L 26*   827 hundred Old] *L 25 (154)* hundred of Old *L 26*   Men *L 26*: Man *L 25 (117) & (154)*   832 Womb? *edd.*: Womb, *L 25 (117) & (154)*: Womb. *L 26*   833 You] *L 26* Your *L 25 (154)*   834 Womb? *L 25 (154)*, *L 26*: Womb, *L 25 (117)*   Margaret, *L 26*: Margt: *L 25 (117)*: Margret *L 25 (154)*   841 thats *L 25 (154)*, *L 26*: that *L 25 (117)*   842 Puppey. *edd.*: Puppey, *L 25 (117)*: Puppy, *L 25 (154)*: Puppy. *L 26*

Lock. Well, Sir, and what is the Result of all this?

Montaigne. That probably neither Robin, John, Margrate You or I,
or any other five Persons alive have either the same Idea's of the
same thing, or the same way of Expressing them. The difference
of Temperament in the Body, Hot, Cold, Phlegmatic or hasty 855
create as Manifest a Variety in the Operations of our hands and
the Conduct of our Lives; and our Conceptions may be as various
as our faces, Bodies and Senses, or Sensations as you call them. If
I like Assafetida I say it has a good Smel, If you cant endure a Rose
you complain it Stinks. In our Taste, may not I nauseate the Food 860
which You Covet, and is it not even a Proverb that what is Meat
to one Man is Poyson to another. If we consider even the Fabric
of the Eye and the Rules of Optic, It can hardly be thought we see
the same; And yet no Words can express this Diversity. So that
there may be as much difference between your Conceptions and 865
mine, as there is between your Band and my Ruff. If so it may
happen I say, that if no Mans Ideas be perfectly the same Locks
Human Understanding may be fit only for the Meditation of Lock
himself, nay further that those very Ideas changing, Lock may be
led into a new Laberinth, or Sucked into another Vortex, and may 870
write a Second Book in order to disprove the first.

Lock. Ay, now I like You, we are come to the very State of the
Question.

Montaigne. Are we so my good Friend? Why then 'tis just time to
break off the Discourse.   875

Intended for Lock.

LOCK, wou'd the Human understanding Show;
    In vain he Squanders Thought and Time and Ink.
People themselves most certainly must know,
    Better than He cou'd tell, how they can think?

I fancy things may quickly be agreed,   5
    If once for All we state our notions right;
And I (thank gracious Heav'n) need never read
    One line that Thou, Friend Lock, did'st ever write.

852 You] *L 25 (154)* your *L 26*   869 changing, *L 26* : changing. *L 25 (117)* : changing
L 25 (154)   871 the] *L 26* His *L 25 (154)*   872 now I] *L 25 (154)* now Sir I *L 26*
Title] Verses intended for Lock & Montaigne '*Contents*' *of L 28*

Sic argumentum pono: if my head
 Had been exactly made, and fill'd like Thine, 10
I shou'd have known what ever thou had'st said
 Tho in Thy I had not read a line.

And if again, pray mind, Thy head and Mine
 Are form'd and Stuff'd quite diff'rent from each other;
I n'er shal understand one Single line, 15
 Thô I shou'd read thy Folio ten times over.

A Dialogue between the Vicar of Bray, and Sir Thomas More.

Vicar. Farewell then to the Dear Vicarage, 'tis gone at last. I held it
bravely out however, Let me see, from the twentieth of Henry the
Eighth, and I Dyed in the twenty-ninth of Elizabeth, just Seven
and Fifty Years; Attacked by Missals and Common Prayer, Acts
of Parliament opposed to Decrees of the Church, Mortuair'es in 5
the Legates Courts, and Præmunire's in Westminster-Hall, Canon
Law and Statutes, Oaths of Obedience to the See of Rome, and
of Supremacy to the King of England, Transubstantiation, real
Presence, Bulls and Premunires and that intricate question of
Divorces. But is not that my good Patron, Sir Thomas, who gave 10
me the Living, and charged the Clerks in his Office to take no
Fees for expediting the Writings, because I was Poor; Indeed I was
so then, but God be thanked, I took care of my Self after, as every
prudent Man should do: Aye, tis he indeed. O Dear Sir Thomas I
was very sorry for your Misfortunes; I was upon Tower-Hill when 15
You sav'd Your Beard, thô You lost Your head, but by our Lady
I did not like such Jesting. I saw you Executed. Oh that ugly Seam,
Sir; that remains stil about your Neck. O Sir a Head Sewed on
again never sits well. I pittyed You Sir, I prayed for You.

12 Thy [*blank*] I *edd.*: Thy I *L 28 (D)*: Thy work I *L 28 (Pope)*
 Title: *A Dialogue between L 26 : om. L 25 (176), L 25 (202) the Vicar . . . More.*] The
Vicar . . . *Moor. L 26 : om. L 25 (202)* 3 twenty-ninth *L 25 (202), L 26* : XXIX
L 25 (176) 4–6 Acts . . . Westminster-Hall,] *om. L 25 (202)* 5 Mortuair'es]
Mortmains *L 26* 6 Westminster-Hall, *L 26* : Westr. Hall *L 25 (176)* 8
Transubstantiation, *L 25 (202), L 26* : Transubstantiacion *L 25 (176)* 9–10 and that
. . . Divorces] *om. L 25 (202)* 10 Divorces. *L 26* : Divorces *L 25 (176)* 12
Writings] *L 25 (202)* Seals *L 26*

More. My Old Acquaintance, in good Truth, the Vicar of Bray very 20 well Friend, I am obliged to You for your Pitty and Your Prayers, but You would have heightned the Obligation had You appeared with Me upon the Scaffold. Your Spiritual Advice might have been of Service to Mee.

Vicar. O Lord, Sir, I would have been there with all my heart, but 25 You remember the Times were so ticklish, and that point of the Supremacy so Dangerous.

More. More Proper therefore for a Divine to have Assisted a Lay-man in so nice a Conjoncture.

Vicar. O, Lord help You, Sir, I thought You had known better than 30 that, (at least since your Death). No Sir, more proper therefore for a Lay-man to have left the nicety of such a Matter to Divines.

More. Well; And did not some of the Clergy suffer upon the same Account with Me?

Vicar. And were they the Wiser for so doing? the greatest part of us 35 were against your Suffering Doctrines, and, in good faith, We of the low Church thought it very Strange that with all your Law and Learning you should not have had Wit enough to keep your head upon your Shoulders.

More. It was that very Law and Learning that made me lay my head 40 down patiently on the Block. My knowledge in Divine and Human Law gave me to understand I was born a Subject to Both. That I was placed upon a Bench not only to expound those Laws to others, but obliged to Observe them my Self with an Inviolable Sanction. That in some cases the King Himself could not change 45 them. That I was commanded to Render to God the things that were of God, before I gave to Cæsar the things that are Cæsars, And when I was Accused upon a point, which I thought Strictly just, My Philosophy taught me to Dispise my Sufferings, and furnished me upon the Scaffold with the same Serenity of Mind 50 and pleasantness of Speech with which I was used to Decide Causes at Westminster-Hall, or Converse with my Friends in my Gardens at Chelsea.

Vicar. Aye, Sir Thomas but it is a sad thing to Dye.

20 Truth] *L 26* troth *L 25 (202)*   23 upon] *L 25 (202)* on *L 26*   28 More Proper] *L 26* Properer *L 25 (202)*   31 Death). *edd.*: Death) *L 25 (176)*, *L 26*: Death, *L 25 (202)*   more proper] *L 26* properer *L 25 (202)*   32 the . . . a] *L 26* that *L 25 (202)*   Divines. *L 26*: Divines *L 25 (176)* & *(202)*   33 Well;] *L 26 om. L 25 (202)* 36 in good faith,] *L 26* faith as to your own particular, *L 25 (202)*   54 Sir *L 25 (202)*, *L 26*: Sir, *L 25 (176)*

More. For ought Men know (I speak to Thee in the Language of 55
People yet alive) it was an uneasy thing to be Born, and for ought
they may know it will be no great Pain to dye. The Friend that
stands by in full health may probably suffer more real Anguish
then the Dying Man who raises His Compassion.

Vicar. Ay Sir Thomas but to Answer You in the same Language to 60
Dye as You did to See the Headsman with the Ax after the Law
had passed your Sentence and demanded the Execution of it.

More. No more than for the Patient to see the Apothecary bring the
Quieting Draught after the Physician has given him over.

Vicar. But that Pomp and Apparatus of Death, the Black cloth and 65
Coffin prepared, Your Relacions and Friends Surrounding You.
You cannot but remember, Sir, Your Dear Daughter Roper fol-
lowing that Father, who always—

More. Hold good Vicar, Ay there indeed you did touch me to the
Quick that beloved Daughter, Beautiful, Innocent, Learned, Pious, 70
That Pride of my Life, that Idol of my Thought, But yet Reason
and Religion soon got the better, and Armed Me as well against
the Softness of Human Nature as against the Apprehension of
Death. You See neither of these could as much as change or
Debase even my good Humor.   75

Vicar. But yet, Sir.

More. But again, but yet what?

Vicar. Why methinks there is a great deal of difference between Dying
and being put to Death. A Man must yeild to the call of Nature.

More. And can he resist the Decrees of Fate. A Man must do his Duty 80
what soever may be the Event of it: in the high Station wherein
I was placed I was keeper of the Kings Conscience, how then could
I possibly dispence with the Dictates of my own?

Vicar. That was a pleasant employment indeed. Keeper of a Mans
Conscience who never knew his own Mind half an Hour. What 85
could the Chancellor think should become of him; if he contra-

55–59] It is a Debt we must all pay to Nature, and some Years sooner or later makes little
difference in the Question compared with the Years either past or to come, which joined
together must make one Eternity for ought we know it was an uneasy thing to be born, and
for ought we may Know, we may not be Sensible of those Pangs of Death under which the
Standers by may think we labor. *L 25 (202)*   55–56 (I . . . alive) *L 26* : I . . . alive.
L 25 (176)   60 Ay . . . Language] *L 26* But *L 25 (202)*   62 Sentence and de-
manded] *L 25 (202)* Sentence stand and Demand *L 26*   it.] *L 25 (202)* it; This sure is
terrible. *L 26*   67–71 You cannot . . . Thought,] *L 26 om. L 25 (202)*   71–74
But . . . could] Reason and Religion will soon get the better of these apprehensions. You see
it did not *L 25 (202)*   74 Death. *L 26* : Death *L 25 (176)*   82–83 then could I]
L 25 (202) could I then *L 26*

dicted his Highness, who Beheaded one of his best Beloved Wives
upon meer Suspition of her being false to him, and had like to have
played the Same trick upon another only for attempting to Instruct
him. You that used to Puzzle Us with your Greek and Latin Should   90
have minded what Your Friend Cicero said *in otio cum dignitate*,
but to be sure *in negocio sine periculo.*

More.   And yet, Vicar, Cicero himself was beheaded as well as I.

Vicar.   Why that is just the thing I have often taken into my consideration, he lost his Life when he forsook his Maxime, to say the   95
Truth on't his Case in some respect was not unlike Yours. He had
his Head cutt off because he would be running it too far into Affairs,
From which he had better to have Receeded. He Spoke so vio-
lently against Anthony that he could never hope in prudence to
be forgiven by him, thô Anthony had good Nature enough, and   100
You contradicted Henry who as to his temper was inflexible, and
in his Anger never forgave any Man.

More.   But did not Anthony deserve that and more from Cicero. And
as to my Case if the King—

Vicar.   Alas, Sir, let People Deserve or not deserve, that is not Sixpence   105
matter, Have they Power or have they not. There's the Question.
If they have, never provoke them. Let me tell You, my late
Lord Chancellor, as there are a hundred Old Womens Receipts of
more real use than any that the Physicians can prescribe by which
the Vulgar live, while the Learned laugh at them, There are as   110
many Common Rules by which We Ordinary People are Directed
which You Wise Men (as You think your selves) either do not
know, or at least never Practice; if you did it would be better for
You.

More.   Prethy good Vicar if thou hast any of these Rules to Spare, let   115
us hear 'em.

Vicar.   Attend then, never Strive against the Stream, always drive the
Nail that will go, eat Your pudding and hold Your Tongue, dont
pretend to be Wiser than your Master, or his Eldest Son.

> *Noli contradicere Priori*
> *Fungere officium taliter qualiter*   120
> *Sine Mundum vadere Sicut vult.*

94–95 have... consideration,] *L 26* was going to Animadvertise upon. *L 25 (202)*   95
Life] *L 26* head *L 25 (202)*   96–97 had ... off] *L 26* lost his head *L 25 (202)*   108 Chancellor *L 25 (202)*, *L 26*: Chanr: *L 25 (176)*   110 them, *edd.*: them. *L 25 (176)*: 'em,
L 25 (202): them: *L 26*   113 Practice; *edd.*: Practice. *L 25 (176)* & *(202)*: Practice, *L 26*
be better] *L 26* be the better *L 25 (202)*   120] *L 26* Nil mali de superiori *L 25 (202)*

and the never failing Reason of that most Excellent precept

Nam mundus vult vadere Sicut vult.

You see I have not forgot all my Latin, will You have any more 125
of them?

More.   No Vicar if the whole hundred be such as these They will make
but One great Tautologie which Signifies no more than take care
of your Self, or keep out of harms way. A Maxim which I presume,
you did most particularly Observe.   130

Vicar.   You are in the Right on't else I should have made a pritty
business of it, I'faith. I might have been Deprived of my Living by
Old Harry, and perhaps not restored by his Son Edward for want
of a Friend to the Protector. I might again have chanced to be
Burned by Queen Mary, and if I had escaped that Storm I had 135
been sure of Starving in the Reign of her Sister Elizabeth.

More.   But what did You think was your business in the World, for
what Cause did You Live?

Vicar.   Why to teach my Parish and Receive my Tythes.

More.   Oh, as to receiving Your Tythes I have no Scruple, but what 140
did you teach your Parish?

Vicar.   What a Question is that, Why, Religion.

More.   What Religion?

Vicar.   Again, Sometimes the Ancient Roman Catholic, sometimes that
of the Reformed Church of England.   145

More.   How came You to teach them the First?

Vicar.   Why my Canonical Obedience, the Order of my Diocessan
Bishop, the Missal and Breviary all injoyned it.

More.   How happened it then that You taught the t'other?

Vicar.   Why New Acts of Parliament were made for the Reformation 150
of Popery. My Bishop was put into the Tower for Disobeying
them, and our Missals and Breviarys were Burnt. You are not
going to Catachise me, Are You?

More.   And You continued Stil in Your Vicarage of Bray.

Vicar.   Where would You have had me been? in Foxes Book of 155
Martyrs?

More.   Soft and fair, Vicar—Only one word more, did you make all

123 precept L 25 (202), L 26 : precept. L 25 (176)   125 You see . . . Latin,] L 26
Deleted in L 25 (202)   136 Starving L 25 (202), L 26 : Staving L 25 (176)   Eliza-
beth. L 26 : Elizabeth L 25 (176) & (202)   144 Sometimes L 25 (202): Sometime
L 25 (176): sometimes L 26   148 it. L 25 (202), L 26 : it L 25 (176)   149
that] L 25 (202) om. L 26   157 Soft . . . Vicar—] L 26 om. L 25 (202)   more,
L 25 (202): more L 25 (176): more. L 26

these leaps and Changes without any previous Examination, as to the Essential good or ill of them.

Vicar.   Why what Should I have done? the King had a mind to fall out 160 with the Pope, would You have a single Man oppose either of these mighty Potentates? His Highness upon the Quarrel bids me read the Mass in English, and I do so. His Son Edward enjoins the same thing, and I continue my Obedience; Queen Mary is in Communion with the Church of Rome, and She commands me to turn 165 my English Mass again into Latin. Why then things are just as they were when first I took Orders. Elizabeth will have it translated back into English, Why then matters stand as they did when I first reformed. You see, Sir, it was the Opinion of the Church of which I was a Member that changed, but the Vicar of Bray re- 170 mained always the same Man.

More.   What Colors do we put upon our Errors and our Fears? And You discharged your Duty all this while.

Vicar.   Exactly: I never mist my Church, was civil to my Parishioners, and gave Something to the poor.   175

More.   And You preached boldly and bravely without respect of Persons. You made Felix tremble.

Vicar.   By Felix I suppose You mean Old Hall; No by our Lady He made us all tremble. To tell You the truth on't Sir Thomas, I always Preached in general at the Vices of the times, but took care 180 not to be too particular upon those of any great Men. Sometimes indeed I ventured a little against Pluralities or Non-residence because if any man was touched he durst not openly show his resentment, and neither of these cases affected my Self, but I always took care to find Texts and deduce Doctrines from them 185 a propos enough. When Harry went to the Seige of Bologne It was David that went out against the Jebusites or the Moabites. When he would be Divorced from Old Kate, and had a mind to Nanny Bullen; Why Vasthi was put away, and Esther was taken unto Ahasuerus into his House Royal. Little Edward was Josiah, who 190 Destroyed the High Places. Then Mary again was Deborah or Judith, who Restored the Ancient Laws and Customs of the People of Israel. Elizabeth as She Succeeded to the Crown, had right to the same Texts, only with New Applications and with

158 these] *L 25 (202)* those *L 26*   164 in] *L 25 (202) om. L 26*   172 upon] *L 25 (202)* on *L 26*   181 Men. *L 26*: Men *L 25 (176)*: Man. *L 25 (202)*   186 enough. *L 26*: enough *L 25 (176)* & *(202)*   190 his] *L 25 (202)* the *L 26*   192 of] *L 26* to *L 25 (202)*

this difference that to Exalt her Praise I always clapt a little of the 195
Jesabell or Athalia upon her Predecessor.

More.   So that all this time You told no Body their Faults; put the
Case now that You had been a Surgeon, you would never have
applyed Medicaments to the proper wound. If You had been a
Mariner you would not have stopped that part of the Ship where 200
the Leake was sprung.

Vicar.   But I was neither a Surgeon nor a Mariner, what Signifies putting cases? I was a Parson and Preached—

More.   Rather Panegyrics I perceive than Sermons.

Vicar.   No not quite So, but they were rather Sermons indeed than 205
Satyrs.

More.   How Sedulously do we endeavor to Shun the Exercise of Virtue,
and what excuses do We make to cover Vice. You never Preach'd
therefore against Ambition or Luxury before Cardinal Woolsey.

Vicar.   No more than before You, I would have preached against 210
Levity of Speech and vain Jesting.

More.   But You ought to have done So, and we should both have
been bound to thank You.

Vicar.   Aye Sir Thomas but would either of You have prefered Me?

More.   That indeed is the main Question. Alas how we Squander away 215
our Days without doing our Duty. Desirous Stil to lengthen life,
while we lose the very Causes for which it was given to Us; and
thus You trifled fourscore Years without doing any good or intending it.

Vicar.   Indeed, Sir, I thought that it was very well that I did not do 220
much harm. Trifled away fourscore Years said You, Aye that I did
indeed, and was very Sorry when they were passed.

More.   But while they were Passing were you not under a thousand
Apprehensions? did You not Suffer continual uneasiness in the
frequent changes that happened as well in the Church as the 225
State?

Vicar.   O Sir, You may be sure I did: Every Body in the World we
lived in had his troubles, I had one particularly that vext me
mightily, the Constant fear of losing my Vicarage.

More.   But I presume you Armed Your self against that fear.   230

Vicar.   As well as I could, Sir, when I could not do as well as I would.

---

200 stopped *L 26* : stoped *L 25 (176)* : Stopd *L 25 (202)*   204] *L 25 (202)*, *L 26* Yours
were rather Panygericks, I find, than Sermons. *Earlier reading in L 25 (202)*   208
Preach'd] *L 26* preach *L 25 (202)*   209 Woolsey. *L 25 (202)* : Woolsey *L 25 (176)* :
Wolsey. *L 26*   230 I presume] *L 26 om. L 25 (202)*

When ever any new Law was made, or any harsh Injunction laid
upon us, away went I to some Clergyman or Casuist who had
a good repute for knowing these kind of things, and had himself
already conformed as to the point in Question, and then I con- 235
stantly carryed with me an Inclination to be convinced, which
You know goes a great way in matters of this Nature, So admit-
ting some things for truth without too Scrupulously Seeking for
Demonstration, and Suppressing some Scruples that might have
been troublesome I generally made the best of a Bad Market, and 240
got safe again out of the Briars. If things looked bad one Day, I
took a cup of Ale, and hoped they would be better the next. When
they were very bad indeed, I concluded they were at the worst,
and So I tell You on I Jogged.

More. How Naturally the Shallowness of thought in this Man in- 245
creases the Severity of it in the mind of a Wiser. When we reflect
upon our past Life, we find it charged with Misfortunes and
Calamities. Yet we never think of the future but in Expectation
of receiving it enlivened with Joy and pleasure. Our whole life all
this while runs like the Current of the same River and to Morrow 250
comes on just as Yesterday past, why therefore do we rather hope
than Dread what it may bring. Why do we not think that in
probability it may rather make us Miserable than happy. How is
it that scarse enjoying the present we turn our thought forward
into a Futurity, which the Will of Heaven in equal Wisdom and 255
Pitty conceals from Us a futurity which may never be Ours; but
suppose it shal be, suppose it coming with all the Delights that
the Wildness of our Imagination can Suggest, Is it more durable
is it less rapid in its course than the past, than the present? while
I am Speaking it approches and while I say it is arrived, Alas it 260
is gone for ever: the fugitive never Stops, but we insensibly follow
it 'till tyred with the pursuit we fall into our Grave.

Vicar. Aye, Sir, that Grave is an ugly hole indeed, when once a Man
Slips his foot into it—

More. You have therefore thought of Death, I am glad at least I have 265
brought you to this point.

234 these kind of] _L 26 om. L 25 (202)_   254 our] _L 26 om. L 25 (202)_   255–6 in . . .
Pitty] _L 26_ wisely _L 25 (202)_   256 Us] _In L 25 (202), followed by:_
                Prudens futuri temporis excitum
                Caliginosa nocte premit Deus
256 Ours; _edd._: Ours _L 25 (176)_: Ours, _L 25 (202)_: Ours. _L 26_   257 coming with]
_L 26_ coming fraught with _L 25 (202)_   258 Suggest, _L 26_: Suggest _L 25 (176)_ &
_(202)_   260 arrived, _L 25 (202)_: arrived. _L 25 (176)_: arrived _L 26_

Vicar. Thought of Death, Sir, aye that I have, and with different Agitations; Sometimes indeed with pleasure enough, for my Parish is of large extent, And when any Body Dyed in it that could pay, I had my Dirge and Funeral Fees, besides my Share of Ale, 270 and the Company of a good many Friends, but then again when any of the poor Dyed whom I was forced to Bury Gratis especially in the Winter time, egad I did not like Death at all.

More. Drole, But did You think of your own Death?

Vicar. Very Seldom, and yet in good troth often enough. You must 275 know I Buryed my Parish twice over, and I strove to forget every One of them as soon as I had laid them under ground. There was one Clergy-man in my Neighborhood who was four Years Older than my Self it was a great Comfort to me to see him in good health. Egad I lived at him. A t'other Side I never was heartily 280 a Friend to my Curate. A lusty Young fellow with large white Teeth and a Vermillion Countenance: I was always apprehensive he'd Outlive me, and put in to be my Successor.

More. Strange Illusion! of which even Death has not cured this Wretch, We join Ideas which in Nature have no Coherence: Our 285 fear of Death gives us not sufficient leizure to consider what Death it self is, we dare hardly think that it makes a total Separation between our Mind and our Body and We provide for our Selves after Death as if that Separation was not to be made. Are we to be alive and Dead at the Same time, Idle and Superstitious way 290 of thinking. What was it to this Vicar who should enjoy that Benefice from which Death has given him an Eternal Quietus. Yet with regret he considers who shall possess the Tythes when he shal neither have Mouth to Receive or Stomach to Digest the produce. Yet with Envy he mentions that Man that shal present 295 the Incense or adorn the Altar when he Shal neither Smel nor See. But why Should I blame him of an Error common to us all. Have not the greatest Men desired Monuments to be raised over them that the Eyes of all the world might gaze on, whilst they have Dreaded the thought that the Dust and Bones hid under the 300 Marble Should be exposed to the Sight of their Surviving Friends.

268 enough, *L 26* : enough. *L 25 (176)* : enough *L 25 (202)* 275 enough. *L 26* : enough *L 25 (176) & (202)* 277 laid them] *L 26* laid him *L 25 (202)* 286–7 what . . . think] *L 26 om. L 25 (202)* 288 and We *edd.* : and We we *L 25 (176)* : and yet we *L 25 (202)* : and we *L 26* 291 thinking. What *L 26* : thinking what *L 25 (176)* : thinking What *L 25 (202)* 292 Yet *L 25 (202)*, *L 26* : yet *L 25 (176)* 293 with regret] *L 25 (202)* with great regret *L 26* 295 Yet *L 26* : yet *L 25 (176) & (202)* mentions] *L 26* mentioned *L 25 (202)* 299 whilst] *L 26* while *L 25 (202)*

Vicar. Why really Sir Thomas You preach very well; I begin to think there was some Mistake in Our Affairs while We were in the troublesome World of which you are Talking. We should e'en have changed Stations; if you had been Vicar of Bray the Parish 305 might have had Excellent Sermons, and if I had been Chancellor of England, I'll give You my word for it, I would have kept my Head.

More. 'Tis true Vicar we Seldom are in life what we seem to be, I jested upon the Bench, yet guarded my Actions with the greatest 310 Severity, and You looked gravely and talked Morally in the Pulpit without any Resolution of Living up to that You taught others, But Vicar what You all this while call Living is only Breathing. Did You think Morality was but Discourse, and that Virtue was not to be practised, did not you know that you must never 315 prefer your Safety to Your Honor, or Your life to your Conscience. You said just now You had not forgot all your Latin, does not Horace tell You that neither the Fury of ill Men in Power nor the Frown of a Tyrant can alter the Resolution or bend the Mind of a Man Strictly just and honest; And Juvenal, that thô Phalaris 320 stood by with his Brazen Bull, The Martyr should rather suffer Flames and Racks than Deviate the least Title from Truth.

> On Her own Worth true Virtue rear'd
> Nor Dreads Disgrace nor seeks reward:
> But from her higher Orb looks greatly down, 325
> On Life or Death, A Scaffold or a Throne.

Vicar. The meer Fancy of Poets, Ah Sir Thomas You are always too much Adicted to that sort of Reading. It is that which spoiled you: Egad those whimsical Fellows have done more Mischief in leading the Minds of Grave People aside by a Contempt of Pain and Death, 330 than in Debauching Youth by too lively Discriptions of Love and Pleasure.

More. Come on then, You shal have some Prose-Men; I'l oblige You if I can: Has not Plato writ a whole Volumn to Explain how reasonable it is that we should rather consent to Die than to do 335 evil? And has not his Imitator Cicero, commenting upon the Text,

---

315 practised,] *L 25 (202)* Preached; *L 26*   316 or . . . Conscience.] *L 26* nor your
Conscience to your Life: *L 25 (202)*   317 now You] *L 25 (202)* now that you *L 26*
323 rear'd *L 25 (202)*, *L 26* : rear'ed *L 25 (176)*   327 are] *L 25 (202)* were *L 26*
329 Fellows] *L 26* Persons *L 25 (202)*   333 Come . . . Prose-Men] Let me give you
some examples in Prose then *L 25 (202)*   Prose-Men; *L 26* : Prose-Men *L 25 (176)*
334–40 Has . . . Brutus?] *L 26 om. L 25 (202)*

Instructed Us that we ought to be so far from fearing Death, in
this case that we should contemn it. What think You of those
Minds who have Practised what these Philosophers taught, of
Socrates, Aristides, and Phocion, of Regulus, Cato and Brutus?   340

Vicar. Heathens, all by the Mass meer Pagan Heathens why I read
Plutarch when I was a Young Man at the University, he is full of
these People, when ever the Game did not go well they always
threw up the Cards, and when they could not rule the World
a Whim took Them that They would Stay no longer in it.   345

More. Now the Doctor is in for it indeed, well I hope Sir since You
came from the University You have read of some Christians who
were of this Opinion too: What think You of St: Polycarp who
asserted what he thought was truth in opposition to the whole
Roman Empire, and a growing Heresy in the Church, and that   350
too in the moment he was sure to Dye for it? What of St Cyprian
who when an Equivoque or Silence it self might have Saved him,
Scorned even Deliberation in asserting his Belief and confirmed it
in the Presence of an angry Judge, and in the Sight of that fire that
was to consume him to Ashes.   355

Vicar. Aye, Sir, and St Laurence was broild on a Gridiron, and St.
Protatius had his head cut off; and a great many more of them:
Lord, there were Females too St: Ursula was Stabbed with a
Poynard, and St: Catharine broke upon the Wheel, why do you
think I am not acquainted with the Army of Martyrs. Oh Dear   360
Sir, as their Holy days came I constantly did 'em Justice in my
Prones, and set out their Relicts to be kist by the People. I had
One Sermon You must know that Mutatis Mutandis did the
Business for a great many of them. I clapt all the Praise I could
upon the Saint of the Day, and e'en let the rest of the Calendar   365
take it as they thought fit.

More. And as You Showed I suppose you respected the Relicks of
these Saints.

Vicar. Aye marry did I.

More. Without any Resolution to follow their Example.   370

Vicar. Lord, Sir, They had their way to Heaven, which in all

341 why I] *L 25 (202)*, *L 26* Why Sir I *Earlier reading in L 25 (202)*   343 these] *L 25
(202)*, *L 26* those *Earlier reading in L 25 (202)*   344 the Cards] *L 26*, *Earlier reading in
L 25 (202)* their Cards *L 25 (202)*   345 a . . . that] *L 26 om. L 25 (202)*   346 well]
L 25 (202), *L 26 om. Earlier reading in L 25 (202)*   347-8 who . . . too] *L 25 (202)*,
L 26 of the same Opinion *Earlier reading in L 25 (202)*   349 was] *L 26 om. L 25 (202)*
opposition to] *L 26* the sight of *L 25 (202)*   361 their] *L 26* the *L 25 (202)*

probability was the nearest; You were pleased to take That; very well, I had mine, it was a little about indeed, why very well again. We were not all Born to be Martyrs any more than Lord Mayors.

More.   Strange is it, that after all that the Wisest and best Men of all 375 Ages have said and writ on this subject of Life and Death, the great Majority of Mankind Stil argue and Act like this poor Vicar. Look You, my Old Friend without entering into any particular points of Religion, I repeat to You that we have two Duties One to our Selves, the other to the public. That either as we are private 380 Persons or Members of the Commonweale our life on many occasions is not our Own, and our Conscience only is the guide, and the Disposer of it.

Vicar.   Well, I do not flatly deny any thing of all this, Sir Thomas, but methinks we should make those many Occasions as few as we 385 could. There may be certain times for those Tryals, but one must not Practise such Dangerous Experiments every Day. Our Duty may be Divided, and in that Case sure we may take the safer side. You that were a Judge Know very well that we are obliged to Conform to the Law of the Land. S'life it would be a Foolish mis- 390 take if a Man should fancy himself a Martyr to Religion, and be trus'd up in Fact as a Traytor to the King. A Man has but one Neck Sir Thomas, and I tell You it is a point that requires very mature Deliberation, good Sir, do but think a little.

More.   Vicar, the beginning, Progress, and Ultimate end of Thought 395 can only inform You that Truth is to Direct all your Actions, and that Courage is only a Virtue as Assistant to Truth, else You wander without a guide, and You Sail without a Compass. Your Caution is but Cowardise, and Your Discretion is double dealing: You scarse can pardon Your own fears to your Self, your Con- 400 science therefore must direct Your prudence, and Your Virtue must be entire that your honor may be unspotted. Life and Death all this while are only things Accidental.

Vicar.   Why Sir Thomas whilst You talk thus you are laying the Model of Your own Utopia. Pray, is not self Preservation a Principle of 405 Nature, is it necessary that we run Absolutely into Danger, should

---

372 were] *L 26* are *L 25 (202)*   377 great Majority] *L 26* Mass *L 25 (202)*   poor] *L 26 om. L 25 (202)*   378 You] *L 26* Ye *L 25 (202)*   into] *L 26* upon *L 25 (202)* 379 points] *L 25 (202)* point *L 26*   382 guide, and] *L 26* guide, the Judge, and *L 25* *(202)*   390 Law] *L 25 (202)* Laws *L 26*   391 and be] *L 25 (202)* and to be *L 26* 404–5 Why ... Utopia] *L 26, Del. in L 25 (202)*: Why these Notions are wilder than any in your own Utopia. *Earlier reading in L 25 (202)*

not we comparatively weigh Circumstances, and may not some
Precepts which You take litterally be understood Figuratively;
and consequently, may not Some Points be Essentiall only in relation to some cases, and may not others be indifferent as to other 410
cases.

More.   What are you got into the Old Cant, lurking behind Distinc-
tions, and arming your Self with Adverbs. I said I would not enter
into any Dispute of Religion with You, But take this at least as an
Axiom that Your Scholemen have not only obscured their Texts 415
but perverted them. Essentially, Absolutely, formally, comparatively, and Figuratively well engrafted upon Interest and Knavery,
are sufficient to divide Five Nations, and produce as many different
Heresies. Once for all Vicar every Man is obliged to suffer for
what is right as to oppose what is unjust.   420

Vicar.   Ay, but a Man may be mistaken in what he thinks Right, as I
fancy you were in the point of the Popes Supremacy. Od Zooks
Sir, to venture ones head in a doubtful cause—

More.   Suppose the Cause to be false; when I had done my best to
inform my self that what I did was Legal, and could not be con- 425
vinced to the Contrary, I had nothing more to do but to Submit
my Self to the Severity of the New made Law, and leave the Event
to the Creator and Disposer of the World, So I tell Thee again that
an Upright and unprejudiced Conscience is our Plea before any
Human Tribunal, Nay, more that it is at once the Law and Judge 430
that must Convict or Absolve Us in all we do or think thô We
stand accused by no Man. The Basis of all Religion and the Bond
of all Society is founded upon this Strict adherence to Truth, and
constancy of Mind in the Defence of it.

> Conscience, Thou Solemn Bond of mutual Trust,   435
> Prop, to the Weak, and Anchor of the Just;
> Fructiferous Root whence human Virtues Spring,
> The Subjects Law, and safety of the King:
> Appeas'd by Thee our inward Tumults cease,
> Thou guid'st our Feet into the Paths of Peace: 440

407 not we] *L 25 (202)* we not *L 26*   418 divide ... many] *L 26* produce five *L 25 (202)*
different] *L 25 (202) om. L 26*   419 Once for all Vicar] *L 26* I tell thee plainly,
Vicar, once more that *L 25 (202)*   420 to oppose] *L 26* much as he is to combat
L 25 (202)   421–30 Ay ... Tribunal] *om. L 25 (202)*   424 false; *edd.*: false
L 25 (176): false, *L 26*   430 Nay ... it] *L 26* And conscience *L 25 (202)*   431
must] *L 26* will *L 25 (202)*   431 Us ... We] *L 26* You thô you *L 25 (202)*

Fair Polar Star, whose influencing Ray
Directs our Toil, and Manifests our way;
Shou'd Cloud or Storm Thy radiant beams obscure
Yet Those who hope They follow Thee are Sure:
Thô tyr'd by Day they pass the Night in rest,   445
And going wrong, yet seeking Right are Blest.

Vicar.   Are those Verses of Your own making Sir Thomas? why really
they are pritty enough but a little hobbling in the Number.
More.   They are not so much to be praised as practised, I'll give You
some translated from a Greek Epigram that carry almost the Same   450
Sense in a Style Something more flowing.

While thrô the Depth of Lifes tempestuous Sea
Our little Vessel cutts its destin'd way,
Now prosp'rous Insolence and wealthy Pride
With rolling Billows swell th'Impetuous Tyde;   455
Now care and want in hollow Tumult roar,
Threatning to Dash us on the Dangerous Shoar.
Around us and above with various rage
High and low Deaths alternately engage;
Fix'd on a Rock upon the distant Strand   460
Bright Virtue does our only Pharos Stand,
Contemns the Winds and Waves, and points us safe to Land.

Vicar.   Pough, hang it, this is all but the Second part of the same tune.
Come Sir Thomas You used to Love a little Mirth, I'll repeat You
some Verses that a Freind of mine brought down heither with him   465
t'other Day.

Your Conscience like a Firy Horse
Shou'd never know His native force
Ride him but with a Moderate Rein
And stroke him down with Worldly gain;   470
Bring him by Management and Art
To every thing that made him Start;
And strive by just degrees to Settle
His native warmth and height of mettle;

---

448 Number. *L 26* : Number *L 25 (176)* & *(202)*   449 I'll *edd.* : Ill *L 25 (176)* & *(202)* :
I'l *L 26*   451 Something] *L 26* a little *L 25 (202)*   464 I'll *edd.* : Ill *L 25 (176)*
& *(202)* : I'l *L 26*   468 never] *L 26 Blotted in L 25 (202)*   473 degrees] *L 26*
Decrees *L 25 (202)*

And when by use he once has got 475
An honest canting low Church Trott
He'll carry You thrô thick and thin
Secure thô dirty to your Inn.
But if You give the Beast his head,
And prick and Spur him to His Speed, 480
The Creature Strait begins his tricks,
He Foams and Neighs Curvets and Kicks,
He gets the Bitt between his Teeth
And runs His Rider out of Breath:
Better You ne'r had rid abroad, 485
For down You come as sure as LAUD.

We may be allowed to know who Laud was thô he lived since our time, for sure it is as reasonable for Us here to mention a Man that was born Since we Dyed as it is for those in the t'other World to quote an Author that Dyed before They were born. 490

More.   I like your thought well enough, but the Verses You repeat were meant as a Satyr upon that very sort of Conduct, which You seem to Commend. You put me in mind of some German Doctors that reading the little Book of my Friend Erasmus fancyed he wrote a real Panegyrick upon the Folly he was laughing at. 495

Vicar.   Be it as it will with the Verses; In honest Prose I must tell You, Sir Thomas, that in difficult cases there must be some Allowances made; if we cannot bring the thing to our Conscience, we must e'en Strive as much as we can to bring our Conscience to the thing. Mahomet and the Mountain seems to me not so unreason- 500 able as some Strait laced Christians think it.

More.   Go to, I contemn You now. If I were to be Chancellor again, and had all the Livings in the Land to dispose I would not give You one of them.

Vicar.   If all Succeeding Chancellors were of Your Opinion your Liv- 505 ings would want Incumbents, and the Civil Power might send out Press Gangs for Priests to supply the Parishes.

More.   How few are there that dare Exercise a true and Active Virtue, too many indeed there are that live in the open Practice of impu- dent and Successful Vice but the Mass of Mankind is a Multitude 510

---

485 You ne'r had] L 26 You'd never L 25 (202)   488–9 a Man that was] L 26 Men that were L 25 (202)   490 an Author] L 26 People L 25 (202)   500 to me not] L 26 not to me L 25 (202)   503 dispose] L 25 (202) dispose of L 26   509 indeed there are] L 25 (202) there are indeed L 26

of Such Animals as this Vicar, the Burden of the Earth, who only feed upon it without endeavoring to deserve the Bread it affords them, Wretches, who in having done nothing have done ill. Negative Ideots who Sink into Folly for want of Courage to aspire to Wisdom, and think nothing bad or hurtfull except they 515 may be Indicted for it at the next Quarter Sessions. This Man now would not commit any famous Wickedness, yet how far is he from being honest; Well; as bad as they say the World is, there are fifty Idle Knaves in it for one determined Villain.

Vicar. Twenty for One is as much as I can grant You; Ah Sir Thomas, 520 tis very true what Dr: Burnet says of You, that you mix't too much Gall with your Ink. Egad with these Maximes of Your's you would raise both Court and Country against You, and if You had as many heads as there are Loops upon Your Gown You might run a fair risk to have 'em all cut off. 525

More. What then! many better heads would have been Confirmed by my Example, and I should have Answered the end for which life was given me.

Vicar. Admirable Philosophy indeed, in the Practice of which you were Beheaded on Tower Hill at fifty-three, whereas without it I 530 Dyed quietly in my bed at eighty. Since I am afraid your Lordship may grow Angry, which would be a little against Your Stoicism, and since You may be assured that if we were to live again I should never be a Convert to your Doctrine, it is time we should part. 535

More. Withal my heart, Adieu, thou poor Spirited Parson with thy Vicarage of Bray.

Vicar. Thou Great Chancellor of England, without a head, Adieu.

A Dialogue between Oliver Cromwell, and his Porter.

Oliver. What a Vicisitude does Death bring to human affairs! No Coronet on my Head, no purple Robe to my back no Scepter in my hand, neither Heralds before nor Guards around me, Justled

---

521 very] *L 26* but too *L 25 (202)*   530 without it I] *L 25 (202)* I without it *L 26*
531 quietly] *L 26 om. L 25 (202)*   533 since] *L 26 om. L 25 (202)*   538 Thou]
L 26 om. L 25 (202)
    Title: *A Dialogue L 26* : Dialogue. *L 25*   *Cromwell, L 26* : *om. L 25*   3 hand, *edd.* :
hand *L 25* : hand! *L 26*

and Affronted by a hundred Cavalier Ghosts whom I ruined in
t'other World. Hist and scoft at by as many Republican Spirits 5
whom I Cajoled and Betrayed—

Porter.   To which You may add the Charges of Your Funeral not paid,
Your Son unable to Sustain the Soveraignty Six Months, The
Lives and Fortunes of all England presented to him in Addresses
now wrapping up Anchovies or lining Old Trunks, and the Sub- 10
scribers ashamed of their own hands. Your Counsellors heads upon
Westminster-Hall, The Royal Family restored, and Public matters
turned again into the Ancient Channel, Your own Dear Carcase
hanged at Tyburn, and your Quondum Subjects striving who can
most imphatically curse your Memory.   15

Oliver.   Who is this that seems to know my Affairs so well, and is so
famillar with my Person? by the length of his Ear and the Sulleness
of his brow it should be my Old Porter: 'Tis he indeed, and glad
am I to find one here that I can command. Hark you Sirrah make
way for me thrô that Croud, and tell those chattering Ghosts who 20
I am.

Porter.   Who You were Friend? but who you are no Ghost alive will
mind. Your Stern look, and your *vultus regibus usque truces* will
fright no body here, in Short, Sir, that Levelling Act which your
Friends above could never obtain has been long since made a 25
Fundamental Law, In these Kingdomes we are all equal.

Oliver.   Show me at least some respect for what I have been.

Porter.   I will as far as You may Merit that respect, and You in your
turn shal render me the same Justice, The Condition of this
Obligation being Such I do not doubt but that I shall have the 30
preference at least by all impartial Judges.

Oliver.   To begin then I raised my Self from a Private Person to the
Dignity of a Prince.

Porter.   And from being Your Porter I made my Self a Prophet.

Oliver.   I was General of the Army, Head of the Parliament, and 35
Supreme Master of Three Kingdoms.

Porter.   I was Senior Inhabitant of Old Bethlem, Prince of the Planets,
and absolute Disposer of every thing I saw or thought of.

Oliver.   Tis true thou wert for many Years locked Up in a little Cell,
Separated from the World by Iron barrs, and no other Furniture 40

15 Memory. *edd.*: Memory *L* 25: Memory! *L* 26   23 mind. Your *L* 26: mind your
L 25   26 Law,] Law here. *L* 26   36 of Three] of the Three *L* 26   37
Bethlem, *L* 26: Bethlem *L* 25

about thee but the torn Leaves of three or Four Bibles, and had not I all this while Splendor and Magnificence, Gardens Parks and Palaces.

Porter.   And is it not as true that I had every thing which I desired or wanted, My Potage well dressed, my Straw fresh and my Coverlet 45 Clean, Whilst in the midst of the Plunder of Three Nations You were always in Necessity, and every Week laying New Taxes upon an opprest People For the Support of an awkward ill founded Greatness, And whilst you were tearing and Confounding the best Libraries in England did not I pick up those leaves you spoke of, 50 which were both the Furniture of my Room and the Comfort of my Life.

Oliver.   But before thou camest to this happy Station, Friend wert Thou ever Seen or heard of otherwise then as my Domestic Servant till thy brains run a Wool gathering, and thou gottest into 55 these Strange Whims of Preaching and Prophecying.

Porter.   And did not I serve you faithfully till I saw You Cheated every Man you had to do with, till You turned those officers out of the Army who had preferrd you, and made use of your Parliamentary Power against those very Persons, who intrusted You with it. I 60 learned to preach from You and indeed am obliged to You for the very distemper that made me turn Prophet. I imitated You, I looked upon You as my Idol till running from your Door with my Staff in my hand one thirtieth of January, I Shal never forget the Day, I saw You order your Master to be brought out of the Win- 65 dow, and Murthered at his own Palace Gate. I confess when You Cut off the Kings head you turned mine into the bargain.

Oliver.   Uncommon Circumstances must Attend great Actions *Pax quæritur bello* was my Motto, yet Sure I made a glorious Figure. The Commons of England prostrate before my Throne, the Peers 70 mingled in the Croud with them, or Submissively retired to Plant Cabbages at their own Country Seats, Citizens and Courtiers conducting Me with Aclamations thrô Cheapside. Ambassadors sent from the greatest Princes in Europe to beg my Friendship, or Soften my Resentments, and the Pope himself trembling for fear 75 that having nothing else to do I might Send my Fleets to Plunder Loretto or destroy Civita Vechia.

Porter.   And while you made all this bustle you were a Slave to your

---

55 and thou] and then thou *L 26*   62 Prophet. *L 26* : Prophet *L 25*   70 Throne, *L 26* : Throne *L 25*   77 Vechia. *L 26* : Vechia *L 25*

own apprehensions, Suspitious of every body that came near You. You durst not Stir out without a Coat of Maile under your Clothes, 80 nor Sleep a nights without a pair of Pistols Loaded by your Bedside. When you Shot the Captain to appease the Mutiny in the Army your hand trembled more than a highway Mans while his tongue has the Insolence to Demand a Purse; And when you were just going to kill Moreland, who Slept Dogs Sleep while you told 85 Your Midnight Secrets to Thurlo, You were more afraid of a Young Clerk than he could Possibly be of an inraged Tyrant. In short you doubted of your Title of Protector, and I rested assured in mine of Prophet, My Mind was divested of all those doubts and fears, which continually disturbed Yours. I cursed my Enemies but 90 never feared or indeed knew them. I excommunicated or blest as I thought proper, And when the Palace of Bethlem from whence I sent out my Soveraign Edicts was on fire I forbid the People under pain of my Displeasure to quench the flames; Told them the Day of Judgement was come, and this was the time when the World 95 must be purged by fire, and so unconcerned I read on. The Pope dreaded your Fleets at Loretto and Civita Vechia did You say? No No, it was I that humbled that high Priest of Baal, I Bombarded his Spiritual Strong holds with my Anathamas, I confounded the Whore of Babylon, the Scarlet Tyrant, Seven heads Ten horns, 100 Gog and Magog.

Oliver. Grant me Patience and I will yet argue meekly with this Whymsicall Person. Observe me friend, My Power was real, Your Authority was only imaginary, I did actually fight in the field, Preached loudly in the Church, and talked vehemently in the Par- 105 liament. Thousands of People can Witness that they Submitted to Me at Dundalk, were Edified by me at Oxford, and frightend out of their Witts at St: Stephens Chappell whilst you only fancy'd—

Porter. Look You Noll, Witnesses may help a Man to recover his Estate in Westminster Hall, but can do nothing towards making 110 him happy in the enjoyment of it. That sort of Testimony must come from within. You Fought You say and were really Victorious, it may be so. I Prophecied and Fancied my Self Inspired But as to the Satisfaction that arose to either of Us from our different ways of Acting or Thinking We our Selves are the only 115 Judges.

Oliver. Pugh prithee this is Frantic Stuff, I appeal to the whole World.

Porter. It is right Philosophy Master, what Signifies Appealing to the World, The Appeal would come too late now, While we were yet alive You suffered a thousand Troubles and Vexations, which you 120 hid from the World, to which You are now so fond of Appealing, and I proclaimed to that World the Raptures and Pleasures I enjoyed in endeavoring to Convert it.

Oliver. But again those who disobeyed Me felt the Effects of my Anger in the loss of their Fortune and Estates. 125

Porter. And those who contradicted me fell under the weight of my Curses; Now while I thought my Censures had as terrible an Effect as you knew Your Arms had I enjoyed as ample Vengeance as ever you did.

Oliver. A pleasant Droll this, So that to Act or not to Act is just the 130 same thing.

Porter. To Act or to think one Acts is just the same. Now how often do we think we Act, when we have lain Stil, and how often in our thought do we jumble things together that never Existed in the same time and Place, and consequently were not, at least were not 135 as we imagined them. In a Dream and without as much as once turning Your Self in your Bed have not You as really, that is as apparently fought the Battel at Marston-Moor, Hectored Your Crop-eared Brethren at Westminster, or thrown Cushons at Your Favorites heads in Spring Garden, as if You had been in these 140 places: The next Morning waking You have thought Your Self Deceived, and So neglected and forgot those Ideas. But if You will imagine Your Life to have been that Dream—

Oliver. Oh, very well then I never did possess any thing, but only Thought that I possest. (This Fellow is extremly Whimsical.) 145

Porter. Aye, most certainly My quondum Lord Protector, what we do in life is but to think we possess, and the Strength and Impulse of that thought does the rest; as the livelyness of that Idea Decays or Changes, the thing it Self is not worth a Straw. Hence it happens that the same Object attracts now, to morrow becomes in- 150 different, and the next day grows Odious. A greater Philosopher Noll than either You or I, States the matter thus, It is not the thing it Self says he that Pleases or disquiets a Man but the Opinion he conceives of the thing. Now I will go a little further with You, and convince you that pleasure or trouble being only the different 155 Effects of your own thought it dos not signify three pence if what you have a fancy for or dislike has its intrinsic Value or not, Nay if it be in the world or No. What you See in a glass is only the effect of an Impression formed in your own brain yet it may either please or put you out of humor, the Sound that you hear is nothing 160 else but a determined motion of Common Air yet a Flute delights, a Trumpet startles and a Bell stuns you. Does not the Lover imagine Charms in his Mistresses face, which no body else ever found, and which indeed She never Possessed, did not Don Quixot (one of Your Predecessors) sigh many years for Dulcinia 165 whom he never saw. What think you of the Poets who hold long Discourses with their Muses and Goddesses, while they believe in their own Conscience there never were Such People upon Earth. Your Mathematicians who plague themselves first and their Correspondents afterwards with the Produce only of Lines and 170 Angles which never did nor will Exist, and Your System makers and World-wrights that as any idle Evening lies upon their hands Stamp an infinite number of New Stars or People a Million or two of Earths.

Oliver.   Why I think these People as mad as ever you were, and that 175 they Deserve as much to be Locked up, but You dont compare these Notional Gentlemen with Heroes and Conquerors who by Superior Sense direct, or by victorious Arms Subdue the rest of Mankind. We Seek for things Solid and visible, and what You desire by your own Confession exists only in meer Speculation.   180

Porter.   Master, take my word for it my Speculations are real, and Your desires but Chimerical. You would have had what never happened to any even from the Result of his own Thought: Peace with Ambition and Tranquility founded upon Injustice. I was pleased with hope in Prophecy and happyness in Expectation. 185 You were never Satisfyed with the Present, I always anticipated and even enjoyed the future. To amuse You no longer Master, every Mortal Man is Mad more or less: The Lover quo ad hanc, The Miser quo ad hoc, but the Ambitious Man quo ad Omnia. Pray observe those miserable People whom You call Heroes, how 190

---

158 What *L 26*: what *L 25*   161 delights, *L 26*: delights *L 25*   165 Your]
Our *L 26*   167 their] the *L 26*   168 own] *om. L 26*   171 nor] or *L 26*
182 had] *om. L 26*   183 Thought: *edd.*: Thought *L 25*: thought, *L 26*   187
Master, *L 26*: Master *L 25*

they go about roaring and crying like Spoiled Children for every
thing they See, throwing away their own and desiring other
Peoples goods, never contented with the common and easy use of
things, and Stil drawing new troubles upon themselves from the
inconsistency and perverseness of their own projects. What think 195
you of Pompey and Cæsar, one could bear no Superior, the t'other
no equal, pritty Fellows! and upon this each plagued that part
of the World where he was. Both by turns Ruined their own
Country, and got themselves Murthered. What do you talk of
being Locked up? That same Cæsar was more confined in Gallia, 200
Alexander in Asia, and You in the Three Kingdoms you usurped
than ever I was in Bethlem. For it is not the Situation of the Body
but of the Mind, my most worthy friend, that either restrains
a Man or gives him Liberty.

Oliver. Ha! there is Some sort of Sense in what this Fellow sayd last. 205
I find he has his lucid Intervalls. I'll humor him a little in his own
way: And So friend as you were Saying every Man is Mad, but in
a different manner, and upon Some particular objects.

Porter. Most certainly, and all We great Men are more emphatically
mad than other people: when You preached, your Head was as 210
hott as an Oven, Mahomed in his Extacys had the falling sickness,
and to tell you truth, in the middle of my Prophecies I was now
and then tyed down to my good behavour.

Oliver. I was therefore mad, but not so mad as You.

Porter. Excuse me, Sir, I never said or thought any thing like That. 215
You were ten times madder, So Mad that no Man durst either
Advise, or tye You, You had brought things to that miserable pass
that Your Counsellors all Dreaded and your Divines all flattered
You, So you run wild about the Streets threatning yet terifyed
Vexing and vexed, till a little bitt of Gravel stop't in your Kidneys 220
took away the relish You had for all the Earth which You Possessed
from Dover Cliff to the Isles of Orkney and a kind Feaver gave you
some relief by taking You out of the World to which you were
a burthen: there is indeed one Difference between you Public
Madmen, and we Sedentary Gentlemen if We happen to be a little 225
Crazed about Love, Learning or Religion while you are ravaging
Nations, and setting the world on fire. You find others bitt with

193 goods, *L 26* : goods *L 25*   196 Cæsar, *L 26* : Cæsar *L 25*   198 Both *L 26* :
both *L 25*   203 but of] but *L 26*   206 I'll *edd.* : Ill *L 25* : I'l *L 26*   220
vexed, till a] vexed. A *L 26*   224 between] *om. L 26*

the same Tarantula who Second your fury pertake of the Plunder and justify your error. Yee all herd together, and it is a very hard thing to catch one of You, but we are fewer in Number, divided, 230 unarmed and different in our Principles. If the least disturbance happens from any impetuosity of our temper the Neighborhood has an Eye upon Us, and away we are hurried the next dark Night to Morefeilds or Hodgdon. In truth whether from the fear or Weakness of Mankind, I shal not argue, but you have commonly 235 the Majority on Your Side, which as your Excellency very well Knows is no Smal advantage in England.

Oliver. Hark you friend; dont talk So loud, yonder stand a Knot of Shabby fellows, whom I dont like, they Seem to Eves-drop.

Porter. O they are very honest Gentlemen take my word for it. There 240 is Diogenes, Epictetus, Peter Aretine, and Guy Patin. Every Man you must know brings a spice of his former Madness down hither with him, These Philosophers are all Reasoning. I'll bring you acquainted with them. Their Discourses may be very Edifying to You.   245

Oliver. No prythee Show me where are the Conquerors and Heroes You named just now. I had rather go to them.

Porter. O they are very far from this quiet part of the Grove, quite a t'other side the River. You may find them there with Spartacus, Massenellio, and Jack Cade, making of Dirt pies or playing at 250 Cudgells for it is not absolutely true what the Poets say of Lethé Waters That they make us forget all we have done, they only cool our Passions and calm the heat of Our Mondane Distempers. Every Man acts in Jeast here what He did in the t'other World in Earnest. You may excercise amongst the Heroes without blowing 255 up Citadells and destroying whole Countries, You may Study among the Lawgivers without being Stark wild about Ordonnances and Proclamations, as I can talk upon Calvins Predestination, the Popes Constitution or any other Theological point without fishing for Leviathans or Slaying Behemoths. But you 260 must previously I tell You take a Course of these Lethé Waters for Six Months at least, for amongst friends You are very far gone.

Oliver. To make me forget any thing of my greatness, I tell Thee I

230 Number, *edd.*: Number *L 25*: number, *L 26*   235 argue, *L 26*: argue *L 25*
239 Eves-drop. *L 26*: Eves-drop *L 25*   242 spice] Piece *L 26*   243 I'll *L 26*:
Ill *L 25*   254 Every *L 26*: every *L 25*   Man] *om. L 26*   255 Earnest. *edd.*:
Earnest *L 25*: earnest. *L 26*   amongst] among *L 26*

wont gargle my Mouth with a drop of it, Mercy on me how 265
extremly mad is this fellow.

Porter.   Glory glory how far beyond all Cure is my quondam Master?

Observations on Ovid's Metamorphoses.

[*Selections*]

OVID in his descriptions and Names of Persons and things must
take it for granted that Even those of his own time and his own
Country must have understood both the Geneologies of the Persons
and the Circumstances of the Stories of which he Treats. For Instance
Actæon is called Nepos Cadmi, Autonœius heros and juvenis Hyantius   5
before You know his Name to be Actæon. The first time he Names the
Muses he calls them Mnemonides, the next, Aonides: So the beginning
of the 7th book,

> Iamque fretum Minyæ Pegasæâ puppe secabant. [VII. 1]

Where you are to understand by Minyæ first people who were of 10
Thessaly, Minos being in that Country, then by those people you must
again understand a part of them Argonautæ who went under the conduct of Jason, who has not yet been mentioned, and by Pegasæâ puppe,
you are to Note that the Ship having wings, ie. sayls was mighty like
the flying horse Pegasus. So L: 7. Tirynthius heros the first time he 15
names Hercules. L: 8. before he Names Castor and Pollux You are to
know who they are by

> Tyndaridæ gemini, spectatus cæstibus alter
> Alter equo: [VIII. 301–2]

* * *

From Multiplicique domo [VIII. 158] Ovid imploys twelve Lines in 20
telling that the Minotaure was putt into a Labyrinth, in the seven next
he tells the whole Story that the Athenians were every nine years to Send
a certain Number of People to be devoured by him, that Ariadne helpt
him with her clew of thred, that He Slew the Monster, ran away with
the Lady, left her upon a desert Island and that Bacchus found her. But 25

266 fellow. *edd.*: fellow *L 25*: Fellow. *L 26*
     Title: *L 28*: Ovids Metam̄ *W*   1 Persons *L 28*: *Partially illeg. in W*   1–2 must
... for *L 28*: *Partially illeg. in W*   2 time] Times *L 28*   4 For *edd.*: for *W*, *L 28*
6 Actæon. *L 28*: Actæon *W*   7 Aonides: *L 28*: Aonides *W*   20 From *L 28*:
from *W*   21 Labyrinth, *L 28*: Labyrinth *W*   23 Number *edd.*: Numbers *W*:
number *L 28*   25 her. But *L 28*: her but *W*

these Matters are so exprest as without knowing the thing before No
Man alive can tell what the author Meant.

* * *

Cytoriaco radium de Monte tenebat.   [vi. 132]

'Twas very well worth while to tell us on what Montaine the shuttle
grew which Pallas threw in Arachne's face. It is greatly the fault of the 30
Ancients to give insignificant Epithetes and dwell too long upon the
description of Trifles.

* * *

Actæon eat by his own doggs

> as it is every Mans Fate
> Whose packs too big for his Estate.   35

* * *

Gnossius Ichnobates, Spartanâ gente Melam.   [iii. 208]

After the Naming these Doggs just before, it is not very Material that
You should know what Country they were of, from hence follow
sixteen lines with the Names only of Actæon's doggs all recounted in
as good order as Homers Ships. Il: 2. after which Ovid makes an Excuae 40
that he does not trouble You with the Names, colours, and Geneology
of the rest of the pack

Quosque referre mora est.   [iii. 225]

and for fear you have not enough of them the eighth line from this

Prima Melanchætes &c   [iii. 232]   45

the three doggs that fasten upon their unfortunate Master were not
named in the forementioned Catalogue.

So afterwards in Lib. 5: naming ignoble people that fought against
Perseus

Inde Semiramio &c.   [v. 85]   50

the great fault of Epic bringing people for whom You have no Concern
in to be killed, you are glad when you are rid of them at the Expence of
their lives: So in a play, when the Hero kills four or five persons who
have not obtained Your good graces by any Character or Merit You
laugh: there is a description of above a hundred lines of a battel without 55
any other variety then that two hundred people with hard Names, and

30 It *L 28*: it *W*   35 too *L 28*: to *W*   Estate. *edd.*: Estate *W, L 28*   36
Melam.] Melampus. *L 28*   37 After *L 28*: after *W*   47 Catalogue. *L 28*: Catalogue *W*   50 Semiramio &c.] Semiramio Polydæmona &c *L 28*

simple Epithetes to them of their Country or their parentage were
killed several ways, some struck thrô the neck, the thigh or the sides
or throat with a Sword, some knockt down with Poles, tankards &c.
after which he tells you   60

> Nomina longa mora est mediâ de plebe virorum
> Dicere.   [v. 207–8]

This I can not like either in Ancient or Modern Epick.

* * *

Ovid gives the same account of the Creation as Moses

· · · · ·

> Sanctius his animal, mentisque capacius altæ   65
> Deerat, adhuc, & quod dominari in cætera posset
> Natus homo est.   [I. 76–78]

> Quam satis Iapeto—
> Finxit in effigiem moderantum cuncta Deorum. [I. 82–83]

Let Us make man in our own Image &c   Gen: I.   70

· · · · ·

Let Us make Man (as before) implyes God advising with himself i.e.
directing his own Action, which direction is to our feeble understandings imparted by the Name of Providence.

· · · · ·

> Flumina jam lactis, jam flumina Nectaris Ibant
> Flavaque de viridi stillabant illice Mella   [I. 111–12]   75

The Notion of the Promised land was a land flowing with Milk and
Honey.

Adam's and Eve's being some time in Paradice is like the time of the
Golden age.

· · · · ·

Neve foret terris &c   [I. 151]   80

The Gyants endeavouring to Scale Heav'n finds Two Stories in Scripture like it, the Angels rebelling, and the building of Babel. Gen: 6: v: 4.
there were Giants in the Earth in those days.

· · · · ·

---

63 This *edd.*: this *W*: These *L 28*   72 Action, *L 28*: Action. *W*   73 Providence.
L 28: Providence *W*   78 Adam's] Adam *L 28*   83 in the] on the *L 28*

Perdendum mortale Genus &c [1. 188] Jupiters speech to the Gods
when he begins to tell them the Story of Lycaon;   85

It repenteth Me that I have made Man   [Gen. vi. 6]

. . . . .

Esse quoque in fatis reminiscitur, affore tempus
Quo mare, quo tellus, correptaque regia cæli
Ardeat, et Mundi moles operosa laboret.   [1. 256-8]

Ovid had plainly the Notion of the general Conflagration.   90

. . . . .

The Deluge is plainly Noahs flood, and some part of the Description
looks as if Ovid had seen the Books of Moses.

—Genus Mortale sub undis
Perdere, et ex omni nimbos dimittere cælo.   [1. 260-1]

Emittitque notum, madidis Notus evolat alis &c   [1. 264]   95
To
—hinc densi funduntur ab æthere Nimbi   [1. 269]

*   *   *

Iphigenia to be Sacrificed for the Success of the Army, and Diana
appeased with Agamemnons piety in giving his daughter, and accept-
ing a Hind in her Stead, has a good deal of Abraham, Isaac and the 100
Ram, the Common comparison, I know is between Agamemnon's
daughter and Jeptha's daughter, and were not long distant in point
of Chronology.

*   *   *

Jupiter and Mercury coming down to Baucis and Philemon has a
good deal of the Angels being entertained by Lott. And the Neighboring 105
Country destroyed for the wickedness of the people answers to the
destruction of Sodom and Gomorrha. When the Gods would punish
they go to Furies, or Evil Spirits, Ceres against Erisicthon makes use
of Fames. God in the holy Scripture is said by means of the Devil to
torment Job: and to putt a lying Spirit into the Mouth of the Prophett. 110

*   *   *

---

91 plainly *L 28: Partially illeg. in W*   Description *L 28: Partially illeg. in W*   101
I know is] is, I know *L 28*   105 And *edd.:* and *W, L 28*   107 Gomorrha. *L 28:*
Gomorrha *W*   109 Scripture] Scriptures *L 28*   110 Prophett. *edd.:* Prophett
W: Prophets. *L 28*

Jupiter declares that Hercules has acted well on Earth, owns him for his Son, says that the fire only consumes the Maternal part of the Hero, that the other part which he has from Him is eternal, cannot dye or be consumed, that He will take him to heaven. Accordingly Hercules's body is burnt, no part of his external form remains, yet he keeps all 115 that he had from his father Jupiter, he puts off his mortal body, is renewed in beauty in Majesty and Strength, and exalted to Heaven in a Chariot. Can any thing speak plainer, that We were Made by a God the father and Creator of the World, that our bodyes are subject to death, that our Souls are Immortal that there is a reward for the good things 120 We do when here on Earth and a certainty of Heaven and Eternity.

*   *   *

Hercules, Cadmus, Jason, St George are upon the Same foot for killing each his Dragon, which Signifies their having subdued famous robbers or Pyrats.

*   *   *

Superstition is the Same in all ages and places, Ovid's Metamorphosis 125 was the Legend of those days, and is full of Miracles, and reliques.

*   *   *

Hercules delivered Hesione from a Sea Monster as Perseus did Andromede, I take it to be the Same Story told in different Countryes, One in Greece, t'other at Troy.

*   *   *

Polyphemus's complaint and Love harangue is a perfect Bucolic, and 130 a great deal of it taken from Theocritus.

*   *   *

et vertice sydera tangam.   [VII. 61]

Sublimi feriam sydera vertice. Horace.   [*Odes*, I. i. 36]

The Storyes of Cadmus and Jason sowing a Serpents teeth and reaping thence a harvest of Armed Men is the Same or very like. Ovids 135 Description of the plague is very fine, its beginning with beasts, and at last affecting Man is the Same with Homers. Il: 1.

Strage canum primâ, volucrumque oviumque boumque
Inque feris &c   [VII. 536-7]

111 on Earth] on all Earth *L 28*   114 consumed, *edd.*: consumed *W*: consumed. *L 28* heaven. Accordingly *edd.*: heaven, accordingly *W*: Heaven accordingly *L 28*   116 body, *edd.*: body *W*: Body, *L 28*   118 Can *L 28*: can *W*   122 Hercules, Cadmus] Cadmus, Hercules *L 28*   123 Dragon, *edd.*: Dragon. *W*: Dragon *L 28*   128 Story] Thing *L 28* Countryes, *edd.*: Countryes *W*: Countries, *L 28*   133 Horace. *L 28*: Hor *W*

compare with at the End of this description   140

    Templa vides &c   [VII. 587]

the five next verses good. How pitiful the sixth

    Inque manu thuris pars inconsumpta reperta est. [VII. 592]

Sprats description of the plague of Athens a good deal taken from
hence.   145

*   *   *

   The Systeme of Pythagoras, from whence Epicurus and Lucretius
took theirs is very fine and shows Ovid to have understood that sort
of Natural Philosophy, he has kept his own Sweetness in the Middle
of his rougher description.

    —Fletque Milon Senior cum spectat inanes   150
    Illos, qui fuerant solidorum mole tororum
    Herculeis Similes, fluidos pendere Lacertos.
    Flet quoque, ut in Speculo rugas aspexit aniles
    Tyndaris et Secum cur sit bis rapta requirit. [XV. 229–33]

          Nascique vocatur   155
    Incipere esse aliud, quam quod fuit ante, morique
    Desinere illud idem.   [XV. 255–7]

*   *   *

   The force of Poetry is very strange, thô Dryope being turned into
a Tree is as silly as imagination can well form a Story, her dying Speech
to her family affects Me when I read it.   160

.   .   .   .   .

   Biblis accusing her self for having too Rashly discovered her passion
to her brother, and the Simile of a Ship carryed away by too much
wind is very good.

*   *   *

   There is a great deal of doubt in the Latin Expression (especially in
Verse,) arising from the Adjectives   165

    —Patrios cum conjuge Muros
    Intrat—   [V. 236–7]

Who knows from that Expression if Perseus went to his fathers country,
or to the Country of his wives father.

*   *   *

<hr>

140 with] which. *L 28*   149 rougher] rough *L 28*

—Animum ad Civilia vertet   170
Jura suum—   [xv. 832–3]

Ovid uses *Suus* more then any other Poet and it is commonly re-
dundant, and sometimes Equivocal

> Primus Ophionides Amycus penetralia donis
> haud timuit spoliare Suis.   [xii. 245–6]   175

One does not know if Suis refers to Amycus, or penetralia, if he gave
these Candlesticks, or if they are only the furniture of the house

—Stamina pollice versant   [iv. 34]

and two lines after

—Deducens pollice filum.   [iv. 36]   180

the nearness makes the Expression very poor

—Poma alba ferebat   [iv. 51]

Pomum is taken for the Fruit of the Mulberry and after

—Nivis uberrima pomis.   [iv. 89]

that Pyramus and Thisbe did not go out of town together only to 185
gather Mulberries.

> —Cruor emicat alte
> Non aliter, quam cum vitiato fistula plumbo
> Scinditur—   [iv. 121–3]

a very poor Simile! Pyramus's blood spouted out like water from a 190
crack't pipe: Ovid might as well have said

He bled like a Stuck Pigg.

> —Exhorruit æquoris Instar
> Quod fremit, exiguâ cum summum stringitur aurâ. [iv. 135–6]

The Simile has Something very pretty and Gentile in it, which I 195
think cannot be well Translated.

*   *   *

170 —Animum *L 28*: animum *W*   172 *Suus*] suum *L 28*   181 the Expression]
this Expression *L 28*   185 that] *om. L 28*   196 Translated. *edd.*: Translated *W*:
translated. *L 28*

Ut canis in vacuuo. &c.   [I. 533]

Of Apollo and Daphne the Simile of a hound and a hare, one pursueing
and tother doubling is but mean when the persons to whom it is
applyed are a God and a beautifull woman.   200

*　*　*

Sic ego torrentem quâ nil obstabat Eunti
Lenius & modico strepitu decurrere vidi
At quacumque trabes obstructaque saxa tenebant
Spumeus, et fervens & ab ojice sævior Ibat   [III. 568–71]

Pentheus raging the more the stronger the advice of his friends com- 205
pared here to a River raging higher the more it is opposed is an
admirable Simile and the Expression of it in these four lines is very fine

—Quod Numen in Isto
Corpore sit dubito, sed corpore Numen in Isto est   [III. 611–12]

Ovid uses this way of Speech a hundred times over.   210

*　*　*

Tmolus who was Judge between Phœbus and Pan removes all ob-
structions to his hearing
—Aures
Liberat arboribus. quercu coma cærula tantum
Cingitur, et pendent circum cava tempora glandes   [XI 157–9] 215

Yet presently after
—Sacer ora retorsit
Tmolus ad os Phœbi, vultum sua sylva secuta est. [XI. 163–4]

I take this to be a wrong Image, to fancy a river God with a whole
wood upon his head, as a God of that Wood he only had, as before, 220
a Wreath of Oak upon his head, as he ceases to be the river himself and
is personated in a Human Shape, We do not bear the Transition of the
figures: for if We Imagine the Judge had a forrest upon his head, we
may think that Phœbus harp and Pan's pipe Were in proportion as
bigg, which Would be a very impertinent Image, and the following Line 225
describes Phœbus with a Lawrell only on his head, (not a Wood) and a
purple robe on his back. ie. he gives You in the god just the figure of a Man.

·　·　·　·　·

198 Of *edd.*: of *W*, *L 28*   200 woman. *edd.*: woman *W*: Woman. *L 28*   206
raging higher] raging the higher *L 28*   210 over. *L 28*: over *W*   220 as
before *L 28*: as as before *W*   221 ceases *L 28*: seizes *W*   224 Pan's] Paris *L 28*
225 Image, *L 28*: Image. *W*   227 Man. *L 28*: Man *W*

It is plain that Ovid in the Story of Ceyx endeavoured to describe the Horror of a Tempest, but the Description is long, and flatt, and the Similies with which he endeavours to heighten it rather Lessen then 230 raise Your Terror, immediately after when he comes to Halcyone's concern he begins again to be Moving, from thence and indeed thrô his whole book We find that tenderness was his Masterpiece but he had no Strength.

* * *

Above two hundred and fifty lines in the battels of the Lapithes, a 235 battel fought with Firebrands, cups, caldrons, Pitchforks, weapons that are ridiculous, the wounds nasty and (the usual Fault) the Conquered or Conquerours so little known that You have no concern for them. I had rather have been author of the Counter Scuffle then of this whole Story.   240

.   .   .   .   .

—Belloque cruentior Ipso
———————————Achilles   [XII. 592–3]

Is by Ovids leave a little upon the Drawcanser.

* * *

Jupiter aut falsus pater est, aut Crimine verus.
Matris adulterio patrem petis, elige, fictum   245
Esse Jovem malis, an Te per dedecus ortum. [IX. 24–26]

The same thing is here according to Ovids usual redundance said three Times and the thought does not rise, Dryden Sometimes commits the Same fault, the four first verses of his Absolom.

* * *

Collecti flores Tunicis cecidere remissis.   250
Tantaque Simplicitas puerilibus ad fuit annis:
Hæc quoque virgineum movit jactura dolorem. [V. 399–401]

Proserpine was indeed very young or very silly that when She was in the hands of Pluto, had her cloaths torn and Squalled out to her Mother was griev'd that She dropt the flowers out of her lap. This was 255 a great while since, Wenches that are bigg enough to be ravish't are not so infinitely concerned for their Nosegays.

* * *

232 thence] hence, *L 28*   234. Strength. *L 28*: Strength *W*   235 Above *L 28*: above *W*   237 Fault *L 28*: fought *W*   240 Story. *L 28*: Story *W*   243 upon] *om. L 28*   Drawcanser. *edd.*: Drawcanser *W*: Draw-canser. *L 28*   246 Jovem] Jovis *L 28*   249 fault, the] fault. —as in the *L 28*   255 This *L 28*: this *W*

Europa was a Trull
that went to Sea with Captain Bull.

*   *   *

Ovid makes his People better bred then his fellow poets usually do 260

—Quæcumque est Causa videndi
Has tibi, Diva, domos, animo gratissima nostro es.   [v. 260–1]

This proceeded from his knowing a Court. So when Ceyx complements
Peleus.

Quod petis omne feres, tuaque hæc pro parte videto   265
Qualiacumque vides, utinam meliora videres.   [xi. 287–8]

Nestor thô he hated Hercules for having killed his brothers and
ravaged his Country, takes no other advantage then passing over in
Silence Hercules's part of the battel against the Centaurs, and answers
Hercules's Son Tlepolemus thereupon with a Complement,   270

—quis enim laudaverit hostem,   [xii. 548]

and presently after

Num videor debere tui præconia rebus
Herculis, o Rhodiæ ductor pulcherrime classis?
Ne tamen ulterius, quam fortia facta silendo,   275
Ulciscor fratres, solida est Mihi gratia tecum   [xii. 573–6]

And Anius describing to Anchises his Son's Cowardise makes him
and Æneas who was present a pretty complement

Non hic Æneas, non qui defenderet Andron
Hector erat per quos decimum durastis in Annum.   [xiii. 665–6] 280

*   *   *

Like Ovid We have all a desire of existing in some Manner, and as
in this life Each subsists mutually by other, the Learned Man and the
Counsellor requiring the courage and conduct of the Seaman and
Souldier, and giving them in exchange the benefit of wholsom laws
and good Maxims, the poor and the rich, the peasant and the Citizens 285
traffiquing fruits for utensils, labour for cloathing assisting each other
in what he has for what he wants and all are helped by the reciprocation
of the Commerce: So is it in this imaginary life which We Seek after

259 Captain Bull. *L 28*: Captn: Bull *W*   263 This] These *L 28*   Court. *L 28*:
Court *W*   280 Annum. *L 28*: Annum *W*   281–95 *om. L 28*   282 other, *edd.*:
other *W*

Death, Heroes and Conquerors perform great Actions which written
and recorded may give them this kind of Immortality, Historians and 290
Poets procure to themselves the Same advantage from the very writing
of these Actions: princes build cities and palaces, Engeneers and
Architects come in for their share of the fame, and he that would be
remembered by a Monument divides the honour with the Sculptor that
Erects it.   295

WORKS OF UNKNOWN DATE

Epigram.

WHEN NELL, giv'n o'er by the Doctor was Dying,
And JOHN at the Chimney stood Decently crying,
Tis in vain Said the Woman, to make Such ado,
For to our long Home we must all of us go.
True NELL reply'd JOHN, but what yet is the worst   5
For Us that Remain, the Best always go first
Remember, Dear Wife, that I said so last Year,
When You lost your white Heifer, and I my brown Mare.

Epigram.

WHEN BIBO thought fit from the World to retreat,
As full of Champaign as an Egg's full of Meat,
He wak'd in the Boat, and to CHARON he said,
He wou'd be set back for he was not yet Dead:
Trim the Boat and sit quiet, stern CHARON reply'd,   5
You may have forgot, You was Drunk when You Dy'd.

Epigram.

O DEATH how Thou spoil'st the best projects of Life,
Said GABRIEL, who stil as He Bury'd one Wife,
    For the sake of Her Family Marry'd her Cousen:
And thus in an Honest Colateral line
He stil Marry'd on till His Number was Nine,   5
    Full sorry to Dye 'till he made up his Dozen.

Title] AN EPIGRAM. *1740*
Title] ANOTHER. *1740*   4 set] row'd *1740*   6 was] were *1740*
Title] ANOTHER. *1740*

Epigram.

QUOTH Richard in jest looking wishly at Nelly
   Methinks Child You seem something round in the Belly:
Nell answer'd him snapishly; how can that be?
My Husband has been more than two Years at Sea.
Thy Husband, quoth Dick, why that matter was carried   5
Most Secretly Nell, I n'er thought thou wert Married.

Cupid in Ambush.

IT oft to many has successful been,
  Upon his arm to let his mistress lean,
Or with her airy fan to cool her heat,
Or gently squeeze her knees, or press her feet.
All public sports to favour young desire,   5
With opportunities like this conspire;
Ev'n where his skill, the Gladiator shows,
With human blood, where the Arena flows.
There oftentimes love's quiver-bearing-Boy,
Prepares his bow and arrows to destroy: 10
While the spectator gazes on the fight,
And sees 'em wound each other with delight.
While he his pretty mistress entertains,
And wagers with her who the conquest gains;
Slily the GOD takes aim and hits his heart,   15
And in the wounds he sees he bears his part.

Song.

HAST my Nannette my lovely Maid
  Hast to the Bower Thy Swain has made.
For Thee Alone I made the Bower
And strow'd the Couch with many a flow'r

Epigram. 1 wishly] wistly *1740*
Song. Title] A Song *L 27, 1740*
1740 : To *M, L 27*

2 Belly: *edd.*: Belly *M*: belly: *1740*
2 made. *1740*: made *M*: maid. *L 27*

3 For

None but my Sheep shal near us come   5
Venus be Prais'd my Sheep are dumb.
Great God of Love take Thou my Crook
To keep the Wolf from Nannetts Flock
Guard Thou the Sheep to her so dear
My own Alas are less my Care   10
But of the Wolf if thou art afraid
Come not to Us to call for Aid
For with her Swain my Love shal stay
Tho the Wolf Strole, and tho the Sheep Stray.

Written in Imitation of a Greek Epigram.

WHEN hungry Wolves had Trespass'd on the Fold,
    And the robb'd Shepherd His sad Story told;
"Call in Alcides, said a crafty Priest,
"Give Him One half and He'l Secure the rest."
No, said the Shepherd, if the Fates decree   5
By ravaging my Flock to ruin me,
To their Commands I willingly resign;
Pow'r is Their Character, and Patience mine:
Tho' troth to me there Seems but little Odds,
Who prove the greatest Robbers, Wolves or Gods?   10

Epigram.

POOR Hall caught his Death standing under a Spout
    Expecting till Midnight when Nan wou'd come out
But fatal his Patience as cruel the Dame,
And curst was the Rain that extinguisht this flame.
"Who e'er thou art that reads these Moral Lines   5
"Make Love at Home, and go to Bed betimes."

---

11 thou art] *L 27* thou'rt *1740*   14 tho] *L 27 om. 1740*
    4 rest." *1740*: rest. *M*   5 No, *1740*: No *M*   9 there *1740*: their *M*
  10 Robbers, *edd.*: Robbers *M*: robbers, *1740*
    Title] AN EPIGRAM. *1740*   4 Rain . . . this] Weather that quench'd the Man's
1740   6 betimes." *1740*: betimes" *M*

Epigram.

P ROMETHEUS forming Mr: D——
  Carv'd something like a Man in Clay.
The Mortals work might well Miscarry;
  He that does Heav'n and Earth controll
  Has only Pow'r to Form a Soul,   5
His hand is Evident in H——.
  Since one is but a moving Clod,
  T'other the lively Form of God,
Squire Ne . . ., You will scarse be able
  To prove all Poetry but Fable.   10

The Wandering Pilgrim.

Humbly Addressed to Sir Thomas Frankland, Bart.
Post-Master, and Pay-Master-General to Queen Anne.

I.

W ILL PIGGOT must to Coxwould go,
  To live, alas! in want,
Unless Sir THOMAS say No, no,
  Th'Allowance is too scant.

II.

The gracious Knight full well does weet,   5
  Ten farthings ne'er will do,
To keep a man each day in meat,
  Some bread to meat is due.

III.

A Rechabite poor WILL must live,
  And drink of ADAM's ale,   10
Pure-Element, no life can give,
  Or mortal soul regale.

Epigram. Title] ANOTHER [EPIGRAM]. *1740*   1 D— *edd.*: D. *M* : DAY, *1740*
5 Pow'r *edd.*: Pow'er *M* : pow'r *1740*   6 H——. *edd.*: H . *M* : HARRY. *1740*   9
Ne...] WALLIS *1740*   scarse] scare *1740*

IV.

Spare diet, and spring-water clear,
    Physicians hold are good;
Who diet's thus need never fear,   15
    A fever in the blood.

V.

Gra'mercy, Sirs, y'are in the right,
    Prescriptions All can sell,
But he that does not eat can't sh* * *
    Or piss if good drink fail.   20

VI.

But pass—The Æsculapian-Crew,
    Who eat and quaff the best,
They seldom miss to bake and brew,
    Or lin to break their fast.

VII.

Could Yorkshire-Tyke but do the same,   25
    Than He like Them might thrive,
But FORTUNE, FORTUNE, cruel DAME,
    To starve Thou do'st Him drive.

VIII.

In WILL's Old master's plenteous days,
    His mem'ry e'er be blest;   30
What need of speaking in his praise,
    His goodness stands confest.

IX.

At His fam'd gate stood Charity,
    In lovely sweet array,
CERES, and Hospitality,   35
    Dwelt there both night and day.

X.

But to conclude, and be concise,
    Truth must WILL's voucher be,
Truth never yet went in disguise,
    For naked still is She.   40

XI.

There is but One, but One alone,
  Can set the PILGRIM free,
And make him cease to pine and moan,
  O! FRANKLAND it is THEE.

XII.

O! save him from a dreary way,   45
  To Coxwould he must hye,
Bereft of thee he wends astray,
  At Coxwould he must dye.

XIII.

O! let him in thy hall but stand,
  And wear a porter's gown,   50
Duteous to what Thou may'st command,
  Thus WILLIAM's wishes crown.

Fragment.

THUS to the Muses spoke the Cyprian Dame;
  Adorn my Altars and revere my Name
My Son shal else assume His potent darts
Twang goes the Bow, my Girls, have at your hearts.
The Muses answer'd, Venus we deride   5
The Vagrants Malice, and his Mothers Pride.
Send him to Nymphs who sleep on Idas shade,
To the loose Dance and wanton Masquerade:
Our Thoughts are settl'd, and intent our look
On the Instructive Verse and Moral book;   10
On Female Idleness his Pow'r relyes
But when he finds Us Studying hard he flyes.

Title] THE ADVICE OF *VENUS. 1740*   1 Cyprian Dame; *edd.*: Cyprean
Dame *M*: CYPRIAN-DAME; *1740*   2 Altars *edd.*: Alters *M*: altars *1740*   5
answer'd, *1740*: answer'd *M*   9 settl'd, *edd.*: settl'd *M*: setled, *1740*   10 book;
1740: book *M*

Cupid a Plowman from Moschus.

His Lamp his Bow and Quiver laid aside,
A rustic Wallet o'er his Shoulders ty'd
Sly Cupid always on new Mischief bent
To the Rich Field and furrow'd Tillage went.
Like any Plowman toil'd the little God,   5
His Tune he whistl'd, and his Wheat he sow'd
Then sat and laugh'd, and to the Skys above
Raising his Eye He thus insulted Jove:
Lay by your Hail your hurtful Storms restrain,
And as I bid You let it Shine or rain   10
Else you again beneath my Yoke shal bow
Feel the sharp Goad, and draw the Servile plough;
What once Europa was Nanet is now.

Epigram.

O With what Woes am I opprest!
—Be stil you Senseless Calf:
What if the Gods shou'd make You blest?
Why then I'd Sing and Laugh.
But if They won't I'll wail and Cry: 5
You'l Hardly Laugh; before You Dye.

Chast Florimel.

No I'll endure ten thousand Deaths
E'er any further I comply
O, Sir, no Man on Earth that breaths
Had ever yet his Hand so high.

Cupid a Plowman. Title: a . . . from] TURNED . . . FROM THE GREEK OF *1740*
1 aside, *1740* : aside *M*   7 Then *1740* : Than *M*   8 Jove: *edd.* : Jove *M* : JOVE.
1740   12 plough; *edd.* : plough *M* : plow, *1740*   13 Nanet] NANNETTE *1740*
    Epigram. Title] HUSBAND AND WIFE. AN EPIGRAM. *1740*   *In 1740, ll. 1*
and 4 are marked H., for 'Husband', and ll. 2 and 6 are marked W., for 'Wife'

O take Your Sword and pierce my heart,　　　5
　　Undaunted see me meet the wound;
O! will you act a Tarquins part?
　　A Second Lucrece you have found.

Thus to the pressing Coridon
　　Poor Florimel unhappy Maid　　　10
Fearing by Love to be undon,
　　In broken Dying Accents said.

Delia, who held the Conscious Door
　　Inspir'd by Truth and Brandy smil'd,
Knowing that Sixteen Months before　　　15
　　Our Lucrece had her Second Child.

And hark ye Madam, cry'd the Bawd
　　None of your flights, your high-rope dodging;
Be Civil here, or march abroad;
　　Oblige the Squire, or quit your Lodging.　　　20

O have I, Florimel went on,
　　Have I then lost my Delia's Aid?
Where shal forsaken Virtue run
　　If by her Friends She is betray'd?

O Curse on empty Friendships Name;　　　25
　　Lord what is all our future view?
Then Dear Destroyer of my Fame,
　　Let my last Succor be to You.

From Delia's rage and Fortunes frown
　　A Wretched Love-sick Maid deliver:　　　30
O tip me but an other Crown,
　　Dear Sir, and make me Yours for Ever.

Partial Fame.

THE Sturdy Man if He in Love obtains,
　　In open Pomp and Triumph reigns;
The Subtil Woman if She shou'd succeed,
　　Disowns the Honor of the Deed.

Tho He for all his boast, is forc'd to yield, 5
Tho She can always keep the Field,
He vaunts his Conquest, She conceals her Shame,
How partial is the Voice of Fame.

Song.

WHITHER wou'd my Passion run
Shal I fly Her or persue her?
Loosing Her I am undone
Yet wou'd not gain Her to undo her.

Yee Tyrants of the Human breast, 5
Love and Reason! cease your War,
And order Death to give me rest;
So Each will Equal Triumph share.

Non Pareil.

I.

LET others from the town retire,
And in the fields seek new delight;
My PHILLIS does such joys inspire,
No other objects please my sight.

II.

In Her alone I find whate'er 5
Beauties a country-landscape grace;
No shades so lovely as Her hair,
Nor plain so sweet as is Her face.

III.

Lilies and roses there combine,
More beauteous than in flow'ry field; 10
Transparent is Her skin, so fine,
To this each crystal stream must yield.

8 Fame.] FAME? *1740*
Song. Title] A SONG. SET BY Mr *PURCEL. 1740* 3 Loosing] Losing *1740*

IV.

Her voice more sweet than warbling sound,
  Tho' sung by nightingale or lark,
Her eyes such lustre dart around,   15
  Compar'd to them the sun is dark.

V.

Both light and vital heat they give,
  Cherish'd by Them my love takes root,
From Her kind looks does life receive,
  Grows a fair plant; bears flow'rs, and fruit.   20

VI.

Such fruit, I ween, did once deceive
  The common parent of mankind;
And made transgress our mother Eve:
  Poison it's core, tho' fair it's rind.

VII.

Yet so delicious is it's taste,   25
  I cannot from the bait abstain,
But to th'inchanting pleasure haste,
  Tho' I were sure 'twou'd end in pain.

Upon Honour. A Fragment.

Honour, I say, or honest Fame,
I mean the substance, not the name;
(Not that light heap of tawdry wares,
Of Ermin, Coronets, and Stars,
Which often is by merit sought,   5
By gold and flatt'ry oft'ner bought.
The shade, for which Ambition looks,
In Selden's or in Ashmole's books:)
But the true glory which proceeds,
Reflected bright from honest deeds,   10
Which we in our Own breast perceive,
And Kings can neither take nor give.

Epigram.

PHYLLIS You boast of perfect Health in vain
     And laugh at those who of their ills complain:
That with a frequent Fever Cloe burns
And Stella's plumpness into Dropsey turns.
O Phyllis while the Patients are Nineteen   5
Little Alas are their Distempers Seen
But Thou for all Thy seeming Health art ill
Beyond thy Lovers Hopes or Blackmores Skill
No Lenitives can thy Disease aswage
I tell Thee tis incurable—'tis Age.   10

Epigram.

LUKE Preach-ill admires what we Laymen can mean
     That thus by our Profit and pleasure are Sway'd.
He has but Three Livings, and wou'd be a Dean,
     His Wife dy'd this Year, He has Marri'd his Maid.

To suppress all his Carnal desires in their Birth   5
     At all Hours a lusty young Hussy is near;
And to take off his thought from the things of this Earth
     He can be Content with Two Thousand a Year.

Pontius and Pontia.

I.

PONTIUS, (who loves you know a joke,
     Much better than he loves his life)
Chanc'd t'other morning to provoke
     The patience of a well-bred wife.

Epigram. Title] THE INCURABLE. AN EPIGRAM. *1740*   2 complain: *1740* :
complain *M*   4 turns. *1740* : turns *M*
     Epigram. Title] THE Insatiable PRIEST. *1740*   1 Preach-ill *edd.* : Preach ill *M* :
PREACH-ILL *1740*

II.

Talking of you, said he, my dear,   5
     Two of the greatest wits in town,
One ask'd, If that high fuzz of hair
     Was, *bona fide*, all your Own.

III.

Her own, most certain, t'other said,
     For NAN, who knows the thing, will tell ye,   10
The hair was bought, the money paid,
     And the receipt was sign'd DUCAILLY.

IV.

PONTIA, (that civil prudent She,
     Who values wit much less than sense,
And never darts a repartee,   15
     But purely in Her own defense)

V.

Reply'd, These friends of your's, my dear,
     Are given extremely much to satire,
But pr'ythee husband, let one hear,
     Sometimes less wit, and more good-nature.   20

VI.

Now I have one unlucky thought,
     That wou'd have spoil'd your friend's conceit;
Some hair I have, I'm sure, unbought,
     Pray bring your brother-wits to see't.

Epigram.

So good a Wife doth Alise make
     That from all Company She flyeth,
Such virtuous Courses doth She take,
     That She all evil Tongues defyeth.
And for her Dearest Spouses Sake   5
     She with His Breth'ren only lyeth.

Title] Cautious ALICE. *1740*   1 Alise] LISSY *1740*

To a Poet of Quality Praising the Lady Hinchinbroke.

O F Thy Judicious Muses Sense
   Young Hinchinbroke so very proud is
That Sacharissa and Hortence
   She looks henceforth upon as Dowdies.

Yet She to One must stil submit   5
   To Dear Mamma must pay her Duty
She wonders praising Wilmots Wit
   Thou shou'dst forget his Daughters Beauty.

Epigram.

L YSANDER talks extremely well;
   On any subject let him dwell,
   His Tropes and Figures will content Yee:
He shou'd Possess to all Degrees
The Art of Talk, he Practices   5
   Full fourteen Hours in four and twenty.

Truth Told at Last. An Epigram.

S AYS PONTIUS in rage,
   contradicting his Wife,
"You never yet told me
   "one Truth in your life:"
Vext PONTIA no way   5
   could this Thesis allow,
"You're a Cuckold, say's she,
   "do I tell you Truth now?"

Epigram. Title] AN EPIGRAM. *1740*

Riddle.

FORM'D half beneath and half above the Earth
We Sisters owe to Art our Second birth.
The Smiths and Carpenters adopted daughters
Made on the land to travel o'er the Waters
Swifter they move as they are straiter bound   5
Yet neither tread the air, the wave or ground:
They serve the poor for Use the rich for whim,
Sink when it rains and when it freezes swim.

Chanson Francoise. Translated.

WHY thus from the Plain does my Shepherdess rove
Forsaking Her Swain and neglecting his love?
You have heard all my Grief, you see how I dye
O give some relief to the Swain whom you fly.

How can you complain or what am I to say,   5
Since my Dog lyes unfed, and my Sheep run astray,
Need I tell what I mean, that I languish alone
When I leave all the Plain, You may guess tis for One.

Human Life.

WHAT trifling coil do we poor mortals keep;
Wake, eat, and drink, evacuate, and sleep.

Riddle. Title: L 28 (*Pope*), 'Contents' *of* L 28: AN ENIGMA. *1740: om. W*, L 28 (D)
1 FORM'D L 28: FORM'D *1740:* form'd *W*   3 The L 28, *1740:* the *W*   Carpenters
L 28: Carpenders *W*: Carpenter's *1740*   4 Made L 28, *1740:* made *W*   o'er] L 28
on *1740, Alt. reading in* L 28   6 the wave] or Wave L 28, *1740*   ground: *1740:*
ground *W*, L 28   7 They L 28, *1740:* they *W*   whim, *1740:* whim *W*, L 28
8] L 28, *1740* & half the Year they sink and half they swim *Earlier reading in W and* L 28
swim. *1740:* swim *W*: Swim L 28
Chanson Francoise. Title] Translated. *Lpo, Harl, Lansd:* A FRENCH SONG. *1740*

Nelly's Picture. A Song.

I.

WHILST others proclaim
   This Nymph, or that Swain,
Dearest NELLY, the lovely, I'll sing;
   She shall grace ev'ry verse,
   I'll her Beauty rehearse,   5
Which lovers can't think an ill thing.

II.

   Her eyes shine as bright
   As stars in the night,
Her complexion's divinely fair;
   Her lips red as a cherry,   10
   Wou'd a Hermit make merry,
And black as a coal is her hair.

III.

   Her breath like a rose,
   It's sweets does disclose,
Whenever you ravish a kiss;   15
   Like iv'ry inchas'd,
   Her teeth are well plac'd,
An exquisite beauty she is.

IV.

   Her plump breasts are white,
   Delighting the sight,   20
There CUPID discovers her charms;
   O! spare then the rest,
   And think of the best:
'Tis heaven to dye in her arms.

V.

   She's blooming as May,   25
   Brisk, lively, and gay,
The GRACES play all round about her;
   She's prudent and witty,
   Sings wond'rously pretty,
And there is no living without her.   30

Prologue.

LADIES, to YOU with pleasure we submit,
 This early offspring of a VIRGIN-WIT.
From your good nature nought our AUTHRESS fears,
Sure you'll indulge, if not the MUSE, her YEARS,
Freely the praise she may deserve bestow,   5
Pardon, not censure, what you can't allow;
Smile on the work, be to her merits kind,
And to her faults, whate'er they are, be blind.

 Let Critics follow RULES, she boldly writes
What NATURE dictates, and what LOVE indites.   10
By no dull forms her QUEEN and LADIES move,
But court their HEROES, and agnize their love.
Poor MAID! she'd have (what e'en no WIFE would crave)
A HUSBAND love his SPOUSE beyond the grave:
And from a second-marriage to deter,   15
Shews you what horrid things STEPMOTHERS are.
Howe'er, to CONSTANCY the PRIZE she gives,
And tho' the SISTER dies the BROTHER lives.
Blest with success, at last, he mounts a throne,
Enjoys at once his MISTRESS and a CROWN.   20
Learn, LADIES, then from LINDARAXA's fate,
What great rewards on virtuous Lovers wait.
Learn too, if Heav'n and Fate should adverse prove,
(For Fate and Heav'n don't always smile on love)
Learn with ZELINDA to be still the same,   25
Nor quit your FIRST for any SECOND flame,
Whatever fate, or death, or life, be given,
Dare to be true, submit the rest to Heaven.

Amaryllis. A Pastoral.

IT was the fate of an unhappy SWAIN
 To love a NYMPH, the glory of the plain;
In vain he daily did his courtship move,
The NYMPH was haughty, and disdain'd to love.

Prologue. Title: edd.: PROLOGUE FOR *DELIA*'s PLAY. *1740 (see commentary)*

Each morn as soon as the SUN's golden ray   5
Dispers'd the clouds, and chaced dark night away,
The sad despairing Shepherd rear'd his head
From off his pillow, and forsook his bed.
Strait he search'd out some melancholy shade,
Where he did blame the proud disdainful MAID,   10
And thus with cruelty did her upbraid:
Ah! SHEPHERDESS will you then let me dye;
Will nothing thaw this frozen cruelty:
But you, lest you should pity, will not hear,
You will not to my sufferings give ear;   15
But adder-like to listen you refuse
To words, the greatest charm that man can use.
'Tis now noon-day, the Sun is mounted high,
Beneath refreshing shades the beasts do lie,
And seek out cooling rivers to asswage,   20
The Lion's sultry heat, and Dog-Star's rage:
The Oxen now can't plow the fruitful soil,
The furious heat forbids the reaper's toil.
Both beast and men for work are now unfit,
The weary'd Hinds down to their dinner sit;   25
Each creature now is with refreshment blest,
And none but wretched I, debarr'd of rest,
I wander up and down thro' desart lands,
On sun-burnt mountain-tops, and parched sands.
And as alone, restless I go along,   30
Nothing but eccho answers to my Song.
Had I not better undergo the scorn
Of JENNY? is it not more easy borne?
The cruelty of angry KATE? altho'
That She is black, and you as white as snow.   35
O! NYMPH don't, too much, to your beauty trust,
The brightest steel is eaten up with rust:
The whitest blossoms fall, sweet roses fade,
And you, tho' handsom, yet may dye a maid.
With THEE I could admire a country life,   40
Free from disturbance, city noise, or strife:
Amongst the shady groves and woods we'd walk,
Of nothing else but love's great charms we'd talk,

15 sufferings *edd.* : suff'rings *1740*

We would pursue, in season, rural sports,
And then let knaves and fools resort to courts;   45
I could, besides, some country-presents find,
Could they persuade you, but to be more kind:
But since with scorn you do those gifts despise,
Another SHEPHERDESS shall gain the prize.
O! AMARYLLIS, beauteous Maid, observe,   50
The NYMPHS themselves are willing THEE to serve,
See where large baskets full of flowers they bring,
The sweet fair product of th'indulgent spring.
See there the Pink, and the Anemony,
The purple Violet, Rose, and Jessamy.   55
See where they humbly lay their presents down,
To make a chaplet thy dear head to crown.
See where the beasts go trooping drove by drove,
See how they answer one another's love:
See where the Bull the Heifer does pursue,   60
See where the Mare the furious Horse does woo:
Each Female to her Male is always kind,
And Women, only cruel Women blind,
Contradict that for which they were design'd.
So CORYDON loves an ungrateful Fair,   65
Who minds not oaths, nor cares for any prayer.
But see the SUN his race has almost run,
And the laborious Ox his work has done.
But I still love without the thought of ease,
No cure was ever found for that disease,   70
But CORYDON, what frenzy does thee seize.
Why dost thou lie in this dejected way?
Why doest thou let thy Sheep and Oxen stray?
Thy tuneful Pipe, why dost Thou throw away.
Had not you better dispossess your mind   75
Of Her who is so cruel and unkind;
Forget Her guile, and calm those raging cares,
Take heart again, and follow your affairs,
For what altho' this NYMPH does cruel prove,
You'll find a thousand other Maids will love.   80

71 seize *edd.*: cease *1740*

Upon Playing at Ombre, with Two Ladies.

I KNOW that FORTUNE long has wanted sight,
And therefore pardon'd, when She did not right;
But yet till then it never did appear,
That as She wanted Eyes, She could not Hear.
I begg'd, that She would give me leave to lose,   5
A thing She does not commonly refuse:
Two Matadores are out against my game,
Yet still I play, and still my Luck's the same:
Unconquer'd in Three suits it does remain;
Whereas I only ask in One to gain;   10
Yet She still contradicting, Gifts imparts;
And gives success in ev'ry suit—but HEARTS.

Cupid's Promise.

Paraphrased.

I.

SOFT CUPID, wanton, am'rous Boy,
The other day mov'd with my lyre,
In flatt'ring accents spoke his joy,
And utter'd thus his fond desire.

II.

O! raise thy voice, One SONG I ask,   5
Touch then th'harmonious string,
To THYRSIS easy is the task,
Who can so sweetly play and sing.

III.

Two kisses from my mother dear,
THYRSIS thy due reward shall be,   10
None, none, like Beauty's Queen is fair,
PARIS has vouch'd this Truth for me.

IV.

I strait reply'd, Thou know'st alone
  That brightest CLOE rules my breast,
I'll sing thee Two instead of ONE,   15
  If Thou'lt be kind, and make me blest.

V.

One Kiss from CLOE's lips, no more
  I crave, He promiss'd me success,
I play'd with all my skill and power,
  My glowing passion to express.   20

VI.

But O! my CLOE, beauteous Maid,
  Wilt thou the wisht reward bestow?
Wilt Thou make good what LOVE has said,
  And by Thy grant, His power show?

Dorinda.

FAREWEL ye shady walks, and fountains,
  Sinking vallies, rising mountains:
Farewel ye crystal streams, that pass
Thro' fragrant meads of verdant grass:
Farewel ye flowers, sweet and fair,   5
That us'd to grace DORINDA's hair:
Farewel ye woods, who us'd to shade
The pressing youth, and yielding maid:
Farewel ye birds, whose morning song
Oft made us know we slept too long: 10
Farewel dear bed, so often prest,
So often above others blest,
With the kind weight of all her charms,
When panting, dying, in my arms.
DORINDA's gone, gone far away,   15
She's gone, and STREPHON cannot stay:
By sympathetic ties I find
That to Her sphere I am confin'd;

My motions still on Her must wait,
And what She wills to me is fate.   20

She's gone, O! hear it all ye bowers,
Ye walks, ye fountains, trees, and flowers,
For whom you made your earliest show,
For whom you took a pride to grow.
She's gone, O! hear ye nightingales,   25
Ye mountains ring it to the vales,
And eccho to the country round,
The mournful, dismal, killing sound:
DORINDA's gone, and STREPHON goes,
To find with Her his lost repose.   30

But ere I go, O! let me see,
That all things mourn Her loss like me:
Play, play, no more ye spouting fountains,
Rise ye vallies, sink ye mountains;
Ye walks, in moss, neglected lie,   35
Ye birds, be mute; ye streams, be dry.
Fade, fade, ye flowers, and let the rose
No more it's blushing buds disclose:
Ye spreading beach, and taper fir,
Languish away in mourning Her;   40
And never let your friendly shade,
The stealth of other Lovers aid.
And thou, O! dear, delightful bed,
The altar where Her maidenhead,
With burning cheeks, and down cast eyes,   45
With panting breasts, and kind replies,
And other due solemnity,
Was offer'd up to love and me.
Hereafter suffer no abuse,
Since consecrated to our use,   50
As thou art sacred, don't profane
Thy self with any vulgar stain,
But to thy pride be still display'd,
The print her lovely limbs have made:
See, in a moment, all is chang'd,   55
The flowers shrunk up, the trees disrang'd,

And that which wore so sweet a face,
Become a horrid, desart place.
Nature Her influence withdraws,
Th'effect must follow still the cause,   60
And where DORINDA will reside,
Nature must there all joy provide.
Decking that happy spot of earth,
Like Eden's-Garden at it's birth,
To please Her matchless, darling Maid,   65
The wonder of her Forming-Trade;
Excelling All who e'er Excell'd,
And as we ne'er the like beheld,
So neither is, nor e'er can be,
Her Parallel, or Second SHE.   70

To Leonora.

IF absence so much racks my Charmer's heart,
Believe that STREPHON's bears a double smart,
So well he loves, and knows thy love so fine,
That in his Own distress he suffers Thine:
Yet, O forgive him, if his thoughts displease,   5
He would not, cannot wish Thee more at ease.

What need you bid me think of pleasures past?
Was there one joy, whose image does not last?
But that One; most extatic, most refin'd,
Reigns fresh, and will for ever in my mind,   10
With such a power of charms it storm'd my soul,
That nothing ever can it's strength controul.
Not sleep, not age, not absence can avail,
Reflection, ever young, must still prevail.
What influence-divine did guide that hour,   15
Which gave to minutes the Almighty Power,
To fix (whilst other joys are not a span)
A pleasure lasting as the life of man.

62 joy *edd.*: gay *1740*   63 happy spot *edd.*: happy, spot *1740*

To Leonora. Encore.

I.

Cease, Leonora, cease to mourn,
Thy faithful Strephon will return.
Fate at thy sighs will ne'er relent,
Then grieve not, what we can't prevent;
Nor let predestinating tears,   5
Increase my pains, or raise thy fears.

II.

'Tis but the last long winter night,
Our Sun will rise to morrow bright,
And to our suff'ring passion bring
The promise of eternal Spring,   10
Which thy kind eyes shall ever cheer,
And make that Season all our Year.

On a Pretty Madwoman.

I.

While mad Ophelia we lament,
And Her distraction mourn,
Our grief's misplac'd, Our tears mispent,
Since what for Her condition's meant
More justly fits Our Own.   5

II.

For if 'tis happiness to be,
From all the turns of Fate,
From dubious joy, and sorrow free;
Ophelia then is blest, and we
Misunderstand Her state.   10

To Leonora. Encore.   12 Year. *edd.*: Year, *1740*

III.

The Fates may do whate'er they will,
   They can't disturb her mind,
Insensible of good, or ill,
Ophelia is Ophelia still,
   Be Fortune cross or kind.   15

IV.

Then make with reason no more noise,
   Since what should give relief,
The quiet of Our mind destroys,
Or with a full spring-tide of joys,
   Or a dead-ebb of grief.   20

Absence.

I.

WHAT a tedious day is past!
   Loving, thinking, wishing, weeping:
Gods! if this be not the last,
   Take a life not worth my keeping.

II.

Love, ye Gods, is Life alone!   5
   In the length is little pleasure:
Be but ev'ry day Our-Own,
   We shall ne'er complain of measure.

The New-Year's Gift to Phyllis.

I.

THE circling months begin this day,
   To run their yearly ring,
And long-breath'd time which ne'er will stay,
Refits his wings, and shoots away,
   It round again to bring.   5

II.

Who feels the force of female eyes,
　And thinks some Nymph divine,
Now brings his annual sacrifice,
Some pretty toy, or neat device,
　To offer at Her shrine.   10

III.

But I can pay no offering,
　To show how I adore,
Since I had but a heart to bring
A downright foolish, faithful thing,
　And that you had before.   15

IV.

Yet we may give, for custom sake,
　What will to both be New,
My Constancy a Gift I'll make,
And in return of it will take
　Some Levity from You.   20

A Song.

I.

FOR God's-sake—nay, dear Sir,
　Lord, what do You mean?
I protest, and I vow Sir,
　Your ways are obscene.

II.

Pray give over, O! fie,   5
　Pish, leave off your fooling,
Forbear, or I'll cry,—
　I hate this rude doing.

9 toy *edd.*: boy *1740*
　6 off *edd.*: of *1740*

III.

Let me die if I stay,
   Does the DEVIL possess You;
Your hand take away,
   Then perhaps I may bless You.

                                                     10

Snuff. An Epigram.

JOVE once resolv'd (the Females to degrade)
  To propagate their Sex without their aid.
His brain conceiv'd, and soon the pangs, and throws
He felt, nor could th'unnatural birth disclose:
At last when try'd, no remedy would do,   5
The God took SNUFF, and out the Goddess flew.

To Celia. An Epigram.

YOU need not thus so often pray,
  Or in devotion spend the day,
Since without half such toil and pain,
You surely Paradise will gain.
Your HUSBAND's impotent and jealous,   5
And CELIA that's enough to tell us
You must inhabit Heaven herea'ter,
Because you are a VIRGIN-MARTYR.

Upon a Friend, Who Had a Pain in his Left-Side.

I.

LAY not the Pain, so near your heart,
  On chance, or on disease,
So sensible, so nice a smart,
  Is from no cause like these.

II.

Your Friends, at last, the truth have found,   5
    Howe'er you tell your story,
'Twas CELIA's eyes that gave the Wound,
    And they shall have the Glory.

'Strephonetta Why d'ye flye me?'

STREPHONETTA *Why d'ye flye me?*
With such Rigour in your Eyes;
O! 'tis cruel to deny me,
Since your Charms I so much prize;
But I plainly see the reason,   5
Why in vain I you pursu'd;
Her to gain 'twas out of Season,
Who before the Chaplain woo'd.

Parting with Flavia.

COME, *weep no more, for 'tis in vain,*
Torment not thus your pretty Heart;
Think, Flavia, we may meet again,
As well as that we now must part.

2

You sigh, and weep, the Gods neglect   5
That precious Dew, your Eyes let fall;
Our Joy, and Grief, with like respect
They mind, and that is, not at all.

3

Wee pray in hopes, they will be kind,
As if they did regard our State;   10
They hear; and the return we find
Is that, no Prayers can alter Fate.

'Strephonetta Why'. Title: edd.: om. *1741*

4

Then clear your Brow, and look more gay,
Do not your-self to Grief resign;
Who knows, but that these Powers may   15
The Pair, they now have parted, joyn?

5

But since they have thus cruel been,
And could such constant Lovers sever;
I dare not trust, least now they're in,
They should divide us two, for ever.   20

6

Then Flavia, come and let us grieve,
Remembring thô upon what Score;
This our last parting Look believe,
Believe, we must embrace no more:

7

Yet should our Sun shine out at last,   25
And Fortune without more deceit,
Throw but one reconciling Cast,
To make two wand'ring Lovers meet

8

How great then would our Pleasure be?
To find Heav'n kinder than believ'd,   30
And we, who had no hopes to see
Each other, to be thus deceiv'd.

9

But, say, Heav'n should bring no Relief,
Suppose, our Sun should never rise;
Why, then, what's due to such a Grief   35
We've pay'd already with our Eyes.

'Let perjur'd, fair, Aminta know'

LET perjur'd, fair, Aminta *know*,
    What for her sake I *undergo*;
Tell her, for her, how I Sustain
A lingring Feaver's wasting pain;
Tell her the Torments I endure,   5
Which only, only, She can cure.

2

But, Oh! she scorns to hear, or see,
The wretch that lies so low as me;
Her sudden greatness turns her Brain,
And Strephon hopes, alas! in vain: 10
For, ne'er 'twas found (tho' often try'd)
That pity ever dwelt with Pride.

To Phillis.

PHILLIS since we have both been kind,
    And of each other had our fill,
Tell me, what Pleasure you can find;
    In forcing Nature 'gainst her will.

2

'Tis true, you may with Art and Pain,   5
    Keep in some Glowings of Desire;
But still, those Glowings, which remain,
    Are only Ashes of the Fire.

3

Then let us free each others Soul,
    And laugh at the dull constant Fool,   10
Who would Love's liberty controul,
    And teach us how to whine by Rule.

'Let perjur'd, fair, Aminta'. Title: edd.: om. 1741

4

Let us no Impositions set,
   Or clogs upon each others Heart;
But as for Pleasure first we met;   15
   So now for Pleasure let us part.

5

We both have spent our Stock of Love,
   So consequently should be free,
Thirsis expects you in yon Grove,
   And pretty Chloris stays for me.   20

'*Phillis this pious talk give o'er*'

PHILLIS *this pious talk give o'er,*
   And modestly pretend no more;
   It is too plain an Art:
Surely you take me for a Fool,
And would by this prove me so dull,   5
   As not to know your Heart.

2

In vain you fancy to deceive;
For truly I can ne'er believe,
   But this is all a sham;
Since any one may plainly see,   10
You'd only save your self with me,
   And with another damn.

'*Still, Dorinda, I adore*'

STILL, *Dorinda, I adore,*
   Think, I mean not to deceive ye;
For, I lov'd you much before,
And alas! now love you more,
Tho' I force my self to leave ye.   5

Title: edd.: om. 1741
Title: edd.: om. 1741

2

Staying I my vows shall fail;
Virtue yeilds, as love grows stronger:
Fierce desires will prevail,
You are fair, and I am frail,
And dare trust my self no longer.   10

3

You my Love too nicely coy,
Least I should have gain'd the treasure;
Made my Vows and Oaths destroy
The pleasing hopes I did enjoy,
Of all my future Peace and Pleasure.   15

4

To my vows I have been true,
And in silence hid my Anguish,
But, I cannot promise too,
What my Love may make me do,
While with her, for whom I languish.   20

5

For, in thee strange Magic lies,
And my Heart is too, too tender;
Nothing's proof against those Eyes,
Best resolves and stricktest tyes
To their force must soon surrender.   25

6

But, Dorinda, you're severe;
I most doating thus to sever;
Since, from all I hold most dear,
That you may no longer fear,
I divorce my self for ever.   30

'Is it, O Love, thy want of Eyes'

Is it, O Love, thy want of Eyes,
  Or by the Fates decreed;
That hearts so seldom sympathize,
  Or for each other bleed?

2

If thou wouldst make two Youthful hearts,   5
  One amorous Shaft obey
'Twould save thee the expence of darts,
  And more extend thy Sway.

3

Forbear alas! thus to Destroy,
  Thy self, thy growing Power;   10
For that, which would be stretch'd by Joy,
  Despair will soon devour.

4

Ah! wound then my relentless Fair,
  For thy own Sake and mine;
That boundless Bliss may be my Share,   15
  And double Glory thine.

A two part Song.

Why Harry? what ails you? Why look you so Sad?
  To think And ne'er drink, Will make you stark mad.
'Tis the Mistress, the Friend, and the Bottle; old Boy,
Which create all the pleasure poor Mortals enjoy,
But Wine of the Three's the most cordial Brother;   5
For one it relieves, and it Strengthens the other.

'Is it, O Love'. Title: edd.: om. 1741

' *Morella, charming without Art* '

M ORELLA, *charming without Art,*
       And kind without design,
Can never lose the smallest part,
    Of such a Heart as mine.

2

Oblig'd a Thousand several ways,   5
    It ne'er can break her Chains:
While Passion, which her Beauties raise,
    My Gratitude maintains.

' *Since my words, tho' ne'er so tender* '

S INCE *my words, tho' ne'er so tender,*
      With sincerest truth exprest,
Cannot make your heart surrender,
    Nor so much as warm your breast:

2

What will move the Springs of nature?   5
    What will make you think me true?
Tell me, thou mysterious Creature,
    Tell poor Strephon what will do.

3

Do not, Charmion, rack your Lover,
    Thus, by seeming not to know,   10
What so plainly all discover,
    What his Eyes so plainly show.

4

Fair one, 'tis your self deceiving,
    'Tis against your reason's laws:
Atheist-like (th' effect perceiving)   15
    Still to disbelieve the cause.

Title: edd.: om. 1741
Title: edd.: om. 1741

'*Love! inform thy faithful Creature*'

*L*OVE! *inform thy faithful Creature,*
   How to keep his Fair ones heart,
Must it be by truth of Nature?
Or by poor dissembling Art?
Tell the secret! show the wonder!   5
How we both may gain our ends;
I am lost, if we're asunder;
Ever tortur'd, if we're friends.

'*Since Moggy I mun bid Adieu*'

*S*INCE Moggy *I mun bid Adieu,*
   How can I help despairing?
Let Fate its Rigour still pursue,
   There's nought more worth my Caring.

'Twas she alone could calm my Soul,   5
   When racking Thoughts did grieve me
Her Eyes my Troubles could controul,
   And into Joys deceive me.

Farewell, ye Brooks no more along
   Your Banks mun I be walking: 10
No more you'll hear my Pipe or Song,
   Or pretty Moggy's Talking.

But I, by Death, an End will give
   To Grief, since we mun sever:
For, who can, after parting, live,   15
   Ought to be wretched ever.

The Divided Heart.

*O*NCE *I was unconfin'd and free,*
   Would I had been so still,
Enjoying sweetest Liberty,
   And roving at my Will.

'*Love! inform*'. Title: edd.: om. 1741
'*Since Moggy*'. Title: edd.: om. 1741

2

But now, not Master of my Heart,
　Cupid does so decide,
That Two she-Tyrants shall it part,
　And so poor me divide.

3

Victoria's Will I must obey,
　She acts without controul;
Phillis has such a taking way,
　She charms my very Soul.

4

Deceiv'd by Phillis's looks and smiles,
　Into her Snares I run:
Victoria shews me all her wiles,
　Which yet I dare not shun.

5

From one I fancy ev'ry Kiss
　Has something in't Divine;
And, awfull, taste the Balmy Bliss,
　That joyns her Lips with mine.

6

But, when with t'other I embrace,
　Tho' She be not a Queen;
Methinks 'tis sweet with such a Lass,
　To tumble on the Green.

7

Thus here you see a shared Heart,
　But I, mean while, the Fool;
Each in it has an equal part,
　But neither yet the whole.

8

Nor will it, if I right forecast,
　To either wholly yield;
I find the time approaches fast,
　When both must quit the Field.

5

10

15

20

25

30

'Some kind Angel, gently flying'

SOME kind Angel, gently flying,
　Mov'd with Pity at my Pain,
Tell Corinna, I am Dying,
　Till with Joy we meet again.

2

Tell Corinna, since we parted,　　　　　　5
　I have never known Delight:
And shall soon be broken hearted,
　If I longer want her Sight.

3

Tell her, how her Lover, mourning,
　Thinks each lazy Day a Year;　　　　　　10
Cursing ev'ry Morn returning,
　Since Corinna is not here.

4

Tell her too, not distant Places,
　Will she be but true and kind,
Joyn'd with Time and change of Faces,　　　15
　E'er shall shake my constant Mind.

'Farewell Amynta, we must part'

FAREWELL Amynta, we must part,
　The charm has lost it's pow'r;
Which held so fast, my captiv'd Heart,
　Untill this fatal Hour.

2

Hadst thou not thus my love abus'd,　　　　5
　And us'd me ne'er so ill;
Thy cruelty I had excus'd,
　And I had lov'd thee still.

Title: edd.: om. 1741
Title: edd.: om. 1741

3

But know, my Soul disdains thy Sway,
    And scorns thy Charms and thee;
To which each fluttering Coxcomb may   10
    As wellcome be as me.

4

Think in what perfect bliss you reign'd,
    How lov'd before thy fall;
And now alas, how much disdain'd   15
    By me, and scorn'd by all.

5

Yet thinking of each happy hour,
    Which I with thee have spent;
So robs my rage of all its Pow'r,
    That I almost relent.   20

6

But pride will never let me bow,
    No more thy Charms can move;
Yet thou art worth my Pity now,
    Because thou hadst my Love.

'Nanny blushes, when I woo her'

NANNY blushes, when I woo her,
    And with kindly chiding eyes,
Faintly says, I shall undoe her,
    Faintly, O forbear, she cries.

2

But her Breasts while I am pressing,   5
    While to her's my Lips I joyn;
Warm'd she seems to taste the Blessing,
    And her kisses answer mine.

Title: edd.: om. 1741   1 woo 'Contents' of 1741: woe Text of 1741

3

Undebauch'd by Rules of Honour,
    Innocence, with nature, charms;   10
One bids, gently push me from her,
    T'other, take me in her Arms.

'*Since we your Husband daily see*'

*S*INCE *we your Husband daily see*
    So jealous out of Season;
Phillis, let you and I agree,
    To make him so with reason.

2

I'm vext to think, that ev'ry Night,   5
    A Sot within thy Arms,
Tasting the most Divine delight,
    Should sully all your Charms.

3

While fretting I must lye alone,
    Cursing the Pow'rs Divine;   10
That undeservedly have thrown
    A Pearl unto a Swine.

4

Then, Phillis, heal my wounded heart,
    My burning Passion cool;
Let me at least in thee have part,   15
    With thy insipid Fool.

5

Let him, by night, his Joys pursue,
    And blunder in the dark;
While I, by day, enjoying you,
    Can see to hit the mark.   20

Title: edd.: om. 1741

Advice to a Lady.

PHILLIS, *give this humour over,*
　We too long have time abus'd;
I shall turn an Errant Rover,
If the favour's still refus'd.

2

Faith, 'tis nonsense out of measure,　　　　5
Without ending, thus to see,
Women forc'd to taste a pleasure,
Which they love as well as we.

3

Let not pride and folly share you,
We were made but to enjoy;　　　　10
Ne'er will Age or Censure spare you,
E're the more for being coy.

4

Never fancy time's before you,
Youth, believe me, will away;
Then, alass! who will adore you,　　　　15
Or to wrinkles tribute pay?

5

All the Swains *on you attending,*
Show how much your Charms deserve;
But Miser-like for fear of spending,
You, amidst your plenty, starve.　　　　20

6

While a thousand freer Lasses,
Who their Youth and Charms employ,
Tho' your Beauty their's surpasses,
Live in far more perfect Joy.

16 *pay?* edd.: *pay.* 1741

'Since, by ill Fate, I'm forc'd away'

SINCE, by ill Fate, I'm forc'd away,
And Snatch'd so soon from those dear **Arms**;
Against my will I must obey,
And leave those sweet endearing charms.

2

Yet still love on, and never fear,   5
But you and Constancy will prove
Enough my present flame to bear,
And make me, tho' in absence, love.

3

For tho' your presence Fate denys,
I feel, alas! the killing Smart;   10
And can, with undiscerned Eyes,
Behold your Picture in my Heart.

'Touch the Lyre, every String'

TOUCH the Lyre, every String,
Touch it Orpheus, I will sing
A Song, which shall immortal be;
Since She I sing's a Deity.
A Leonora whose blest birth   5
Has no relation to this Earth.

'In vain alas! poor Strephon trys'

IN vain alas! poor Strephon trys,
To ease his tortur'd breast;
Since Amoret the cure denys,
And makes his Pain a jest.

Title: edd.: om. *1741*
Title: edd.: om. *1741*
Title: edd.: om. *1741*

2

Ah! Fair one, why to me so coy,   5
   And why to him so true?
Who with more coldness slights the joy,
   Then I with Love pursue.

3

Die then, unhappy Lover, Dye;
   For since She gives thee Death;   10
The World has nothing that can Buy,
   A minute more of Breath.

4

Yet tho' I could your Scorn outlive,
   T'were folly, since to me
Not love it self a Joy can give,   15
   But, Amoret, in thee.

'Well—I will never more complain'

WELL—I will never more complain,
   Or call the Fates unkind;
Alas! how fond it is, how vain!
But self conceittedness does reign
   In every mortal mind.   5

2

'Tis true they long did me deny,
   Nor would permit a Sight;
I rag'd, for I could not Espy,
Or think that any harm could lye
   Disguis'd in that delight.   10

3

At last my Wishes to fullfill,
   They did their Pow'r resign;
I saw her, but I wish I still
Had been obedient to their will,
   And they not unto mine.   15

Title: edd.: om. 1741

4

Yet I by this, have learnt the Wit,
  Never to grieve or fret;
Contentedly I will submit,
And think that best, which they think fit;
  Without the least regret.   20

'*Chloe Beauty has and Wit*'

CHLOE *Beauty has and Wit,*
  And an Air that is not common;
Ev'ry Charm does in her meet,
Fit to make a handsome Woman.

2

But we do not only find   5
Here, a lovely Face or Feature,
For she's mercifull and kind,
Beauty's answer'd by good Nature.

3

She is always doing good,
Of her Favours never sparing,   10
And, as all good Christians shou'd,
Keeps poor Mortals from despairing.

4

Jove the pow'r knew of her Charms,
And that no man cou'd endure 'em,
So providing 'gainst all harms,   15
Gave to her the pow'r to cure 'em.

5

And 'twould be a cruel thing,
When her black Eyes have rais'd desire,
Shou'd she not her Bucket bring,
And kindly help to quench the Fire.   20

Title: edd.: om. 1741

Verses in Lady How's Ovids Epistles.

HOWEVER high, however cold the fair,
However great the dying Lover's care,
Ovid Kind Author, found him some relief,
Rang'd his unruly sighs and sett his grief:
Taught him what accents had the pow'r to move,   5
And always gain'd him pitty—sometimes Love:
But oh! what pangs torment the destin'd heart,
That feels the wound, yet dare not show the Dart.
What Ease could Ovid to his Sorrows give
Who must not Speak, and therefore cannot live.   10

Simile.

THE worthless Cypher when Alone
Is in himself much less then One
But plac't behind more cunning Men
Exalts Each figure up to Ten
And when two thoughtless Noughts have blunder'd   5
The Knave before becomes a hundred.

So by the aid of worthless fools
The Man who knows to use his tools.

The Courtier.

AND Courtiers traffick for their fame
Like Nymphs for what I need not name.
If this and that time they hold out
Is It their virtue? yes—no doubt:
In short they happen to dispise   5
The Lover now and now the price:

Title: *Verses edd.*: Mr Prior's Verses *Lpo*: Mr Priors Verses wrote *Harl*
     Title: *L 28 (Pope)*: om. *W, L 28 (D)*   3 But *L 28*: but *W*   7 by the] *L 28 (D)*
rise, by *L 28 (Pope)*   8 The *L 28*: the *W*   Man ... knows ... his] *L 28 (D)* Men
... know ... their *L 28 (Pope)*   tools. *edd.*: tools *W*: Tools. *L 28*
     Title: 'Contents' *of L 28 (D)*: The Courtier | Fragment. 'Contents' *of L 28 (Pope)*, *Text of*
L 28 (Pope): om. *W*   1 AND *L 28 (D)*: and *W*: Our *L 28 (Pope)*   2 Like *L 28*:
like *W*   4 Is It] It is *L 28*   6 The *L 28*: the *W*

But be the Youth gallant, the Sum
Sufficient, what reply they—Mum.
Nature and Interest must prevail
And flesh and blood you know are frail.   10

To charm the fair, to cheat the wise
To lure us to the proffered vice:
'Tis all but coming to our price.

Narcissus.

OH happy Youth, what can destroy
   The long excesses of thy Joy
For nothing in the whole Creation
Will prove a rival to thy passion.

To Cloe.

THERE'S all Hell in her Heart and all Heaven in her Eye
He that sees her must love, he that loves her must Dye.

To a Painter.

THE Pride of Babel that confus'd our tongues
   To narrow bounds confines the Poet's Songs.
The Painters meaning thrô the Earth may fly
For Babels curse afflicted n'er the Eye.
Unequal is our labour and our fame   5
Whilst men talk different but they See the Same.

<hr>

7 But *L 28*: but *W*   8 what reply they—] *L 28* and the word is *Earlier reading in*
W   11, 12 To *L 28*: to *W*   11 wise *edd.*: wis *Torn off in W*: Wise *L 28*   13
'Tis *L 28*: 'tis *W*   price. *edd.*: pr *Torn off in W*: Price. *L 28*
   Title: 'Contents' *of L 28*: *om. W, L 28*   1 Oh *edd.*: oh *W*: O *L 28*   2 The *L 28*:
the *W*   3 For *L 28*: for *W*   4] *L 28* but for thy self thou hast a passion *Earlier*
reading in W   passion. *edd.*: passion *W, L 28*
   2 he *edd.*: yᵉ *L 29*
   Title: L 28 (Pope): Poetry and Painting 'Contents' *of L 28 (D)*: The pride of Babel 'Contents'
of L 28 (Pope): *om. W, L 28 (D)*   1 THE . . . Babel *L 28*: the . . . babel *W*   confus'd . . . tongues] confin'd . . . Tongue *L 28*   2 To *L 28*: to *W*   Songs. *edd.*:
Song *W, L 28*   3 The *L 28*: the *W*   4 For Babels *L 28*: for babels *W*   afflicted
n'er] afflicted *L 28 (D)*: affected not *L 28 (Pope)*   5–6 In *L 28*, marked for deletion (by
Pope?)   6 Same. *edd.*: Same *W*: same *L 28*

Should adverse fortune banish Me or Pope
What could our pens from France or Holland hope?
With cruel *je n'entens pas* we should meet
Or soft *varacht'et ik verstaen ye neet*   10
But thou mayst go to Athens or to Rome
And in each region think thy Self at home.

Song.

THOU arm'st thy Self in Celia's Eyes
      Great Love, when Reason would rebell
And every time I dare be wise
Thy rage more terrible I feel.

Repeated thoughts present the Ill   5
Which Seeing I must still endure
They tell Me Thou hast darts to Kill
And Wisdom has no power to cure.

Let reason therefore leave the breast
Which vainly he would strive to hold   10
And Try his Strength in Celias breast
Severe and disengag'd, and cold:

There bid him all his arts imploy
And showing thy eternal Slave
Convince Her, Victors may destroy   15
But legal Sovereigns always save.

8 France or Holland *L 28*: france or holland *W*   hope? *L 28*: hope *W*   9–10 *Italics
supplied from L 28*   11–12 *In L 28, these precede l. 7, and are marked for deletion (by
Pope?)*   11 But *L 28*: but *W*   12 And *L 28*: & *W*   each] *L 28 (Pope)*: om.
L 28 (D)   home. *edd.*: home *W*: Home *L 28*

Title: edd.: om. *L 29 (P), L 29 (D), W*   1] *L 29 (D)* om. *W*   arm'st *L 29 (D)*:
arms't *L 29 (P)*   2] *L 29 (D)* when weaker reason *W, Alt. reading in L 29 (D)*   3
And *L 29 (D)*: and *L 29 (P)*: & *W*   4 Thy] *L 29 (D)* His *W, Alt. reading in L 29
(D)*   feel. *L 29 (D)*: feel *L 29 (P), W*   5 Repeated . . . present *L 29 (D)*: repeated
. . . present *L 29 (P)*: Avails it ought to see *W, Alt. reading in L 29 (D)*   6 Which
W, L 29 (D): wch *L 29 (P)*   7 They . . . hast] *L 29 (D)* to know that Love has *W,
Alt. reading in L 29 (D)*   8 And . . . no] *L 29 (D)* While Wisdom wants the *W, Alt.
reading in L 29 (D)*   cure. *edd.*: cure *L 29 (P), W*: Cure. *L 29 (D)*   9–16] *Earlier
version in L 29 (P) and L 29 (D) reads:*

                    let reason then her arts imploy
                    let Her convince thee doubtfull maid
                    That Venus is the Queen of Joy
                    And Thou art gentle when obey'd:

9 Let *L 29 (D)*: let *L 29 (P)*   10 Which *L 29 (D)*: wch *L 29 (P)*   he] we *L 29 (D)*
13 There *L 29 (D)*: there *L 29 (P)*   him . . . his] her . . . her *L 29 (D), Alt. reading in
L 29 (P)*

Song.

LET us, my Dear, my Life, be friends
  Forget all fears and troubles past:
Our pleasure on this hour Depends
Would heaven and Thee but make it last.

Stil to improve each opening day   5
Be all our future thought employ'd
Nor more e'er let our Tombstone Say
Than That we liv'd and Lov'd and Joy'd.

Those Ills which were before too great
We still augment whilst we complain.   10
Our Sorrows why should we relate
If Memory but renews our pain?

Mankind whose various action strives
Each others blessing to destroy
Would smile malicious if our lives   15
Knew any Interval of Joy.

Invocation to Fortune.

ETERNAL powers, who turn this restless ball
  And say when Empires shall arise or fall
Assist my cause with Honor, Justice, Truth,
And Thou great fortune wont to favor Youth:

Title: edd.: om. Both MSS. 2 past: *edd.: past Both MSS.* 4 Would . . . make]
Ever mayst thou make Alt. reading in L 29 (D & P): And hence for ever may *Earlier reading
in both MSS.* 7 Nor . . . our] *L 29 (D)* And let our faithful *Earlier reading in both
MSS.* 8 Than] *L 29 (D) om. in earlier version* 9–10] *L 29 (D)*
Since all our deed was done by fate
We vainly of the events complain: *Earlier reading in both MSS.,
except that L 29 (D) has* indeed *for* our deed 9 Those *L 29 (D):* those *L 29 (D & P)*
which] that *L 29 (D)* 10 complain. *edd.:* complain *Both MSS.* 12 our] the
L 29 (D) pain? *edd.:* Pain *L 29 (D):* plain *L 29 (D & P)* 16 Joy. *edd.:* Joy *Both
MSS.*
Title: 'Contents' of L 28: om. W, L 28 (153ᵛ), L 28 (324) 1–2 *In all MSS., these
follow l. 8* 1 powers . . . turn] Pow'r . . . turns *L 28 (153ᵛ), L 28 (324)* 2 or]
L 28 (153ᵛ) and L 28 (324) 3 Honor, Justice, Truth, *L 28 (153ᵛ), L 28 (324):* honr:
Justice truth *W*

For once thy Godhead by thy mercy prove 5
Chain cruell rage, and aid afflicted love
Great Heavn's decrees undaunted lett me try
And live with Empire, or with virtue dye.

Fragment.

THY King O may I call him by that Name
But he shall be the last that e're shall bear it.

No Man more heartily shall hate his wife
Then he shall Thee. Nor fly with more Impatience
Into a yeilding Mistress dear Embraces 5
Then he to Belgia's shore, Belgia thy rival
In Empire and in Interest, she shall triumph
Shal to the furthest East send forth
New colonies and build her towring abodes
On Ganges and in India, she shall have treatyes 10
Made for her sake alone, and Kingdom given.

Thy Miters shal be worn by Men at best
Stupid and Ignorant, scarce capable
To guide a Parish flock, by others famous
For rapes, and outlaw'd from their Native country 15
For having by vile treasons given up
The Masters that had fed them, fools and Madmen
That prophecy false dreams, that take distemper
For revelation
And comment Blasphemy on sacred Scripture 20
These, these shall rule thy Clergy.

Thou shalt have Preists immers't in lust and gluttony
And bishops three times married, thy cathedrals

6 Chain *L 28 (153ᵛ)*, *L 28 (324)*: chain *W*   8 dye. *edd.*: dye *W*, *L 28 (153ᵛ)*, *L 28 (324)*
  Title: L 28 (Pope): Fragment in blank Verse '*Contents*' *of L 28*: *om. W*   1 THY ...
O *L 28*: thy ... o *W*   2 But *L 28*: but *W*   4 Then *L 28*: then *W*   fly] *L 28*
from her *Earlier reading in W*   6 Then *L 28*: then *W*   8 to *L 28*: to in *W*
9 towring] *L 28 (D)*: proud *L 28 (Pope)*   abodes *L 28*: *Illegible in W*   10 Ganges
L 28 (Pope?) Gandes *W*, *L 28 (D)*   11 Made *L 28*: made *W*   12 Thy *L 28*:
thy *W*   14 To *L 28*: to *W*   15, 16 For *L 28*: for *W*   17 The *L 28*: the *W*
18 That *edd.*: that *W*: Shal *L 28*   19 For *L 28*: for *W*   21 These *L 28*: these *W*
Clergy. *L 28*: Clergy *W*   22 Thou *L 28*: thou *W*   23 And *L 28*: and *W*

The Seats where Prayer and hospitality
Should dwel, shall be the taverns   25
Where Drunken bowles incessantly goe round
In leud debauch and midnight dice are hurld,
The beds wherein the wearied Pilgrim us'd
To ease his crippled Limbs, he now shall find
Possess't with Women, nurses, she attandants,   30
And a Dishonest brood of ugly children.

Fragment.

O DEAR to God and Man O Prince approv'd
  And tryd by heav'n, by Earth confest and lov'd
Oh for our good ascend thy Native seat:
In thee lett Judah once again be great
Let the glad oyl from thy anointed head,   5
Upon a bleeding Nations wounds be shed:
Pardon and rule, lett Kindness grace thy power
The throne on mercy founded stands secure.

Epigram.

A T Noble Mens table Ned every day Eats
  And rails against all but the Bubble that treats.
To what real Use does He manage his Sence
Who ne'r opens his mouth but at others Expence?

24 The *L 28*: the *W*   25 taverns] Taverns of the Land, *L 28 (Pope?)*   27 In
L 28: in *W*   28 The *L 28*: the *W*   29 To *L 28*: to *W*   31 And *L 28*: and
W   children. *edd.*: children *W*: Children. *L 28*
    Title: edd.: *om. L 29 (P), L 29 (D)*   1 O Prince *L 29 (D)*: o P *L 29 (P)*   2
heav'n *edd.*: heav'en *L 29 (P)*: Heav'n *L 29 (D)*   4 thee *edd.*: the *L 29 (P)*: Thee
L 29 (D)   5 Let *L 29 (D)*: let *L 29 (P)*   8] *L 29 (D)* and bless thy people to
make the throne secure *Earlier reading in L 29 (P)*   secure. *edd.*: secure *L 29 (P)*:
Secure. *L 29 (D)*
    Title: edd.: *om. W*   2 treats. *edd.*: treats *W*   4 ne'r . . . Expence? *edd.*:
ner . . . Expence *W*

The Normans Wish.

WHEN Eve did with the Snake dispute
  O had they both been dumb
The Apple, of all Sin the root,
  O had it been a Plumb!
And Adam when Thou Eat'st the Fruit   5
  O had Thou suck'd Thy Thumb.

Epigram.

TOM's Sickness did his Morals mend;
  His Health impair'd, his mind grew stronger.
Bad his Beginning Good his End
  He Dy'd when He cou'd live no longer.

Epigram.

RISE not till Noon, if Life be but a Dream,
  As Greek and Roman Poets have Exprest:
Add good Example to so grave a Theme,
  For he who Sleeps the longest lives the best.

3 Apple, . . . Sin *edd.* : Apple . . . Sin, *M*
1 mend; *edd.*: mend *M*   2 impair'd, . . . stronger. *edd.*: impair'd . . . stronger *M*
2 Exprest: *edd.*: Exprest *M*

PRINTED IN GREAT BRITAIN
AT THE UNIVERSITY PRESS, OXFORD
BY VIVIAN RIDLER
PRINTER TO THE UNIVERSITY